Second Edition

AUTOMATIC
RANSMISSIONS

MATHIAS F. BREJCHA

Professor
Automotive Department
Ferris State College
Big Rapids, Michigan

PRENTICE-HALL, INC.
Englewood Cliffs, New Jersey   07632

Library of Congress Cataloging in Publication Data

BREJCHA, MATHIAS F.
    Automatic transmissions.

    Includes index.
    1. Automobiles—Transmission devices, Automatic.
    2. Automobiles—Transmission devices, Automatic—
Maintenance and repair.   I.   Title.
TL263.B74   1982   629.2'446   81-21010
ISBN   0-13-054577-5   AACR2

Editorial/production supervision
    and interior design by *Virginia Huebner*
Manufacturing buyer: *Joyce Levatino*
Cover design by *Frederick Charles, Ltd.*

Printed in the United States of America

10   9   8   7   6   5   4   3   2   1

ISBN 0-13-054577-5

Prentice-Hall International, Inc., *London*
Prentice-Hall of Australia Pty. Limited, *Sydney*
Prentice-Hall of Canada, Ltd., *Toronto*
Prentice-Hall of India Private Limited, *New Delhi*
Prentice-Hall of Japan, Inc., *Tokyo*
Prentice-Hall of Southeast Asia Pte. Ltd., *Singapore*
Whitehall Books Limited, Wellington, *New Zealand*

CONTENTS

PREFACE

Automatic Transmissions had its first printing in 1973. This second edition has been completely revised with in-depth new material that represents the developments of recent years, especially in connection with fuel economy and front wheel drive adaptations. The new family of transmissions primarily feature converter clutch and direct mechanical drive systems in the torque converter that eliminates fluid slip, the use of a fourth gear overdrive and lightweight construction. For the near future, electronically controlled automatic transmissions will be a reality and this is given some attention in the text.

A considerable amount of obsolete material has been eliminated. Changes and additions have been made in each chapter to keep in line with new design developments or to improve the presentation. The following chapters, in particular, have undergone extensive changes as indicated in the Table of Contents.

VII. THE HYDRAULIC CONTROL SYSTEM— FUNDAMENTALS OF OPERATION
IX. PRINCIPLES OF DIAGNOSIS
X. AUTOMATIC TRANSMISSION SERVICE
XI. SUMMARY REVIEW OF CURRENT AUTOMATIC TRANSMISSIONS

This edition contains over seven hundred new and improved supporting art and photographic illustrations along with a corresponding amount of new text. Input from highly skilled transmission mechanics and field service technicians provides information not readily available elsewhere. Metric and English units of measurements are combined throughout the text with a direct reading English/Metric conversion table provided in the Appendix.

AUTOMATIC TRANSMISSIONS still remains comprehensive in nature dealing with basic fundamentals of operation, diagnosis and service. It supports the factory service manuals or their equivalent and is not intended to eliminate their need. The book is written for the auto mechanics student and those journeyman mechanics and related service personnel who want to upgrade their knowledge and skills with more concise and comprehensive information. Automotive engineers will find the text a useful reference book.

AUTOMATIC TRANSMISSIONS is listed as recommended reading for auto mechanics by the National Institute for Automotive Service Excellence as preparation for the NIASE Certification Examination in the area of automatic transmissions. The author is certified as a NIASE General Automobile Mechanic and has participated in several NIASE test workshops to help in the development of this examination.

The author gratefully acknowledges the following companies and organizations for their special contributions in compiling AUTOMATIC TRANSMISSIONS:

AMERICAN MOTORS CORPORATION
BORG-WARNER CORPORATION
CHRYSLER MOTORS CORPORATION
FERRIS STATE COLLEGE
FORD MOTOR COMPANY
GENERAL MOTORS CORPORATION
SOCIETY OF AUTOMOTIVE ENGINEERS

MATHIAS F. BREJCHA

Big Rapids, Michigan

AUTOMATIC
TRANSMISSIONS

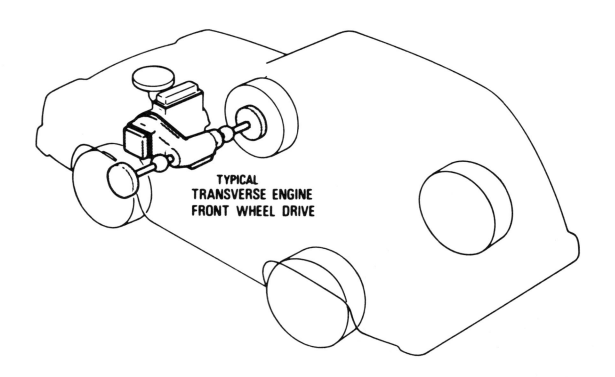

TYPICAL
TRANSVERSE ENGINE
FRONT WHEEL DRIVE

AUTOMATIC TRANSMISSION—POWER TRAIN

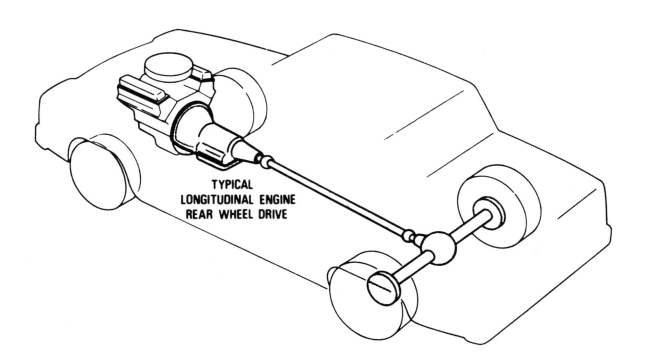

TYPICAL
LONGITUDINAL ENGINE
REAR WHEEL DRIVE

1

DEVELOPMENT OF AUTOMATIC TRANSMISSIONS

Hydra-Matic, TorqueFlite, and Cruise-O-Matic are some of the familiar names used for automatic transmissions in the auto trade. To understand how each operates might seem to be a monumental task. However, the purpose of this book is to present a simple, comprehensive study of the fundamentals of automotive transmissions that covers operation, diagnosis, and servicing. This background will add immeasurably to your automotive knowledge in preparation for earning a living in an expanding service industry.

The ultimate goal of this text is to create an awareness that automatic transmissions are more alike in design and operation than they are different. The differences that do exist are primarily in component sizes and structure and some minor variations in hydraulic control systems. This should not interfere in applying fundamental principles to individual transmissions.

The differences that exist in both operation and service among the various manufacturers are best learned by studying their current operation and service manuals. Although specific transmissions are not presented in detail, the text deals with current production units when applicable to the discussion. Although concentration is on passenger car automatic transmissions, there should be an awareness that they are also used in light and heavy-duty truck applications.

The study of this text is but one in a series of steps needed for a complete understanding of automatic transmissions. The individual should learn to apply his knowledge of fundamentals, then review service manuals for particular transmissions, drive passenger cars equipped with the various transmissions to get the feel of how they perform, and finally get involved in the actual diagnosis and servicing of transmissions.

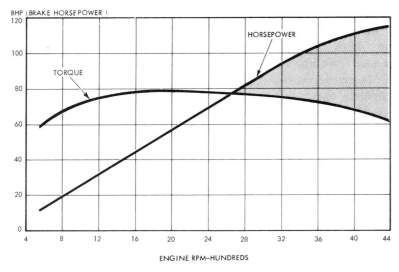

BHP (BRAKE HORSEPOWER)

ENGINE RPM—HUNDREDS

Fig. 1-1. Relationship of brake horsepower (bhp) to torque.

In keeping with the objective of presenting fundamentals, this book briefly reviews the theory of automotive power transmission and the evolution of transmission design. Then it discusses the fluid torque converter, planetary gearing, and hydraulic control systems in order to build toward an understanding of total transmission operation. Later chapters deal with trouble diagnosis, general overhaul practices, and a comprehensive study of current production passenger car automatic transmissions.

A review of transmission fundamentals for students who have not had previous training is appended at the end of the text. Because manual transmissions are still a small part of the transmission market, it is assumed that they can be studied in a basic level text and so are not included in our discussions here.

THE POWER TRAIN

The term *power train* includes all the drive components between the engine flywheel and the drive wheels. Typically, this includes a clutch assembly, a transmission or gear box, u-joints and drive shaft, a ring and pinion drive, differential unit, and the drive axles and wheels.

In this power train, the gear ratio(s) of the transmission and rear axle drive are used to control engine rpm and provide the necessary torque. The transmission acts as the torque and speed changer.

Because the engine output changes directly in proportion to changes in vehicle load and speed, the transmission must provide suitable gear ratio changes, usually three or four, that permit the engine to efficiently move the load. As shown in Fig. 1-1, the ideal transmission gear ratios should adjust the engine's load to produce the same torque curve at all speeds. Optimum engine performance is the objective, and the transmission is designed to make a significant contribution to engine performance as well as to transmit power.

ENGINE CHARACTERISTICS

The primary function of the internal combustion engine is to produce torque (turning or rotational effort) for powering the automotive vehicle. Horsepower, a term that is often loosely used to describe the output of an engine, is simply the product of torque and speed (motion per unit of time). That is, torque and speed produce horsepower. A specific horsepower can be the result of high torque and low speed or low torque and high speed.

Figure 1-1 shows a typical relationship of horsepower to torque. As engine rpm increases, both torque and horsepower increase together until the midrange is reached in engine speed. It is at this midrange that engine efficiency reaches a maximum before gradually decreasing, with a resulting decrease in torque. Although absolute horsepower may continue to rise, effective utilization or performance drops off. Torque is thus seen to be the prime performance factor.

Another engine characteristic is that the engine will not produce any more output than is demanded by the vehicle load. For example, at 2,500 rpm, with the transmission in neutral, little torque is produced. This is because of the small throttle opening required and the resulting high engine vacuum. When a load (weight of vehicle x friction) is placed on the engine, a wider throttle opening is required to maintain the same rpm. Consequently, engine vacuum drops due to the increased volumetric efficiency (the ability of the atmosphere to charge the cylinders with a quantity of air/fuel mixture). The net result is an increase in engine power output.

Another observation of engine characteristics can be made. Figure 1-1 shows that when an engine's crankshaft turns too fast and develops too litte torque, it is less effective in accelerating the vehicle. For best vehicle performance, the engine must be linked with a power train that will utilize and adapt engine output to the road load (weight, speed, and road terrain).

TRANSMISSION FUNCTIONS

A typical drive shaft torque curve (engine torque × transmission gear ratio(s) against road load on full throttle acceleration to 100 mph) is shown in Fig. 1-2 for a three-speed automatic transmission. Road load in this case refers to the drive shaft torque required to keep the vehicle moving at a particular speed. Observe the drive shaft torque curve; the greatest amount of torque is available at start because engine torque is multiplied by the torque converter (the converter ratio being greatest at start) and by the transmission first gear ratio. Because the converter ratio decreases rapidly once the vehicle begins moving, the drive shaft torque decreases rapidly up to 20 mph.

During first-gear operation, this converter effect gives a smooth transition in torque drop when com-

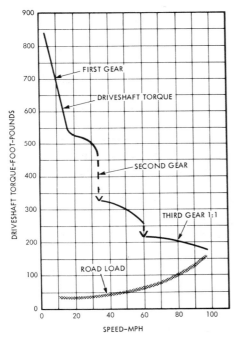

Fig. 1-2. Torque curve of a typical driveshaft showing its relationship to gear ratios.

pared to the sudden torque changes observed for second and third gears. If the vehicle is to accelerate, the drive shaft torque must exceed the road load requirement. When the condition is such that the drive shaft torque and road load are equal, the vehicle speed is then fixed. Figure 1-2 shows the torque curve of a typical drive shaft and its relationship to gear ratio changes.

At 5 mph, the road load torque of 25 lb-ft and the drive shaft torque of 850 lb-ft gives a reserve of 825 lb-ft for acceleration. As the vehicle continues to accelerate to 100 mph, the road load increases and the drive shaft torque decreases until finally the transmission (1) shifts into third gear, (2) the engine rpm is at

maximum but at less than full torque, and (3) the road load and drive shaft torque reach an equilibrium. No further vehicle speed is possible. It should be rather evident from Fig. 1-2 that engine and transmission work together to provide this performance.

TRANSMISSION DEVELOPMENT

The role of the automobile transmission has not changed throughout the years. Although its main function is that of a torque and speed changer, it also provides for reverse and neutral and engine braking. Great strides have taken place in its design and development to keep pace with the evolution of the automobile.

The American passenger car got along nicely for the first 30 to 40 years of its existence with one basic transmission structure, a manually-shifted three-or four-speed sliding gearbox (Fig. 1-3) equipped with a foot operated friction clutch for engaging and disengaging engine power during shifts. The early versions were very simple and usually rugged in construction and operation.

During the same period, manually-operated transmissions with planetary gears were also being developed—a three-speed version was used in the 1904 Cadillac, and of more popular vintage, the old Model

Fig. 1-3.

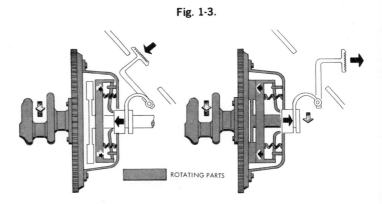

ROTATING PARTS

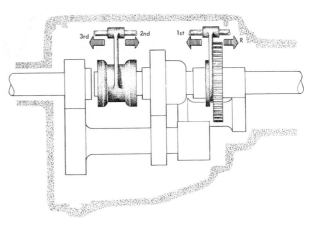

T Ford used a two-speed planetary gearbox design that saw years of popularity until it was dropped in 1928.

Despite these early successes, auto industry engineers were searching for the ideal transmission, one that would provide ease of driver operation, smooth shifts, and infinitely variable ratios to give the engine the ultimate in performance assist. The fully automatic transmission was the answer, and the industry proceeded to pass through several important stages.

1928 Cadillac introduced the synchromesh transmission.

1933 Reo brought out a semi-automatic transmission. This unit had planetary gear sets that used centrifugal weights to control them. This permitted the gears to shift automatically from low speed into drive once the car was moving. A single-plate, conventional friction clutch was still used.

1934 Chrysler introduced automatic overdrive.

1937 Oldsmobile introduced the next semi-automatic transmission design. Planetary gears were used and controlled by a combination of hydraulic and mechanical devices. The friction clutch was used, as were conventional gears for reverse operation.

1938 Chrysler Fluid Drive was introduced, thus making it possible to idle the engine with the transmission in gear. It consisted of a fluid coupling for starting, a conventional dry-disc clutch and fully synchronized four-speed constant mesh transmission (Fig. 1-4). With the foot clutch disengaged, either a low or high range could be selected manually by use of the shift lever on the steering column. Automatic gear changing occurred between 1st and 2nd gears and be-

tween 3rd and 4th gears. The automatic gear change was carried out by a vacuum servo cylinder system. Shifting between the two ratios in each speed range was controlled by the accelerator pedal at the driver's option at speeds above governor cut-in. This early design was also known as the Simplimatic and Vacuumatic.

Later design units (1949) used a hydraulic servo shift system in place of the vacuum system and the transmission was known by various trade names; Chrysler Prestomatic, De Soto Tiptoe, and Dodge Gyromatic. The Plymouth Hy-Drive represented a further variation and employed a three-speed gearbox with a torque converter.

In 1951, all fluid coupling units were replaced by a fluid torque converter and called the Chrysler Torque-Drive (Fig. 1-5). The same four-speed gearbox was used.

1940 General Motors Hydra-Matic first appeared in Oldsmobile. This design marked the first use of a fluid coupling in combination with a four-speed planetary, fully automatic transmission (Fig. 1-6). Both front and rear planetary sets provided for neutral and the forward gears. In reverse, the front planetary gave a reduction, the rear planetary reversed the power flow, and the reverse planetary added a further reduction. Note that the power flow from the flywheel must pass through the front planetary before turning the coupling drive member. When the rear planetary is in direct drive, the front planetary output has a split delivery between the fluid coupling and rear clutch. This minimizes coupling slip in 3rd and 4th gears. The fluid coupling transmits 40% of the front planetary

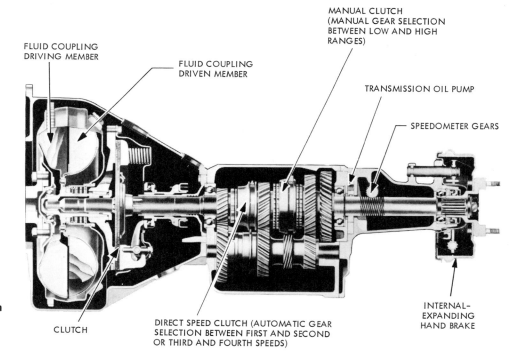

Fig. 1-4. **Fluid coupling with manual gear box.** (Chrysler Corp.)

4

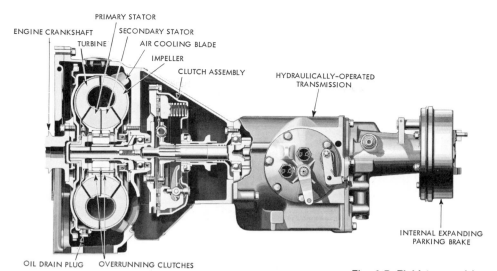

PRIMARY STATOR
ENGINE CRANKSHAFT
SECONDARY STATOR
TURBINE
AIR COOLING BLADE
IMPELLER
CLUTCH ASSEMBLY
HYDRAULICALLY-OPERATED TRANSMISSION

INTERNAL EXPANDING PARKING BRAKE

OIL DRAIN PLUG   OVERRUNNING CLUTCHES

Fig. 1-5 Fluid torque-drive with manual and hydraulically operated gear box. (Chrysler Corp.)

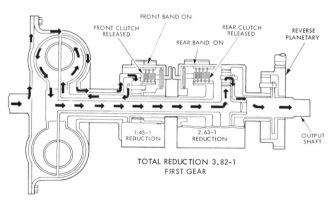

FRONT BAND ON
FRONT CLUTCH RELEASED
REAR CLUTCH RELEASED
REAR BAND ON
REVERSE PLANETARY

1:45-1 REDUCTION   2.63-1 REDUCTION   OUTPUT SHAFT

TOTAL REDUCTION 3.82-1
FIRST GEAR

Fig. 1-6. The original Hydra-Matic transmission.

POWER FLOW SUMMARY

	FRONT BAND	FRONT CLUTCH	REAR BAND	REAR CLUTCH	REVERSE ANCHOR LOCK TO INTERNAL GEAR
NEUTRAL ENGINE RUNNING	OFF	OFF	OFF	OFF	OFF
DRIVE 1ST GEAR	ON REDUCTION	OFF	ON REDUCTION	OFF	OFF
2ND GEAR	OFF	ON DIRECT	ON REDUCTION	OFF	OFF
3RD GEAR	ON REDUCTION	OFF	OFF	ON DIRECT	OFF
4TH GEAR	OFF	ON DIRECT	OFF	ON DIRECT	OFF
LOW 1ST GEAR	ON REDUCTION	OFF	ON REDUCTION	OFF	OFF
2ND GEAR	OFF	ON DIRECT	ON REDUCTION	OFF	OFF
REVERSE	ON REDUCTION	OFF	OFF POWER FLOW REVERSAL	OFF	ON REDUCTION
PARK ENGINE OFF	Move Selector Lever to R Position REAR BAND IS (ON), ANCHOR IS ENGAGED TRANSMISSION OUTPUT SHAFT IS MECHANICALLY LOCKED				

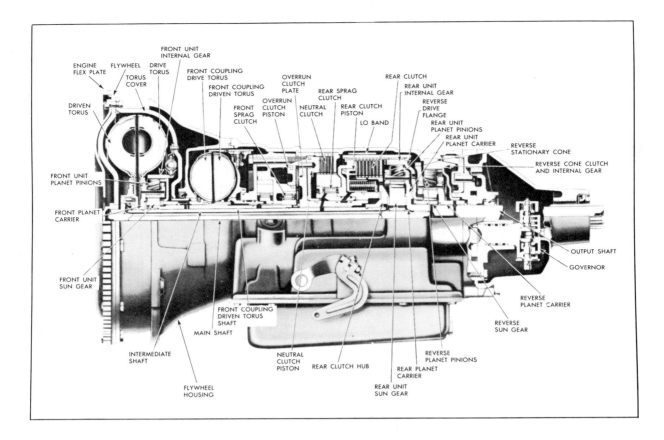

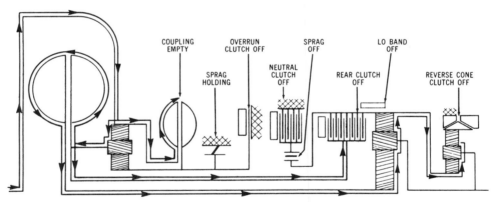

Fig. 1-7. Cross section of controlled coupling Hydra-Matic, powerflow—neutral.

output to the rear sun gear while 60% is mechanically transmitted to the rear internal gear.

The Hydra-Matic transmission was subject to considerable design change mostly related to the hydraulic control system and the control elements. Most of the changes concerned the improvement of gear engagement and shift quality.

The original 1940 design underwent the following changes:

•1951   A cone clutch was used for reverse gear in

place of the mechanical reverse anchor or pawl. With the engine off, a park pawl still engaged the reverse unit when the selector was placed in Reverse (R).

•1952   A Dual Range selection provided for two operating ranges; Drive Left (DL) and Drive Right (DR). Drive Left provided the full four speeds for all normal driving. Drive Right was the three-speed range for better performance in congested traffic and long mountain grades.

A variable capacity vane pump replaced the original IX gear front pump.

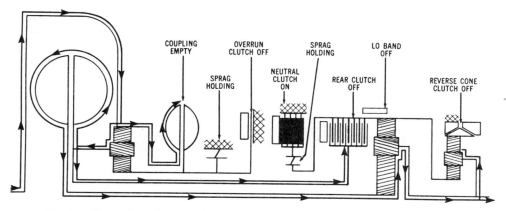

Fig. 1-8. Power flow-first speed-drive left. (Pontiac Division, General Motors Corp.)

•1954 Twin Hydra-Matic or "Twinburger." Two transmissions were "piggybacked" in one case design to achieve seven forward speeds and a reverse gear for commercial vehicle application.

•1955 Part throttle 4-3 downshift was available in Drive Left below 29 mph. Hydra-Matic was the first to introduce this feature.

•1956 The original design saw limited production for use in the Oldsmobile and Pontiac. The Controlled Coupling Hydra-Matic was introduced. It was basically a complete redesign of the original Hydra-Matic and was also identified by the trade names of Strato-Flight (Pontiac) and Jetaway (Oldsmobile). The same three planetary gear sets were used to provide four forward speeds and reverse. The dual range feature Drive Left and Drive Right was retained; however, the selector range pattern now included a park position (P N DR Lo R). A separate park gear mechanism was part of the redesign. Some of the significant changes were as follows:

1. A quick fill and exhaust miniature fluid coupling (or fluid clutch) replaced the multiple disc front clutch.
2. The front and rear bands were eliminated and replaced by sprag clutches.

The same large fluid coupling was used for the transmission of power as in the original Hydra-Matic. Forward ratios are: first, 3.97:1; second, 2.55:1; third, 1.55:1; and fourth, 1:1. Reverse ratio is 4.31:1.

The powerflow in neutral, the forward gears, and reverse are shown in Figs. 1-7 to 1-12. The powerflow in the forward gears are illustrated as it happens in the Drive Left range.

In Drive Right, in which the transmission operation is limited to the first three gears, the overrun clutch would be applied in first and third gears for coast braking.

In Lo range, in which the transmission is limited to first and second gears, the overrun clutch is applied in first gear and the low band in both first and second gears for coast braking.

The Controlled Coupling Hydra-Matic was used by Oldsmobile from 1956 thru 1960 and Cadillac and Pontiac from 1956 thru 1964.

•1961 The Roto Hydra-Matic was added to the family. Known in the trade as "Slim Jim," this transmission consisted of a fluid coupling with a torque multiplier and a fully automatic three speed gearbox.

Fig. 1-9. Power flow-second speed-drive left. (Pontiac Division, General Motors Corp.)

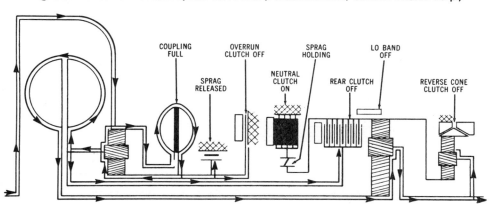

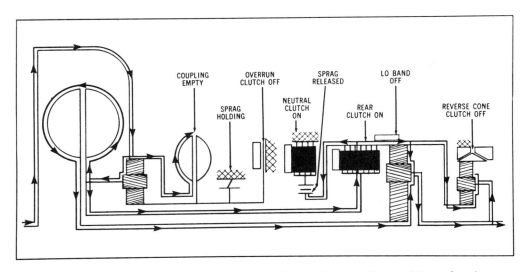

Fig. 1-10. Power flow-third speed-drive left. (Pontiac Division, General Motors Corp.)

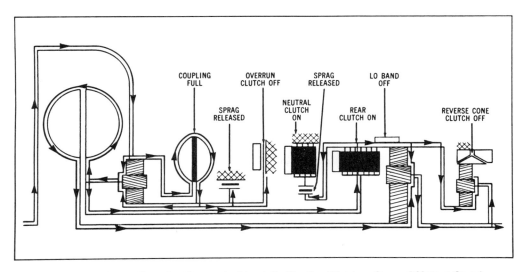

Fig. 1-11. Power flow-fourth speed-drive left. (Pontiac Division, General Motors Corp.)

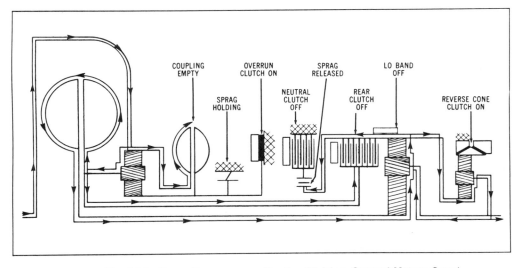

Fig. 1-12. Power flow-reverse. (Pontiac Division, General Motors Corp.)

PARK AND NEUTRAL—ENGINE RUNNING

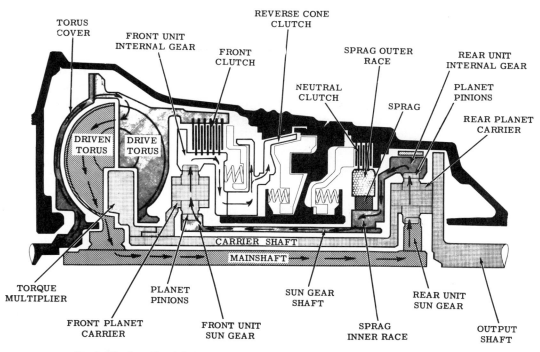

Fig. 1-13. Coupling-full; front clutch—released; neutral clutch—released; sprag—off; reverse clutch—released. (Oldsmobile Division, General Motors Corp.)

FIRST SPEED

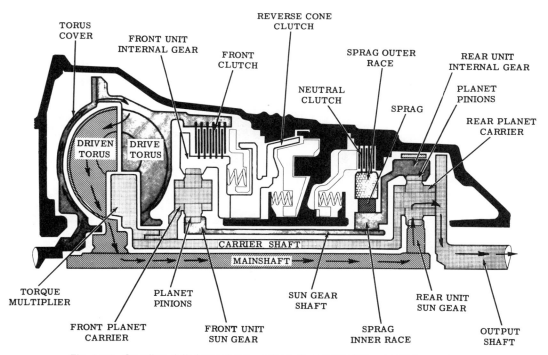

Fig. 1-14. Coupling-full; front clutch—released; neutral cloth—applied; sprag—on; reverse clutch—released. (Oldsmobile Division, General Motors Corp.)

With a torque-multiplying fluid coupling, the equivalent ratio coverage of a four speed transmission was achieved using only two gear ratio changes. The coupling actually functioned as a variable ratio torque multiplier for added performance in first and reverse.

The powerflow in neutral, the forward gears, and reverse are shown in Figs. 1-13, 1-14, 1-15, 1-16, and 1-17. The powerflow in the forward gears are illustrated as it happens in (D) range. Forward ratios are as follows: first, low gear ratio (2.93:1) plus the effect of the torque multiplier in the fluid coupling results in maximum starting torque of 3.56:1; second, 1.56:1; and third, 1:1. Reverse ratio is 3.45:1. The total reverse reduction is due to the 1.3 coupling torque ratio times the 2.42 gear ratio plus a .3 engine torque acting on the torque multiplier and output shaft in the reverse direction.

In the Intermediate and Low operating ranges, the overrun band is applied for coast braking. Note in Fig. 1-18 that the power from the engine is mechanically transmitted through the flywheel and damper assembly before driving the coupling torus cover.

The Roto Hydra-Matic was used by Oldsmobile and Pontiac from 1961 through 1964. A special small size unit was produced for the smaller class car. Internally it elminated the sprag in the rear planetary in favor of a double wrap band. An external band adjust screw provided for periodic adjustment of the band.

1948 Buick introduced the Dynaflow (Fig. 1-19), which was the first passenger car automatic transmission to successfully use the fluid torque converter. The dual pinion Ravigneaux planetary gear box provided direct, low, and reverse gear ratios. The drive range selection of the transmission connects the fluid converter to the output shaft with no additional gearing. This was the first attempt to use a pure fluid converter drive as transmission drive power; automatic shifting was not used. The maximum torque multiplication of converter is 2.25:1. A low gear ratio of 1.82:1 is provided for extra pulling power or engine braking. To improve car acceleration in the lower speed range, several interesting design variations were made in the 1948-52 converter design.

•1953 The five-element polyphase configuration was replaced with a twin turbine four element polyphase converter incorporating a planetary gear set (Fig. 1-20). This layout shows the first turbine T_1 connected to the internal gear while the second turbine T_2 is connected to the planet carrier member and the transmission input shaft. The sun gear is part of the stator member and is mounted on a freewheel sprag clutch.

SECOND SPEED

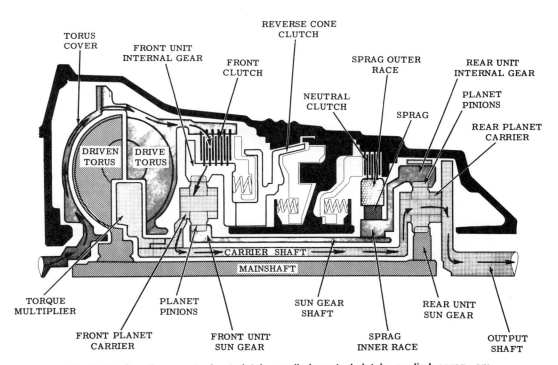

Fig. 1-15. Coupling-empty; front clutch—applied; neutral clutch—applied; sprag—on; reverse clutch—released. (Oldsmobile Division, General Motors Corp.)

THIRD SPEED

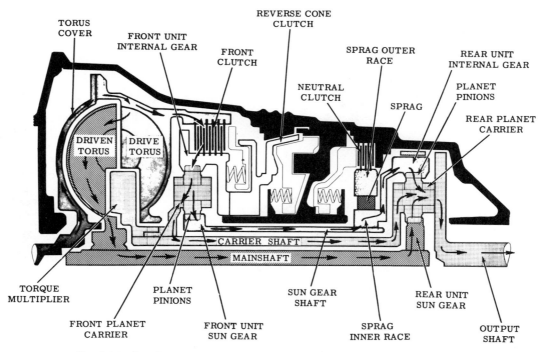

Fig. 1-16. Coupling-full, front clutch—applied; neutral clutch—applied; sprag—(overruns-ineffective); reverse clutch—released. (Oldsmobile Division, General Motors Corp.)

REVERSE

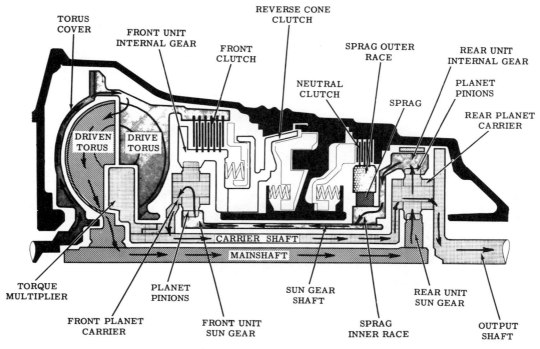

Fig. 1-17. Coupling-full; front clutch—released; neutral clutch—released; sprag—off; reverse clutch—applied. (Oldsmobile Division, General Motors Corp.)

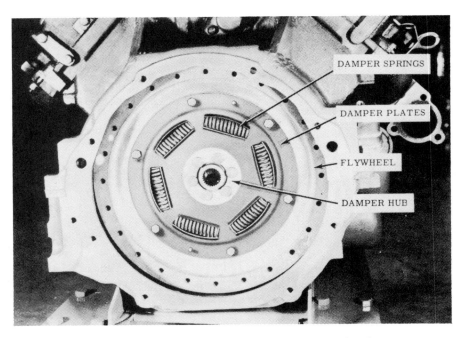

Fig. 1-18. (Oldsmobile Division, General Motors Corp.)

Fig. 1-19. First design Buick Dynaflow with polyphase converter.
(Buick Division, General Motors Corp.)

POWER FLOW SUMMARY

	DIRECT CLUTCH	LOW BAND	REVERSE BAND
NEUTRAL	OFF	OFF	OFF
DRIVE	ON	OFF	OFF
LOW	OFF	ON	OFF
REVERSE	OFF	OFF	ON

NOTE: NO AUTOMATIC SHIFTING

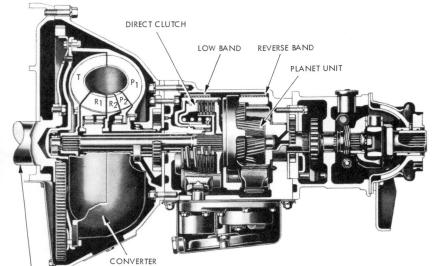

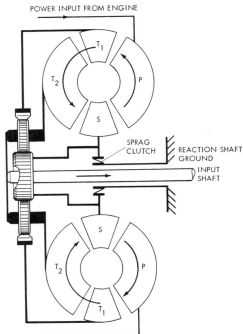

Fig. 1-20. 1953-54 four-element polyphase; twin turbine dynaflow.

By combining the gearing with the two turbine elements, the turbines could operate under different conditions. At low road speeds, turbine T_1 rotates faster than turbine T_2, which also makes the gear set effective. The gear reduction on turbine T_2 rotates T_2 at ⅝ths the speed of T_1. The torque output of T_1 increased by the gearing ratio of 1.60 to 1 gives a maximum stall ratio of 2.45 to 1. At higher output speed, the larger T_2 member develops a larger torque and accelerates to match the speed of T_1. When turbine T_2 has the capability to exceed ⅝ths the speed of turbine T_1, then the sun gear and stator are released by the freewheel sprag clutch. The output torque is now the function of turbine T_2. The converter provides a coupling phase when T_2 reaches 90% pump speed.

Although a gear set is included in the fluid unit, an actual gear change does not happen or is felt as in the usual manner. Because the gearing is operated according to fluid flow conditions no noticeable gear change occurs with converter conditions.

•1955 A Variable Pitch Dynaflow made the scene. The layout of the converter was similiar to the 1953 design with the exception of the stator and sun gear, which are now detached (Fig. 1-21). Both the stator and sun gear were mounted as separate parts with their own one-way sprag clutch. This arrangement had no great effect on the normal operation of the Twin Turbine. However, the variable angle stator permitted a faster fluid flow in the converter when

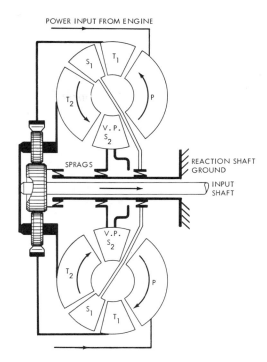

Fig. 1-22. 1956 five-element polyphase two stage converter with variable pitch stator; twin turbine dynaflow.

switched to the high angle position. This permitted an increase in engine rpm for added acceleration. The vane angle was controlled by external throttle linkage to the transmission. Extra movement of the throttle linkage at wide open throttle triggered a hydraulic valve in the stator circuit that resulted in selection of high angle and a maximum stall speed ratio of 2.5:1. For normal acceleration and cruising conditions the stator blades are positioned at low angle. The maximum converter ratio with the blades at low angle was 2:1. Chapter 2 discusses the effect of the variable angle stator concept in more detail.

•1956 As a final converter configuration change, the Dynaflow featured a five-element, two-stage Twin Turbine (Fig. 1-22). The use of the variable pitch stator and planetary gear set was retained. However, an extra stator was added between turbine T_1 and turbine T_2 for still more performance. The additional stator increased the maximum stall torque ratio for starting to 3.5:1 for stator blades in high angle position and 3.2:1 for low angle.

The last production year of the Turbine Drive Dynaflow was 1963 (Buick LeSabre, Wildcat, Electra, and Riviera).

1950 The Chevrolet Powerglide was introduced as a companion to the Buick Dynaflow. This fluid transmission was a small size version of the Dynaflow and basically was not different in construction and operation. The converter, as well as the gearbox, was identical to the early design Dynaflow.

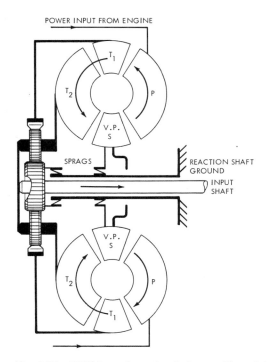

Fig. 1-21. 1955 four-element polyphase with variable pitch stator; twin turbine dynaflow.

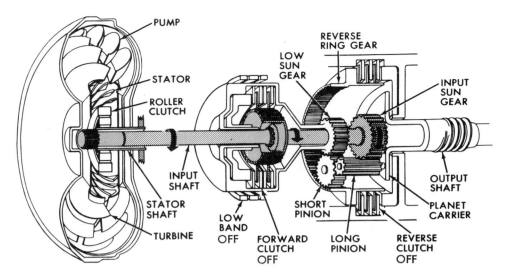

Fig. 1-23. Powerglide operation—neutral. (General Motors Corp.)

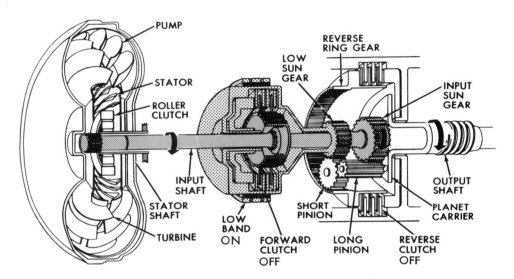

Fig. 1-24. Powerglide operation—low. (General Motors Corp.)

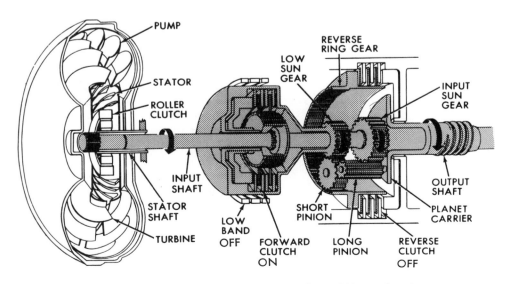

Fig. 1-25. Powerglide operation—direct. (General Motors Corp.)

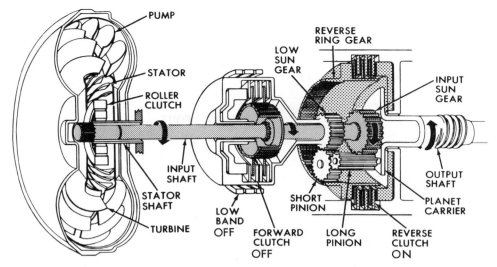

Fig. 1-26. Powerglide operation—reverse. (General Motors Corp.)

The Powerglide was a real workhorse and enjoyed a service life of 23 years with some significant design changes occurring.

•1953 The Powerglide was converted into a two speed automatic transmission using a basic three-element torque converter. The original gearbox was retained and modified to provide a low ratio (1.82:1) start in Drive range. The automatic gear change depended on throttle opening and car speed.

With the automatic shift system, forced downshifts (direct to low) were available within the proper vehicle speed range.

The transmission could be manually locked in low range for extra pulling power and engine braking. The transmission remained basically the same unit from 1953 through 1962. In 1963 the cast iron case Powerglide was entirely discontinued in favor of the aluminum case Powerglide design.

•1962 The Aluminum Powerglide came of age and was used concurrently in 1962 production with the cast iron unit on the full size Chevrolet, depending on the engine application. The aluminum Powerglide used a one piece aluminum case and bolt on extension housing that resulted in a 35% weight saving over the comparable cast iron Powerglide. Operating characteristics remained the same, with the single shift occurring between low and drive. Also, the basic planetary gear set did not change; however, a reverse multiple-disc type clutch did replace the reverse band in the rear of the transmission case. A three-element welded converter unit provided the drive torque.

The Powerglide powerflow is illustrated in Figs. 1-23, 1-24, 1-25, and 1-26. The reverse and low ratios were the same—1.82:1 or 1.76:1—depending on the engine application. A powerflow summary and transmission cutaway illustration is provided in Fig. 1-27.

TABLE 1-1. General Motors Two-Speed Applications

Transmission Type	G.M. Passenger Car Application	Production Year Introduced	Last Production Year
ALUMINUM[1] POWERGLIDE	Chevrolet, Monte Carlo, Chevelle, Chevy Nova, Camaro, Corvair, and Vega	1963; EXCEPT CORVAIR—1961	1973
SUPER TURBINE 300[2]	Buick Special, Skylark GS, and LeSabre	1964	1969
PONTIAC 2-SPEED[3]	Pontiac Tempest, GTO, Firebird, and Venturi II	1961	1973
JETAWAY[2]	Oldsmobile F-85, 4-4-2, and Jetstar 88	1964	1969

[1]The Aluminum Powerglide is so-called to distinguish it from its ancestor, the Cast Iron Powerglide.

[2]The Super Turbine 300 and Jetaway used a three element converter designed with a VP reactor(stator) from 1964 through production year 1967. The maximum torque multiplication of the converter in low pitch angle was 1.95:1 (1.8 on V-8's), and in the high pitch angle 2.75:1 (2.45 on V-8's).

[3]Tempestorque 1961-63; Tempest T-300, 1964-69 (no VP); Tempest M-35, 1970-73.

The last production year of the aluminum Powerglide was 1973. Pontiac used the transmission from 1970-73 on their small size cars and it was referred to as the M-35.

General Motors used other two-speed transmissions using the same basic gear train and transmission design. These are summarized in Table 1-1.

1957-58 General Motors continued its efforts to develop improved fluid converter drives. The Turboglide (1957, Chevrolet) and Flight Pitch Dynaflow (1958, Buick) were introduced. The two transmissions were very similar in operation and construction with the Flight Pitch being physically larger. To simplify the discussion, references relate to the Turboglide.

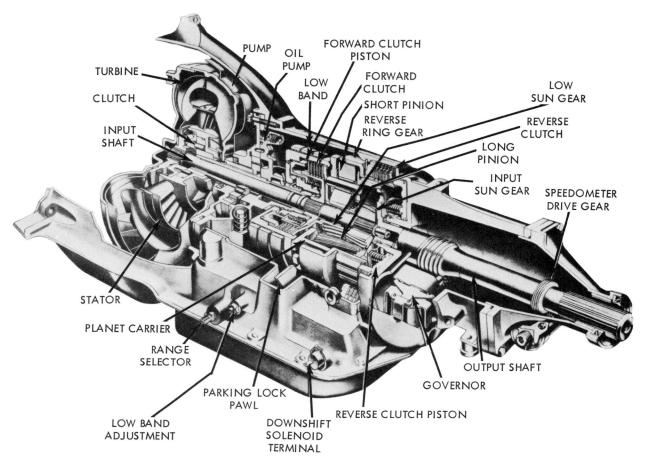

POWERFLOW SUMMARY FOR SUPER TURBINE 300, JETAWAY, POWERGLIDE, AND PONTIAC 2-SPEED

SELECTOR LEVER PATTERN P R N D L

RANGE	GEAR	FORWARD CLUTCH	REVERSE CLUTCH	LOW BAND	PARK PAWL
PARK		OFF	OFF	OFF	IN
REVERSE		OFF	ON	OFF	OUT
NEUTRAL		OFF	OFF	OFF	OUT
DRIVE	LOW	OFF	OFF	ON	OUT
	HI	ON	OFF	OFF	OUT
LOW	LOW	OFF	OFF	ON	OUT

Fig. 1-27. Typical G.M. 2-speed transmission. (General Motors Corp.)

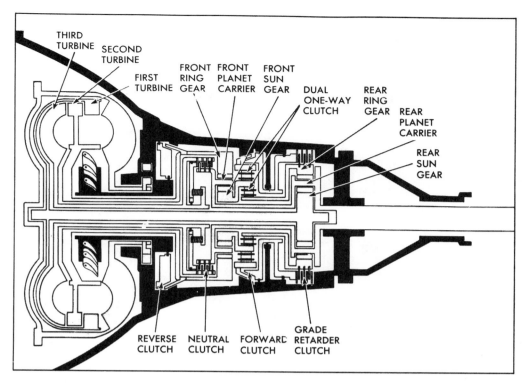

Fig. 1-28. Turboglide gear case cross section. (Chevrolet Division, General Motors. Corp.)

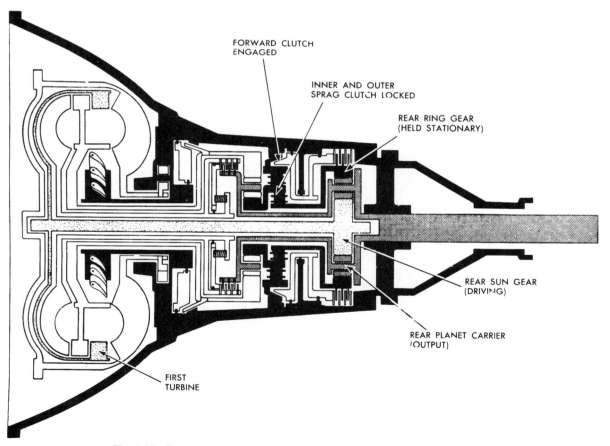

Fig. 1-29. First turbine phase powerflow. (Chevrolet Division, General Motors Corp.)

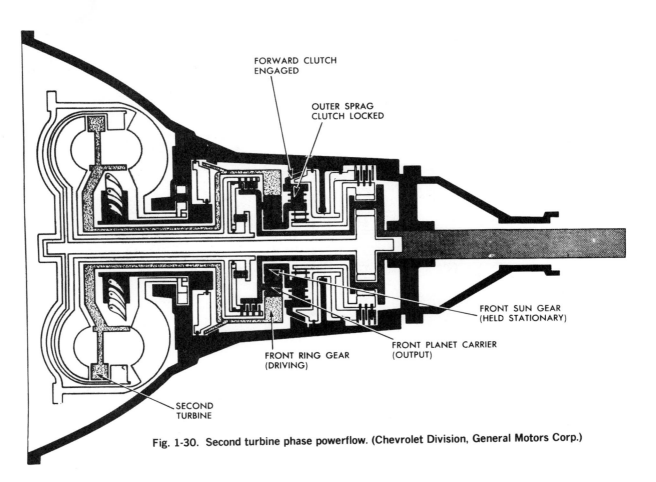

Fig. 1-30. Second turbine phase powerflow. (Chevrolet Division, General Motors Corp.)

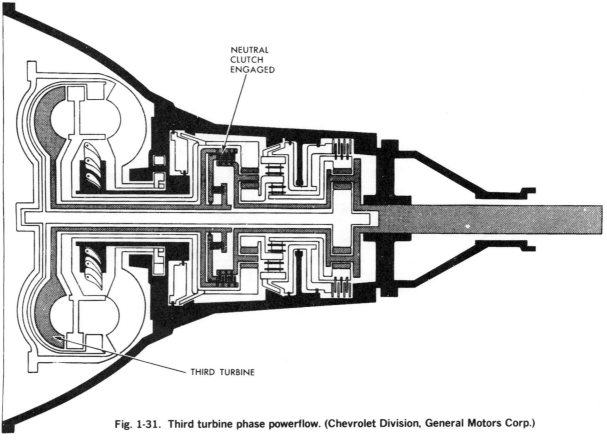

Fig. 1-31. Third turbine phase powerflow. (Chevrolet Division, General Motors Corp.)

The Turboglide transmission used a five-element polyphase torque converter. It consisted of three turbines, a variable pitch stator, and a pump (Fig. 1-28). Each turbine drives a separate shaft. As shown in Fig. 1-28, the first turbine drives the rear planetary sun gear, the second turbine drives the front planetary ring gear, and the third turbine is connected directly to the output shaft. With this arrangement, gear ratio changes occurred in absence of an automatic shift system or shift feel.

The maximum torque multiplication of the converter was 4.2:1 in the high stator position and 3.8 in the low position. In comparison, the Flight Pitch Dynaflow variable pitch action was unique from the Turboglide. It used a multiple-pitch stator that provided an infinite number of positions from low to high angle in response to throttle position.

When starting from rest, the first turbine rotated at the fastest speed and transmitted the greatest torque. This geared the first turbine to the propeller shaft at 2.67:1 (rear planetary gear set, Fig. 1-29). Because of the considerable difference in the blade angles, the second turbine rotated at $\frac{5}{8}$ and the third turbine at $\frac{3}{8}$ of turbine T_1 speed. As the speed difference between T_1 and the converter pump becomes less,

it is easier for the fluid to drive turbine T_2 and turbine T_3. The torque on the second turbine takes command and gears T_2 to the propeller shaft at 1.63:1 (front planetary gear set, Fig. 1-30). The first turbine no longer carries the torque and is released by the free-wheeling action of the rear ring gear. More progressive fluid action in the converter phases out T_2 as it approaches converter pump speed. The second turbine now freewheels as it is released by the sprag action on the front sun gear. With turbine T_1 and turbine T_2 phased out, turbine T_3 becomes effective and produces a hydraulic lock with the converter pump for a final 1:1 drive through the transmission (Fig. 1-31). The interaction between the turbines produce no "cut-in" sensation during ratio changes.

A "hill retarder" or coast clutch is included in the transmission to make the rear planetary effective during overrun conditions of the sprag clutches.

Chart 1-1 summarizes the Turboglide operation. Note that T_2 is locked in Reverse range and acts as another stator. The fluid flow is redirected by T_2 to produce a reverse torque on T_3. This converter action is combined with the use of both planetary sets for reverse operation (Fig. 1-32).

Fig. 1-32. Reverse powerflow. (Chevrolet Division, General Motors Corp.)

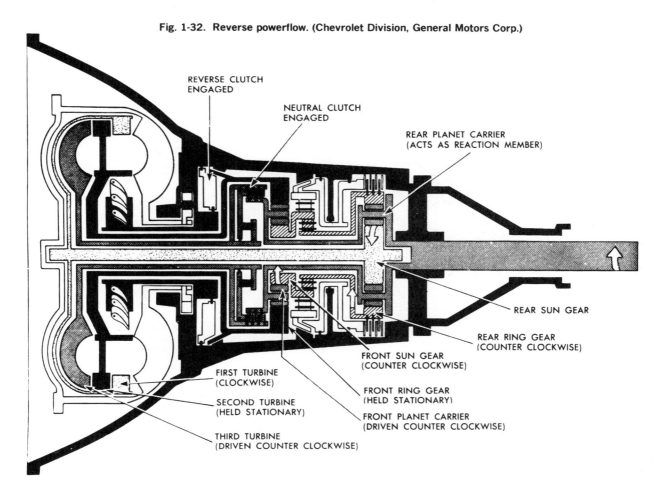

RANGE	APPROX. MPH	TURBINE ACTION			CLUTCH APPLICATION				SPRAG CONDITION		PLANETARY ACTION	
		T1	T2	T3	Reverse	Neutral	Forward	Grade Retard	Inner	Outer	1.6 Front	2.67 Rear
Drive	0-30	D	1	1	UA	A	A	UA	L	L	R	R
Drive	30-65	FW	D	1	UA	A	A	UA	UL	L	R	N
Drive	65—up	FW	FW	Coupling stage	UA	A	A	UA	UL	UL	N	N
Grade Retarder	45-0	Drives conv. pump	FW	FW	UA	UA	UA	A	UL	UL	N	R
Reverse	0—up	D	Locked	1 (In reverse)	A	A	UA	UA	L	UL	R	REV
Neutral	0	0	0	0	UA	UA	UA	UA	N	N	N	N
Park	0	0	0	0	UA	UA	UA	UA	N	N	N	N

D—Decreasing
I—Increasing
A—Applied
UA—Unapplied
L—Locked
UL—Unlocked
R—Reduction
N—Neutral
FW—Freewheeling

(Chevrolet Division, General Motors Corp.)

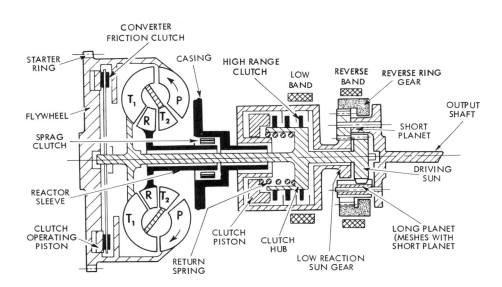

POWERFLOW SUMMARY CHART

	CONVERTER CLUTCH	HIGH CLUTCH	LOW BAND	REVERSE BAND
NEUTRAL	OFF	OFF	OFF	OFF
DRIVE CONVERTER & HIGH RANGE	OFF	ON	OFF	OFF
HIGH RANGE	ON	ON	OFF	OFF
LOW	ON	OFF	ON	OFF
REVERSE	OFF	OFF	OFF	ON

Later versions provided for low ratio in automatic drive range

Fig. 1-33. Packard Ultramatic transmission.

The last production year for the Turboglide was 1961 and for the Flight Pitch Dynaflow, 1959. The Flight Pitch was also known as the Triple Turbine.

Although General Motors did a considerable amount of pioneering in automatic transmissions, other car manufacturers made their contribution.

1949 The Packard Ultramatic made its entry with a four-element, two-stage converter drive featuring a lock-up clutch. Behind the converter was a Ravigneaux planetary gearbox identical to the Buick Dynaflow (Fig. 1-33).

The powerflow in forward drive is passed through the converter to the output shaft without additional gearing assists. The direct drive lock-up clutch in the converter, however, was affected by an automatic shift. For part-throttle and cruising conditions, the direct clutch was applied to provide a solid drive through the converter. For performance conditions, the converter direct clutch was off and could provide a maximum torque multiplication of 2.4:1. Low range, 1.82:1 gear ratio, could be manually engaged for extra power and engine braking.

1950 The Studebaker automatic transmission was manufactured by Borg-Warner. It featured a basic three-element converter with a lock-up clutch and three-speed planetary gearbox (Fig. 1-34).

Normal drive started through the converter (maximum torque multiplication 2.15:1) and intermediate gear ratio and then shifted to solid direct drive both in the converter and gear set. The gear ratios were as follows: first, 2.31:1; second, 1.43:1; and third, 1:1. Low range was manually engaged for extra pulling power or engine braking.

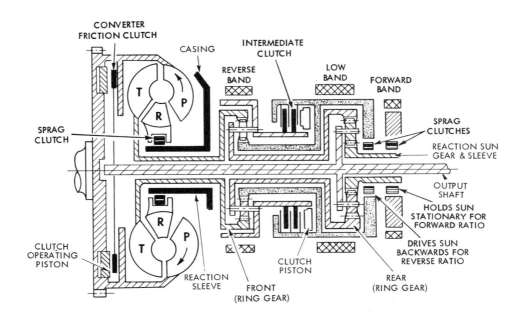

STUDEBAKER (BORG WARNER) EARLY DESIGN
3 SPEED TRANSMISSION

POWER FLOW CHART

	CONVERTER CLUTCH	INTERMEDIATE CLUTCH	FORWARD BAND	FORWARD SPRAG	LOW BAND	REVERSE BAND	REVERSE SPRAG
NEUTRAL	OFF	OFF	OFF	OFF	OFF	OFF	OFF
DRIVE INTERMEDIATE	OFF	ON	ON	ON	OFF	OFF	OFF
DIRECT DRIVE	ON	ON	ON	OFF	OFF	OFF	OFF
LOW	OFF	OFF	ON	ON	ON	OFF	OFF
REVERSE	OFF	OFF	OFF	OFF	OFF	ON	ON

Later versions provided for low range ratio in automatic drive range.

Fig. 1-34. Studebaker (Borg-Warner) transmissions.

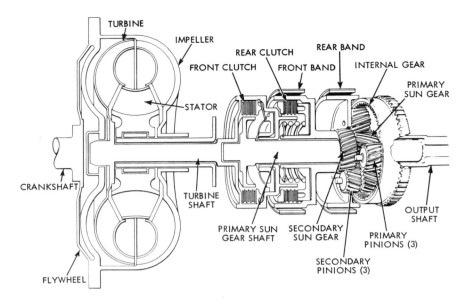

Fig. 1-35. Planetary gear train.

POWER FLOW SUMMARY CHART

OPERATING RANGE	FRONT BAND	FRONT CLUTCH	REAR BAND	REAR CLUTCH
NEUTRAL	OFF	OFF	OFF	OFF
DRIVE				
INTERMEDIATE	ON	ON	OFF	OFF
HIGH	OFF	ON	OFF	ON
LOW	OFF	ON	ON	OFF
REVERSE	OFF	OFF	ON	ON

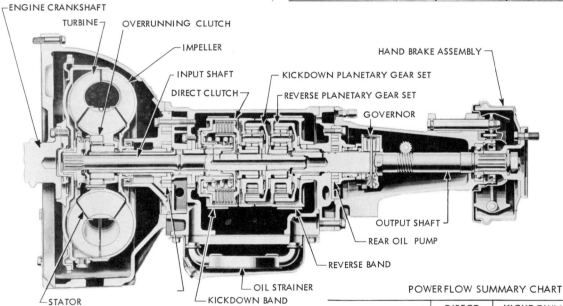

Fig. 1-36. PowerFlite transmission.
(Chrysler Corp.)

POWER FLOW SUMMARY CHART

	DIRECT CLUTCH	KICKDOWN BAND	REVERSE BAND
NEUTRAL	OFF	OFF	OFF
DRIVE AUTOMATIC LOW DIRECT DRIVE	OFF ON	ON OFF	OFF OFF
LOW	OFF	ON	OFF
REVERSE	OFF	OFF	ON

1951 Ford Motor Company introduced its three-speed Ford-O-Matic. Produced by Borg Warner, it used a basic three-element converter and dual pinion Ravigneaux gear system (Fig. 1-35). The converter provided a maximum torque multiplication of 2.1:1.

Normal drive started through the torque converter and intermediate gear ratio, 1.48:1, and automatically shifted to direct or converter drive only. A manual low range, 2.44:1 gear ratio, was used for extra pulling power or engine braking.

1953 The Chrysler Corporation Powerflite was a two-speed transmission that used a four-element polyphase converter and two planetary gear sets compounded together (Fig. 1-36). This provided for low, direct, and reverse gear ratios.

For forward drive operation, the powerflow started through the converter (maximum torque multiplication 2.7:1 and low gear ratio of 1.72:1) and automatically shifted to direct or converter drive only. The transmission could be manually locked in low range for extra pulling power or engine braking.

Although the original torque converter used a primary and secondary stator mounted back to back, the basic three-element design was later adopted.

TABLE 1-2. Introduction of Early Transmissions

Car Make	Transmission Trade Name	Model Year
		GENERAL MOTORS
Oldsmobile	Hydra-Matic	1940
Cadillac	Hydra-Matic	1941
Pontiac	Hydra-Matic	1948
Buick	Dynaflow	1948
Chevrolet	Powerglide[1], Cast Iron	1950
Chevrolet	Turboglide	1957
		FORD MOTOR COMPANY
Lincoln	GM Hydra-Matic	1950
Mercury	Merc-O-Matic[2] (Fig. 1-35)	1951
Ford	Ford-O-Matic	1951
		CHRYSLER CORPORATION
Chrysler and Imperial	Powerflite (Fig. 1-36)	1953
Dodge, DeSoto, and Plymouth	Powerflite	1954
Chrysler and Imperial	Torqueflite, Cast Iron	1956
Dodge, DeSoto, and Plymouth	Torqueflite, Cast Iron	1957
		OTHER MANUFACTURERS
Packard	Ultramatic (Fig. 1-33)	1949
Nash	GM Hydra-Matic	1950
Studebaker	Studebaker (Fig. 1-34)	1950
Kaiser-Frazer	GM Hydra-Matic	1951
Rambler	GM Hydra-Matic	1953
Willys	GM Hydra-Matic	1953

[1]The first design Powerglides, 1950-52, were almost exact copies of the early Buick Dynaflow. Automatic shifting was not introduced in the Powerglide until 1953 when the fluid torque converter and hydraulic control system were redesigned to produce a two-speed automatic shift transmission. The planetary gear train remained the same.

[2]The Merc-O-Matic and Ford-O-Matic transmissions were identical in design and operation. Produced by Borg-Warner, they differed only in torque capacity.

This chapter has described some of the major automatic transmission designs and innovations that occurred in their early development (summarized in Table 1-2). When comparing these transmissions with current production models, several conclusions can be drawn.

1. The automatic transmission was an almost instant success with the consumer. By 1955 it had firmly established itself and was offered as a standard or optional item by all automobile manufacturers. In today's car market, over 80% of the automobiles sold are equipped with automatic transmissions.

2. The attempt to develop a pure fluid converter drive has been abandoned. It lacked the competitive acceleration required at low speeds even when additional gearing was introduced.

3. The two-speed transmission did not offer the ideal compatibility with engine torque output and was also dropped.

4. The car manufacturers have apparently compromised the early design work. They now all favor an automatic transmission with a three-element torque converter augmented by a three-speed gearbox using either a Ravigneaux or Simpson planetary train. It is interesting to note that this concept was introduced in the early Borg-Warner Studebaker and Ford transmissions.

Transmission design and innovation had reached a peak by 1965-66 and nothing really significant happened until the demand for lighter cars and full economy became a serious factor in the 1970s. New transmissions began to appear and design modifications featuring light-weight construction in the traditional models has generated some excitement. Contributing to light-weight construction has been the application of electron beam welding in the manufacturing process of basic parts. Traditional cast iron clutch drums can now be fabricated from stampings that are joined together by the new welding process. The contrast in drum structure is shown in Figs. 1-37 and 1-38.

The following key developments have occurred since 1976. Summary details are fully discussed in Chapter 11.

• 1976 General Motors introduced its metric three-speed THM-200 (Fig. 1-39).

• 1978 Chrysler Corporation featured a torque converter lock-up clutch in a majority of its Torque-Flite 727 and 904 applications (Fig. 1-40).

• 1978 The Chrysler A-404 Automatic Transaxle combined a basic three-speed TorqueFlite with a differential assembly in one compact unit for its transverse mounted front-wheel drive Omni/Horizon (Figs. 1-41 and 1-42).

Fig. 1-37. Forward clutch drums.

Fig. 1-38. Direct clutch drums.

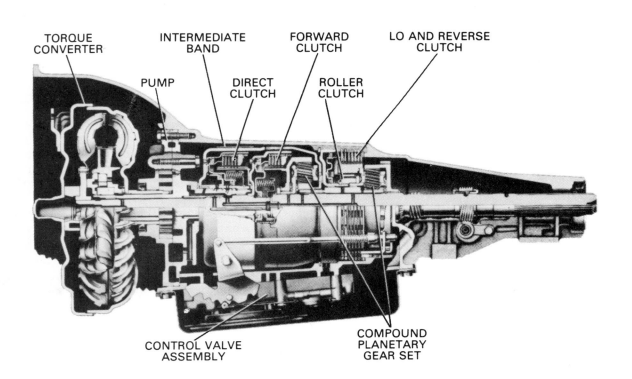

Fig. 1-39. THM 200 cut-away view. (Hydra-Matic Division, General Motors Corp.)

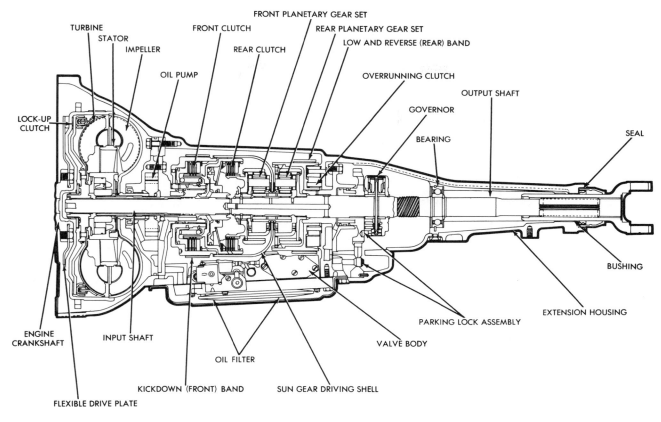

Fig. 1-40. Torqueflite transmission (A-904). (Chrysler Corp.)

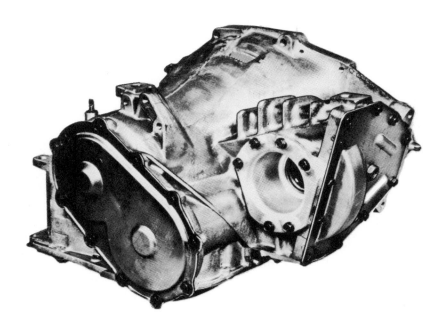

Fig. 1-41. A-404 case assembly. (Chrysler Corp.)

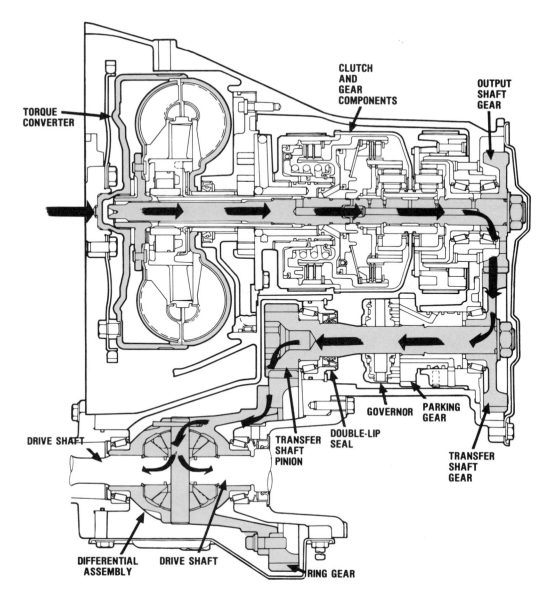

Fig. 1-42. Transmission to differential powerflow.

• 1979 The General Motors THM-325 used an adaptation of the THM-200 for a front-wheel drive application in the El Dorado, Riviera, and Toronado (Fig. 1-43).

• 1980 The General Motors THM 125 three-speed Automatic Transaxle was developed for use in its transverse mounted front-wheel drive applications used with small engines and light cars (Figs. 1-44 and 1-45).

• 1980 To eliminate converter slippage, General Motors developed a Torque Converter Clutch (TCC) for its family of automatic transmissions used on various intermediate and full-sized cars. The new con-

verter design is very similar to the Chrysler Lock Up Converter.

• 1980 Ford Motor Company took a bold step forward and introduced its AOT Transmission (Fig. 1-46). It was the first in the automotive industry to feature a built-in overdrive. The AOT is a four-speed transmission that achieves fourth gear overdrive using the basic gear set found in the three-speed cast iron FMX. Another notable feature is the direct mechanical drive (engine crankshaft to transmission overdrive clutch) provided in fourth gear. The converter hydraulic drive to the transmission is by-passed.

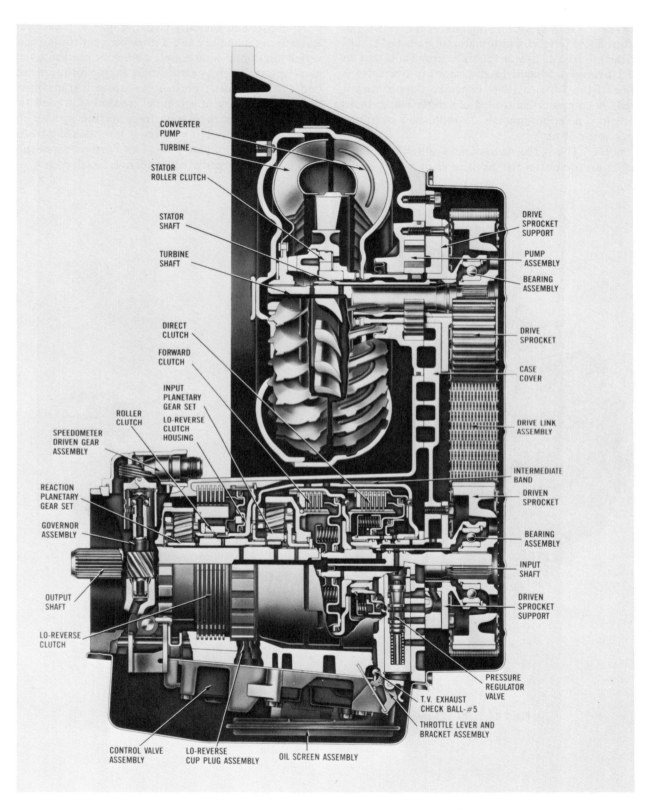

Fig. 1-43. THM-325 cut-away view. (Oldsmobile Division, General Motors Corp.)

•1981   General Motors introduces the THM 200-4R four-speed overdrive automatic for its B and C full-size car models. It uses a 1:1 third gear ratio and an 0.67:1 overdrive fourth. Engine speed in overdrive is reduced from 14% to 19%, depending upon the car model. A computer-controlled converter clutch locks up in third at approximately 25 mph, and overdrive fourth above 35 mph.

•1981   The ATX Automatic Transaxle is developed as an option on the 1.6-liter engine used in the Ford Escort and Mercury Lynx. It uses a three-speed Ravigneaux planetary and a three-element torque converter incorporating a simple planetary gearset acting as a "splitter". This gearset splits engine torque in second and third gears. Part of the torque is transmitted mechanically, like in a manual transmission, and the remainder by the hydraulic force on the turbine. In second gear 62% of the power is mechanically transmitted and in third gear 93%. This Ford patented split torque concept greatly reduces converter slippage.

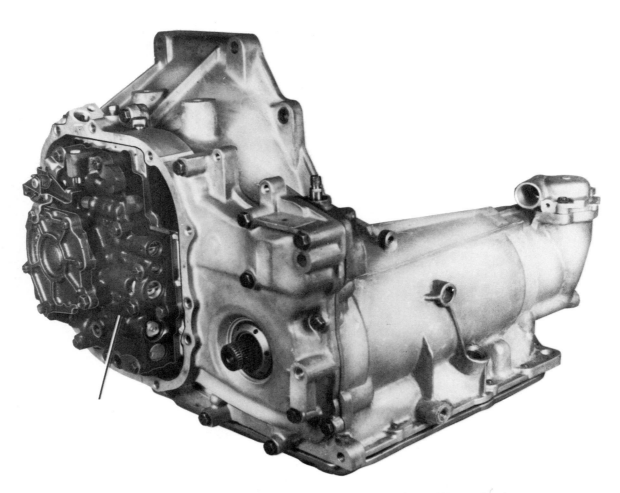

Fig. 1-44. THM-125 case assembly. (Hydra-Matic Division, General Motors Corp.)

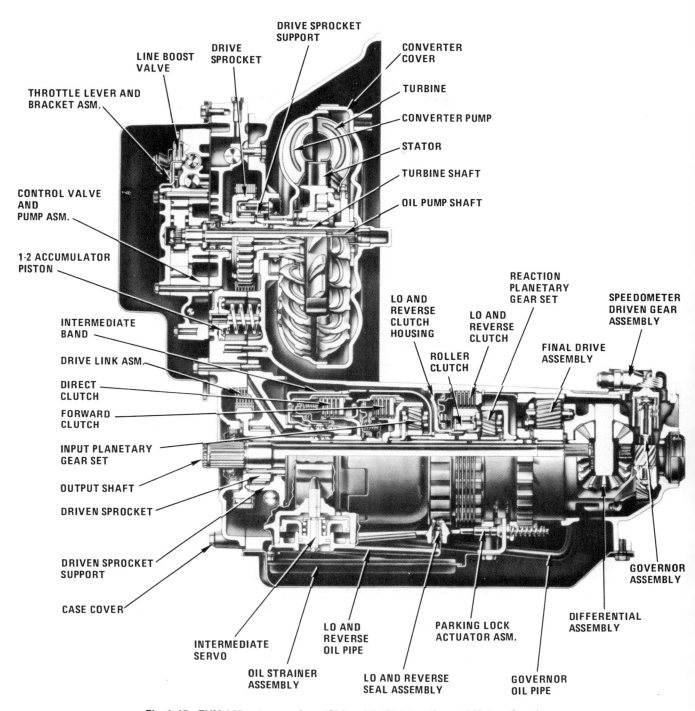

LINE BOOST VALVE

DRIVE SPROCKET

DRIVE SPROCKET SUPPORT

CONVERTER COVER

TURBINE

CONVERTER PUMP

STATOR

TURBINE SHAFT

OIL PUMP SHAFT

THROTTLE LEVER AND BRACKET ASM.

CONTROL VALVE AND PUMP ASM.

1-2 ACCUMULATOR PISTON

INTERMEDIATE BAND

DRIVE LINK ASM.

DIRECT CLUTCH

FORWARD CLUTCH

INPUT PLANETARY GEAR SET

OUTPUT SHAFT

DRIVEN SPROCKET

DRIVEN SPROCKET SUPPORT

CASE COVER

LO AND REVERSE CLUTCH HOUSING

ROLLER CLUTCH

REACTION PLANETARY GEAR SET

LO AND REVERSE CLUTCH

FINAL DRIVE ASSEMBLY

SPEEDOMETER DRIVEN GEAR ASSEMBLY

GOVERNOR ASSEMBLY

DIFFERENTIAL ASSEMBLY

INTERMEDIATE SERVO

OIL STRAINER ASSEMBLY

LO AND REVERSE OIL PIPE

LO AND REVERSE SEAL ASSEMBLY

PARKING LOCK ACTUATOR ASM.

GOVERNOR OIL PIPE

Fig. 1-45. THM 125 cut-away view. (Oldsmobile Division, General Motors Corp.)

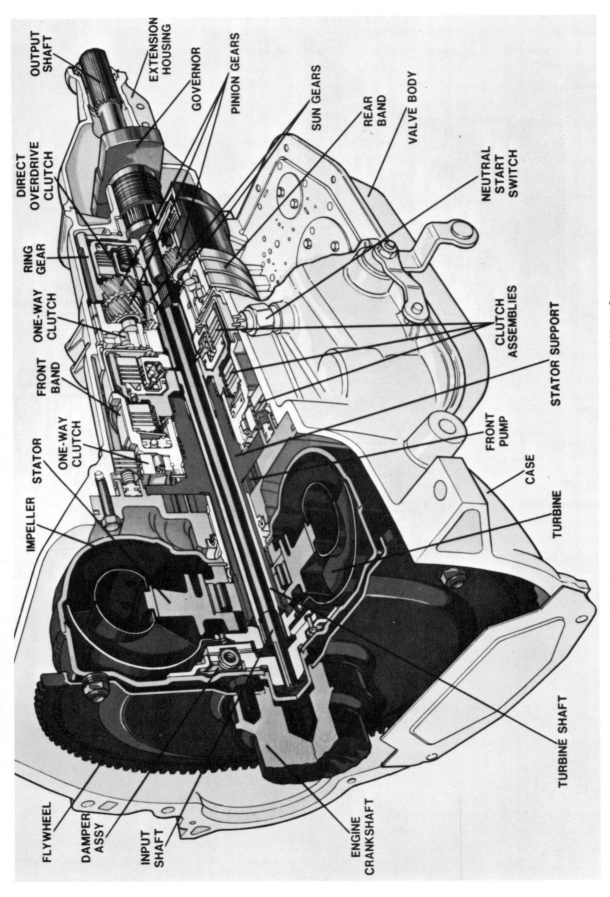

OUTPUT SHAFT

EXTENSION HOUSING

GOVERNOR

PINION GEARS

SUN GEARS

REAR BAND

VALVE BODY

NEUTRAL START SWITCH

DIRECT OVERDRIVE CLUTCH

RING GEAR

ONE-WAY CLUTCH

FRONT BAND

ONE-WAY CLUTCH

STATOR

IMPELLER

CLUTCH ASSEMBLIES

STATOR SUPPORT

FRONT PUMP

CASE

TURBINE

FLYWHEEL

DAMPER ASSY

INPUT SHAFT

ENGINE CRANKSHAFT

TURBINE SHAFT

Fig. 1-46. Ford automatic overdrive cut-away view. (Ford Motor Co.)

BRIEF OPERATIONAL DESCRIPTION

How an automatic transmission operates is an exciting story. The basic principles of operation can best be learned by a brief overview of how a typical automatic transmission works. This is easy because all self-shifting automatic transmissions operate in basically the same manner: a fluid torque converter is combined with a planetary gear set whose various gear ratios are automatically selected by a hydraulic control system (Fig. 1-47).

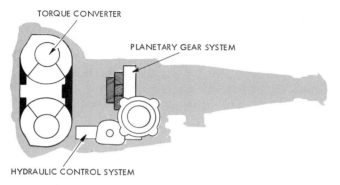

Fig. 1-47. Automatic transmission systems.

One of the great advantages of automatic shifting is that it takes the gear selection job away from the driver, who is not always skilled in sensing the correct gear ratio needed by the engine at a particular throttle opening and road load (road load is a function of weight, speed, and road grade). Whether the result is overspeeding or lugging the engine, the engine or the drive train is eventually damaged by an unskilled driver. There is also the direct hazard to a manual gearbox by the uncoordinated operator or the unorthodox speed shifter. The driver of an automatic-

Fig.1-48. Only the pressure on the accelerator is needed to operate the completely automatic transmission.

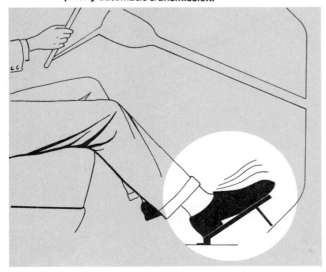

transmission-equipped automobile needs only to select an operating range and step on the accelerator, as in Fig. 1-48.

Control Systems

Here's how it works. The transmission has a system of controls that link it (1) to the engine and vehicle speed for influencing automatic shifts and (2) to the driver for manual selection of an operating range. These controls are respectively referred to as the throttle, governor, and manual control systems and will respectively have the following functions.

MANUAL CONTROL SYSTEM. Through linkage movement, the driver positions a manual valve in the valve body of the hydraulic control system and thus programs the transmission for the selected operating range (Fig. 1-49).

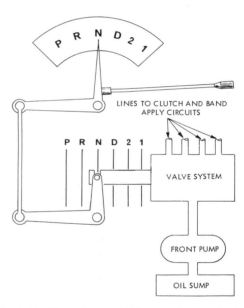

Fig. 1-49. Manual control linkage and manual valve establishes the selected operating range.

THROTTLE CONTROL SYSTEM. This system senses engine torque and hydraulically sends a pressure signal to the hydraulic control system valve body. It directly affects the shift schedule and shift quality.

The throttle control system consists of a regulator valve assembly within the valve body. It receives its input torque signal either by external mechanical linkage responding to gas pedal movement or by engine vacuum connected to an external vacuum control unit at the transmission (Fig. 1-50).

One more link-up for the transmission is necessary if automatic shifting is to take place. A governor system is provided to make the transmission sensitive to the road speed of the vehicle.

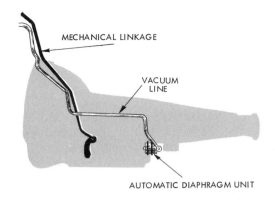

Fig. 1-50. Two methods are employed to send torque signals to the transmission: a mechanical linkage, or diaphragm control.

The manual, throttle, and governor links are part of the overall make-up of a much larger assemblage known as the hydraulic control system.

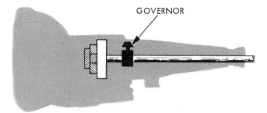

Fig. 1-51. Governor picks up road speed signal from the transmission output shaft.

GOVERNOR CONTROL SYSTEM. This system senses the variations in road speed from the transmission output shaft rpm and, like the throttle system, sends a hydraulic pressure signal to the hydraulic control system valve body. The governor signal causes the automatic shifts to occur. The system is made up of a regulating valve assembly equipped with centrifugal weights (Fig. 1-51).

HYDRAULIC CONTROL SYSTEM. This system consists of an engine-driven hydraulic pump and pressure regulator valve for supplying the necessary oil charge to the torque converter and to the valve body for distribution to the clutch and band apply circuits. The clutches and bands are the transmission working elements. They couple and hold planetary gear members to achieve ratio changes.

The valve body is the "brain" of the hydraulic control system and normally houses the manual valve, the throttle valve, a detent valve for forced downshifts by the driver's choice, and the automatic shift valve assembly (Figs. 1-52 and 1-53).

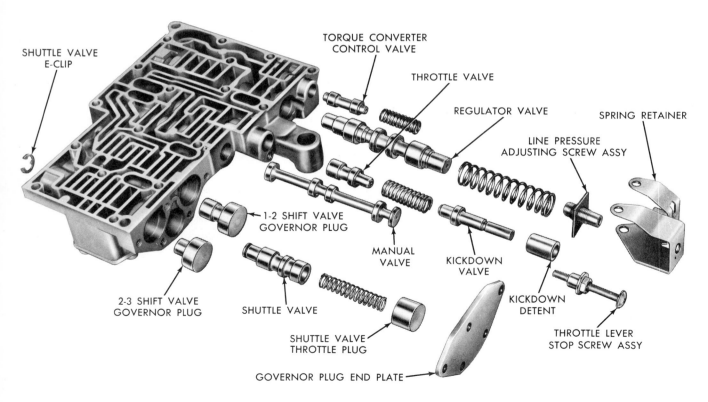

Fig. 1-52. Control valve assembly, right side. (Chrysler Corp.)

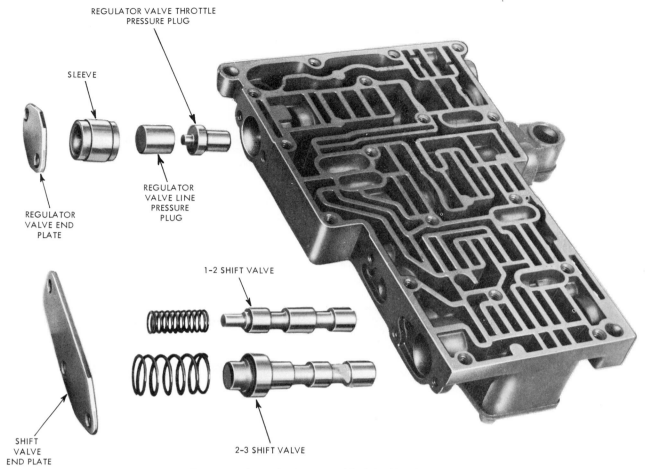

REGULATOR VALVE THROTTLE PRESSURE PLUG

SLEEVE

REGULATOR VALVE LINE PRESSURE PLUG

REGULATOR VALVE END PLATE

1-2 SHIFT VALVE

SHIFT VALVE END PLATE

2-3 SHIFT VALVE

Fig. 1-53. Control valve assembly, left side. (Chrysler Corp.)

Automatic Shift Operation

With the system controls defined let's consider how a typical automatic transmission shift system works. In Fig. 1-54, a simple block diagram illustrates the shift system make-up. The throttle pressure is a variable-regulated engine torque signal and represents the driver intent; governor pressure is a variable-regulated vehicle speed signal and will cause the shift to happen. These two pressure signals are transmitted to a shift control containing the shift valves, whereby an engineered shift schedule dictates the proper gear ratio for the vehicle operating conditions.

Figures 1-55, 1-56, 1-57 and 1-58 represent a typical shift system used in a three-speed automatic transmission. The main supply oil to the manual valve is provided by the transmission pump and will be used for working the bands and clutches to attain the proper gear ratio.

In neutral, the manual valve shuts off the mainline oil to the operating ranges and all friction elements remain released (Fig. 1-55). When the manual valve is indexed for *automatic drive,* the forward clutch is applied and the shift valve circuits are charged with mainline oil (Fig. 1-56). The torque converter and transmission low gear combine to multiply engine torque in response to engine throttle opening and the vehicle moves smoothly forward. Note that the forward clutch circuit is controlled by the manual valve and is not an automatic shift function. The intermediate and direct drive circuits, however, are controlled by the shift valves (Figs. 1-57 and 1-58).

SHIFT SYSTEM BLOCK DIAGRAM WITH VACUUM THROTTLE CONTRL

MANIFOLD VACUUM

UPSHIFT DIRECTION

GOVERNOR (ROAD SPEED)

SHIFT VALVE

THROTTLE PRESSURE

VACUUM DIAPHRAGM UNIT

DOWNSHIFT DIRECTION

MAINLINE OPERATING PRESSURE

Fig. 1-54.

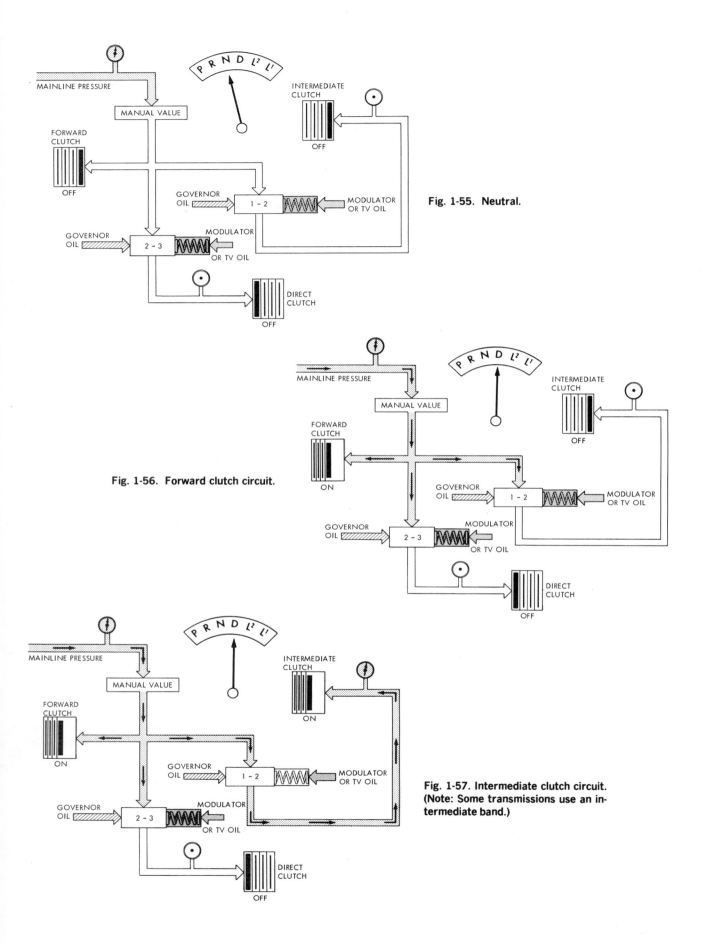

Fig. 1-55. Neutral.

Fig. 1-56. Forward clutch circuit.

Fig. 1-57. Intermediate clutch circuit.
(Note: Some transmissions use an intermediate band.)

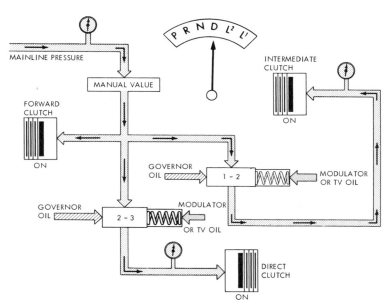

Fig. 1-58. Direct clutch circuit.

Keeping in mind the purpose of the throttle and governor systems, 1–2 and 2–3 shift timing is achieved in the following manner. If acceleration takes place at a light throttle opening, the regulated throttle pressure at the shift valve spring end is light. This combined throttle and spring pressure keeps the shift valves in a closed position. Because a gear ratio change depends on engine torque versus road speed, the regulated governor pressure opposes the throttle and spring resistance at the opposite end of the shift valve and tries to open the valve.

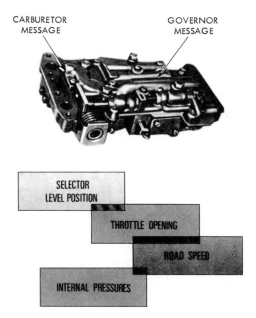

Fig. 1-59. The valve body receives signals from the throttle and the governor and shifts automatically.

Thus, at light throttle, a minimum of governor pressure will move the shifter valves from the closed to the open position and cause the shifts to occur at relatively low vehicle speeds. When the 1–2 and 2–3 shift valves open in sequence, mainline oil charges the intermediate and direct clutch circuits. Although the 1–2 and 2–3 shift valves receive the same throttle and governor signals, internal valve and spring dimensions are designed to provide an appropriate shift spread.

Heavier throttle conditions required for rapid acceleration or hill grades add more throttle pressure to the normal resistance of the shifter valve spring. This means that more vehicle speed is required to raise the necessary governor pressure to open the shift valve. This interaction between the throttle and governor pressures is engineered to give a variable shift pattern to match any throttle and road load condition. The valve body, or brain, works like a computer. It is programmed for the operating range by the manual valve and receives two signals, one from the throttle system and another from the governor system. These signals are then transmitted to an automatic shift valve to determine the shift point (Fig. 1-59).

On closed throttle, such as when braking for a stop, throttle pressure is zero and governor pressure is simply overcome by spring tension and the transmission shifts back to low gear just before the vehicle stops.

Within safe vehicle speed ranges that will permit the engine to accelerate and not over-speed itself, the shift valves can be overruled for a forced downshift by driver's choice. The accelerator is simply depressed to the wide open throttle position and the transmission shifts 3–2 or 3–1 for added performance.

Electronic Shift Control

Soon to become a reality is the application of electronic programming for transmission shift schedule control. A proposed production configuration is illustrated in Fig. 1-60. In brief, the system still must interpret a vehicle speed and throttle signal to trigger the shifts. Vehicle speed is measured from a magnetic pick-up located at the transmission park gear and engine load is measured by a three-contact wiper switch mounted just above the throttle pedal. When the shifts are to occur, the solenoids open the valves. This operation is described in more detail in Chapter 7.

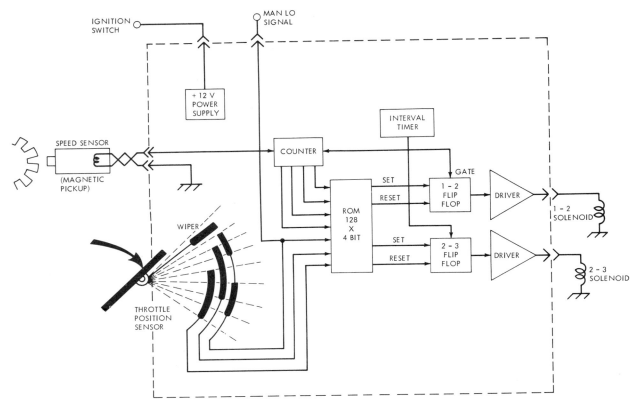

Fig. 1-60. Futuristic electronic shift control. (S.A.E.)

REVIEW QUESTIONS

CHAPTER 1
DEVELOPMENT OF AUTOMATIC TRANSMISSIONS

Completion:

1. The term *Power Train* includes all the drive components between the engine _____ and the _____ _____ wheels.

2. Starting with the flywheel name in sequence the typical components that make-up the *Power Train* using a manual transmission.

REAR WHEEL DRIVE

a. Engine flywheel

b. _____

c. _____

d. _____

e. _____

f. _____

g. _____

3. List the functions of the transmission:

   a. _____

   b. _____

   c. _____

   d. _____

4. The ability of the atmosphere to charge the engine cylinders with a quantity of air/fuel mixture is called

   _____.

5. Name the three factors that produce the driveshaft torque for vehicle acceleration.

   a. _____

   b. _____

   c. _____

6. Name the three factors that determine the road load on the engine.

   a. _____

   b. _____

   c. _____

7. To attain third gear, the transmission should shift gears 1-2 and 2-3 just before the driveshaft torque drops below the _____.

8. An early turn of the century car that used a manually operated transmission with planetary gears:

   _____.

9. The first manually operated synchromesh transmission was introduced by Cadillac in production year _____.

10. The first manually operated transmission equipped with automatic overdrive was introduced by Chrysler in production year _____.

11. The introduction of the fluid coupling for transmission application in domestic passenger cars was pioneered by

    _____ in production year _____.

12. The first fully automatic transmission was introduced

    by _____ in production year _____.

    It utilized a fluid coupling and_____ speed planetary system.

13. List the production year in which the following G.M. Hydra-Matic transmissions were introduced.

    _____ Controlled Coupling Hydra-Matic

    _____ Roto Hydra-Matic

14. Name the Hydra-Matic transmission that featured the use of two fluid couplings. _____.

15. Name the Hydra-Matic transmission that featured the use of a fluid coupling incorporating a torque multiplier. _____.

16. Name two early historical transmissions that featured the use of a converter with a lock-up clutch.

    a. _____ b. _____

17. Name three early historical G.M. transmissions that pioneered in polyphase converter drivers.

    a. _____

    b. _____

    c. _____

18. The variable pitch stator was a design feature introduced in the _____ production year Dynaflow.

19. For improved low speed acceleration the 1953 Buick Dynaflow converter drive design used a_____ turbine, four element converter incorporating a

    _____.

20. In efforts to develop improved fluid converter drives, General Motors introduced the Chevrolet _____ _____ in 1957 and Buick _____ in 1958.

21. The Chevrolet Powerglide was introduced as a fluid converter drive in production year _____. It was converted into a two-speed automatic transmission using a three-element torque converter in production year _____. The aluminum case Powerglide came of age in production year _____ and gave many years of dependable service. The last production year of the aluminum Powerglide was _____.

22. Chrysler Corporation introduced its first fully automatic transmission in production year _____. It was a two-speed design named the _____.

23. Ford Motor Company entered its first automatic transmission in production year _____. It was a three-speed Borg-Warner unit called the _____

    _____.

24. In what production year were the following automatic 3-speed transaxles introduced for small size car applications.

_____ Chrysler A-404

_____ General Motors THM 125

_____ Ford ATX

25. The Ford 4-speed automatic overdrive transmission was introduced in production year _____ and is referred to as the _____ Transmission.

26. The General Motors 4-speed automatic overdrive transmission was introduced in production year _____ and is referred to as the _____ Transmission.

AUTOMATIC TRANSMISSION SHIFT OPERATION

1. The control system that selects or programs the transmission operating range. _____

2. The control system that senses engine torque and sends a regulated hydraulic pressure signal to the shift valves. _____

3. The control system that senses vehicle speed and sends a regulated hydraulic pressure signal to the shift valves.

_____

4. The control system that provides the hydraulic signal to open the shift valves. _____

5. The control system that provides the hydraulic signal to delay the shifts. _____

6. Generates the necessary operating pressure and fluid supply to the torque converter and to the clutch/band circuits. _____

7. Name the two types of external controls that are used to relay the engine torque signal to the transmission throttle control system. _____

and _____.

8. The force that closes the shift valve on closed throttle downshifts. _____

9. The valve that controls the forward clutch circuit.____

_____

10. The valve that controls the reverse circuit._____

_____

11. The valve that controls the intermediate circuit.____

_____

12. The valve that controls the direct circuit._____

_____

2

HYDRODYNAMIC

UNITS

Hydrodynamic drive units, the fluid coupling, and the fluid torque converter have been used in semi- and fully-automatic transmissions on millions of American passenger cars since the introduction of the fluid coupling in 1938 and the fluid torque converter in 1948. At least one such hydrodynamic unit has been used since in all past and present automatic passenger car transmissions.

Hydrodynamic drive units are a European and not an American development. Dr. Hermann Fottinger, a German engineer working with the Vulcan shipyards in Stettin, Germany, built the first experimental fluid drive unit, a torque converter, in 1908. This was developed and used as a speed reducer for high horse-power steam turbines for ship propulsion (Fig. 2-1, left). A modern version with a stator is shown in Fig. 2-1, right.

Fig. 2-1. The Fottinger torque converter; the guide wheel, now called the reactor or stator, is the name used by the inventor; and a modern three element converter coupling used in passenger cars. (Ford Motor Co.)

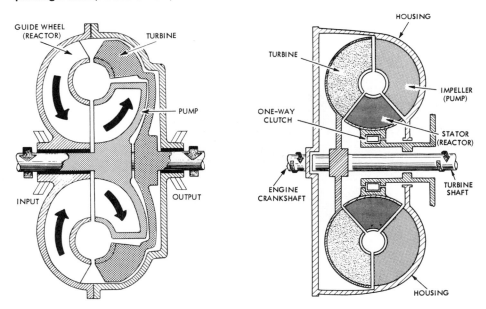

Fottinger's torque converter gave a speed reduction of 5:1 and operated at an efficiency of 85%. His converter, however, was soon replaced by the geared turbine drive, which was less expensive and even more efficient.

Further progress on fluid drives continued at the Vulcan yards along with marine application of the diesel engine. Diesel engines had then reached a stage at which they were beginning to be used for very large marine installations. However, these engines had an objectionable torsional vibration that was imparted to the gear drives and into the ship structure.

In order to dampen these vibrations, a fluid drive unit was designed that was a modification of the original Fottinger converter. It was found that by eliminating the reaction member, a functional two-member fluid coupling was created that developed no extra torque but had a very high efficiency of 98% (Fig. 2-2). Marine hydraulic couplings continue to be used today.

The coupling and the converter in their early stages were two distinct and separate units and were not combined as a single unit, as is common in current practices. The greater efficiency of the fluid coupling over the converter was the reason for its wider use.

Some attempts were made, however, to take advantage of both the coupling and converter characteristics. The Fottinger drives were applied to some locomotive transmissions that used a converter and a fluid coupling in series. The transition from converter drive to coupling drive was made by emptying the fluid from the converter and then filling the coupling that had previously been empty.

In the years between World War I and World War II, much of the work on fluid drives took place in England and Germany. Alan Coats, a young engineer with Vickers in England, made a significant discovery

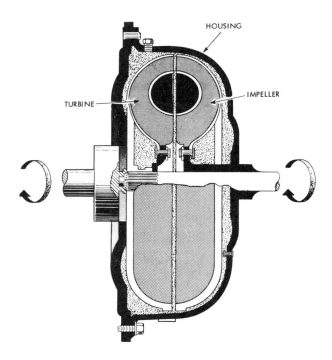

Fig. 2-2. Simplified fluid coupling.

when he saw the possibility of using roller clutches or freewheeling devices on the reaction member for transforming a fluid converter into a fluid coupling within a single drive unit. He obtained a U.S. patent in 1930 and is considered to be the inventor of the converter-coupling. Coats died while his work was still in the experimental stages but his invention is employed in modern converters. The converter–coupling concept continued to be developed in Europe following the Vickers-Coats development, with several other patents being filed.

In the meantime, extensive work by Harold Sinclair, a British engineer, led to a successful drive application of the two-member fluid coupling in motor

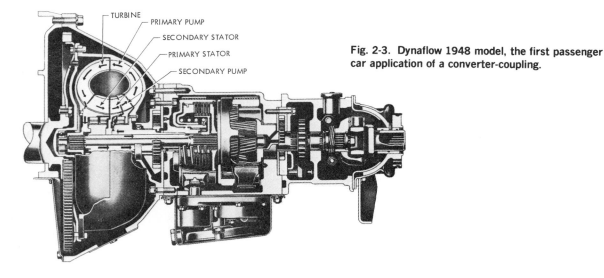

Fig. 2-3. Dynaflow 1948 model, the first passenger car application of a converter-coupling.

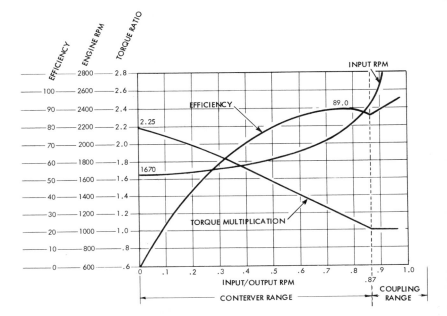

Fig. 2-4. A torque converter performance curve. (Chrysler Corp.)

buses and automobiles. Eventual adoption of his fluid coupling in the United States by Chrysler Corporation occurred under license in 1938.

It was not until after World War II that a converter-coupling was applied to an American passenger car. In 1948, the Buick Motor Division of General Motors Corporation introduced a five element fluid unit on its newly designed Dynaflow transmission (Fig. 2-3).

Following the Dynaflow development, most of the success with converter work has occurred in the United States. Converter applications are now used extensively in domestic and foreign passenger cars, trucks, and buses. A wide variety of heavy-duty construction machinery also uses converters, such as wheeled and track-laying tractors, loaders, cranes, lift trucks, graders, earth movers, and large farm tractors.

In modern passenger cars, the torque converter has gradually taken over as the prime fluid drive unit. The fluid coupling has not been used in American automatic transmissions since 1965. When using the term torque converter in connection with automatic transmissions, it is understood that it has the dual function. It must act as a torque multiplier with infinitely variable ratios from its maximum engineered torque output to unity (1:1) where it acts as a fluid coupling (Fig. 2-4).

The converter offers several desirable operating features. It is a simple, rugged unit that operates as a clutch in a constant oil bath that gives unlimited life and requires no maintenance, in contrast to the foot-operated friction clutch that it eliminated. Because it is a fluid unit, it provides a silky, smooth attachment of the engine power to the vehicle that eliminates any sudden engagement shock to the power train components and results in their longer life and reduced repair costs.

Another dividend is the excellent dampening of engine vibration that is taken up by the fluid before it extends into the transmission and drive line. The converter can be likened to a cushion that protects the power train from shocks and vibrations and prevents lugging or stalling of the engine.

Although a variety of fluid torque converter designs have been used in automatic transmissions, the simple three-element unit (impeller, turbine, and stator) is currently used. The discussion of converter operation concentrates on this unit.

TERMINOLOGY—HYDRODYNAMIC DRIVES

Before engaging in a discussion of the fluid coupling and torque converter, some of the common terminology that is used later to describe the make-up and operation of these units now follows for review and quick reference.

ELEMENT. An element is a vaned member with a single row of flow directing blades. In a simple torque converter, the impeller, the turbine, and the stator each have a single row of flow directing blades, thus the term three-element converter.

FLUID COUPLING. The simplest form of hydrodynamic drive. It consists of two look-alike members referred to as the impeller (pump) and turbine. Input torque is always equal to the output torque; maximum efficiency is unity or 1:1.

HYDRODYNAMIC DRIVE. A drive that transmits power solely by the action of a kinetic fluid flow in a closed recirculating path. An impeller energizes the fluid and discharges a high speed jet stream into a turbine, which transfers the fluid force to the turbine for power output.

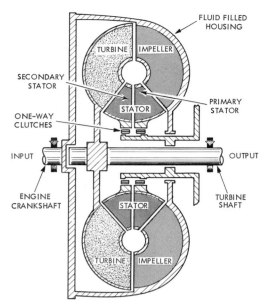

Fig. 2-5. Three member, four element converter; the stator member is made of two elements mounted on separate overrunning clutches that can freewheel independently; used in early converters.

IMPELLER.   This is the power input member of a hydrodynamic drive. It acts as a centrifugal pump and puts the fluid in motion. An impeller is sometimes called a pump, which is technically correct; use of the word *impeller* is recommended, however, to avoid confusion with pressure and other kinds of pumps.

MEMBER.   A member is an independent component of a hydrodynamic unit such as an impeller, a stator, or a turbine. It may comprise one or more elements (Fig. 2-5).

ONE-WAY CLUTCH.   A mechanical device that transmits or holds torque in one direction only. The roller design application is favored for use with converter–stator operation (Fig. 2-6).

Fig.2-6. Viewed from front, typical cross section of one-way roller clutch. (Buick Division, General Motors Corp.)

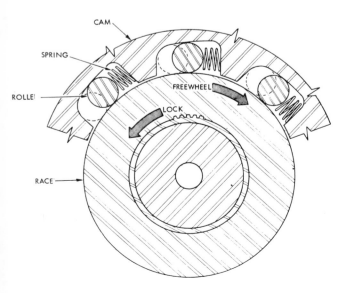

REACTOR (stator).   The reaction member of a fluid torque converter. It is commonly called a stator. In engineering language, the term *reactor* is preferred because the word describes its function.

STAGE.   Refers to the number of turbine sets separated by a stator. A turbine set may be made-up of one or more turbine members. A three element converter would be classified as a single stage.

STATOR.   (See REACTOR.)

TORQUE CONVERTER.   A hydrodynamic drive that has the ability to multiply torque. In automatic transmission applications, it is more correct to refer to the converter as a converter–coupling. It is designed to also perform as a fluid coupling.

TURBINE.   The driven or output member of a fluid coupling or fluid torque converter.

Hydrodynamic drives have involved a lot of brainstorming that has resulted in a collective experience of different designs and developments. Although it is not the objective of this chapter to be involved with the properties and characteristics of all these fluid drive forms, it is desirable to briefly get acquainted with terminology used in their classification. Five classifications are generally used, the first three having just been defined.

1. Fluid Coupling.
2. Fluid Converter.
3. Converter-Coupling.
4. Multi-stage Converter. It is used to attain the highest torque ratios. This is accomplished by using the circulating fluid to drive two or more turbine members, which are separated by a stator member. The first-stage conversion occurs when the fluid has discharged from the pump through the first turbine and is redirected by the stator to drive the second turbine. Examples are given in Table 2-1.
5. Polyphase Converter–Coupling. A polyphase converter–coupling is a variation of the basic three-element fluid unit. One or more of the three members is divided into further elements. Examples are given in Table 2-1.

In describing a fluid drive unit it is also the practice to make reference to the number of elements and stages that make up the unit.

Table 2-1 reviews the several fluid drive classifications as they apply to design configuration used in the development of automatic transmission.

TABLE 2-1
Classification of Hydrodynamic Drives
Early Development Designs

Name of Transmission	Classification	Fluid Flow Circuit Diagram
1948 Buick Dynaflow	5-element polyphase converter-coupling	T, P, S, P
1953 Buick Twin Turbine Dynaflow	4-element polyphase converter-coupling	T_1, T_2, P, S
1955 Buick Variable-Pitch Dynaflow	4-element polyphase converter-coupling w/variable pitch stator	T_1, T_2, P, V.P.S
1956 Buick Variable-Pitch Two-Stage Dynaflow	5-element two-stage converter-coupling w/variable pitch stator	S, T_1, T_2, P, V.P.S
1958 Buick Flight Pitch Dynaflow	5-element polyphase converter-coupling w/variable pitch stator	T_2, T_1, T_3, P, V.P.S
1950 Chevrolet Powerglide	5-element polyphase converter-coupling	T, P, S, P
1953 Chevrolet Powerglide	3-element converter-coupling	T, P, S
1957 Chevrolet Turboglide	5-element polyphase converter-coupling w/variable pitch stator	T_2, T_1, T_3, P, V.P.S
1938 Chrysler Fluid Drive	2-element coupling	T, P
1951 Chrysler Fluid Torque — 1954 Chrysler Powerflite	4-element polyphase converter-coupling	T, P, S, S
1956 Chrysler Powerflite — Chrysler Torqueflite	3-element converter-coupling	T, P, S
1951 Ford Fordomatic (Borg-Warner)	3-element converter-coupling	T, P, S
1949 Packard Ultramatic	4-element two-stage converter-coupling	T_1, P, S, T_2
1950 Studebaker (Borg-Warner)	3-element converter-coupling	T, P, S

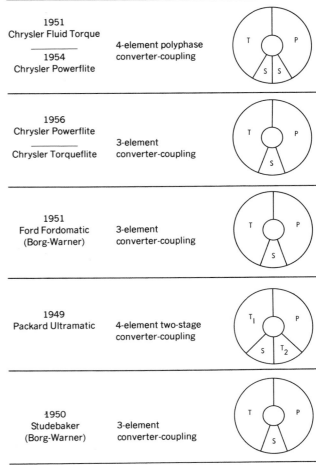

THE FLUID COUPLING

Because the fluid coupling is the simplest form of fluid drive unit, the principles of fluid coupling operation serve as an ideal introduction to how a fluid force can put a solid object into motion. Some of these working principles will apply later to the discussion on the fluid converter-coupling operation.

Fig. 2-7. Coupling members (impeller and turbine) are identical. (Pontiac Division, General Motors Corp.)

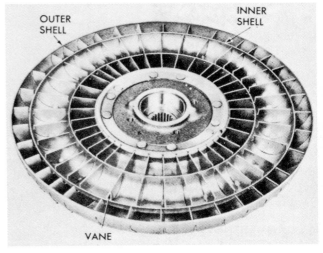

OUTER SHELL INNER SHELL VANE

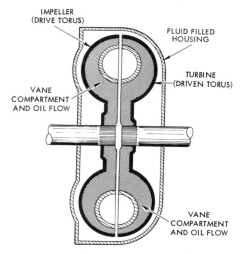

Fig. 2-8. Coupling turbine and impeller member in a housing. (Pontiac Division, General Motors Corp.)

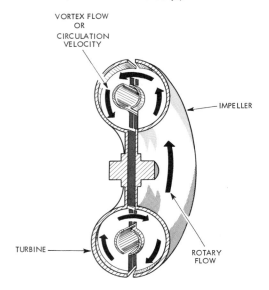

Fig. 2-9. Rotary and vortex flow shown. (Chrysler Corp.)

Fig. 2-10. Swinging bucket shows both rotary and vortex forces.

The construction of a fluid coupling is very simple. It consists of impeller and turbine members of indentical structure contained in a housing filled with oil (Figs. 2-7 and 2-8). The coupling members face one another closely with the impeller driven by the engine and the turbine driving the wheels through the transmission and axle.

Operation

The following describes what happens inside a fluid coupling when starting the car, or accelerating under heavy load. As the engine drives the impeller, it sets the fluid mass into motion creating a fluid force. The path of the fluid force strikes on a solid object, the turbine. The impact of the fluid jet stream against the turbine blades sets the turbine in motion. An energy cycle has been completed; mechanical to fluid and back to mechanical.

The fluid action that takes place between the impeller and turbine is an interesting science. When the impeller spins-up, two separate forces are generated in the fluid. One is *rotary flow,* which is the rotational effort or inertia of the impeller rotation. The other is *vortex flow,* which circulates the fluid between the coupling members and is caused by the centrifugal pumping action of the rotating impeller (Fig. 2-9). The vortex flow is the fluid exist velocity from the impeller.

The rotary and vortex flows can also be explained by using a bucket of water as an example. Any time there is a spinning mass, the mass (in the case of a transmission, the oil) follows the rotational movement but it also creates a centrifugal force. This dual effect is illustrated by swinging a bucket of water in a circle (Fig. 2-10). As the bucket is swinging, the water is following the circular path of the bucket. At the same time it is developing a centrifugal force that keeps the water in the bucket as it passes through the overhead position. The water is confined by the solid side and bottom of the bucket and cannot discharge (fly) outward, so it is forced to follow the bucket rotation only.

In a fluid coupling, however, the centrifugal force of the oil is not confined. The oil at the center of the spinning impeller follows the curved shell and is discharged along the outer diameter and into the turbine to establish a circular path between the impeller and the turbine (Fig. 2-11 top and bottom). The combination of rotary and vortex flow causes an oil motion that follows the course of a rotating corkscrew. It is like watching the blade tips of a rotating pinwheel at the end of a stick with the stick itself turning about a center (Fig. 2-12).

With the corkscrew oil action created by the rotation of the engine driven impeller, the turbine is pushed around ahead of the oil, striking on the turbine

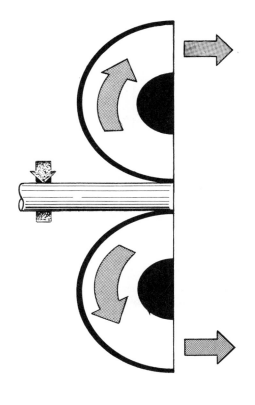

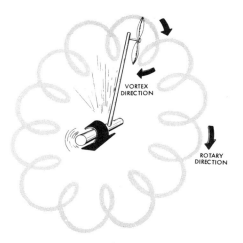

Fig. 2-12. Explanation of rotary vortex motion.

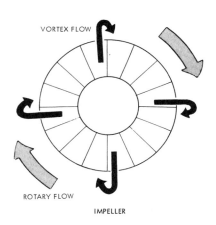

Fig. 2-11. View of oil discharged from impeller-vortex flow; side and front views of impeller showing pumping action on fluid.

blades. A fluid clutch is thus established, with the turning torque on the turbine never exceeding impeller input torque.

Let's define these two flows:

VORTEX FLOW. The crosswise or circulatory flow of oil between the blades of the members caused by the centrifugal pumping action of the impeller.

ROTARY FLOW. The flow of the fluid trapped between the blades of the members assumes the direction of the impeller rotation (rotational inertia).

Speed Ratio

The striking force of the fluid on the turbine can be explained from a slightly more technical viewpoint. In doing this it become necessary to define another term that reflects the efficiency of a fluid coupling or a torque converter.

The number of revolutions that the turbine makes relative to one rotation of the impeller is its *speed ratio*, which is expressed in percentages. For example, if the impeller rotation is 1,000 rpm and turbine rotation 900 rpm the speed rotation is 90%.

$$\text{speed ratio} = \frac{\text{turbine rpm}}{\text{impeller rpm}} \text{ or } \frac{900}{1,000} = 90\%$$

Just when the car starts to move there is an instant moment when the impeller is rotating and the turbine has not begun to move, a condition of zero speed ratio. During this situation the following rotary and vortex flow conditions are in effect:

1. Because the turbine is stationary the vortex flow cycles through the turbine unopposed, giving a massive cross circulation between the coupling members (Fig. 2-13).

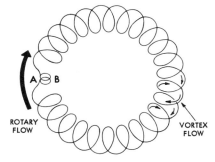

Fig. 2-13. Rotary and vortex flow during the condition of zero speed ratio.

2. The stationary turbine also opposes the rotary flow and the moving oil does not favor rotary flow (also Fig. 2-13).

The direction of the oil striking on the turbine is determined by the strength of the respective oil flows. This is illustrated by the vector diagram in Fig. 2-14. The diagram shows the movement of both the vortex flow and the rotary flow and the obvious fact that the direction of impact cannot move in two directions at the same time. The direction of fluid thrust that results from the two flows will be at a resultant angle to the rotary and the vortex action, as determined by the speed ratio, or drive condition.

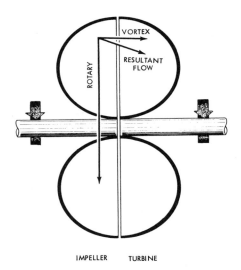

Fig. 2-15. Vortex and rotary impact angle with turbine stationary.

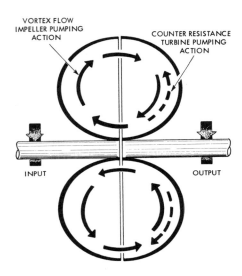

Fig. 2-16. As the turbine begins to turn a counter pumping action builds up.

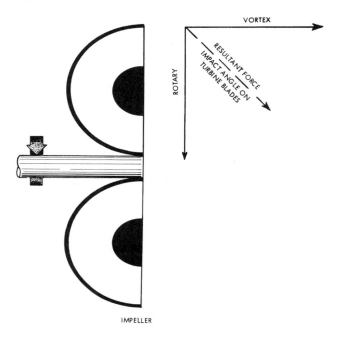

Fig. 2-14. Vector diagram of impact force of rotary and vortex flow.

Going back to the coupling start condition, it is evident that the high rate of vortex flow does not have a favorable oil impact on the turbine blades; however, it is sufficient to get the turbine moving, as shown in Fig. 2-15. Considerable slipping takes place because the fluid impact is only striking a glancing blow on the straight blades of the turbine.

As the turbine begins to rotate and catch up to impeller speed, the vortex flow gradually slows down because of the counter pumping action of the turbine (Fig. 2-16). This permits the rotary action to become the greater influence on the fluid and the resultant thrust becomes more effective in propelling the turbine. Finally, at 90% speed ratio the rotary inertia or momentum of the fluid and coupling members form a hydraulic lock and turn at unity. The fluid coupling is now operating at its coupling point and maximum efficiency. Figures 2-17 and 2-18 illustrate the vortex and rotary flow conditions and their effect on the resultant fluid thrust at the coupling point.

The change from a state of coupling slip to a state of coupling full torque occurs quite rapidly and is effective in controlling excessive engine run-up in the process. In all instances, whether within a coupling or a converter, no torque is transmitted unless there is a circulation of oil through the members (vortex flow). This circulation is necessary to keep the bladed sections pumped full of oil so that the effect of the rotary thrust is realized. At maximum efficiency the coupling or converter must operate with some slippage. If the turbine turned at exactly impeller speed, vortex flow would cease and coupling action would be lost.

Another feature of a coupling or converter is the ability to keep the vehicle drive wheels coupled to the engine for braking action. On deceleration, the turbine becomes an impeller and drives the oil against the normal impeller rotation and engine compression. The impeller fluid thrust is ineffective at idling speed and this results in a desirable automatic disengagement of engine power to the drive wheels.

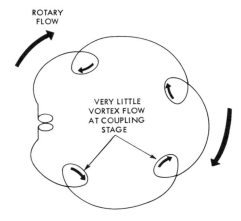

Fig. 2-17. At the coupling point.

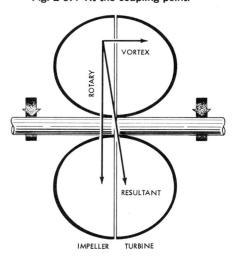

Fig. 2-18. Vortex and rotary impact with turbine at coupling point.

THE FLUID TORQUE CONVERTER

The behavior of the fluid action in a coupling can be applied to the operation of a fluid torque converter. The very same vortex and rotary forces are generated by a moving impeller that puts the fluid in motion. To multiply torque, however, a different make-up of the fluid unit is necessary. Although more complicated designs have been used, the current practice in automatic transmissions is to use a basic three-element converter-coupling unit; an impeller, a turbine, and a stator (Fig. 2-19).

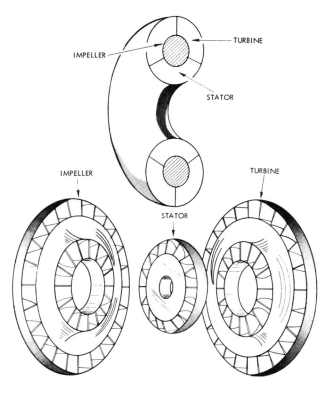

Fig. 2-19. Torque converter of the three element type.

A split guide ring (Fig. 2-20) is built into the impeller and turbine for greater operational efficiency. Because the center of the vortex flow sets up a turbulence that results in a loss of efficiency, the guide ring is used to provide a smooth, uniform flow between the impeller and turbine.

Figure 2-21 shows the impeller as an integral part of the housing, which in manufacturing production is welded to the cover and encloses the turbine and the stator. The stator incorporates a one-way clutch and mounts on a stationary support shaft that is integral with the transmission front pump assembly.

Another construction feature is the design of the impeller and turbine blades, as illustrated in Fig. 2-22. The curved shape of the impeller blades in a backward direction gives added acceleration and energy to the oil as it leaves the impeller, while the curved shape of the turbine vanes is designed to absorb as much energy as possible from the moving oil as it passes through the turbine.

Turbine vane curvature has two functions that give the turbine its excellent torque-absorbing capacity. It reduces shock losses due to sudden change in oil direction between the impeller and turbine (Fig. 2-23). It also takes advantage of the hydraulic principle that the more the direction of a moving fluid is diverted, the greater the force that the fluid exerts on the diverting surface. The two functions are illustrated in Fig. 2-24.

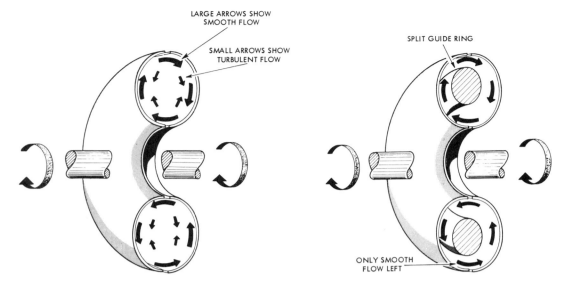

Fig. 2-20. Guide ring part of converter.

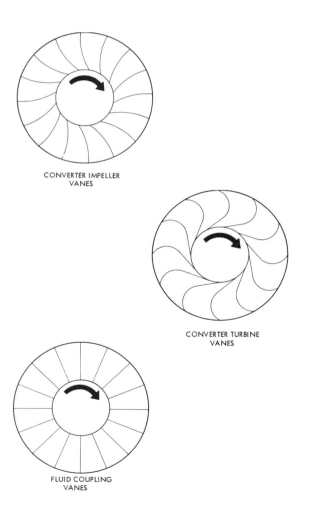

CONVERTER IMPELLER
VANES

CONVERTER TURBINE
VANES

FLUID COUPLING
VANES

Fig. 2-22. Comparison of converter impeller and turbine blades to coupling blades. (Buick Division, General Motors Corp.)

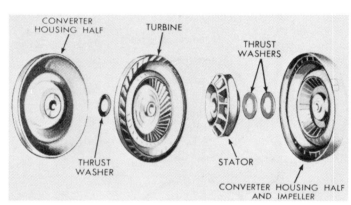

Fig. 2-21. Impeller as part of housing. (Ford Motor Co.)

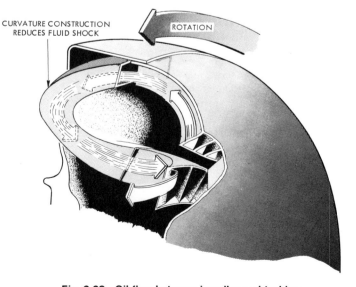

Fig. 2-23. Oil flow between impeller and turbine modified by vessel curvature. (Chrysler Corp.)

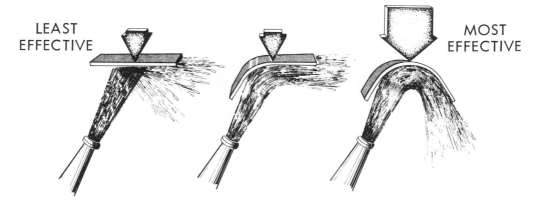

LEAST EFFECTIVE

MOST EFFECTIVE

Fig. 2-24. Path of diverted fluid under various conditions.

A fluid jet stream directed against a flat surface exerts a force on the plate but not without a shock loss caused by the breakdown of the smooth fluid flow (Fig. 2-24, left). By curving the inlet side (Fig. 2-24, center) the shock loss is reduced considerably but the force on the flat surface remains the same. The plate surface (Fig. 2-24, right) is curved at both inlet and outlet, keeping the fluid flow smooth and greatly increasing the force of the fluid jet stream on the plate.

Figure 2-25 shows this effect on a curved turbine vane. Note that the fluid impact is absorbed along the full length of the vane surface.

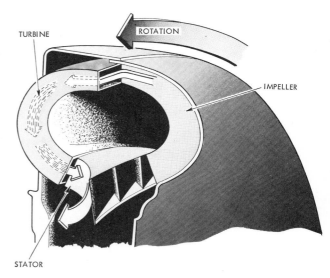

Fig. 2-26. Stator design redirects fluid flow to assist impeller rotation. (Chrysler Corp.)

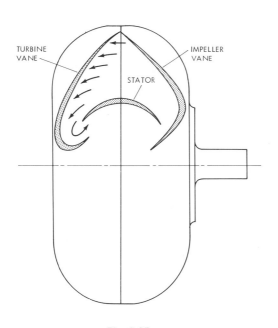

Fig. 2-25.

The third bladed member of the converter is the stator. Its function is to redirect the fluid as it leaves the turbine and re-enters the impeller (Fig. 2-26). The stator performs the same function in the converter circuit as the fulcrum in a lever arm or gear system.

Converter Operation

To assist in the discussion, the powerflow relationship between the engine crankshaft, fluid torque converter, and transmission input shaft is illustrated in Fig. 2-27.

IMPELLER AND TURBINE. The converter operation starts with the impeller putting the fluid in motion, with the engine furnishing the energy input. The rotating impeller creates a centrifugal pumping head or vortex flow. At the same time, the fluid must follow the rotational inertia or effort of the impeller. These two fluid flows combine to produce a resultant force in the form of an accelerated jet stream against the turbine vanes (Fig. 2-28).

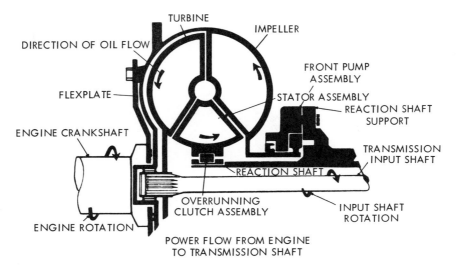

Fig. 2-27.

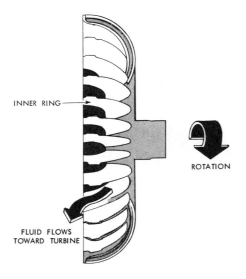

Fig. 2-28. Impeller operation-fluid flow.

The curved turbine blades absorb energy from the fluid until the force of fluid is great enough to overcome the turbine resistance to motion (4,000 lbs of automobile). The force on the turbine vane is actually working on the end of a rotating lever arm attached to the transmission input shaft. The lever arm represents the mean radius of the turbine (Fig. 2-29). The mean radius is the distance from the transmission input shaft center to a point on the turbine vane that equally divides the effect of the fluid force on the vane above and below the point.

Figure 2-30 shows that at this point of operation the impeller and turbine are attempting to act as a fluid coupling. It should be noted that the turbine vanes have reversed the fluid flow. Although the curved turbine blades provide for efficient energy transfer, the reverse flow of fluid back to the impeller would work against impeller rotation and lug the engine.

Fig. 2-29. Turbine lever arm represented by mean radius of turbine.

Fig. 2-30. Fluid coupling action at point at which reversal of turbine flow occurs.

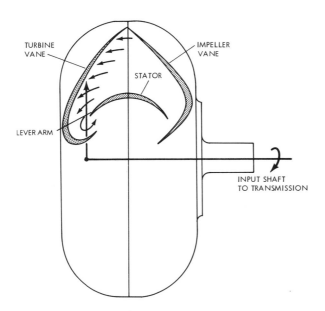

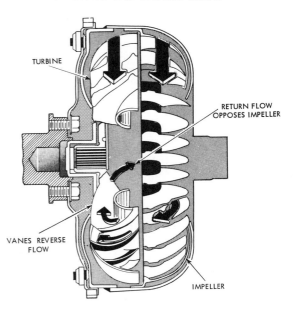

STATOR (REACTOR). To correct this condition a stator or reactor is employed between the turbine outflow and the impeller inflow to reverse the direction of the oil and make it flow in the same direction as the impeller rotation (Fig. 2-31). Instead of the fluid bucking the impeller, the unexpended energy in the oil now assists the impeller. The stator becomes a reaction member aiding the function of the impeller. Through this boost, the impeller has another and easier opportunity to accelerate the same fluid and develop greater

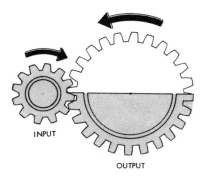

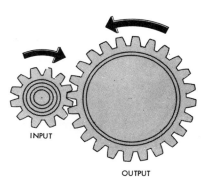

Fig. 2-32. Fluid torque multiplication gives the same effect as gear reduction.

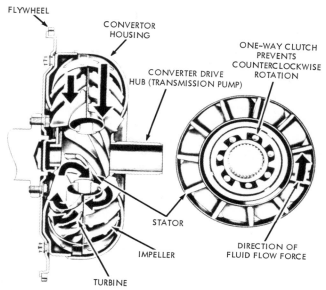

Fig. 2-31. Stator operation with converter in torque multiplication stage.

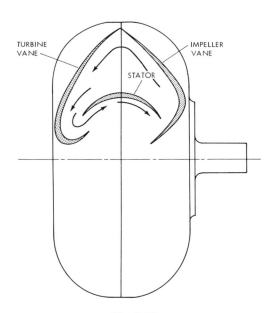

Fig. 2-33.

TORQUE MULTIPLICATION. The recycling of the fluid permits more of the impeller input from the engine to be used in increasing the jet stream velocity and the turning effort on the turbine. It should be noted that the stator, by helping the impeller to accelerate the fluid stream, provides the basis for torque multiplication. This is similar to torque multiplication by gear reduction (Fig. 2-32).

The maximum torque conversion occurs with the engine at wide open throttle (W.O.T.) and zero turbine speed. This is commonly referred to as the stall torque ratio. For passenger car applications, engineering design of the three-element converter keeps the torque output within the general range of 2:1 to 2.5:1.

The stall torque stabilizes at its design point when the impeller reaches its capacity for pumping. It cannot take on any more volume of fluid nor can it further increase the fluid velocity or thrust. Ideally, this occurs at the peak of the engine torque curve.

During torque multiplication, vortex flow predominantly moves the fluid through the impeller, to the turbine, to the stator, and back through the impeller (Fig. 2-33). It is the acceleration of the vortex

movement that results in torque multiplication. Because vortex flow is greatest at stall conditions, the greatest torque boost takes place at this time. As the turbine and the 4,000 lb automobile starts to move, it becomes easier for the working fluid to spin-up the turbine. With the turbine increasing in speed, the vortex flow decreases and rotary flow increases. As the rotary influence becomes stronger, the angle at which the fluid exits the turbine starts to favor the impeller rota-

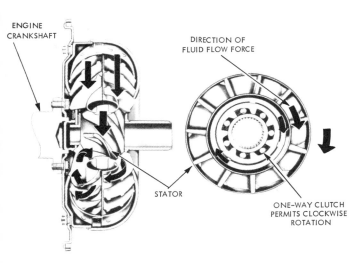

Fig. 2-34. Coupling phase of converter operation. (Ford Motor Co.)

tion. This means that the fluid exiting the turbine needs less and less redirection. This effect reduces the torque multiplication. At about a 90% speed ratio, or when the turbine speed is 9/10 of impeller speed, there is no longer any torque multiplication. The converter enters its coupling phase of operation and the stator is no longer needed (Fig. 2-34). The rotating inertia of the fluid mass, the impeller, and the turbine form a hydraulic lock. The rotary thrust of the fluid mass strikes the back side of the stator and releases the roller clutch. The stator can now freewheel and not interfere with the coupling action or fluid flow.

Once the turbine starts moving it is no longer a stationary target and its lever arms require less and less fluid thrust to move the vehicle as the turbine approaches impeller speed. Therefore, converter torque output begins to drop off from maximum torque to 1:1 as the turbine buries itself in the rotary inertia of the fluid.

NEWTON'S LAW. The ability of the torque converter to multiply torque can also be approached by applying Newton's Law of Physics, "For every action there is an equal and opposite reaction." In the converter, the impeller, the turbine, and the reactor are points of action and reaction with respect to oil flow. During the period of torque multiplication, the reaction of the stationary reactor (stator) blades to the oil is in the same direction as the impeller rotation (Fig. 2-35). In accordance with Newton's Law, the reaction of the turbine blades on the oil must be equal to the combined reactor and impeller torque $(A + B = C)$. Turbine torque, therefore, is greater than impeller torque by the amount of the reactor (stator) reaction torque. Therefore $C - B = A$.

Using Newton's Law again, it is obvious why a coupling cannot increase torque. Without a stator or reactor, the fluid coupling has only two points of action and reaction—the impeller and the turbine. The

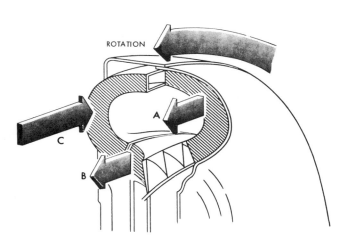

(A) ACTION FORCE OF IMPELLER
(B) REACTION FORCE OF STATOR
(C) REACTION FORCE OF TURBINE

$A = C - B$
THEREFORE:
$C = A + B$

Fig. 2-35. Newton's law as applied to converter torque multiplication. (Chrysler Corp.)

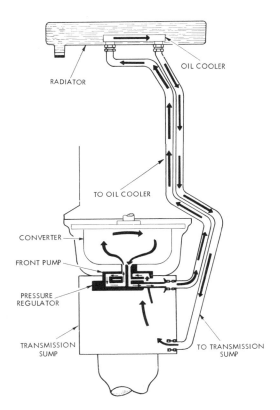

Fig. 2-36. Oil cooling circuit for the converter, bottom tank of radiator. (Ford Motor Co.)

impeller action on the fluid is opposed only by the reaction of the turbine, so the action–reaction between the two must always equal one another.

COOLING THE HYDRAULIC FLUID. When the converter is multiplying torque, a shearing action of the fluid occurs between the impeller and turbine because of the strong recirculating vortex flow and converter slipping. Considerable heat is generated and it becomes necessary to provide some type of cooling to keep the fluid from overheating. This differs from the coupling phase, in which heating is not a factor. Two types of cooling systems are used, oil-to-air and oil-to-water.

In both types, feed oil from the transmission pump regulator valve is constantly cycling oil into and out of the converter, with the outflow returning to the transmission for lubrication purposes and return to the sump. In the oil-to-water system used with larger engines, the oil is simply routed through the water cooler lower tank or side tank (Figs. 2-36 and 2-37).

The oil-to-air system requires a cooling shroud cover, tacked over the rear half of the converter and ventilation ports in the transmission converter housing

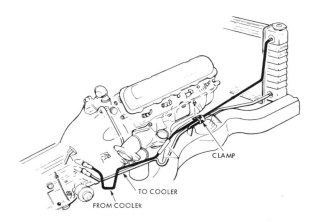

Fig. 2-37. Another converter oil cooler circuit, side tank design. (Oldsmobile Division, General Motors Corp.)

(Fig. 2-38). As the converter revolves, a centrifugal air pump action develops. A low pressure area is formed between the shroud and converter shell, which allows outside air to enter the space and absorb the converter heat. After the air passes over the converter it is expelled by centrifugal force through the case housing outlets back to the atmosphere.

Converter Operating Characteristics

In operation on the road, the converter provides effortless driving characteristics.

1. At engine idle, the converter acts as an automatic clutch and permits the engine to run and the car to stand still.

2. The converter automatically adjusts its torque output to drive shaft torque requirements within its design limits. It acts as a fluid coupling for level road, constant speed conditions, but when performance is needed for acceleration or hill climbing it responds with the necessary extra torque dictated by the slowdown of the turbine from increased drive shaft torque.

3. As the converter is a fluid unit, it acts as a natural shock absorber during gear ratio changes and adds to shift smoothness.

Converter Capacity or Size

When discussing converters, it is important to note another characteristic. A mechanical gear transmission will take on any amount of torque up to the clutch slip point; a torque converter will, however, absorb only a given amount of engine torque and no more. For example, as the throttle control opens and engine torque starts to rise, the engine will be permitted to speed up only to the point where engine torque reaches converter torque capacity. When converter torque capacity is reached, engine rpm stabilizes and the converter slips. This is referred to as the converter stall speed. (Converter stall speed will be explained later when stall speed testing is covered).

It should be apparent that the converter has the added job of controlling engine rpm and, in essence, must be carefully designed to take advantage of the engine torque output for most efficient operation (the converter and engine must be matched). As another approach, the engine rpm, by virtue of converter design, is controlled by the load that the impeller imposes on the engine as it attempts to drive the turbine. Naturally, as the vehicle picks up momentum and turbine speed increases, the engine torque required to drive the impeller falls off and engine speed steadily rises.

If too small a converter is used for a particular application, the engine will operate at higher rpm than desired before the converter can transmit maximum torque.

In the situation in which too large a converter is used, the engine would not have the ability to drive the impeller at a speed that would permit it to operate at maximum power. Both size extremes result in an undesirable overspeed or underspeed condition. The normal practice is to match the converter and engine at

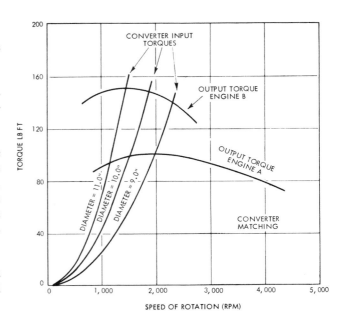

Fig. 2-39. Matching of converter design to the engine.

a stall speed that enables the engine to reach its maximum torque (Fig. 2-39).

From the preceding discussion, it should be apparent that the field mechanic should not alter the converter-engine size match engineered by the manufacturer.

Variable Capacity Converts

In the design of a torque converter, a compromise is usually made between the performance characteristics of a high-capacity and a low-capacity converter.

A high-capacity converter absorbs engine torque with a minimum of slippage. A low-capacity converter absorbs engine torque with greater slippage, but produces more fluid torque for acceleration. A high-capacity converter gives pleasing light throttle starts and a low coupling point for excellent highway cruising efficiency. A low-coupling point means that the torque multiplication under heavy throttle cannot stretch itself over a wide vehicle speed range. The converter, for example, may be designed to reach coupling phase under full throttle at 40 mph (65 km/h). The automatic gear ratios continue to function to give engine performance. With the low coupling point and the low engine speed inherited from a high-capacity converter, full throttle engine performance is not at optimum.

When acceleration performance is improved by decreasing converter capacity, light throttle feel and coupling tightness suffer, causing the condition commonly called excessive engine run-up. However, the converter torque multiplication covers a wider vehicle speed range with improved engine acceleration.

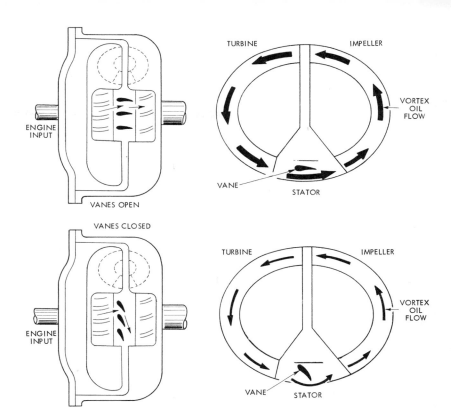

Fig. 2-40. Variable stator vane open, and closed. (Allison Division, General Motors Corp.)

This presents one drawback: the coupling point does not rapidly achieve highway cruising efficiency. To eliminate the dilemma of choosing between a high-capacity and a low-capacity converter, some converters were designed with variable pitch stator blades. A simple illustration of variable pitch stator blades is shown in Fig. 2-40.

Figure 2-41 shows how the exit angle of the stator blades affects the converter capacity. This is directly related to the amount of fluid acceleration that must take place in the impeller to bring the velocity of the fluid at the stator exit to match the velocity of the fluid exiting from the pump. The greater the change, the greater is the capacity.

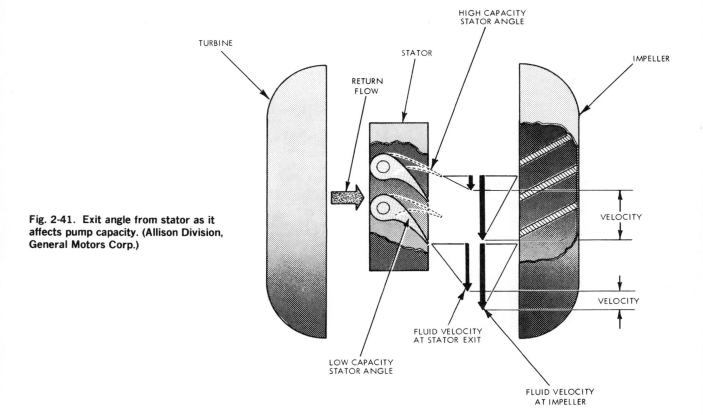

Fig. 2-41. Exit angle from stator as it affects pump capacity. (Allison Division, General Motors Corp.)

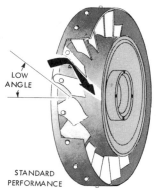

LOW
ANGLE

STANDARD
PERFORMANCE

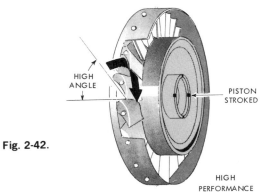

HIGH
ANGLE

PISTON
STROKED

Fig. 2-42.

HIGH
PERFORMANCE

As shown in Fig. 2-42, the high angle position causes the re-entry oil from the stator to have greater momentum and a more favorable thrust angle for impeller propulsion. The stator assembly still mounts on a stator shaft and uses a one-way roller clutch (Fig. 2-43). The individual stator blades are fixed to a crankshaft that fits into a cage and moveable piston. Stroking the piston moves the blades to their high angle and low angle positions (Fig. 2-44).

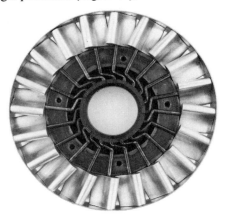

Fig. 2-44. Top (low angle). Bottom (high angle).

Fig. 2-43.

Another factor works to lower converter capacity as the stator blades are moved to high angle. The blades cause a restriction in flow, which decreases the amount of fluid passing through the impeller. As a result, the impeller can add more energy to the fluid. Because the quantity of fluid is less, it can be accelerated at a faster rate and thus improve engine performance.

ADVANTAGES. A torque converter with a variable stator offers these advantages:

1. In the high-capacity range, the tighter converter allows starts with a minimum of engine speed.

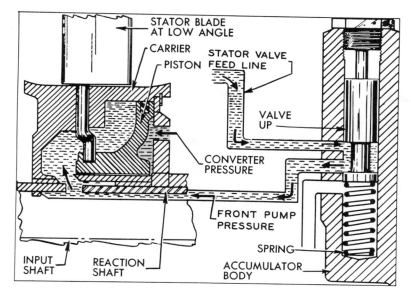

Fig. 2-45. Typical variable pitch control circuit. Top. (stator in low angle position). Bottom. (stator in high angle position). Although not shown in the illustration the stator valve position can be mechanically controlled by external linkage to the transmission or by hydraulic pressure. Stator feed line pressure is the same as transmission operating pressure with converter pressure being less. Note that the back side of the piston is constantly exposed to the converter pressure. (Buick Division, General Motors Corp.)

2. The high capacity also gives a very efficient coupling.

3. In the low-capacity range, engine speed is allowed to increase for high performance starts, giving more input to the converter.

4. Extension of the torque multiplication range is increased to higher speeds in the low-capacity range. High performance engines with low axle ratios have had coupling points as high as 90 mph (150 km/h).

5. A transition from the high capacity converter to low capacity converter and vice versa can be easily and smoothly accomplished, as seen in Fig. 2-45.

The variable capacity converter was first introduced in the Buick Dynaflow and was subsequently adopted for use in the other multiturbine converter drives that were soon to follow. After more than a decade, the multiturbine converter drives faded from the scene; however, the variable capacity concept was kept alive and was used in some of the three-element converter-type applications through production year 1967.

Lock-Up Converters

Although not new in concept, the lock-up converter is making a comeback. A number of years ago it was built into some of the converters as a high-cost feature and consequently was dropped. With the current cost of gasoline and the scramble for good fuel economy, the lock-up converter becomes a desirable feature. For 1978, Chrysler incorporated the lock-up converter in most of their 727 and 904 Torqueflite transmission applications. The new unit boosts fuel

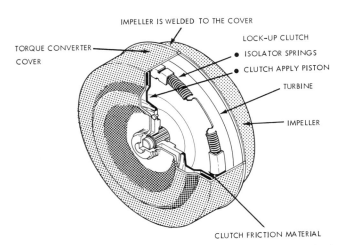

Fig. 2-46.

economy by 4% in city driving and 6% in country driving. In production year 1979, some AMC Torque Command automatic transmissions began to feature the same converter lock-up system. The converter design is illustrated in Fig. 2-46, and lock-up power flow operation in Fig. 2-47.

The principle of the lock-up is very simple. A single disc clutch locks the turbine member directly to the converter housing cover, providing a direct mechanical drive to the transmission. The normal fluid drive of the converter is bypassed. This is the equivalent of a direct drive in a manual transmission.

The lock-up mode occurs in direct drive only. To prevent engine lugging, the engagement and disengagement points are set at approximately 25–40 mph (40-65 km/h), depending on engine size and axle ratio. At light throttle, the 2–3 shift will occur before the minimum lock-up shift.

The lock-up feature is not used in first and second gears because converter torque multiplication is

needed for full-time acceleration. Lock-up and unlock are completely automatic and controlled by new circuits in the valve body (Fig. 2-48).

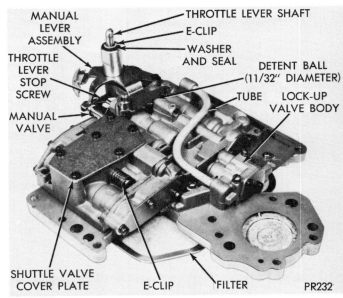

Fig. 2-48. (Chrysler Corp.)

1. The torque converter control valve used in earlier models has been modified to control both the *on* and *off* oil pressures to move the lock-up piston. The torque converter control valve, therefore, is now called the *switch valve*.

The switch valve is controlled by two other valves housed in a lock-up control valve body. They are the *lock-up valve* and *fail-safe valve*.

2. A lock-up valve sensitive to governor pressure (road speed) will prevent lock-up at speeds below 40 mph (65 km/h).

3. A fail-safe valve sensitive to throttle pressure permits lock-up in high gear only after the transmission front (direct) clutch circuit pressure is satisfied.

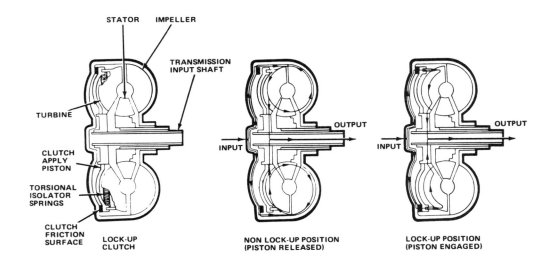

Fig. 2-47. Lockup torque converter operation. (American Motors Corp.)

The fail-safe valve also allows a fast lock-up release for kickdown (forced downshift) performance.

The switch valve, lock-up valve, and fail-safe valve are coordinated relay valves.

Figures 2-49 and 2-50 feature the control circuit in the *unlock mode.* The fail-safe valve is held into position by spring tension and throttle pressure. This insures that line pressure from the manual valve does not affect the spring-loaded switch valve. Converter feed oil from the regulator valve is applied through a center oil passage in the transmission input shaft. The oil flows around the front of the lock-up piston and through the converter and out again for cooling and lubrication. This flow arrangement keeps the lock-up piston disengaged. The lock-up clutch apply piston and torsional isolator springs rotate with the converter turbine element.

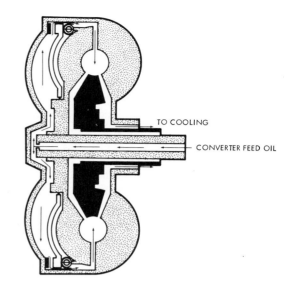

Fig. 2-49. Converter circuit in unlock mode.

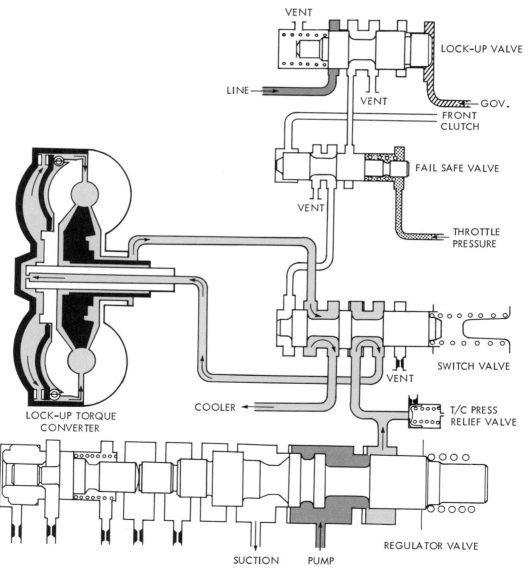

Fig. 2-50. Hydraulic circuit controls in unlock mode.

When the circuit valving controls dictate the *lock-up* mode in high gear (Figs. 2-51 and 2-52), front (direct) clutch oil is relayed through the lock-up valve and repositions the fail-safe valve. If the vehicle speed is right, governor pressure moves the lock-up valve and permits line pressure oil from the manual valve to be relayed to the switch valve. The switch valve's new position vents the input shaft converter feed oil on the front side of the piston. Transmission line pressure is relayed past the switch valve and enters the converter through what was the converter out circuit. The line pressure moves the piston against the friction surface that is bonded to the torque converter cover. The turbine is now locked to the engine crankshaft. The contacting surface between the friction material and piston plus an O-ring at the I.D. of the piston provides a seal across the piston area to insure firm clutch holding power.

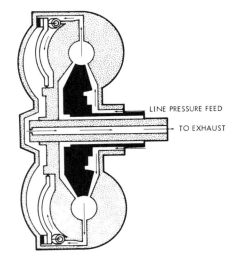

LINE PRESSURE FEED

TO EXHAUST

Fig. 2-51.

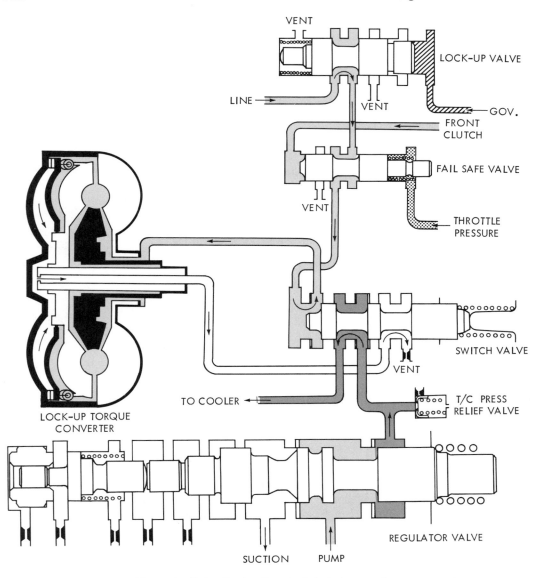

VENT

LOCK-UP VALVE

LINE

VENT

GOV.

FRONT CLUTCH

FAIL SAFE VALVE

VENT

THROTTLE PRESSURE

SWITCH VALVE

VENT

LOCK-UP TORQUE CONVERTER

TO COOLER

T/C PRESS RELIEF VALVE

SUCTION   PUMP

REGULATOR VALVE

Fig. 2-52. Hydraulic circuit controls in lock-up mode.

During lock-up there is no need to exchange the converter oil for cooling because heat is not a factor. The switch valve short-circuits the normal converter feed and sends fluid directly to cooling and lubrication.

During a kickdown 3–2 or 3–1, throttle pressure equals transmission line pressure. The throttle pressure, with a spring assist, will move the fail-safe valve against front (direct) clutch oil. Transmission line pressure is cut-off and an unrestricted vent provides a quick lock-up release.

Figures 2-53, 2-54, 2-55, 2-56, 2-57, 2-58, 2-59, and 2-60 shows a sequence of the actual lock-up parts and their relationship. Note that torsional dampers are added between the lock-up piston and the turbine. This is necessary because the lock-up mode by-passes the dampening effect of a fluid coupling on engine torsional vibration. The mechanical power flow passes through the damper springs before driving the turbine.

Ford and General Motors lock-up systems are discussed in Chapter 11.

Fig. 2-53. External converter—appearance is the same as a standard converter. Chrysler provides a converter decal identification for approximately 12 different lock-up converters.

Fig. 2-54. Clutch disc lining bonded to converter cover.

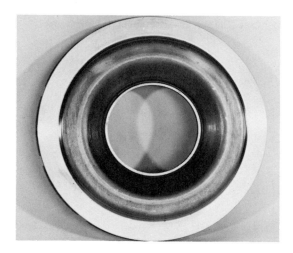

Fig. 2-55. Front view; lock-up piston with machined clutch contacting surface.

Fig. 2-56. Rear view; lock-up piston with torsional spring cage.

Fig. 2-57. Front side of turbine illustrated with torsional damper spring inserts. The input shaft lip seal in the turbine hub prevents internal leakage past the transmission input shaft.

Fig. 2-58. Front view; lock-up piston mounts on turbine hub with O-ring at the I.D. providing a pressure seal.

Fig. 2-59. Rear view; lock-up piston fit to turbine damper springs.

Fig. 2-60. Close-up of turbine damper spring fit to lock-up piston damper cage. The link-up is like a floating brake caliper.

REVIEW QUESTIONS

CHAPTER 2
HYDRODYNAMIC UNITS

Completion:

1. The name given to the input or drive member of a fluid coupling. _____

2. The name given to the output or driven member of a fluid coupling. _____

3. The name given to the input or drive member of a fluid torque converter. _____

4. The name given to the output or driven member of a fluid torque converter. _____

5. The name given to the torque multiplier of a fluid torque converter. _____

6. The reference made to the fluid flow from the centrifugal pumping action of the converter or coupling input member. _____

7. The reference made to the fluid flow from the inertia effect of the rotating converter or coupling input member. _____

8. The reference made to the effective directional thrust of the fluid between the drive and driven members of a coupling or converter. _____

9. List in sequence the converter members through which the fluid cycles in a torque converter during the torque phase.

   a. _____

   b. _____

   c. _____ and back to the

   d. _____

10. The non-rotating converter shaft is referred to as the _____ shaft.

11. The torque converter member or element that is driven by the engine. _____

12. The member of the torque converter that puts the fluid into motion. _____

13. The two types of fluid cooling systems used with converter operation are oil-to-_____ and oil-to-_____.

14. Fluid torque converters used on current passenger cars are usually described by using the following terminology: _____ element, _____ stage.

15. The input shaft of an automatic transmission is attached to the member of the torque converter called the _____.

16. Name the converter element that makes up part of the converter housing. _____.

17. A fluid coupling may also be correctly called a fluid_____.

18. A fluid coupling cannot transmit a torque ratio of more than _____.

19. A fluid torque converter acts as both a _____ and _____.

20. A term used to reflect coupling or converter efficiency. _____

21. The converter front is supported and aligned to the engine crankshaft by a _____ in the crankshaft end.

22. The converter drive hub is supported and aligned by a _____ located in the transmission pump body.

23. The transmission pump is driven by the converter _____.

24. The crankshaft is attached to the converter cover with a plate referred to as the _____ plate.

25. The stator one-way roller clutch locks when the fluid effort is attempting to rotate the stator in a _____ direction.

26. At engine idle, transmission in (D) and vehicle stationary; the stator is: locked ☐ freewheeling ☐.

27. For more torque and acceleration the stator blades in a variable capacity converter are positioned in their _____ angle position.

28. Chrysler introduced their converter lock-up for the 727 and 904 Torqueflite Transmissions in production year _____.

29. (Chrysler) Converter lock-up mode occurs in _____ gear only with the minimum vehicle speed requirement falling between a range of ____ to ____ mph depending on engine size and axle ratio.

30. (Chrysler) The lock-up features a _____ disc clutch that locks the converter _____ member directly to the converter cover or drive housing.

31. (Chrysler) To dampen crankshaft torsional vibrations, _____ _____ are added between the lock-up piston and the turbine.

32. (Chrysler) Name the three valves that control the lock-up circuitry for the "on" and "off" modes.

    a. _____

    b. _____

    c. _____

33. (Chrysler) Name the valve that prevents "lock-up" at speeds below 40 mph. _____

34. (Chrysler) Name the valve that switches the circuitry for the unlock and lock-up modes. _____

35. For lock-up to occur, governor pressure opens the _____ valve and front (direct) clutch oil opens the _____ valve to relay mainline oil to the switch valve. The mainline oil switches the _____ valve and the following occurs:

    a. Converter feed oil is cut off and vented at the _____ valve.

    b. Mainline oil enters the converter through the converter _____ and applies the clutch piston to the converter housing.

36. During the unlock mode, converter feed oil enters the converter through the _____ and exits out through the converter _____.

3

PLANETARY GEARS IN TRANSMISSIONS

Planetary gears have been associated with the American automobile since its very beginning at the turn of the century. They were among the first type of gearing used in passenger car and light truck transmissions and offered the advantage of minimum driver skill when changing gears (gear ratios). The sliding gear boxes in the early years did not feature synchronized shifts and it was a skillful art to change gears on the move.

Design restrictions confined the planetary gear boxes to two speeds and a reverse, although it is on record that the 1906 Cadillac used a three-speed planetary transmission. These early versions were not without their problems. They were noisy, had short bearing life (the practice at that time was to use bushing mounted pinions), and at times chattered or grabbed during shift changes because of uneven brake band application.

Advances in the sliding gear transmission design eventually lead to its popularity over the planetary designs and the almost universal use of sliding gear transmissions in passenger cars and trucks. The Ford Model T, however, used a planetary transmission until the year 1928.

Planetary gears staged a comeback in the 1930s with the introduction of the Borg-Warner automatic overdrive and the General Motors' Hydra-Matic transmission. Research and development in helical gears, alloy steels, heat treatment of metal, and needle bearings eliminated many of the deficiencies of the early types of planetary gears.

Planetary gears today have a wide range of applications, varying from passenger car and truck automatic transmissions to steering and final drive mechanisms of track-and wheel-driven construction machinery, and as reduction gears for aircraft propeller drives. These are just a few modern examples of the planetary gear applications in power transmission.

THE PLANETARY GEAR ASSEMBLY

The heart of the automatic transmission is the planetary gear system. It is therefore essential to review the basic construction of a simple planetary gear set as an introduction to how planetary gears operate.

A simple planetary gear set (Figs. 3-1 and 3-2) consists of a sun gear or center gear that is surrounded and in constant mesh with the planet or pinion gears. The pinion gears are mounted and free to rotate on their support shafts, which are pinned to a planet carrier. The internal or ring gear is in constant mesh with the planetary pinions and surrounds the entire assembly. It should be noted that the sun gear, planet carrier, and internal gear rotate on a common center while the planet pinion gears rotate on their own independent centers. For clarification, the planet pinion gears are considered to be part of the planet carrier.

The planetary gear set gets its name from the action of the planet pinion gears. As can be observed in later discussion, they have the ability to turn on their own centers and at the same time revolve around the sun gear. This is similar to the earth turning on its axis and rotating around the sun.

By studying Figs. 3-1 and 3-2, several major advantages of planetary gears are realized:

1. All members of the planetary gear set share a common axis, which results in a structure of compact size.
2. Planetary gears are always in full and constant mesh, eliminating the possibility of gear tooth damage from gear clash or partial engagement. The full and constant mesh feature also permits automatic and quick gear ratio changes without power flow interruption.

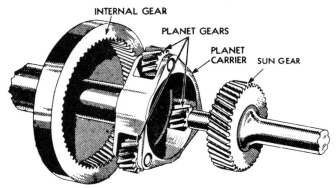

Fig. 3-2. Planetary gear assembly—exploded view. (Pontiac Division, General Motors Corp.)

3. Planetary gears are strong and sturdy and can handle larger torque loads for their compact size in comparison to other gear combinations in manual transmissions. This is because the torque load as it passes through the planetary set is distributed over the several planet pinion gears, which in effect allows more tooth contact area to handle the power transmission.

4. The location of the planetary members makes it relatively easy to hold the members or lock them together for ratio changes.

Gearing Definitions

Whether a gear train is set up as a conventional or planetary system, they all perform the same function in a transmission gear box.

1. Provide a neutral
2. Provide a reverse
3. Provide for a direct drive ratio 1:1
4. Provide for gear ratio changes that increase or decrease the torque input with proportional changes in output speed

To understand how a planetary gear train operates, it is important to review some gearing definitions that are fundamental to all power train systems.

GEAR RATIO. The number of revolutions the input gear makes to one revolution of the output gear. In a simple gear combination, three revolutions of the input gear to one of the output gear gives a ratio of 3:1.

GEAR REDUCTION. Torque is multiplied and speed decreased by the factor of the gear ratio. For example, a 3:1 gear ratio will change an input torque of 180 lb-ft and an input speed of 2,700 rpm to 540 lb-

Fig. 3-1. Simple planetary gear assembly. (Pontiac Division, General Motors Corp.)

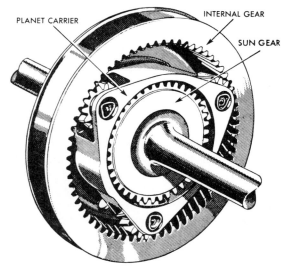

ft and 900 rpm respectively. (No account is taken for frictional losses, which are always present).

OVERDRIVE. It produces the opposite effect of a gear reduction. Torque is reduced and speed is increased by the factor of the gear ratio. A 1:3 gear ratio would change the previously mentioned input torque and speed used for gear reduction to 60 lb-ft and 8,100 rpm.

DIRECT DRIVE. The gear ratio is 1:1 with no change occurring in the torque and speed input.

FREEWHEELING. There is a power input with no transmission of power output.

REACTION MEMBER. In a planetary gear set, reference is made to the stationary planetary member grounded to the transmission case. This is accomplished through the use of friction and wedging devices known as bands, disc clutches, and one-way clutches. These are discussed and illustrated later in the chapter.

THE LAWS OF PLANETARY GEAR OPERATION

The operation of a planetary gear train is governed by five basic laws that provide the key to understanding the various power flows in all automatic transmissions. They are the laws of neutral, reduction, overdrive, direct drive, and reverse. Carefully study them one at a time.

Law of Neutral

When there is an input, but no reaction member, the condition is neutral.

In Fig. 3-3, the sun gear serves as the driving input member and the internal gear is free to rotate because it is not grounded to any part of the transmission. The planet carrier is held stationary by the weight of the car on the rear wheels. This causes the planet pinion gears to rotate on their pins and drive the internal gear opposite the sun gear or input direction.

In automatic transmissions, neutral is achieved with the gear set, or by declutching the transmission input shaft to the gear set. The most popular method is to declutch the input shaft and avoid using the gear set. Although no longer in production, the General Motors two-speed automatic transmissions used the gear set planetary action for neutral. More recently, the General Motors (MD-3) 180 Automatic Transmission introduced in midyear 1977 also achieves neutral through the planetary set.

Law of Reduction

When there is a reaction member and the planet carrier is the output, the condition is gear reduction.

There are two reduction possibilities that meet the requirements for the law of reduction. In Fig. 3-4, a brake or friction band used typically in automatic transmissions is applied to the internal gear and holds it against rotation. The band itself is rigidly anchored to the transmission case when applied and serves as the grounding medium for the reactionary internal gear.

Fig. 3-3. Planetary gear set during neutral operation.

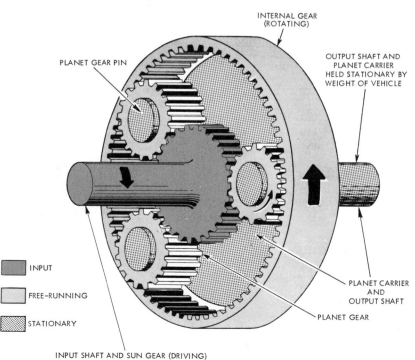

INTERNAL GEAR (ROTATING)

OUTPUT SHAFT AND PLANET CARRIER HELD STATIONARY BY WEIGHT OF VEHICLE

PLANET GEAR PIN

PLANET CARRIER AND OUTPUT SHAFT

PLANET GEAR

INPUT

FREE-RUNNING

STATIONARY

INPUT SHAFT AND SUN GEAR (DRIVING)

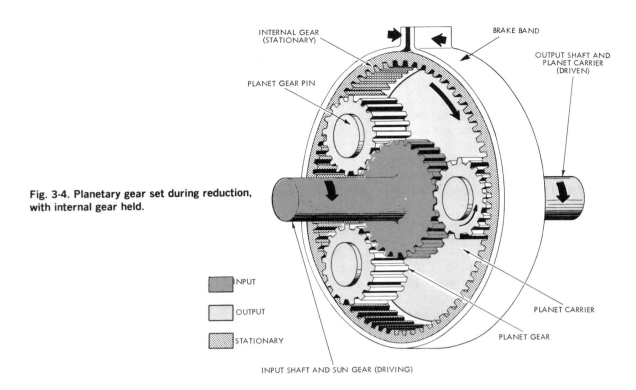

INTERNAL GEAR
(STATIONARY)

BRAKE BAND

OUTPUT SHAFT AND
PLANET CARRIER
(DRIVEN)

PLANET GEAR PIN

Fig. 3-4. Planetary gear set during reduction,
with internal gear held.

INPUT

OUTPUT

STATIONARY

PLANET CARRIER

PLANET GEAR

INPUT SHAFT AND SUN GEAR (DRIVING)

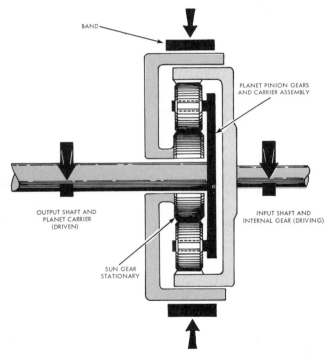

BAND

PLANET PINION GEARS
AND CARRIER ASSEMBLY

Fig. 3-5. Planetary gear set during reduction,
with sun gear held.

OUTPUT SHAFT AND
PLANET CARRIER
(DRIVEN)

INPUT SHAFT AND
INTERNAL GEAR (DRIVING)

SUN GEAR
STATIONARY

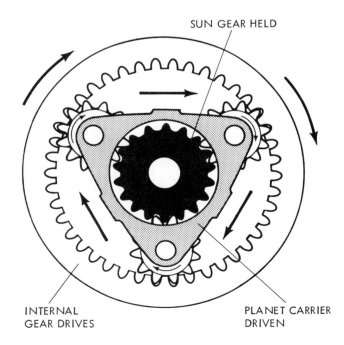

SUN GEAR HELD

INTERNAL
GEAR DRIVES

PLANET CARRIER
DRIVEN

This *first method* of reduction shows the input sun gear driving the pinion gears on their pins opposite the input direction. Because the pinion gears cannot move the stationary internal gear, a reaction force is created that causes the pinions to walk around the internal gear as they rotate and to move the carrier in a forward direction at a reduced speed. If the input torque is 100 lb-ft and the gear reduction is 2.5:1, then the output torque is increased to 250 lb-ft.

The *second reduction method* is set up with the sun gear stationary and power input applied to the internal gear (Fig. 3-5). The planet pinions now rotate on their pins and walk around the sun gear to produce another forward reduction effect on the carrier. This planetary gear reduction power flow is used for second-gear operation in the current series Chrysler Torque-Flite 727 and 904, Ford C-3, C-4, C-6 and JATCO, and General Motor's 400, 350, 250, 200, and 125.

Instead of using a band to connect a selected planetary reaction member solidly to the transmission case, the sprag clutch, the roller clutch, and the multiple-disc clutch are also used as grounding components for reduction. The sprag and roller clutches are both classified as one-way clutches and are rather interesting devices. They are self-initiating in the exact timing of their hold and freewheeling actions and require no hydraulic controls. They operate solely by mechanical means, and both use a wedging action when they self-apply. This self-operating feature permits simplified and space-saving transmission design with no band adjustment requirement.

The freewheeling action of the one-way clutch is used to an advantage to improve shift quality. When ratio changes are made, it eliminates a timing problem during band-to-band or band-to-clutch shifts.

In automatic transmissions, one-way clutches have two general applications. They are used in:

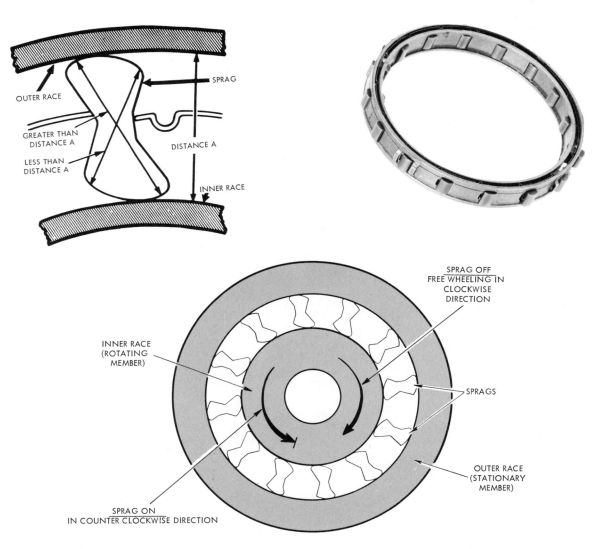

Fig 3-6.(a) Sprag configuration. (b) Sprag and cage assembly. (c) Sprag clutch action with stationary outer race—viewed from front.

1. Torque converter units to control the stator member action.
2. The gearset of the transmission for forward gear reduction ratios. Although the sprag clutch pioneered the use of the one-way clutch in automatic transmissions, the roller clutch is now favored.

A study of Figs. 3-6 and 3-7 will show the wedging (ON position) and freewheeling (OFF position) action of these clutches. Both illustrations could be reversed to show the inner race as the stationary member and the outer race as the rotating or drive member. In actual practice, the stationary race is either bolted, riveted, or clutched to the transmission case, as indicated in Figs. 3-8 and 3-9.

Another behavior pattern is peculiar to both sprag and roller clutch operation. They are effective as long as the engine powers the vehicle. If coasting occurs when gear reduction is in effect, the sprags and rollers will unwedge and allow freewheeling to take place. The planetary gear set is then in neutral, making it impossible to relay the power flow to the torque converter and engine for braking.

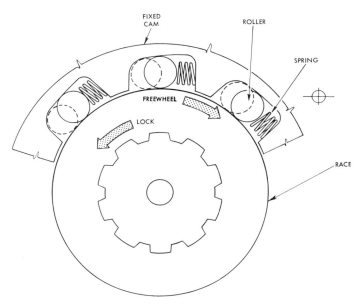

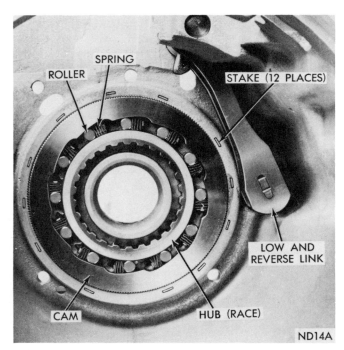

Fig. 3-7. Roller clutch action with stationary outer cam—viewed from the front.

Reviewing Figs. 3-8 and 3-9 in respect to coasting action, the output shaft and planet carrier now become the input member to the planetary set, causing the internal gear in Fig. 3-8 and the sun gear in Fig. 3-9 to rotate in the input direction and to release the one-way clutch.

For future reference in determining the gearing power flow in automatic transmissions, it is important to know that any time the input race is rotating in a clockwise (engine) direction, the sprag or roller clutch will freewheel. Lock-up occurs when the input race is rotated counter-clockwise.

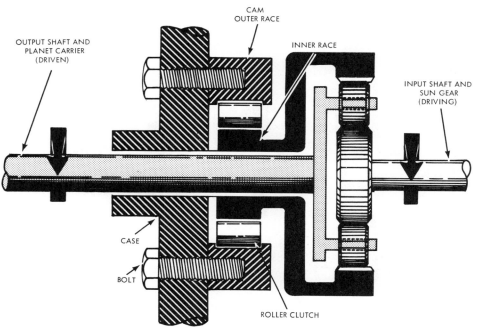

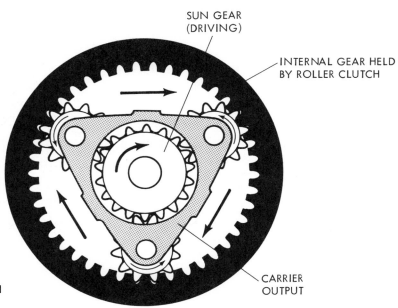

Fig. 3-8. Planetary gear set in reduction, internal gear held by roller clutch action.

Although the freewheeling action of a sprag or roller clutch is an asset to closed-throttle downshift quality when the vehicle transmission performs in the normal drive range, it is definitely unsafe when the transmission gear reduction needs to be used for controlling vehicle speed on decending steep hills or mountain grades. To overcome this deficiency, the driver can select an operating range, such as manual low, which will eliminate the freewheeling and return positive gearing action to the engine for braking and a safe descent.

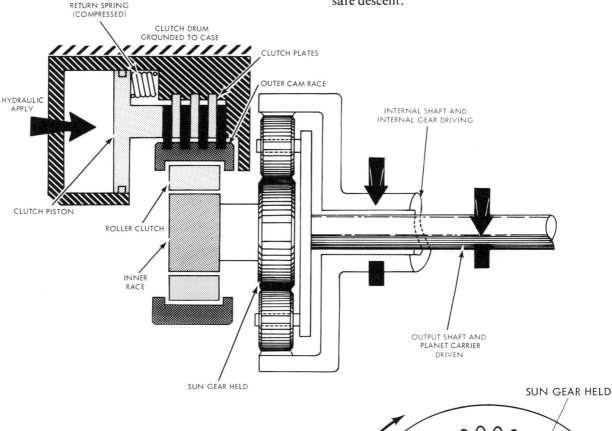

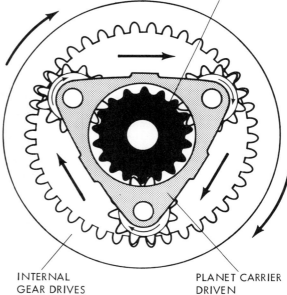

Fig. 3-9. Planetary gear set in reduction. Sun gear clutched to transmission case by multiple disc clutch apply and one-way clutch action.

To illustrate, Fig. 3-10 is a redesign of Fig. 3-8 and shows the addition of a coast band that would be applied in the case of manual low operation. While the vehicle is under power from the engine, such as in climbing a steep grade or while using manual low for maximum performance, the applied band is not really holding against the drive torque because the roller clutch is effective. During grade descent or decelera-tion, however, the band already applied holds up against coasting torque and keeps the internal gear reactionary. With the planet carrier serving as the input to the gear set during coasting it is now possible to transfer an overdrive speed to the converter turbine when the fluid attempts to overspeed the impeller against engine compression.

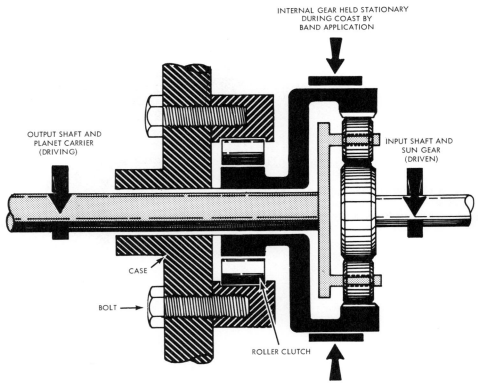

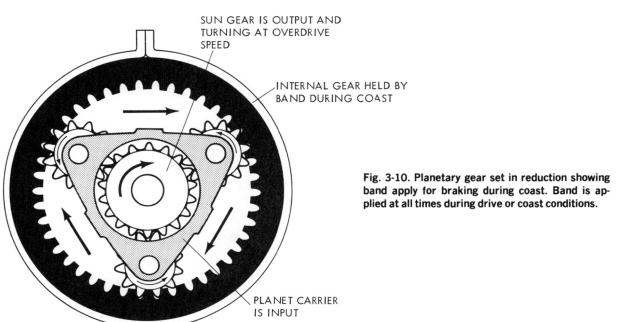

Fig. 3-10. Planetary gear set in reduction showing band apply for braking during coast. Band is ap-plied at all times during drive or coast conditions.

Although the band and one-way clutch are widely used for the reduction function, on occasion a multiple-disc clutch is used for this purpose. Figure 3-11 shows the internal gear clutched to the transmission case and the sun gear acting as the input drive.

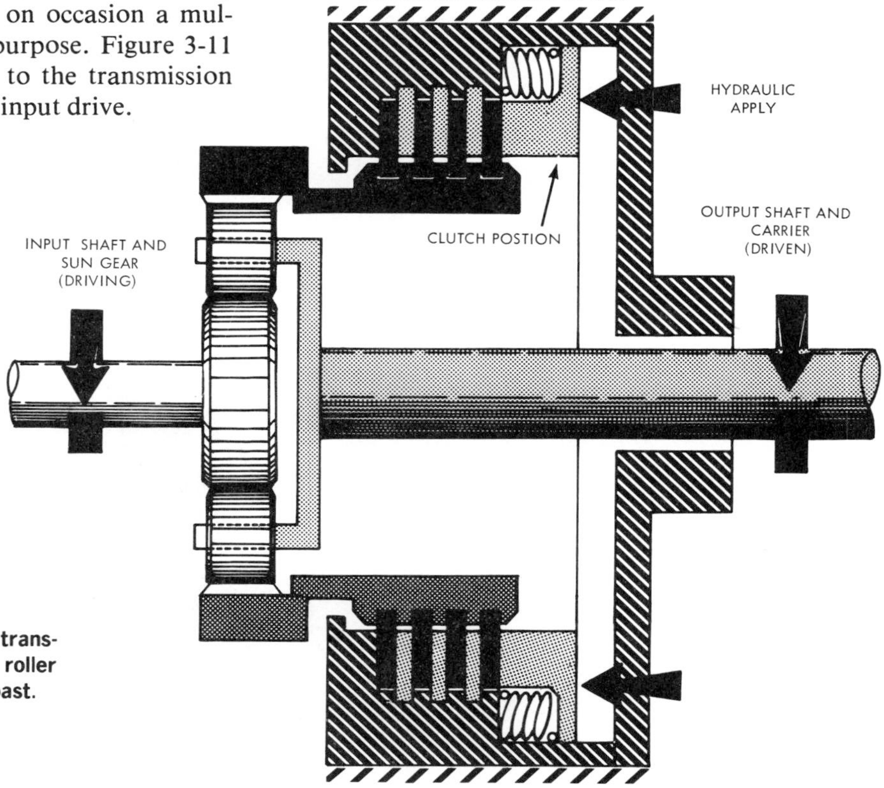

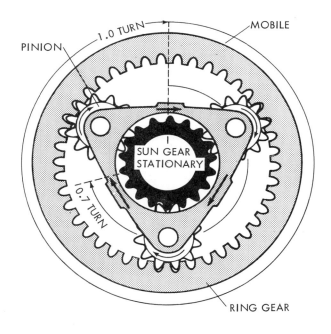

Fig. 3-11. Internal gear clutched to the transmission case, with sun gear driving. No roller clutch or band is needed for drive or coast.

Law of Overdrive

When there is a reaction member and the planet carrier is the input, the condition is overdrive.

Because overdrive gives the opposite effect of gear reduction, the planet carrier serves as the input rather than as the output member, with either the sun gear or the internal gear held stationary (Figs. 3-12 and 3-13). It should be noted that even with the planet carrier as the power input, the pinions are still free to rotate on their pins and to walk as they react to the fixed planetary member. This time, the turning and walking action moves the output member at an increased speed and at reduced torque.

During coast or deceleration, overdrive effects are encountered in the gearing power flow with the reversal of the power thrust (rear wheels to engine).

Overdrive planetary outputs have been avoided and deemed not necessary for automatic transmission applications until Ford introduced its new four-speed AOT (Automatic Overdrive) unit in 1980. The cost of fuel versus the added cost of integrating an overdrive is now a sound economic cost exchange. For 1981, General Motors introduced its own four-speed overdrive automatic transmission for rear wheel drives; the 200-4R.

Fig. 3-12. Planetary gear set in overdrive, with sun gear stationary—showing pinion carrier versus ring gear travel.

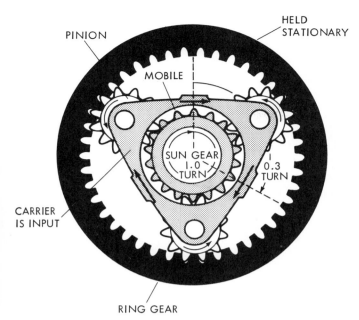

Fig. 3-13. Planetary gear set in overdrive, with ring gear stationary—shooting pinion carrier.

Law of Direct Drive

Direct drive or high gear is obtained by clutching or locking any two members of the gear set together. This can also be interpreted to mean that driving any two members at the same relative speed and in the same direction will give the same effect.

The principle of direct drive is shown and explained in the following sequence of illustrations, Figs. 3-14, 3-15, and 3-16. In automatic transmissions, a multiple-disc clutch or fluid clutch is used to lock any two members of a planetary gear set for direct drive.

Although the fluid clutch was used for years in the G.M. Hydra-Matic controlled coupling, it has no current application. Its uniqueness, however, is worthy of attention.

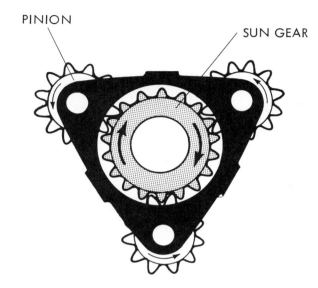

Fig. 3-15. Planetary gear set in direct drive sequence with sun gear driving. Clockwise power applied to planet pinions.

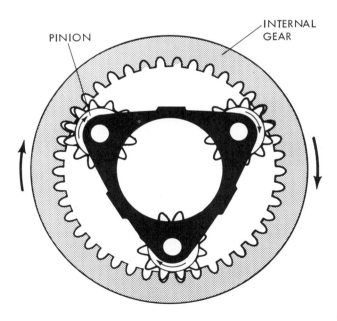

Fig. 3-14. Planetary gear set in direct drive sequence, with internal gear driving. As clockwise power is applied to the internal gear the planet pinions are rotated clockwise.

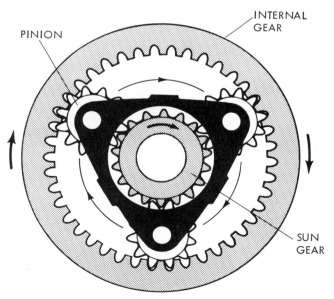

Fig. 3-16. Planetary gear set in direct drive. Clockwise power applied to the sun gear and the internal gear meets at the planet pinion preventing the pinions from rotation on their centers. If the pinions cannot rotate on their centers, it is obvious that the planet pinions are trapped solidly between the sun gear and the ring gear and must turn with them at the same relative speed.

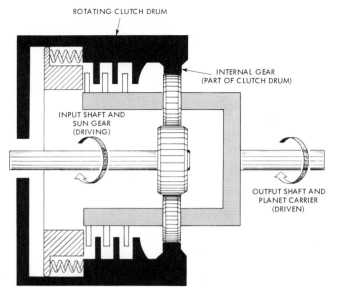

ROTATING CLUTCH DRUM

INTERNAL GEAR
(PART OF CLUTCH DRUM)

INPUT SHAFT AND
SUN GEAR
(DRIVING)

OUTPUT SHAFT AND
PLANET CARRIER
(DRIVEN)

Fig. 3-17. Multiple disc clutch for locking internal gear and planet carrier in direct drive.

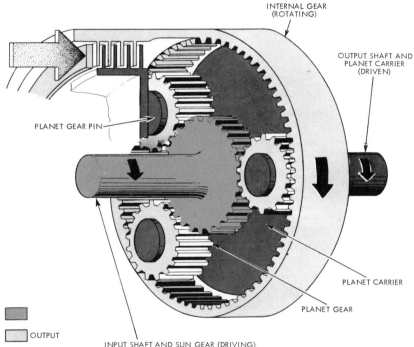

INTERNAL GEAR
(ROTATING)

OUTPUT SHAFT AND
PLANET CARRIER
(DRIVEN)

PLANET GEAR PIN

PLANET CARRIER

PLANET GEAR

INPUT SHAFT AND SUN GEAR (DRIVING)

OUTPUT

Figure 3-17 shows a typical multiple-disc clutch, which in this case locks the internal gear and planet carrier together. Apply and release of the clutch is controlled by the transmission valve body.

Figure 3-18 illustrates how a fluid clutch is used for direct drive. The fluid clutch is nothing more than a fluid coupling with a drive and a driven member enclosed in a housing.

When the housing is filled with oil, the drive member transmits power through the oil to the driven member for direct drive. In this case the internal gear (input) through the fluid clutch drives the sun gear at the same relative speed.

The exhaust valve is used to empty the coupling when direct drive is not needed, (Fig. 3-19). When the hydraulic close signal is released from the exhaust valve, spring pressure and the rotating force of the coupling opens the valve. At the same time, the oil supply for the coupling fill is cut-off by the valve-body control, and the centrifugal effect of the rotating coupling dumps the coupling oil out through the exhaust valve.

For coupling fill, the exhaust valve is closed by a hydraulic signal followed by coupling feed oil. Essentially, the exhaust and fill operations are controlled by the transmission valve body.

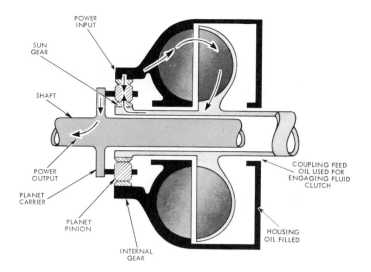

Fig. 3-18. Fluid clutch filled and engaged for direct drive.

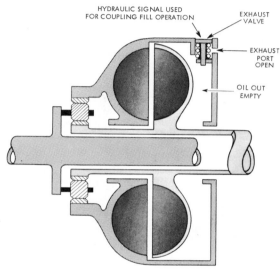

Law of Reverse

When the planet carrier, but not the planet gears, is held against rotation, reverse is the result (for simple planetary set only).

Reverse rotation (and one that is popularly used in most current three-speed automatic transmissions) is shown in Fig. 3-20. With the planet carrier held by a band application, the sun gear input rotation is reversed by the planet gears, with the reverse motion then picked up by the internal gear and output shaft at a reduction. In place of a band, it is common to find the use of a multiple-disc clutch for holding the carrier.

If the internal gear was used as the input in Fig. 3-20, then the sun gear would rotate in reverse overdrive.

Fig. 3-19. Fluid clutch emptied and disengaged for gear reduction.

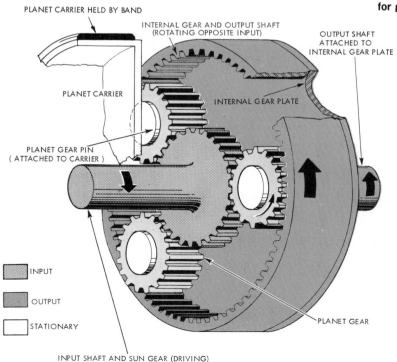

Fig. 3-20. Typical reverse gear operation.

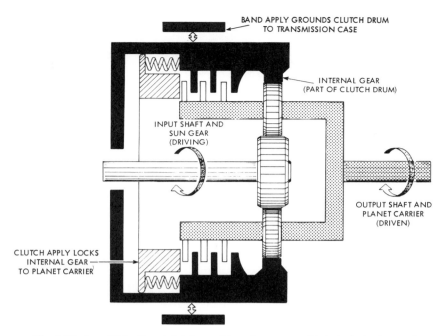

Fig. 3-21. A multiple disc clutch is used in a drum assembly to lock the internal gear to the planet carrier for direct drive. The clutch is oil applied and spring released. For gear reduction the band is APPLIED and the clutch is OFF.

COMBINING GEAR REDUCTION AND DIRECT DRIVE

It is possible to use a single planetary gear assembly as a two-speed transmission if the basic requirements for reduction and direct drive are satisfied. A band and multiple-disc clutch are combined in Fig. 3-21 to illustrate the possibility. The band is used for holding the internal gear for reduction and the multiple disc clutch ties the internal gear and planet carrier together for direct drive.

It is the valve body controls that coordinate the apply and release of these friction units so that they do not fight one another or cause a powerflow interruption during a gear change.

Figure 3-22 shows how a sprag clutch and fluid clutch are combined for two-speed operation. For gear reduction, the fluid clutch is empty and therefore cannot transmit a power flow. The clockwise input rotation of the internal gear will attempt to turn the sun gear counter-clockwise (Fig. 3-23), applying the sprags that will lock the inner race to the outer race (Fig. 3-24). But because the outer race is grounded to the transmission case, the sprag clutch assembly now holds the sun gear and the end result is gear reduction.

Fig. 3-22. When the coupling is empty and the sprag is ON the condition is reduction. When the coupling is full and the sprag is OFF the effect is direct.

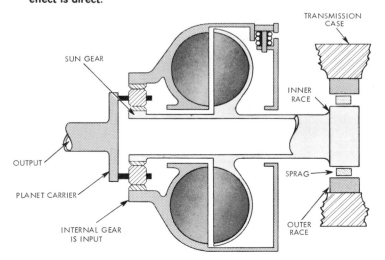

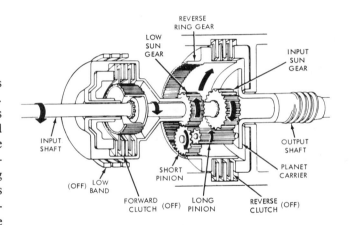

COUNTERCLOCKWISE MOTION
LOCKS SUN GEAR AND SPRAG

INTERNAL
GEAR DRIVES

Fig. 3-23. Sun gear reversal locks inner sprag race
to outer race and holds the sun gear stationary.

When the fluid clutch is filled, direct drive occurs as previously explained under the Law of Direct Drive. The important point is to note that the sprag releases independently of any valve body control. The oil-filled clutch forces the sun gear and also the inner sprag race to rotate in a clockwise direction, along with the internal gear. This clockwise motion of the inner sprag race releases the wedging action of the sprags and it is free to rotate independently of the outer race (Fig. 3-24). This release action does not take place until the fluid clutch is capable of picking up the torque load during its oil fill.

COMBINING PLANETARY SETS

To achieve a two-speed, three-speed, or four-speed gear train, planetary sets can be arranged mechanically in a variety of ways.

In a two-speed set-up, one planetary is used, with the shift from low to direct usually accomplished as a band to clutch transition. Figure 3-25 illustrates a two-speed gear train arrangement using a Ravigneaux planetary. It is a compound single planetary whereby a dual pinion planet carrier and two sun gears are integrated in the assembly. The band is applied and holds the low sun gear for reduction. On the low to direct shift the band is released and the direct clutch is applied, locking the low sun gear and input sun gear together. The Ravigneaux planetary configuration is also adaptable for three-speed and four-speed applications used in the Ford FMX and AOT transmissions and the General Motors (MD-3) 180. These are discussed in Chapters Four and Eleven.

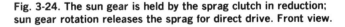

Fig. 3-25. 2-speed planetary.
(Courtesy General Motors Corp.)

Fig. 3-24. The sun gear is held by the sprag clutch in reduction;
sun gear rotation releases the sprag for direct drive. Front view.

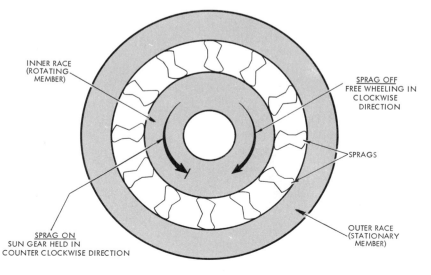

INNER RACE
(ROTATING
MEMBER)

SPRAG OFF
FREE WHEELING IN
CLOCKWISE
DIRECTION

SPRAGS

SPRAG ON
SUN GEAR HELD IN
COUNTER CLOCKWISE DIRECTION

OUTER RACE
(STATIONARY
MEMBER)

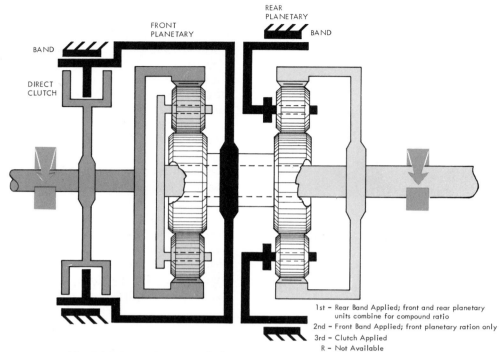

Fig. 3-26. 3-speed compound planetary arrangement. Front planetary
internal gear is a constant input.

A three-speed arrangement can be achieved by compounding two planetaries. As illustrated in Figs. 3-26 and 3-27, the planetaries are integrated by sharing two common members together. Both illustrations are configurations of the popular Simpson planetary, which is widely used in current three-speed automatics.

The operation of the three-speed planetary arrangements are not discussed at this time.

Operational details and applications are covered in Chapters 4 and 11.

Two simple planetaries can be put together in series for four-speed operation. The planet sets share one common member. In Fig. 3-28, the output member of Planetary A is the input member of Planetary B.

Fig. 3-27.   3-speed compound planetary arrangement. Rear internal gear is a constant input.

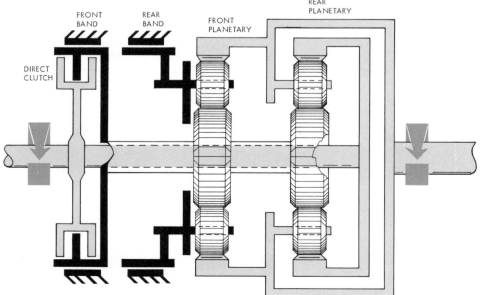

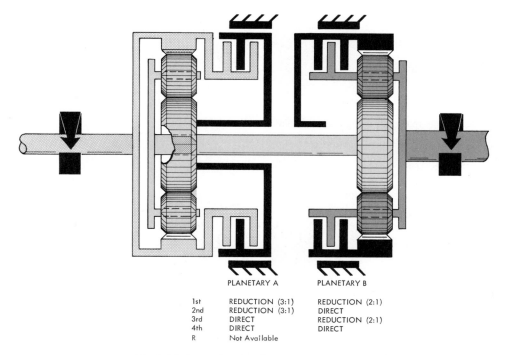

	PLANETARY A	PLANETARY B
1st	REDUCTION (3:1)	REDUCTION (2:1)
2nd	REDUCTION (3:1)	DIRECT
3rd	DIRECT	REDUCTION (2:1)
4th	DIRECT	DIRECT
R	Not Available	

Fig. 3-28. 4-speed series planetary arrangement.

PLANETARY GEAR RATIOS

The gear ratio equals the number of revolutions the driving member makes while the driven member makes one revolution. The gear ratios may also be expressed as the number of teeth on the driven member divided by the number of teeth on the drive member.

$$\text{Gear Ratio} = \frac{\text{rpm driving}}{\text{rpm driven}} = \frac{N \text{ teeth driven}}{N \text{ teeth drive}}$$

A gear ratio can be applied to any gear set—simple, compound, or planetary. In a simple gear set-up, the calculation of the gear ratio is easily determined by using a direct comparison of the number of gear teeth. However, for planetary gear set ratios, a modified ratio formula must be used because the planet pinions rotate about two centerpoints at the same time. During reduction or overdrive, the pinion gears rotate on their own centers and they walk around the common rotational center of the sun and internal gears. The following formulas and examples should clarify how gear ratios are calculated for single planetary gear sets.

Ns equals number of teeth on the sun gear (20)
Ni equals the number of teeth on the internal gear (50)

Example:

$$\text{Reduction} \atop \text{(carrier driven)} = \frac{N_\text{s} + N_\text{i}}{N \text{ driving}}$$

With sun gear driving and internal gear fixed

$$\text{Reduction} = \frac{20 + 50}{20} = 3.5{:}1 \text{ ratio}$$

Example:

$$\text{Overdrive} \atop \text{(carrier driving)} = \frac{N \text{ driven}}{N_\text{s} + N_\text{i}}$$

With internal gear driven and sun gear fixed

$$\text{Overdrive} = \frac{50}{20 + 50} = .71{:}1 \text{ ratio}$$

Example:

$$\text{Reverse} \atop \text{(carrier fixed} = \frac{N \text{ driven}}{N \text{ driving}}$$

With sun gear driving and internal gear driven

$$\text{Reverse} = \frac{50}{20} = 2.5{:}1 \text{ gear ratio}$$

Example:

$$\text{Reduction} \atop \text{(carrier driven)} = \frac{N_\text{s} + N_\text{i}}{N \text{ driving}}$$

With internal gear driving and sun gear fixed

$$\text{Reduction} = \frac{20 + 50}{50} = 1.4{:}1 \text{ ratio}$$

REVIEW QUESTIONS

CHAPTER 3
PLANETARY GEARS IN TRANSMISSIONS

Completion:

1. Identify the basic parts make-up of a simple planetary gear assembly.

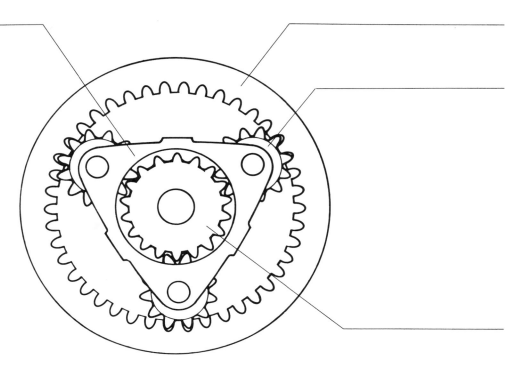

NOMENCLATURE
PLANETARY GEAR ASSEMBLY

2. In Figures 1, 2, 3, 4, and 5 use the following color code to indicate the input, output, and stationary members of a simple planetary gear assembly in neutral, reduction, overdrive, direct, and reverse modes.

    Red - Input   Blue - Output

    Black - Stationary
     Member

Indicate with arrows the direction of rotation of the planetary members.

<u>NEUTRAL</u>

SUN GEAR DRIVING

PLANET CARRIER ATTACHED TO OUT-PUT SHAFT AND CAR WEIGHT

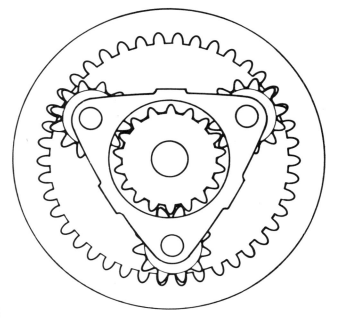

FIGURE 1

REDUCTION

RING GEAR DRIVING

SUN GEAR STATIONARY

FIGURE 2

OVERDRIVE

PLANET CARRIER DRIVING

SUN GEAR STATIONARY

FIGURE 3

DIRECT

SUN GEAR AND RING GEAR LOCKED
TOGETHER

FIGURE 4

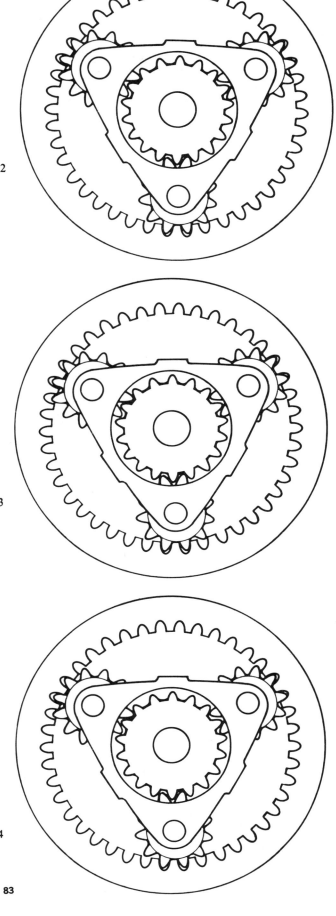

REVERSE REDUCTION

SUN GEAR DRIVING

PLANET CARRIER STATIONARY

FIGURE 5

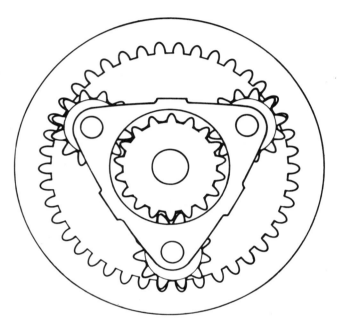

Completion:

1. When there is a reaction member and the planet carrier is the output, the planetary unit is operating in

   _____ .

2. When there is a reaction member and the planet carrier is the input, the planetary unit is operating in

   _____ .

3. Three devices that are used in automatic transmissions to hold a planetary member stationary.

   a. _____

   b. _____

   c. _____

4. Two types of one-way clutch designs used in controlling planetary gear action.

   a. _____   b. _____

5. Calculate the gear train torque output when:
   a. engine torque is 180 lb/ft
   b. converter torque ratio is 2 to 1
   c. the gear ratio is 2.5 to 1

6. For a one-way clutch to be effective and hold a planetary member stationary, the input effort to the one-way

   clutch must be in a _____ direction.

7. When any two planetary members are clutched together

   the resulting effect is _____ .

8. Overdrive gear ratios _____ speed and

   _____ torque.

9. Reduction gear ratios _____ speed and

   _____ torque.

10. The ring gear may also be referred to as an internal gear

    or _____ gear.

11. A one-way clutch will hold against _____

    torque and freewheel against _____ torque.

12. The reaction of the rotating planetary pinions to a fixed

    sun or ring gear results in a _____ motion.

13. The function of the planetary pinions in reverse is to act

    as _____ gears and reverse the power flow.

4

PLANETARY GEAR SYSTEMS IN AUTOMATIC TRANSMISSIONS

The preceding chapter served as the basis for understanding the fundamentals of planetary gears, their function, construction, and operation. The objective in this chapter is to discuss the application of these fundamentals to modern planetary gear systems used in three-speed and two-speed passenger car automatic transmissions.

The Powerglide two-speed, although no longer in production, is still being used in a significant number of second- and third-generation owned cars and therefore warrants discussion. In studying three-speed designs, 13 of the current passenger car transmissions use the Simpson planetary gear set while only three use the Ravigneaux planetary. It should be obvious that the task of learning how the gear train works in 13 different transmissions should not be too difficult, considering that 90% of the gear trains are the same. The main task is to study the minor product variations used in controlling the gear trains. In second gear, for example, some transmissions will hold the sun gear reactionary with an intermediate band, while in another transmission the same sun gear is held reactionary by an intermediate roller clutch. For maximum effect, the reader should study this chapter in conjunction with Chapter 11.

The Chrysler TorqueFlite is selected for a detailed study of how a three-speed Simpson planetary gear set operates (Fig. 4-1). This same planetary system is also common to the Ford C-6, JATCO, C-4 and C-3, American Motors Torque Command, and the General Motors 400, 350, 250, 200, 200-4R, and 125 Turbo Hydramatics. The new General Motors (MD-3) 180 automatic transmission and Ford FMX is used to illustrate the operation of a three-speed Ravigneaux planetary gear set. Some interesting comparisons can be made with the Powerglide two-speed Ravigneaux configuration.

When trouble shooting an automatic transmission, it is an advantage to know what gear sets are operational for each gear ratio and also what band and clutch combinations control these individual gears. With this knowledge, noise and friction element problems can be isolated to one area of the transmission.

SIMPSON PLANETARY SYSTEM (THREE-SPEED CHRYSLER TORQUEFLITE)

The TorqueFlite Transmission combines a three-element lock-up torque converter with a fully automatic three-speed planetary system. The transmission consists of two multiple-disc clutches, an overrunning roller clutch, two servos (a hydraulic piston that converts hydraulic force to mechanical force), two bands, and a compound planetary gear system consisting of two planetary gear sets sharing a common sun gear shaft and output shaft. This design provides three forward gear ratios, reverse, and neutral (Fig. 4-1).

Various versions of the TorqueFlite are manufactured: the A-904 for six-cylinder and low-torque V-8 engines, the A-727 for high torque V-8 engines or heavy duty six cylinder applications, and the A-404, A-413, and A-470 series for subcompact FWD vehicles. The basic difference between the A-904 and A-727 is the physical size. The A-404, A-413, and A-470 units have only slight differences in the case castings.

Operating Characteristics

The transmission operation is programmed by the traditional manual control at the steering column or on-the-floor console selector. The selector ranges are: P (park), R (reverse), N (neutral), D (drive), 2 (second), and 1 (low). For safety, the engine cannot start in other than the park or neutral positions.

In D, the transmission shifts through all three ratios automatically. Shift points are determined by throttle opening and car speed. If additional acceleration is desired while in Drive, the transmission will downshift (depending on vehicle speed) to second or breakaway (first gear) when the accelerator pedal is completely depressed. On closed throttle downshifts, the transmission shifts 3-1, taking advantage of the smooth, freewheeling action from the overrunning roller clutch during coast. For controlled acceleration at low speeds, a part throttle 3-2 downshift is available.

2 position is used to operate the transmission in the first two gears only—third gear is blocked out of operation. The 1-2 automatic shift occurs in the same manner as in D. This range is suitable for heavy city traffic, when the driver may desire to use part throttle second-range operation for more precise control. It may also be used on long down-grades, when additional engine braking is needed, or for extra pulling power.

1 position keeps the transmission in first gear only. It provides added braking and handling ease in

Fig. 4-1. Torqueflite transmission (A-904). (Chrysler Corp.)

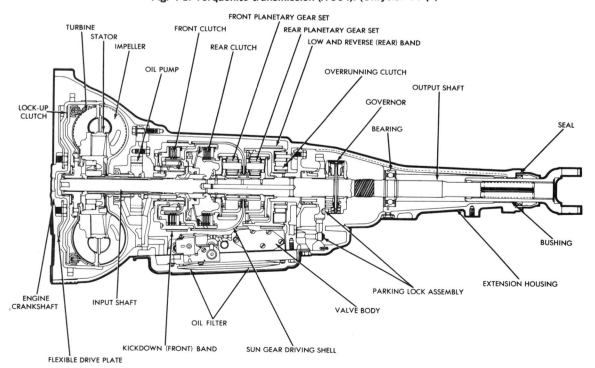

Range	Gear	Front Clutch	Rear Clutch	Front Kickdown Band	Rear Low-Reverse Band	Over-Running Clutch	Park Pawl
Park							in
Reverse		on			on		
Neutral							
D-Drive	first		on			holds	
	second		on	on			
	third	on	on				
2-Drive	first		on			holds	
	second		on	on			
1-Low	first		on		on	holds	

mountain driving and exceptional pulling qualities in sand and snow. If low range is selected at an excessive car speed, the transmission shifts to second gear and remains until the vehicle is slowed to a safe speed range. Once low gear is engaged, the transmission cannot upshift again.

Planetary Power Flow

Before proceeding with the details of operation, some basic facts need to be mentioned as a background for understanding the planetary system power flow. The power input to the transmission comes from the engine torque output through the converter to the transmission input shaft and the clutch units in the transmission. The power flow through the planetary gear train will depend on the application of the clutches, bands, and the overrunning roller clutch. Chart 4-1 provides a summary of the Torqueflite powerflow and range operation.

NOTE: Of special concern to the reader is that all reference to direction of rotation in describing the gearing power flows is based on viewing from the transmission front.

Neutral

In N (neutral), none of the clutches are engaged or bands applied. There is a power feed to the input shaft; however, with the front and rear clutches disengaged, no power is transmitted to the planetary gear set and to the output shaft. The powerflow dead-ends at the clutches.

Breakaway (First)

With the selector in either the D or 2 range, the rear clutch is engaged and the overrunning clutch holds (Figs. 4-2 and 4-3). The rear clutch has the same function as the forward clutch in other Simpson powerflows.

The torque flows from the converter turbine through the input shaft to the rear clutch. With the rear clutch engaged, the torque flow is able to turn the annulus gear (terminology preferred by Chrysler to

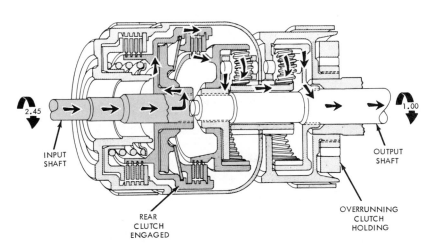

Fig. 4-2. Power flow in breakaway. (Chrysler Corp.)

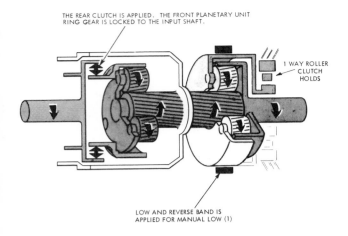

THE REAR CLUTCH IS APPLIED. THE FRONT PLANETARY UNIT RING GEAR IS LOCKED TO THE INPUT SHAFT.

1 WAY ROLLER CLUTCH HOLDS

LOW AND REVERSE BAND IS APPLIED FOR MANUAL LOW (1)

Fig. 4-3. Simplified power flow—breakaway.

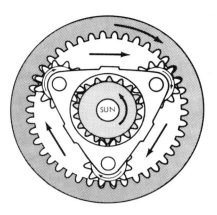

Fig. 4-4. Front planetary breakaway. The carrier will rotate with the output shaft once the gearing action begins, thus the annulus gear and the planet carrier are inputs to the front planetary. This results in a reverse overdrive effect on the sun gear which is the input to the rear planetary.

describe the internal gear) of the front planetary in a clockwise direction. Because the front planet carrier is splined to the output shaft and the weight of the car, the annulus gear drives the front planetary pinions, rotating them in the same direction. The pinions, in mesh with the sun gear, rotate the sun gear counterclockwise (Figs. 4-3 and 4-4).

The front and rear planetary sets share the same sun gearshaft; therefore, the sun gear turns the rear planet pinions in clockwise rotation. The planet pinions, in mesh with the rear annulus gear, turn the annulus gear and output shaft in a clockwise direction. The rear planet carrier is held by the overrunning clutch because of the action of the pinions as they rotate the rear annulus gear. The pinions must rotate the annulus gear against the weight of the car, which makes the annulus gear reactionary. This results in the pinions attempting to walk the rear carrier counterclockwise, which results in a lock-up of the roller clutch (Figs. 4-3 and 4-5).

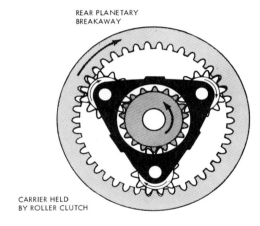

REAR PLANETARY BREAKAWAY

CARRIER HELD BY ROLLER CLUTCH

Fig. 4-5. Rear planetary breakaway, with carrier held by the roller clutch.

Fig. 4-6. Power flow in second gear. (Chrysler Corp.)

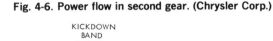

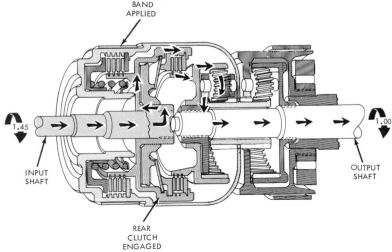

KICKDOWN BAND APPLIED

1.45

INPUT SHAFT

REAR CLUTCH ENGAGED

1.00

OUTPUT SHAFT

Lock-up of the overrun clutch is effective as long as the car is under drive power. On coast, with the rear wheels and the weight of the car working against the engine compression, the planetary gear action forces the rear carrier to turn clockwise and release the roller clutch. This results in a neutral gear condition, and therefore engine braking is not possible during coast breakaway.

In summary, breakaway is a result of the compound gearing action of both the front and rear planetary gear sets. The gear sets share a common sun gearshaft and integrated front carrier and rear annulus with the output shaft. The effective compound torque ratio is 2.45:1.

Second

With the selector in D or 2 (second), the rear clutch remains engaged while the kickdown band is applied to hold the driving shell and sun gear stationary (Figs. 4-6, 4-7, and 4-8).

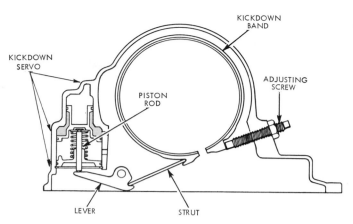

Fig. 4-8. Rear view; Torqueflite servo and linkage mechanism is used for applying the kickdown around the front clutch drum.

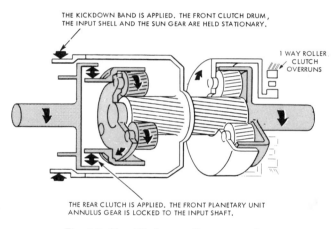

THE KICKDOWN BAND IS APPLIED. THE FRONT CLUTCH DRUM, THE INPUT SHELL AND THE SUN GEAR ARE HELD STATIONARY.

1 WAY ROLLER CLUTCH OVERRUNS

THE REAR CLUTCH IS APPLIED. THE FRONT PLANETARY UNIT ANNULUS GEAR IS LOCKED TO THE INPUT SHAFT.

Fig. 4-7. Simplified power flow—second.

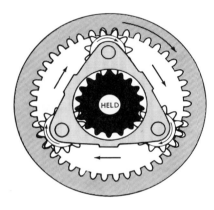

Fig. 4-9. The front planetary carrier is splined to the output shaft and turns at reduced speed. The sun is held by the kickdown band.

With the rear clutch engaged, the front annulus gear and front planetary pinions all rotate in a clockwise direction. Applying the law of reduction, the rotating planet pinions react on the stationary sun gear and walk the front planetary carrier and output shaft at a reduced speed (Fig. 4-9).

The rear planetary in second gear goes along for the ride. The rear annulus gear attached to the output shaft drives the rear planet pinions in a clockwise direction. These pinions react on the stationary sun gear and walk the carrier in a clockwise direction, resulting in a freewheeling overrun clutch (Fig. 4-10).

In summary, second gear is a result of a simple reduction action from the front planetary—when there is a reactionary member and the planetary carrier is the output, the condition is gear reduction. The torque ratio result is 1.45:1.

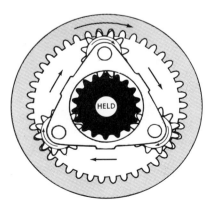

Fig. 4-10. The rear planetary-carrier and overrun clutch freewheel, and the planetary is ineffective. The sun gear, also common to the front planetary, is held by the kickdown band.

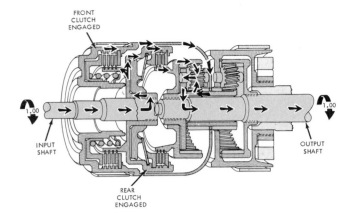

FRONT CLUTCH ENGAGED

1.00   1.00

INPUT SHAFT   OUTPUT SHAFT

REAR CLUTCH ENGAGED

Fig. 4-11. Power flow in D (drive) range—direct. (Chrysler Corp.)

Fig. 4-12. Simplified power flow in D (drive) range—direct. (Chrysler Corp.)

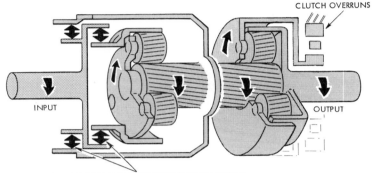

1 WAY ROLLER CLUTCH OVERRUNS

INPUT   OUTPUT

BOTH THE REAR AND FRONT CLUTCHES ARE APPLIED. ALL PLANETARY GEAR MEMBERS ARE LOCKED TO EACH OTHER AND ARE LOCKED TO THE OUTPUT SHAFT.

Direct (Third)

D (direct) occurs when the front and rear clutches are engaged and both bands are released (Figs. 4-11 and 4-12). The front clutch has the same function as the direct clutch in other Simpson powerflows.

With both clutches engaged, the torque from the input shaft takes a dual path, one through the front clutch to the drive shell and sun gear and the other through the rear clutch to the front planetary annulus gear. This dual input to the front planetary prevents the pinions from rotating and locks the front and rear

gear set to the output shaft at a 1:1 ratio. The overrun clutch continues to freewheel.

In summary, the planetary gear train behaves in accordance to the Law of Direct Drive—when two members of a planetary gear set are clutched together or driving at the same speed, the pinion gears are trapped and kept from rotating on their centers; this results in a planetary lock-up.

Typically, in all automatic transmissions, direct drive locks-up the drive clutches and planetary gears so that all motion within the power train is essentially at

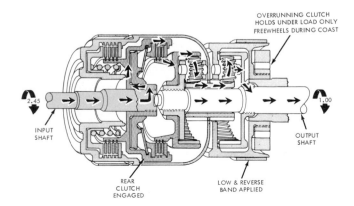

OVERRUNNING CLUTCH HOLDS UNDER LOAD ONLY FREEWHEELS DURING COAST

2.45   1.00

INPUT SHAFT   OUTPUT SHAFT

REAR CLUTCH ENGAGED   LOW & REVERSE BAND APPLIED

Fig. 4-13. Power flow in (1) manual low—low or retarding. (Chrysler Corp.)

the same speed. When troubleshooting noise problems that are audible in direct drive or high gear, it is not likely that the planetary gears or clutch assemblies are at fault.

It is interesting to note that neither the front or rear clutch handles the full input torque to the planetary set. Because of the dual path input, the torque to the planetary set is divided between the clutch units. The holding power of the front and rear clutch units is more than adequate for high gear operation.

Manual Low

In 1 (manual low), the rear clutch is engaged and the low and reverse band applied (Figs. 4-13 and 4-14).

A comparison of Fig. 4-2 and Fig. 4-13 shows that the power flow in breakaway and manual low is the same. Although the low/reverse band is applied, it is not effective when manual low is used for sustained pulling power; the roller clutch holds. The band, however, assures that, upon a coast condition, the holding force remains on the rear planetary carrier as the overrun clutch attempts to freewheel. Hence, the planetary gear unit remains effective for engine braking during deceleration or when coasting down hilly or mountainous terrain.

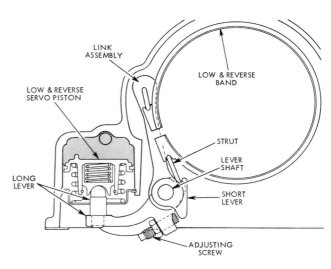

Fig. 4-14. Rear view; Torqueflite servo and linkage used for applying the low/reverse band around the low/reverse drum which is part of the rear planet carrier.

Reverse

In R (reverse), the front clutch is engaged to the drive shell and the sun gear. The low and reverse drum and rear planetary carrier are held stationary by the low/reverse band (Figs. 4-15 and 4-16).

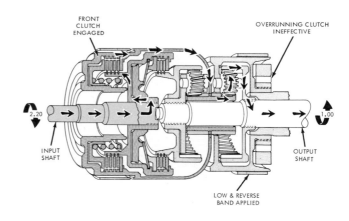

Fig. 4-15. Power flow in reverse. (Chrysler Corp.)

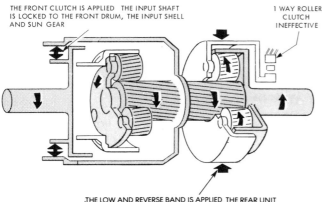

Fig. 4-16. Simplified power flow— reverse position.

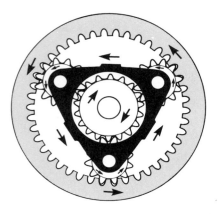

Fig. 4-17. Reverse—rear planet carrier held by low/reverse band. Planet pinions reverse the motion of the sun gear and drive the rear annulus gear and output shaft in reverse.

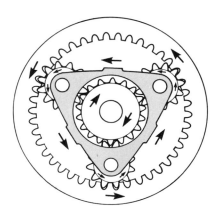

Fig. 4-18. Reverse-front planetary action. Powerflow dead-ends at the annulus gear which is rotating at an overdrive speed.

Engagement of the front clutch drives the shell and sun gear in a clockwise direction. With the rear carrier held stationary, the sun gear drives the rear planet pinions counterclockwise. This reversing motion of the planet pinions also drives the rear annulus gear (splined to the output shaft) in the reverse direction at a reduced speed (Fig. 4-17). The front planetary gears during reverse operation are active but do not enter into the power flow picture. The rear clutch is OFF and the power flow dead-ends (Fig. 4-18).

In summary, reverse is a result of a simple reduction action from the rear planetary with the pinion gears acting as reverse idlers—when the planetary carrier (but not the planet gears) is held against rotation, reverse is the outcome. In this case, the sun gear is the input member that gives a reverse reduction of 2.20:1.

Park

In P (park), the transmission gear train remains in neutral. A manually-activated linkage engages a spring loaded pawl in the parking lock gear assembly, which is splined to the output shaft to lock the rear wheels to the transmision case as shown in Fig. 4-19.

Fig. 4-19. (Chrysler Corp.)

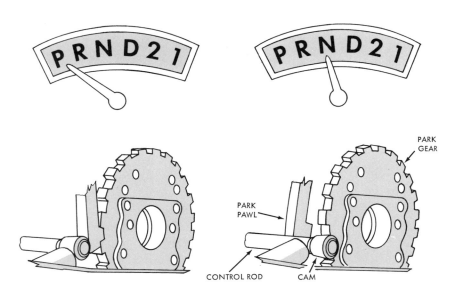

ENGINE RUNNING
NEUTRAL AND PARK

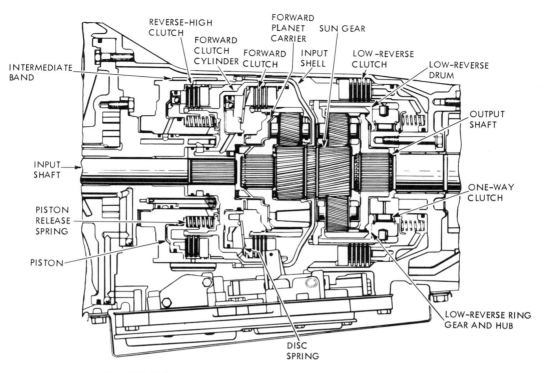

Fig. 4-20. C-6 gear train, clutches and band. (Transmission converter is not shown.) (Ford Motor Co.)

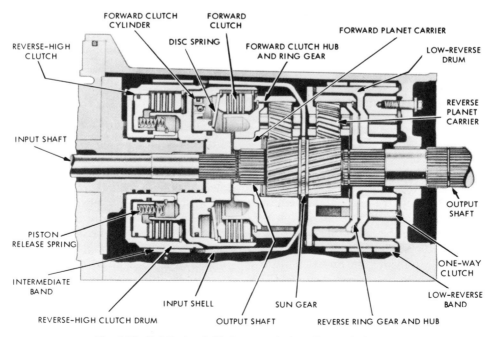

Fig. 4-21. C-4 Cruise-O-Matic transmission. (Transmission converter is not shown.) (Ford Motor Co.)

SIMPSON LOW GEAR FORMULA
(COMPOUND REDUCTION)

Formula:

Planetary Set I

I_1 = number of teeth on internal gear

S_1 = number of teeth on sun gear

Planetary Set II

I_2 = number of teeth on internal gear

S_2 = number of teeth on sun gear

Formula I:

$$\left[\frac{I_2}{S_2}\right]\left[\frac{\left(\frac{S_2}{I_2}\right)(I_1+S_1) + S_1}{I_1}\right] = \begin{array}{c}\text{First Gear}\\\text{Compound Ratio}\end{array}$$

This formula will be accurate if the carrier of set 1 is connected to the internal gear of set 2, with the sun gears coupled, and set 2 carrier held reactionary. This is a true formula and will work even if the planetary gear sets are not identical.

SIMPSON PLANETARY SYSTEM
(FORD C-6 AND C-4 THREE-SPEED)

The Ford C-6 and C-4 Cruise-O-Matic transmissions (Figs. 4-20 and 4-21) closely resemble the Chrysler TorqueFlite. The gear trains are of the same design, and so are the clutch and band combinations, with one exception. The C-6 has a low-and-reverse multiple disc clutch in place of the low-and-reverse band used in both the C-4 and the TorqueFlite. The C-4 was introduced in 1964 and the C-6, which is a larger version design for higher torque engines, in 1966.

Within the Ford family, the JATCO is a small size version of the C-6, and the C-3 is a small size version of the C-4. Both the JATCO and C-3 are manufactured overseas.

Operating Characteristics

The C-6 and C-4 use either the standard steering column or a console shift selector with six positions. Figures 4-22 and 4-23 show the early and late design selector patterns. The change in selector design patterns was to accommodate the Select-Shift feature of the transmissions in 1967. The Select-Shift had previously been available only in the Sports-Shift C-6 Cruise-O-Matic on the high performance Comet GTA and Fairlane GTA models. The selector illustrated in Fig. 4-22 offers two drive ranges, D2 and D1.

In the normal drive range (D1), full automatic shifting takes place. The car starts in low and upshifts automatically to second and high depending on

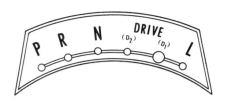

Fig. 4-22. Early selector pattern used for Dual Range automatic transmission, C-4 and C-6. (Ford Motor Co.)

Fig. 4-23. Later selector pattern used for Select Shift automatic transmissions, C-4 and C-6. (Ford Motor Co.)

throttle opening and road speed. The usual 3–2 and 3–1 wide open throttle-forced downshifts and part throttle 3–2 downshift are available.

D2 range starts out in second gear and automatically upshifts to high. The 3–2 wide open throttle-forced downshift and 3–2 part throttle downshift feature is maintained.

The current Select-Shift (Fig. 4-23) gives the driver more manual control over the transmission.

The (1) range keeps the transmission in low gear and the (2) range gives second gear operation only. In D range, the transmission is fully automatic, starting in first gear, shifting into second, and then into high gear. With this selector arrangement, the driver can elect to start in D and have fully automatic shifting, or start in 1, then shift to 2, and then into D at any speed or peak engine rpm.

On manual downshifting by the driver for braking or added performance, full engine–transmission protection is built in. Shifting from D to 2 immediately downshifts the transmission to second gear, while the shift from the D or 2 position into 1 downshifts the transmission to low. If the road speed is too high when shifting to 1, the transmission selects second gear until road speed is at a safe level for the downshift into low.

The usual 3–2 and 3–1 wide open throttle-forced downshifts and part throttle 3–2 downshift are available in D. The closed throttle downshift sequence is 3–1 at 10 mph. This avoids using the intermediate band, and the transition back to first gear is extra smooth because of the freewheeling roller clutch action.

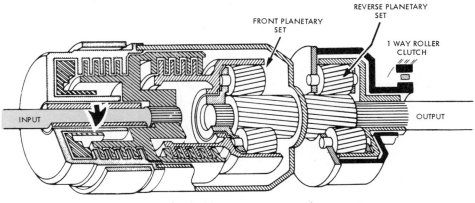

FRONT PLANETARY SET

REVERSE PLANETARY SET

1 WAY ROLLER CLUTCH

INPUT

OUTPUT

CLUTCHES AND THE BAND ARE RELEASED
NEUTRAL

Fig. 4-24. Neutral—with bands and clutches in the OFF position, there is no input to the gear sets. (Ford Motor Co.)

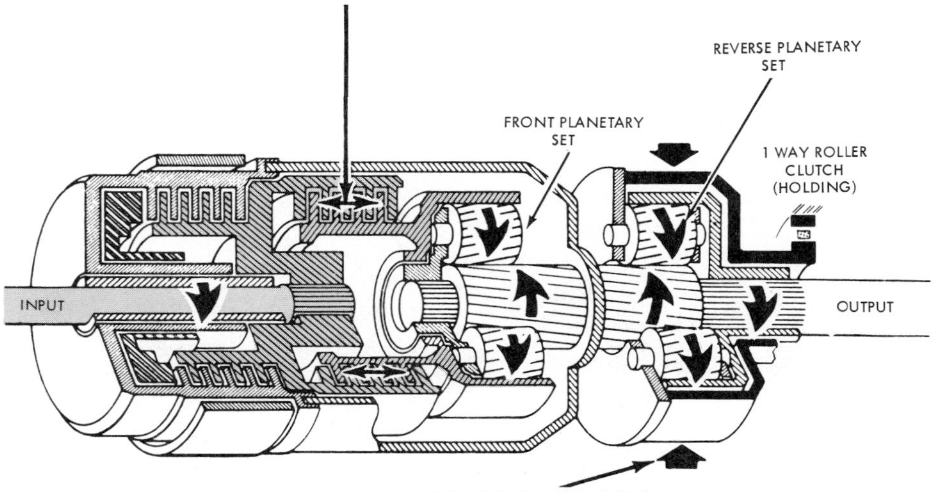

THE FORWARD CLUTCH IS APPLIED THE FRONT PLANETARY UNIT RING GEAR IS LOCKED TO THE INPUT SHAFT

REVERSE PLANETARY SET

FRONT PLANETARY SET

1 WAY ROLLER CLUTCH (HOLDING)

INPUT

OUTPUT

THE LOW AND REVERSE BAND IS APPLIED FOR LOW RANGE (1)
FIRST GEAR

Fig. 4-25. Drive—first gear is a function of the front and the reverse planetary sets. (Ford Motor Co.)

Fig. 4-26. Drive—second gear is a function of the front planetary gear set. (Ford Motor Co.)

THE INTERMEDIATE BAND IS APPLIED THE REVERSE AND HIGH CLUTCH DRUM, THE INPUT SHELL AND SUN GEAR ARE HELD STATIONARY

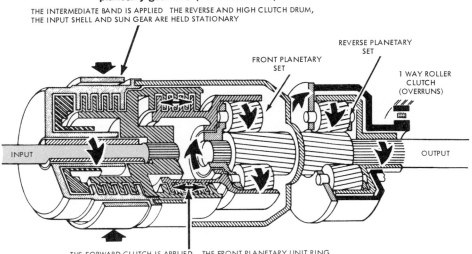

FRONT PLANETARY SET

REVERSE PLANETARY SET

1 WAY ROLLER CLUTCH (OVERRUNS)

INPUT

OUTPUT

THE FORWARD CLUTCH IS APPLIED THE FRONT PLANETARY UNIT RING GEAR IS LOCKED TO THE INPUT SHAFT

SECOND GEAR

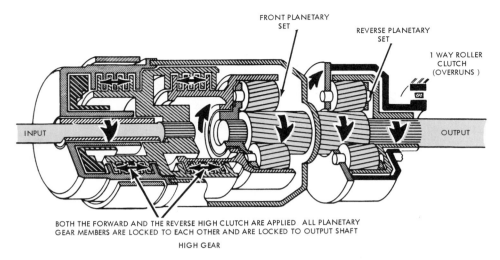

FRONT PLANETARY
SET

REVERSE PLANETARY
SET

1 WAY ROLLER
CLUTCH
(OVERRUNS)

INPUT

OUTPUT

BOTH THE FORWARD AND THE REVERSE HIGH CLUTCH ARE APPLIED   ALL PLANETARY
GEAR MEMBERS ARE LOCKED TO EACH OTHER AND ARE LOCKED TO OUTPUT SHAFT

HIGH GEAR

Fig. 4-27. Drive—in high the locking of the planetary gears is a result of the forward clutch driving the front internal gear and the reverse/high clutch driving the sun gear.

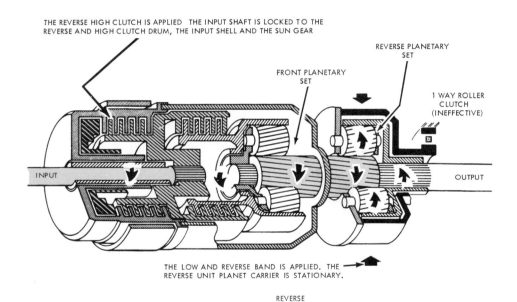

THE REVERSE HIGH CLUTCH IS APPLIED   THE INPUT SHAFT IS LOCKED TO THE
REVERSE AND HIGH CLUTCH DRUM, THE INPUT SHELL AND THE SUN GEAR

REVERSE PLANETARY
SET

FRONT PLANETARY
SET

1 WAY ROLLER
CLUTCH
(INEFFECTIVE)

INPUT

OUTPUT

THE LOW AND REVERSE BAND IS APPLIED. THE
REVERSE UNIT PLANET CARRIER IS STATIONARY.

REVERSE

Fig. 4-28. Reverse is the function of the reverse planetary unit. (Ford Motor Co.)

CHART 4-2
Ford C-6 Select Shift
Powerflow Summary and Range Reference
Selector Pattern P R N D 2 1

Range	Gear	Forward Clutch	Reverse High Clutch	Intermediate Band	Low Reverse Clutch	One-Way Clutch	Park Pawl
Park							in
Reverse			on		on		
Neutral							
D-Drive	first	on				holds	
	second	on		on			
	third	on	on				
2-Drive	second	on		on			
1-Low	first	on			on	holds	

Range	Gear	Forward Clutch	Reverse High Clutch	Intermediate Band	Low Reverse Clutch	One-Way Clutch	Park Pawl
Park							in
Reverse			on		on		
Neutral							
D-Drive	first	on				holds	
	second	on		on			
	third	on	on				
2-Drive	second	on˙		on			
1-Low	first	on			on	holds	

Planetary Power Flow

Because the C-6 and C-4 planetary power flows are identical to the Chrysler TorqueFlite, it should be necessary only to compare Figs. 4-24, 4-25, 4-26, 4-27, and 4-28 with the previous TorqueFlite sequence of power flow illustrations and detailed discussion. The overrunning clutch used in the C-6 and C-4 (shown in the illustrations) functions as in the TorqueFlite. Also note that the reverse/high clutch has the same function as the TorqueFlite front clutch and the forward clutch has the same function as the TorqueFlite rear clutch.

Charts 4-2 and 4-3 give the power flow and range summaries of the Select-Shift C-6 and C-4.

RAVIGNEAUX PLANETARY SYSTEM (G.M. MD-3 180)

The Ravigneaux planetary system utilizes a dual pinion planetary carrier, two sun gears, and a ring gear (Fig. 4-29). The planet carrier is made-up of three dual pinion sets. The short pinions are in constant mesh with both the input (front) sun gear and the long planet pinions. The long planet pinions are in constant mesh with the reaction (rear) sun gear, the short planet pinions, and the ring gear. Cross section and schematic views are illustrated in Figs. 4-30 and 4-31.

Ravigneaux planetary systems can be arranged for three-speed operation with either the planet carrier or ring gear as the output member.

In the General Motors 180 transmission, the planet carrier is arranged as the output member (Figs. 4-30 and 4-31). The planetary set is controlled by three multiple-disc clutches, a one-way sprag clutch, and a band.

NEUTRAL. The band and clutches are not applied. The sprag is locked, however, and there is an input to the planetary set. Because there is no reactionary member, the planetary gears spin-up but cannot provide an output (Fig. 4-31).

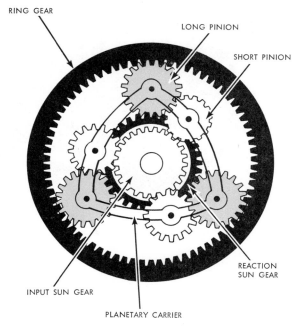

Fig. 4-29. Ravigneaux planetary set. (Chevrolet Division, General Motors Corp.)

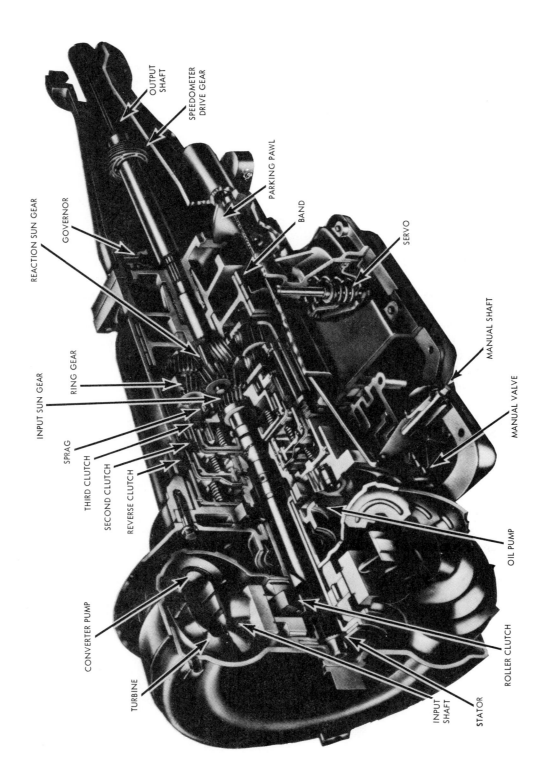

Fig. 4-30. MD-3 180 sectional view. (Chevrolet Division, General Motors Corp.)

OUTPUT SHAFT

SPEEDOMETER DRIVE GEAR

PARKING PAWL

BAND

SERVO

REACTION SUN GEAR

GOVERNOR

MANUAL SHAFT

INPUT SUN GEAR

RING GEAR

MANUAL VALVE

SPRAG

THIRD CLUTCH

SECOND CLUTCH

REVERSE CLUTCH

OIL PUMP

CONVERTER PUMP

TURBINE

ROLLER CLUTCH

INPUT SHAFT

STATOR

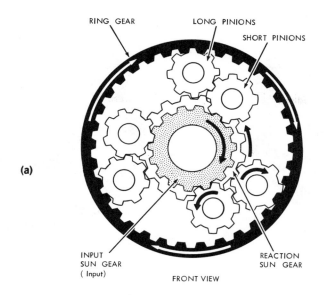

(a)

RING GEAR — LONG PINIONS — SHORT PINIONS

INPUT SUN GEAR (Input) — REACTION SUN GEAR

FRONT VIEW

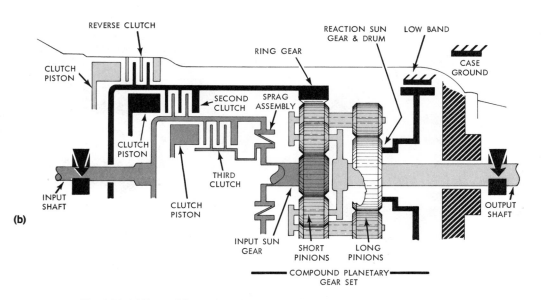

(b)

REVERSE CLUTCH — REACTION SUN GEAR & DRUM — LOW BAND

CLUTCH PISTON — RING GEAR — CASE GROUND

CLUTCH PISTON — SECOND CLUTCH — SPRAG ASSEMBLY

THIRD CLUTCH

INPUT SHAFT — CLUTCH PISTON — OUTPUT SHAFT

INPUT SUN GEAR — SHORT PINIONS — LONG PINIONS

COMPOUND PLANETARY GEAR SET

Fig. 4-31. (a) Neutral-Power input but no reactionary gear member. (b) Schematic.

FIRST GEAR. The reaction sun gear is held stationary. The input sun gear rotates in a clockwise direction, turning the short pinions counterclockwise and the long pinions clockwise. The long pinions walk around the held reaction sun gear, driving the planet carrier and output shaft in a forward reduction. A compound gear ratio of 2.40:1 is provided. The ring gear in mesh with the long pinions rotates clockwise but has no function in the power flow. First gear is illustrated in Figs. 4-31 and 4-32.

SECOND GEAR. The reaction sun gear remains stationary. The ring gear is the input member that drives the long pinions in a clockwise direction. The long pinions walk around the reaction sun gear and drive the planet carrier and output shaft at a forward

reduction. A simple gear ratio of 1.48:1 is provided. The long pinions are also driving the short pinions counterclockwise. The input sun gear in mesh with the short pinions is driven in a clockwise direction. The effect of the planet carrier rotation causes the short pinions to drive the input sun gear at an overdrive speed, which results in the release of the sprag clutch. Second gear is illustrated in Figs. 4-31 and 4-33.

THIRD GEAR. The ring gear and input sun gear are common input members turning at the same speed. The long and short pinions are, therefore, trapped between the ring gear and input sun gear and cannot rotate on their shafts. This results in a lock-up of the planetary members and a 1:1 ratio. Third gear is illustrated in Figs. 4-31 and 4-34.

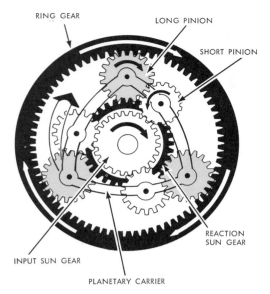

Fig. 4-32. First Gear. Input sun gear driving and reaction sun gear stationary. (Chevrolet Division, General Motors Corp.)

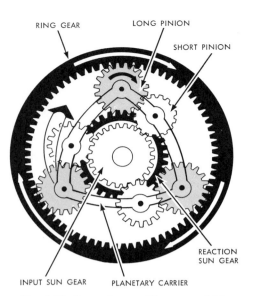

Fig. 4-33. Second gear. Ring gear driving and reaction sun gear stationary. (Chevrolet Division, General Motors Corp.)

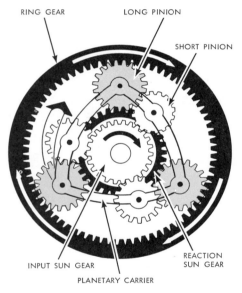

Fig. 4-34. Third gear. Ring gear and input sun gear driving. (Chevrolet Division, General Motors Corp.)

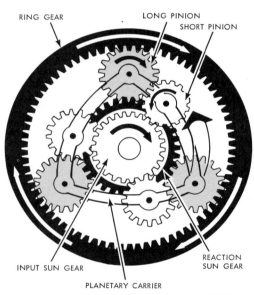

Fig. 4-35. Reverse. Input sun gear driving and ring gear stationary. (Chevrolet Division, General Motors Corp.)

CHART 4-4
(MD-3) 180 Automatic Transmission
Power flow and Range Summary Chart
Selector Pattern P R N D L$_2$ L$_1$ or P R N D 2 1

Range	Gear	Reverse Clutch	Second Clutch	Third Clutch	Low Band	Sprag
Park-Neutral						Locked
Reverse		on		on		Locked
D	First				on	Locked
	Second		on		on	
	Third		on	on		
L$_2$	First					Locked
	Second		on		on	
L$_1$	First			on	on	Locked

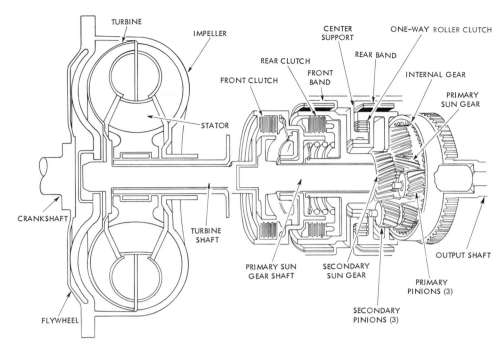

Fig. 4-36. FMX planetary gear train. Cross section. (Ford Motor Co.)

REVERSE. The ring gear is held and the input sun gear drives the planetary pinion gears. The short pinions turn counterclockwise and the long pinions clockwise. The long pinions in mesh with the stationary ring gear walk around the inside of the ring gear and drive the planet carrier and output shaft in a counterclockwise direction. A simple reverse reduction of 1.91:1 is provided. Reverse is illustrated in Figs. 4-31 and 4-35.

Chart 4-4 summarizes the powerflow and range operation of the 180 transmission.

RAVIGNEAUX PLANETARY SYSTEM (FORD FMX)

In the Ford Motor Company FMX transmission, the ring gear is the output member (Fig. 4-36). The planetary set is controlled by two multiple-disc clutches, a one-way roller clutch, and two bands.

Fig. 4-37. FMX operation—neutral. (Ford Motor Co.)

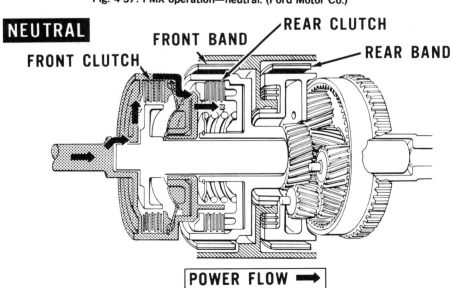

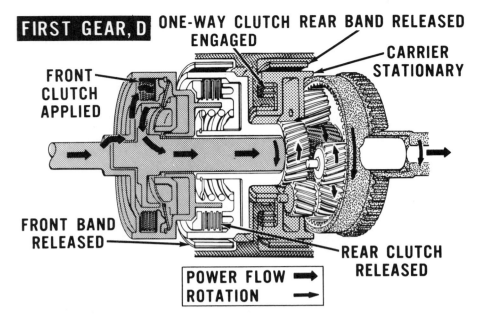

Fig. 4-38. FMX operation—first gear, D. (Ford Motor Co.)

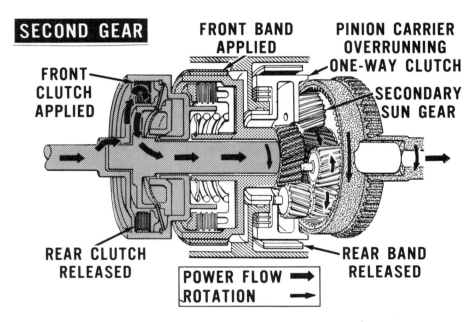

Fig. 4-39. FMX operation—second gear. (Ford Motor Co.)

CHART 4-5
Ford FMX
Powerflow Summary and Range Reference
Selector Pattern P N R D 2 1

Range	Gear	Front Clutch	Rear Clutch	Front Band	Rear Band	One-Way Clutch	Park Pawl
Park							in
Reverse			on		on		
Neutral							
D-Drive	First	on				holds	
	Second	on		on			
	Third	on	on				
2-Drive	Second	on		on			
1-Low	First	on			on	holds	

The FMX gear train operation is illustrated in Figs. 4-37, 4-38, 4-39, 4-40, 4-41, and 4-42. Note that the dual pinion planetary carrier is mounted on a one-way roller clutch. When reviewing the planetary action it is important to know that the short pinions are meshed with the primary sun gear and long pinions, but not the ring gear. The long pinions mesh with the short pinions, secondary sun gear, and the internal gear. The power flow and range operation is summarized in Chart 4-5.

For 1980, the FMX has been redesigned to incorporate a fourth gear overdrive. It is referred to as the AOT (Automatic Overdrive Transmission).

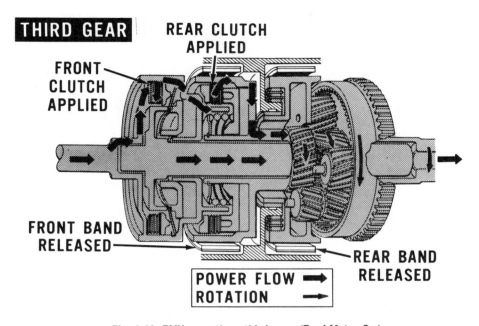

Fig. 4-40. FMX operation—third gear. (Ford Motor Co.)

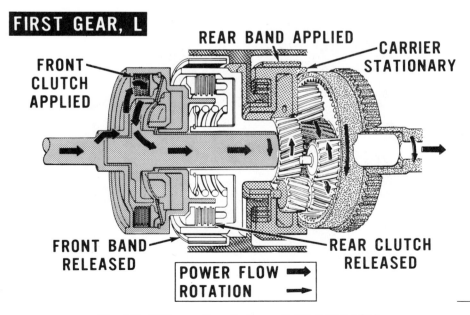

Fig. 4-41. FMX operation—first gear, 1. (Ford Motor Co.)

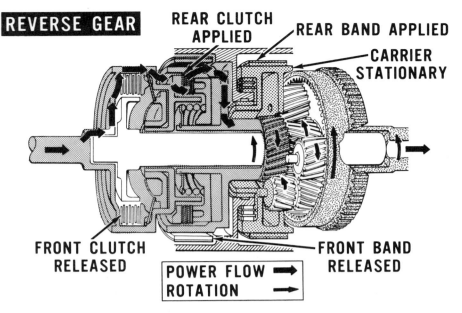

REVERSE GEAR

REAR CLUTCH APPLIED

REAR BAND APPLIED

CARRIER STATIONARY

FRONT CLUTCH RELEASED

FRONT BAND RELEASED

POWER FLOW ➡

ROTATION ➡

Fig. 4-42. Cruise-O-Matic operation—reverse gear. (Ford Motor Co.)

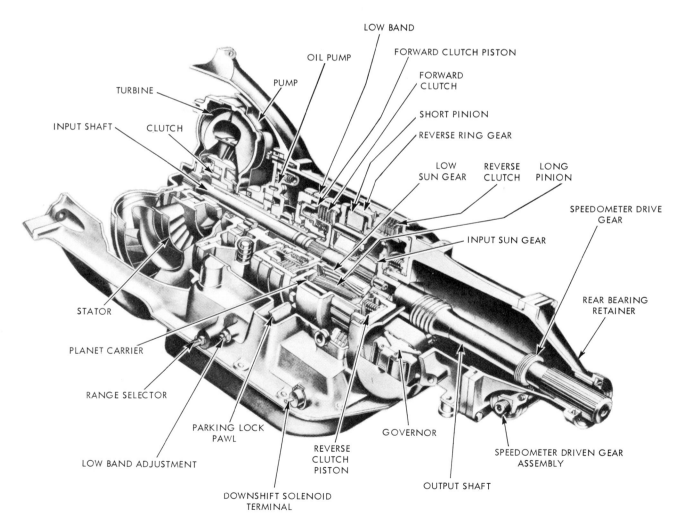

LOW BAND

OIL PUMP

FORWARD CLUTCH PISTON

PUMP

FORWARD CLUTCH

TURBINE

SHORT PINION

REVERSE RING GEAR

INPUT SHAFT

CLUTCH

LOW SUN GEAR

REVERSE CLUTCH

LONG PINION

SPEEDOMETER DRIVE GEAR

INPUT SUN GEAR

REAR BEARING RETAINER

STATOR

PLANET CARRIER

RANGE SELECTOR

PARKING LOCK PAWL

GOVERNOR

SPEEDOMETER DRIVEN GEAR ASSEMBLY

LOW BAND ADJUSTMENT

REVERSE CLUTCH PISTON

OUTPUT SHAFT

DOWNSHIFT SOLENOID TERMINAL

Fig. 4-43. Typical 2-speed Ravigneaux. (General Motors Corp.)

RAVIGNEAUX PLANETARY SYSTEM
(TWO-SPEED)

The Ravigneaux planetary system is adaptable to two-speed operation. When two-speed automatic transmissions were in production, this planetary system was employed by Ford, General Motors, and Packard (Fig. 4-43). The planetary set is controlled by a band and two multiple-disc clutches. Early design units, however, did use two bands and one multiple-disc clutch.

The two-speed gear train operation is illustrated in Figs. 4-44, 4-45, 4-46, and 4-47. The power flow and range operation is summaried in Chart 4-6.

CHART 4-6
2-Speed Ford and G.M. Super Turbine 300,
Jetaway, Powerglide, and Pontiac 2-Speed
Powerflow Summary and Range Reference
Selector Pattern P R N D L

Range	Gear	Direct Clutch	Reverse Clutch	Low Band	Park Pawl
Park					in
Reverse			on		
Neutral					
Drive	Low			on	
	Hi	on			
Low	Low			on	

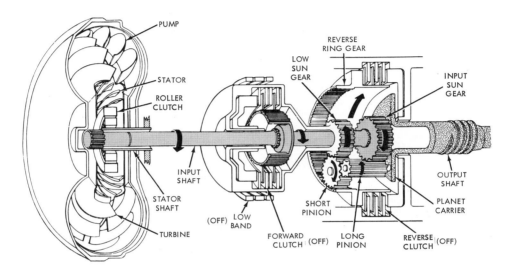

Fig. 4-44. Neutral. (General Motors Corp.)

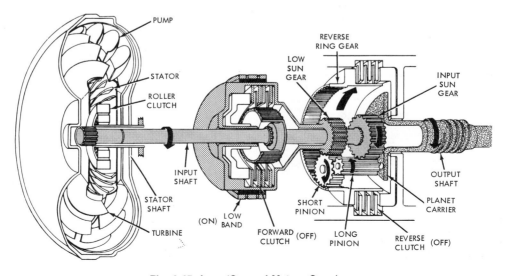

Fig. 4-45. Low. (General Motors Corp.)

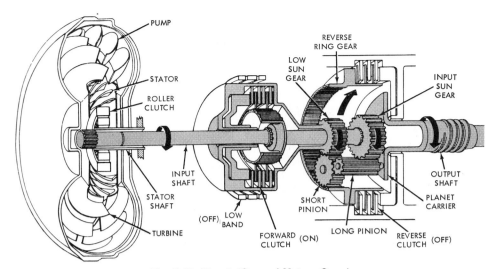

Fig. 4-46. Direct. (General Motors Corp.)

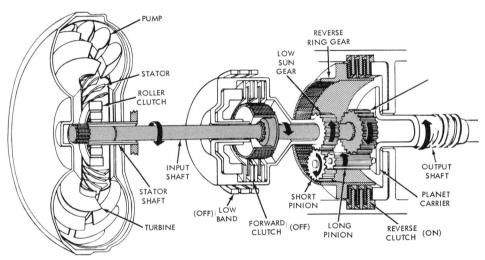

Fig. 4-47. Reverse. (General Motors Corp.)

REVIEW QUESTIONS

CHAPTER 4
PLANETARY GEAR SYSTEMS IN AUTOMATIC TRANSMISSIONS

Completion:

1. The name given to a compound single planetary configuration integrating a dual pinion planet carrier and two sun gears. _____

2. The name given to a compound planetary configuration using two single planetary sets sharing the same sun gear shaft and output shaft. _____

3. Review Chapters 4 and 11 and check mark the following transmissions that use a Simpson compound planetary gear unit.

GENERAL MOTORS

_____ THM 125	_____ THM 325
_____ THM 200	_____ THM 400
_____ THM 200-4R	_____ MD-3 180
_____ THM 250	_____ Powerglide
_____ THM 350	

FORD MOTOR COMPANY

_____ C-3	_____ ATX
_____ C-4	_____ FMX
_____ C-6	_____ AOT
_____ JATCO	

CHRYSLER

_____ 727	_____ 904	_____ 404
_____ 413	_____ 470	

MECHANICS OF OPERATION
SIMPSON 3-SPEED PLANETARY
WITH TORQUEFLITE TERMINOLOGY

Use the given choices and select the one best answer for the following questions. Indicate your choice by placing the letter code in the question blank. A choice may be used more than once.

GROUP I

A.	Front Annulus Gear	**E.** Sun Gear
B.	Rear Annulus Gear	**F.** Front Planetary Unit
C.	Front Planet Carrier	**G.** Rear Planetary Unit
D.	Rear Planet Carrier	**H.** Compound Planetary Unit

_____ Provides the second gear ratio.

_____ Provides the reverse gear ratio.

_____ The stationary planet member in second gear.

_____ The stationary planet member in first gear.

_____ The stationary planet member in reverse.

_____ The output planetary member in first gear.

_____ The output planetary member in second gear.

_____ The output planetary member in reverse gear.

_____ The planet member motion related to the overrun clutch.

GROUP II

A. Front Clutch	**D.** Low and Reverse Band
B. Rear Clutch	**E.** Overrunning Clutch
C. Kickdown Band	

_____ Holds the sun gear.

_____ Drives the sun gear.

_____ Drives the front annulus gear.

_____ Holds the stationary planet member first gear acceleration.

POWER FLOW QUESTIONS
SIMPSON 3-SPEED PLANETARY
TORQUEFLITE TERMINOLOGY

NEUTRAL

All clutches and bands are _____; therefore, the torque converter turbine cannot drive the planetary gear assembly and output shaft.

DRIVE OR (2) RANGE—FIRST GEAR (Breakaway)

The _____ clutch is applied and the input shaft delivers turbine torque to the _____ annulus gear in a clockwise direction. The clockwise rotation of the annulus gear causes the planetary pinions to rotate in a _____ direction and drive the sun gear _____. The sun gear causes the rear planetary pinions to rotate _____ and drive the rear annulus gear and output shaft clockwise at a first gear reduction ratio. The reaction of the rear planetary pinions working against the rear annulus gear and car weight results in a pinion gear "walking" action that attempts to rotate the planet carrier _____. This reaction effort results in a lock-up of the _____ clutch and the rear planet carrier is held stationary.

DRIVE OR (2) RANGE—SECOND GEAR

The _____ clutch remains "on" and the _____ band is applied to hold the _____ clutch drum, _____ shell, and _____ gear stationary against counterclockwise rotation. Turbine torque driving through the _____ clutch rotates the _____ annulus gear in a clockwise direction. The clockwise rotation of the annulus gear causes the front planet pinions to "walk" around the stationary _____ gear in a _____ direction. This causes the front planet carrier and the output shaft to turn clockwise at an intermediate reduction ratio. Second gear ratio is a function of the _____ planetary unit.

Because the rear annulus gear is splined to the output shaft it drives the rear planet pinions in a _____ _____ direction. The rotating planet pinions react against the stationary _____ gear and "walk" the rear planet carrier in a _____ direction. This releases the _____ clutch and the rear planetary unit freewheels.

DRIVE RANGE—THIRD GEAR

In third gear the _____ and _____ clutch units are applied. Turbine torque is transmitted through the rear clutch and drives the _____ annulus gear, and also through the front clutch and drives the _____ gear. Essentially, the front and rear clutches lock the front annulus and sun gears together permitting the turbine to rotate the two gears in a _____ direction at the same speed. This traps the planet pinion gears in both front and rear units and the planetary gear sets are locked and turn as one unit providing a direct drive ratio of 1:1.

MANUAL LOW—FIRST GEAR

The _____ clutch is applied and the roller clutch holds the rear planet carrier against _____ _____ rotation during acceleration or power conditions. The planetary gear action is identical to Drive Range—First Gear. Manual Low features the added application of a _____ band to guarantee engine braking. Coast torque from the vehicle drive wheels is now the input to the transmission. The reaction of the rear pinion gears against the rear annulus gear (splined to the output shaft) imposes a clockwise effort on the roller clutch. This would cause the roller clutch to _____ and disengage the engine from the drive wheels. With the _____ band already applied, the rear planet carrier remains fixed and overrun breaking is provided.

REVERSE

The _____ clutch is applied and the _____ band holds the rear planet carrier stationary. The turbine torque is transmitted through the _____ clutch to the _____ _____ shell, and sun gear. Clockwise rotation of the sun gear causes the rear carrier pinions to turn _____. Because the planet carrier is held by the _____ band, the rear pinions act as idler gears and drive the _____ annulus gear and output shaft counterclockwise to achieve a reverse reduction ratio. Reverse reduction is a function of the _____ planetary unit.

In other Simpson planetary units, the Torqueflite rear clutch is referred to as the _____ clutch and the front clutch is called the _____ clutch.

MECHANICS OF OPERATION
RAVIGNEAUX 3-SPEED PLANETARY
FORD FMX

Use the given choices and select the one best answer for the following questions. Indicate your choice by placing the letter code in the question blank. A choice may be used more than once.

GROUP I

A.	Primary Sun Gear	D.	Planet Carrier
B.	Secondary Sun Gear	E.	Primary (Short) Pinions
C.	Internal Gear	F.	Secondary (Long) Pinions

_____ The common output planetary member of the FMX Ravigneaux Assembly.

_____ The larger sun gear.

_____ The smaller sun gear.

_____ The stationary planet member in first gear.

_____ The planet member motion related to the overrun clutch.

_____ The stationary planet member in second gear.

_____ Meshes with the secondary sun gear.

_____ Meshes with the internal gear.

GROUP II

A. Front Clutch   D. Front Band
B. Rear Clutch   E. Rear Band
C. Overrun Clutch

_____ Connects the primary sun gear to the input shaft.

_____ Connects the secondary sun gear to the input shaft.

_____ Holds the planet carrier in reverse.

_____ Serves as the forward clutch.

_____ Serves as the intermediate band.

_____ Holds the planet carrier in manual low (coast).

RAVIGNEAUX 3-SPEED PLANETARY FORD FMX POWERFLOW

1. Label the planetary members in the following Ford FMX planetary unit.

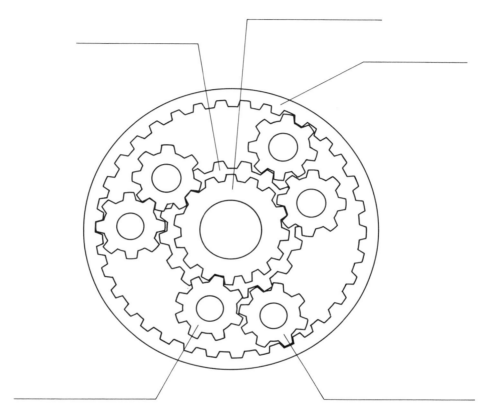

In other Ravigneaux planetary units, the secondary pinions

are referred to as the _____ pinions and the pri-

mary pinions are called the _____ pinions.

2. In Figures 1, 2, 3, and 4 use the following color code to indicate the input, output, and stationary members in 1st Gear, 2nd Gear, 3rd Gear, and Reverse.

Red—Input   Blue—Output   Black—Stationary
                                                Member

Indicate with arrows the direction of rotation of the planetary members. Be sure to indicate carrier rotation.

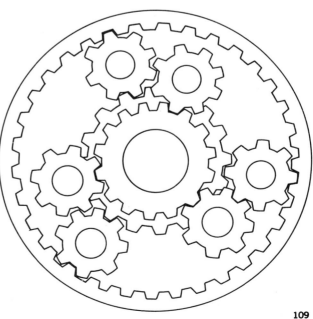

FIRST GEAR   Figure 1

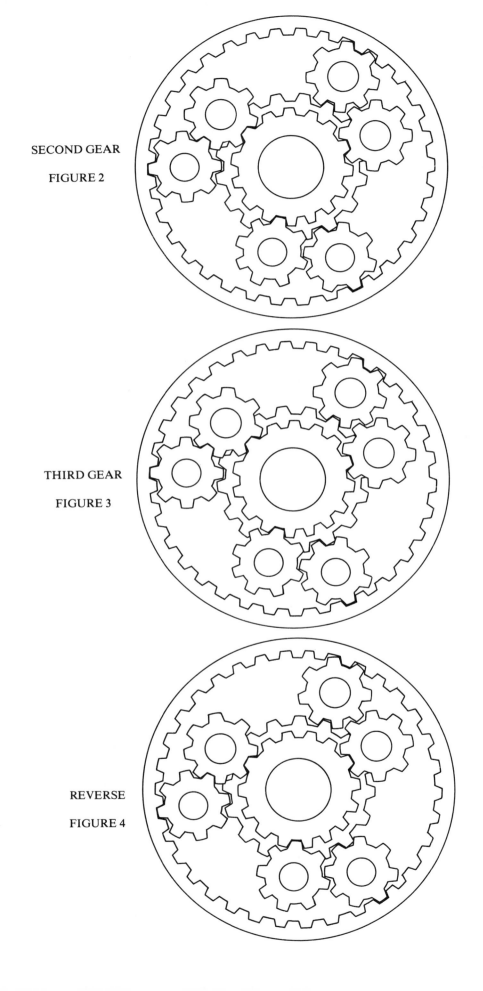

SECOND GEAR

FIGURE 2

THIRD GEAR

FIGURE 3

REVERSE

FIGURE 4

5

HYDRAULIC SYSTEM FUNDAMENTALS*

The principal objective in the development of automatic transmission units was to relieve the driver of the physical effort and coordination required to operate a clutch pedal and a shift lever for gear changes. For full automatic shifting, the transmission must start the car in motion smoothly, swiftly, and silently. It must select the proper gear ratio for any given engine torque and vehicle speed combination. It must also respond immediately to the will of the driver.

To provide the automatic gear ratio changes, fluid energy through a valve control system is used to apply the friction band and multiple-disc clutch combinations that work the planetary gear set. The hydraulic system used for this automatic control consists of the following (Fig. 5-1):

- Fluid
- Fluid reservoir (pump)
- Pressure source from a hydraulic pump

*Based on training publications of the Chrysler Corporation.

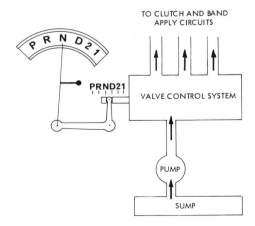

Fig. 5-1. Basic hydraulic control system.

- Hydraulic operating units (actuators) to apply the bands and clutches.
- Control or valve system for regulating pressures and directing fluid flows for automatic and manual gear engagements.
- Mechanical control to allow for driver selection of the operating ranges.

Operational details of the hydraulic system involves the use of pump gears, pistons, spool valves, regulating valves, relay valves, and a host of supporting parts and controls. Before proceeding with these details, it is important to know the science of pressure hydraulics.

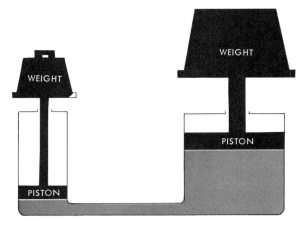

Fig. 5-2. Pressure is transmitted by fluids. (Chrysler Corp.)

FLUID AND THE HYDRAULIC LEVER

The word hydraulic comes from the Greek word for water. For many years the science of hydraulics was nothing more than storing water, moving it from place to place, and operating water wheels. The machine age changed all of this simplicity. Today's modern hydraulics involves a lot more science and machine applications than ever dreamed by the ancient Greeks.

Hydraulics involves the use of a fluid, so let's proceed to ''de-Greek'' hydraulics and begin with what a fluid is:

FLUID. A fluid can either be a liquid or a gas. Because our subject matter is hydraulics, the media for transmitting force and motion takes place through the use of a liquid. In automatic transmissions, a mineral oil fortified with additives is used.

An essential part of pressure hydraulics is understanding the basic nature of a fluid and how it acts as a lever arm in transmitting force and motion. This is defined in Pascal's Law.

Pascal's Law

In the seventeenth century, Pascal, a French scientist, discovered the hydraulic lever. In laboratory experiments, he proved that force and motion could be transferred by means of a confined liquid. Experimenting with weights and pistons of varying size, Pascal also found that mechanical advantage or force multiplication could be obtained in a pressure system, and that the relationships between force and distance were exactly the same as with a mechanical lever (Fig. 5-2). From the data Pascal collected, he formulated a law, which states:

Pressure on a confined fluid is transmitted equally in all directions and acts with equal force on equal areas.

To the novice learning hydraulics this may sound like a mass of complicated words. Therefore, let's break it down into easy-to-understand parts, demonstrating it with the kind of equipment Pascal used in his experiments. To simplify the discussion of Pascal's Law, it is important to review two terms that are commonly used when talking about hydraulics; force and pressure. Actually, force and pressure are units of measurement used in hydraulics.

FORCE. For our purposes, force can be defined as a push or pull on an object.

A classic example of a kind of force is gravity. The force of gravity is nothing more than the weight of an object. If you weigh 175 lb (778 N), you exert a downward force of 175 lb (778 N) on the floor on which you are standing.

In hydraulics, another type of force often encountered is spring force (Fig. 5-3). Spring force is the tension in the spring when it is compressed or stretched.

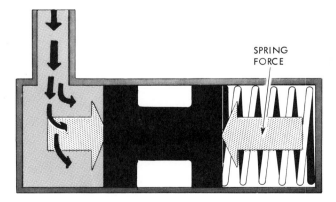

Fig. 5-3. Hydraulic force versus spring force. (Chrysler Corp.)

The reader by now has probably deduced that the engineering and household unit for force is the pound (lb). Force can be measured, then, on any scale designed to measure weight.

In the Metric-English conversion, force is measured by *newtons*. Pounds of force can be converted to equivalent newtons by multiplying pounds by a factor of 4.448; 100 lb equals 444.8 newtons. The abbreviation for newtons is N.

PRESSURE. Pressure is force divided by area, or force per unit area.

To illustrate pressure (Fig. 5-4), a uniform weight of 1,000 lb (4,448 N) rests on a surface 100 in² (645 cm²). The total force is 1,000 lb (4,448 N), the weight of the object; however, the force on each square inch of area is 1,000 lb (4,448 N) divided by 100 in² (645 cm²), or 10 lb (44.5 N) of pressure on the surface per square inch:

POUNDS PER SQUARE INCH. This is the unit for measuring pressure. It is abbreviated psi.

In the Metric-English conversion, lb/in² is measured by *kilopascals*. lb/in² can be converted to kilopascals by multiplying lb/in² by a factor of 6.895; 100 psi equals 689.5 kilopascals. The abbreviation for kilopascals is kPa.

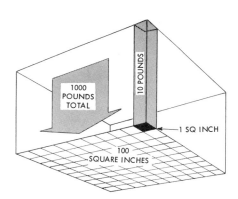

PRESSURE = 10 POUNDS PER SQUARE INCH

Fig. 5-4. Force is pressure divided by area. (Chrysler Corp.)

Pressure on a Confined Fluid

Pressure is exerted on a confined fluid by applying a force to some area in contact with the fluid. For example, if a cylinder is filled with fluid, and a piston closely fitted to the cylinder has a force applied to it, pressure will be created in the fluid (Figs. 5-5 and 5-6).

If the fluid is not confined, no pressure will be created but a fluid flow will result. There must be a resistance to flow to create pressure. (In the illustrations, the applied forces used are that of gravity, or weight

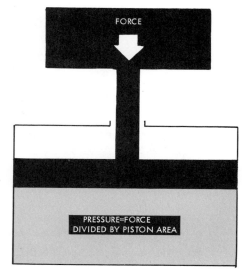

Fig. 5-5. Pressure is force on a confined liquid. (Chrysler Corp.)

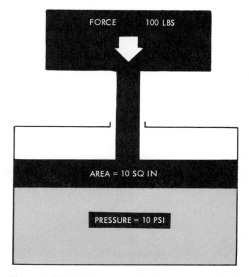

Fig. 5-6. Pressure is equal to the force applied. (Chrysler Corp.)

applied downward. The principle, however, is the same, no matter in what direction the force is applied.)

Figures 5-5 and 5-6 show that the pressure created in the fluid is equal to the force applied divided by the piston area. If the force is 100 lb (444.8 N) and the piston area is 10 in.², pressure equals 10 psi (69 kPa). According to Pascal's Law, this pressure of 10 psi (69 kPa) is equal everywhere in the trapped fluid (Fig. 5-7).

Pressure on a confined fluid is transmitted undiminished in all directions.

No matter what shape the container is, no matter how large, this pressure will be maintained throughout, as long as the fluid is confined.

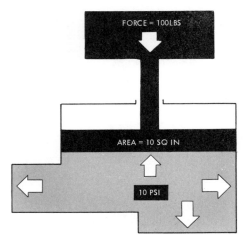

Fig. 5-7. Pressure is equal in all directions. (Chrysler Corp.)

Force on an Area

Another part of Pascal's Law states:

Pressure acts with equal force on equal areas.

The greater the area, however, the greater the force; in fact, the total force on any area equals the pressure multiplied by the areas (Fig. 5-8). In the illustration, 10 psi (69 kPa) is created and applied to a piston with a 100 in² (645 cm²) area; thus, a total of 10 times 100, or 1,000 lb (4,448 N) of force, is exerted. In fact, input force may be multiplied 100 to 1, or even 1,000 to 1 by increasing the size of the output piston.

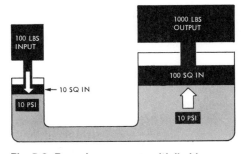

FORCE ON LARGE PISTON = 1000 LBS

Fig. 5-8. Force is pressure multiplied by area. (Chrysler Corp.)

The servo and clutch pistons in an automatic transmission are working examples of how hydraulic pressure is transformed into a mechanical force to apply the bands and clutches (Figs. 5-9 and 5-10). If the transmission apply pressure is 100 psi (689.5 kPa), then a 5 in² servo piston and 10 in² (64.5 cm²) clutch

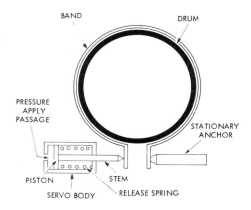

Fig. 5-9. A servo is a hydraulic piston used for band application.

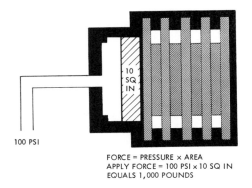

FORCE = PRESSURE × AREA
APPLY FORCE = 100 PSI × 10 SQ IN
EQUALS 1,000 POUNDS

Fig. 5-10. A hydraulic piston used for clutch application.

piston would develop 500 lb (2224 N) and 1,000 lb (4,448 N) of apply force respectively.

Conservation of Energy and the Hydraulic Lever

The old law of conservation of energy says that "energy can neither be created nor destroyed." The only way to get a large output force with a small input force is to make the input force travel farther.

In a mechanical set-up using the fulcrum and lever principle (Fig. 5-11), a 100-lb (444.8 N) weight is used to move a 1,000-lb (4448 N) weight with a lever. It should be obvious that to get an output ten times the input lever, the input lever arm has to be ten times as long. Thus, for every foot the 1,000 lb (4448 N) weight moves, the 100-lb (444.8 N) weight has to move 10 ft. The energy transfer in this system can easily be measured in foot-pounds (ft-lb). The 1,000-lb (4,448 N) weight moves 1 ft, and therefore it also has 1,000 ft-lb of energy. (Work is measured in ft-lb, but torque is measured in lb-ft.) In summation, if friction losses are ignored, 1,000 lb (4,448 N) of energy is transferred in the system with no loss or gain, thus proving the law of conservation of energy.

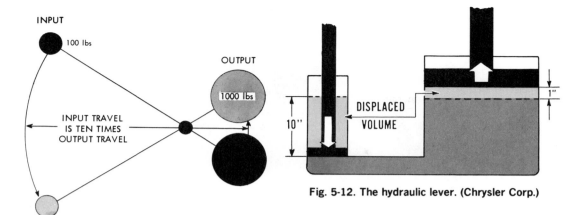

Fig. 5-11. The story of the lever. (Chrysler Corp.)

Fig. 5-12. The hydraulic lever. (Chrysler Corp.)

The law of conservation of energy can be related to hydraulics. Returning to a small and large piston illustration (Fig. 5-12), the same weight-to-distance relationship is established as with the lever. In this case, if the values are used from Fig. 5-8, the input piston has to travel 10 in. to displace enough fluid to move the output piston 1 in., a lever ratio of 10:1. In this example, the energy transfer is calculated in inch-pounds (in.-lb). It works out to 1,000 in.-lb (work may be measured in in.-lb as well as ft-lb) at each piston if you ignore friction loss in the system.

A BASIC HYDRAULIC SYSTEM

Now that you have been introduced to Pascal's Law and the principles of the hydraulic lever, let's look at how a simple hydraulic system works. Every pressure hydraulic system has certain basic components (Fig. 5-13); even the seemingly complex control system in an automatic transmission has the same basic units.

First a Reservoir

The reservoir (or sump) is a storehouse for fluid until it is needed in the system. In some systems in which there is constant circulation of the fluid, the reservoir aids cooling by transferring heat from the fluid to the container and ultimately to the atmosphere.

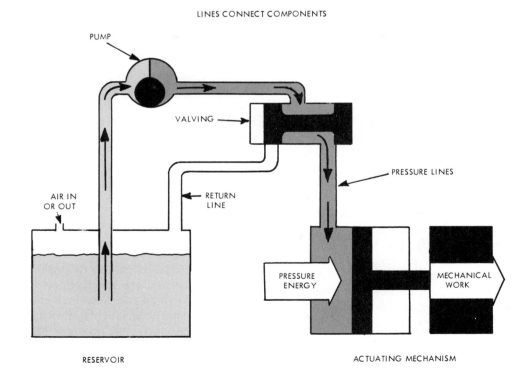

Fig. 5-13. A basic hydraulic system. (Chrysler Corp.)

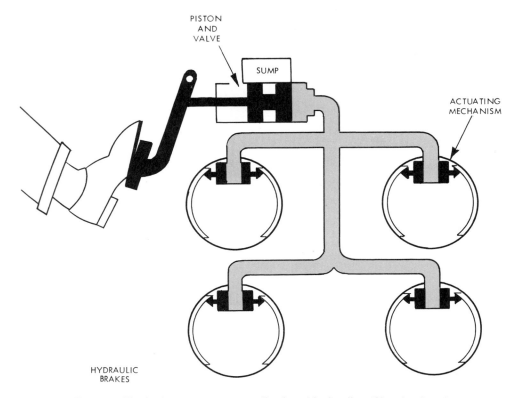

Fig. 5-14. The brake system as an application of hydraulics. (Chrysler Corp.)

In a brake system, the reservoir is part of the master cylinder (Fig. 5-14). In power steering, the power steering reservoir surrounds the pump housing. In automatic transmissions, the control system reservoir is the oil pan.

Then a Pump

The pump creates flow and applies force to the fluid. It pushes the fluid into the system and pressure is built-up when the fluid encounters resistance.

Here's an important point to remember. The pump cannot create pressure by itself; it can only create flow. If the flow does not meet any resistance, it is referred to as a free flow, and there is no pressure build-up. There must be a blind alley, a dead end, or a resistance to flow in the system to create pressure.

Pumps can be the reciprocating piston type (as in a brake master cylinder), or they can be rotary (like the front pump in an automatic transmission). In hydraulics, piston pumps are usually operated manually and rotary pumps are driven by an engine or an electric motor. In automatic transmissions, the front pump is driven by the engine through the converter hub, or if the transmission is also designed with a rear pump, it is driven by the output shaft.

Then Valving

Valving regulates and directs the fluid. Some valves just interconnect passages, telling the fluid where to go and when. Other valves control or regulate pressure and flow. In a brake system, for instance, valving is made up of the piston and ports in the master cylinder. In automatic transmissions, the valving for controlling the shifts and shift quality is housed in a control valve body.

An Actuating Mechanism

The working or actuating mechanism changes pressure energy to mechanical force. This is where the flow from the pump runs into a dead end and causes pressure to build-up. The pressure works against a surface and causes a force to be applied. In a brake system, there are eight actuating mechanisms, the wheel cylinder pistons (Fig. 5-14). In automatic transmissions, there are the servo pistons and clutch pistons to apply the bands and clutches.

Finally the Lines

The individual components of a hydraulic system need to be tied together for the system to operate. These components are interconnected by tubing, hoses, or passages that are machined or cast in the system housing and attachments. Pressure lines carry fluid from the pump to the actuating mechanisms and return lines release fluid to the sump when pressure is released. In many systems, such as brakes and automatic transmissions, the same lines perform both functions.

The Complete System

The preceding basic components make up any hydraulic system, whether it is simple or complex. An understanding of how these components work, and of some basic facts about hydraulic systems, will let you approach any system with confidence. No matter how many lines and how many valves in the system, each has a basic function that can be studied apart from the rest.

Flow in a Circuit

Flow has been mentioned several times without giving it too much attention. Flow is what is coming out of the pump when it is pumping and is commonly measured in gallons per minute, abbreviated gpm.

If the system output is force and motion, there is continuous flow to the actuating mechanism. If the output is force only, there is very little flow in the system, only enough to maintain pressure and make up for normal leakage. The pump is still delivering fluid, but it is bypassed to the sump by a regulator valve.

In any pressure hydraulic system, the components are kept full of fluid at all times. Thus, response to flow, or pressure build-up, is instantaneous. This is one reason that air, which is compressible, cannot be tolerated in a pressure system and must be bled out for proper operation of the system.

THE HYDRAULIC JACK

Let's look at a hydraulic jack circuit, examine it for basic component make-up, and study how it works (Fig 5-15).

The small piston is the pump and the large piston is the actuating mechanism. The large piston is used to raise a load; therefore its output will be force and motion. The system makes use of pressure and flow; pressure to supply force and flow to supply motion.

A reservoir and valving is needed to permit repeated stroking of the pump, which results in raising the output piston another notch with each stroke. Two check valves are needed, one to keep the load from lowering on the intake stroke, the other to prevent pressure loss on the power stroke.

The component make-up of the hydraulic jack circuit meets the basic hydraulic system requirements. We are now ready to see how it operates; but first, let's look at two terms that need to be defined.

ATMOSPHERIC PRESSURE. This is the pressure exerted on everything around us because of the weight of the air. If a 1 in² column of air as high as the atmosphere goes could be isolated, it would weigh 15 lb at sea level. Because air is a fluid and is confined to the earth's atmosphere, 15 psi is exerted equally over everything on the earth's surface.

Atmospheric pressure does vary with altitude and weather conditions. A pressure of 15 psi is often referred to as 1 atmosphere. Denver, the mile-high city, has an atmospheric pressure of less than 1 atmosphere.

VACUUM. Technically, a vacuum is the absence of pressure. Actually, any condition in which pressure is less than 1 atmosphere is referred to as a vacuum. For example, when you sip on a straw, the pressure in the straw is less than 1 atmosphere. The liquid in your glass, though, is still at atmospheric pressure; it is the pressure difference that forces the liquid up through the straw.

Atmospheric pressure and vacuum will play an important part in a later discussion of hydraulic pump operation.

Intake Stroke

As we study the pump system in Fig. 5-16, we see that as the pump piston is stroked upward, a partial vacuum is created below it. Atmospheric pressure in the reservoir forces fluid past the reservoir check

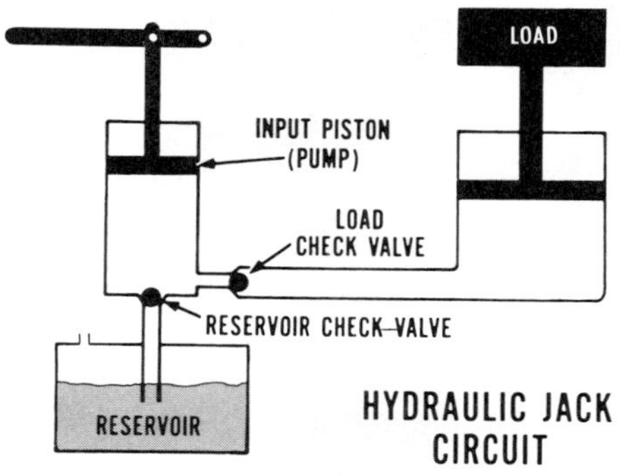

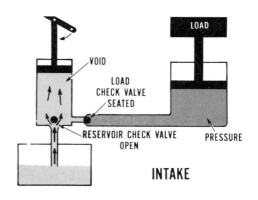

Fig. 5-15. Diagram of hydraulic jack circuit.
(Chrysler Corp.)

Fig. 5-16. Intake stroke in a jack. (Chrysler Corp.)

valve, which is unseated by the flow. The load is prevented from coming down by high pressure seating the load check valve and preventing any back flow.

Power Stroke

When the pump piston is stroked downward (Fig. 5-17), the pressure builds up below it, seating the reservoir check valve and preventing return of the fluid to the sump. The load check valve opens and fluid is forced under the large piston, raising the load another notch.

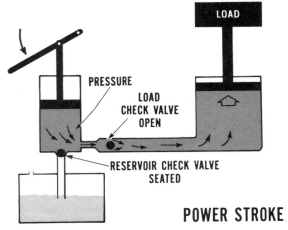

Fig. 5-17. Pressure stroke in a jack. (Chrysler Corp.)

Lowering

To lower the load, a third valve is connected, a manually-controlled needle valve between the large piston and the reservoir (Fig. 5-18). The load is trying

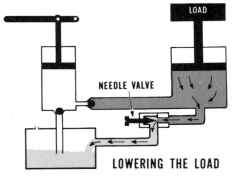

Fig. 5-18. Lowering a jack. (Chrysler Corp.)

to push fluid back past the needle valve to the sump. Slightly opening the needle valve meters the fluid back to the reservoir, permitting gravity to bring the load down.

THE HYDRAULIC HOIST

The hydraulic hoist is another simple system similar in function to the hydraulic jack. The hoist uses a rotary pump driven by an electric motor instead of the hand-powered piston pump. This gives a smooth, constant flow of fluid. One three-position spool valve, controlled by the operator, raises, holds, and lowers the load, depending on the valve position (Fig. 5-19).

Raise Position

The valve has three ports; these are connected to the pump output, the hoist cylinder, and the sump. In one position of the valve handle, flow from the pump

Fig. 5-19. A hydraulic hoist system.

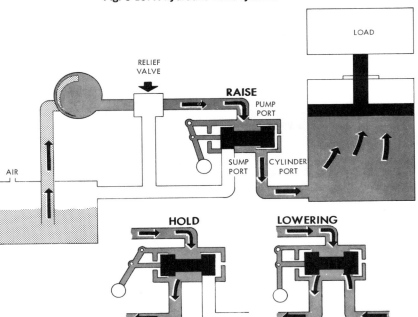

is directed under the cylinder. The weight of the load causes pressure to develop and the hoist is raised. The reservoir port is blocked by a valve land.

Hold Position

In the hold position of the valve, the line to the hoist cylinder is blocked by one of the valve lands. This prevents the hoist from lowering or raising. The reservoir port is uncovered and pump delivery is by-passed to the tank.

Lowering Position

For lowering, all three ports are open to each other. Pump delivery is bypassed to the reservoir along with the fluid under the hoist cylinder and gravity lowers the load.

Relief Valve

A relief valve is needed in the hydraulic hoist system to protect the system from overloading. For instance, if the control valve is left in the raise position when the cylinder is all the way up, there is no place for additional fluid to go. The pump, however, is still pumping and, if no relief is provided, pressure increases until something breaks or the motor stalls. The relief valve by-passes pump delivery to the reservoir and also maintains system pressure under the cylinder to prevent it from lowering.

The hydraulic jack and hydraulic hoist are simple but basic examples of the hydraulic lever. We can now build upon this basic background in the next two chapters, getting a more detailed look at hydraulic pumps and valving. Finally we look into the working of an automatic transmission hydraulic control system.

REVIEW QUESTIONS

CHAPTER 5
HYDRAULIC SYSTEM FUNDAMENTALS

Completion:

1. A fluid can either be a _____ or a

_____ .

2. Force is defined as a _____ or _____ ef-fort. The English unit measure for force is the

_____ . In the Metric-English conver-

sion, force is measured in _____ and

its metric abbreviation is _____ .

3. Convert 500 pounds of force to its metric equivalent. Show your work.

4. Pressure _____ per unit area. The English

unit for measuring pressure is _____

and is abbreviated _____ . In the Metric-English con-

version, pressure is measured in _____

_____ and its metric abbreviation is _____ .

5. Convert 60 psi to its metric equivalent. Show your work.

6. Calculate the pressure on the confined fluid in the following problem illustration. Show your work.

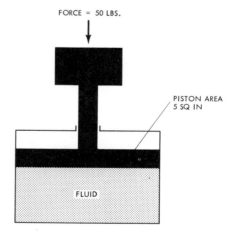

FORCE = 50 LBS.

PISTON AREA 5 SQ IN

FLUID

7. Using the following illustration and data calculate the following:

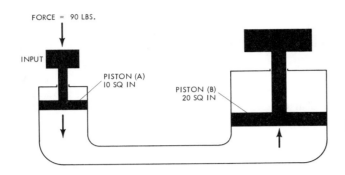

FORCE = 90 LBS.

INPUT

PISTON (A)
10 SQ IN

PISTON (B)
20 SQ IN

a. Pressure on the confined fluid.

b. Pressure on piston (B).

c. Force on piston (B).

d. Piston (B) travel when Piston (A) travels one inch.

8. Pressure on a confined fluid is _____ everywhere in all directions.

9. In a hydraulic system, the _____ creates the fluid flow. If the flow doesn't meet any resistance, it is referred to as a _____ _____, and there is no pressure build-up. To create a hydraulic pressure head the fluid flow must encounter a _____ _____ such as a dead end against a hydraulic piston.

10. To convert hydraulic force to mechanical force, _____ pistons and _____ pistons are used in automatic transmissions to apply the bands and cluthes.

11. The pressure exerted on everything around us because of the weight of the air is referred to as _____ _____ pressure.

12. An absence of atmospheric pressure; a pressure that is less than atmosphere is referred to as a _____ _____.

13. Every hydraulic system needs a reservoir or sump for fluid storage. In an automatic transmission, the fluid supply for the system pump is stored in the _____.

6

HYDRAULIC SYSTEM FUNDAMENTALS— PUMPS AND VALVES*

HYDRAULIC PUMPS

A hydraulic pump is a mechanism through which an external source of power is used to apply force to a liquid. In automatic transmissions, the front pump drive (Fig. 6-1) is keyed to the converter hub; therefore, the external source of power is the engine.

In most cases, a hydraulic pump must provide a flow of fluid and pressure head from which force and motion are transmitted. The pump is the heart of any pressure hydraulic system. When it fails to operate to specifications, the system encounters partial or total failure.

Rotary hydraulic pumps are widely used in pressure hydraulic systems. Although there are many types of rotary pumps, we confine our discussion to those used in current automatic transmission applications.

All rotary pumps used in pressure hydraulic systems work on the same operating principle. Fluid is trapped in chambers that are constantly expanding and contracting—expanding at the pump inlet to draw fluid into the pump and contracting at the outlet to force fluid into the system under pressure (Fig. 6-2).

Most of these pumps have two round members, with the inner drive member turning inside the outer. The members are on different centers; therefore, at one point of rotation they are in mesh and provide no clearance. As the members continue to turn, they will separate to a point of maximum clearance and then come back together (Fig. 6-3).

The pumping mechanism lobes, or gears, form sealed chambers between the members. These pumping chambers are carried around by rotation of one or both members.

*Based on training publications of the Chrysler Corporation.

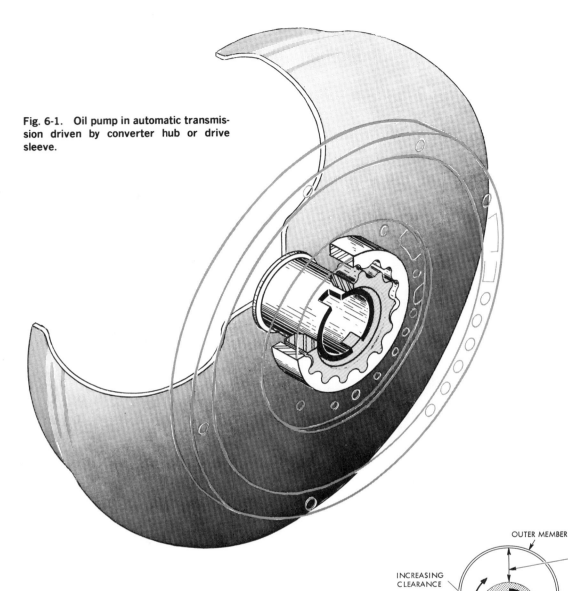

Fig. 6-1. Oil pump in automatic transmission driven by converter hub or drive sleeve.

Using Fig. 6-2, here is how the pumping action takes places. At the point where clearance begins to increase, the pumping chamber expands in size, creating a void. The inlet is located at this void and atmospheric pressure in the sump forces fluid into the void.

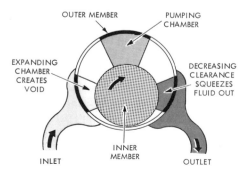

Fig. 6-2. Diagram of a rotary pump. (Chrysler Corp.)

Fig. 6-3. Rotary pumps have two round members or different shaft centers. (Chrysler Corp.)

The size of the chamber continues to increase until rotation carries it past the inlet to the point of maximum clearance. For a few degrees of travel at maximum clearance, the chamber neither increases nor decreases.

The outlet is located where the clearance is decreasing. Here, the pumping chamber decreases in size and fluid is squeezed out of the chamber and into the system under pressure. Succeeding chambers follow each other closely so a smooth, continuous output is obtained.

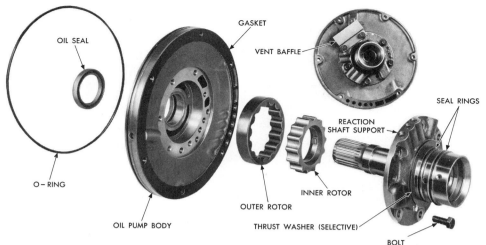

Fig. 6-4.   Internal-external rotor pump, Torque Flite. (Chrysler Corp.)

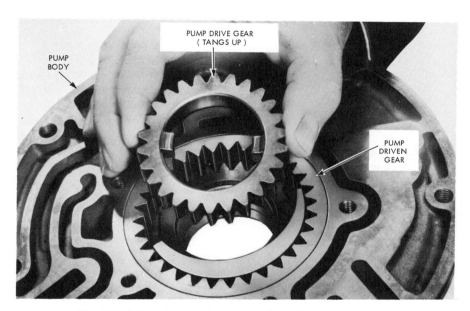

Fig. 6-5.   Internal-external gear pump, Turbo Hydra-Matic 350.
(Oldsmobile Division, General Motors Corp.)

INTERNAL—EXTERNAL ROTARY PUMPS—
ROTOR AND GEAR DESIGN

The two pumps under discussion are commonly referred to as the IX rotor pump and the IX gear pump; the term IX is used as an abbreviation for the internal–external pumping elements, Fig. 6-4 and 6-5.

In the IX rotor pump design, both rotor members turn together. The inner rotor is the drive member and carries the outer rotor by meshing of the lobes (Fig. 6-6). A pumping chamber is formed between the lobes. As the lobes separate from the mesh, the chamber increases at the inlet. At the outlet, the lobes are meshing again, decreasing the chamber size and squeezing the fluid out into the system (Fig. 6-7). The inlet is sealed from the outlet by the close clearance between the lobe tips at the point of maximum displacement.

The pumping action of the IX rotary gear pump is similar to the IX rotary lobe pump (Fig. 6-8). As the inner gear drives the outer gear, the space between the gears increases as the gear teeth separate and pass the inlet port and then decreases as the gear teeth come together and pass the outlet port. There is a crescent-shaped divider between the two gears. In this case, oil is trapped between the divider and the gear teeth of both gears and carried to the outlet.

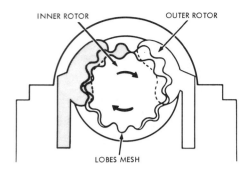

Fig. 6-6. Internal-external rotor design.
(Chrysler Corp.)

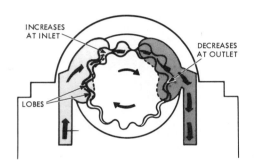

Fig. 6-7. Internal-external rotor design flow pattern.
(Chrysler Corp.)

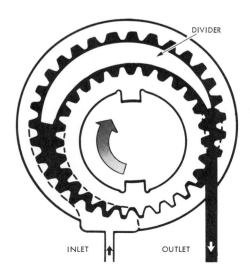

Fig. 6-8. IX gear pump.

Positive Delivery

The IX rotor and IX gear pumps are classified as positive delivery or positive displacement. This means that the pump has a continuous delivery characteristic. Once the hydraulic system demands have been satisfied, the pump will then continue to deliver against the system pressure no matter how high the pressure. This pressure build-up could have no end; therefore, it is necessary to provide a relief valve to protect against pressure overloads on the hydraulic circuits. Circuit pressure overloads could easily fracture the transmission case as well as clutch and servo pistons, in addition to blowing-out seals and gaskets.

The volume delivery or output of positive displacement pumps is simply determined by the speed of the pump drive. Because of the positive delivery characteristic, these pumps can waste energy by pumping more oil than is needed.

VARIABLE CAPACITY VANE PUMP

A variable capacity pump will vary its output according to the need requirements of the transmission, thereby conserving energy. It offers the advantage of delivering a large capacity when the demand for fluid is great, especially at low pump speeds. At high speeds, the pump load is not usually high and the transmission volume demand is low. The variable capacity pump, therefore, requires very little effort to drive at high speeds when compared to a positive displacement pump.

A typical variable capacity vane-type pump design is illustrated in Figs. 6-9 and 6-10. The rotor of the pump is engine-driven and carries the slipper-type vanes. A slide is incorporated in the pump to automatically control pump output to transmission needs.

Variable output is obtained in the following manner. When the priming spring moves the slide in the full extended position, the slide and rotor are not on the same centers (Fig. 6-9). As the rotor and vanes rotate within the slide, the expanding and contracting areas form suction and pressure chambers. Fluid trapped between the vanes at the suction side is moved to the pressure side. When the slide moves toward the center, a greater quantity of fluid is moved from the pressure side back to the suction side (Fig. 6-10). When the slide and rotor are both centered, a neutral or no volume condition is attained.

The priming spring keeps the slide in the fully extended position so that, when the engine is started, full output is immediate. Movement of the slide against the priming spring occurs when the pump pressure regulator valve reaches its predetermined value. At the regulating point, the pressure regulator valve opens a port feed to the pump slide and results in a slide movement against the priming spring to cut back on the volume delivery and maintain regulated pressure.

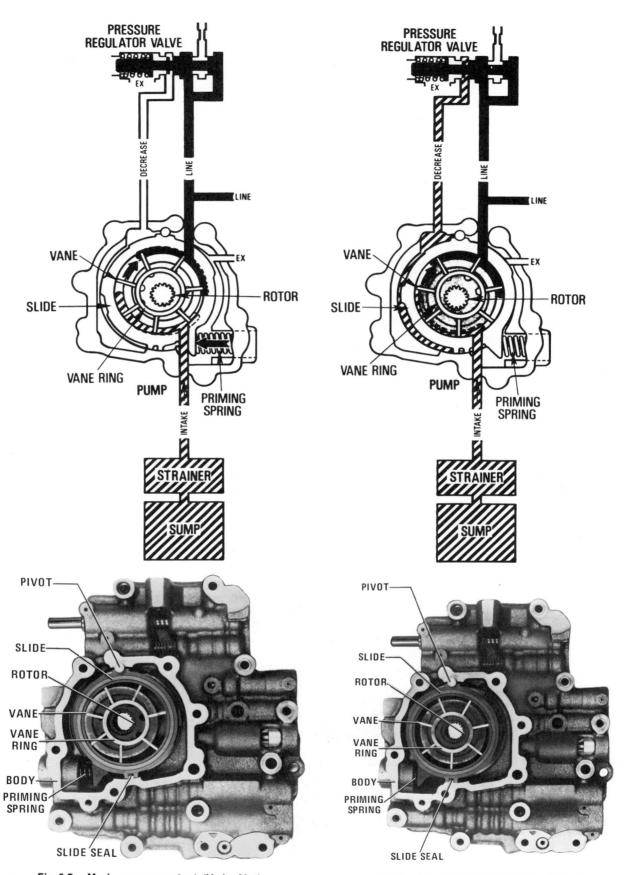

PRESSURE
REGULATOR VALVE

EX

DECREASE

LINE

LINE

VANE

EX

SLIDE

ROTOR

VANE RING

PUMP

PRIMING
SPRING

INTAKE

STRAINER

SUMP

PIVOT

SLIDE

ROTOR

VANE

VANE
RING

BODY

PRIMING
SPRING

SLIDE SEAL

Fig. 6-9.   Maximum pump output. (Hydra-Matic
Division, General Motors Corp.)

PRESSURE
REGULATOR VALVE

EX

DECREASE

LINE

LINE

VANE

EX

SLIDE

ROTOR

VANE RING

PUMP

PRIMING
SPRING

INTAKE

STRAINER

SUMP

PIVOT

SLIDE

ROTOR

VANE

VANE
RING

BODY

PRIMING
SPRING

SLIDE SEAL

Fig. 6-10.   Minimum pump output. (Hydra-Matic
Division, General Motors Corp.)

Hydraulic System Fundamentals   **125**

ORIFICE

The simplest means of controlling flow and pressure is by an orifice. An orifice is a restriction. It slows down fluid flow either to create back pressure or to delay pressure build-up downstream.

When fluid is pumped to an orifice, there is not enough room for it to go through all at once, and a back pressure is created on the pump side. If there is a flow path on the downstream side, a pressure difference is maintained across the orifice; pressure is lower on the downstream of the orifice (Fig. 6-11) as long as fluid continues to flow in the circuit. In hydraulic circuits, the orifice is a simple means of lowering pressure.

When flow is blocked on the downstream side, Pascal's Law then applies and pressure equalizes on both sides of the orifice (Fig. 6-12). The pressure does not equalize, however, until flow across the orifice stops. The orifice then is used to delay pressure build-up.

Figure 6-13 shows a clutch piston with two apply chambers, inner and outer. Note how the inner chamber gets a rapid feed to apply the clutch for initial engagement while the outer chamber apply is delayed by an orifice. By not engaging the clutch with full force, a harsh clutch apply is not experienced by the driver. Eventually, the flow across the orifice ceases and full pressure in both chambers apply against the clutch piston for maximum holding power.

In automatic transmissions, the change from one gear ratio to another requires a delicate control of the rate of release of one friction clutch or band in favor of an alternative friction device also requiring a precise rate of application. Small restriction orifices are engineered and used throughout the hydraulic paths to obtain a timed sequence for a quality shift so that the engine does not flare up nor the two gear ratios fight one another.

The density of automatic transmission fluid does not vary appreciably, thus a rate of flow through an orifice can be considered to depend solely on the apply pressure in spite of small variations in viscosity from temperature changes.

Fig. 6-11. An orifice acts as a fixed or metered opening. (Chrysler Corp.)

Fig. 6-12. Pressure equalizes when flow through orifice stops on the blocked side. (Chrysler Corp.)

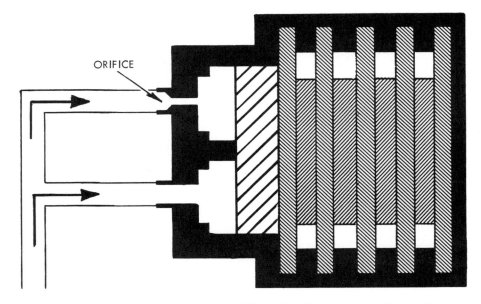

Fig. 6-13. An orifice gives delaying action. (Oldsmobile Division, General Motors Corp.)

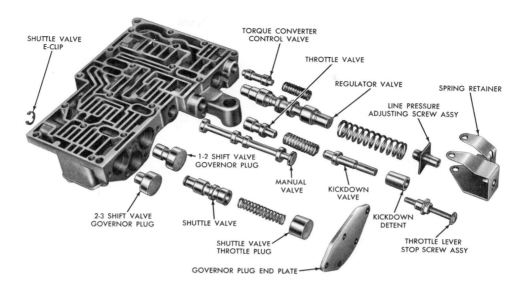

Fig. 6-14. Control valve body assembly. (Chrysler Corp.)

HYDRAULIC VALVES

Valves are used for the control of hydraulic circuits. They exercise their control in the circuit by regulating pressure, by creating special pressure conditions, by deciding how much fluid will flow in portions of the circuit, and by directing the fluid traffic to the servo and clutch circuits.

It is common to refer to a group of valves built into a single assembly as the control valve body assembly (Fig. 6-14). In construction, they vary from a simple ball and seat to a multiple spool valve train.

Hydraulic valves can be divided generally into two classes, those that direct flow and pressure and those that regulate or control flow and pressure.

Valves that direct flow and pressure are like an ON/OFF switch. They simply connect or disconnect interrelated passages without restricting the fluid flow or changing the pressure. These valves are usually called directional or relay valves and perform the simple function of turning the circuit on and off.

Regulator valves are valves that change the pressure of the oil as it passes through the valve. It does this by bleeding-off (or exhausting) some of the volume of oil supplied to it.

Let's look at some of the directional control and regulating valves typically used in automatic transmissions. It will help in understanding hydraulic circuits if it can be determined which control valves function as the directional or regulating components.

Check Valves

A check valve is a simple one-way directional valve. It permits flow in a hydraulic line in one direction only. The two most common kinds of check valves are the ball check and poppet check.

The ball check valve (Fig. 6-15) consists of a steel or nylon ball and a seat. When pressure is applied on the seat side, the ball is forced off the seat and permits flow. Pressure on the opposite side holds the ball against its seat and blocks flow in the reverse direction.

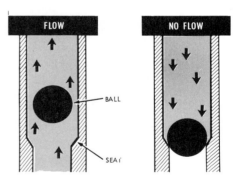

Fig. 6-15. One-way ball type check valve. (Chrysler Corp.)

In automatic transmission valve control body assemblies, the ball check plays an important part in directing the many flow patterns of the fluid (Fig. 6-16). Some of the ball checks have two seats to control the fluid traffic between interconnecting hydraulic circuit

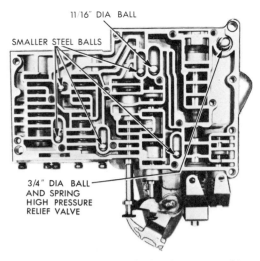

Fig. 6-16. Ball type check valves are used to direct flow patterns in transmissions.

paths. In this arrangement, the check ball is seated against the low pressure line by the high pressure circuit (Fig. 6-17).

The poppet check valve is a flat disc that seals around a hole smaller than the disc. A light spring guides the disc and holds it seated when no pressure is applied (Fig. 6-18). The operation is the same as a simple ball check valve.

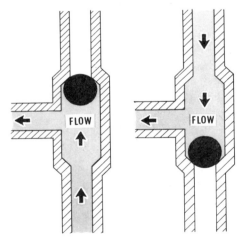

Fig. 6-17. Two seat ball type check valve.

Fig. 6-18. Poppet valves use discs for sealing. (Chrysler Corp.)

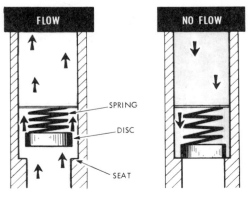

Relief Valves

A relief valve is a spring-loaded, pressure-operated valve that bypasses pump delivery to the sump, thereby limiting system pressure to a predetermined maximum value. It is always connected between the pump outlet and sump and it meters pump delivery back to the sump when the desired pressure has been reached in the system.

A simple relief valve (Fig. 6-19) is like a check valve in construction except that it has a heavier spring to hold it seated against pressure. The spring tension can either be fixed or adapted to an adjusting screw to vary the spring tension, which will thereby vary the pressure at which the valve relieves. Once the spring tension is set, it cannot be varied in operation. System pressure will be determined by the spring tension.

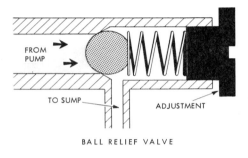

BALL RELIEF VALVE

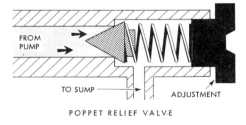

POPPET RELIEF VALVE

Fig. 6-19. A relief valve is a check valve with a heavy spring exerting a fixed pressure to one side. (Chrysler Corp.)

In operation, the spring holds the valve seated against pump delivery until system pressure is high enough to overcome the spring. The valve unseats and meters fluid from the pump or main circuit back to the sump. It adjusts itself automatically so just enough fluid is bypassed to the sump to maintain proper system operating pressure.

The pressure regulation in an automatic transmission requires a regulation system capable of giving variable values, and therefore the relief valve is not used for pressure regulation. Rather, it is sometimes incorporated as a safety device (Fig. 6-20). If the normal regulation system fails and permits the pump to build up excessive pressure, the relief valve will open and prevent damage to the transmission.

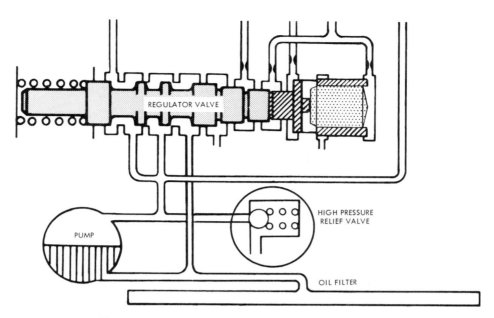

Fig. 6-20. High pressure relief valve used in Torque Flite to protect against excessive pressure.

Fig. 6-21.

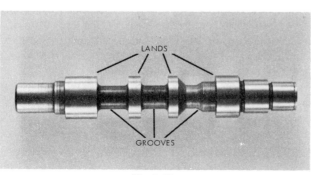

Fig. 6-22.

Spool Valves

The check valve and relief valve are the simplest kinds of hydraulic valves, both in construction and operation. They are, however, limited in the means of control and the number of flow paths that can be handled. When a valve must interconnect several passages or react to more than one pressure, a spool valve is usually used.

A spool valve (Fig. 6-21) is a precision-machined, cylindrically-shaped valve made-up of *lands* and *grooves* (illustrated in Fig. 6-22). The valve is closely fitted to a round bore, with the valve lands sliding on a pressurized film of fluid. Fluid passages are indexed to each other depending on the position of the valve lands and the fluid is passed through the valve at the grooves (Fig. 6-23). Spool valves can be positioned manually, by springs, or by pressure (Fig. 6-24).

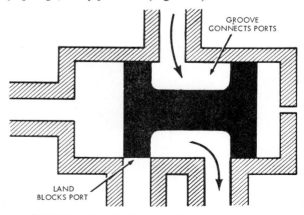

Fig. 6-23. Spool valves are widely used to control flow direction. (Chrysler Corp.)

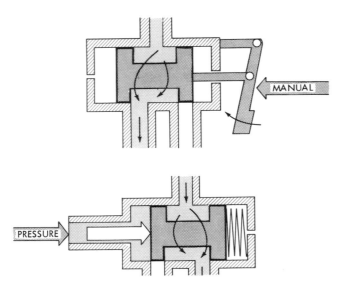

Fig. 6-24. Spool valves may be operated manually or by pressure. (Chrysler Corp.)

When a valve is acted upon by a spring and by pressure, the spring exerts force in one direction; the pressure that opposes the spring is called a reaction pressure, and the area on which it acts is called a reaction area.

Pressure can be resolved into force by multiplying the pressure and the reaction area. The valve will always move in the direction of the greater force. For example, a valve has a reaction area of ½ in² (3.23 cm²) and a spring with a 20-lb (90 N) force. If the reaction pressure is 25 psi (172 kPa), the force from this pressure is 25 psi (172 kPa) multiplied by ½ in², or 12½ lb (56 N). This is less than spring force and the spring holds the valve closed. If reaction pressure rises above 50 psi (344 kPa), its effective force is greater than 25 lb (111 N). This will overcome the spring and the valve will shift.

When two adjacent lands of a spool valve have different diameters and pressure is applied between the lands, a differential force results (Fig. 6-25). The force

on the larger land is greater than that on the small land and this results in a differential force in the direction of the large land.

Regulator Valves

A regulator valve is used for pressure control and in this respect performs the same function as a relief valve. Both valves meter fluid from the pump to the sump and maintain system pressure. The difference is that a relief valve controls pressure at a set value depending on spring tension, while a regulator valve can change the pressure in response to auxiliary hydraulic or mechanical forces.

All regulator valves use the transmission mainline operating pressure as the input feed. This mainline feed is then regulated to a specified working pressure and passed on into the circuit. The regulator valve works on the balanced valve principle. Following is a simple example of how it operates when used as a pressure regulator for the pump.

A study of Fig. 6-26 will show that the valve has connections from the pump, to the system, to the sump, and from the system to a reaction area that is opposite the valve spring. It should be noted that the system pressure will oppose the spring force.

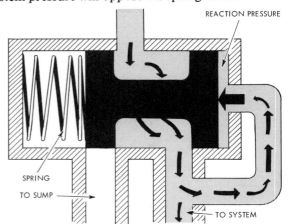

Fig. 6-26. Regulator or balanced valve system. (Chrysler Corp.)

Before fluid begins to flow (Fig. 6-27), there is no reaction pressure. The spring is the only positioning force and it holds the valve in the extreme position of a wide open feed to the system and a completely blocked sump port. All the pump delivery goes to the system until pressure begins to build-up.

As pressure builds up in the system, it reacts against spring force. When it starts to exceed the spring force, the valve moves and bleeds-off part of the pump flow back to the sump (Fig. 6-28). The bleed-off causes the pressure build-up to drop. Because the spring force is sensitive to the pressure drop, it immediately moves the valve back to close down the

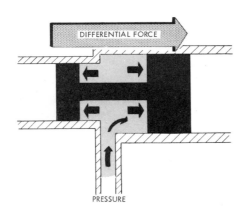

Fig. 6-25. Spool valves can be made to operate on a differential force. (Chrysler Corp.)

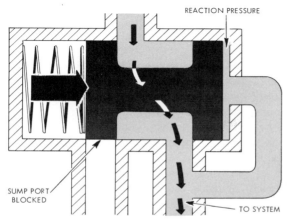

Fig. 6-27. Regulator valve is closed by spring force before fluid flow. (Chrysler Corp.)

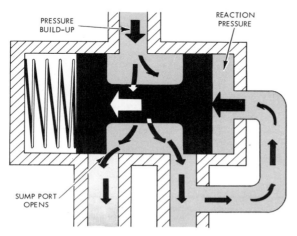

Fig. 6-28. Regulator valve opens when pressure in system builds up and overcomes spring tension. (Chrysler Corp.)

bleed-off. The system pressure very rapidly recovers and a regulated pressure output equal to the spring force is maintained.

The valve is poised between the spring force and reaction pressure. It is, therefore, continuously cycling back and forth, acting as a variable bleed orifice to attain an equilibrium or *balance* between the two forces

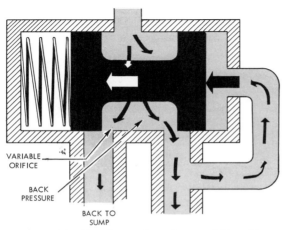

Fig. 6-29. Regulator valve acts as variable orifice. (Chrysler Corp.)

(Fig. 6-29). If the reaction area of the valve was 1 in² and a spring force of 90 lb (400 N) was used, then the valve would balance or regulate at 90 psi (621 kPa).

The regulator valve just described is really nothing more than a sophisticated relief valve. To become a true regulator valve, a variable pressure signal must be added to change the system pressure, as shown in Fig. 6-30. The variable auxiliary pressure assists the spring and regulated pressure is increased (boosted).

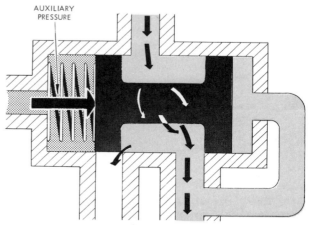

Fig. 6-30. Auxiliary pressure assists the spring to control regulator valve. (Chrysler Corp.)

A typical pressure regulator valve assembly used in automatic transmissions is illustrated in Fig. 6-31. Note that the reaction area is on the top end of the valve and that line pressure is regulated according to a fixed spring force and auxiliary fluid pressure on the boost valve.

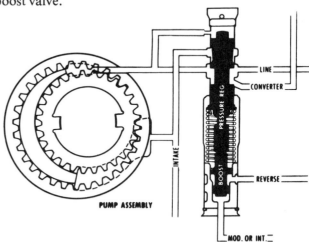

Fig. 6-31. Typical pressure regulator valve. (Oldsmobile Division, General Motors Corp.)

In an automatic transmission hydraulic control system, the pressure regulator valve, modulator and throttle valves, and the governor valve are classic examples of regulating valves. The balanced valve principle is critical to the understanding of how these regulating valves work. They are discussed in Chapter 7.

Relay Valve

The relay valve is a circuit control valve having two positions, ON and OFF. They are used in hydraulic control systems to give direction to fluid traffic without changing pressure. The valve is held in one position by spring force or by spring force plus an auxiliary pressure. When pressure opposing the spring rises high enough, the valve shifts and interconnects the porting for proper circuit flow. The relay valve is not designed for metering; it either opens or closes like a circuit switch. Figure 6-32 shows a relay valve, triggered by hydraulic pressure, overcoming spring force and the auxiliary pressure.

The automatic transmission manual valve and shift valves are examples of relay valve application. A typical manual valve that establishes the operating range of the transmission is illustrated in Fig. 6-33. Movement of the manual valve interconnects the line pressure with the various range circuits.

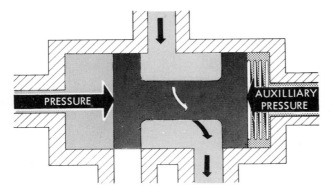

Fig. 6-32. Relay valve position ON or OFF is controlled by opposing force. (Chrysler Corp.)

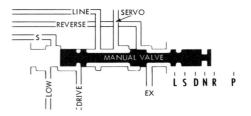

Fig. 6-33. Manual relay valve is used to establish operating range in automatic transmissions. (Oldsmobile Division, General Motors Corp.)

REVIEW QUESTIONS

CHAPTER 6
HYDRAULIC SYSTEM FUNDAMENTALS
PUMPS AND VALVES

Completion:

1. In a hydraulic system the _____ creates flow and applies force to the fluid.

2. In automatic transmissions, the pump drive is usually keyed to the converter _____ and will always turn with the speed of the _____ which is the external source of power.

3. Name three types of rotary pump designs common to automatic transmissions.

    a. _____

    b. _____

    c. _____

4. The rotation of the hydraulic pump produces a pumping action from the expanding and contracting action taking place between the inner and outer pump members. When the clearance between these members is expanding, a _____ is created and _____ _____ pressure in the sump forces the fluid into the pumping chambers. As the clearance between the inner and outer members decreases the fluid is squeezed into the system creating the system _____.

5. A pump design that uses a crescent shaped divider.

    _____

6. A pump design that uses a rotor with slipper vanes contained within a slide member. _____

    _____

7. A pump that has a continuous delivery characteristic is called a positive _____ or positive _____ pump.

8. A variable capacity pump has the ability to adjust its output volume to the transmission needs. For maxi-

mum output a _____ spring moves the pump slide in the full extended position. To cut-back on

pump output the _____ valve relays regulated pump output to the pump slide which results

in a slide movement against the _____ spring. When the slide is centered with the rotor and vanes, pump output is cycled back to the _____

_____ side of the pump.

9. A fluid pressure that can move a spool valve against a mechanical force such as a spring or a combination of a mechanical force and an auxilliary fluid pressure is

called a _____ pressure. The spool

valve area on which it acts is called a _____

_____ area.

10. A popular type of check valve used in hydraulics is the

_____ check.

Use the following choices and select the one best answer for the following questions. Indicate your choice by placing the letter in the question blank. A choice may be used more than once.

ANSWER CODE

A. Spool Valve   **D.** Relief Valve
B. Relay Valve   **E.** Check Valve
C. Regulator Valve   **F.** Orifice

_____ A one-way directional valve used for directing fluid traffic between inter-connecting hydraulic circuits.

_____ Engineered to control the rate of fluid flow and pressure build-up time.

_____ The reference made to a valve design cylindrically shaped with two or more lands separated by annular grooves.

_____ A simple spring loaded ball check used as a safety device to protect the hydraulic system when system pressure exceeds engineered values.

_____ Controls the porting that connects and disconnects a hydraulic circuit from its fluid supply source. It could easily be called a "switch" valve.

_____ Works on the balanced valve principle.

_____ Provides a variable pressure control.

Check mark the following valves that are used in an automatic transmission hydraulic control system and are classified as a regulating valve.

_____ Pressure Regulator   _____ Throttle or
        Valve   Modulator Valve
_____ Manual Valve   _____ Shift Valve
_____ Governor Valve

7

THE HYDRAULIC CONTROL SYSTEM: FUNDAMENTALS OF OPERATION

The hydraulic control system is responsible for the release and apply of the band-clutch combinations, which determine the select action of the planetary gear train. Although the design of the system is very complex, it is made-up of individual clutches, servos, accumulators, and valving that is interrelated and easy to understand.

The hydraulic control systems for all automatic transmissions are basically alike. There are some minor product design differences, but this should not interfere with our discussion of the basic working of the system. Hydraulic system features peculiar to a transmission can always be found in the manufacturer's service or training manual. The objective, therefore, is to discuss the subject matter of the hydraulic control system based on the technical information that is common and necessary to know about all automatic transmissions. Of course, this includes the fundamentals of automatic shifting.

For discussion purposes, let's apply our knowledge of hydraulic fundamentals, Chapters 5 and 6, and gradually build-up an automatic transmission hydraulic control system.

First, we introduce the several basic systems that make-up a typical hydraulic control package, learn about their job function, and explain how they work. We then illustrate how they all work together in making up a total system.

THE PRESSURE SUPPLY SYSTEM

The pressure supply system is responsible for pressure development and control. This system incorporates a front or engine-driven pump and sometimes an additional rear or output shaft-driven pump, both of which are controlled by a main regulator system to meet the engineered pressure schedule for transmission operation.

All transmissions require the pressure supply system to perform these functions:

1. Establish and maintain a main line pressure (a feeder) for operation of all the individual hydraulic circuits.
2. Fill and maintain a charge pressure to the converter.
3. Supply and circulate fluid for cooling.
4. Supply and circulate fluid for lubrication of the gears, bushings, thrust washers, clutch plates, sprag, and roller clutches.
5. Supply fluid to a valve control body and a governor for the regulation of apply and release of the clutches and bands.

If a rear pump is used, it would perform three additional functions:

1. Provide a working pressure for the transmission during push starts.
2. At a designed vehicle speed, it cuts into the main regulating circuit and takes over the duties of the front pump.
3. Provide a source of fluid supply to the governor.

The current practice is to eliminate the use of the rear pump. This trend started in 1959 and continued until no rear pumps appeared in any transmission in the production year 1968.

Because there is still interest in how a rear pump works, let's briefly look at a front and rear pump regulating system (Figs. 7-1 and 7-2). The front pump is larger and is needed to supply the transmission hydraulic demands under the most severe conditions. This would be during stall and low-speed operation or whenever pressure requirements are high and the pump speed is low.

Note the position of the check valves and the regulating valve when the front pump is working the system (Fig. 7-1). As the vehicle gains speed, the output delivery of the front pump becomes more than adequate and the excess is bled-off back through the regulator valve to the suction side of the circuit. Meanwhile, the rear pump is building up its pressure with increased vehicle speed. When its pressure is sufficient to overcome the line pressure, the rear pump check valve is opened and the front pump check valve is closed (Fig. 7-2). The rear pump cuts in at a slightly higher pressure than the line pressure because of check valve design—the effective hydraulic area is larger on the check valve spring side.

Note in Fig. 7-2 that the regulator valve has repositioned itself for regulation of the rear pump output and the recycling of the entire front pump output back to the suction side of the circuit. Reducing the

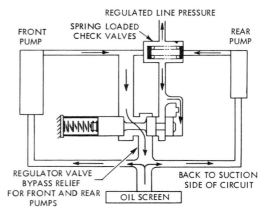

Fig. 7-1. Front pump pressure is regulated by a regulator valve by-pass.

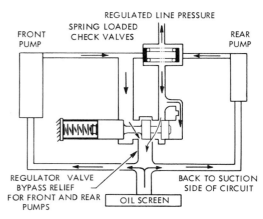

Fig. 7-2. Rear pump regulation. Note the position of the regulator valves and check as compared to Fig. 7-1.

front pump operating pressure to 0 psi results in increased efficiency—it takes less power to operate the smaller rear pump. If for any reason the rear pump fails to meet the transmission hydraulic demands, the front pump immediately cuts back into the system.

In systems using a rear pump, it is common practice to supply the governor feed oil directly from the rear pump output. In cases of a no-shift or delayed-shift operational complaint, the technician should be aware that the rear pump circuit may be at fault—no rear pump pressure results in governor pressure of 0 psi and a no-upshift pattern. Low rear pump pressure results in low governor pressure, delayed upshifts and a high closed-throttle downshift pattern.

In a typical single pump pressure supply system (Fig. 7-3), the pump output is sensed by a pressure regulator valve. The regulator valve works on the balanced valve principle and regulates the main transmission line pressure according to a fixed spring force and auxiliary oil pressures on the boost valve. Note in Fig. 7-3 how the force of a fluid on top of the regulator valve moves the valve against the spring force and

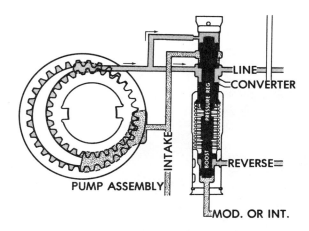

Fig. 7-3. Pressure supply system with single pump. The differential fluid force on top of the valve balances against the spring tension and boost valve auxiliary pressures. (Oldsmobile Division, General Motors Corp.)

boost valve. A bleed-off back to the suction side of the circuit is provided for valve balancing.

Depending on transmission design, main line or control pressure usually varies between a range of 55 psi (375 kPa) to 280 psi (1930 kPa).

If you recall the discussion in Chapter 6, a regulator valve is used for pressure control just like a relief valve. The difference is that a relief valve controls pressure at a set value depending on spring tension, but a regulator valve can change the pressure response according to other hydraulic pressure signals. This change of pressure response is typically brought about by use of a booster valve that is sensitive to hydraulic pressure signals and that varies the pressure regulation (Fig. 7-3). These boost signals are supplied by:

1. A regulated throttle or modulator pressure that varies with engine torque.

2. Regulated main line pressure for reverse operation.

Throttle and modulator pressures come from the same source and are discussed later in the chapter. By using throttle and modulator pressures, the transmission line pressure can be feathered between a minimum and a maximum to give the clutch and servo pistons the necessary holding force in relation to engine and converter torque. This means that, for power performance, the line pressure is high and the shift sequence is aggressive, whereas cruising or light throttle conditions require lower operating pressures. Operating at minimum pressures means less horsepower-loss in driving the pump and soft shift quality is maintained as a bonus.

The boost valve is also used in reverse for increasing the line pressure to ensure adequate fluid pressure for additional torque-holding requirements. Shown in Fig. 7-3, reverse pressure (line pressure) is directed to the boost valve that, in addition to the throttle or modulator booster signal, provides the necessary increase in line pressure. Increased line pressure for reverse operation is required for all automatic transmissions to keep the reverse band, or clutch, from slipping. The torque reaction on the reverse carrier opposing reverse direction is much greater than the reaction force to the forward torques in first and second gears.

In addition to controlling the pump pressure, the regulator valve is usually assigned the additional job of feeding a constant oil supply to the converter when the engine is running and prevents oil from draining back out of the converter through the pressure regulator valve when the engine is stopped (Fig. 7-3 and 7-4). If the converter were to drain whenever the engine stopped, an undesirable delay would be experienced when operation resumed.

Fig. 7-4. Typical pressure regulator valve and converter cooling-lube circuit. Cooler by-pass valve is not always included.

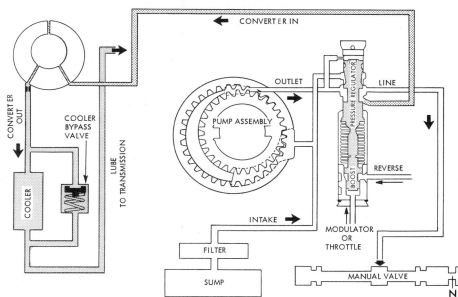

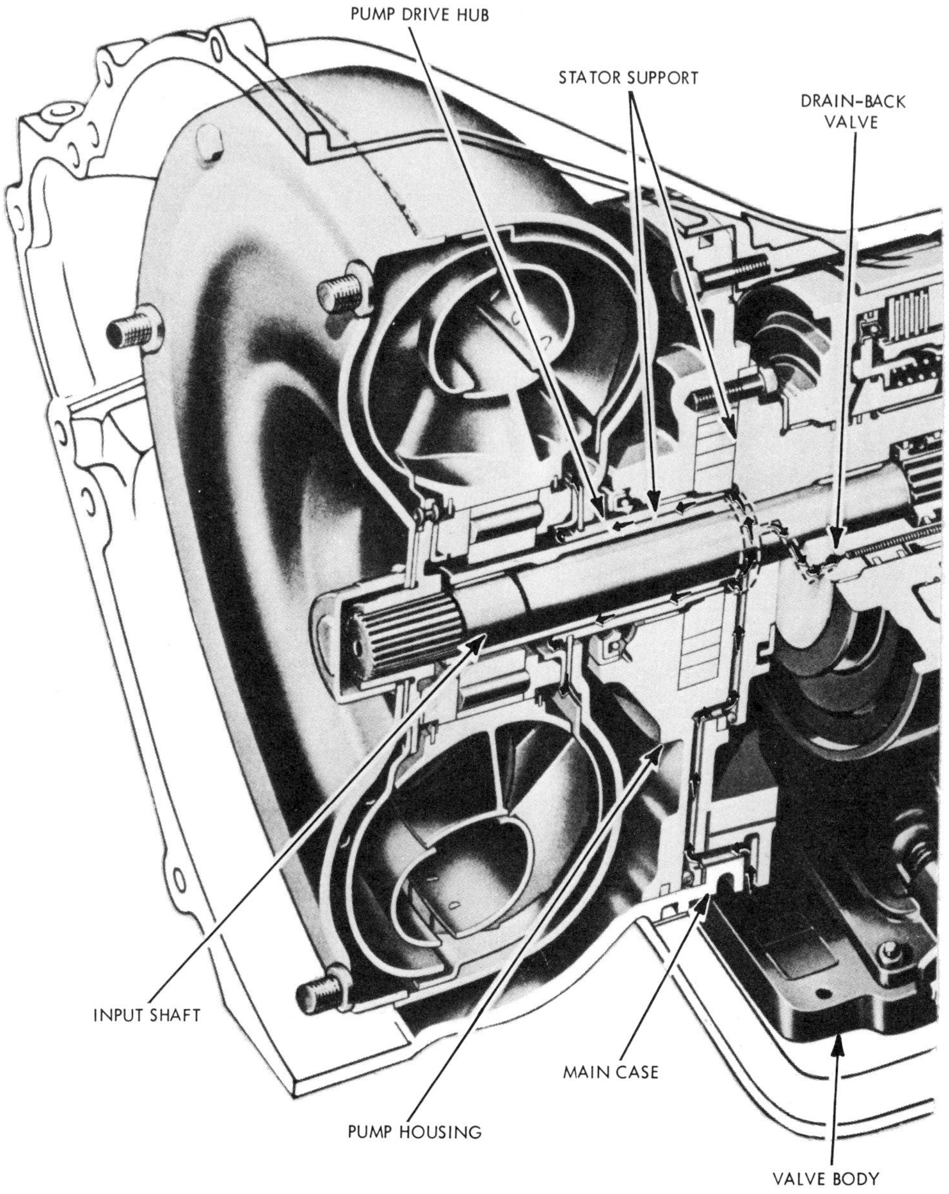

STATOR SUPPORT BUSHING

CONVERTOR CHECK VALVE

INPUT SHAFT

STATOR SUPPORT

TO COOLER CONNECTION

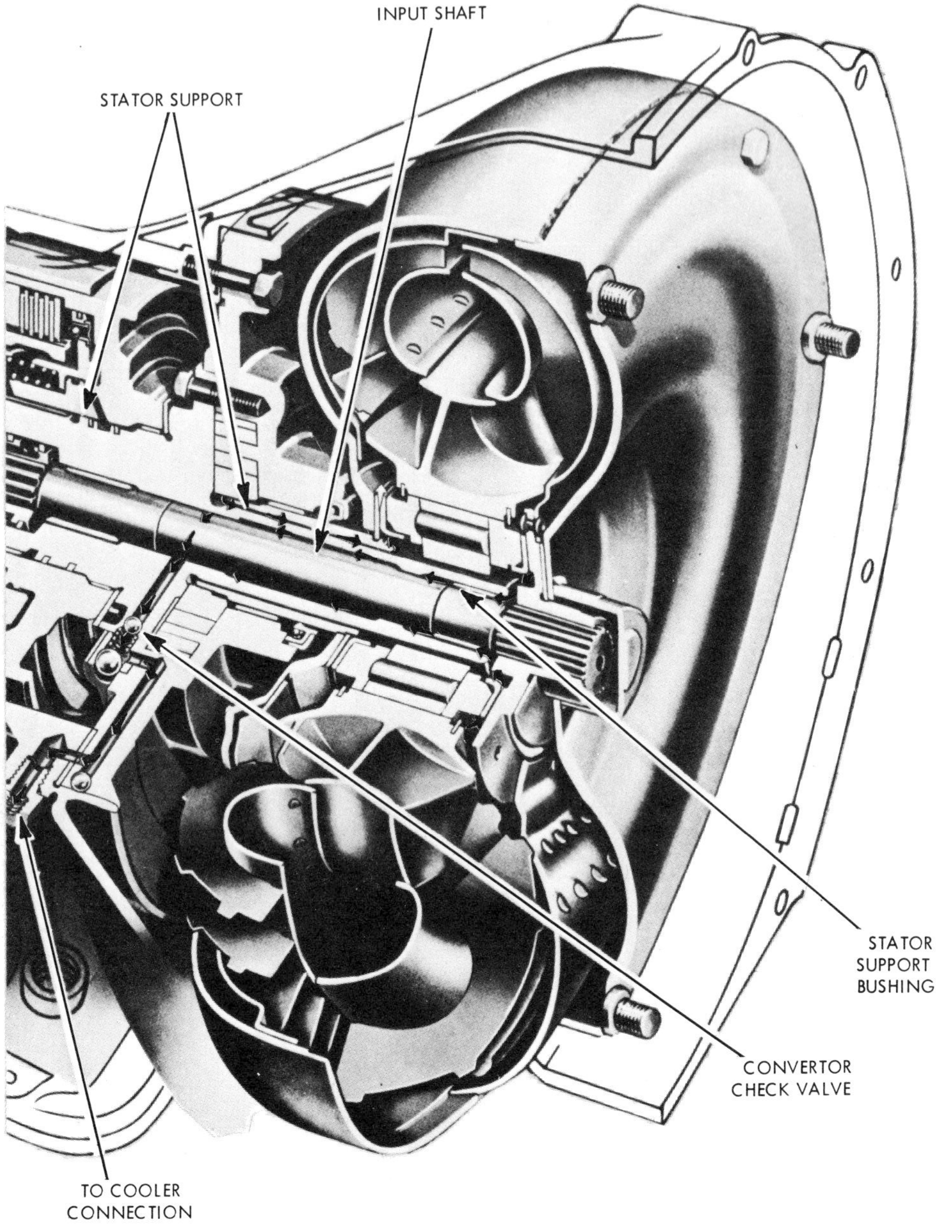

Fig. 7-6.   Converter—out circuit. (Ford Motor Co.)

DRAIN-BACK VALVE

STATOR SUPPORT

PUMP DRIVE HUB

VALVE BODY

MAIN CASE

PUMP HOUSING

INPUT SHAFT

Fig. 7-5.   Converter—in circuit. (Ford Motor Co.)

The Converter, Cooler and Lube System

The converter, cooler, and lube system is illustrated in Fig. 7-4. It represents three separate circuits, linked together in series, that maintain the life line of the transmission.

When the pressure regulator valve is at rest, it is bottomed in its bore by the spring and the converter feed opening is sealed. During operation, the regulator valve moves from its rest position and, before regulation begins, it uncovers a port to feed the converter; thus, oil from the mainline pressure is permitted to flow into the converter circuit (Figs. 7-3 and 7-4). The port opening is sometimes designed with a metered orifice to assist converter pressure regulation. Converter pressure regulation is concerned with maintaining a minimum of charge pressure to prevent converter cavitation and the limitation of maximum charge pressure to prevent converter ballooning.

The converter regulation system usually consists of a simple arrangement of restricting orifices that give an engineered bleed-down of the regulated line pressure. The converter, cooler, and lube circuit are in series with the lube part of the circuit open-ended. Because the circuit is open, the fluid flow does not stop moving and, therefore, a controlled fluid pressure drop is effective throughout the circuit. Depending on the transmission design, converter pressures operate in a range of 10 psi (69 kPa) to 90 psi (622 kPa). Lubrication pressures may vary from 5 psi (35 kPa) to 50 psi (343 kPa).

In observing Fig. 7-4, it is obvious that the converter fluid could drain out the lube end of the system when the engine is off. A very small amount does drain out until a void or suction pocket is formed in the converter. The regulator valve has the other end of the circuit sealed off. Some converter circuits require check valves and a pressure relief valve. The check valves trap the converter fluid along with the regulator valve when the engine is off. The converter pressure relief valve limits the maximum converter pressure (Figs. 7-5 and 7-6).

Getting the oil flow in and out of the converter is quite an engineering stunt. In observing Fig. 7-5, note how the converter fluid slips through the clearance provided between the stator support and converter pump drive hub to feed the converter. For the converter out-flow (Fig. 7-6), the fluid goes past the outside of the front bushing of the stator support and exits between the input shaft and stator support, through the pump housing and transmission case. From the transmission case it is then piped to and from the cooler through steel tubing (Fig. 7-6). The return line from the cooler is coupled to the transmission case, where the fluid is used for lubrication of the planetary gear train, clutch plates, bushings, and thrust surfaces. When the job of lubrication is completed, the fluid gravitates to the sump. Notice in Fig. 7-7 that the line to the cooler enters at the bottom. This prevents cavitation of the circuit, because the fluid must be pushed to the top.

There is an almost constant flow of oil through the system whenever the engine is running. On occasion, however, this flow is interrupted when severe demands are made on the transmission pump. For example, a manual shift into reverse at engine idle will usually cause a temporary drop in main line system pressure because of the oil volume demanded to apply the friction elements. To restore the main line pressure back to normal, the pressure regulator valve temporarily cuts off converter feed until the friction elements are applied.

All hydraulic systems use a regulator valve tap as the source of oil feed to the converter, cooling, and lubrication circuits. These circuits are unaffected by the manual valve position and function the same in each operating range of the transmission. Keep in mind that design variations do exist.

In this particular illustration (Fig. 7-5), a front lube circuit is tapped from the converter inflow and used for lubrication of the clutch friction plates, bushing supports, and thrust washers located in the forward section of the transmission case. A drain-back

Fig. 7-7.   Converter cooler lines. (Oldsmobile Division, General Motors Corp.)

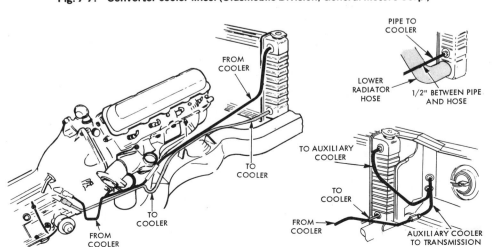

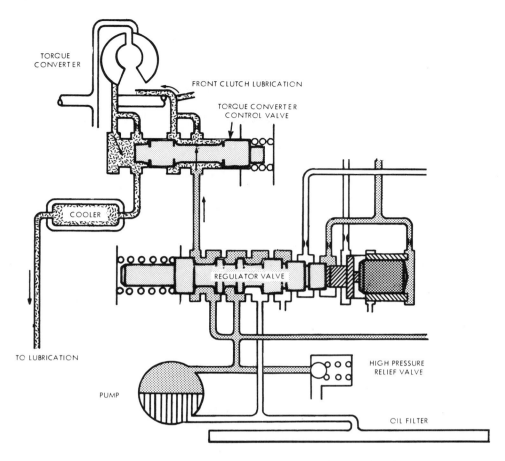

Fig. 7-8. Converter feed circuit using a control valve. (Chrysler Corp.)

valve is incorporated to prevent oil from draining from the converter into the front lube circuit when the engine stops. To keep the lube circuit from diverting too much oil from the converter inflow, the lubrication feed is orificed.

Another system variation is shown in Fig. 7-8. Note that the charge pressure from the pressure regulator valve is controlled by a torque converter control valve.

THROTTLE/MODULATOR VALVE SYSTEM

The two terms *throttle* and *modulator* have the same meaning and the systems perform the same job functions. The use of either term depends on the language used by the car manufacturer. Either system generates a regulated engine torque signal for the following functions:

1. It supplies a boost pressure to the primary or main regulator valve train. When engine breathing changes, the torque signal changes, as does the main line operating pressure. This is an instant chain reaction.

2. In the shift system it provides for a wide range of automatic shift points by delaying the shifts in relation to engine requirements.

3. It may be used in an accumulator system to control the shift quality on a clutch or band application.

The Throttle System

The throttle valve is another example of a regulating or balanced valve application. Again, we discuss a hydraulic force balancing against a variable spring force. There are three methods of obtaining a throttle signal in current transmission designs: vacuum, mechanical linkage, and mechanical cable control. Let us consider a vacuum controlled system (Fig. 7-9). The function of the vacuum unit is to instantly sense changes in intake manifold vacuum and convert the manifold vacuum signal to a proper spring force on the throttle value.

There are three forces acting within the vacuum unit: the absolute pressure and spring tension on the manifold side of the diaphragm, working toward the throttle valve, and the atmospheric pressure that acts on the diaphragm away from the valve. These forces

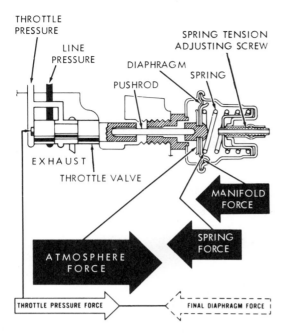

Fig. 7-9. Vacuum diaphragm control unit. (Ford Motor Co.)

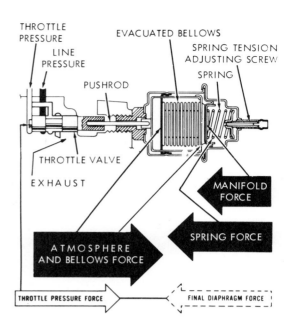

Fig. 7-10. Compensated vacuum diaphragm control unit. (Ford Motor Co.)

balance out the diaphragm and determine the amount of spring tension that will oppose the throttle valve movement. The throttle valve regulated output, therefore, is determined by the effective spring force on the valve. Keep in mind that atmospheric pressure is acting on the diaphragm to control the spring force on the valve relative to engine vacuum conditions. Below approximately 3 in. of vacuum, the spring force is completely unloaded on the throttle valve. This extreme condition keeps the valve position wide open and line pressure passes through the valve unregulated (throttle pressure equals line pressure unless the system is designed with a pressure relief valve limiting maximum TV pressure). During high vacuum conditions, there is no effective spring force and the throttle pressure output equals 0 psi.

The vacuum throttle unit just described is generally referred to as the vacuum modulator control unit. It is noncompensated for the effects that high altitudes will have on its operation. With an increase in altitude, atmospheric pressure falls as well as the engine manifold pressure (vacuum). Referring again to Fig. 7-9, it is apparent that when identical engine throttle conditions are compared, Chicago and Denver, the throttle pressure output increases with the altitude. This effect raises the minimum shift points and causes the shift quality to be more aggressive. The engine is now detuned with the shift system. At high altitudes, the engine torque output has dropped and the shifts are occurring after the engine torque has peaked. For ideal performance, gear ratio changes should occur at the peaks of the engine torque output.

To compensate for the high altitude effect, an altitude-compensated vacuum diaphragm is used for some of the transmissions (Fig. 7-10). This unit incorporates an evacuated spring bellows that is sensitive to barometric pressure.

The throttle pressure schedule is the same at sea level for both noncompensated and altitude-compensated vacuum units. However, at higher altitudes, the barometric pressure decreases and the crush effect on the bellows is less. This permits the bellows to expand and to assist the atmospheric force on the diaphragm to decrease the effective spring force on the throttle valve. In effect, the bellows reprograms the throttle system so that shifts occur slightly sooner to match the lower-peak engine torques related to high altitude.

In the mechanical version of throttle pressure control, a linkage or cable system actuated by the accelerator pedal movement is used to vary the spring load on the end of the throttle valve. A throttle valve lever shaft within the transmission is rotated in proportion to the amount of throttle opening of the carburetor. This means that a mechanical linkage hook-up between the transmission and carburetor throttle movement must be accurately coordinated (Fig. 7-11).

As the carburetor throttle opening increases, the throttle valve spring exerts a greater force on the throttle valve and a corresponding increase in throttle pressure. In the wide open position, the throttle valve (TV) is mechanically bottomed-out in the bore and line pressure will pass through the valve unregulated (throttle pressure is equal to line pressure). At closed throttle, TV pressure is 0 psi.

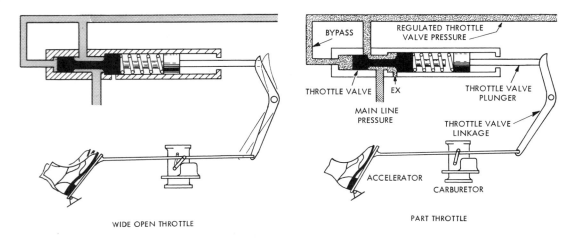

WIDE OPEN THROTTLE

PART THROTTLE

Fig. 7-11. TV pressure in wide-open and part throttle positions.

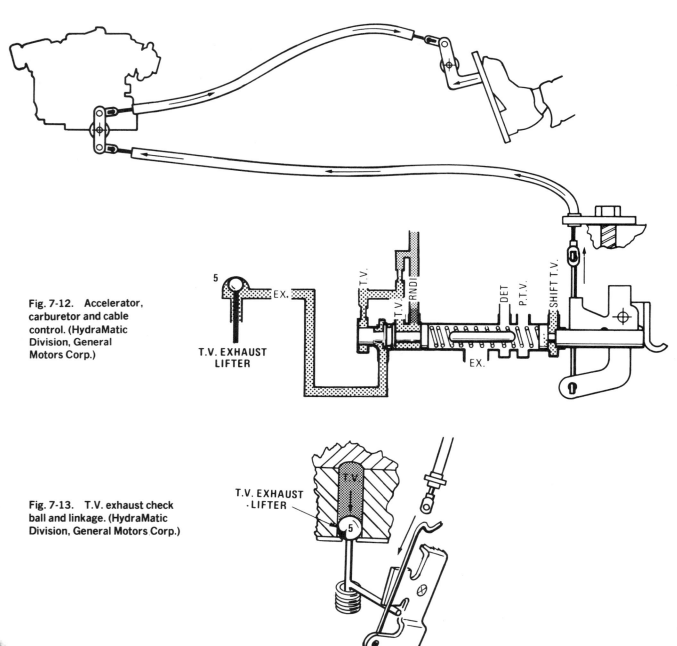

Fig. 7-12. Accelerator, carburetor and cable control. (HydraMatic Division, General Motors Corp.)

Fig. 7-13. T.V. exhaust check ball and linkage. (HydraMatic Division, General Motors Corp.)

The cable-controlled TV system works similar to the mechanical linkage TV system (Fig. 7-12). The cable movement coordinates the carburetor throttle opening with the transmission TV plunger movement. In this particular TV system, a spring-loaded lifter and exhaust check ball is featured (Fig. 7-13). Should the cable disconnect or get broken, the TV exhausted lifter pin drops and permits the check ball to seal the TV exhaust passage. A disconnected or broken cable would normally result in 0 psi throttle pressure and low operating line pressure, resulting in a burned or damaged transmission. Sealing the TV exhaust forces the TV pressure to equal line pressure regardless of carburetor throttle opening. This does cause delayed shift system problems, but the transmission is saved until the problem is resolved.

General Motors refers to their vacuum-operated throttle system as a modulator system (Fig. 7-14). It performs the same functions as any other throttle system and also works very similar to other vacuum-controlled TV systems. As a special feature, the modulator valve is sensitive to both engine vacuum and governor pressure (Fig. 7-15).

In observing the illustration, it is shown that line pressure serves as the supply oil for the modulator system. The modulator valve itself must balance against spring force in the vacuum unit and is assisted by governor pressure to help it move against the

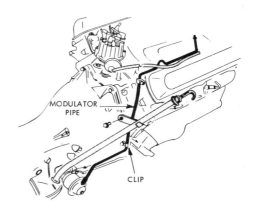

Fig. 7-14. Modulator unit and vacuum attachment.

spring. Governor pressure at the valve acts to decrease the modulator pressure relative to car speed. High speed cruising, therefore, will produce a slightly lower modulator and line pressure for a given vacuum. The transmission pressure requirements to hold the bands and clutches decrease as the car speed increases.

The Modulator System

Vacuum modulator systems are generally identified with General Motors transmissions, and also produce a regulated torque sensing oil as described under the throttle system: High vacuum produces a low modu-

Fig. 7-15. Modulator system used for line pressure control and shift scheduling. (HydraMatic Division, General Motors Corp.)

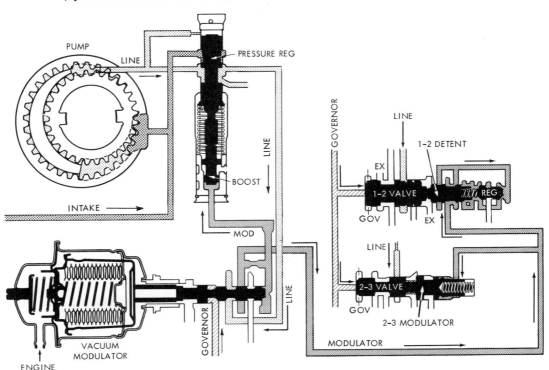

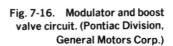

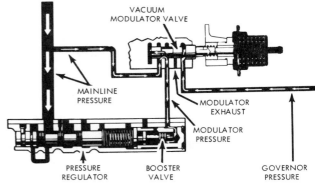

Fig. 7-16. Modulator and boost valve circuit. (Pontiac Division, General Motors Corp.)

MAINLINE PRESSURE

VACUUM MODULATOR VALVE

MODULATOR EXHAUST

MODULATOR PRESSURE

PRESSURE REGULATOR

BOOSTER VALVE

GOVERNOR PRESSURE

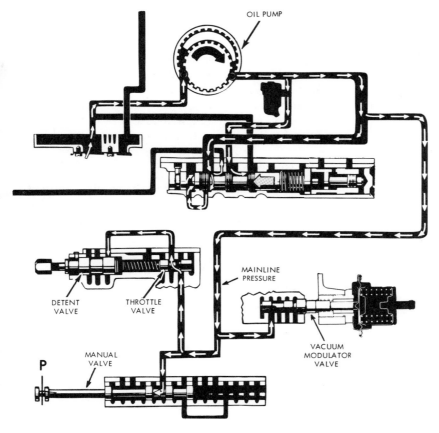

OIL PUMP

Fig.7-17. Main line pressure circuit illustrating separate throttle and modulator systems. (Pontiac Division, General Motors Corp.)

DETENT VALVE

THROTTLE VALVE

MAINLINE PRESSURE

VACUUM MODULATOR VALVE

MANUAL VALVE

P

Fig. 7-18. (Buick Motor Division, General Motors Corp.)

Fig. 7-19. (Chevrolet Motor Division, General Motors Corp.)

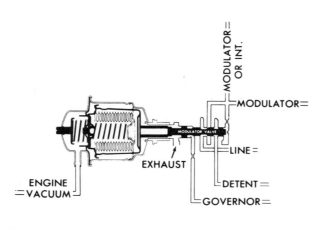

MODULATOR OR INT.

MODULATOR

LINE

DETENT

GOVERNOR

ENGINE VACUUM

EXHAUST

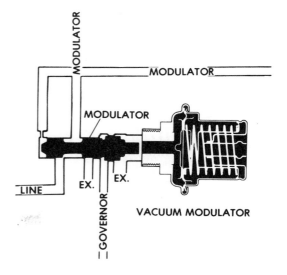

MODULATOR

MODULATOR

MODULATOR

LINE

EX.

EX.

GOVERNOR

VACUUM MODULATOR

lator pressure and low vacuum produces a high modulator pressure. The system also uses non-compensated and altitude-compensated vacuum modulator control units.

In the GM Chevrolet two-speed Powerglide and Pontiac two-speed (M-35) transmissions, the vacuum modulator system is used strictly for line pressure boost (Fig. 7-16). A separate, mechanically-controlled throttle system is added to provide the necessary shift scheduling (Fig. 7-17). Samples of GM vacuum modulator controls are illustrated in Figs. 7-18 and 7-19.

The vacuum, linkage, or cable-controlled systems each offer their own advantages. In the vacuum control, no periodic adjustments are required of the system after the transmission leaves the factory. If the diaphragm fails or the vacuum line develops a leak, high line pressure will result, whereas an incorrect linkage or cable adjustment can cause low line pressure and permit clutch or band slippage. If not immediately corrected, the excessive friction element slippage leads to transmission failure.

Although the periodic adjustment requirement of linkage or cable is subject to human error and wear, the vacuum system is not entirely fail-safe. A leaky diaphragm will actually permit the manifold vacuum to pull the transmission fluid into the engine for consumption. This loss of fluid is usually not picked up until transmission slippage is evident to the driver and that might be too late. In addition, a pinched vacuum line will cause a temporary delay in line pressure build-up during quick acceleration, resulting in transmission slippage, especially during forced downshifts. The pinched line prevents the vacuum unit from sensing an immediate change in manifold pressure.

Chart 7-1 summarizes the types of throttle/modulator system control used on current and recent production transmissions.

CHART 7-1
Throttle/Modulator Summary Chart

Transmission	Type of Control	Transmission	Type of Control
American Motors A904, A727, and 998	Linkage	Ford FMX, C-3, C-4, C-6, JATCO	Vacuum
		AOT and ATX	Linkage
Chrysler A904 and A727	Linkage	General Motors T-425, T-400, T-350, T-250, and (MD-3) 180	Vacuum
A404	Cable	T-325, T-200, and T-125	Cable

With the introduction of EGR (Exhaust Gas Recirculation) systems in 1973 production cars, the vacuum modulator units had to undergo design changes if the shift schedules were to be properly maintained. The inherent low manifold operating vacuum would cause late and harsh shifting. General Motors simply changed to a larger diameter modulator; however, Ford went to a dual diaphragm design (Fig. 7-20). In viewing the cross section, note that the effective left diaphragm area (A) is smaller than the effective right diaphragm area (B). Connector "A" is direct engine manifold vacuum and connector "B" is ported EGR carburetor vacuum, which is much lower than manifold vacuum. The differential area of the large diaphragm permits the atmospheric pressure to put an EGR vacuum-related push against the modulator spring. During warm-up, engine vacuum is not effective at connector "B," nor anytime at closed throttle.

Fig. 7-20. Ford dual diaphragm vacuum modulator. Photograph on right is the assembly view. (Ford Motor Co.)

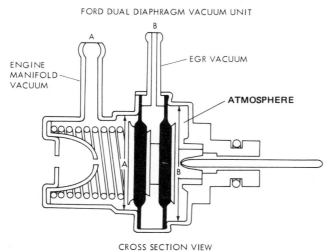

CROSS SECTION VIEW

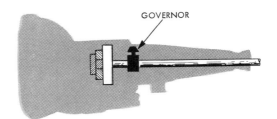

Fig. 7-23. Governor picks up road speed signal from the transmission output shaft.

MANUAL CONTROL SYSTEM

The manual control system programs the operating ranges of the transmission. It consists of a valve that is mechanically connected to a selector lever and enables the driver to choose the appropriate mode of operation (Fig. 7-21).

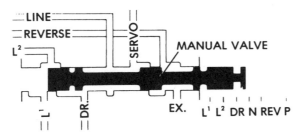

Fig. 7-21.

A typical selector quadrant might read P—R—N—D—2—1 (Fig. 7-22). The letters denote: Park, Reverse, Neutral, Drive, Intermediate, and Manual First. N and P cuts off all operating circuits and inhibits gear engagement. In P the output shaft is mechanically locked to the case by a pawl.

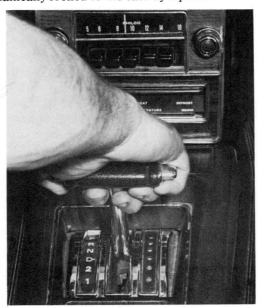

Fig. 7-22.

GOVERNOR SYSTEM

The governor is a hydraulic speedometer that is driven by the output shaft of the transmission, Fig. 7-23. It receives fluid from the main line pressure and produces a regulated governor pressure signal that is proportional to vehicle speed. It is used primarily for scheduling the transmission shifts along with throttle

or modulator pressures. It is also used as a pressure signal for auxiliary or supporting control valves in the valve body. We concentrate on its use for shift scheduling, in which capacity it opens the shift valve and causes the shift to happen.

There are several types of governor valve assembly designs in current use but they all rely on the centrifugal effect of a rotating mass (weights).

Illustrated in Fig. 7-24 is a case mounted governor assembly. When the transmission output shaft drives the governor assembly, the governor weights fly outward and exert a centrifugal force on the governor valve. Drive oil, which is actually mainline oil from the transmission pump, feeds the governor valve until sufficient pressure build-up on top of the valve balances the centrifugal force of the weights. The greater the vehicle speed, the greater the centrifugal force of the weights, and hence the greater the governor pressure

Fig. 7-24. Case mounted governor assembly. Top photo shows governor case installation. (Oldsmobile Division, General Motors Corp.)

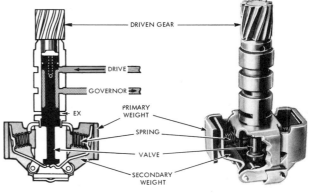

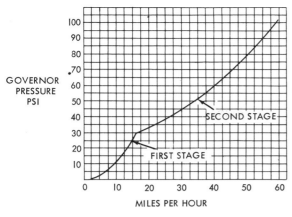

Fig. 7-25. Typical two-stage governor pressure curve.

Fig. 7-26. Output shaft mounted governor.

necessary to balance the centrifugal force. Eventually vehicle speed reaches a point at which the governor valve cannot balance itself against the centrifugal force of the weights. When this happens, the governor valve is permanently in the open position and governor pressure equals the mainline supply pressure.

The governor weight assembly is made-up of two sets of weights, primary and secondary, plus two springs. These parts are combined to produce a two stage output curve, Fig. 7-25, that provides a pressure range that will produce shifts at desired speeds. The primary and secondary weights have their own independent action; however, the primary weights are arranged to act on the secondary weights through the preload force of the springs. At low speeds, both weights act together, with the result that small changes in vehicle speed give comparatively large changes in centrifugal force and regulated governor pressure. As vehicle speed and governor rpm increases, the centrifugal force of the primary (heavy) weights exceeds the spring force and then moves out against a stop. The primary weights are now disengaged from the secondary (light) weights and are ineffective on the

governor valve. The governor valve now balances against centrifugal force of the secondary weights plus the spring force.

Governor assemblies are also designed to mount over the output shaft, Fig. 7-26. Again, the balance between the hydraulic pressure acting on the governor valve and the centrifugal force produced by the rotating primary and secondary weights and the compression of a coil spring results in a regulated governor pressure, Fig. 7-27.

Fig. 7-28 shows a relatively new design of a case mounted governor. Notice that the governor valve has been eliminated. Regulated governor pressure is determined by the amount of drive oil (regulated line) that is exhausted past the check balls. The centrifugal force of the governor weights acts to seat the check balls and seal the exhaust. At low speeds the secondary check ball is seated and the bleed-off of drive oil to balance the system is through the primary check ball. This is because the combined spring force and centrifugal force of the light secondary weight is greater than the combined spring and centrifugal force of the heavy primary weight (secondary spring force is greater than

Fig. 7-27. Cross section views of governor operation in secondary phase. Left: Governor valve open to line feed by centrifugal force. Right: Governor valve moved out over exhaust port to balance pressure.

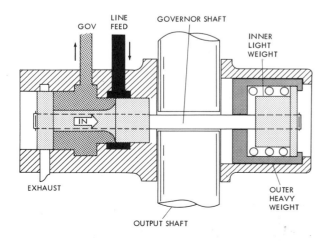

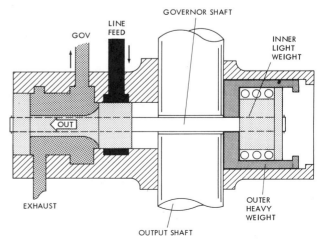

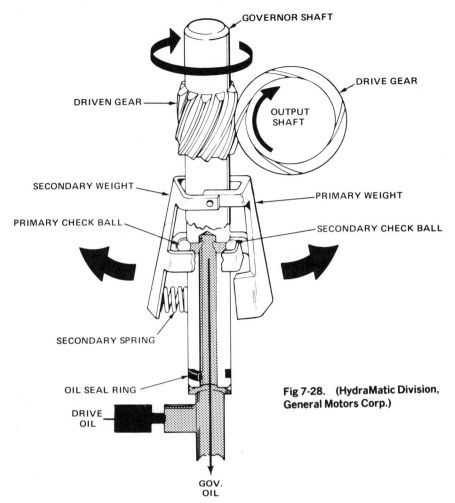

GOVERNOR SHAFT

DRIVE GEAR

DRIVEN GEAR

OUTPUT
SHAFT

SECONDARY WEIGHT

PRIMARY WEIGHT

PRIMARY CHECK BALL

SECONDARY CHECK BALL

SECONDARY SPRING

OIL SEAL RING

DRIVE
OIL

GOV.
OIL

Fig 7-28. (HydraMatic Division,
General Motors Corp.)

primary spring force). The secondary check ball is
seated and the bleed-off of drive oil to balance the
system is through the primary check ball. As vehicle
speed increases the centrifugal force on the primary
(heavy) weight greatly increases over the centrifugal
force of the secondary (light) weight. This effect
switches the governor action to the secondary weight
and checkball.

SERVO AND CLUTCH ASSEMBLIES

The use of hydraulic power to apply the bands and
clutches is confined to a single device, the hydraulic
piston. The pistons are housed in cylinder units known
as servo and clutch assemblies. The function of the piston is to convert the force of fluid into a mechanical
force capable of handling large loads. Hydraulic pressure applied to the piston strokes the piston in the cylinder and applies its load. During the power stroke, a
mechanical spring or springs are compressed to provide a means of returning the piston to its original
position. In some cases, fluid pressure may be applied
to the opposite side of the piston to assist the spring
force.

SERVO ASSEMBLY. A servo unit provides the
method of application and disengagement of the
bands. The band is applied by the piston force acting
on one end of the band while the other end is anchored
to the transmission case, which absorbs the reaction
forces (Fig. 7-29).

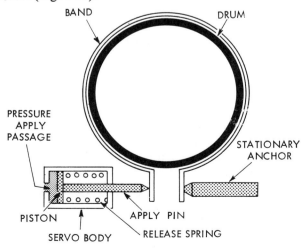

BAND

DRUM

PRESSURE
APPLY
PASSAGE

STATIONARY
ANCHOR

PISTON

APPLY PIN

SERVO BODY

RELEASE SPRING

Fig. 7-29. A servo is a hydraulic piston used for band
application. (Chevrolet Division, General Motors Corp.)

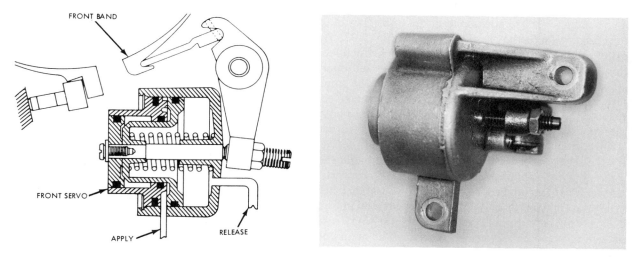

Fig. 7-30. Bolted servo to case.

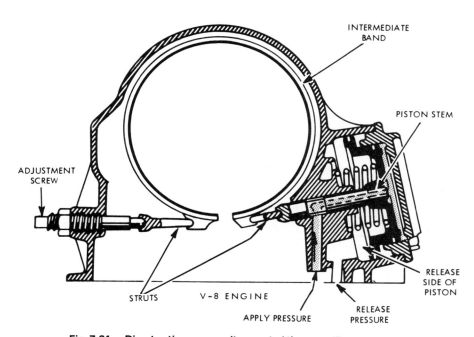

Fig. 7-31. Direct acting servo unit as part of the case. (Ford Motor Co.)

The servo unit consists of a piston in a cylinder and a piston return spring. It may be a separate cylinder assembly bolted to the transmission case or the cylinder can be designed as an integral part of the case (Figs. 7-30 and 7-31). Through suitable linkage and lever action, the servo is connected to the band it operates. The servo force acts directly on the end of the band with an apply pin or through a lever arrangement that provides a multiplying force. These arrangements are illustrated in Figs. 7-31 and 7-32.

The servo unit band application must rigidly hold and ground a planetary gear member to the transmission case for forward or reverse reduction. To assist the hydraulic and mechanical apply forces, the servo

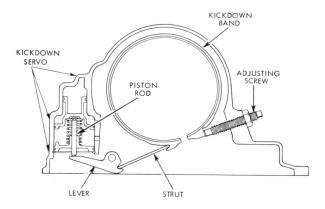

Fig. 7-32. Servo unit lever arrangement.

and band anchor are positioned in the transmission to take advantage of the drum rotation. In Fig. 7-32, the drum rotational effort is in the counterclockwise direction. When the band is applied, it becomes self-energized and wraps itself around the drum in the same direction as drum rotation. This self-energizing effect reduces the force that the servo must produce to hold the band. The principle is the same one used to describe the action of self-energized drum brakes.

To release the servo apply action on the band, the servo apply oil is exhausted from the circuit or a servo release oil is introduced on the servo piston that opposes the apply oil (Fig. 7-33). The servo piston in Fig. 7-33 is shown in the apply position. When servo release oil is introduced on a 2–3 shift, the hydraulic main line pressure acting on the top side of the piston plus the servo return spring will overcome the servo apply oil and move the piston downward.

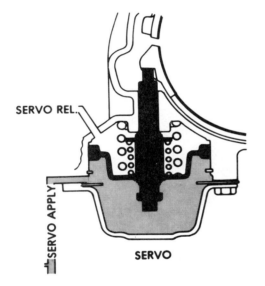

Fig. 7-33.

BAND DESIGN. Band designs in automatic transmissions use a flexible contracting band and are classified as single-wrap (Fig. 7-34) or double wrap (Fig. 7-35). The double wrap offers the advantage of having the greater holding force should the drum rotation provide for a self-energizing effect.

Fig. 7-35.   Double wrap band.

The composition of the friction lining is either *semimetallic* or *organic*. The semimetallic materials can withstand high unit pressures but have a tendency to scrape away the drum surface. Therefore, semimetallic applications are limited to conditions that require a high static torque and minimum of dynamic service. This explains why the semi-metallic band is usually confined to use as a reverse band. A favored organic material is paper pulp or cellulose based compound. It is a soft material that has very little wear effect on a drum and will show better uniform contact to the drum surface. Grooving of the friction surface provides for a controlled escape of fluid and vapor during engagement.

Fig. 7-34.   Samples of single wrap bands.

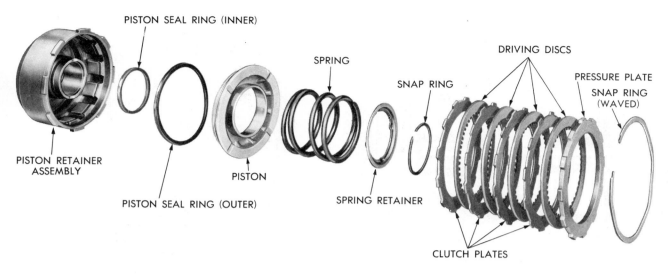

Fig. 7-36. Disc clutch assembly. (Chrysler Corp.)

Soft organic materials are used when the band is operating under dynamic conditions. Drum surface speeds over 6,000 rpm can be encountered prior to band application.

Critical to the proper band action is the drum material, hardness, and surface finish. Most drum material is a soft iron that cannot use a high finish surface. This combination would have a tendency to cause glazing of the band and drum. In service practice, it is recommended that any polished surface on a soft iron drum be deglazed with 120–180 grit emery cloth. In contrast, a smooth finish on a hard surface drum is optimum for the right band action.

In summary, consistent shift quality depends on the following factors:

1. Friction material
2. Grooving in the friction material
3. Drum material and hardness
4. Drum surface finish
5. Proper adjustment of band clearance
6. Transmission fluid type and condition

CLUTCH ASSEMBLY. The multiple-disc clutch is the favored clutch unit used in automatic transmissions. It offers the following features:

1. Multiple discs give the clutch a sufficient area of frictional or torque-holding capacity in an overall small diameter drum.
2. Unlike bands, disc clutches can easily be used as rotating engagement members.
3. Once the proper running clearance has been established during factory or field service assembly, there is no adjustment requirement for wear.
4. The disc clutch can be used as a reaction member by connecting a rotating part to a stationary component. For example, the low–reverse clutch in a T-350 or C-6 connects the reaction carrier to the transmission case. In a T-350 or T-200, the intermediate clutch connects the one-way roller clutch outer race to the transmission case.

A typical clutch unit is made up of the following components and is illustrated in Fig. 7-36.

1. Friction plates or drive discs with internal splines that fit on a torque transmitting hub.
2. Steel discs or plates that mate with the friction plates. The external drive lugs of the steel plates fit into a torque transmitting drum or cylinder.
3. A reaction or pressure plate at the end of the clutch pack.
4. A hydraulic apply piston to engage the clutch pack.
5. A spring-loaded piston release.
6. A retainer or drum that houses the complete assembly.

When the piston is applied, it will squeeze the clutch pack together against the pressure plate and snap ring. The snap ring fits in front of the pressure plate and into a snap ring groove in the clutch drum.

In Fig. 7-37, a pair of multiple disc clutch assemblies show a more exact relationship to a transmission power flow. Both clutches are oil-applied and spring-released. With both clutches OFF, there is no power to the gear set, whereas a front clutch apply drives the primary sun gear and a rear clutch apply drives the secondary sun gear. This is how power enters the gear set for forward speeds and reverse. In high gear, the front and rear clutches are applied and drive both sun gears together.

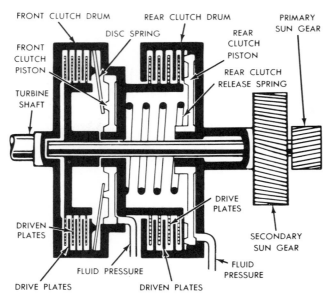

Fig. 7-37. Front and rear disc clutch assemblies controlling power input to planetary gear train. (Ford Motor Co.)

Fig. 7-39. Clutch piston return springs; small coil springs shown without spring seat and retainer in place.

To return or release a clutch piston there are several spring designs that are used:

1. A large single coil spring (Fig. 7-38)
2. A series of small coil springs (Fig. 7-39)
3. A belleville or disc spring (Fig. 7-40)

Notice the cross section view of the disc spring in the front clutch as shown in Fig. 7-37. The spring acts as a lever arm to gain additional apply force as it moves about the pivot ring, or fulcrum point, of the inner pressure plate. This arrangement will require the piston to take a longer apply stroke, which results in cushioning the clutch apply. Clutch units will also use a steel-waved plate or waved snap ring to cushion the clutch apply if desirable (Figs. 7-40 and 7-41).

In rotating clutch units, a problem usually arises when the clutch is not engaged. With the clutch OFF, the clutch drum or housing still spins; as a matter of fact, the spin-up may be at an overdrive speed. The high speed rotation could create sufficient centrifugal force in the residual or remaining oil in the clutch-apply cylinder to partially engage the clutch. This creates an unwanted rubbing effect between the clutch plates. To prevent this problem, a clutch relief valve (Fig. 7-42) is incorporated in the clutch drum or sometimes in the clutch piston.

The relief valve is a steel check ball that operates in a cavity with a check ball seat. A small hole or orifice is tapped from the seat for pressure relief. In the clutch drum example, when the clutch unit is applied, oil pressure holds the ball on its seat and blocks off the orifice. In the released position, the centrifugal force created by the rotating clutch drum moves the ball off its seat, allowing the trapped oil behind the clutch piston to be discharged.

Fig. 7-38. Clutch piston return spring, large single coil.

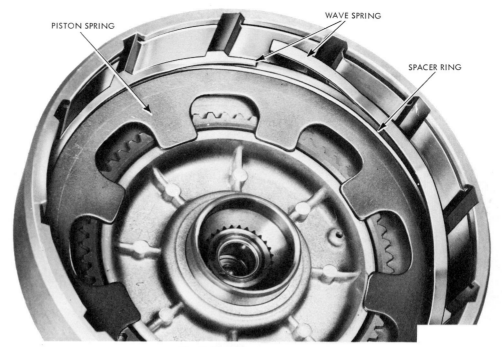

PISTON SPRING

WAVE SPRING

SPACER RING

**Fig. 7-40. Disc spring installation.
(Chrysler Corp.)**

COMPOSITION
PLATES

STEEL
PLATES

STEEL
WAVED
PLATE

**Fig. 7-41.
(HydraMatic Division, General Motors Corp.)**

FORWARD
CLUTCH
HOUSING

**Fig. 7-42.
(Oldsmobile Division, General Motors Corp.)**

EXHAUST
CHECK BALL
SEATED

EXHAUST
CHECK BALL
UNSEATED

CLUTCH APPLIED

CLUTCH RELEASED

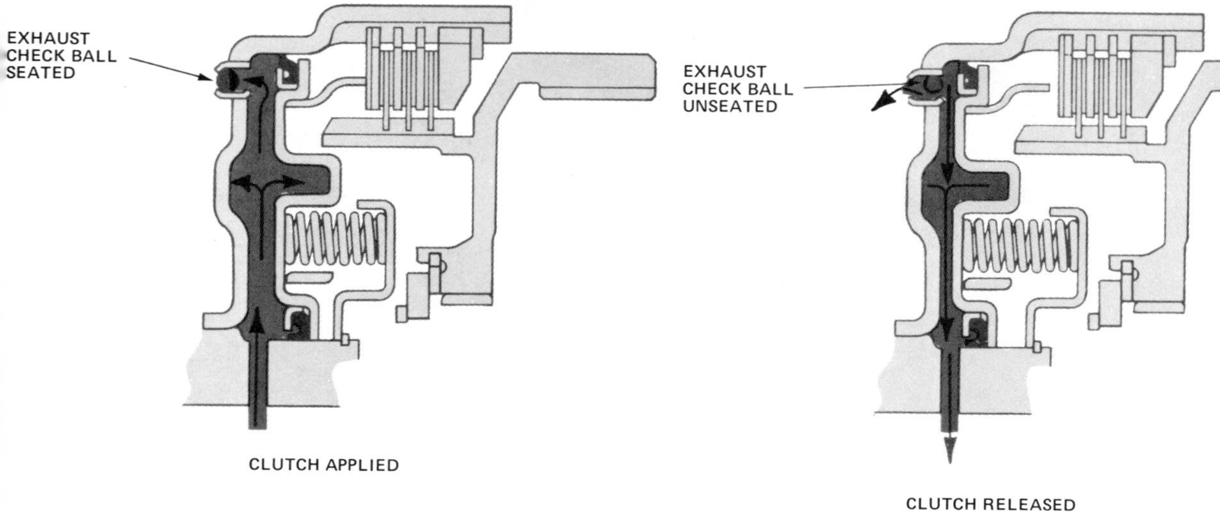

Fig. 7-43. Typical friction disc grooving pattern.

ular friction material that is sometimes processed with asbestos fibers.

There is a final process of grooving and grinding. In Fig. 7-43, some typical grooving patterns are illustrated. Although all friction facings do not require grooving, the purpose of the grooving is to provide a controlled fluid wiping action and vapor escape as the clutch contacting surfaces are squeezed together. Grooving is very effective in cooling the clutch. The best groove pattern is determined by the friction material used, surface conditions, engagement speeds, and type of fluid. These factors determine shift quality and clutch life.

The steel plates are made from carbon steel rolled stock. The rolled stock is run through straightening rolls and then blanked into clutch discs. As a final process, the blanked discs are tumbled to produce a dull or mat surface finish. The surface finish breaks-in the mating composition fiction-faced discs. After the break-in period, the steel discs become polished; however, they should never be used with replacement friction discs. It should be obvious that the new friction plates are likely to develop surface glazing and cause lazy or slipping shifts.

CLUTCH PLATE DESIGN. The clutch composition or friction discs are made-up of a steel plate core, faced with a friction material of either sintered metal or paper cellulose.

The *full-metallic* friction material is usually made from a powder mix of copper and graphite. A *semimetallic* material is also used and consists of copper powder compounded with lead powders, asbestos, and resin binders. *Organic* or paper cellulose is a very pop-

VALVE BODY ASSEMBLY

The valve body assembly is the heart of the hydraulic control system. It is an intricate network of interrelated passages, precision valves, springs, check balls and orifices (Figs. 7-44, 7-45, and 7-46). The assembly normally contains the manual valve, the throttle and kickdown valves, shift valves, and a pressure regulator valve.

Fig. 7-44. Manual shift body disassembled.

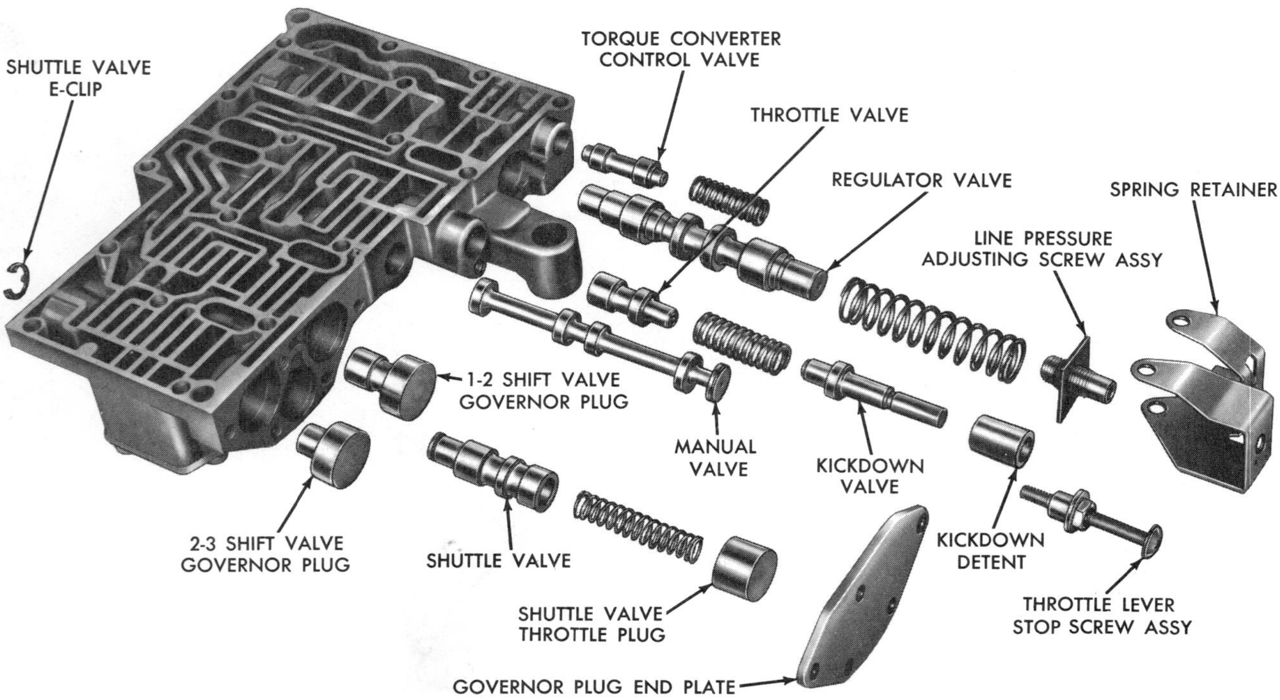

SHUTTLE VALVE E-CLIP

TORQUE CONVERTER CONTROL VALVE

THROTTLE VALVE

REGULATOR VALVE

SPRING RETAINER

LINE PRESSURE ADJUSTING SCREW ASSY

1-2 SHIFT VALVE GOVERNOR PLUG

MANUAL VALVE

KICKDOWN VALVE

2-3 SHIFT VALVE GOVERNOR PLUG

SHUTTLE VALVE

KICKDOWN DETENT

SHUTTLE VALVE THROTTLE PLUG

THROTTLE LEVER STOP SCREW ASSY

GOVERNOR PLUG END PLATE

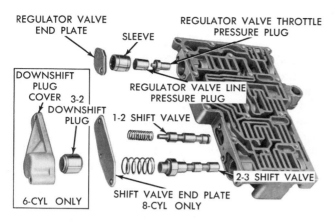

Fig. 7-45. Automatic shift body disassembled.

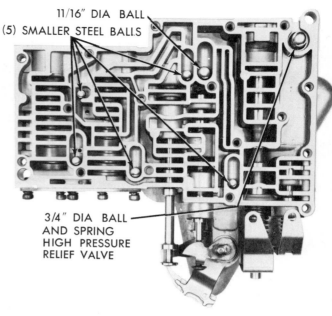

Fig. 7-46. Valve body ball check valves.

The valve body, or brain, works like a computer. It is programmed for the operating range by the manual valve and monitors two hydraulic signals, one from the throttle system and another from the governor system. These signals are evaluated by the automatic shift system to determine the shift points and by the pressure regulation system to determine line pressure modulation (Fig. 7-47).

A third signal is provided by the kickdown or detent mechanism. The system is driver controlled and provides a hydraulic command to overrule the shift valves for either a 3–2 or 3–1 forced downshift.

ACCUMULATOR

Accumulators are used in the servo and clutch apply circuits for the purpose of controlling the 1–2 and 2–3 shift feel or quality. This is done by controlling the rate at which the band or clutch fully applies. It is a spring-loaded piston device that cushions the shift engagement according to engine torque output. It does this by absorbing a certain amount of fluid flow in the circuit during a band or clutch application.

A series of illustrations will show how a typical accumulator system works. First, let's look at a simple clutch circuit without provisions to cushion the automatic shift (Fig. 7-48). With this arrangement, the clutch engagement is sudden and the car jerks forward. The shift sensation is similar in effect to "popping" the clutch pedal on a manual transmission. The driver gets a kick in the back.

To smooth the shift, an accumulator is designed into the clutch apply circuit (Fig. 7-49). In the first stage, initial rapid flow of apply oil and pressure build-up is permitted in the circuit. The clutch piston return springs are overcome and the slack or clearance is taken up between the discs. As soon as the clutch slack is removed and the discs begin to tighten up, the pressure build-up in the circuit is rapid. At a point just be-

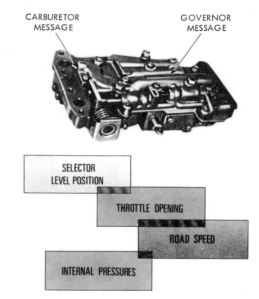

Fig. 7-47. The valve body receives signals from the throttle and the governor and shifts automatically.

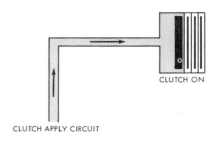

Fig. 7-48. Clutch circuit without accumulator.

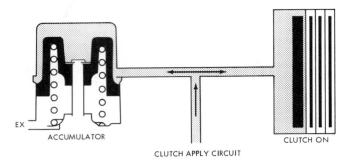

Fig. 7-49. Simple accumulator with spring load.

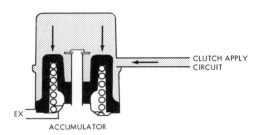

Fig. 7-50. Simple accumulator with piston fully stroked.

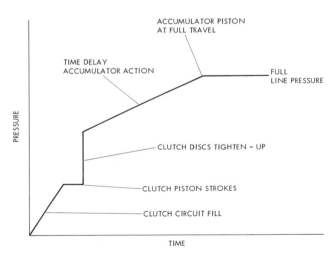

Fig. 7-51. Typical pressure rise and accumulator action in clutch circuit.

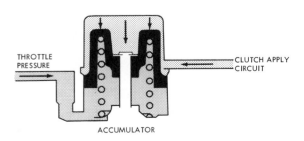

Fig. 7-52. Throttle sensitive accumulator.

fore maximum pressure is reached, the accumulator piston is stroked against the spring force (Fig. 7-50). Because the accumulator absorbs fluid as the piston strokes, the final pressure build-up in the clutch circuit is more gradual and a smooth engagement is attained. The complete sequence of events is shown in Fig. 7-51 and can be compared to engaging the clutch with a manually-operated transmission. Through driver foot control, the clutch pedal is let out rapidly until the clutch slack is removed and starts to apply. At this point the pedal travel is slowed down to cushion the final lock-up.

The accumulator in Fig. 7-49 would be adequate if all shifts were made at the same engine torque, whereby the spring tension in the accumulator would provide a fixed rate of pressure build-up time for final clutch lock-up. When shifts are made under heavy throttle conditions, it is necessary to increase the initial circuit apply pressure on the clutch discs before the accumulator piston strokes; otherwise, clutch spin-up would occur. Refer to Fig. 7-51.

To vary the pressure at which the accumulator action begins, a throttle-sensitive oil pressure is introduced to oppose the stroking of the piston. This oil pressure could be the same as the existing throttle pressure used for shifting the valves or a modified throttle pressure for the best shift feel. This arrangement is illustrated in Fig. 7-52. Some accumulators use the mainline operating pressure as the throttle sensitive pressure. The accumulator piston and spring arrangement, however, work in a slightly different manner (Fig. 7-53). When the accumulator piston is stroked, the spring force decreases. This permits an increase in

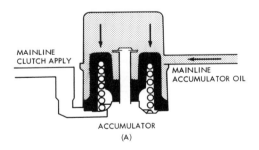

(A)

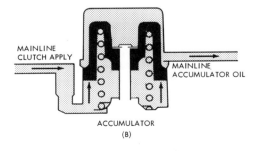

(B)

Fig. 7-53. Accumulator action with mainline used as the accumulator oil.

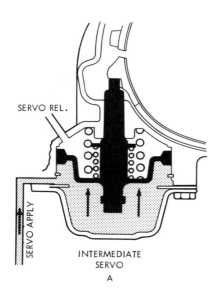

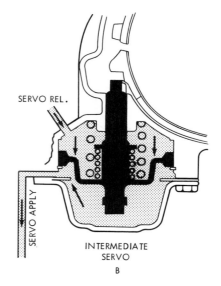

Fig. 7-54.

oil pressure during the piston stroke or clutch apply time.

Using a throttle-sensitive oil in the accumulator makes it behave like a variable shock absorber. With light throttle shifts, the accumulator allows for a soft engagement of the clutch or band. Under heavy throttle, the shift feel is quick, firm, and aggressive.

It is common practice to build-in an accumulator action with the servo unit. A servo piston in the apply position for intermediate gear operation is shown in Fig. 7-54. On the 2–3 shift, direct clutch apply oil is routed into the servo release side of the piston. The release oil plus the release springs overcome the servo apply force and the piston strokes downward. This action releases the band while the clutch is being applied. Note that the servo release, or downward piston movement, provides an accumulator action for the direct clutch. The intermediate band adjustment is therefore critical to the accumulator action because it controls the servo release spring load. A loose band adjustment, for example, will result in a longer piston apply stroke. The band apply is not affected but the release spring load is increased. Therefore, during direct clutch apply, the servo is released too early and the accumulator action occurs too early. The end result is an engine flare-up on the 2–3 shift.

SHIFT SYSTEM

The shift system provides both automatic and non-automatic gear selection. The non-automatic selections are provided by the manual valve and typically include neutral, reverse, and forward range plus the operating ranges used for engine braking. Automatic gear selection provides for gear ratio changes that are compatible to the vehicle speed and available performance desired by the driver. In a three-speed system, the shift schedule is programmed for a 1–2 and 2–3 shift in full automatic drive range.

The shift system can be viewed as a hydraulic computer. Through driver selection, the manual valve is properly indexed in the valve body and programs the transmission for the desired operating range. In full automatic drive range, the two shift valve arrangements digest a hydraulic road speed signal and a hydraulic torque signal. The shift valves evaluate the information and automatically trigger ON and OFF to provide the best gear ratio for the driving load.

The essential hydraulic support systems for transmission operation have already been discussed: the pressure supply system, converter, cooling and lube system, throttle and modulator systems and the governor system. Add to these the manual valve, servos and bands, clutches, and accumulators and you are ready to tie it all together with the shift system operation. A gradual build-up of a three-speed hydraulic control system shows how a seemingly complex subject is made-up of a number of simple circuits and assorted devices that are easy to understand. Our control system uses the standardized range selection P—R—N—D—2—1 as it relates to a typical Simpson planetary gear train.

Neutral and Park (N—P)

The manual valve blocks the line pressure to the clutch and band apply circuits (Fig. 7-55). With the forward and direct clutches both disengaged, the transmission is isolated from the engine and torque converter.

The line pressure control continues to function. A steady supply of regulated operating oil is maintained and the constant requirement to feed the converter and lubrication circuits and maintain cooling is satisfied (Fig. 7-55).

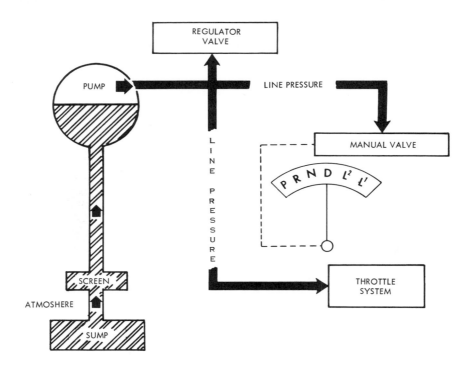

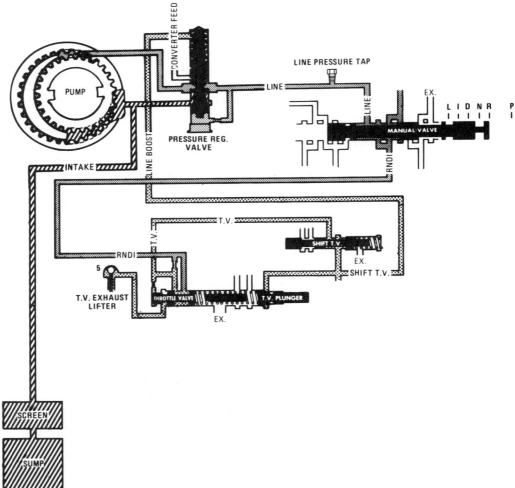

Fig. 7-55. (A and B). (HydraMatic Division General Motors Corp.)

Automatic Drive Range (D)

When the selector lever is positioned in (D), the manual valve connects the line pressure to the forward clutch circuit (Fig. 7-56). The oil is usually metered through an orifice for a smooth clutch apply.

Application of the forward clutch mechanically connects the gear train to the engine and torque converter. The compound planetary gear action causes the low roller clutch assembly to lock-up and initiate first-gear operation. The vehicle is now ready for 1st gear operation.

As the vehicle accelerates, progressive shifts to second and third gears are determined by automatic

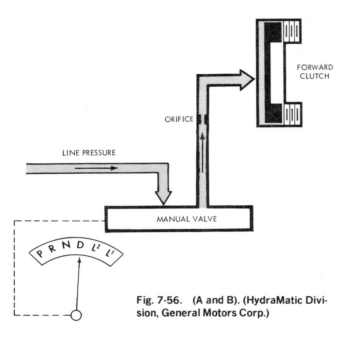

Fig. 7-56. (A and B). (HydraMatic Division, General Motors Corp.)

FORWARD CLUTCH

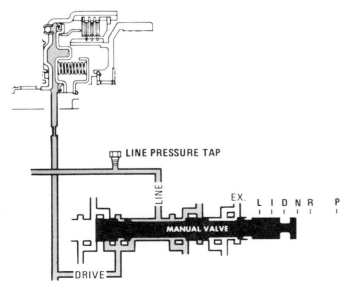

shift valve movement. A shift valve is a relay valve and acts as a simple type of hydraulic circuit selector. Its movement or position is determined by pressures from its supporting controls, the governor and throttle systems (Fig. 7-57). Governor pressure, a regulated vehicle-speed-sensitive signal, acts on one end of the shift valve and works to *open* or upshift the valve. The governor pressure causes the shift to happen. Opposing governor pressure is throttle pressure that is a regulated engine-torque-sensitive signal. The throttle pressure will act to *delay* the upshift movement of the valve. In most cases, throttle pressure is modified by a regulating valve in the shift valve train before acting upon the shift valve. In addition, a fixed spring load is used on the throttle side of the shift valve to determine the closed throttle downshift point. The line pressure at the shift valve is distributed from the manual valve. It will serve as the prime mover for the entire shift when it occurs.

A gear change is decided by the acting forces of governor pressure vs. throttle pressure. At light throttle openings, a small throttle signal is received by the shift valve. To overcome the throttle pressure resistance, only a low vehicle speed is required to generate a sufficient governor force to shift the valve. An early shift, therefore, takes place.

If the driver wants medium and heavy throttle performance, the shift is delayed. The throttle opening produces a correspondingly larger throttle signal, which in turn dictates higher vehicle speeds to generate the necessary governor signal for the shift. The maximum shift point, therefore, occurs at wide open throttle and within the engineered safe speed limit. Typically, for V-8 applications, the 1–2 shift spread is 10–50 mph (16-80 km/h) and the 2–3 shift spread is 18–70 mph (29-112 km/h).

The 1–2 shift circuit is illustrated in Figs. 7-58 and 7-59. In Fig. 7-59, note how the accumulator regulates the build-up time of line pressure on the intermediate servo piston for proper shift feel. Stroking of the intermediate servo piston compresses the servo cushion spring and applies the intermediate band. The band apply holds the planetary sun gear and causes the low roller clutch to release. Second gear ratio is provided by the front planetary only.

The 2–3 shift circuit is illustrated in Figs. 7-60 and 7-61. When the shift valve opens (Fig. 7-61), line pressure flow in the circuit applies the direct clutch and releases the intermediate servo piston. The direct clutch apply oil, acting on larger servo piston surface area, and the compressed servo cushion spring force overcome the intermediate apply oil. The servo piston moves and the band is released. The stroking of the servo piston absorbs direct clutch oil and provides an accumulator action against the torque-sensitive intermediate apply oil.

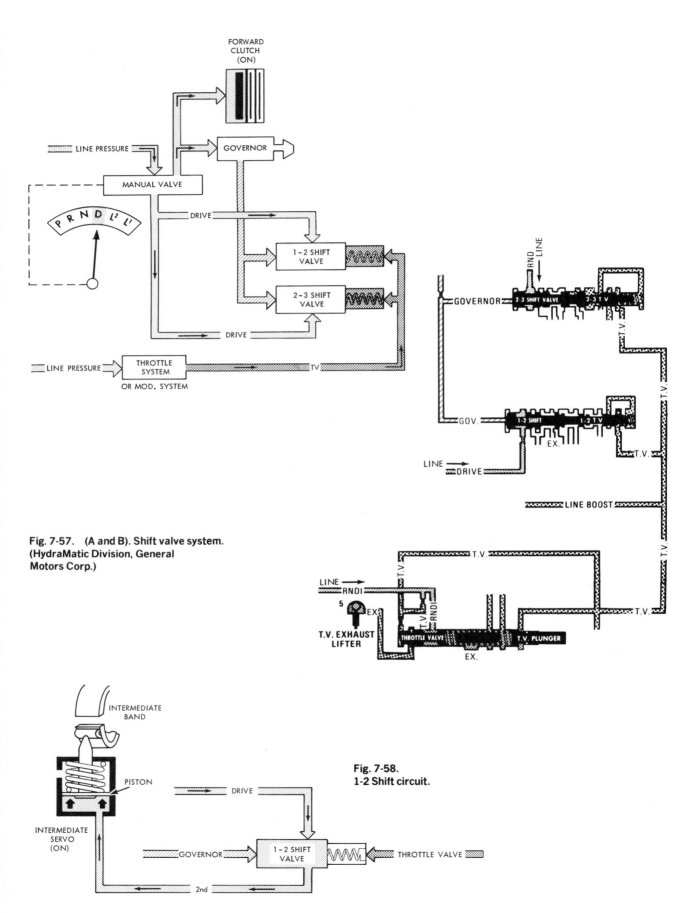

FORWARD
CLUTCH
(ON)

LINE PRESSURE

GOVERNOR

MANUAL VALVE

P R N D L² L¹

DRIVE

1-2 SHIFT
VALVE

2-3 SHIFT
VALVE

DRIVE

LINE PRESSURE

THROTTLE
SYSTEM

OR MOD. SYSTEM

TV

RND
LINE

GOVERNOR

2-3 SHIFT VALVE

2-3 T V

T.V.

GOV.

1-2 SHIFT

1-2 TV

EX.

T.V.

LINE

DRIVE

LINE BOOST

T.V.

Fig. 7-57. (A and B). Shift valve system.
(HydraMatic Division, General
Motors Corp.)

T.V.

T.V.

LINE

RNDI

5

EX.

T.V.

RNDI

T.V.

T.V. EXHAUST
LIFTER

THROTTLE VALVE

T.V. PLUNGER

EX.

INTERMEDIATE
BAND

PISTON

Fig. 7-58.
1-2 Shift circuit.

INTERMEDIATE
SERVO
(ON)

DRIVE

GOVERNOR

1-2 SHIFT
VALVE

THROTTLE VALVE

2nd

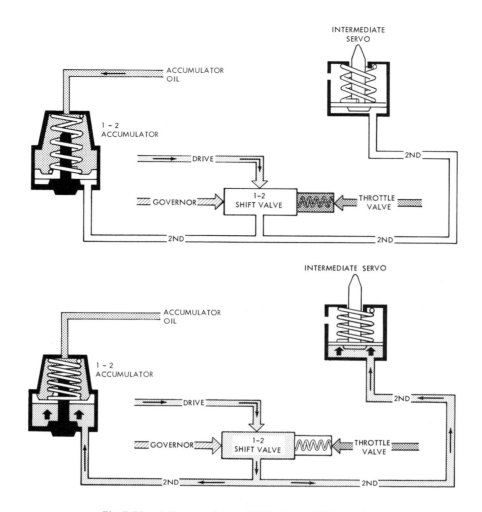

Fig. 7-59. 1-2 accumulator—(A) First gear. (B) Second gear.

Fig. 7-60. 1-2 accumulator—third gear.

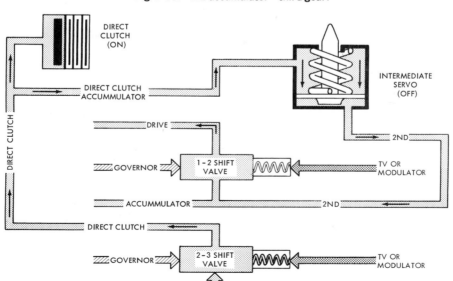

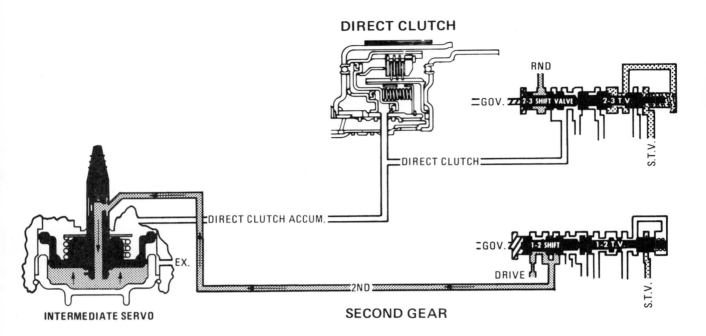

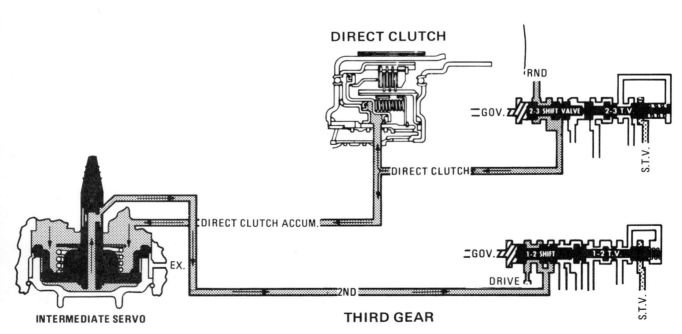

Fig. 7-61. (a) Second gear; intermediate servo apply. (b) Third gear; direct clutch apply and intermediate servo release. Servo piston release stroke provides (2-3) accumulator action.

COAST OR CLOSED THROTTLE DOWN-SHIFT. In reviewing the 1–2 and 2–3 shift valve movement, notice that the TV pressure is cut-off from the end of the shift valves when they open. This sudden exhaust of TV pressure gives the shift valves a snap action on the upshift and eliminates any hunting or indecision of the valves to shift and stay shifted, especially if the vehicle speed is maintained at or near the shift point. Once the shift is made, spring tension alone opposes governor pressure on the shift valves. As the vehicle slows down on closed throttle, governor pressure is reduced at the shift valves. When governor pressure is less than the opposing fixed spring force, the shift valves close with a snap action. The direct and intermediate circuits are then exhausted at the shift valves. At closed throttle, TV pressure is 0 psi and has no effect on the shift valves when they close.

In a shift system in which the closed throttle sequence is 3–2 and 2–1, the 3–2 shift generally occurs between 8–12 mph (13–19 km/h) and the 2–1 shift between 3–5 mph (5–8 km/h). On Ford shift systems using a 3–1 closed throttle pattern, the governor cuts out at 10 mph (16 km/h) and both shift valves close simultaneously. Chrysler closed throttle shift patterns are also 3–1. A hydraulic interlock between the shift valves does not permit the 2–3 shift valve to close until the 1–2 shift valve closes. At approximately 5 mph (8 km/h), both shift valves close together.

PART THROTTLE 3–2 DOWNSHIFT. Most shift systems feature a part throttle 3–2 downshift for extra performance during moderate acceleration at low speeds. The accelerator pedal needs only to be partially depressed to cause the shift. The transmission will automatically return to third gear as car speed increases or the accelerator is released. Depending on the vehicle make and engine application, a part throttle 3–2 downshift can be accomplished at speeds as high as 50 mph, (81 km/h) while others may require the road speed to drop below 30 mph (48.5 km/h).

Although each automatic transmission has its own part-throttle design system, they all provide a throttle pressure by-pass circuit to the 2–3 shift valve. Illustrated in Figs. 7-62 and 7-63 are two part throttle systems with different circuit approaches. Featured in Fig. 7-62 is a mechanically operated throttle system tied in with the part throttle 3–2 downshift circuit. By depressing the accelerator pedal far enough, the TV plunger opens the PT circuit to TV pressure. When the TV plunger moved, it also raised the TV pressure, which can now act upon the 2–3 shift valve train. If the vehicle speed is right, the TV pressure moves the 2–3 valve train against governor pressure and the transmission shifts to second gear.

The part throttle system shown in Fig. 7-63 also ties into the throttle system. A throttle plug is designed into the 2–3 shift valve train and can keep the 2–3 shift valve throttle pressure sensitive. After the valve has made the 2–3 upshift, it butts up against the end of the 3–2 throttle plug, which is shown with a throttle pressure load (Fig. 7-63). The throttle pressure load at the 3–2 throttle plug, however, is switched ON and OFF by a limit valve (Figs. 7-64 and 7-65). The limit valve is a relay valve and is controlled by spring force and governor pressure. At low road speeds, the spring force on the limit valve is greater than the governor force and the valve will be moved to its ON position (Fig. 7-64). This permits the throttle pressure supply to

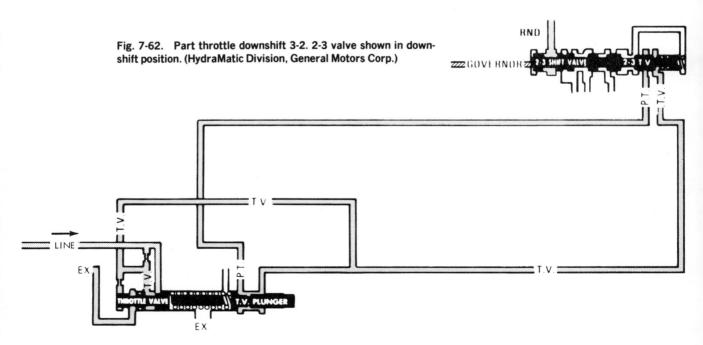

Fig. 7-62. Part throttle downshift 3-2. 2-3 valve shown in downshift position. (HydraMatic Division, General Motors Corp.)

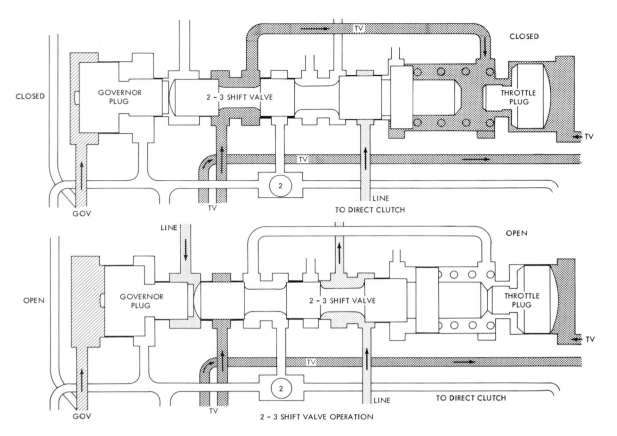

CLOSED

CLOSED

GOVERNOR PLUG

2 - 3 SHIFT VALVE

THROTTLE PLUG

TV

TV

②

TV

TV

GOV

LINE

TO DIRECT CLUCH

LINE

OPEN

OPEN

GOVERNOR PLUG

2 - 3 SHIFT VALVE

THROTTLE PLUG

TV

②

TV

TV

LINE

GOV

TO DIRECT CLUTCH

2 - 3 SHIFT VALVE OPERATION

Fig. 7-63.

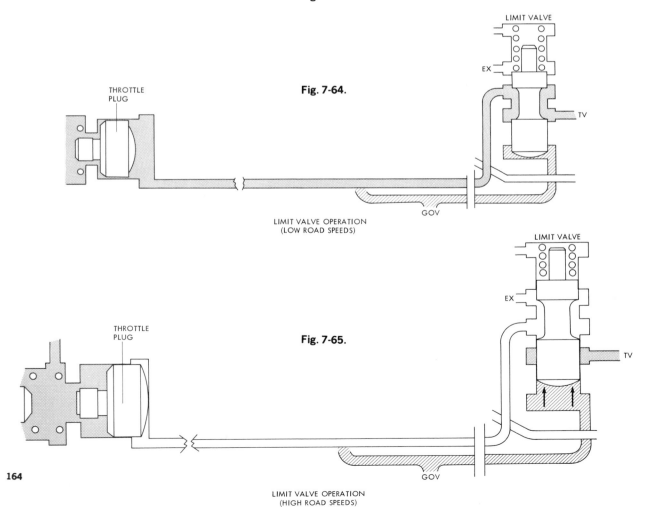

Fig. 7-64.

LIMIT VALVE

EX

TV

THROTTLE PLUG

GOV

LIMIT VALVE OPERATION
(LOW ROAD SPEEDS)

LIMIT VALVE

EX

TV

THROTTLE PLUG

Fig. 7-65.

GOV

164

LIMIT VALVE OPERATION
(HIGH ROAD SPEEDS)

load the 3-2 throttle plug. Any moderate accelerator pedal depression will raise the throttle pressure and push the throttle plug against the 2-3 shift valve and opposing governor pressure. The 2-3 shift valve closes and the direct clutch circuit is exhausted for a 3-2 part throttle downshift. At higher vehicle speeds, the part throttle 3-2 downshift feature would be annoying and not desirable. The limit valve prevents this from happening. As vehicle speed increases, the governor pressure builds-up to the point at which its force on the limit valve is greater than the spring force. This moves the limit valve to the OFF position, and the throttle pressure supply to the 3-2 throttle plug is cut-off (Fig. 7-65). The 3-2 part throttle plug is now inactive. At high road speeds, the only 3-2 downshift that can occur is a wide-open throttle downshift.

FULL THROTTLE FORCED DOWNSHIFT. This term is also referred to as detent, kickdown, or forced downshift operation. The function of the forced downshift is to overrule the governor system control of the shift valves. At full throttle, the downshift system provides a by-pass circuit to the shift valves loaded with throttle or line pressure. By temporarily helping the regular throttle pressure at the shift valves, the W.O.T. upshifts can be delayed longer or a forced downshift can be promoted. Maximum upshifts are usually delayed by 5-10 mph (8-16 km/h) and, depending on the vehicle speed, forced 3-2 and 3-1 downshifts will occur.

In a mechanically-operated throttle system, linkage or cable-controlled, a downshift valve or plunger works in tandem with the throttle valve (Fig. 7-66). By

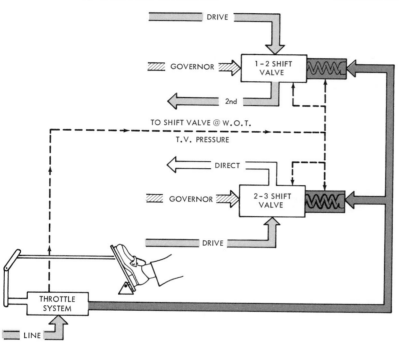

Fig. 7-66. Detent (full throttle) downshift 3-2, valves in second gear position.

fully depressing the accelerator pedal, the TV plunger movement bottoms the throttle valve to provide maximum TV pressure. The detent and part throttle circuits are also opened up to full TV pressure, which is directed to the shift valves to signal a downshift. Full TV pressure can now act upon both shift valves even though they are in the upshifted position. Figure 7-66 shows that the 2–3 shift valve was closed against the governor pressure and the direct clutch circuit was exhausted. The 1–2 shift valve remains open simply because the vehicle speed is too high and the opposing governor pressure is in command. When the vehicle speed is slowed to the safe range, the 1–2 shift valve will be forced to close for a 3–1 or 2–1 downshift effect. Should the vehicle speed be too high, the downshift or detent system will fail to close the 2–3 shift valve against governor pressure and no forced downshift will occur.

Although the speed range at which the forced downshifts occur varies with the engine application, axle ratio, and tire size, the following guide line can be used. The 3–2 shifts are usually available below 65 mph (105 km/h) and the 3–1 or 2–1 shifts below 40 mph (64.5 km/h). On some applications the 3–2 shift can happen below 90 mph (145 km/h) and the 3–1 or 2–1 below 55 mph (88.5 km/h).

If the throttle pressure control uses engine vacuum, then an independent downshift valve must be used. This valve is usually controlled by an external mechanical connection to the accelerator linkage. Some transmissions, however, use an electrical solenoid control on the valve, which is used in the THM-400 and JATCO.

Illustrated in Figs. 7-67 and 7-68 are two block diagrams showing variations of forced downshift systems used when the throttle system is vacuum-controlled. Figure 7-67 shows the TV pressure as the sup-

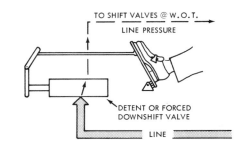

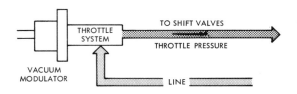

Fig. 7-68.

ply oil to the downshift valve. At wide-open throttle, the mechanical linkage triggers the valve, and TV pressure charges the downshift circuit and signals the shift valves. The same action takes place in Fig. 7-68; however, line pressure is substituted for T.V. pressure.

Intermediate and Manual Low

Intermediate and manual low operation are a function of the manual valve. The manual valve controls the hydraulic loading of the shift valve trains when the selector lever is placed in the 1 or 2 position. This arrangement can prevent the 1–2 shift valve from initiating a change into second gear or the 2–3 shift valve can be prevented from initiating a change into high gear.

The block diagrams in Figs. 7-69, 7-70, 7-71, 7-72, and 7-73 give a condensed summary of how the shift valves can be inhibited.

Figure 7-69 is representative of an intermediate system that allows a first-gear start and an automatic shift into second gear. In this instance, the manual valve opens the 2 circuit to line pressure, which charges the 2–3 shift valve train and hydraulically locks the valve closed. If the car is in high gear when the 2 range is selected, the transmission will downshift to second regardless of vehicle speed. The 1–2 shift valve performs the same as it did in automatic drive range. A variation of the same intermediate system will find the manual valve cutting off the line pressure feed to the 2–3 shift valve and producing the same results (Fig. 7-70). The intermediate circuit can also be arranged to provide a second gear start (Fig. 7-71). The manual valve cuts off the line pressure feed to the 2–3 shift valve and allows line pressure to charge the 2 circuit leading to the 1–2 shift valve train. The line pressure rules and the 1–2 shift valve is immediately blocked open.

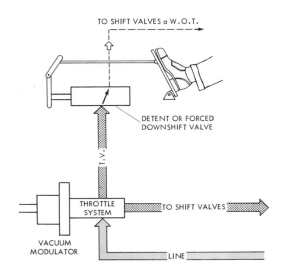

Fig. 7-67.

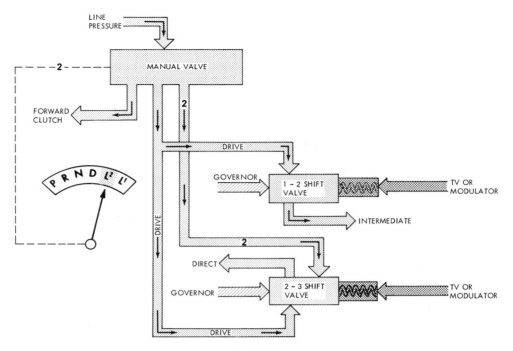

Fig. 7-69.

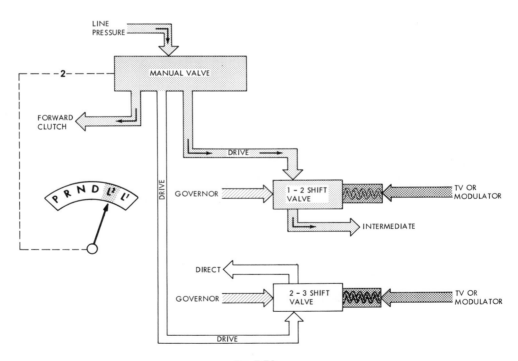

Fig. 7-70.

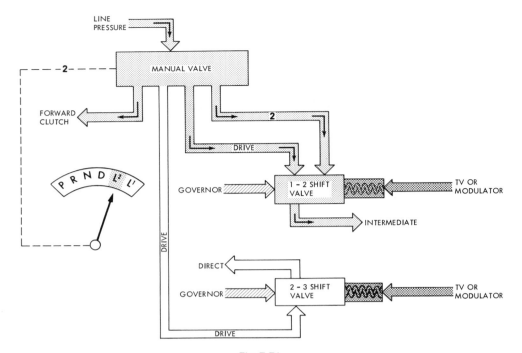

Fig. 7-71.

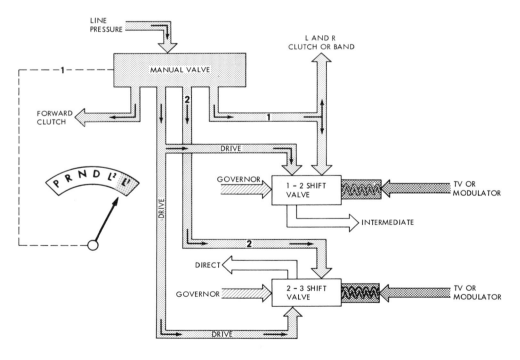

Fig. 7-72.

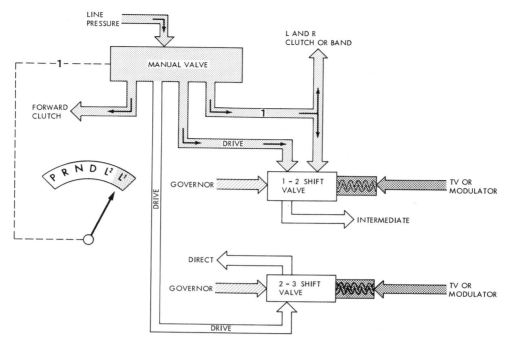

Fig. 7-73.

The manual low system in Fig. 7-72 has the 2 and 1 circuit lines charged with line pressure and leading to the 1–2 and 2–3 shift valve trains. With the TV line at the shift valves also carrying line pressure, both shift valves are hydraulically locked closed and upshifts cannot occur. Should the vehicle speed be too high when manual low is engaged, the 1 circuit in the shift valve train is ineffective until a safe vehicle speed is reached. Once first gear is locked-in, the transmission cannot upshift unless it is part of a "hot dog" package. Under these circumstances, some systems will allow a 1–2 shift between 60–90 mph (96–145 km/h). The above system can be modified to produce the same results and is illustrated in Fig. 7-73. The TV pressure in this setup remains effective at the shift valves. The 1–2 shift valve is hydraulically locked closed by the combination of line pressure and throttle pressure. The 2–3 shift valve is permitted to open, however, the manual valve has eliminated the line pressure feed to the direct clutch circuit.

Although not illustrated in the diagrams, some intermediate and manual low systems send a line pressure boost to the pressure regulator valve. During coast conditions, TV pressure is at 0 psi and very little line pressure would be available to hold the friction elements against coast torque.

Reverse Range

A simplified illustration (Fig. 7-74) shows a typical reverse circuit. When the manual valve is moved into (R) position, the reverse and direct clutch circuits are charged with line pressure and the clutches are applied. Note that a line boost is routed to the pressure regulator valve to double the regulated line pressure. Reverse boost pressures can run as high as 250–300 psi (1,725-2070 kPa). The extra pressure is required to prevent slipping of the reverse clutch or band. In reverse, the torque reaction on the planet carrier exceeds 3.0 times the engine torque. Although first gear has the largest gear ratio, the torque reaction on the very same planet carrier is much less. Forward gear reductions produce much less torque reaction and, therefore, the stress on a band or clutch to hold is considerably lower than for reverse.

Semi-Automatic Shifting

This term simply means that the transmission has been stripped of its automatic shift controls and the manual valve is used for individual gear selection. A clutch pedal is not needed because the torque converter is still part of the power flow. Essentially, the transmission operation remains the same with the driver in full control. Changing gears is a matter of moving the selector lever to the desired position.

For example, a limited amount of early production Ford C-4 transmissions in the 1960s were converted for semi-automatic operation and used in the small-size cars. General Motors did the same with the two-speed Powerglide in the early 1970s. These semi-automatics were respectively referred to as the Ford C-4 Semi-Automatic (P—R—N—H_i—2—1) and the Chevrolet Torque Drive (P—R—N—H_i—L).

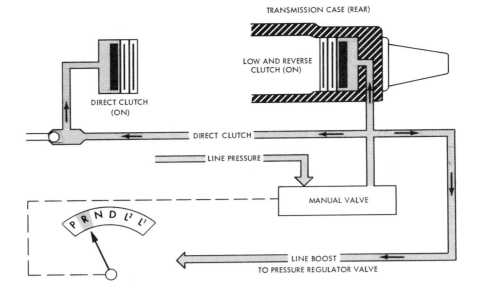

Fig. 7-74.

Electronic Shift Control

Electronic shift control is now in an advanced phase of development and should make its grand entry in production transmissions for the 1980s. It replaces the hydraulic-mechanical control components now employed for programmed shift scheduling. The use of a valve body is entirely eliminated by an electronic control unit mounted above the throttle pedal.

In operation, it still must measure engine torque and vehicle speed. This input data is electronically analyzed and a shift command is delivered to trigger the shift. The shift valves are solenoid-operated.

A proposed system configuration is illustrated in simple diagram form (Fig. 7-75). The system is easy to understand when the function of the individual components is defined.

Fig. 7-75.   (S.A.E.)

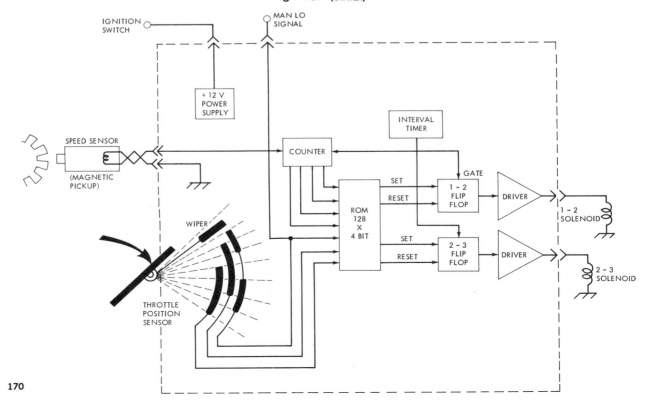

Counter: Determines where we are in terms of vehicle speed and sends the appropriate signals to the ROM.

ECU: Electronic Control Unit. It is the microprocessor.

Flip flop: A device that stores a continuous updated command from ROM. Through power drivers, the flip flops in Fig. 7-75 control the 1–2 and 2–3 shift solenoids in the transmissions.

Interval timer: Dictates to the flip flop the necessary amount of shift time to conclude a shift. When the shift time is up, the interval timer resets the flip flop and counter. This is the same as clearing the machine.

The interval timer is selfgenerating and sends out built-in time pulses at an engineered specified time interval. It gives the ECU sufficient time to execute the shift command before accepting new inputs.

Microprocessor: Micro means superminiaturized. A microprocessor is an Electronic Control Unit (ECU) that has the ability to make decisions based on input data. It evaluates the input data and generates the required command or output signal that causes the function to happen.

In an electronic shift schedule the function is to shift the valves.

Read only memory (ROM): It is the heart of the microprocessor which may already be on board the vehicle for the control of other electronic systems. The ROM compares the vehicle speed and throttle signals and dictates appropriate command signals to the flip flops. The ROM output signals tell the flip flops what to do. The ROM signals only one flip flop at a time.

Solenoids: An electro-mechanical device that causes shift valve movement from a flip-flop signal.

Solenoid power driver: It is a transistor that amplifies the low power flip-flop outputs to satisfy the solenoid load requirements.

Speed sensor: Uses a magnetic pick-up located by the transmission park gear. Low voltage impulses are transmitted to a *counter* indicating vehicle speed.

Throttle position sensor: A three-contact wiper switch mounted just above the throttle pedal. It provides eight throttle position signals to the ROM. It tells the ROM where the driver wants to be.

REVIEW QUESTIONS

**CHAPTER 7
THE HYDRAULIC CONTROL SYSTEM—
FUNDAMENTALS OF OPERATION**

I. COMPLETION: The Pressure Supply System

1. List five functions of the pressure supply system.

   a. _____

   _____

   _____

   b. _____

   _____

   _____

   c. _____

   _____

   _____

   d. _____

   _____

   _____

   _____

   e. _____

   _____

   _____

2. Provides the main oil supply to satisfy all the operating needs of the transmission. _____

3. The mainline operating pressure is controlled by the _____ valve.

4. The regulator valve works on the _____ valve principle. The regulated pressure is determined by a fixed _____ force and hydraulic auxiliary boost forces from the _____ and _____ pressures.

5. When the regulating valve "bleeds off" excess fluid to control line pressure, the fluid is dumped back into the

_____ line of the pump circuit.

6. The regulator valve controls the fluid feed that charges the _____ circuit. When the fluid cycles out of the converter it enters the _____ circuit and is relayed back to the transmission for _____.

II. COMPLETION: Throttle and Modulator Systems

1. The two terms *throttle* and *modulator* have the _____ meaning and the systems perform the _____ job functions.

2. The throttle system produces a regulated hydraulic pressure that reflects engine _____. The throttle valve in the system re-regulates the transmission line pressure feed according to a variable _____ force that is controlled by an engine torque signal transmitted externally by either; (1) mechanical linkage, (2) _____ or (3) _____.

3. In every automatic transmission, throttle pressure is distributed to the shift valves to _____ the shifts and to the pressure regulator valve train to provide an engine torque sensitive _____ pressure. Therefore, any change in throttle pressure will effect a change in the regulated _____ pressure.

4. In a vacuum operated throttle system, the engine manifold vacuum is opposed by _____ pressure at the modulator diaphragm to control the _____ force on the throttle valve. A high vacuum signal results in a *(low) (high)* throttle pressure.

5. In mechanical linkage or cable controlled throttle systems, wide throttle openings result in (low) (high) throttle pressures.

6. With closed throttle or high manifold vacuum conditions, throttle pressure output is _____ psi.

7. At wide open throttle or extreme low vacuum conditions, throttle pressure is usually the same as _____ pressure.

8. As altitude increases, atmosphere pressure *(increases) (decreases)* with a resulting *(increase) (decrease)* in manifold vacuum.

9. Higher altitudes cause the throttle output to be *(higher) (lower)* than normal resulting in delayed and harsh shifts.

10. In an altitude compensated vacuum modulator the vacuum sealed spring bellows *(expands) (contracts)* with increased altitude. The bellows action works with the atmospheric force on the modulator diaphragm and *(increases) (decreases)* the spring force on the throttle valve, thus, producing *(higher) (lower)* level throttle pressures and an *(earlier) (later)* shift schedule as the altitude gets higher.

11. In a General Motors vacuum modulator system, _____ pressure assists the modulator valve to balance out against the spring force. This results in an *(increase) (cutback)* of modulator output relative to car speed.

III. COMPLETION: Governor System

1. The governor system produces a regulated hydraulic pressure that is proportional to _____ speed. The governor valve in the system re-regulates the transmission line pressure feed according to the _____ force acting on the governor weights.

2. In every automatic transmission, governor pressure is distributed to the shift valves where its function is to oppose throttle pressure and *(open) (close)* the shift valves.

3. The governor valve is another example of a regulating valve that works on the _____ valve principle.

4. Regulated governor pressure has a variable output range from _____ psi to full _____ pressure.

5. A governor usually has two sets of weights. The heavy weights are called the _____ weights and the light weights are called the _____ weights.

6. The weights work together and make it possible to generate an adequate governor output at low speeds up to approximately 20 mph. At this point the

force against the governor valve is through the

_____ weights.

7. Governor units that are gear driven off the output shaft are referred to as _____ mounted governors.

8. When the governor unit turns with the output shaft it is referred to as an _____ mounted governor.

IV. COMPLETION: Servo and Clutch Assemblies

1. The purpose of a servo unit is to change a hydraulic force into a _____ force. It functions to apply a _____ around a drum to rigidly hold a planetary gear member stationary for a forward or reverse reduction.

2. The servo piston apply force can act directly on the band or through a _____ arrangement that provides a multiplying force.

3. When a band is applied, it is designed to wrap around the drum in the *(same) (opposite)* direction as drum rotation. This produces a _____ effect that assists the servo piston force in holding the band.

4. Band designs are classified as single-wrap or _____-wrap. The _____-wrap provides the greater holding force.

5. The material composition of the band friction lining is either organic or _____. The _____ material is used where high drum speeds are encountered prior to band application.

6. A planetary gear member can be locked to the transmission case by either a band, _____, or _____.

7. Multiple-disc clutches are used for two functions in controlling the planetary gear train.

   a. _____

   _____

   b. _____

   _____

8. The clutch is hydraulically applied and released by _____ force.

9. The thick reaction plate that absorbs the end force of the apply piston is usually referred to as the _____ plate.

10. In a rotating clutch drum assembly, the friction plates have _____ splines that fit on a torque transmitting hub. The steel plates have _____ drive lugs that fit into the torque transmitting drum or cylinder.

11. Name three spring designs that are used to release the clutch piston.

   a. _____

   b. _____

   c. _____

12. When a disc type spring arrangement is used in a clutch unit, it flexes on a pivot ring and acts as a mechanical _____ that adds to the hydraulic force on the piston.

13. (CLUTCH OFF) To prevent partial engagement of a rotating clutch unit by the centrifugal force effect on the residual oil, a steel check ball is placed in either the clutch _____ or clutch _____.

14. To assist in cushioning the clutch apply, clutch units sometimes use a _____ steel plate as part of the clutch disc pack.

V. COMPLETION: Accumulator

1. The purpose of an accumulator is to control the shift feel by controlling the rate of pressure build-up in the circuit during a _____ or _____ application. The pressure build-up rate is keyed to engine _____ output.

2. An accumulator essentially is made-up of a piston and cylinder bore, plus a piston _____.

3. When the accumulator piston strokes it _____ _____ fluid from the clutch or band circuit and delays the final pressure build-up in the circuit.

4. To vary the firmness of the clutch or band engagement the clutch/band apply oil must work the accumulator against a torque sensing oil. Depending on circuit design the torque sensing oil could be (1) _____ (2) _____ or (3) _____.

5. A clutch piston will stroke and take-up the slack between the discs when the circuit pressure build-up overcomes the force of the _____ return springs.

6. The accumulator piston starts to stroke *(before) (after)* the clutch piston is applied.

7. When the intermediate band is released during a 2-3 shift, it is common practice to use the intermediate servo piston assembly as a direct clutch _____

_____ .

8. When the accumulator piston completes its stroke, then the clutch/band apply pressure equals _____ pressure.

VI. COMPLETION: Shift System

Use the following three choices and indicate the letter code (A), (B), or (C) as it applies to the question.

A. Governor   C. Spring
B. Modulator/Throttle   D. Manual

_____ The control system that enables the driver to program the transmission operating range.
_____ The control system that senses vehicle speed.
_____ The control system that senses engine torque.
_____ The force that works to open the shift valve.
_____ The force that works to delay the upshifts.

_____ The force that closes the shift valve on closed throttle downshifts.

1. A shift valve is classified as a *(regulating) (relay)* valve.

2. On typical V-8 engine applications the minimum to full throttle shift spread is approximately _____ to _____ mph for the (1-2) shift and _____ to _____ mph for the (2-3) shift.

3. To eliminate any hunting or indecision of the shift valve to stay shifted, _____ pressure is usually cut off from the end of the shift valve.

4. The shift valve spring is located on the _____ pressure side of the shift valve. Its main function is to _____ the shift valve on closed throttle downshifts.

5. On very light throttle upshifts, throttle pressure is usually at _____ psi, therefore, the minimum shift points are determined by the resistance of the shift valve _____ to the governor oil.

6. In a 3-speed system, the forward clutch circuit is controlled by the _____ valve, the intermediate circuit by the _____ valve, and the direct circuit by the _____ valve.

7. In (N) and (P) the _____ valve blocks the regulated line pressure feed to the clutch and band apply circuits.

8. In a 3-speed system the manual valve typically has _____ selector positions.

9. Depending on the transmission "make", the closed throttle downshift sequence can be (3-2 and 2-1) or _____ .

10. To provide for extra performance during moderate low speed acceleration most shift systems feature a part throttle _____ downshift. This is usually achieved by providing a by-pass circuit that routes _____ pressure oil to the _____ shift valve to overrule the _____ pressure oil at the shift valve.

11. Full throttle forced downshifts are also referred to as _____ or _____ shifts.

12. Depending on the vehicle speed range, full throttle forced downshifts 3-2, _____, and _____ are available in the typical 3-speed shift system.

13. At full throttle the downshift system provides a by-pass circuit to the shift valves loaded with either _____ or _____ pressure to overrule the _____ pressure at the shift valves.

14. If the transmission has a vacuum controlled modulator/throttle system then an independent external control to the transmission is needed to trigger the downshift valve with full throttle opening. This external control can be mechanical or _____ .

Mechanical systems use either _____ or _____ control. The downshift valve works (in a different valve bore) (the same valve bore) as the modulator/throttle valve.

15. If the transmission has a linkage or cable controlled throttle system, the downshift valve or plunger works (in a different valve bore) (in the same valve bore) as the throttle valve.

VII. COMPLETION: Intermediate, Manual Low, and Reverse Ranges

1. The intermediate and manual low operating ranges

   are established by the _____ valve.

2. To inhibit the 2-3 shift valve in intermediate range, line pressure from the manual valve is introduced into the 2-

   3 shift valve train and _____ locks the 2-3 valve against governor pressure. In another type circuit the 2-3 shift valve is permitted to open with the manual valve arranged to "cut-off" the

   _____ pressure feed to the shift valve and direct clutch circuit.

3. Some intermediate ranges provide a second gear start. Line pressure from the manual valve is introduced into

the 1-2 shift valve train and _____

locks the 1-2 valve in the _____ position.

4. To inhibit the 1-2 shift valve in manual low range, line pressure from the manual valve is introduced into the 1-

   2 shift valve train and _____ locks the 1-2 shift valve against governor pressure.

5. Should the vehicle speed be too high when moving the selector from (D) to (1) the transmission will function in

   _____ gear until a safe vehicle speed is reached for manual low engagement. Once the transmission is locked into manual low it cannot

   _____.

6. In reverse, the torque reaction on the stationary reac-

   tion carrier exceeds _____ times the engine torque. For extra clutch/band holding power, maximum reverse boost pressures can run the mainline pressure as

   high as _____ psi.

8

AUTOMATIC TRANSMISSION FLUIDS AND SEALS

THE FLUID

The hydraulic fluid used in automatic transmissions is a special fluid because it is required to do more things than ordinary lubricating oils.

The term *fluid* is applied to the liquids used in hydraulics to avoid confusion with ordinary engine and lubricating oils. The most important job of any hydraulic fluid is to transmit force and do it immediately. Therefore, a liquid is used because it is noncompressible.

The automatic transmission fluid mixture performs four main functions:

1. It transfers power from the engine to the drive line via the torque converter.

2. It absorbs and transmits heat from the torque converter to the cooler. Even in air-cooled automatic transmissions, the fluid acts as a heat-transmitting medium; fluid to air.

Within the transmission, the fluid must act as the friction element coolant. It absorbs and dissipates the heat energy generated by a clutch or band engagement.

3. It transmits hydraulic pressure through a hydraulic control system, which utilizes the fluid in the complex array of pumps, valves, lines, servos, and clutch cylinders.

4. It is a multipurpose lubricant for the gears, thrust bearings, bushing supports, clutches, bands, and so on. Like an engine oil, it must lubricate, cool, seal, and clean; however, it is subject to more severe service.

To meet the above requirements, automatic transmission fluids (ATF) use a selected mineral oil fortified with a precise blend of additives. These additives, as many as ten different types and comprising approximately 10% of the volume of the ATF, give necessary additional properties needed for transmission operation, such as:

OXIDATION STABILITY. ATF has high resistance to varnish and sludge build-up that occurs from excessive heat that is primarily generated in the torque converter. Local temperatures as high as 600°F (315°C) can occur at the clutch plates during engagement and this must be absorbed and dissipated. If the fluid cannot withstand the heat, it burns or oxidizes, resulting in an almost immediate destruction of friction materials, clogged filter screen and hydraulic passages, and sticky valves in the transmission.

VISCOSITY INDEX IMPROVERS. Using viscosity index improvers keeps the viscosity more nearly constant with changes in temperature. This is especially important at low temperatures, when the oil needs to be thin to aid in shifting and for cold weather starting. Yet it must not be so thin that at high temperatures it will cause excessive hydraulic leakage so that pumps are unable to maintain the proper pressures.

COMPATIBILITY. It must be compatible with the materials used in the transmission. It cannot react chemically with the metals, seal materials, or friction materials.

OTHER PROPERTIES. Other chemical properties reduce wear and corrosion, prevent foaming, and act to slightly swell the seals and keep them from leaking. Friction modifiers are also added to help control the quality of clutch/band engagement.

DEVELOPMENT OF TRANSMISSION FLUIDS

A great quantity of fluids of various kinds has been poured into automatic transmissions since they were introduced to American passenger cars in 1939. Over the years, much research has gone into the development and improvement of these hydraulic fluids to meet the changing requirements of the various transmission designs and the types of operational service encountered.

For example, a typical model car in 1946 with a 150-hp engine was coupled with an automatic transmission that had a fluid capacity of 13.5 qts. This meant that each quart of fluid had to handle 11 hp. In later years, on the very same model car, horsepower had been upped to 375 hp and the transmission fluid capacity cut to 10.5 qts. Each quart of fluid must now handle 36 hp or carry three times the load it did over 30 years ago. It is obvious that the transmission fluid had to continuously change character, especially in oxidation inhibitors, to keep from breaking down and also to accommodate transmission design changes.

Even with the current downsizing of vehicles and their smaller power plant/transmission combinations, the fluid volume is still proportionately taxed with handling heat.

In the beginning, automatic transmissions were generally fed straight mineral oil, exactly the same type used in the engines. In some cases, an oxidation inhibitor was added to the motor oils. As automatics took hold with the motoring public, service experience soon indicated that these oils had definite shortcomings. It became necessary to develop an oil with properties more compatible with actual automatic transmission needs.

An automatic transmission fluid specification was first developed by General Motors in 1949 and labeled Type A Specification, for automatic transmission fluid (ATF). This fluid was adopted industry-wide for automatic transmissions with policing of the specification assigned to the Armour Research Foundation, Illinois Institute of Technology (now I.I.T. Research Institute). If the individual petroleum suppliers met the Type A Specification, they were approved and given an AQ (Armour Qualification) number.

The approved suppliers were licensed to carry the AQ-ATF General Motors trademark. These letters, along with the suppliers' numbers and brand names, appeared on the containers they sold on the market.

Since the original 1949 formula, the fluid specifications have been revised several times to accommodate changes in transmission design and the increased size of engines and cars. The use of options such as air conditioning, the rise in the number of recreational trailers, and the increase in city traffic have imposed additional thermal loads on automatic transmission fluids.

In 1957, field reports, especially with respect to varnish build-up, dictated the first modification of Type A fluid. The new specification was simply retabbed Type A Suffix A and replaced the original Type A. It was adopted for use by all the major car manufacturers in their automatic transmissions.

Ford Motor Company, however, developed its own Type F fluid under Ford Specification (M-2C33-D) in 1961 for the initial factory fill. In 1964, Ford specified that Type F must also be used for all refills in their automatics. Other car manufacturers continued to use Type A Suffix A fluid.

1968 brought about some major changes as new, long-life transmission fluids were introduced, and it is the newer fluids that are of main concern. Ford Motor Company developed an improved Type F fluid (M-2C33-F) for all its transmissions and General Motors introduced a new formula, Dexron (Fig. 8-1). Both fluids were upgraded in their capacity to resist oxidation. The Dexron formula was also adopted by Chrysler and American Motors. Chart 8-1 summarizes

Fig. 8-1.

In model year 1977, Ford introduced a new CJ fluid (M-2C138CJ) for use in various production transmissions, (Fig. 8-2) with Type F fluid still required for some transmissions. The new CJ fluid is red with an orange tint compared to the dark red of Type F. The CJ fluid is available only through Ford dealers. While CJ fluid is tailored for Ford, it has a close frictional characteristic to Dexron and, therefore, Dexron may be used in place of CJ. All 1976 and prior Ford transmissions still require Type F fluids; consult Chart 8-1 for Ford fluid recommendations after 1976.

Fig. 8-2.

the latest factory service recommendations regarding the use of ATF. (I.I.T. Research Foundation no longer certifies automatic transmission fluids marketed by major oil companies. Ford Motor Company and General Motors Corporation are their own authorizing agents for Type F and Dexron.) The main difference between these fluids is in the friction characteristics. Dexron fluids use a friction modifier while Type F fluids do not.

Dexron had to undergo a change because of the United States ban on killing whales in December, 1971. The sperm whale supplied the oil additive used as the friction modifier in Dexron fluids. The whale oil was substituted with a chemical and Dexron II was developed as the new long-life fluid. The change in the formula resulted in a corrosive action between the solder used by General Motors in their tubular type transmission coolers and the new additives used in Dexron II. Available now is a new Dexron II "D" and it is required on all GM vehicles from 1969 on. It may be used in all GM transmissions before and after 1969 or anywhere that Dexron is called for. This would include American Motors, Chrysler, and Ford special applications.

Although Dexron is packaged with a distinctive red dye, some original factory fills may not contain red dye. It has a clear brown like varnish appearance and smells like burnt fluid. All current Dexron fluid has a

CHART 8-1
Passenger Car ATF Recommendations

Dexron II, Series D	
All American Motors Models	Mercedes Benz—All Models
All General Motors Models	Opel—All Models
All Chrysler Corporation Models	Peugeot—All Models-
Audi—All Models	Porsche—All Models
BMW—All Models	Subaru—All Models
Datsun—1972 and Later	Triumph—All Models
Fiat—All Models	Volkswagon—All Models
Honda—All Models	

Ford Motor Company	
AOT—CJ or Dexron II-D	JATCO—CJ or Dexron II-D
*ATX—CJ or Dexron II-D	FMX—Type F
C3—CJ or Dexron II-D	
C4—March 8, 1979 and prior models; Type F	
After March 8, 1979; CJ or Dexron II-D	
C6—1976 and prior models; Type F	
1977 and later; CJ or Dexron II-D	

*A new fluid to be released by Ford will replace the CJ/Dexron II-D requirement. It is a multi-viscosity fluid development.

Type F	
Datsun—1971 and Prior Models	Toyota—All Models
Mazda—All Models	Volvo—All Models
Saab—All Models	

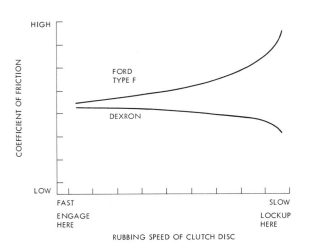

Fig. 8-3. Dexron and Type F friction curves. Type F produces a higher friction rise especially during final lockup.

slight burnt odor characteristic. Dexron is used where the friction material formulation requires the fluid to be insensitive to the slip speed between the clutch discs until the clutch nears complete lock-up. To prevent a grabbing action during the final lockup stage, Dexron fluid reacts to the apply pressure and lowers the coefficient of friction. Type F fluid is used with friction material compounding requiring a continuous coefficient of friction rise from initial clutch engagement, where slip speed is the highest until final lock-up occurs. Typical Dexron and Type F fluid curves are compared in Fig. 8-3.

Transmission fluid has a definite influence in producing desirable shift feel and durability. Transmis-

sion manufacturers, therefore, recommend using only the fluid type compatible with the friction materials in their transmission design. Type F, CJ,, and Dexron fluids should be used in the transmissions for which they are intended. For the future, it can be expected that one transmission fluid will be developed to meet all specifications. The current trend is to favor Dexron.

Transmission Additives

The use of transmission additives or conditioners in the fluid must be done on a selective basis. A good quality conditioner has no harmful or destroying effect. It revitalizes the friction and seal materials and can give the transmission new life. It cannot, however, compensate for burned friction plates or seals that have become worn or brittle. A conditioner works well with a fluid change to cure a varnish condition which has caused slipping or drawn out shifts.

SEALING THE FLUID

The job of the transmission seals is to control the external and internal bleeding of the fluid. The many uses of the fluid and the number of places to which it must travel make for an enormous sealing task—especially when external bleeding is obvious and annoying to the car owner. Any fluid spill on the garage floor or driveway is classified as a transmission failure. Internal leakage is less obvious and is usually tolerated by the owner as long as the vehicle moves forward and provides reverse.

Fig. 8-4.

The number of seals used in today's automatic transmission averages more than 25 per transmission (Fig. 8-4). Although seals were once classified as the weak links in the transmission, their durability is no longer a serious problem. Improved sealing material and fluid compounding have made this possible. Cleanliness of the fluid is another factor affecting seal life. The fluid must be free of dirt, water, and other foreign material. Otherwise, undesirable chemical processes like rust, corrosion, and fluid oxidation attack the seals.

Sealing applications are classified as static or dynamic. In a static application, the parts being sealed do not move in relation to each other. In dynamic applications, there is rotating or reciprocating motion between the parts. Static and dynamic conditions are illustrated in Figs. 8-5, 8-6, 8-7, and 8-8.

Seals provide *positive* or *nonpositive* sealing. In *positive* sealing, the sealing method completely prevents leakage. *Nonpositive* sealing allows some minor leakage for lubrication.

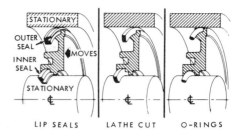

Fig. 8-8. Dynamic seal application to pistons. (SAE)

Synthetic Rubber Seals

Today, all modern automatic transmissions use synthetic rubber seals, especially where positive sealing is required. Synthetic rubber seals are used for either static or dynamic applications involving both recipro-

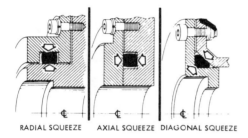

Fig. 8-5. Static seal application for sealing case to cover. (SAE)

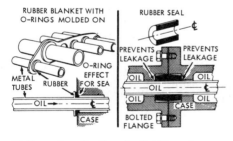

Fig. 8-6. Static seal applications for fluid transfer passages. (SAE)

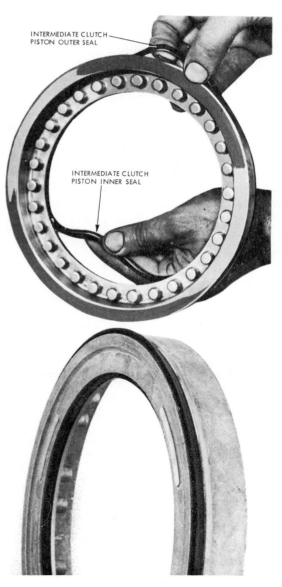

Fig. 8-9. Clutch piston lip seals, Turbo Hydra-Matic 350. (Oldsmobile Division, General Motors Corp.)

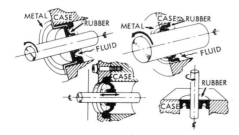

Fig. 8-7. Dynamic seal application to rods. (SAE)

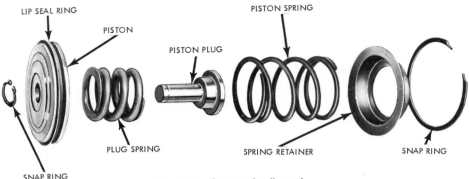

Fig. 8-10. Servo using lip seal.

cating and rotary motion. There are three basic types of synthetic rubber seals used in the automatic transmission: (1) lip, (2) lathe or square-cut O-ring, (3) round O-ring (Fig. 8-8).

LIP SEAL. The lip seal is a molded seal and can seal against high pressure, but in one direction only. It is primarily used on piston applications in the clutch and servo units (Figs. 8-9 and 8-10).

The lip seal works on the deflection principle (Fig. 8-11). The installed lip tip diameter, which is larger than the cylinder bore, is deflected during installation into the cylinder, resulting in lip tension against the cylinder wall. The compressing of the free lip position (maximum diameter) thus gives an oil-tight seal. Furthermore, in piston applications, the seal lip is installed toward the pressure source and the piston apply-fluid exerts a pressure against the lip. This flares the lip out and aids sealing.

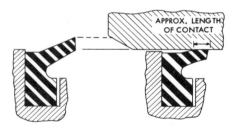

Fig. 8-11. Lip seal. (SAE)

In Fig. 8-12, it is interesting to note the flexibility of the lip seal in adapting itself to changes in bore and piston clearances.

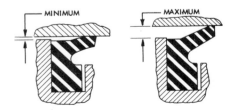

Fig. 8-12. Lip seal provides flexibility. (SAE)

Lip seals are also used as rotating shaft seals (Fig. 8-13). There are only two main rotating shaft seals required for the automatic transmission: the front pump seal and extension housing seal (Figs. 8-19 and 8-20). Sealing is accomplished by the spring-loaded flex section maintaining a lip contact pressure on the rotating hub or shaft.

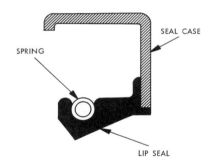

Fig. 8-13.

Rotating shaft lip seals are not designed to seal against high pressure. They function to retain the fluid as it escapes past the pump and extension housing bushings and to keep external contaminants from entering the transmission.

LATHE CUT O-RING SEAL. The lathe cut O-ring seal is square in cross section and used for both dynamic and static applications. It is often referred to in the trade as a square-cut O-ring seal. The seal is generally extruded or molded in a tube shape, but it is always cut into individual rings on a lathe.

In dynamic applications, the lathe cut seal is used on servo, accumulator, and clutch pistons (Figs. 8-14 and 8-15). In order to seal, the lathe cut seal requires a squeeze when installed in its cylinder bore. Note in Fig. 8-16 how the lathe cut seal is squeezed into the piston groove because its outside diameter is larger than the cylinder bore into which it is installed. Complete installation in the cylinder bore shows that the seal is squeezed and under compression. The reaction force

Fig. 8-14. Servo piston with lathe cut (square) O-ring seal.

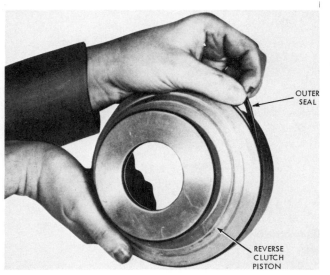

OUTER SEAL

REVERSE CLUTCH PISTON

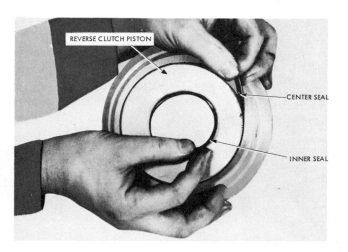

REVERSE CLUTCH PISTON

CENTER SEAL

INNER SEAL

Fig. 8-15. Clutch piston using lathe cut (square) O-ring seal. (Oldsmobile Division, General Motors Corp.)

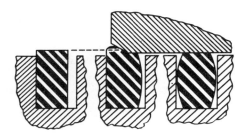

Fig. 8-16. (SAE)

created by the compression tries to return the seal section to its original size and shape, thereby creating a sealing effect on the contact area of the cylinder bore and bottom of the piston groove.

Figure 8-17 illustrates how a typical O-ring seal behaves in a cylinder bore. Note that the seal is compressed forming a seal against the contacting surface of the bore and bottom of the piston groove. When pressure is applied, it forces the seal against the side of its groove and, in effect, packs it into a corner. The end result is a positive seal on three sides capable of withstanding very high pressure. The O-ring also has the ability to seal effectively from both directions (Fig. 8-18).

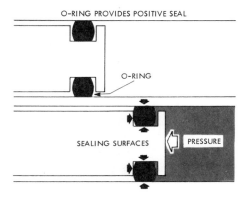

O-RING PROVIDES POSITIVE SEAL

O-RING

SEALING SURFACES

PRESSURE

Fig. 8-17. O-ring is compressed on three sides.

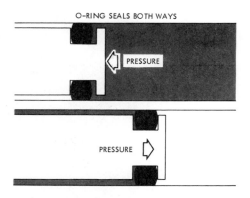

O-RING SEALS BOTH WAYS

PRESSURE

PRESSURE

Fig. 8-18. O-ring is forced against walls and seals from either direction.

EXTENSION HOUSING TO CASE OIL SEAL

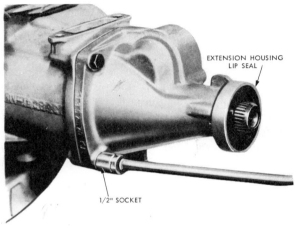

EXTENSION HOUSING LIP SEAL

1/2" SOCKET

Fig. 8-19. Lathe cut seal used on extension housing. (Oldsmobile Division, General Motors Corp.)

PUMP O.D. TO CASE (SQUARE CUT) O-RING

PUMP LIP SEAL

Fig. 8-20. Lathe cut seal used on front pump housing to case. (Oldsmobile Division, General Motors Corp.)

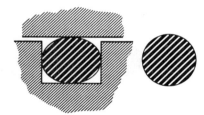

Fig. 8-21.

Fig. 8-22. Strainer pipe to case O-ring seal. (Oldsmobile Divisions, General Motors Corp.)

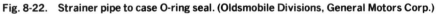

STRAINER ASSEMBLY

O-RING SEAL

VACUUM MODULATOR
TO CASE SEAL

**Fig. 8-23. Modulator tube to case O-ring seal.
(Oldsmobile Division, General Motors Corp.)**

Static applications of lathe cut seals on an extension housing and a front pump housing assembly are shown in Figs. 8-19 and 8-20.

ROUND O-RING SEAL. The round O-ring seal is a molded seal and has a round circle for a cross-sectional area. Like a lathe cut seal, it is squeezed during installation, forming a seal against the contacting surface (Fig. 8-21).

This type of seal is primarily used as a static seal for tubes, pipes, or shafts (Figs. 8-22 and 8-23). In dy-namic applications, its use is limited to piston action requiring short and slow strokes (Fig. 8-24). The reason is that the round O-ring has a tendency to roll or twist in its groove, either on installation or while stroking.

Metal Seal Rings

Metal seal rings do not give positive sealing. They are used for sealing rotating shafts or clutch drums that carry fluid under pressure and where some fluid leakage is needed to lubricate the shaft journals and

Fig. 8-24. Servo piston using round O-ring seals.

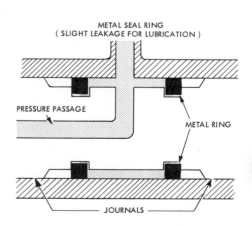

METAL SEAL RING
(SLIGHT LEAKAGE FOR LUBRICATION)

PRESSURE PASSAGE

METAL RING

JOURNALS

Fig. 8-25. Metal seals allow some leakage for lubrication.

Fig. 8-26. Butt type metal seal rings used on servo and accumulator pistons, Chrysler TorqueFlite. (Chrysler Co.)

The sealing effect of the metallic ring is accomplished by the fluid pressure head working the ring against the side of the groove and bore wall (Fig. 8-28).

Transmission oil rings use two types of joint ends. They are (1) butt joint and (2) hook lock joint (Figs. 8-26 and 8-27). The butt joint is used where small leakage past the joint is not important or where the leakage is utilized for lubrication. A lock joint is used where improved control of fluid leakage is required and when compression is needed initially to fit the ring to its bore during installation. The lock joint is designed with small tangs that hold the ring in compression.

bushings (Fig. 8-25). Although the largest usage is found in rotary applications, metallic seals are frequently used in reciprocating applications on accumulator pistons and servo pistons (Figs. 8-26 and 8-27). The metal ring may also be used as a static seal; however, these applications are very limited. The basic metallic ring used in automatic transmissions is designed or shaped like the common piston ring. Depending on the application, these piston-type rings are made from cast iron or aluminum. Cast iron rings are made from the same kind of piston ring iron used for automotive piston rings or small castings and, where required, are coated with nickel, chrome, or tin.

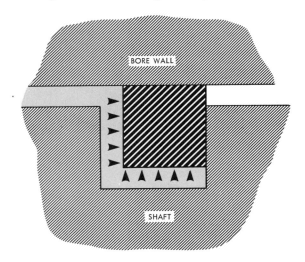

Fig. 8-28

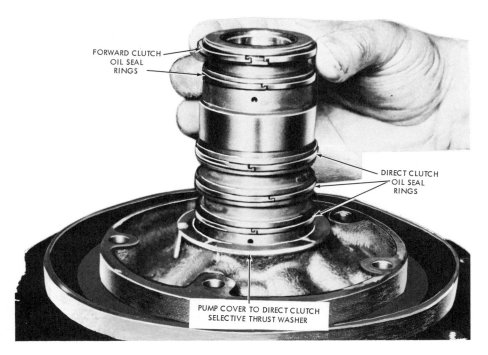

Fig. 8-27. Metal hook type oil rings used on THM-350. (Oldsmobile Division, General Motors Corp.)

Fig. 8-29. Teflon seal rings with angle seal joints used for the direct clutch and intermediate roller lubrication, Turbo HydraMatic 400.

Fig. 8-30. One piece teflon seals used in top grooves for forward clutch THM-350.

Teflon Seals

Teflon seals perform the same function as metal seals and are becoming more popular in automatic transmissions. It is not unusual to see teflon rings used in places on accumulator pistons and shafts (rotating and nonrotating) where metal rings were once used.

Teflon rings are highly heat resistant, offer a cost reduction over metal rings, and provide excellent sealing. The material is soft, however, and is very sensitive to scratching and penetration from the fine metallic particles.

Effective sealing is made possible by the use of an angle seal joint, which allows minimum leakage under fluid pressure (Fig. 8-29) and by the ability of the soft material to conform to cylinder bore irregularities. Where it is practical, the joint is eliminated and a one-piece teflon ring is stretched and placed into the groove (Fig. 8-30).

REVIEW QUESTIONS

CHAPTER 8
AUTOMATIC TRANSMISSION FLUIDS AND SEALS

I. COMPLETION: Fluids

1. What are the four main functions of automatic transmission fluid?

   a. _____

   _____

   _____

   b. _____

   _____

   _____

   c. _____

   _____

   _____

   _____

   d. _____

   _____

   _____

2. DEXRON formula fluids are a development of

   _____.

3. The most current DEXRON formula fluid is specified

   as DEXRON _____.

4. A qualified container of DEXRON fluid must be labeled _____.

5. DEXRON *(can) (cannot)* be used in older transmissions that required Type A, or Type A, Suffix A fluids.

6. Type F formula fluids are a development of _____.

7. The most current Type F formula fluid is identified under Ford specification _____.

8. Type CJ fluid is available only through _____ dealers.

9. Ford Motor Company permits _____ fluid to be used in place of Type CJ.

10. DEXRON and Type F fluids are usually colored with a _____ dye.

11. Type CJ fluid has a base color of _____ with an _____ tint when compared to DEXRON or Type F.

12. Type F and DEXRON fluids primarily differ in their frictional characteristics. During the final lock-up phase of a band or clutch apply, Type F *(lowers) (increases)* the coefficient of friction between the contacting surfaces while DEXRON produces the opposite effect.

13. The recommended fluid for all General Motors automatic transmissions through 1981 is _____ _____.

14. The recommended fluid for all American Motors and Chrysler automatic transmissions through 1981 is _____.

15. The recommended fluid for the following Ford automatic transmissions through 1981.

_____ FMX   _____ JATCO

_____ ATX

_____ C3   _____ AOT

_____ C4 Before March 8, 1979

_____ C4 Beginning with March 8, 1979

_____ C6 Before Production Year 1977

_____ C6 Beginning with Production Year 1977

II. COMPLETION: Seals

1. The lip type seal is a molded seal that provides *(positive) (non-positive)* sealing.

2. Lip type seals work very effectively on applications involving reciprocating and _____ motion.

3. There are two main rotating lip seal applications external to the transmission. They are the extension housing seal and _____ seal. The seal lip contact pressure on the hub or shaft is maintained by a _____ load on the flex section.

4. Rotating shaft lip seals external to the transmission must retain fluid, plus, keep external _____ from entering the transmission.

5. For high pressure applications, the lip seal is used on piston applications in _____ and servo units.

6. Lip seals are installed with the lip facing *(toward) (away)* from the pressure or fluid source.

7. A lathe cut O-ring seal is usually referred to in the trade as a _____ O-ring seal.

8. To seal effectively, both lathe cut and round O-ring seals depend on a proper _____ fit against the contacting surface.

9. The lathe cut and round O-ring seals provide *(positive) (non-positive)* sealing.

10. Metal sealing rings used in automatic transmissions are made from _____ or _____ metal.

11. Metal sealing rings are primarily used for *(rotary) (static)* applications where fluid pressure for example is transferred between a _____ and clutch drum.

12. Metal seal rings provide *(positive) (non-positive)* sealing.

13. Metal seal rings in automatic transmissions use two types of joint ends. They are the (1) _____ joint and (2) _____ joint.

14. Teflon seals are a relatively new development for automatic transmissions and are widely used in some current production units in place of _____ _____ seal rings.

9

PRINCIPLES OF DIAGNOSIS

Diagnosis involves a scientific or logical step-by-step plan, an orderly procedure that produces accurate information that the technician can use as clues to pinpoint the most probable cause of trouble. A diagnostic procedure follows a definite sequence of steps that accomplishes the most results with the least amount of unnecessary time and labor. From the technician's viewpoint, diagnosis cannot be a shotgun approach. The procedure must cover the likeliest causes of trouble first and eliminate every possibility that does not require opening the transmission before you start taking things apart.

Accurate diagnosis of transmission problems is not complicated. You must, however, have a reasonable understanding of the basic transmission mechanical and hydraulic functions and the relationship of engine performance to proper transmission operation. Diagnosis is simply a matter of tying together the basics you already know and applying them to a logical problem solution.

Although the transmission has an intricate maze of hydraulic circuits and clutch/band mechanical units, diagnosis can be simplified by (1) emphasizing what is *right* about the transmission before the usual approach of what is *wrong* and (2) confining or isolating your problem to the individual hydraulic or mechanical system with the fault. If the problem area is not isolated, then diagnosis becomes a hit and miss proposition, time consuming and frustrating. The problem may never get solved and then we hear the old familiar "I tried everything." If you tried everything, shouldn't the problem be fixed or is it a matter of record that you just couldn't out think a metal casting.

Diagnosis represents a key phase in the service cycle (Fig. 9-1). It not only isolates the problem but also serves as a basis for the type of service work to be performed. Most importantly, take note that the service performed must always be followed-up and tested to validate the correction of the problem. Did the diagnosis and service work do what it was supposed to do? If not, why not?

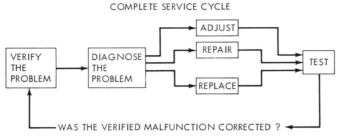

COMPLETE SERVICE CYCLE

Fig. 9-1.

In the final analysis, it is you who must make the decision as to what is the problem, what caused it, and what must be done to repair it. You will need to depend upon your own good built-in diagnosis tools that nature gave you—your eyes, your ears, your nose, and some common sense.

GENERAL DIAGNOSIS

Automatic transmission problems are usually caused by six basic conditions: mechanical malfunction, hydraulic malfunction, friction element failure, con-

verter failure, poor engine performance or improper engine signal to transmission, and improper adjustments. Diagnosis of these conditions and related problems follow an exact six step procedure that gives excellent results. The success of the procedure, however, depends on the accuracy of the data or information collected. Your task is to methodically and accurately stick with the procedure until enough information is gathered for a diagnosis decision.

Diagnosis Procedure

   I. Listen to customer and verify complaint
  II. Check fluid level and condition
 III. Quick check engine idle, vacuum lines, transmission and carburetor linkage
 IV. Stall test (optional)
  V. Road test
 VI. Pressure test

The above procedure is discussed in depth with practical applications made in isolating friction element failures and erratic shift problems.

STEP I: Listen to Customer and Verify Complaint

An often overlooked but important aspect of diagnosis is to find out the exact nature of the customer complaint. It is your job to kindly listen to the customer (Fig. 9-2). The customer may not always know what he is talking about with regard to what is really wrong; however, he can relate to you his impression of the transmission's performance.

Fig. 9-2. Listen to the customer for symptoms and clues to malfunctions.

If the customer's verbal description is doubtful and does not apparently identify the problem, then a road test is in order. Take the customer along to demonstrate the problem. Be sure to perform Steps II and III in the diagnosis procedure before road testing. The road test may simply prove the customer's misunderstanding of how the transmission should operate, and show that what he wants corrected is normal.

While your customer is still a captive audience, do some detective work. A trailer hitch can tip you off to the fact that the transmission has been under heavy-duty service. The same is obvious when odometer mileage is higher than average for the age of the car, or an inspection of the right rear or spare tire may tip the hot rodder.

Get the customer to talk about it. You may need to set up a transmission preventive maintenance program with the customer to fit the type of service his/her transmission encounters.

Some common sense driver education pertaining to transmission life may also be included. This not only adds up to trouble-free miles for the customer, but also protects the reliability of the repair, especially when band and clutch failures have occurred.

The objective of Step I is to avoid the same plight as the dentist who just pulled the wrong tooth.

STEP II: Check the Fluid Level and Fluid Condition

Fluid level and fluid condition are very basic to proper transmission operation. Checking the dipstick can give the technician some immediate and important clues to the general condition of the transmission. In many cases the diagnosis procedure stops here and a service recommendation is made to cure the problem. Improper fluid level alone can be responsible for over 20 malfunctions. You can expect the transmission to act up when only one pint low on fluid.

Fluid Level Check. The fluid level check is technically not a difficult task. Yet, a significant number of car owners and even technicians are not accurately following recommended factory fluid check procedure. This results in false dipstick readings and contributes to a misdiagnosis. Rule number one is never assume that someone else's fluid level check is right. Do it yourself and you will be surprised at some of the differences between what you are told and what you actually find.

Ideally, the fluid level should be checked with the transmission at normal operating temperature. Normal operating range is considered to be approximately 180°F (85°C). To reach this temperature range it takes at least 20 minutes of expressway driving or equivalent heavy city driving. Don't expect to reach operating temperature with the transmission in Neutral or Park

and engine set at a fast idle. The fluid is at operating temperature when the sample fluid on the dipstick is too hot for the fingers to handle.

Because it isn't always convenient to check the fluid at operating temperature, most dipsticks give a hot and cold measurement (Fig. 9-3). The fluid level can rise as much as one inch from cold or hot. When the fluid is overheated from severe service operation, expect a reading over the full mark.

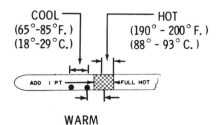

Fig. 9-3. (Oldsmobile Division, General Motors Corp.)

There is a variance in checking procedure between different transmissions. For accurate results, follow these guidelines. For safety measures, be sure to set the park brake.

Chrysler 727, 904, 998, and 999

- Engine at curb idle.
- Move the selector lever through all of the ranges to fill all clutch and servo cavities.
- Place the selector in Neutral only and check.

NOTE: The manual valve opens the pump circuit to exhaust in the Park position. This results in loading the pan area with extra fluid. If the correct level is based on using the Park position, then the transmission will be operating over one quart low on fluid.

Chrysler 404 FWD Transaxle

NOTE: Same procedure as other Chrysler automatic transmissions. Selector lever, however, can be positioned in Park or Neutral. Park is preferred for safety.

Ford family

- Engine at curb idle.
- Move the selector lever through all of the ranges to fill all clutch and servo cavities.
- Place the selector in Park and check.

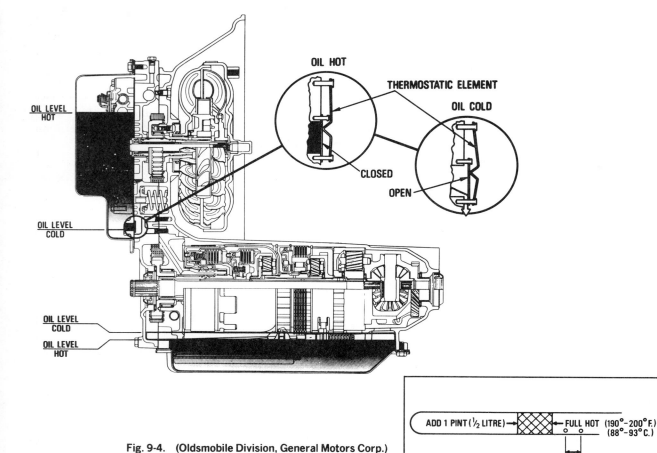

Fig. 9-4.   (Oldsmobile Division, General Motors Corp.)

ADD 1 PINT (½ LITRE) ➞ ◄— FULL HOT (190°-200°F.)
(88°-93°C.)

COLD (65°-85°F.)
(18°-29°C.)

NOTICE: 'Cold' reading is ABOVE 'Full' mark

OX7A264

General Motors 400, 350, 250, 200 and 180

- Engine at curb idle
- Move the selector lever through all of the ranges to fill all clutch and servo cavities.
- Place the selector in Park and check.

General Motors 125 FWD Transaxle

- Place selector in Park and leave in Park. Do not move selector through the ranges.
- Start engine and run at curb idle.
- Check fluid level.

NOTE: The THM 125 has a separate valve body reservoir in addition to the oil pan area. A thermostatic element controls the amount of fluid that is trapped in the valve body area depending on hot or cold operation. During hot operation fluid is drawn from the pan area and added to the valve body reservoir. A cold check of the fluid level will actually read above the full mark (Fig. 9-4).

Foreign cars

NOTE: Consult the manufacturer's service manual for procedure. Some checks will be made with the engine not running.

Some problems do arise in reading the fluid level. When the fluid is new and very clear it is sometimes difficult to read where it is on the dipstick. As a trick of the trade, rub down the end of the dipstick with typewriter carbon paper and you'll easily pick-up the level reading. The effect of the carbon treatment is illustrated in Fig. 9-5 using the dipstick on the same transmission fluid.

On occasion the wrong dipstick is used. You'll find this to occur in both new and used cars. A slip-up at the factory or on a replacement can play tricks on your diagnosis. The wrong dipsticks are usually too long, therefore, a full reading could mean one or more quarts low on fluid. If this is suspect, add a quart of fluid and road test. A short dipstick results in an overfill and causes fluid to spew out the filler tube.

Low level. Low fluid level can result in the oil pump taking in air along with the fluid. In any hydraulic system, air bubbles will make the fluid spongy and compressible. This can result in a slow build-up of pressure in the transmission hydraulic system.

Low fluid level will cause delayed engagement in drive and reverse, and slipping on upshifts. You may also get disturbing noises such as pump whine and regulator valve buzz. The slipping action adds to the troubles by causing overheating and rapid wear of clutches and bands. With air in the fluid, the pump can not provide an adequate supply of fluid for converter feed and lubrication, so more overheating is generated and other transmission parts will wear to destruction.

The "Add" mark on the dipstick means add one pint of fluid only. This seems to be ignored at times as being insignificant in a problem cause. Don't be fooled. When the selector is dropped into Drive, the forward clutch circuit fills and moves the car with no problems. On the shift to second gear, the intermediate circuit takes on more volume of fluid and still no apparent problem. On the shift to third, however, the transmission is one pint short and is struggling to satisfy the direct clutch circuit. It is common then to get a drawn out shift or slight engine flare-up during direct clutch apply.

If the fluid level is down, the low level may be the result of an external leak, a leaky vacuum modulator diaphragm, or improper filling. If there is no evidence of an external leak, or inspection and testing of the vacuum modulator shows no sign of a leaky diaphragm, then in all probability someone failed to refill and properly check the fluid level. If the fluid condition looks normal, simply add enough fluid to reach the full cold or hot mark and it is a good bet that the transmission will perform normally again. Don't forget to perform a road test before giving the final OK.

High level. When the fluid level is too high, the planetary gear train is riding in the sump fluid, which is not necessary. The gear train has its own lubrication feed system. The gear train action will actually whip the fluid into a foam and typically cause the same conditions as low fluid. The combination of foam (aeration) and overheating causes rapid oxidation and fluid varnishing, which interferes with normal valve, clutch, and servo operation. Overfilling, therefore, doesn't exactly "treat" the transmission.

To avoid overfills, check with the manufacturer's refill recommendations when replacing the fluid during an overhaul or fluid change. Overhaul fluid requirements are based on the total transmission, which includes the converter and oil pan. Oil pan requirements only are given for fluid change purposes as a preventative maintenance item. In most cases, the pan fluid is all that can be changed for preventative maintenance. General Motors has not provided converter drain plugs for years, and since midyear 1977 Chrysler has eliminated converter drain plugs. Ford Motor Company thru 1981 is still using converter drain plugs and the fluid from the converter should be drained as part of its preventative maintenance package.

When refilling for an overhaul or preventative maintenance schedule, consider the manufacturer's recommendation as only a guideline. It is impossible to determine how much fluid was added for lubrication during an overhaul or how much did not drain out for just a fluid change. Therefore, always stop at least one quart short of the recommended refill and check the dipstick. Because this is a cold check, bring the fluid into the cold zone or no further than the "Add" mark.

Fig. 9-5. (A) Fluid check without carbon treated dipstick. (B) Fluid check with carbon treated dipstick.

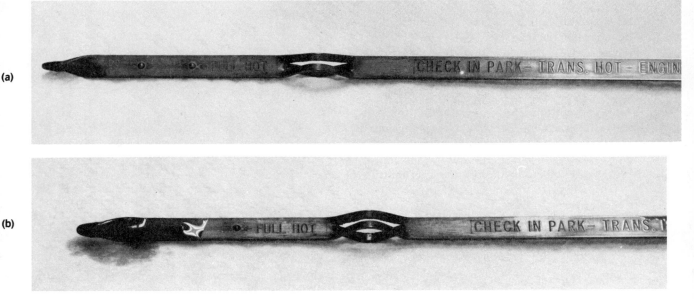

FLUID CONDITION. When checking the fluid level, examine the fluid condition. It should be clean and carry a normal color. Transmission fluids Dexron and Type F are treated with a deep red dye, while Type CJ carries an orange-tinted red color. The fluids will change to a darker color at an early stage, which may look like a clear varnish and also take on a strong odor. Although these signs are usually associated with overheated transmission fluid, it is a normal condition. This is not a positive sign of required maintenance or transmission failure.

To help analyze fluid condition, the sample fluid off the dipstick can be placed on a white ink blotter or a white paper type shop cloth (Fig. 9-6). Should the following conditions exist, then an overhaul diagnosis is required to determine the cause.

ATF oxidation rates and useful ATF life, Table 9-1. Fluid heating caused from severe service is discussed in Chapters 8 and 10.

TABLE 9-1 Kendall ATF Oxidation Rate Data

ATF Operating Temperature	Projected ATF Useful Life in Miles
175° F	100,000
195° F	50,000
215° F	25,000
235° F	12,000
255° F	6,250
275° F	3,000
295° F	1,500
315° F	750
335° F	325
355° F	160
375° F	80
390° F	40

Fig. 9-6.

- Fluid smells burned like a rotten egg or burned electrical coil. The fluid takes on a very dark or even black color.
- Fluid is contaminated with solid residue particles of metal or friction material.
- Fluid is heavily varnished and discolored to a dark brown.
  The varnish even glues itself to the dipstick.

Varnish formation is an indication that the transmission was overheated. Heat is the major enemy of the transmission. It oxidizes the fluid and produces the by-product, varnish. Once automatic transmission fluid breaks down from oxidation, the internal transmission parts life suffers as they easily fatigue and fail. The friction, bearing, and seal materials are all affected in addition to the valving and piston operation. Kendall Oil and Refining has produced some interesting research data related to the temperature effect on

- Fluid is discolored a milky pink. This means that engine coolant has leaked into the ATF. The water and glycol content swells the transmission seals and softens the friction material. It is not uncom-

Fig. 9-7.

mon to find friction facing material unglued from its backing. The only cure is to seal the coolant leak and completely overhaul the transmission, clean the converter, and flush cooler lines.

If in doubt about the fluid condition and residue, the transmission pan should be dropped for inspection and an evaluation (Fig. 9-7). There will always be some residue in the pan, which is normal. Excessive deposits will be obvious and an overhaul necessary.

Varnish conditions do not always dictate an overhaul. When the pan is dropped, it may be determined that a transmission tune-up is likely to produce successful results. This means an oil and filter change, flushing the cooler lines, valve body overhaul, and external linkage adjustments. In many cases, fluid condition tells the story and the diagnostic process stops here. No further information is needed.

STEP III: Quick Check Engine Idle, Vacuum Lines, Transmission and Carburetor Linkage

In keeping with the diagnosis objective of reaching the end result with the least amount of effort, we are going to use our eyes and ears for some quick checks in preparation for a road test. The transmission fluid is at the correct level and fluid condition is normal, and we are in need of further testing.

ENGINE IDLE. Set the engine fast and hot idle rpm to manufacturer's specifications using a reliable tachometer (Fig. 9-8). When the engine idle is too high, the forward or reverse clutch engagement is harsh and usually associated with a drive line "clunk." Settling down the idle rpm can also eliminate that closed throttle downshift "clunk."

Dropping the idle 25 or 50 rpm can sometimes make a noticeable difference.

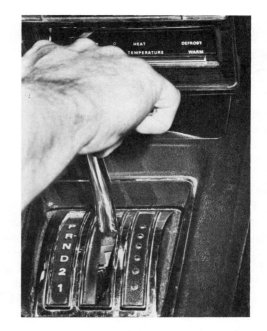

Fig. 9-9. Checking manual linkage for accuracy of selector positions.

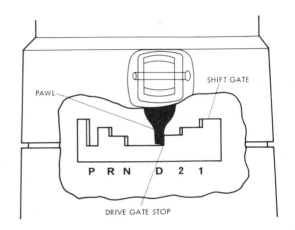

Fig. 9-8. Setting idle with tachometer.

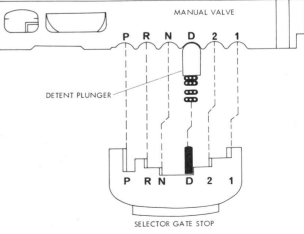

Fig. 9-10.

MANUAL LINKAGE. This check takes place from the driver's seat. It is a simple matter of running the selector through all the ranges and feeling for the spring loaded transmission detent dropping into the notches of the manual valve (Fig. 9-9). Are they coordinated with the markings on the shift selector? This is more accurately illustrated in Fig. 9-10.

Each operating range has a gate stop position in the selector mechanism that indexes with the markings on the selector. If the markings are slightly off with the detents in the transmission, it is still considered acceptable. If the selector indexing is noticeably off target, then an adjustment is necessary. Drivers by nature will usually move the selector to the stop gate position where, technically, the transmission detents are properly positioned. If the detents are not synchronized, then the manual valve is out of position and cross feeds into another circuit. In observing Fig. 9-11, it is obvious that the Drive circuit line pressure is partially exhausting out the Neutral circuit. This results in a loss of pressure apply and subsequent clutch and band failure. When the manual linkage is not properly adjusted, it can even cause the vehicle to creep forward or in reverse with the selector in Neutral, Fig. 9-12.

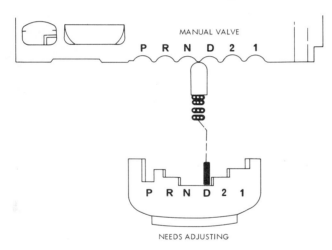

NEEDS ADJUSTING

Fig. 9-11.

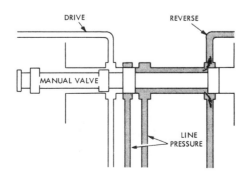

Fig. 9-12. Manual not in adjustment and line pressure bleeding into reverse circuit (neutral).

Manual linkage adjustment is simple but too often neglected. The linkage adjustment is usually coordinated with the selector against the Drive gate stop and transmission manual valve in its Drive detent. Refer to the car manufacturer's service manual or equivalent for correct procedure.

THROTTLE LINKAGE AND VACUUM LINE CONNECTIONS. It is in this area where most of the problems that cause erratic shift conditions and even complete transmission failure are found. Engine performance and the torque signal to the transmission must be right if the transmission is to work properly. It would be interesting to know how many transmissions have been removed and disassembled unnecessarily in desperation when the problem's cause was actually in the engine torque signal. There will be no attempt at this time to discuss the subject matter in detail. This is reserved for a separate discussion involving erratic shift situations later in the chapter. The emphasis here is to treat carburetor and throttle linkage and vacuum line connections as a quick check item, unless road testing and pressure testing point to a detailed involvement.

A quick check involves mostly a close visual inspection to verify that the connections between the engine and transmission are properly attached, not worn or loose, and there is no evidence of tampering.

On vacuum lines leading to modulator units, look for pinched and leaky tubing, especially at the connections. Give special attention to the vacuum hose connection at the modulator. It tends to become disconnected or leak and many shift complaints can be easily solved. With the maze of vacuum line plumbing under the hood, it is essential to make sure the transmission is attached to the proper vacuum source fitting. On manifold vacuum trees, be positive that the vacuum line is not coupled to a metered fitting. You will even find unusual situations where the vacuum line has been attached to carburetor venturi and ported vacuum.

CARBURETOR AND EGR. Because the transmission is engine torque sensitive, the carburetor and EGR system are important check-out points. They both affect engine vacuum and can cause shift problems.

The carburetor needs to be checked for wide open throttle (Fig. 9-13). For accurate results, an assistant should depress the accelerator pedal with his foot while you make the observation. Make the needed correction before road testing.

For an EGR operational inspection:

- Let the engine run at hot idle in Park.
- While increasing the engine speed to 1,500 rpm, watch for movement in the valve stem (Fig. 9-14).

Fig. 9-13. Carburetor inspection for full throttle travel.

If the valve stem doesn't move, the valve is stuck or the EGR vacuum is not operating the system. Make the necessary corrections to the system. A restriction check and procedure is demonstrated in Fig. 9-15.

DOWNSHIFT SYSTEM. Automatic transmissions use three types of external controls on the downshift systems.

- Mechanically activated where a separate rod to the transmission is used or sometimes is incorporated in the same rod linkage movement that controls the throttle system.
- Mechanically activated where a separate cable is used or sometimes is incorporated in the same cable control for the throttle system.
- Mechanically activated where an electrical switch is closed and a downshift solenoid valve is energized.

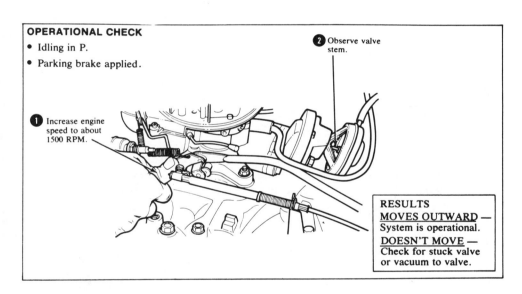

OPERATIONAL CHECK
- Idling in P.
- Parking brake applied.

❷ Observe valve stem.

❶ Increase engine speed to about 1500 RPM.

RESULTS
MOVES OUTWARD —
System is operational.
DOESN'T MOVE —
Check for stuck valve or vacuum to valve.

Fig. 9-14.
(Ford Motor Co.)

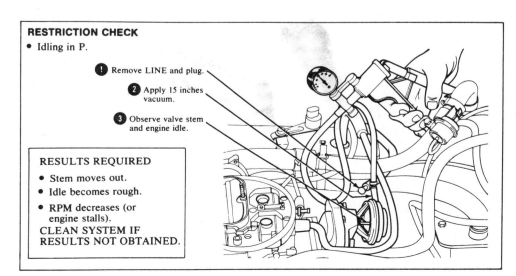

RESTRICTION CHECK
- Idling in P.

❶ Remove LINE and plug.
❷ Apply 15 inches vacuum.
❸ Observe valve stem and engine idle.

RESULTS REQUIRED
- Stem moves out.
- Idle becomes rough.
- RPM decreases (or engine stalls).
CLEAN SYSTEM IF RESULTS NOT OBTAINED.

Fig. 9-15.
(Ford Motor Co.)

CHECK THROTTLE LINKAGE FIRST

- Must be set properly for downshift linkage to operate.

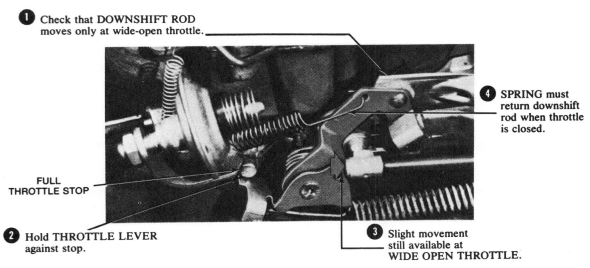

1 Check that DOWNSHIFT ROD moves only at wide-open throttle.

4 SPRING must return downshift rod when throttle is closed.

FULL THROTTLE STOP

2 Hold THROTTLE LEVER against stop.

3 Slight movement still available at WIDE OPEN THROTTLE.

Fig. 9-16. (Ford Motor Co.)

Because there is a wide variety in check-out procedures, it is best to consult the car manufacturer's service manual when in doubt about the procedure. Check points on a typical Ford downshift (throttle) linkage set-up are illustrated in Fig. 9-16. An electrically-controlled system can easily be checked-out as follows:

- Turn on the radio and tune in to the local radio station with the final setting de-tuned on the high frequency side of the broadcast, engine off.
- Depress the accelerator pedal to energize the solenoid.
- Release the accelerator pedal and listen for a speaker sound caused by a magnetic induction from the solenoid.

Step III is very vital in diagnosis and can lead to a quick correction of a transmission problem without getting involved with major service. Conditions found to be improper must be corrected at this time.

STEP IV: STALL TEST (Optional)

The stall test works full engine power against the stationary weight of the vehicle. The purpose of the test is to determine band and clutch holding ability, torque converter operation and engine performance. This procedure must be used with caution, however, because the test produces severe heat and twisting stress. Vehicles with neglected cooling systems could burst a hose. How do you explain $12 worth of antifreeze and a $10 hose plus added labor costs to the customer?

Perform the stall test when you feel that it is needed as an additional diagnostic tool, especially when the complaint is power performance. When slippage is not a factor, the test can be very useful in isolating power loss to either the engine or converter. The stall test can be compared to a full power dynamometer test.

STALL TEST PROCEDURE. The engine coolant, engine oil and transmission fluid levels must be correct and at normal operating temperatures.

WARNING: The full weight of the vehicle must be on the wheels and the vehicle must be positively prevented from moving. It will be necessary to apply the park and service brakes and block the vehicle. NO PERSON is to stand in front of the vehicle during the test.

Procedure

1. Connect the tachometer and position it so you can read it from the driver's seat.
2. Shift the selector lever to the (D) range.
3. Accelerate the engine to full throttle.
4. Note the maximum rpm attained by the engine and record (Fig. 9-17.)

CAUTION: This operation must not take over five seconds or severe overheating and damage to the transmission will result.

5. Return the selector lever to neutral and operate the engine at fast idle for a minimum of 30 seconds for cooling.
6. Repeat the above procedure for each test run.

Fig. 9-17.   Stall test tachometer reading.

If engine speed exceeds the maximum limits of the stall specification, release the accelerator immediately, because slippage is indicated and further damage to the transmission must be avoided. The test should also be stopped when unusual noises occur. A churning noise or even a whining noise from the converter fluid action is normal during a stall test. However, any metallic type noise in the assembly indicates a defective torque converter.

STALL TEST INTERPRETATION. For interpretation of test results, a comparison is made against the manufacturer's test specifications. In Chart 9-1, typical stall speed specifications are listed for the Torque-Flite transmission. Allowances should be made for altitude changes; engine power decreases with higher altitude levels. Be sure to record test results and com-

CHART 9-1
TorqueFlite Transmission Stall Speed

Engine Cu. In.	Transmission Type	Converter Diameter	Stall R.P.M.
225	A-904	10¾″	1800-2100
318 CAL./Hi. Alt.	A-904-LA	10¾″	2125-2425
318 FED.	A-904-LA	10¾″	1700-2000
225	A-904-HD	10¾″	1800-2100
318 CAL./Hi. Alt.	A-727	10¾″	2125-2425
318 FED.	A-727	10¾″	1700-2000
360-4 H.D.	A-727	10¾″	2150-2450
360-2	A-904-LA	10¾″	1775-2075
360-2	A-727	10¾″	1775-2075
360-4 CAL./Hi. Alt.	A-904-LA	10¾″	2150-2450
400-4	A-727	10¾″	1850-2150
400-4 H.D.	A-727	10¾″	2300-2600
440-4	A-727	10¾″	1950-2250
440-4 H.P.	A-727	10¾″	2500-2800

Engine Litre	Transmission Type	Converter Diameter	Stall R.P.M.
1.7	A-404	9½ inches (241 millimetres)	2000-2400

TABLE 9-2. TORQUEFLITE STALL TEST SUMMARY

	STALL SPECIFICATION			
RANGE	ACTUAL	CONDITION AS TESTED		
		LOW	NORMAL	HIGH
DRIVE				
(2)				
(1)				
REVERSE				

OPERATING RANGE	HOLDING MEMBERS APPLIED
D	REAR CLUTCH AND ONE-WAY CLUTCH
2	REAR CLUTCH AND ONE-WAY CLUTCH
1	REAR CLUTCH AND LOW-REVERSE BAND
R	FRONT CLUTCH AND LOW-REVERSE BAND
KICKDOWN BAND IS NOT USED DURING STALL TESTS.	

pare them to the manufacturer's specifications, Chart 9-2.

Variations in test speed results are interpreted as follows:

- Stall speed is 200–300 rpm higher than normal. The transmission is not holding and the probable cause is a slipping clutch. Aerated transmission fluid or low operating pressure could be another suspect area.
- Stall speed is extremely high and runs away; the test run has to be stopped. A likely suspect is still a slipping clutch or low operating pressure; however, don't overlook sheared turbine splines on the input shaft.
- Stall speed is 200–300 rpm lower than normal. It is an indication of engine power loss. Typically, the customer already has noticed a drop in engine performance and a tune-up is in order.
- Stall speed is 33% lower than normal. A free-wheeling stator is the suspect. The converter during a stall test is producing full torque; the stator is normally in a locked condition. If the stator roller clutch fails to take hold, then the fluid action works against the impeller and engine rotation. The engine power is drastically lost in working against the converter fluid. Car performance in the low speed range, 0–30 mph (0–48 km/h), is dead and has almost no pulling power or acceleration.

- Stall speed is normal. This means that the engine power is normal, the transmission is holding and the converter stator is holding. It does not prove, however, whether the stator can release and permit the converter to act as a fluid coupling.

A frozen stator can be suspected when the top vehicle speed at W.O.T. (wide-open throttle) is greatly reduced; usually 33%. Low-speed acceleration and performance is normal, but when the converter wants to operate in coupling phase, the frozen stator acts as a dam or brake against the rotary fluid motion. The side effects are overheating of transmission fluid and possible loss of transmission pump pressure. The car usually travels 15–20 miles (24–32 km/h) down the road and then the transmission loses pressure and holding power.

As another test for a frozen stator, place the manual selector in (N) and push the accelerator to W.O.T. If the engine indicates a normal no-load condition and easily exceeds 3,000 rpm, stop the test; the stator is freewheeling and turning together with the impeller and turbine in the fluid flow. If the engine cannot exceed approximately 3,000 rpm at W.O.T., then the stator roller clutch is frozen. The stator acts as a brake against the rotary fluid force and lugs the engine.

STEP V: Road Test

Road testing starts with recognizing normal transmission performance. This is a must before you can give an opinion on abnormal conditions. If you are not completely familiar with the normal performance, take time to get acquainted. If possible, drive several low-mileage, well-tuned, current model cars equipped with the transmission.

During a road test, try all of the operating ranges. Compare the shift schedule and quality under light, medium and heavy throttle. Test the downshift or detent performance. And perhaps most important of all, learn to visualize which band or clutch is applied for each gear.

On complaints relating to erratic shifts with delayed and harsh shift quality, don't overlook the condition of the engine, particularly if the stall test was omitted. Idle and engine performance should be up to specifications. The shift pattern and shift quality of the transmission is tailored to normal engine performance. If the engine is not functioning properly, the transmission has no way of knowing.

When the engine output is low, the driver has to step on the gas harder to accelerate; in effect, the throttle is opened further than normal (Fig. 9-18). If the transmission has a mechanically-operated throttle system, the throttle pressure will be too high in relation to actual engine torque because the throttle linkage

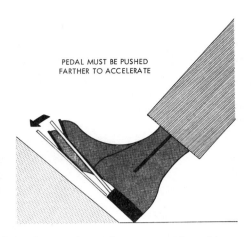

Fig. 9-18. Poor engine performance requires wider openings and upsets the shift pattern and shift quality.

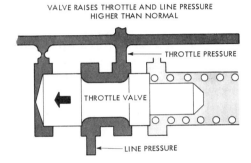

Fig. 9-19.

and valve is advanced too far (Fig. 9-19). In applications where vacuum modulator or vacuum throttle systems are incorporated, the below-normal engine vacuum will produce higher values in these systems in relation to the throttle opening. The end result of low engine output in relation to transmission operation is delayed and harsh upshifts—the line pressure is higher for clutch-band application, and it will take more vehicle speed to generate the necessary governor pressure for the upshift pattern.

Always correct an untuned engine condition before the road test starts. More than one shift quality complaint has been corrected by correcting engine performance and not touching the transmission.

A properly conducted road test is a valuable diagnostic tool. The objective is to gather exact information on transmission performance from which the technician can get more evidence to help pinpoint the transmission problem area.

It should be used when:

- The customer complaint is not clearly defined.
- The problem cause is not obvious and/or has not been found up to this point in the diagnosis procedure.

Test Summary Guide.

Transmission Model _____   Axle Ratio _____   Engine Displacement _____

INITIAL CLUTCH AND BAND ENGAGEMENTS AT ENGINE IDLE

RANGE	ENGAGES		QUALITY		
	YES	NO	HARSH	DELAYED	NORMAL
DRIVE					
(2)					
(1)					
REVERSE					
NEUTRAL	CAR CREEPS _____			O.K. _____	

MINIMUM THROTTLE UPSHIFTS AND CLOSED THROTTLE DOWNSHIFTS

RANGE		SHIFT POINTS (MPH)		SHIFT QUALITY			
		Actual	Mfg. Spec.	Harsh	"Mushy" (Drawn Out)	Slips	O.K.
DRIVE	1-2						
	2-3						
	3-1						
(2)	1-2						
	2-1						

TRAFFIC THROTTLE UPSHIFTS WITH MODERATE THROTTLE

RANGE			SHIFT QUALITY			
			Too Harsh	"Mushy" (Drawn Out)	Slips	O.K.
DRIVE	1-2	— At 30-40 MPH —				
	2-3					
(2)	1-2	At 15-25 MPH				

WIDE OPEN THROTTLE UPSHIFTS
NOTE: This test is limited to prevailing road and traffic conditions

RANGE		SHIFT POINTS (MPH)		SHIFT QUALITY			
		Actual	Mfg's Spec.	Too Harsh	"Mushy" (Drawn Out)	Slips	Firm and O.K.
DRIVE	1-2						
	2-3						

(KICKDOWN) WIDE OPEN THROTTLE FORCED DOWNSHIFTS
NOTE: This test is limited to prevailing road and traffic conditions

RANGE		VEHICLE SPEED LIMITS (MPH)		SHIFT QUALITY			
		Actual	Mfg's Spec.	Too Harsh	"Mushy" (Drawn Out)	Slips	O.K.
DRIVE	3-2						
	2-1						

PART THROTTLE 3-2 DOWNSHIFT

RANGE	VEHICLE SPEED LIMITS (MPH)		SHIFT QUALITY			
	Actual	Mfg's Spec.	Too Harsh	"Mushy" (Drawn Out)	Slips	O.K.
DRIVE						

MANUAL LOW
MANUAL CLOSED THROTTLE DOWNSHFT FROM 3rd GEAR (DRIVE) AT 25 MPH TO TEST BRAKING ACTION.
O.K. _____   NO BRAKING _____

REVERSE
HOLDS _____   SLIPS _____   CHATTERS _____

CHART 9-3
TorqueFlite A-904 and A-727
Automatic Shift Speed
(Approximate Miles and Kilometers Per Hour)

Carline	HNFG		HNFG				XSJET		SXJET	
Engine	225		225	318		318	360-4		360-2	
Transmission Ratio	Standard		Wide	Standard		Wide	Standard		Standard	
Axle Ratio	2.76		2.76	2.45		2.24	3.21		2.45	
Standard Tire	DR78 x 14			FR78 x 15			GR78 x 15		GR78 x 15	
	Mph	Km/hr.	Mph	Km/hr.	Mph	Km/hr.	Mph	Km/hr.	Mph	Km/hr.	Mph	Km/hr.
Closed Throttle 1-2	9-11	14-18	8-10	13-16	11-13	18-21	10-12	16-19	9-11	14-18	11-14	18-23
Closed Throttle 2-3	13-15	21-24	12-15	19-24	15-18	24-29	15-18	24-29	12-15	19-24	16-19	26-31
Closed Throttle Lock-up	27-36	43-58	24-33	39-53	32-43	51-69	32-43	51-69	—	—	26-30	42-48
Detent 1-2	23-30	37-48	20-28	32-45	27-35	43-56	26-34	42-55	22-33	34-53	28-36	45-58
Detent 2-3	46-66	74-106	45-57	72-92	55-78	89-126	55-77	86-124	49-69	79-109	56-80	90-129
W.O.T. 1-2	36-46	43-74	30-42	48-68	42-54	68-87	40-52	64-84	39-48	63-77	43-55	69-89
W.O.T. 2-3	63-73	101-117	57-68	92-109	74-87	119-140	75-87	121-140	65-75	105-121	76-88	122-142
Kickdown limit 3-2	58-68	93-109	52-64	84-103	69-81	111-130	69-81	111-130	60-70	97-113	70-83	113-134
Kickdown limit 3-1	28-38	45-61	21-31	34-50	33-44	53-71	29-39	47-63	31-40	50-64	33-45	53-72
Closed Throttle 3-1	9-11	14-18	8-10	13-16	11-13	18-21	10-12	16-19	9-11	14-18	11-14	18-23
Part throttle 3-2 Kickdown limit	30-41	48-66	33-34	53-71	35-49	56-79	33-45	53-71	33-44	53-71	36-50	58-80

NOTE: Figures given are typical for other models. Changes in tire size or axle ratio will cause shift points to occur at corresponding higher or lower vehicle speeds.

The road test will be used to analyze slipping and erratic shift conditions caused by clutch/band partial failures, throttle system, or governor system failures.

ROAD TEST PROCEDURE. The engine coolant, engine oil, and transmission fluid must be correct and at normal operating temperature. A quick check and any necessary corrections should be made on engine idle, vacuum lines, and transmission and carburetor linkage.

To road test the transmission, it should be operated in each selector range to check for clutch /band slipping and engagement quality and any abnormal variations in the shift schedule. Performance testing should be made at minimum, medium, and heavy throttle modes.

During the performance testing, observe whether the shifts are harsh or long and drawn out. Check the speeds at which the upshifts and downshifts occur. Look for an engine flare-up during a shift especially on medium and heavy throttle testing.

To attain your minimum shift points, the throttle should be teased just enough to keep the vehicle moving through 20 mph (32 km/h). Engine manifold vacuum must be kept high. For best results find a flat stretch of road or one that has a slight downgrade. What is usually considered mild acceleration from a stop is too aggressive for a check-out on the minimum shifts. The minimum shift pattern check-out requires a careful and very easy throttle manipulation by the technician for accurate test results. It takes a little practice to master the technique.

The road test requires collecting information and data; therefore, reference must be made to the manufacturer's applicable shift speed specifications and an account recorded on transmission behavior. Because of the many items being tested, it is best to record the test results rather than to depend on memory. A comprehensive road test program for the TorqueFlite transmission and related shift speed data are shown in Test Summary Guide 9-1 and Chart 9-3. The test summary guide can be modified and adapted for other automatic transmissions. The road test results can effectively be used for:

- Clutch and band slip analysis
- Mechanical noise analysis
- Erratic shift analysis

CLUTCH AND BAND SLIP ANALYSIS. If the road test indicates any slipping or engine flare-up condition, it usually means clutch, band, or overrunning clutch problems. By the process of elimination, any friction units that slip can be verified, as well as those that are in good working order.

It must be emphasized that the clutch/band slip analysis during the road test is meaningless unless Steps II and III have been completed in the diagnosis process. Conditions not found or corrected in Steps II and III can cause slipping and flare-up. The idea is to find and correct external conditions that may cause the slip before it is too far advanced and an overhaul is needed to restore normal operation. And that's just what the road test reveals.

The key to a band and clutch analysis is in using a summary clutch/band apply chart. Experienced technicians need only to make mental notes. To illustrate how the technique works, a TorqueFlite Clutch/Band Apply Summary is given in Chart 9-4. Most three-speed automatic transmissions use the same basic combinations.

Range	Gear	(Direct) Front Clutch	(Forward) Rear Clutch	(Front) Kickdown Band	(Rear) Low-Reverse Band	Low Roller Clutch
Park						
Reverse		On			On	
Neutral						
D—Drive First	(Breakaway)					
			On			Holds
	Second		On	On		
	Third	On	On			
2—Drive	First		On			Holds
	Second		On	On		
1—Low	First		On		On	Holds

Rear (forward) clutch slipping

The rear clutch is in constant apply for all forward gears. With a slipping condition:

- There will be a slip or no drive in all forward gears. (D), (2), and (1).
- If the rear clutch is the only affected unit, then the transmission will have a working (R).
- Should the clutch greatly delay engagement when cold and work normal when hot, the suspect area is hard or worn clutch piston seals.

Front (direct/reverse) clutch slipping

With a slipping front clutch, high gear and reverse is affected.

- The slip will be first noticeable in high gear with an engine flare-up on the 2–3 shift. When the condition is far advanced, reverse slip also becomes noticeable. (R) works at almost three times the line pressure required in (D), and therefore, may not slip in early stages of clutch failure.
- Worn or hard piston seals first act up under cold conditions. The shift into high is drawn out or may not occur until the fluid is warm. Advanced conditions prevent total engagement of high gear, cold or hot.
- First and second gears will not be affected.

Kickdown (front or intermediate) band slipping

Kickdown band trouble is easy to spot because the band applies only in second gear.

- When the band completely fails to hold, second gear is skipped and a 1–3 upshift will occur. With the kickdown band not applying, the overrunning clutch will hold in first gear (breakaway) until the road speed is high enough for the shift into direct (Fig. 9-20).
- If the kickdown band slip is not in an advanced condition, then there will be a short upshift delay

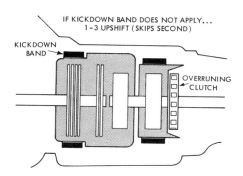

IF KICKDOWN BAND DOES NOT APPLY...
1–3 UPSHIFT (SKIPS SECOND)

KICKDOWN BAND

OVERRUNNING CLUTCH

Fig. 9-20. 1-3 upshift skips second if kickdown band does not apply; overrunning clutch remains effective on 1-2 shift.

accompanied by a bump as the band takes over from the overrunning clutch.
- When the selector is moved to (2) from (D) range or 3–2 forced downshift is attempted, there will be a slipping or no downshift. On the 3–2 forced downshift attempt, the engine will race trying to catch-up with the first gear ratio.

Overrunning clutch slipping

This will affect the D and 2 ranges.

- The transmission will fail to engage first gear and, therefore, a vehicle start-up is not possible in D or 2.
- In manual low, the vehicle can start-up. The low/reverse band substitutes for the overrunning clutch. Manual low start-ups with a slipping overrun clutch causes severe band wear. The band operation is not engineered to hold against pulling power in this operating range.

Low/Reverse (rear) band slipping

Manual 1 and R uses the low/reverse band. Indications of a slipping band are:

- A slipping or complete loss of reverse drive.

- No engine braking in manual 1 during coast. The holding ability of the band cannot be checked under acceleration or power. Should the band slip, the overrunning clutch is not affected. It should hold under drive conditions. For a band check-out in 1, accelerate to 30 mph (48 km/h) and quickly decelerate and feel for engine braking (Fig 9-21).

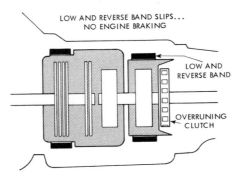

Fig. 9-21. When low and reverse band slips there is no engine braking or reverse.

Rear (forward) clutch fails to release

It does not happen as an everyday event. The following conditions, however, will prevail.

- The transmission will operate normal in all forward drive ranges.
- The transmission will move forward in neutral and lock-up in reverse.

The clutch/band road test analysis just described can be adapted to any automatic transmission providing the technician is aware of operating characteristics and construction differences. For example, a clutch may be substituted for the low/reverse band or an intermediate roller clutch system substituted for the intermediate band. In Ford transmissions, the 2 range starts out in second gear; would an intermediate band failure prevent a forward drive?

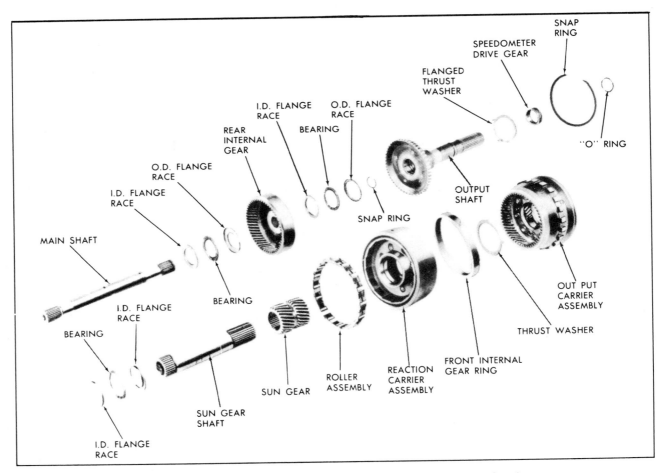

Fig. 9-22. THM-400 gear unit. (Oldsmobile Division, General Motors Corp.)

MECHANICAL NOISE ANALYSIS. Mechanical noises are usually analyzed on a road test. They can cover a wide variety of items, which could include rare cases of clutch plate rattle in P and N or cooler line vibration. Most of the noise problems, however, take place within the planetary gear train and this will be the area of concentration. The potential gear train noises will come from the planetary gears, needle-type thrust washers located in many of the gear units, or the overrunning clutch rollers (Fig. 9-22).

It is important to verify that the noise is in the planetary gear assembly. When the transmission is disassembled, it then gives the technician a specific area for inspection, location, and correction of the problem.

Planetary gear train noise is related to speed changes that take place with changes in the gear ratios. First gear, for example, provides the greatest speed difference between the planetary input and output. This means that the relative motion between the gear train parts is at its greatest. The noise analysis basically involves listening to the rhythm or noise level change as the transmission shifts gears.

The following examples illustrate the idea.

- If the noise factor is most noticeable in first gear, cuts back in second gear, and then eliminates itself in Direct, then the problem is confined to the gear train unit. In Direct Drive, the clutch and planetary units are locked at 1:1 and any internal planetary assembly noise should disappear.

It is not uncommon to find the cause related to worn or brinneled races used with needle-type thrust bearings employed in the gear assembly (Fig. 9-23).

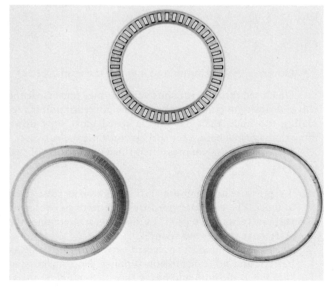

Fig. 9-23.

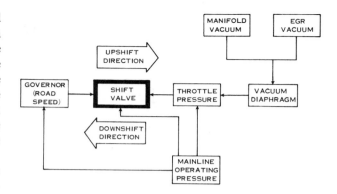

Fig. 9-24.   Shift system block diagram with vacuum controlled throttle system.

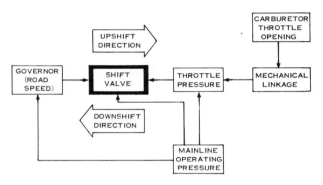

Fig. 9-25.   Shift system block diagram with mechanically controlled throttle system.

- If the unusual noise is not a factor in first gear or reverse but starts in second gear and continues with more intensity and speed rhythm in Direct, then the low roller clutch assembly is the high suspect area.

The low roller clutch has no overrunning action in first and reverse. In second gear, its freewheel speed is less than the output shaft speed and then, with the shift into direct drive, the freewheel speed gets a sudden jump to equal output shaft speed.

ERRATIC SHIFT ANALYSIS. Erratic shifts simply mean that the shift points are incorrect and they may be accompanied by incorrect shift quality. Again, the road test can be used to verify the complaint and analyze the probable shift system cause.

Road testing for erratic shift analysis will require the technician to be knowledgeable of shift system theory of operation. Two block diagrams in Figs. 9-24 and 9-25 illustrate in brief a typical shift system makeup. The only variance shown is in the type of throttle system control, either vacuum or mechanical. The essentials of shift system operation are as follows:

1. A throttle or modulator system produces an engine torque-sensitive pressure used at the shift valve to delay shifting.
2. A governor system produces a vehicle speed-sensitive pressure used at the shift valve to open the valve or cause the shift to happen.
3. Once the shift is made, only spring tension opposes the governor force. Throttle pressure is cut-off from the shift valve assembly.
4. The shift valve spring determines the closed throttle downshifts against governor force.

Most erratic shifts occur from an out-of-balance governor or throttle system, which causes the following problems.

- The upshifts are delayed or, in extreme cases, will not occur regardless of vehicle speed.
- The upshifts occur too soon or, in extreme cases, the transmission starts out already in high gear.

The throttle and governor systems can be analyzed on a road test to determine which system is at fault, and then you must locate the problem within the system. What you are going to find is entirely unknown, but at least the problem is confined to a system.

Some of the throttle and governor system fault analysis is obvious. For example:

- When the transmission starts out in high gear, the 2–3 shift valve must be open. This means that the governor system has not been able to regulate or shut down the line pressure feed to the shift system. Governor pressure equals line pressure at all times. The throttle system is ruled out because its function is to delay the shift.
- When the transmission will not upshift at any speed, it rules out the throttle system and indicates a governor system problem. The simple reasoning is that even maximum throttle pressure will permit an upshift if the car is driven fast enough.

But what about those in between shift problems when the transmission quick-shifts or the shifts are moderately delayed but noticeable. Here is how the road test can be used. It is preferred to use shift data provided by the manufacturer; however, in the absence of shift data, use the following guidelines:

Minimum Upshifts at Almost Closed Throttle

1–2 Upshift at 8–12 mph (13–19 km/h)

2–3 Upshift at 15–20 mph (24–32 km/h)

Closed Throttle Downshift

3–2 at 10–12 mph (16–19 km/h)

2–1 at 5–8 mph (8–13 km/h)

or

3–1 at 5–8 mph (8–13 km/h)

CASE PROBLEM:
Minimum upshift pattern is delayed. The 1–2 shift occurs at 20 mph (32 km/h) and 2–3 shift at 35 mph (56 km/h). On the closed throttle test run the downshift 3–1 happens at 10 mph (16 km/h), which can be considered close enough for normal.

Cause:

- It could be low governor system output.
- It could be high throttle system output.

Because throttle pressure is not a factor at the shift valve once the shift happens, the closed throttle downshift 3–1 is determined by spring tension working against governor pressure. If the closed throttle shift is correct, then it verifies that the governor system is proper. The problem is isolated to the throttle system. If, in the very same problem, the closed throttle downshift 3–1 happened at 18 mph (29 km/h), then the throttle system is ruled out. The early downshift was caused by the shift valve springs overcoming governor system output, which was too low for the road speed.

CASE PROBLEM:
Minimum upshift pattern is too early. The 1–2 shift occurs at 5 mph (8 km/h) and 2–3 shift at 10 mph (16 km/h). A medium and heavy throttle shift sequence shows that the shifts are delayed, with no transmission slipping but that they still occur early. On the closed throttle test run, the downshift 3–1 happens at almost a dead stop, which is very late.

Cause:

- Governor system output too high for the road speed.

On closed throttle, the shift valve springs must close the valves against governor pressure. If the governor unit is regulating too high, then the vehicle speed must slow down more than normal before the springs can close the valves.

Low throttle system pressure is ruled out because of two factors:

1. TV pressure at minimum shift conditions is close to or at 0 psi. The governor pressure only needs to overcome shift valve spring tension. In this case, it overcomes the shift valve springs too soon.
2. Even though the shifts occurred early, there was a delay pattern and no transmission slipping. No transmission slipping at medium and heavy throttle is a good indication that the TV signal to the pressure regulator valve is right.

CASE PROBLEM:

Minimum upshift pattern is correct. The 1–2 shift occurs at 10 mph (16 km/h) and the 2–3 shift at 18 mph (29 km/h). Under medium and heavy throttle testing, the shift system does not respond and the shift points remain the same. Transmission slipping also becomes part of the problem with medium and heavy throttle.

A check on the closed throttle shift 3–1 finds that it occurs correctly at 5 mph.

Cause:

The throttle system output is remaining close to or at 0 psi. It does not respond to changes in engine performance.

Because the minimum shift points and closed throttle 3–1 shift are right, then the governor system has to be right.

Without a shift valve throttle signal:

- The governor pressure needs only to overcome the shift valve springs, which offer the same fixed resistance from closed to wide open throttle.
- The line pressure regulator valve fails to receive a torque signal for pressure boost. The pressure regulating point stays at a minimum fixed value as determined by the regulator valve spring.

STEP VI: Pressure Testing

Pressure testing is usually avoided by most technicians. In most cases, this can be attributed to a lack of expertise in hydraulic system operation or a misunderstanding of what pressure testing can and what it cannot tell you.

Pressure testing is most valuable for use in special problem situations, especially diagnosis of shift complaints and slip conditions that remain unresolved. When a malfunction still exists after ordinary diagnosis test checks have proven to be right or resulted in correction of discrepancies that failed to solve the problem, then the final step is to make the oil pressure checks. The pressure tests will pinpoint problem areas such as the pump, throttle, and governor systems.

Avoid the error of pulling the transmission from the vehicle for disassembly and inspection on a chance that you might find the problem. What are you going to find if you do not know where to look? It is too late once the transmission is apart. Let the pressure tests tell you where to look. In most cases, you will find that the problem solution can be handled by an in-the-car repair.

Pressure tests will not identify if servos or clutches work properly. They will, however, eliminate key hydraulic systems as a possible cause of trouble when the readings are right. Specifically, pressure testing checks the pulse of the following systems:

- Pump
- Throttle
- Governor

Pressure testing consists of reading the transmission pressures in each of the operating ranges under specific conditions spelled out by the manufacturer. The validity of the test results will depend on the following factors:

1. Transmission fluid level and condition checks out.
2. Transmission fluid is at operating temperature.
3. Manual linkage is set properly.
4. Test instruments are known to give accurate readings.
5. Exact test procedures are followed.
6. Test results are recorded for comparison with specifications and not left to memory.

TEST EQUIPMENT. For test equipment, a portable automatic transmission tester is a helpful device. It contains a pressure gauge, a vacuum gauge, and a

Fig. 9-26. Automatic transmission tester. Shelf holds transmission tester during in-place tests.

tachometer. The tester has extra long instrument attachments to permit mounting of the unit on the car front-door glass (Fig. 9-26). This permits the technician to easily take test readings with the car on the road or in the shop.

In Fig. 9-27, the pressure gauge hose and adapter are connected to the main pressure tap of an automatic transmission. In most cases, this is the only pressure take-off available. If you recall the basic theory of pressure control, you know that operating line pressure is always sensitive to engine torque and sometimes to vehicle speed. Therefore, from the one mainline pressure tap, the pump, modulator, and governor systems can be monitored, as they will be reflected in the mainline pressure test readings.

Although the single pressure tap is used in most transmissions, you will find, for extra convenience, that some makes provide several pressure gauge outlets. Example transmissions are the Chrysler Torque-Flite family (Fig. 9-28) and the General Motors THM-350 and THM-250 (Fig. 9-29).

Be sure to use a 300 psi gauge for any pressures reflecting reverse operation. For single pressure taps, it is a must.

On transmissions equipped with vacuum modulators, the vacuum gauge hose is tied into the manifold vacuum line at the modulator with a tee fitting (Fig. 9-30). This is done to insure that we are working with the exact vacuum at the modulator for accurate test re-

sults. If the vacuum gauge is hooked directly to the intake manifold, you will have no way to determine if the vacuum signal is interrupted on its way to the modulator.

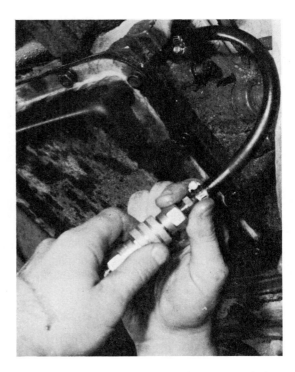

Fig. 9-27. Pressure gauge connection to transmission.

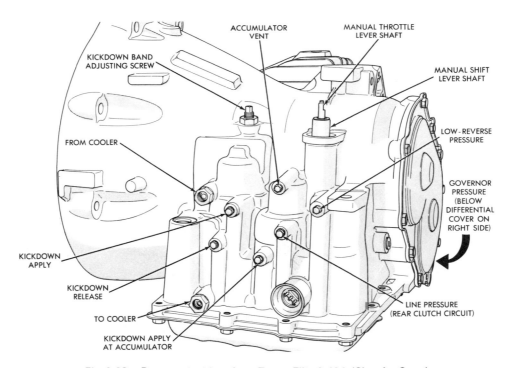

Fig. 9-28.   Pressure test tap plugs, TorqueFlite A-404. (Chrysler Corp.)

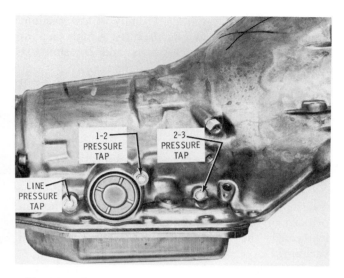

Fig. 9-29. Pressure test tap plugs, THM-350 and THM-250. (Oldsmobile Division, General Motors Co.)

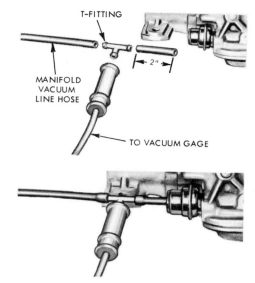

Fig. 9-30. T-fitting for vacuum line connection to gage.

Manifold vacuum represents the engine torque or load signal to the transmission. If the signal is not right, then the modulator regulated output is not right. This means that the transmission will definitely have the wrong line pressure, and the shift schedule and shift quality will also be upset. Many slipping transmissions have been overhauled when the actual cause was in the vacuum supply.

It makes sense then to do a first-class investigation and correction of the vacuum supply if the pressure tests are to reveal true internal transmission problems.

VACUUM SUPPLY SYSTEM CHECK-OUT PROCEDURE

1. Evaluate the vacuum source at the manifold. Acceptable vacuum depends on altitude, engine design, and emission control equipment. Most engines should pull 16 in. of vacuum or better at sea level. Perform engine tune-up if necessary to correct engine breathing problem.

2. Because the EGR affects manifold vacuum, it should be tested for proper operation. For an opera-

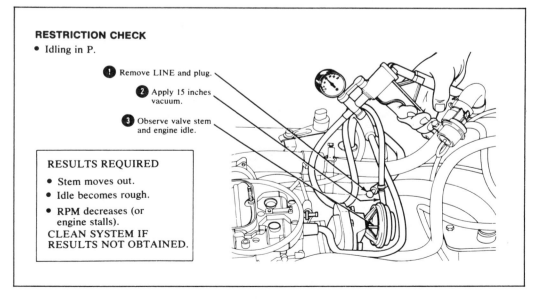

Fig. 9-31. (Ford Motor Co.)

tional check, crack open the throttle and attain an approximate engine rpm of 1,500. Observe the EGR valve stem (Fig. 9-31). The valve stem should move outward. Next, remove the vacuum line hose from the EGR valve diaphragm and plug the end of the hose. Then apply 15 in. of vacuum to the EGR valve at idle with a vacuum tester (Fig. 9-32). The EGR diaphragm should hold vacuum. Engine idle should get rough and engine rpm drop. The engine may even stall.

If the EGR system does not produce the proper test results, then it must be removed for cleaning or replacement.

Should the EGR system be disconnected by a "do-gooder," keep in mind that the modulator at the transmission is no longer in tune with the manifold vacuum. Medium and heavy throttle performance will result in quick shifts and a slipping transmission.

3. On the engine top side, examine the modulator vacuum line and hoses for the following defects:

- Loose connections.
- Hard, brittle, and cracked hoses, especially on high-mileage cars.
- Collapsed, spongy, stretched, or pinched hoses.

When hoses are connected to a fire-wall-mounted vacuum tree, they need enough slack to prevent stretching and closing when the engine rolls on its mounts during heavy throttle shifting.

Be aware of the fact that the hose line to the intake manifold vacuum tree may not collapse and close until the engine gets hot. Depending on when it occurs, a low or high vacuum signal can be trapped on the modulator side of the fault. Usually, a low vacuum trap is producing late and harsh shifts. A high vacuum trap causes sudden quick shifts and transmission slipping.

Modulator vacuum hoses must be a good grade of reinforced hose to prevent collapse problems. Absolutely avoid the use of windshield washer hoses.

- Check the vacuum hoses for correct routing. Are they attached to the proper vacuum fittings?

For example, on a manifold tree, is the modulator hose connected to a large open fitting and not an orificed or metered fitting? Has someone by chance connected the modulator to carburetor venturi vacuum?

In some cases, the modulator vacuum source comes from the distributor vacuum advance supply line. Therefore, any leak in the distributor vacuum diaphragm would upset the vacuum signal to the transmission modulator, resulting in a hard closed throttle downshift clunk and sometimes delayed upshifts. It is essential in this case that a leak down test of the distributor vacuum advance diaphragm becomes part of the check-out procedure.

The vacuum supply to the modulator can be easy to find or it can also be very elusive. The very nature of the vacuum plumbing on top of the engine makes all vacuum circuits interrelated. A leak in a vacuum circuit entirely divorced from the transmission modulator could have an effect on how the modulator controls the transmission. For example, a leak in the distributor vacuum advance or in the headlight door circuit or any vacuum accessory will fool the modulator.

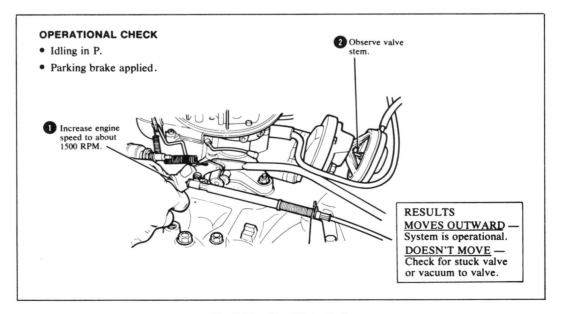

OPERATIONAL CHECK
- Idling in P.
- Parking brake applied.

❷ Observe valve stem.

❶ Increase engine speed to about 1500 RPM.

RESULTS
MOVES OUTWARD — System is operational.
DOESN'T MOVE — Check for stuck valve or vacuum to valve.

Fig. 9-32. (Ford Motor Co.)

The engine load signal can always be by-passed with a "cheating" instrument. A combined hand-operated vacuum pump and gauge applied to the modulator will simulate any desired vacuum condition (Fig. 9-33). The instrument can be extended into the car front seat and manipulated by the technician for road testing and pressure checks. When the normal vacuum supply to the modulator is in doubt, vacuum substitution is a good back-up procedure to verify if the normal supply system is playing games.

Fig. 9-33.   (Ford Motor Co.)

In concluding the discussion on the vacuum supply, let's look at the restricted-line and iced-line affect on the load signal. A healthy supply line is shown in Fig. 9-34, delivering 15 in. of vacuum. When the line is restricted, there is a time delay to changes in engine vacuum on the modulator side of the restriction.

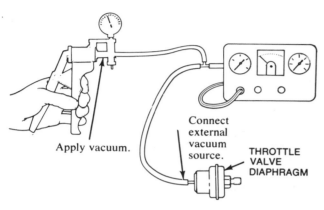

Fig. 9-34.   Healthy vacuum modulator, external circuit.

Eventually, both sides of the restriction will equal engine vacuum if given enough time. Here's what can happen. While waiting at a stoplight, both sides of the restriction are stabilized. With a medium or heavy throttle on the green light, engine vacuum is close to 0 in. and the modulator is temporarily stuck with 15 in. of vacuum. The result is low line pressure and a slipping transmission. This delayed vacuum action is illustrated in Fig. 9-35. The same theory can be applied with forced downshifts.

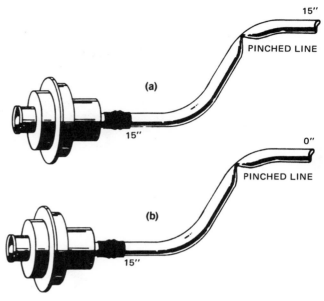

Fig. 9-35.   (a) Vacuum stabilized. (b) Acceleration or load change—delayed vacuum signal.

On icing, the condensation or water accumulation in the vacuum line and modulator will obviously freeze after the engine is shut down. This holds the modulator so that the diaphragm will not function and shuts off the vacuum signal. Modulator vacuum is now 0 in. until the engine and transmission warm-up and thaw the ice (see Fig. 9-36). In the meantime, line pressure is high and the shift schedule is working at its maximum limits. Modulator icing can cause the line pressure to exceed its engineered maximum limits and result in a cracked transmission case or serve cover.

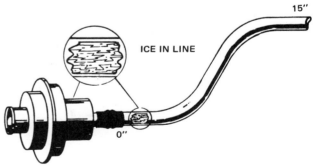

Fig. 9-36.   Modulator at constant zero vacuum.

4. At the modulator, check the physical condition of the vacuum tube and hose connections. Examine the nipple connector between the metal vacuum tube and modulator (Fig. 9-37). Connector ends should be tight and the hose firm but not brittle. If the hose is brittle and cracked or is soft and spongy then a replacement is necessary. Do not use straight hose where molded elbows are required for proper routing (Fig. 9-

Fig. 9-37.

vacuum waves. Should the tube appear satisfactory, send a shot of air through the tube line and recheck the results. The unwanted restriction must be located and eliminated.

Another method that is effective in testing the vacuum response at the modulator is the use of the vacuum gauge. It represents a more scientific approach and leaves no margin of error. With the instrument connected in the modulator line, the idle vacuum at the modulator should be the same as manifold vacuum. If the gauge does not read manifold vacuum, then a misrouted line or vacuum leak is the probable cause. Snap the throttle and observe the gauge needle. The gauge needle must drop and recover with the instant response to engine breathing (Fig. 9-39). If the needle action lags behind throttle action then a vacuum restriction is indicated.

Fig. 9-38.

38); you will pinch the straight hose when it bends the corner and build-in another problem.

5. At the transmission, check the modulator vacuum supply. With the engine running at hot idle, pull the nipple connection off the modulator and listen to the engine response. The engine should speed up or idle rough. If the engine fails to respond, then a restriction exists in the modulator line back to the source of vacuum. If a pinch in the metal tube line is found, it must be replaced. Be careful not to confuse factory built-in tube restrictions designed to dampen modulator diaphragm oscillations caused by manifold

Fig. 9-39.   (Ford Motor Co.)

MANIFOLD VACUUM TO DIAPHRAGM

RESULTS REQUIRED

- AT IDLE — Steady engine vacuum as specified for test altitude.

- MOMENTARY ACCELERATION — Drop quickly; return to idle vacuum.

CHECK VACUUM LINES FOR BREAKS, RESTRICTION, ROUTING IF RESULTS NOT OBTAINED.

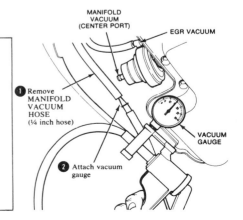

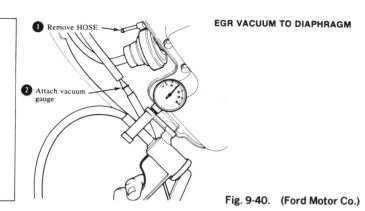

EGR VACUUM TO DIAPHRAGM

1 Remove HOSE

2 Attach vacuum gauge

RESULTS REQUIRED

- AT IDLE — Zero vacuum.

- UP TO HALF-THROTTLE —
  Vacuum increase with
  throttle opening.

CHECK EGR VACUUM SYSTEM
IF RESULTS NOT OBTAINED.

Fig. 9-40. (Ford Motor Co.)

On the dual diaphragm modulators used by Ford with EGR-equipped engines, disconnect the EGR vacuum hose at the modulator and test for vacuum (Fig. 9-40). Vacuum at the EGR port (front diaphragm) should be 0 psi at engine idle and then show a reading at ¼ to ½ throttle. Be sure that the engine is at operating temperature. There is no part throttle specified vacuum reading. The only requirement is that a reading is indicated. EGR system or ported carburetor vacuum is what you are reading. The front diaphragm should work when the EGR system is working.

If the gauge reads a vacuum at idle, then look for a misrouted EGR line.

6. At the transmission, check the modulator unit. At the vacuum port make an analysis of contaminants that may have settled in the diaphragm area. A pipe cleaner inserted into the vacuum port (Fig. 9-41) is effective for gathering contaminant samples.

- Transmission fluid indicates that the diaphragm leaks and must be replaced.
- Water may have accumulated from condensation or been pulled through a loose or cracked hose during a rain storm.

Fig. 9-41.

Once water enters the diaphragm area the spring begins to rust and lose its calibrated tension. A modulator replacement is in order.

- If gasoline is found without the presence of transmission fluid, the modulator should not be changed.

The gasoline gravitated into the area either from an overchoked carburetor or failure of the modulator tube to be routed uphill from the manifold, as illustrated in Fig. 9-42.

If transmission fluid contamination was not found, do not assume the diaphragm is not leaking.

Fig. 9-42.

Attach a vacuum tester to the modulator and draw 20 in. of vacuum. The diaphragm should hold 20 in. for a period of 1 minute (Fig. 9-43). Then test the diapragm at 10 in. for one minute even though it held at 20 in.

Should the vacuum diaphragm check-out prove positive, you may then procede to pressure testing. You must be aware, however, that even though a modulator passes a diaphragm condition analysis, it is not conclusive evidence that the modulator is right.

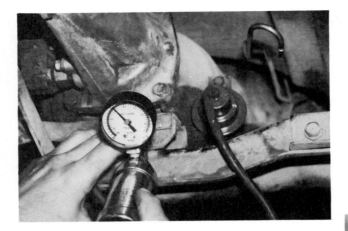

Fig. 9-43.

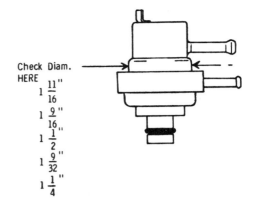

Check Diam.
HERE
$1\frac{11}{16}$"
$1\frac{9}{16}$"
$1\frac{1}{2}$"
$1\frac{9}{32}$"
$1\frac{1}{4}$"

Other considerations are the modulator-calibrated spring tension and diaphragm diameter. They must also be right for the transmission application.

A tight modulator spring results in a higher than normal hydraulic torque signal for the engine vacuum. This will cause high line pressures, late/harsh shifts, and downshift clunks. A soft modulator spring produces an opposite effect and causes low line pressure and early shifts. Medium and heavy throttle shifts result in transmission slipping or sometimes a chatter, and, consequently, burned clutches.

Diaphragm diameters do make a difference. When the diameter is too large for the engineered modulator system, the applied vacuum has an extra draw on the diaphragm. This makes the modulator spring work too light for the engine vacuum signal. End results are low line pressures and early/slipping shifts. Diaphragm diameters on the small side will have the opposite effect—high line pressures accompanied by harsh/late shifts.

How can you absolutely be sure that the modulator spring tension and diameter is right for the transmission? Simply measure the diaphragm diameter on the vacuum can and weigh the spring tension. Ford modulators use four diameter sizes, $1\frac{11}{16}$ in., $1\frac{9}{16}$ in., $1\frac{9}{32}$ in., and $1\frac{1}{2}$ in.; while General Motors uses two diameter sizes, $1\frac{11}{16}$ in. and 2 in. The measurement checkpoints for Ford and GM modulators are illustrated in Figs. 9-44 and 9-45.

Using GM modulators as an example, all $1\frac{11}{16}$ in. and 2 in. vacuum cans will not necessarily have the same calibrated spring tension and, to add to the woes, the $1\frac{11}{16}$ in. and 2 in. vacuum cans are interchangeable. It may not be right for the transmission but they do interchange. Ford has similar problem conditions.

The spring tension is weighed on a common kitchen scale. The technique consists of preconditioning the spring by flexing the diaphragm on the bench

Fig. 9-44. Checking Ford modulator diameters.

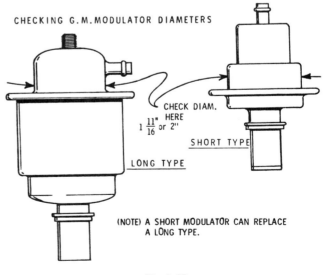

CHECKING G.M. MODULATOR DIAMETERS

CHECK DIAM.
HERE
$1\frac{11}{16}$" or 2"

LONG TYPE

SHORT TYPE

(NOTE) A SHORT MODULATOR CAN REPLACE A LONG TYPE.

Fig. 9-45.

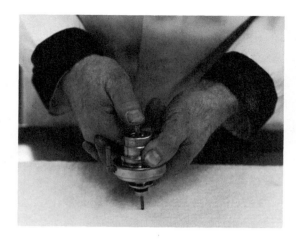

Fig. 9-46.

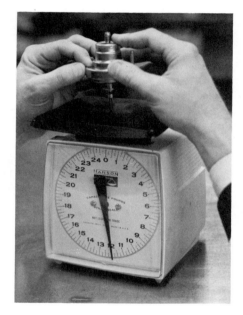

Fig. 9-47.

with thumb on vacuum port (Fig. 9-46) and then pushing the modulator down on the scale (Fig. 9-47) until the push rod just begins to move. This modulator tips the scales at 12 lb.

Measuring and weighing vacuum modulators is a development of Trans Go/Research.* They provide the modulator specifications for all Ford and GM transmission applications.

For GM modulators, a factory-recommended comparison test can be used to check the load of the modulator in question. A Kent-Moore comparison gauge J24466 or an equivalent self-made gauge, as shown in Fig. 9-48, can be used on both the long and short modulators.

*Research, 2621 Merced Avenue, El Monte, CA 91733

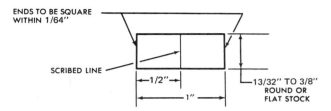

Fig. 9-48. (Hydra-Matic Division, General Motors Corp.)

Check the modulator load as follows, using the gauge in Fig. 9-48.

1. Use a known good modulator with the same part number as the modulator in question. The part numbers are located on the back of the vacuum can.
2. Install the gauge between the ends of the known good modulator and the questionable modulator.
3. Hold the modulators in a horizontal position and gradually squeeze them together on the gauge pin until either modulator sleeve end just touches the center line of the gauge. The gap between the opposite modulator sleeve and the gauge line should be $\frac{1}{16}$ in. or less (Fig. 9-49). A distance greater than $\frac{1}{16}$ in. means that the modulator in question must be replaced (Fig. 9-50).

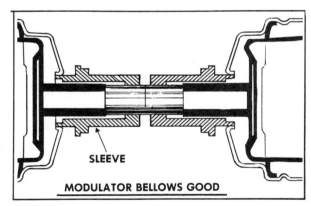

Fig. 9-49.

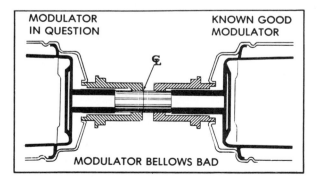

Fig. 9-50.

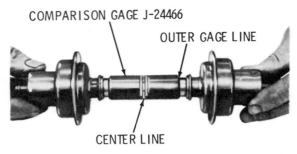

COMPARISON GAGE J-24466

OUTER GAGE LINE

CENTER LINE

Fig. 9-51. (Oldsmobile Division, General Motors Corp.)

The use of comparison gauge J-24466, shown in Fig. 9-51, produces the same results.

Just like its vacuum supply system, modulator vacuum unit faults can be elusive. Even new replacement modulators have proven to be faulty. You might diagnose a faulty modulator, but the replacement might create the same problem or a new problem in the system. You will even find that some adjustable modulators can not be adjusted to specifications. For reliable results, make it a practice to check each replacement modulator for (1) vacuum leaks, (2) correct diameter and transmission application, and (3) correct spring load.

In concluding the discussion on modulators, absolutely avoid setting the diaphragm spring load (adjustable type) out of the specification range for a "softer" shift feel. Any change in the modulator setting not only affects shift feel but also transmission operating pressure. A light spring load, therefore, will result in low operating pressure and major clutch/band failure. The transmission is likely to slip under medium and heavy throttle operation.

PRESSURE TEST PROCEDURE. It has already been emphasized that pressure tests must follow the manufacturers' procedures. Because instrument hookups and test procedures vary between transmission makes, there will be no attempt to discuss individual transmission test requirements except for selected examples. Always consult with the applicable service manual or equivalent for exact procedures and specifications.

PRESSURE TEST INTERPRETATIONS. For discussion purposes, the Ford C-6 and General Motors THM-350 transmissions are selected to feature pressure testing highlights. The C-6 has only one pressure take-off port for testing, which taps into the mainline operating pressure. It is located at the left side of the case in front of the control levers (Fig. 9-52). The THM-350 has three pressure take-off ports, all located on the right side of the case; they are identified in Fig. 9-53. All THM-350 pressure test readings are taken

Fig. 9-52.

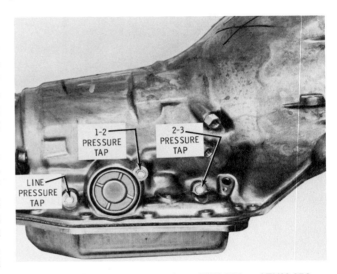

Fig. 9-53. Pressure test tap plugs, THM-350 and THM-250. (Oldsmobile Division, General Motors Corp.)

from the mainline pressure tap. The intermediate and direct clutch circuit taps are used for auxillary testing and are sampled as a back-up to the mainline pressure tests when the intermediate or direct circuits are under suspect.

Mainline pressure readings in both the C-6 and THM-350 will provide a check-out of the pump, throttle or modulator, and governor systems.

Pressure test Chart 9-5 gives the pressure test procedure and applicable specification data for a C-6 transmission. Note that the engine is used as the vacuum source. The drive wheels must be held stationary with the car brakes applied and the car weight on the wheels. Operation below 3 in. of vacuum is a wide-open throttle stall condition; therefore, each test run must be limited to a maximum of 5 sec. followed by a cooling cycle. To cool the transmission, place the

CHART 9-5
Ford C-6 Typical Line Pressure Specifications*

| Trans. Type | Vacuum Diaphragm Type and Ident. | Range | Manifold Vacuum | | | | | | W.O.T. Thru Detent |
| | | | Idle | | | | | | |
			15" & Above	14"	13"	12"	11"	10"	
C6	SAD 1 Black Stripe	D, 2, 1	53-88	74-94	80-100	86-106	92-112	98-118	151-180
		R	66-138	116-147	125-156	135-166	144-175	153-184	236-295
		P, N	53-88	74-94	80-100	86-106	92-112		
C6	SAD 1 Purple Stripe	D, 2, 1	53-75	62-82	69-89	76-96	83-102	89-109	150-180
		R	66-118	97-128	108-139	119-149	129-160	140-171	235-295
		P, N	53-75	62-82	69-89	76-96	83-102		
C6	SAD 1 Green Stripe	D, 2, 1	53-60	53-60	53-72	61-80	69-88	77-97	149-180
		R	66-88	70-100	82-113	95-126	108-138	120-151	233-295
		P, N	53-60	53-60	53-72	61-80	69-88		
C6	HAD Plain Sea Level Bar = 29.5	D, 2, 1	53-75	62-82	69-89	76-96	83-102	89-109	150-180
		R	66-118	97-128	108-139	119-149	129-160	140-171	235-295
		P, N	53-75	62-82	69-89	76-96	83-102		

*Line Pressure Specifications (Control PSI) With Governor Pressure at Zero (Oil Temperature — 150°-200°F)
SAD: Single Area Diaphragm
S-SAD: Extra Large Single Area Diaphragm
HAD: High Altitude Diaphragm
S-HAD: Extra Large High Altitude Diaphragm
Using absolute barometric pressures:
(1) Determine the difference between the baseline, absolute barometric pressure of 29.25 and the absolute barometric pressure for the area.
(2) For the HAD device, multiply the result of (1) by 3. (C4) or by 3.62 (C6). For the S-HAD device, multiply the result of (1) by 4. (C4).
(3) For an absolute barometric pressure greater than the baseline barometric pressure, add the result of (2) to the given "D" and "P, N" specifications for the 29.75 to 28.75 barometric pressure range.
For an absolute barometric pressure less than the baseline barometric pressure, subtract the result of (2) from the given "D" and "P, N" specifications for the 29.75 to 28.75 barometric pressure range.

Pressure Test

| Engine RPM | Manifold Vacuum In-Hg | Throttle | Range | PSI | |
				Record Actual	Record Spec.
Idle	Above 15	Closed	P		
			N		
			D		
			2		
			1		
			R		
As Required	10	As Required	D,2,1		
As Required	Below 3	Wide Open	D		
			2		
			1		
			R		

selector in (N) and run the engine at 1,000 rpm for at least 30 sec.

As an alternate method for setting the required vacuum levels, tee a hand-operated vacuum pump tester into the transmission tester vacuum line where it can be adjusted and controlled from the driver seat (Fig. 9-54). Using the vacuum pump tester avoids running the pressure tests at the high stall engine rpm required to pull the vacuum down to the 10 in. or 3 in. levels. Transmission heating and the cooling time between tests is reduced. The idle speed pressure tests remain the same. At 10 in. and 3 in., however, the test runs are made at 1,000 engine rpm.

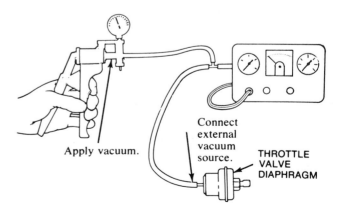

Apply vacuum.

Connect external vacuum source.

THROTTLE VALVE DIAPHRAGM

Fig. 9-54. (Ford Motor Co.)

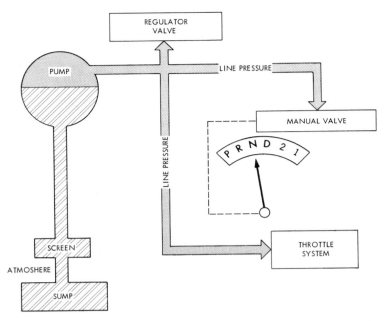

Fig. 9-55. Basic neutral circuit.

Once accurate test results are obtained, the test data can be analyzed to identify the problem area and to verify the parts of the hydraulic system that are meeting specifications and working right. When test results show abnormal pressure, referral can be made to the applicable pressure diagnosis chart provided by the manufacturer. Chart 9-6 applies to Ford transmissions. Chart interpretation and location of the problem still depends on your knowledge of hydraulic system operation and some common sense deductions.

Because the hydraulic systems of all automatic transmissions are closely alike, a general analysis of the information that C-6 pressure tests provide can be applied to other transmissions.

At engine idle. The tests at idle produce the biggest stress on the pump circuit for delivering volume and operating pressures; therefore, engine idle or low rpm conditions are excellent for analyzing the pump circuit for pump wear or circuit leaks.

Beginning or existing pump circuit problems can be detected with an isolation test in P and N. The manual valve has the pump output shut-off from distribution to all clutch/band circuits and the governor circuit (Fig. 9-55). In the C-6, the throttle circuit must be cancelled out to eliminate any possibility of a TV boost at the regulator valve. This is done by drawing the vacuum down to 20 in. With TV pressure now at 0 psi, the pump is strictly working against the fixed spring tension of the regulating valve. Pressure readings should be at the low side of the specifications; refer to Chart 9-5. The reason for the high and low side of the specifications is the fact that the throttle

system is still delivering a boost signal to the regulator valve up to 18 in. of vacuum in most cases. You cannot allow a TV boost signal for an isolated pump circuit test.

If the pressure readings in P and N are normal, then the following is right about the hydraulic system.

- The suction side of the pump circuit is OK
- The pump gears and assembly casting are OK
- The pressure delivery side of the circuit is OK
- The pressure regulator valve is OK

It is important in pressure testing to establish that the pump system has normal capabilities. If the pump system is not right, then other systems and circuits will not be right and can falsely be diagnosed as the problem area.

If the P and N pressure readings are low, the other ranges can also be expected to read low. Refer to the diagnosis Chart 9-6 for suggested problem cause in the pump circuit. Be sure the filter is not restricted and re-torque the valve body to the case bolts to check for looseness. Should it be necessary to pull the transmission for further investigation, re-torque the pump to the case bolts to check for looseness. All parts of the pump system must be treated as a potential suspect area. Be careful to approach the problem solution starting with the easy and accessible checkout points first.

Don't be fooled if the pressure readings at the 10 in. and 3 in. vacuum level are normal. The higher engine or pump rpm can sometimes overcome the pump circuit pressure deficiency indicated at idle.

CHART 9-6, TROUBLE SHOOTING CHART (FORD MOTOR CO.)

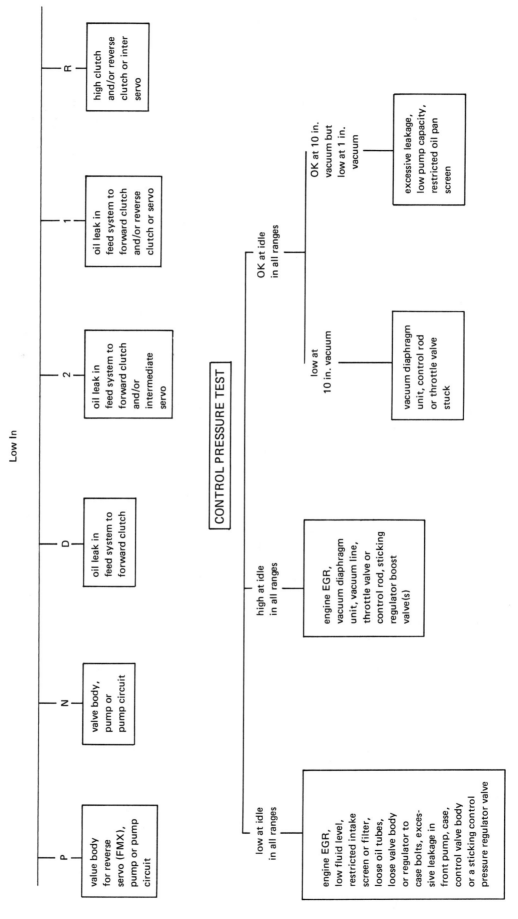

CONTROL PRESSURE TEST

Low In

P
value body for reverse servo (FMX), pump or pump circuit

N
valve body, pump or pump circuit

D
oil leak in feed system to forward clutch

2
oil leak in feed system to forward clutch and/or intermediate servo

1
oil leak in feed system to forward clutch and/or reverse clutch or servo

R
high clutch and/or reverse clutch or inter servo

CONTROL PRESSURE TEST

low at idle in all ranges
engine EGR, low fluid level, restricted intake screen or filter, loose oil tubes, loose valve body or regulator to case bolts, excessive leakage in front pump, case, control valve body or a sticking control pressure regulator valve

high at idle in all ranges
engine EGR, vacuum diaphragm unit, vacuum line, throttle valve or control rod, sticking regulator boost valve(s)

OK at idle in all ranges

low at 10 in. vacuum
vacuum diaphragm unit, control rod or throttle valve stuck

OK at 10 in. vacuum but low at 1 in. vacuum
excessive leakage, low pump capacity, restricted oil pan screen

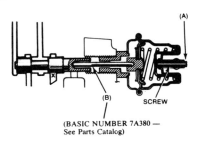

CHANGING DIAPHRAGM PRESSURE SETTING

- Adjust ONLY if all pressures are high or low.

- Do not set below specified pressure for shift feel.

SCREW-IN DIAPHRAGM

- In to increase; out to decrease (A).

- One turn = 2-3 psi.

PUSH-IN DIAPHRAGM

- Change selective rod (B).

- Longer to increase; shorter to decrease.

- Each rod increment = 5-6 psi.

(BASIC NUMBER 7A380 —
See Parts Catalog)

Fig. 9-56. (Ford Motor Co.)

Should the P and N idle pressures read 0 psi or almost 0, the most likely problem area is the pressure regulator valve stuck in the exhaust position. A worn pump will always develop a pressure head even though it cannot meet specification requirements. Low pressures cannot furnish the muscle to hold a band or a clutch and the transmission slips. Obviously, at 0 psi the vehicle fails to move.

Idle pressure tests in P and N can be used as a checkout of the throttle system regulated output. Because the pressure boost valve is sensitive to throttle pressure, it makes sense that a mainline pressure reading isolated from the clutch and band circuits can reflect throttle system output.

If test pressure is high at idle in P and N, the other ranges can be expected to read high. Even at 20 in., the throttle system has not cancelled out. Consult the diagnosis Chart 9-6 for suggested problem causes in the throttle circuit. Do not overlook an improper vacuum modulator application or calibrated modulator spring tension. Don't let the modulator fool you. What you are going to find is unknown but you must hunt until the cause is found. At least you know that the transmission does not need to be removed and disassembled for inspection. This is an in-the-car fix. And, hopefully, the modulator diaphragm was checked for leakage before going through all this trouble.

It is also important to verify at what point the throttle system cuts-in. Gradually drop the vacuum from 20 in. until it is observed that the mainline pressure starts to rise from the throttle boost effect. The throttle system cut-in point should occur before the vacuum drops below 17 in. on the C-6 transmission.

The cut-in point can be adjusted by changing the modulator spring load setting (Fig. 9-56). If the adjustment cannot be attained, then you should consider installing a new modulator.

Further check-out of the throttle system continues with the pressure rise checks.

Pressure rise check at 10 in. If the pressure does not increase as the vacuum drops to 10 in., then the push rod to the throttle valve is probably missing. This means that the spring force cannot be relayed to the throttle valve and TV pressure is 0 psi.

If the pressure does increase but remains low, then a modulator adjustment might correct the problem. The modulator cut-in point, however, must remain correct; otherwise, a replacement modulator unit must be considered.

With a good cut-in point and proper operating pressure at 10 in., it is reasonable to believe that the pump and throttle systems are both right.

Pressure rise check at 1 in. Correct pressures at 10 in. will usually mean good pressures at 1 in. Should the pressures prove to be low, then a restricted suction screen is a high suspect item, or possibly excessive leakage in the pump circuit resulting in low pump capacity. The pump is not worn out. The extra high boost pressures can open up hairline fractures in the pump or valve body castings or even blow past defective or loose gasket areas, for example, the pump to case gasket.

Special pressure test considerations. Low pressures at idle in the D, 2, and 1 ranges (only) can be caused by excessive leakage in the governor circuit. In D, 2, and 1, the manual valve routes mainline pump pressure to the governor (Fig. 9-57). Severely worn governor rings, stuck governor valving, loose governor body bolts, or loose valve body to case bolts represent possible problem areas.

Clutch and band circuits are usually metered before the apply oil reaches the clutch or servo unit. Where the mainline pressure test is supposed to be reading the circuit, it will tell you what is happening up to the orifice but nothing about the circuit from the orifice to the clutch or servo unit. For example, at idle

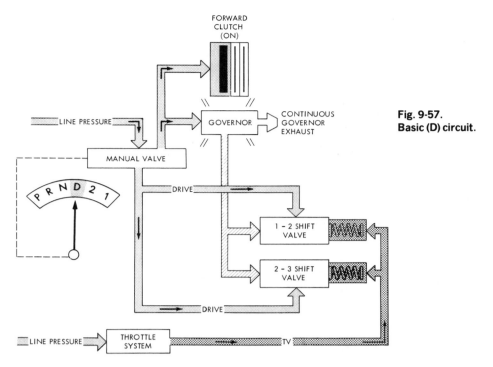

Fig. 9-57.
Basic (D) circuit.

in D range, the forward clutch circuit is introduced into the mainline pressure reading (Fig. 9-58). The pressure will read normal and will not show any pressure losses from leaking piston seals or oil rings beyond the control orifice. The orifice makes it possible for the pump to maintain its pressure head. A good reading in this case only identifies that a good pressure head is feeding the forward clutch circuit up to the orifice.

C-6 governor system test. A branch of the throttle pressure circuit to the pressure regulator boost valve is routed through a cut-back control valve. At the cut-back valve, the throttle pressure holds the valve up against governor pressure and is relayed to the pressure boost valve (Fig. 9-59). Depending on the aggressiveness of the throttle foot, the governor pressure shifts the cut-back control valve at some point between 10–50 mph (16–81 km/h)

Fig. 9-58. Basic forward clutch circuit.

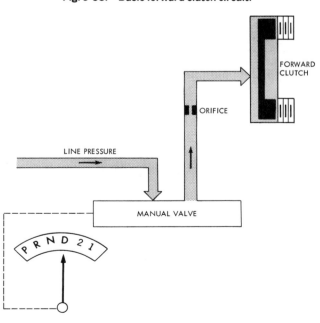

Fig. 9-59. Throttle boost circuit. (Ford Motor Co.)

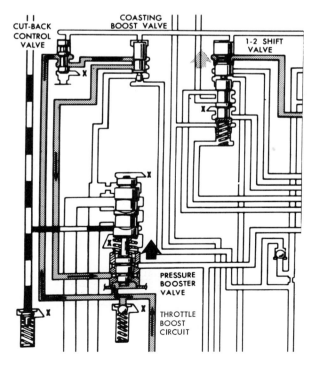

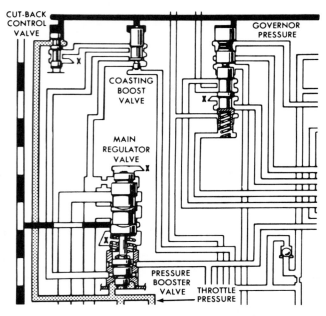

Fig. 9-60. Cut-back control valve operation.

When the cut-back control valve is shifted, throttle pressure is cut-off from part of the pressure boost valve and the mainline pressure drops (Fig. 9-60). This pressure drop can be identified on the pressure gauge and, therefore, the governor system operation can be tested in the shop off the mainline pressure tap.

To prepare for the test:

1. Hook-up the transmission tester or equivalent instrumentation as described earlier under pressure testing.

2. Isolate the engine vacuum from the modulator and provide an external vacuum control (Fig. 9-61).

3. Support the rear axle on a hoist or floor stands to clear the drive wheels off the ground. Drive wheels must be free to turn.

To run the test:

1. Never exceed 60 mph (96 km/h)

2. Place the selector in the 2 range and procede to test the governor system under moderate and heavy loads as outlined in Fig. 9-62.

If the cutback speeds check-out OK, then the governor system is right.

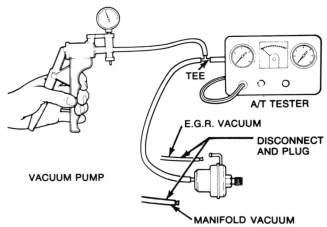

Fig. 9-61. (Ford Motor Co.)

Fig. 9-62. (Ford Motor Co.)

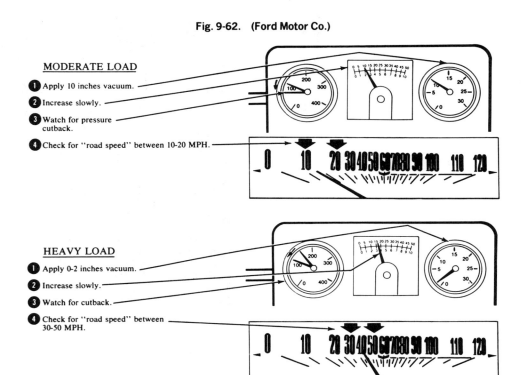

The same test procedure and test results are applicable to the C-3 and C-4 transmissions.

THM 350. Pressure test Chart 9-7 gives the pressure test procedure and applicable specification data for a THM-350 transmission. Refer to Fig. 9-53 for location of pressure take-off ports. Again, all pressure test data will basically come from the mainline pressure port.

There will be no attempt to expand into a detailed discussion but only to point out some test features. We have here another example when mainline pressure test readings can be used to analyze the pump, modulator, governor, detent, and clutch circuits. The modulator valve output is sensitive to the governor and detent system pressures and, therefore, they can be reflected in the mainline pressures (Fig. 9-63) and Chart 9-7.

In working with the THM-350 pressure tests, you will find that you can run an isolated pump and modulator check-out. At 20 in. of vacuum, selector range in N, and preferably using idle rpm:

• *Pump Test.* Modulator pressure is 0 psi and pump system is closed off from the clutch and band circuits. The pump only needs to work against the regulator valve spring. Even at idle, the pump system should read 60–70 psi (412–482 kPa).

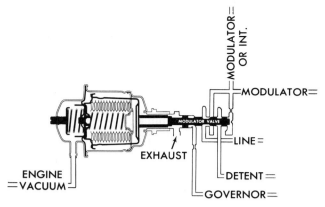

Fig. 9-63. THM-350 modulator valve system. (Oldsmobile Division, General Motors Corp.)

• *Modulator Test.* Gradually drop the vacuum while observing the pressure gauge. Although there is no available data, note when the modulator cuts-in and the mainline pressure begins to rise. The cut-in point must be right and can only be determined by your own data collected from experience with known comparable systems. Cut-in points will vary from approximately 17.5–12.8 in. As the vacuum continues to drop, the mainline pressure should rise steadily until it peaks at about 4 in. The pressure reading should be approximately 160 psi (1,100 kPa).

CHART 9-7,
THM-350 Typical Transmission Malfunction Related to Oil Pressure

Drive Brakes Applied 1000 RPM	Reverse Brakes Applied 1000 RPM	Super or Lo Brakes Applied 1000 RPM	Neutral Brakes Applied 1000 RPM	Drive 1000 RPM Brakes on Detent* Activated	Drive Idle	(1) Drive 30 MPH Closed Throttle	0" vacuum to modulator. Drive—from 1000 to 3000 RPM Wheels free to move	Pressure Test Conditions
60-70	90	90	60-70	90-110 20"vacuum	60-70	60-70	Pressure drop of 10 PSI or more	Normal Results Note (2)
160	250	160	160 LINE OFF 0" VACUUM		160		DROP	Malfunction in Control Valve Assembly
							NO DROP	Malfunction in Governor or Governor Feed System
ALL HIGH BUT LESS THAN 35 PSI							—	Malfunction in Detent System
ALL HIGH MORE THAN 35 PSI							—	Manfunction in Modulator
	Low				—	Low to Normal	—	Oil Leak in Feed System to the Direct Clutch
Low	Low to Normal		Low to Normal		—	Low to Normal	—	Oil Leak in Feed System to the Forward Clutch
			Low				—	Detent System

A blank space = Normal pressure
A dash (—) in space = Pressure reading has no meaning
 (1) Coast from 30 mph — read before reaching 20 mph
 (2) If high line pressures are experienced see "High Line Pressures" note.
 * Cable pulled or blocked thru detent position

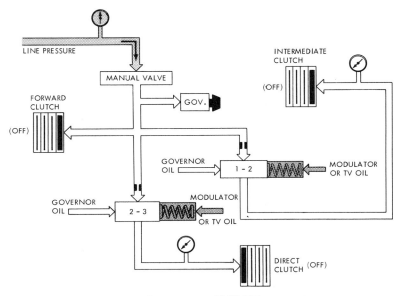

Fig. 9-64. Pressure test THM-350—neutral.

Although pressure readings are given for vacuum conditions above 15 in., run them also at 0 in. to verify the complete boost action at the regulator valve. For example, if the modulator circuit check ball was missing, it would be difficult to diagnose because all the readings above 15 in. would still be normal.

For a complete analysis on the clutch circuits, pressure take-off ports are provided for the intermediate and direct clutch circuits. These circuits are metered and the only way to know what is happening between the orifice and clutch is to make pressure tap provisions. A series of simplified illustrations shows how all three gauges working together can make a check-out of the clutch circuits to determine if they are hydraulically right.

• *Neutral* (Fig. 9-64). Pressure gauge (1) reads the pump system pressure head. Line pressure to the clutches is isolated by the manual valve.

• *Drive* with brakes applied (Fig. 9-65). Pressure gauge 1 reads the forward clutch circuit and governor feed circuit. The THM-350 forward clutch circuit is not metered through an orifice; however, experience has proven that the pressure gauge will not usually reflect conditions at the clutch oil rings and piston seals. Line pressure to the intermediate and direct clutches is isolated at the shift valves.

• *Drive* or *L2* with rear wheels off the ground (Fig. 9-66). Pressure gauge 1 reads the line pressure to the intermediate circuit metering orifice. Pressure

Fig. 9-65. Pressure test—THM-350—forward clutch circuit.

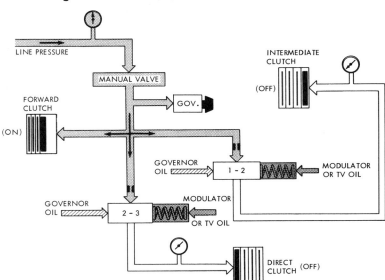

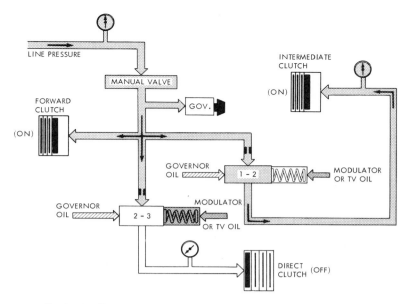

Fig. 9-66. Pressure test—THM-350—intermediate clutch circuit.

gauge 2 reads line pressure from the metering orifice to the clutch and verifies that the shift valve has opened. Preferably gauges 1 and 2 should read the same or within 3 psi (22 kPa). Excessive pressure loss indicated on gauge 2 usually indicates defective piston seals. Other possibilities are defects in the pump casting or pump gasket to case.

• *Drive* with rear wheels off the ground (Fig. 9-67). Pressure gauge 1 reads the line pressure to the direct clutch circuit metering orifice. Pressure gauge (3) reads line pressure from the metering orifice to the clutch and verifies that the shift valve has opened. Preferably gauges 1 and 3 should read the same or within 3 psi. Excessive pressure loss usually indicates defective piston seals or clutch oil rings. Other possi-

bilities are defects in the pump casting or pump gasket to case.

In a special problem situation, a THM-350 had normal shift patterns and performance for the first 5–10 road miles (8–16 km). It would then downshift 3-2 while cruising and the shift patterns became unstable. Eventually, the transmission would not even engage high gear. After a rest period, the same sequence of events would repeat. The fluid level was OK and fluid condition healthy. A pressure test in the shop using all three gauges was performed. This included a check-out of modulator and governor systems in addition to the pump and clutch circuits. Pressure tests met specifications, but keep in mind that the vehicle had an opportunity to rest before pressures were taken. The

Fig. 9-67. Pressure test—THM-350—direct clutch circuit.

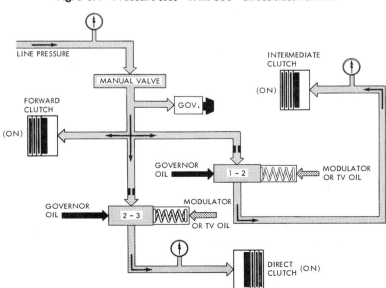

decision was to take the car on the road with the gauges in place and extended in the car front seat for observation. When the critical road mileage was reached, the transmission downshifted 3–2, only this time the direct clutch pressure gauge produced the necessary clue. The pressure gauge reading dropped to 0 psi. So what did this mean? Let's look at some deductions and the final conclusion.

1. It is a certainty that the shift valve has good movement and is not stuck.

2. The problem is related to the direct clutch circuit.

3. With a pressure drop to 0 psi, the shift valve had to shut the circuit down. Even extensive leakage at the clutch piston seals or oil rings would not produce a 0 psi pressure condition.

4. If the 2–3 shift valve closed, the shift valve spring had to close the valve against governor pressure. Modulator pressure is not effective on the shift valve once the shift is made; therefore, modulator oil is not a factor in the problem.

It should be evident that the governor system is at fault. A healthy governor pressure dropped significantly to allow the 2–3 valve spring to close the valve, but not low enough for the 1–2 shift valve to close. Investigation into the governor circuit found contaminants in the governor filter screen. The problem was located and corrected with the transmission in the car.

REVIEW QUESTIONS

CHAPTER 9
PRINCIPLES OF DIAGNOSIS

I. Diagnosis Procedure

Outline the basic six step approach to automatic transmission problem diagnosis.

- _____
- _____
- _____
- _____
- _____
- _____

II. Fluid Level and Fluid Condition

1. Rule number one is: Never assume that another's fluid

   check is _____. Do it yourself.

2. Outline the basic three step procedure for checking the fluid level.

   - _____
   - _____
   - _____

3. Some fluid level check procedures might deviate from the basic procedure.
   - The Chrysler 727 and 904 Torqueflite transmissions

   must be checked with the selector in _____.
   - The General Motors THM-125 is checked with the

   selector in _____ without moving through the operating ranges.
   A cold check in this transmission will read (above) (below) the add mark.

4. When the sample fluid on the dipstick is too hot for the

   fingers, it is at _____ temperature.

5. The "Add" mark on the dipstick means add one (quart) (pint) of fluid.

6. List some typical problems that can be caused by low fluid level.

   - _____
   - _____
   - _____
   - _____

7. When the fluid color looks like a strawberry milkshake,

   it is contaminated with _____.

8. Fluid contaminated with engine coolant requires a complete overhaul of the transmission. True ☐ False ☐

III. Quick Check of Engine Idle, Vacuum Lines, Transmission and Carburetor Linkage

1. List some typical problems caused by abnormally high engine idle.

   • _____

   • _____

2. When inspecting linkage be sure to check the carburetor

   for wide open _____.

3. List some quick check point items when inspecting the vacuum line routing to modulator.

   • _____

   • _____

   • _____

4. On manifold vacuum trees, the modulator vacuum line must be coupled to a (metered) (wide open) fitting.

5. The manifold EGR system can be checked out with the engine hot or cold. True ☐ False ☐

6. The EGR valve stem should begin to move when engine speed is increased from idle to approximately (1,500 rpm) (2,500 rpm).

7. Electrically controlled forced downshift or detent systems can be checked out with the car radio. True ☐ False ☐

IV. Stall Test

1. The purpose of the stall test is to determine:

   _____ a. Transmission band and clutch holding ability.

   _____ b. Engine power output.

   _____ c. Torque converter operation.

   _____ d. All of the above choices; a, b, and c

2. Each stall test run must be limited to:

   _____ a. 5 seconds

   _____ b. 10 seconds

   _____ c. 15 seconds

   _____ d. 30 seconds

3. Between each stall test run, the transmission must be run in (N) with the engine at fast idle for at least:

   _____ a. 5 seconds

   _____ b. 15 seconds

   _____ c. 30 seconds

   _____ d. one minute

4. The stall test specification for an engine is given as 1,800—2,000 rpm.

   The actual stall speed test reading is 950 rpm.

   What is the likely problem?

   _____

5. Briefly explain why a frozen stator cannot be determined with a stall test.

   _____

   _____

6. Very poor low speed acceleration or performance is very likely caused by a (frozen) (freewheeling) stator.

7. When top vehicle speed at W.O.T. is greatly reduced, the likely cause is a (frozen) (freewheeling) stator.

8. A frozen stator can be determined by placing the

   manual selector in _____ and depressing the accelerator to W.O.T. If the engine cannot exceed ap-

   proximately _____ rpm then the stator is frozen.

9. Extreme fluid temperatures are caused by a (frozen) (freewheeling) stator.

V. Road Test—Clutch and Band Diagnosis

TYPICAL 3-SPEED CLUTCH AND BAND APPLICATION CHART

Operating Range	Forward Clutch	Direct Clutch	Intermediate Band	L & R Band	Low Roller Clutch
Park/Neutral					
Reverse		ON		ON	
Drive—1st	ON				HOLDING
2nd	ON		ON		
3rd	ON				
(2) —1st	ON				HOLDING
2nd	ON		ON		
(1)	ON			ON	HOLDING

RELATED CLUTCH/BAND PROBLEMS

PROBLEM 1

• Transmission engagement is soft in all forward ranges (D), (2), (1).

• Transmission slips in all forward ranges (D), (2), (1) and in advanced stages there is no drive in the forward ranges.

• The transmission performs OK in (R).

Likely failure?

_____

PROBLEM 2

- Transmission slips or fails to move the vehicle in (D) or (2) ranges, only.
- Manual (1) provides a good start.
- The transmission performs OK in (R).

Likely failure?

_____

PROBLEM 3

- Transmission forward ranges (D), (2), (1) test OK.
- Vehicle moves forward in (N).
- Transmission locks-up in (R).

Likely failure?

_____

PROBLEM 4

- The transmission has a positive first gear start in (D), (2), (1).
- The transmission skips second gear (D) and shifts 1-3. Should the 1-2 shift occur it may be drawn out, slip or bump.
- When the selector is moved from (D) range to (2) range there will be no downshift to second gear. A freewheeling coast sensation is felt in the, "seat of the pants".
- 3-2 forced downshifts will slip entirely or result in a slip and bump affair while engaging second gear.
- The transmission performs OK in (R).

Likely failure?

_____

PROBLEM 5

- The transmission 1st and 2nd gears give good positive action.
- On the 2-3 shift in (D) an engine flare-up might occur before engagement, the shift may be long and drawn out, or it may not occur.
- Reverse may slip, chatter, have a no drive condition, or even appear to work normal.

Likely failure?

_____

PROBLEM 6

- Transmission starts out in 2nd gear (D) range and locks-up on the 2-3 shift.
- The transmission also locks-up in (R) range and (1) range.
- (2) range starts out in second gear.
- (N) range is OK.

Likely failure?

_____

PROBLEM 7

- Slip, chatter, or no drive in (R).
- Manual low (1) range has no braking during coast.

Likely failure?

_____

PROBLEM 8

- On Ford Motor Company 3-speed rear drive transmissions, the practice is to have a second gear start in the (2) range and keep the transmission locked into 2nd. Should the intermediate band fail to hold then the transmission would fail to move the vehicle in (2). True ☐ False ☐

Briefly explain:_____

_____

V. Road Test—Mechanical Noise Analysis

PROBLEM 1

- Transmission unusual noise factor is very audible in first gear all forward ranges.
- In second gear the noise factor cuts back and in direct drive it disappears.
- Reverse operation may or may not produce an unusual noise.
- (N) may or may not produce an unusual noise.

Likely problem area?

_____

PROBLEM 2

- Transmission produces no unusual noise in first gear all forward ranges and in (R) range.
- The noise factor starts in second gear and continues with increase intensity and speed rythm in direct.
- (N) may or may not produce an unusual noise.

Likely problem area?

_____

V. Road Test—Erratic Shift Analysis

In the absence of shift data, the following guidelines can be used.
Minimum Upshifts at Almost Closed Throttle;

1-2 Upshift at _____ mph; 2-3 Upshift at _____ mph
Closed Throttle Downshifts

3-2 at _____ mph; 2-1 at _____ mph or 3-1 at

_____ mph

PROBLEM 1

- The minimum 1-2 and 2-3 shift speeds are higher than normal.
- The closed throttle downshift 3-1 occurs at 5 mph.

Likely shift system problem area?

_____

PROBLEM 2

- Transmission starts out in high gear.

Likely shift system problem area?

_____

PROBLEM 3

- The minimum 1-2 and 2-3 shift speeds occur at 10 mph and 18 mph.
- The closed throttle downshift 3-1 occurs at 5 mph.
- Medium and heavy throttle shifts occur early along with transmission slipping.
- Attempts at part throttle and forced downshifts results in transmission slipping.

Likely shift system problem area?

_____

PROBLEM 4

- Transmission minimum 2-3 shift occurs erractically between 30-60 mph.
- It is not unusual for the transmission to downshift to 2nd gear when the vehicle speed drops to 40 mph.

Likely shift system problem area?

_____

PROBLEM 5

- Transmission stays in first gear and fails to upshift regardless of vehicle speed.

Likely shift system problem area?

_____

VI—Pressure Testing

If mainline pressure regulation is sensitive to vehicle speed then it is possible to analyse three systems from a single mainline pressure tap. They are:

- _____
- _____
- _____

CHECKING THE VACUUM SUPPLY AND MODULATOR AS A PRELIMINARY TO DIAGNOSING ERRATIC TRANSMISSION OPERATION AND PRESSURE TESTING.

1. When checking for the effective vacuum on the modulator it should be checked with a vacuum gauge at the (modulator) (engine manifold).
2. When the vacuum line is disconnected at the modulator, engine idle rpm should (increase) (decrease).
3. Windshield washer hose is an acceptable substitute for modulator vacuum hose. True ☐ False ☐
4. With a 15 inch vacuum supply applied to the EGR valve at idle, engine idle rpm should (increase) (decrease).
5. When the vacuum line is connected to a vacuum tree connector it should be connected to a (metered) (wide open) fitting.
6. It is acceptable to connect the vacuum line to carburetor venturi vacuum. True ☐ False ☐
7. It is acceptable to connect the vacuum line to the vehicle vacuum reservoir supply. True ☐ False ☐
8. Evidence of fuel at the modulator diaphragm means that the modulator should be replaced. True ☐ False ☐
9. A leaky diaphragm in the distributor vacuum advance might have an effect on the modulator vacuum signal. True ☐ False☐
10. To prove that a modulator unit is right for the transmission it must pass a three point checkout. List the checkout points.

- _____
- _____
- _____

11. On dual diaphragm Ford modulators 1973-76; the EGR vacuum at the modulator should read zero at closed throttle. True ☐ False ☐
12. A modulator application using too large a diaphragm diameter will cause late and harsh shifting. True ☐ False ☐
13. If the modulator spring weight or tension is too weak, then the transmission will shift early and slip. True ☐ False ☐
14. If the modulator part number is right for the transmission application, then the spring weight or tension can be considered to be right. True ☐ False ☐
15. An iced modulator would typically cause a maximum delayed shift pattern. True ☐ False ☐
16. An unwanted restriction in the vacuum line would typically cause a delayed shift pattern. True ☐ False ☐
17. A disconnected vacuum line at the modulator will cause maximum delayed shifts. True ☐ False ☐
18. An unwanted restriction in the vacuum line would cause transmission slippage with medium and heavy throttle performance. True ☐ False ☐

19. (Altitude compensated) A punctured bellows would cause delayed and harsh shifts. True ☐ False ☐

20. Modulator operation has a direct bearing on the transmission shift schedule and quality. True ☐ False ☐

21. Modulator operation has a direct bearing on the transmission operating pressure. True ☐ False ☐

22. A poor performing engine will result in an early shift schedule and slipping transmission. True ☐ False ☐

23. Most erratic shift problems are modulator system problems. True ☐ False ☐

BRIEFLY EXPLAIN:

How could you prove that the vacuum delivery system to the modulator is not right.

VI—Pressure Test Interpretations

1. If the mainline pressure tests in all ranges meet specifications it identifies for sure that two basic systems or circuits are right. They are:

    ● _____

    ● _____

2. To run an isolated pump circuit test in (P) and (N) the throttle or modulator systems must be arranged to produce (zero) (full) output.

3. During the isolated pump circuit test in (P) and (N) the mainline operating pressure is determined by the fixed

    _____ on the pressure regulator valve.

4. If the pressure reading is too high during an isolated pump circuit test in (P) and (N) the probable cause is an

    internal problem in the _____ circuit.

5. If the (P) and (N) pressure readings are low, the other range pressures can also be expected to read low. True ☐ False ☐

6. If test pressure is high during an isolated pump circuit test in (P) and (N), the other range pressures can also be expected to read high. True ☐ False ☐

7. If the pressure doesn't increase as vacuum is dropped or throttle travel is increased, then the probable cause is an

    internal problem in the _____ circuit.

8. The highest pressure readings occur when testing

    _____ operating range.

9. When the governor circuit can be tested from the transmission mainline pressure tap, specifications will call for a pressure (drop) (increase).

10. If the operating pressure is zero or almost zero, the most likely cause is a _____.

BRIEFLY EXPLAIN:

A mainline pressure tap reading will not usually show a low reading because of a pressure loss or excessive leakage at a clutch or servo unit.

10

AUTOMATIC TRANSMISSION SERVICE

Automatic transmission service requires a high standard of reliable workmanship. The technician must be able to give attention to detail, use proper tooling, follow exact specifications, and work in extra clean surroundings. The technician will find that automatic transmissions are easy to service. The same basic skills developed in the servicing of engines, manual transmissions, and clutches are definite assets and easily transfer over to automatic transmission service. Your work habits will be directly related to your success: how often do you fix the problem on the first try.

The chapter does not eliminate the need for factory repair manuals. For detailed step-by-step instructions and specifications on the repair and overhaul of a particular automatic transmission, the best policy is to consult the manufacturer's shop manual or equivalent. Our goal is to add to the shop manual instruction, highlighting basic overhaul practices and tricks of the trade that will insure a winner.

TRANSMISSION OVERHAUL

If driving conditions were always ideal, the transmission would easily last 100,000 miles. An overhaul would seldom be needed. Ideal conditions, however, seldom prevail and thousands of automatic transmissions break down every year. Most of these failures are caused by excess heat build-up, which attacks the transmission fluid and forms gum and varnish contaminants. Typical end results are no forward, no reverse, slipping shifts, and so on.

Many driving conditions considered to be normal can be quite severe and contribute to overheating. Daily bumper to bumper traffic to and from work, pulling trailers and a full house of passengers and overflow luggage strapped to roof racks are just some examples of everyday traffic. The transmission cooler located in the radiator cannot always handle these severe conditions. Depending on the overheating temperature, a slow or sometimes sudden breakdown of the transmission can occur. Rocking a stuck car back and forth in snow or mud for just a few minutes can generate extremely high temperatures at the friction elements and destroy a transmission. Automatic transmission overhaul is a needed service and a big business. Your skills are needed.

In most cases, it is obvious when a transmission suffers a serious problem and requires an overhaul. The most common tipoff comes from a foul smelling dipstick and varnished fluid, which means that the clutches and bands have already suffered overheating and damage. If the fluid has its normal color and is at the correct level the transmission problem can usually be fixed with an in-the-car repair. Under these circumstances, avoid any quick decision to overhaul and try to discover the exact problem through systematic diagnosis.

Fig. 10-2.

TRANSMISSION REMOVAL

The transmission and converter are removed as an assembly (Fig. 10-1). When removing the transmission, here are some important guidelines to follow:

1. As a safety precaution, remove the starter ground cable.

2. It is preferred to drain the fluid from the transmission pan. Because most pans do not have a drain plug, the following procedure can be used. Loosen the front pan bolts and then remove all the remaining bolts. The oil pan can simply be pried loose and tilted over a drain container without losing control of the fluid (Fig. 10-2).

The converter is not usually drained because it is more practical to perform this operation when the transmission is out of the car. Besides, most converters do not have drain plugs.

3. Scribe mark or use a light paint spray from an aerosol can for marking the drive shaft and companion flange for correct assembly. This should be standard practice whenever removing the drive shaft to insure that the drive shaft runout is not disturbed. Otherwise, an unwanted driveline vibration may result.

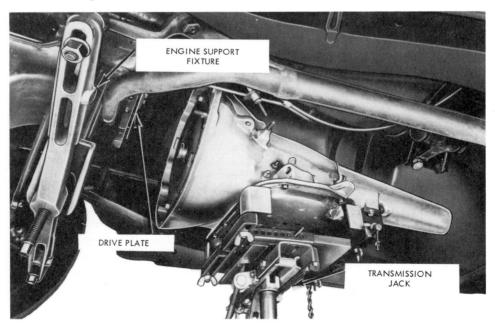

Fig. 10-1 .

4. Mark the drive plate (also referred to as the flex plate) and converter so they can be installed in the same position for balance purposes. A light paint spray from an aerosol can offers a quick method of marking. Punch marks may be used.

5. Remove the converter attaching bolts (or nuts) before removing the transmission to engine block bolts; otherwise, the weight of the transmission will rest on the converter drive plate, resulting in possible damage to the drive plate, front pump bushing, or front pump seal.

It is easy to distort the flex plate. Do not pry on the converter or flex plate during removal operations. To gain access to the converter attaching bolts, rotate the engine from the front of the crankshaft (Fig. 10-3).

Fig. 10-4.

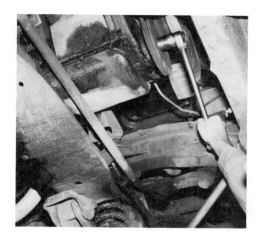

Fig. 10-3.

6. Although engine support fixtures are available, the engine can safely hang on its motor mounts. Because the engine will have a slight drop at the rear when the transmission is removed, make sure the fan doesn't wedge into the radiator and radiator hoses are not overly strained. If the distributor is mounted at the engine rear, remove the distributor cap if there is any doubt about leaning against the firewall. It may be necessary to use a wood block between the engine block and firewall.

7. When the transmission is ready to be removed and lowered out of the car, a word of caution: Keep the front of the transmission tilted slightly up to prevent the converter from falling out. As a safety precaution, you may want to design a hold-in clamp that can bolt onto the opening of the transmission converter housing. Mechanics wire strapped across the converter front can also do the job (Fig. 10-4).

Once the transmission is removed, make an immediate inspection of the flex-plate and check for cracks (Fig. 10-5). A cracked flex plate causes the converter drive hub to run off center with the transmission pump drive gear and causes quick pump damage.

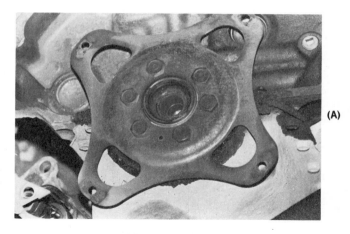

(A)

(B)

Fig. 10-5 . (A) Typical Chrysler flex plate.
(B) Typical Ford flex plate.

Fig. 10-6.

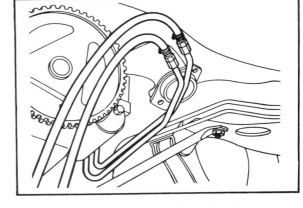

Fig. 10-7.   (General Motors Corp.)

If the flex plate is cracked be sure to check for the following:

1. Missing engine to case dowel pins.
2. Damage to the crankshaft converter pilot hole and the converter pilot itself.

If the alignment between the engine and transmission case is not maintained, the replacement flex plate will soon develop cracks and cause a repeat pump failure. Although cracked flex plates occur infrequently, they are often overlooked. It is a good practice to spot this condition before transmission overhaul begins and installation of the transmission. A cracked flex plate is shown in Fig. 10-6.

TRANSMISSION INSTALLATION

Installation of the transmission and converter assembly basically requires reversing the removal procedure. Some key points, however, need to be reviewed and also added.

1. To protect your overhaul, flush the cooler lines if the following was part of the transmission problem:

a. Engine coolant in the transmission fluid.
b. Severely varnished transmission fluid.
c. Damaged transmission pump.
d. Internal converter wear, producing a fluid with an "aluminum paint" appearance.

If the cooler lines are not flushed, the contaminated fluid will be cycled back into the transmission through the lube circuit. Return contaminants frequently cause seizing of the pressure regulator valve and loss of operating pressure. The governor filter screen can get clogged or the governor valve can seize,

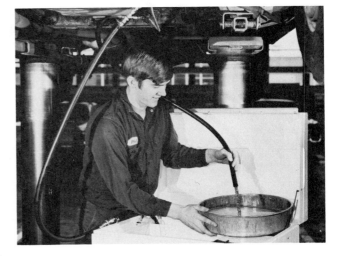

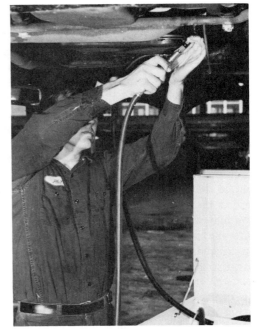

Fig. 10-8.

causing shift problems. The fine powdered metal floating in the lube circuit also attacks the bushing and thrust washer areas. Discovery of clogged cooler lines at this time can prevent immediate overheating and transmission failure.

If the shop is blessed with a converter flusher, it is usually equipped to flush cooler lines. Hose attachments from the flusher are connected to the lines and the cleaning solvent under low pressure is charged into the cooler feed line (Fig. 10-7). The technician watches for a clear flow of solvent from the cooler return line and then stops the operation (Fig. 10-8). The recommended flushing time is 20 minutes. Compressed air at no more than 50 psi is used to clear solvent from cooler lines.

A solvent tank pressure pump used in the shop can also be used for the flushing operation (Fig. 10-9).

Fig. 10-11.   (Chrysler Corp.)

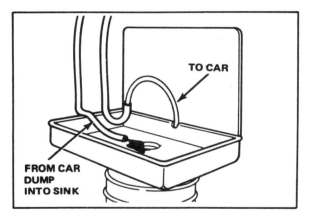

Fig. 10-9.   (General Motors Corp.)

Another effective method for flushing cooler lines is the use of a suction gun (Fig. 10-10). With this technique, fill the cooler with solvent. Reload the gun and procede to work the gun handle back and forth to surge the solvent for the best cleaning effect.

2. When installing the converter, be sure that the converter drive fully engages the oil pump drive gear. Figure 10-11 illustrates the usual measurement procedure, from the face of the housing to the converter weld nut in this case, to insure that the converter drive hub is seated. Refer to the individual manufacturer's specifications for the dimension.

When installing the converter, be aware that the converter drive hub slipping through the pump bushing and butting against the pump gear gives a false feeling of full engagement. With a slight forward pressure, spin the converter and feel that final drop into the pump drive gear.

If full engagement is not established, the pump will be damaged when the transmission is bolted to the engine. The converter is butted against the flex plate with the drive hub wedged against the pump drive gear. Figure 10-12 shows what can happen even before the engine is started (Ford application).

Fig. 10-12.

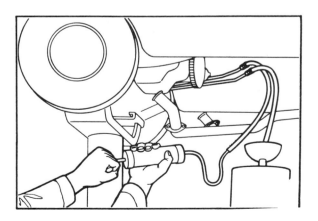

Fig. 10-10.   (General Motors Corp.)

3. Full converter engagement must be maintained during installation. Keep the front of the transmission tilted slightly upward and work the transmission onto the alignment dowels at the back of the engine block (Fig. 10-13).

Fig. 10-13.

When the transmission case is secured, there should be a ⅛–¼ in. clearance between the flex plate and converter. If the converter cannot slide forward and stays wedged against the flex plate, the converter drive hub has not engaged the pump. You may already have caused pump damage.

4. Align the balance marks between the drive plate and converter. Use your own established marks or those furnished by the manufacturer. Figure 10-14 illustrates the usual marking system for Chrysler applications. Hand start the converter bolts or nuts and finger tighten, then torque to specifications. This will insure proper converter alignment.

Fig. 10-14. (Chrysler Corp.)

⅛ INCH HOLE

STAMPED "O"

ND10B

5. Make sure the drive shaft is bolted to the yoke or companion flange in its original position. If this practice is not followed, there may be problems with vibration due to shaft run-out.

6. If the transmission has a vacuum modulator, examine the vacuum line for a pinched tube. The rubber tube used at the modulator and sometimes at the engine must be replaced if it is deteriorated and does not have a snug fit.

Do not use straight hose where a 90° molded hose is used. The straight hose crimps and restricts the vacuum signal.

7. Fill the transmission with four quarts of the correct fluid. Start the engine and bring the fluid level to the add or cold mark on the dipstick using proper level check method.

8. Road test and make any necessary external linkage adjustments for proper shift feel and kickdown performance.

9. Make a final check for external fluid leaks and proper fluid level.

TRANSMISSION DISASSEMBLY

Automatic transmission disassembly and reassembly techniques follow similar patterns between the various makes of transmissions. A few product design differences do exist, but will only require slight variations in procedure. Special tooling required for the job does not require excessive investment. After carefully researching the requirements, you will find that many tools are interchangeable between AMC, Chrysler, Ford and GM. With a little thought, you can also engineer some of your own special tools at little or no expense. Figure 10-15 shows some of the basic tools that you will need for major transmission work.

Good shop practice techniques are the same for all the transmissions. Before disassembly of the unit, thoroughly clean the exterior using either a steam clean or mineral spirits wash (Fig. 10-16). A clean outside condition avoids contaminating the work area and makes handling and disassembly of the transmission easier. As you are aware, whenever working with hydraulic units, cleanliness cannot be overemphasized, as a little dirt can undo many hours of careful work. Therefore, keep your work bench, tools, and parts clean at all times.

There are highly polished and precision mating surfaces in the transmission, and careful handling of parts is required. Avoid using tools or techniques that will cause nicks or scores or distortion of parts. For example, do not groove or score the inside of a front pump seal housing by carelessly extracting the oil seal with a chisel or screwdriver. Use proper tru-arch and snap-ring pliers to remove snap rings without distorting. Avoid nicking ring grooves.

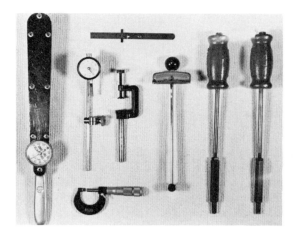

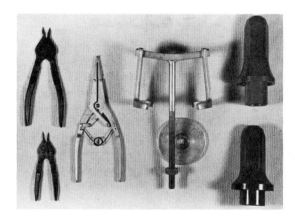

Fig. 10-15.   (A) and (B). Tools for major transmission repairs.

Fig. 10-16.   Steam cleaning exterior.

In line with the industry commitment to convert to the metric system, some of the current transmission fasteners are dimensioned all metric. On transmissions still using the S.A.E. fasteners, certain bolts are sometimes used with metric dimension. The manufacturer's service manual usually will identify these special metric applications. Metric and traditional inch fasteners should not be interchanged or substituted.

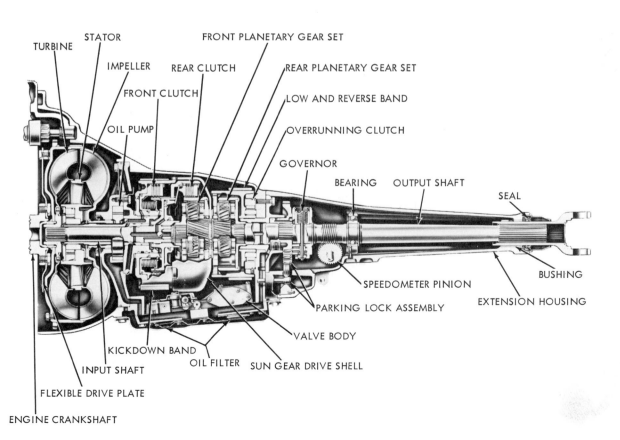

TURBINE

STATOR

IMPELLER

FRONT CLUTCH

OIL PUMP

REAR CLUTCH

FRONT PLANETARY GEAR SET

REAR PLANETARY GEAR SET

LOW AND REVERSE BAND

OVERRUNNING CLUTCH

GOVERNOR

BEARING   OUTPUT SHAFT

SEAL

BUSHING

EXTENSION HOUSING

SPEEDOMETER PINION

PARKING LOCK ASSEMBLY

VALVE BODY

KICKDOWN BAND

OIL FILTER   SUN GEAR DRIVE SHELL

INPUT SHAFT

FLEXIBLE DRIVE PLATE

ENGINE CRANKSHAFT

The Chrysler TorqueFlite is selected to feature disassembly highlights, Fig. 10-17. Remove the converter with a firm pull, Fig. 10-18. Be sure to keep the drive hub tilted up to avoid fluid spill at this time. Mount the transmission in a repair stand (Fig. 10-19) and follow the general sequence for subassembly removal.

Fig. 10-18.

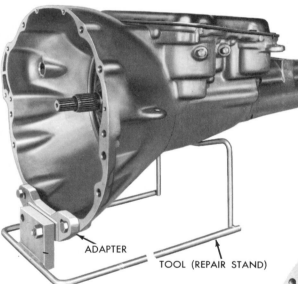

ADAPTER

TOOL (REPAIR STAND)

Fig. 10-19.

Fig. 10-20. (Chrysler Corp.)

Repair stands or fixtures are available for all transmissions and offer the advantage of working convenience to save repair time. Some of these fixtures can easily be homemade fabrications. After all, the name of the game is "speed, reliability, and profit."

Disassembly Procedure

1. Measure the front endplay of the transmission off the input shaft movement using a dial indicator (Fig. 10-20). This is a requirement for all automatic transmissions and is usually controlled by a selective thickness thrust washer in the case assembly. Internal part damage is generally indicated at the thrust washers and related thrust surfaces if endplay is excessive.

Most specifications permit an army tank to drive between the low and high limits of the input shaft endplay. By taking a reading at this time, it will permit you to set the endplay at the low limits during reassembly. For the more experienced technician, the endplay can be preferably set below the minimum specification to almost zero. The main criteria for setting-up front endplay is to keep the input shaft endplay to a minimum and still maintain freedom of shaft rotation. During acceleration and deceleration the clutch drums move back and forth in the case as permitted by the controlled front endplay. This action scuffs the oil rings in the drum bores and shortens ring life. This action also imposes a high load against the ring groove sides, resulting in a combination of ring and groove wear.

2. Remove the oil pan, screen, valve body assembly, and accumulator (Figs. 10-21, 10-22, 10-23, and 10-24).

3. Remove extension housing seal (Fig. 10-25).

4. Remove extension housing to case bolts (Fig. 10-26).

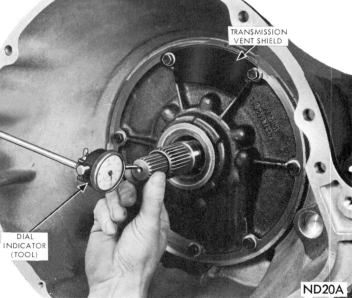

TRANSMISSION VENT SHIELD

DIAL INDICATOR (TOOL)

ND20A

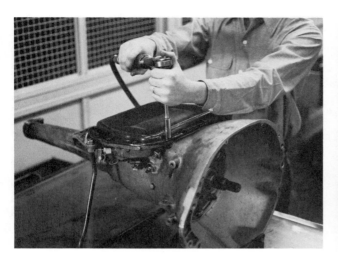

Fig. 10-21. Oil pan.

Fig. 10-22. Filter screen.

Fig. 10-23. Valve body.

Fig. 10-24. Accumulator.

Fig. 10-25. Extension housing seal.

Fig. 10-26. Extension housing.

Fig. 10-27.   Output shaft bearing snap ring.

Fig. 10-28.   Output shaft bearing.

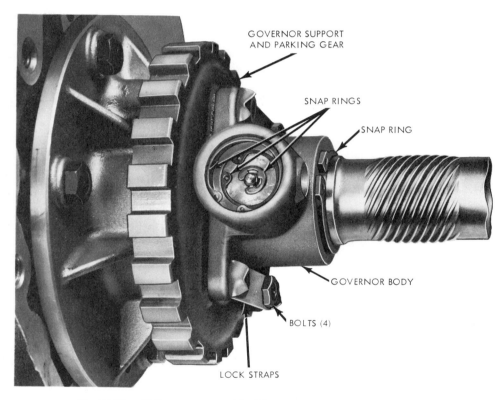

GOVERNOR SUPPORT
AND PARKING GEAR

SNAP RINGS

SNAP RING

GOVERNOR BODY

BOLTS (4)

LOCK STRAPS

Fig. 10-29.   (A) Governor assembly. (Chrysler Corp.) (B) Governor removal.

5. Remove small cover plate located over output shaft bearing and spread output shaft bearing snap ring retainer (Fig. 10-27). Carefully tap extension housing off output shaft and bearing.

6. Remove the output shaft bearing. Use heavy duty tru-arc pliers on the front and rear snap rings (Fig. 10-28).

7. Observe the snap rings at the governor assembly (Fig. 10-29A). Only two snap rings need to be removed to slide the governor assembly off the output shaft (Fig. 10-29B); (a) carefully pry E-clip from weight end of governor shaft and slide governor valve and shaft out of governor body; (b) remove snap ring on output shaft from behind governor body.

Once the valve body assembly, extension housing, and governor assembly have been removed, the re-

Fig. 10-30. Front pump to case attaching bolts.

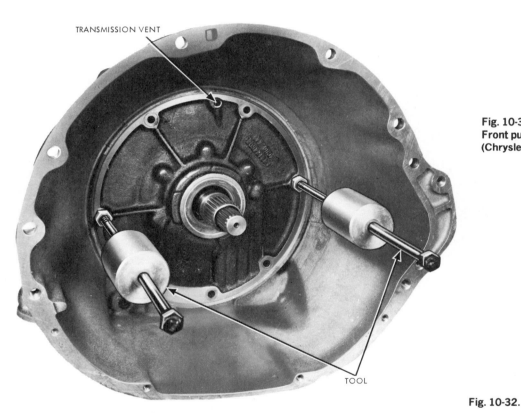

Fig. 10-31.
Front pump removal.
(Chrysler Corp.)

TOOL

Fig. 10-32.

mainder or internal subassemblies will come out the front of the transmission.

8. Remove front pump to case attaching bolts (Fig. 10-30).

9. Tighten front band and remove front pump. This usually requires a pair of slide hammers (Fig. 10-31). The long bolts are provided with tapped holes in the pump casting. On some transmissions, an extra large screwdriver blade can be used behind the pump to pry it out of the case (Fig. 10-32).

Fig. 10-33. Front band.

10. Loosen front band adjusting screw and remove band and strut (Fig. 10-33).

11. Grasp input shaft and remove front and rear clutch units together, Fig. 10-34.

12. Support and carefully slide output shaft and planetary gear assembly forward and out of case, Fig. 10-35.

13. Remove low-reverse drum, rear band and overrunning clutch rollers, Figs. 10-36A and 36B. Thread a ¼ inch bolt into actuating lever pin and remove. O-ring seal on pin must be replaced.

14. Remove low-reverse servo assembly. The low low-reverse servo spring retainer can easily be held down against spring tension and the snap ring removed, Fig. 10-37.

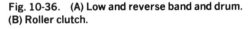

Fig. 10-36. (A) Low and reverse band and drum. (B) Roller clutch.

Fig. 10-34. Front and rear clutch units.

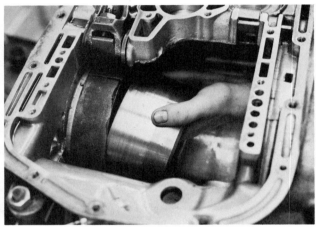

(A)

Fig. 10-35. Output shaft and planetary assembly.

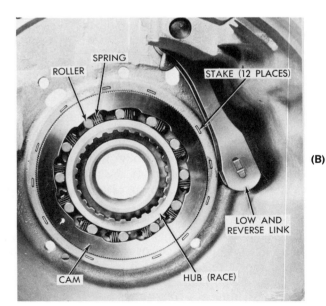

(B)

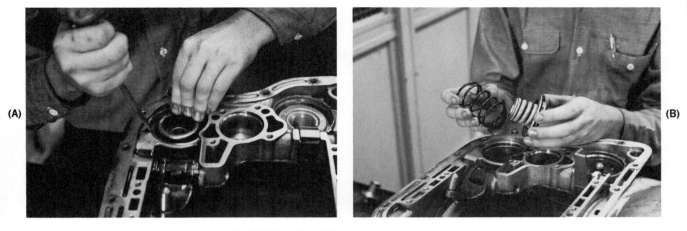

Fig. 10-37. (A) and (B). Low and reverse servo.

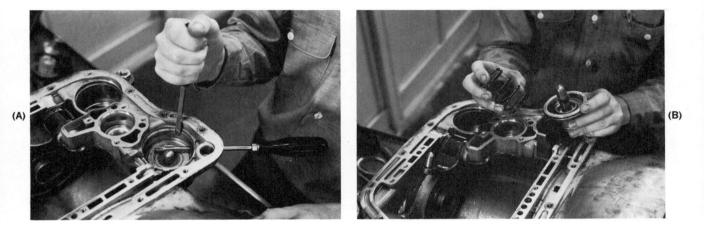

Fig. 10-38 (A) and (B). Kickdown (front) servo.

Fig. 10-39.

15. Remove kickdown servo assembly. To relax the spring tension on the snap ring hold down on the piston rod guide. Since the spring force is quite high, insert a Phillips screwdriver thru the pressure test plug hole over the guide, Fig. 10-38A & 10-38B.

All the subassemblies and minor parts are now removed from the transmission. Notice in Fig. 10-39 how they are organized in exact order of removal. Special attention should be given to the location of thrust washers and spacers. The use of a muffin tin will help to keep small items such as bolts, screws and snap rings in order.

You have just witnessed a brief lesson in dismantling an automatic transmission. Essentially, after the valve body and extension housing pieces have been removed, the internal case subassemblies are all removed out the front of the case. Keep in mind, however, that there are product differences between transmissions and minor variations in disassembly requirements prevail. The manufacturer's service manual or equivalent should be consulted for each transmission.

GENERAL TRANSMISSION AND SUBASSEMBLY OVERHAUL PRACTICES

During an overhaul, it is standard practice to discard and replace certain part items with new ones. Others are replaced according to need when inspected and evaluated to be worn excessively or damaged.

Discard and Replace	Replace as Needed
Gaskets	Gears
O-rings	Bands
Oil seals	Bushings and thrust washers
Metal or teflon sealing rings	Pump
Clutch steel plates	Converter
Clutch friction plates	Governor
Modulators	Clutch housings
Fluid intake filter	Roller or sprag units
Pump body bushing	Minor parts

When servicing subassemblies, work with one unit at a time; disassembly, cleaning, inspection, and reassembly of each unit should be completed before tackling other units. This avoids unnecessary mix-up of parts and their order of assembly. Figures 10-40, 10-41, 10-42, and 10-43 show four major disassembled TorqueFlite subassembly units. It does not take much imagination to realize the mass mix-up and extra needed bench space should all units be disassembled at one time. More experienced technicians, however, may prefer to disassemble all units and keep the assembly parts stacked together. This permits a quicker evaluation of part needs and cost estimate to the customer.

A typical make-up of an overhaul kit is shown in Fig. 10-44. It contains all the necessary replacement gaskets, rubber seals, metal and teflon sealing rings, clutch plates, and sometimes the intake filter. The vacuum modulator is a non-kit item as well as bushings and thrust washers.

Fig. 10-40. Pump assembly. (Chrysler Corp.)

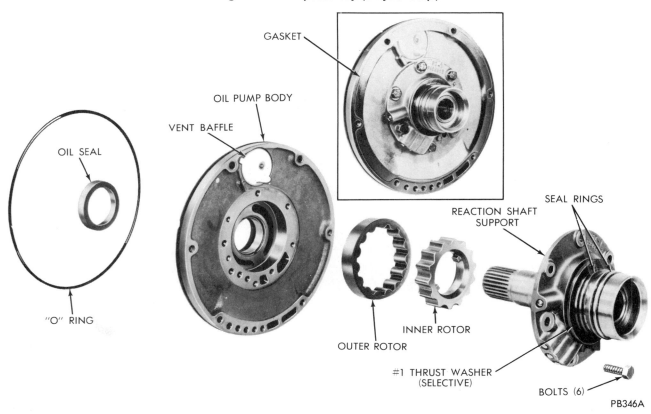

OIL SEAL
"O" RING
VENT BAFFLE
OIL PUMP BODY
GASKET
REACTION SHAFT SUPPORT
SEAL RINGS
OUTER ROTOR
INNER ROTOR
#1 THRUST WASHER (SELECTIVE)
BOLTS (6)

PB346A

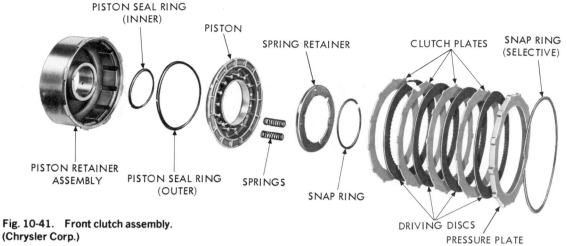

PISTON SEAL RING (INNER)

PISTON

SPRING RETAINER

CLUTCH PLATES

SNAP RING (SELECTIVE)

PISTON RETAINER ASSEMBLY

PISTON SEAL RING (OUTER)

SPRINGS

SNAP RING

DRIVING DISCS

PRESSURE PLATE

Fig. 10-41. Front clutch assembly. (Chrysler Corp.)

Fig. 10-42. Rear clutch assembly. (Chrysler Corp.)

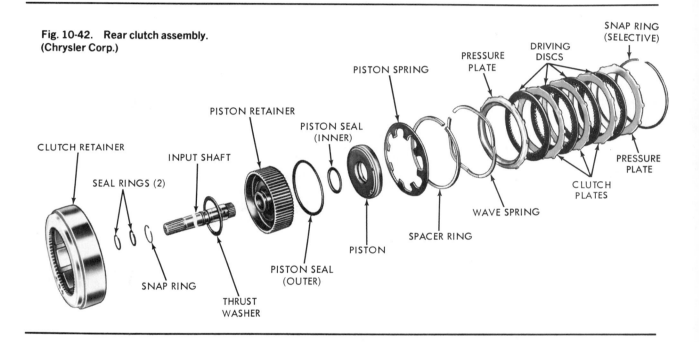

PISTON SPRING

PRESSURE PLATE

DRIVING DISCS

SNAP RING (SELECTIVE)

PISTON RETAINER

PISTON SEAL (INNER)

CLUTCH RETAINER

INPUT SHAFT

SEAL RINGS (2)

PRESSURE PLATE

CLUTCH PLATES

PISTON

SNAP RING

PISTON SEAL (OUTER)

WAVE SPRING

THRUST WASHER

SPACER RING

Fig. 10-43. Planetary gear assembly. (Chrysler Corp.)

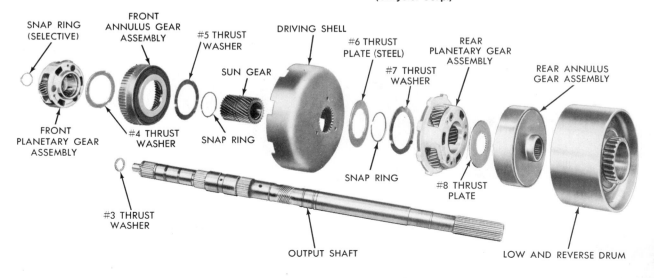

SNAP RING (SELECTIVE)

FRONT ANNULUS GEAR ASSEMBLY

#5 THRUST WASHER

DRIVING SHELL

#6 THRUST PLATE (STEEL)

REAR PLANETARY GEAR ASSEMBLY

REAR ANNULUS GEAR ASSEMBLY

SUN GEAR

#7 THRUST WASHER

FRONT PLANETARY GEAR ASSEMBLY

#4 THRUST WASHER

SNAP RING

SNAP RING

#8 THRUST PLATE

#3 THRUST WASHER

OUTPUT SHAFT

LOW AND REVERSE DRUM

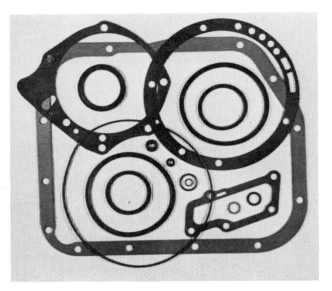

Fig. 10-44.

The parts furnished in an overhaul kit must be checked for proper sizing and fit and prepared for installation. Each metal sealing ring, rubber seal, and gasket should be given a final quality control check to make sure they are going to work. This is a critical part of the transmission overhaul and serious attention must be given to the preparation and installation of these items.

Preparation and Installation Guidelines

• Use a thin coating of nonhardening seal compound on all metal encased seals. These are used in the front pump, extension housing, and transmission case. Prelube the lip seal area with transmission fluid or petroleum jelly (vaseline or equivalent).

• All paper gaskets are installed dry. Do not use any sealing compounds or treat with lubricant.

• Prelube all rubber seals with transmission fluid, petroleum jelly, or a silicone wax such as Door Ease®. Absolutely avoid using white lube. Its high melting point makes it incompatible with transmission fluid. The white lube can get caught in the fluid stream and clog filter screens or small metered orifices.

• Remove all the dirt and old materials before installing new gaskets and seals. Be careful not to scratch or groove gasket and seal surfaces.

• Check for the correct valve body gaskets. Compare the old to the new gaskets or check them out against the separator plate. If the gaskets are right, all separator plate holes will have an opening through the gasket (Fig. 10-45).

Fig. 10-45.

• Presoak new friction plates for 30 minutes in transmission fluid before installation (Fig. 10-46). If new bands are installed, they must also be soaked. (Refer to Clutch Service)

Fig. 10-46.

• Torque tighten valve body, pump, and extension housing bolts.
• Check the fit of the metal oil rings in bore and grooves.

Inside the bore (Fig. 10-47), the ring must have good tension and conform to the bore diameter. Test the ring for any side motion with your fingers. Side motion in the ring cannot be tolerated. The ring gap should not exceed .012 inch. If an oversized ring is installed, it will break-up when slipped into the bore. An undersized or nonconforming ring will obviously leak between ring and bore. Undersized rings will actually fall through the bore.

Fig. 10-47. Sizing ring and gap in Ford C-6 governor sleeve bore.

Fig. 10-48.

To check for ring and groove fit, place the ring in the groove as illustrated in Fig. 10-48. Ring and groove clearance should not exceed .005 inch. With the ring in place, be sure to check the grooves for step and taper wear and ridging (Fig. 10-49). When the ring is installed, make sure that it rotates freely in the groove. Nicks or minor damage at the groove that bind the ring can be removed with a file.

Fig. 10-49.

RING GROOVE WEAR PATTERNS

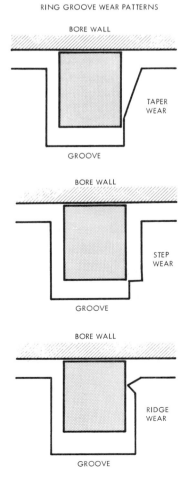

Ring gap and groove clearance measurements are not normally required. These specifications can be used for making a quick visual judgment if the ring is right for the bore and groove, or if wear is the problem. If there is a ring-to-bore or ring-to-groove problem, the clearances will greatly exceed specifications and measurements will generally not be necessary.

Ring-to-bore and ring-to-groove conditions are too often taken for granted or overlooked. Be sure to make this a regular part of your overhaul practice and avoid a repeat clutch failure. Every new ring should be quick checked in the bore and groove.

• Check the fit of the rubber seals. This is especially critical where they are used on clutch and servo piston applications. Occasionally a seal will be found that does not meet dimensional standards.

O-RING SEALS. On round or square cut O-ring seals, the seals must meet a criteria for (1) correct diameter and (2) correct thickness.

Standard manufacturing tolerances require that the O-ring seal diameter must be within 3% ± of the bore size. Check this dimension by placing the seal in its bore (Fig. 10-50). The seal should have a slight drag without losing its configuration or fit loosely within the 3% limit. For example, a 2½ in. or 2.50 servo piston bore will require that the seal clearance be no more than approximately 5/64 in. (.03% x 2.50). Because we are working with a circle, the maximum clearance to the bore on all sides of the seal is ½ of 5/64 in., or slightly more than 1/32 in. Although O-ring clearance measurements are not required during overhaul, the above problem can give you a basis for quick checking a seal for correct diameter. A correct diameter seal should not fit loosely on the piston, nor should it need to be overstretched to be put in place.

Fig. 10-50.

The O-ring seal thickness determines the amount of squeeze or compression on the rubber when it is installed and is related to the ability of the rubber to seal (refer to Chapter 8). Seal thickness in the servo piston can be checked by sampling the drag in the assembly unit (Fig. 10-51). With the seal installed on the piston and lubricated, round-type seals should have a firm drag, while square type seals give only a light drag. Round seals have a tendency to return to their normal set and will get looser, and therefore require the heavy drag.

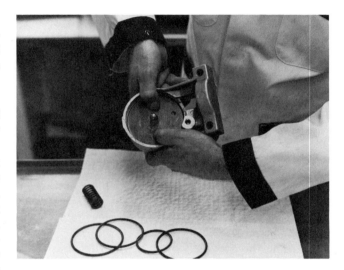

Fig. 10-51.

There are usually two or more seals involved with a piston installation. This makes it necessary to test and remove each seal one at a time so they can be individually checked.

A small diameter seal with good thickness sometimes gets wrongfully overstretched into place in the piston groove. The seal sticks out of groove and looks like it will have a good drag. The only problem is that the overstretched seal wants to return to its original size and what was a good drag eventually is nonexistent. The so-called good seal becomes a leaker. O-rings will shrink .001 inch for every 1% stretched.

LIP TYPE SEALS. These seals can be individually checked with the clutch piston in the drum cylinder. Because these seals depend on hydraulic pressure for sealing, they will only provide a very light drag. (Refer to Chapter 8.)

The seals will need to be lubricated for check out. Start with the inner seal by holding the drum upside down and letting the piston free fall against your hand. Work the piston up and down in the cylinder and feel for a light drag (Fig. 10-52). If there is an absence of a drag, the seal is undersized.

Fig. 10-52.   Checking TorqueFlite rear clutch piston drag.

Leave the inner seal in place and install the outer seal on the piston. Using the same procedure with both seals, a definite increase in a seal drag should be felt. The piston may even stay in the cylinder and not free fall.

When the piston uses a center or third seal, then each seal should be checked one at a time only.

• Paper-based friction bands that are burned or heavily discolored in black should be replaced. A black discolored band has picked-up a heavy carbon surface from the cast iron drum, which probably has a glazed surface to compliment the band. If this combination is reused, long drawn out 1–2 shifts or 1–3 skip shifts will be built back into the transmission. When new bands are used, the drum surface should be deglazed with a medium-coarse grit paper or emery cloth to break-in the friction surfaces. Always work-in drum rotation (Fig. 10-53). Working back and forth across the drum will cause considerable band wear.

On smooth, hard-surfaced drums such as the TorqueFlite front drum, deglazing is not required. This type surface is engineered with the band to give the desired 1–2 shift feel and must not be upset. Hard-surfaced drums are easily identified when the medium-coarse grit has very little effect on deglazing the drum surface.

Where the drum surface has been scored by metal to metal contact with the band, the drum must be replaced. In cases where an oversized band is available, the drum can sometimes be salvaged by centering it in a brake drum lathe and using the grinding attachment (Fig. 10-54). Hard-surfaced cast iron or stamped drums cannot be salvaged in this manner.

Fig. 10-54.

• After complete disassembly of a unit, all metal parts should be washed in clean mineral spirits and dried with compressed air (Figs. 10-55 and 10-56).

Fig. 10-53.

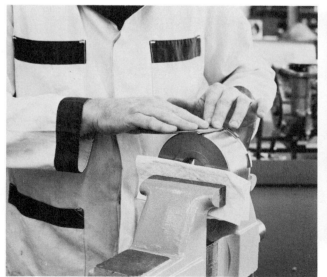

Fig. 10-55.

Fig. 10-56.

Fig. 10-57.

Fig. 10-58.

Shop towels or rags should not be used to wipe parts after cleaning because of the lint that would adhere to the parts. This lint accumulation has been known to clog filter screens and cause valve seizing.

During the drying process, be sure to blow out the fluid passages to remove any existing obstructions. In Fig. 10-57, the technician is blowing out and checking the output shaft lube holes. Extra small orificed passages may need to be checked with tag wire (Fig. 10-58).

Be sure to do an extra good job of cleaning the case. After the mineral spirits bath, use hot water to flush the case and then air dry (Fig. 10-59). The case passages must all be blown out.

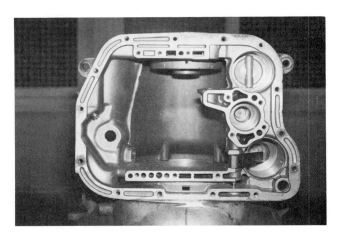

Fig. 10-59.

The unit parts are ready to be inspected to determine their condition for reuse or replacement. Figure 10-60 shows a technician inspecting planet pinion gears for loose or worn pins and chipped or worn gears. Give extra attention to bushings and thrust washers and their contact surfaces. Needle-type thrust washers need to be observed closely for brinneling (Fig. 10-61).

Fig. 10-60.

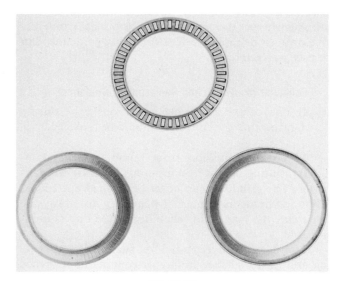

Fig. 10-61.

• When installing one-way sprag clutch units in some of the older transmissions, follow the exact manufacturer's instructions for installation. Sprag cage assemblies can easily be installed backwards and this results in the wrong freewheeling action.

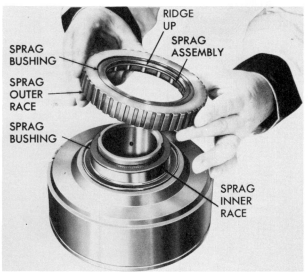

Fig. 10-62. (Oldsmobile Division, General Motors Corp.)

In Fig. 10-62, the intermediate sprag assembly (early design THM-400) is shown in its outer race. One side of the sprag assembly has a shoulder that must face down to give the correct freewheeling direction, as illustrated in Fig. 10-63, when mounted on the direct clutch housing.

If the sprag cage was installed backwards, the transmission would start in first gear, miss second gear, and lock-up in third gear. The engine lugs down until the transmission downshifts back to first gear. The cycle then repeats itself.

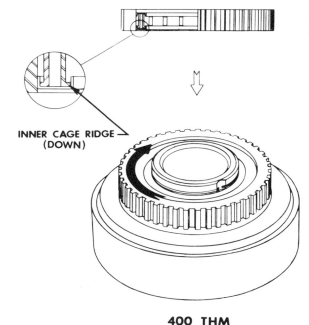

400 THM

Fig. 10-63. (Oldsmobile Division, General Motors Corp.)

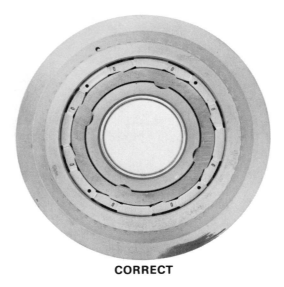

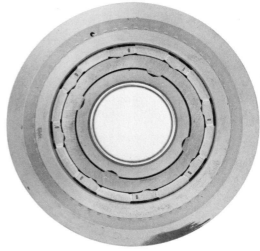

CORRECT   INCORRECT

Fig. 10-64.   Roller clutch installation.

The one-way roller clutches usually pose no special installation problem; however, they also can be improperly installed. It is almost impossible to do but it can be done. A correct and incorrect assembly installation is shown for a THM-350 intermediate roller clutch (Fig. 10-64). Notice how the cage and cam configurations are matched and mismatched. An incorrect installation would give a freewheeling action in both directions; the rollers would fail to hold.

• If tapped aluminum threads are stripped or damaged, they should be made serviceable again with the use of a helicoil or equivalent (Fig. 10-65). This should be done before any assembly work begins.

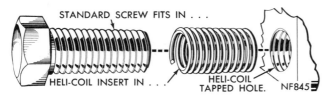

STANDARD SCREW FITS IN . . .

HELI-COIL INSERT IN . . .   HELI-COIL
                                 TAPPED HOLE.   NF845

Fig. 10-65.   (Chrysler Corp.)

CONVERTER SERVICE

Converter service must be considered as part of the overhaul. This is an often neglected service along with the cooler lines, which, if overlooked, can lead to a quick repeat failure of the transmission. Contaminants not removed from the converter or cooler lines will cycle back into the transmission through the lube circuit, attacking bushing and thrust washer surfaces. Should the cooler lines be restricted, overheating occurs in the converter and total transmission.

Today's modern converters are of welded design and therefore cannot be disassembled in field service for cleaning and inspection. There are bench check procedures, however, that can be used by the technician to evaluate and determine converter serviceability. The converter is a high-cost item that many times is needlessly replaced. Studies have shown that over 50% of replacement converters are not defective and are serviceable. It should be obvious that it is important to understand the various conditions that determine whether the converter can be put back into service or must be replaced. The following guidelines can be used as a reference.

Converter Inspection and Replacement Guidelines

If one of the following conditions exist during bench inspection the converter should be replaced.

1. The transmission front pump is badly damaged, resulting in cast iron grindings entering the converter. The grindings can never be flushed out 100%. Although immediate internal wear may not always be apparent, the long term reliability of the unit is questionable.

2. Internal converter failure, such as thrust bearing and thrust surface failure or running interference between the member elements. Internal wear failures are usually associated with "aluminized" oil from the converter sampling.

3. Stator roller clutch failure. It is either frozen or freewheels in both directions.

4. A scored or damaged hub, which could cause a repeat front pump seal or bushing failure (Fig. 10-66). Fretting wear on the end of the hub is a normal condition and not a reason to replace the converter (Fig.

Fig. 10-66.

Fig. 10-67.

Fig. 10-68.

10-67). Minor scuff marks and grooving are acceptable but should be hand-polished with crocus cloth (Fig. 10-68).

5. External leakage, such as at the hub weld area (Fig. 10-69).

6. The drive studs on the converter cover are loose, have damaged pilot shoulders or stripped threads (Fig. 10-70). These studs mate the converter to the crankshaft drive plate to (1) drive the converter and (2) pilot the converter to run true with the crankshaft. Any misalignment of the converter with the engine and transmission would run the drive hub off center to the pump and wipe out the bushing and the pump gears.

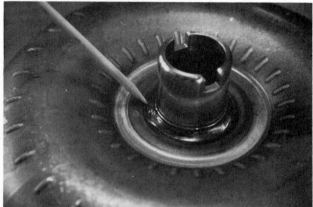

Fig. 10-69.

Fig. 10-70.

Converters using threaded bolt holes should not be rejected for stripped or crossed threads. A heli-coil installation can usually correct the situation.

To determine the internal condition of the converter, some simple bench checks can be performed by the technician to evaluate thrust wear and the stator one-way roller clutch action.

The converter can be checked for wear by several methods.

1. Observe the internal parts through the hub (Fig. 10-71). If a thrust washer is observed out of place, excessive endplay exists and the converter must be replaced. If a thrust washer is not observed out of place, it cannot be assumed that the endplay is not excessive. You must procede to use either check method 2. or 3. for a back-up.

Fig. 10-73.

Fig. 10-71.

Fig. 10-74.

2. If special tooling is available, the internal endplay can be measured with a dial indicator (Fig. 10-72). Procedure details are available in the shop manual. The endplay should not exceed .050 in. New converters will be considerably tighter.

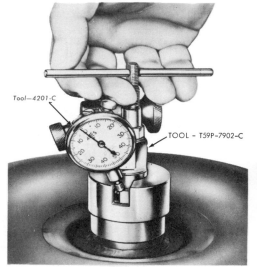

END PLAY CHECK

Fig. 10-72.   (Ford Motor Co.)

3. In the absence of special tooling, snap ring pliers can be extended into the hub opening and clutched to the stator hub splines (Fig. 10-73). A firm up and down movement should not exceed $\frac{1}{16}$ in. (Fig. 10-74). This technique produces good results. If the converter has objectionable wear, the endplay exceeds the $\frac{1}{16}$ in. limit without question.

4. Internal interference inside the converter should be checked as follows:

Stator-to-turbine and turbine-to-cover interference

a. Position the converter face down on the bench.
b. Insert the transmission pump and input shaft into the converter and engage the splines of the stator and turbine. See Figs. 10-75 and 10-76.

Fig. 10-75.

Fig. 10-76.

c. Hold the pump and converter and rotate the input shaft in both directions (Fig. 10-77). Any binding or scraping indicates internal wear and interference.

Fig. 10-77.

Stator-to-impeller interference

a. Invert the pump and converter on the bench as shown in Fig. 10-78. With the converter in this position, the stator will drop against the impeller thrust washer.
b. Hold the pump fixed and rotate the converter in both directions. Check for any binding or scraping, which would indicate a worn thrust washer or thrust surface.

Fig. 10-78.

5. To test the action of the stator one-way clutch, a dummy stator shaft can be inserted in the converter to engage the one-way clutch race (see Fig. 10-79). The inertia of a counterclockwise snap action should produce a freewheeling sensation and a clockwise snap action a lock-up sensation (Fig. 10-80). A freewheeling action or lock-up action in both directions indicates a faulty one-way clutch. For best results, the converter should be full with fluid.

Fig. 10-79.

Fig. 10-80.

Snap ring pliers can be used to hold the splines of the one-way clutch race in place of the stator shaft. The same rotational snap action will check-out the one-way clutch (Fig. 10-81).

Fig. 10-81.

Most converters will pass the bench checks and are reusable. Before putting the unit back into service, however, drain as much of the used oil from the converter as possible. On converters without drain plugs, a limited amount of oil can be drained through the hub. If the converter has been run with heavily varnished, discolored, or engine-coolant-contaminated oil, then the unit should be flushed with a mechanically-agitated cleaner. Engine coolant contamination turns the oil into a milky-pink color and is easily identified. Because this type of contamination will attack the friction material in the transmission, a complete drain and flush operation is a must along with the cooler lines.

Converters without drain plugs must be drilled for complete draining and flushing. To drill a converter, center punch and drill a ⅛ in. hole close to the converter weld bead. Fig. 10-82 shows the location for General Motors applications.

Once the converter is completely drained, it is ready for mounting in a converter flusher (Fig. 10-83). This piece of equipment slowly rotates the converter while a cleaning solvent is cycled in and out of the converter to purge the old oil and contaminates. The machine automatically adds timed blasts of compressed air to the solvent for agitation as it enters the converter.

After the flushing operation, install a ⅛ in. closed-end pop rivet in the drilled hole. This is a special rivet that can be purchased at the jobber outlets (Fig. 10-84). The completed rivet installation is shown (Fig. 10-85). Should the correct pop rivets not be available, a

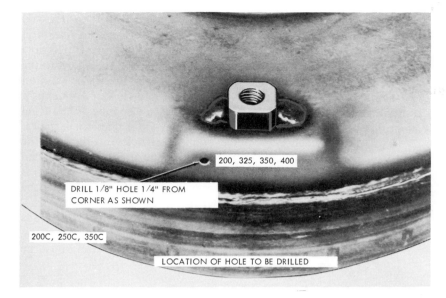

Fig. 10-82. Location of holes to be drilled. (Oldsmobile Division, General Motors Corp.)

200, 325, 350, 400

DRILL 1/8" HOLE 1/4" FROM CORNER AS SHOWN

200C, 250C, 350C

LOCATION OF HOLE TO BE DRILLED

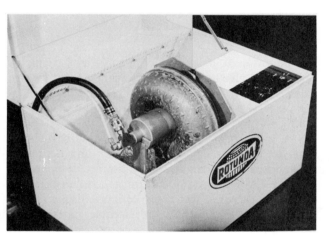

Fig. 10-83.

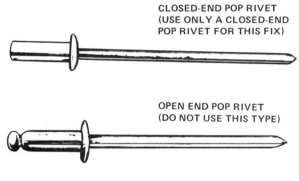

CLOSED-END POP RIVET (USE ONLY A CLOSED-END POP RIVET FOR THIS FIX)

OPEN END POP RIVET (DO NOT USE THIS TYPE)

Fig. 10-84. (Oldsmobile Division, General Motors Corp.)

0-85. (Oldsmobile Division, General Motors Corp.)

CLOSED-END POP RIVET (COVER WITH SEALER)

TIG weld does produce excellent results (Fig. 10-86). As a final reliability check, the converter should be tested for leakage. The converter is submerged in a water tank and pressurized with a minimum of 80 psi. In Fig. 10-87, the technician has clamped a water hose to the converter hub and uses a rubber check ball with a steel tube insert on the top end for pressurizing. If the converter has a leak area, it is easily identified by air bubbles in the water.

Fig. 10-86.

Fig. 10-87.

When a converter is designed with a lock-up clutch, it is difficult to evaluate the internal condition of the friction lining. If the friction lining is deteriorated, loose friction particles enter the fluid flow to the cooler and will accumulate at the line fitting junction to the cooler and restrict the fluid flow or even shut it down. It should be a practice to disconnect the fitting and inspect for any clogging from friction particles. Evidence of clutch friction particles means that the converter must be replaced. The friction material can usually be removed with a miniature screwdriver. It is recommended, however, that the cooler outlet be tested for a free flow. If the return flow to the transmission is intermittent or takes longer than 20 seconds to collect one quart of fluid, separate reverse flushing operations of the cooler and cooler lines must be made.

PUMP SERVICE

The pumps used in automatic transmissions are highly reliable and give long life service with very little wear. They seldom need to be replaced. Only conditions of very excessive wear and damage require replacing the pump.

A typical gear-type and rotor-type pump is shown in Figs. 10-88 and 10-89. To service and determine whether the pump can be reused, it must be separated, all parts cleaned with mineral spirits, and air dried. In most cases a close, visual inspection will pick-up excessively worn parts. The serviceable parts of the pump assembly are the stator support bushings, body seal, and bushing. If the body or gears need replacement, a new pump must be usually installed. It is not common practice to sell the body and gears as separate parts, although there are exceptions.

Pump Unit Inspection Guidelines

Because visual inspection is very critical in evaluating pump wear, it is advantageous for the technician to know where to look. This means that we can put our knowledge of how the pump works into locating logical wear points.

Figure 10-90 identifies the suction and pressure pockets of a gear-type pump. Note that the pressure side has the small-size pocket. The fluid in the pressure pocket will (1) exert a side thrust on the drive gear and converter drive hub toward the suction pocket and (2) exert a side thrust on the driven internal gear opposite the suction pocket. These forces result in the following wear patterns.

Fig. 10-88.   Gear type pump.

Fig. 10-91.

Fig. 10-89.

• The side thrust on the drive gear and converter hub puts constant pressure on one side of the pump body bushing. This wear area is located by the suction side (Fig. 10-91). Perhaps you have always wondered why this bushing wore on one side only.

• Should the body bushing wear be excessive, then the drive gear will undercut the crescent or divider. This damage area will be located at the leading edge of the divider, suction side (Fig. 10-92). This type of wear produces fine metallic particles that can severely damage the pump and contaminate the converter, cooling, and lube circuits.

Fig. 10-92.

Fig. 10-90.

• The side thrust on the internal gear produces a wear area in the body on the pressure side (Fig. 10-93).

• Should the internal gear-to-pump body wear be excessive, then the internal gear will undercut the divider in the area of the leading edge, suction side (Fig. 10-94).

Fig. 10-95.

Fig. 10-93.

Fig. 10-94.

The following items will also need your special attention during inspection of the pump assembly.

• Examine the land area between the pressure and suction pockets. The location will depend on pump design (Fig. 10-95). If the area is grooved or undercut, part of the pump pressure head is lost back to the suction side.

• Inspect the gears or rotors for cracks, scoring or galling. A cracked drive member usually is an indication that the transmission was bolted to the engine with the converter drive hub not engaged in the drive member (Fig. 10-96).

• A production practice is to apply a black lubrite coating on the pump gears for initial break-in. It is normal for the lubrite coating to wear off unevenly and is not a reason to replace the pump body assembly.

• Inspect the pump cover or stator support for scoring or galling (Fig. 10-97).

• A usually neglected item is the stator shaft bushings (Fig. 10-98). Although they seldom need replacement, they must be inspected very closely for out-of-round or eccentricity. Excessive worn stator shaft bushings can affect the converter, cooling, and lubrication circuits. It may also be the cause of fluid foaming and fluid loss out the filler tube.

(A)

Fig. 10-96.   (A), (B), and (C)

(B)

(C)

Fig. 10-98.   (A) Stator shaft front bushing.
(B) Stat shaft rear bushing.

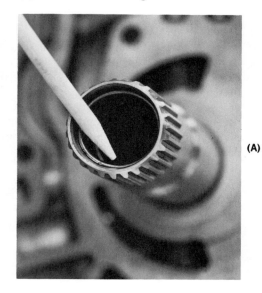

(A)

(B)

Fig. 10-97.

• Inspect oil ring grooves and clutch bushing supports on the oil delivery sleeve for damage or wear (Fig. 10-99). New oil rings can be used to size the groove condition if necessary.

Fig. 10-99.

• A severely damaged pump is usually an indication of an external problem such as a cracked or loose flex plate. If this inspection is overlooked, your overhaul will soon fail.

• Check the pump body bushing for tightness. If the bushing is loose and spins, be sure that the replacement bushing fits tight, otherwise, the pump body will need to be replaced.

Evaluation of the pump assembly is usually a matter of performing a good visual inspection. Any damage or excessive wear will be obvious. If there might be some doubt about the pump wear, you can perform some clearance checks outlined in the manufacturer's service manual. Figure 10-100 illustrates the technician making a pump-body-to-gear-face clearance check.

Pump Unit Assembly Guidelines

• To prepare for assembly, begin with thoroughly cleaned and dried assembly parts.

• Always replace the pump bushing.

• To replace the pump seal, the outside seal body should be treated with a nonhardening sealer. To install the seal, the use of a seal driver is preferred (Fig. 10-101). In the absence of a seal driver, the weight of a heavy hammer carefully striking the outside shoulder of the seal can be used (Fig. 10-102).

Fig. 10-101.   (Oldsmobile Division, General Motors Corp.)

Fig. 10-100.   (Oldsmobile Division, General Motors Corp.)

Fig. 10-102.

• Dip the drive and driven gears or rotors in transmission fluid and install into the pump body. Gear type pumps must have the pump gears installed in the same position in which they were removed for two reasons: (1) the gears have established a wear pattern that cannot be upset, otherwise, pump gear noise would become a problem; (2) the drive gear must definitely be installed with the drive tangs or drive slots in the correct relationship to the converter drive hub. Incorrect drive gear installation wedges the flex plate, converter, and drive gear when the transmission is bolted to the engine. Refer to the manufacturer's directions for correct installation. The current practice is to provide production marks in the gear faces to identify correct installation position. Shown in Fig. 10-103 are the gear marks provided for a THM-350 pump assembly. Note

that the drive gear is positioned with the converter drive tangs facing up. The driven gear mark may face up or down as required by the manufacturer. In the absence of production marks, the gears can be installed by matching the wear pattern of the teeth. The gear teeth will show wear on one side only.

• When the pump design matches a pump cover to the pump body, the two halves must be bolted together on center. If this is not done, then the pump assembly may not fit into the transmission case. By using the machined transmission case opening, the pump halves can be assured of alignment. Loosely bolt the pump body and pump cover together and install the assembly in its machined case bore without the pump body O-ring seal (Fig. 10-104). Procede to torque tighten the pump cover bolts.

• When the new pump-body-to-case O-ring seal is installed, check it for correct size. You should feel a slight lip edge extending from the seal groove (Fig. 10-105). If the lip edge is not felt, it means that the O-ring does not extend out of the groove and is undersized.

Fig. 10-103.

Fig. 10-105.

Fig. 10-104.   THM-350 pump alignment.

CLUTCH SERVICE

Clutch servicing requires some special attention and know how. When a clutch unit is disassembled, it is good practice to keep the clutch plates and related assembly parts in order (Fig. 10-106). This provides a guidance for assembly sequence. What you have apart may not always match the service manual pictorial view, should it be needed for a reference. Even keep the clutch plates that will be discarded in the line up. Typical clutch assembly pictorial views are shown in Figs. 10-107, 10-108, and 10-109.

Fig. 10-106.   TorqueFlite rear clutch.

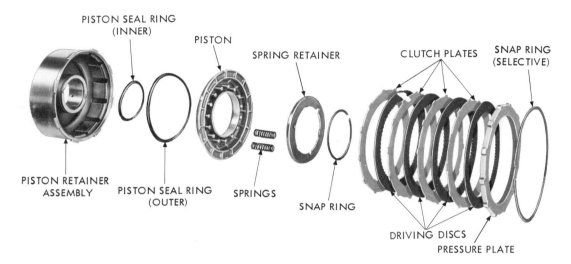

PISTON SEAL RING
(INNER)

PISTON

SPRING RETAINER

CLUTCH PLATES

SNAP RING
(SELECTIVE)

PISTON RETAINER
ASSEMBLY

PISTON SEAL RING
(OUTER)

SPRINGS

SNAP RING

DRIVING DISCS

PRESSURE PLATE

Fig. 10-107.   TorqueFlite front clutch assembly. (Chrysler Corp.)

Fig. 10-108.   TorqueFlite rear clutch assembly. (Chrysler Corp.)

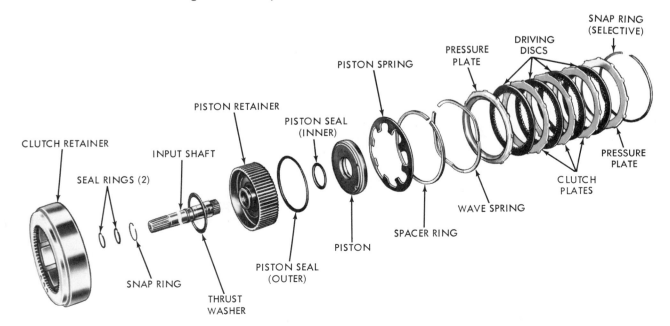

SNAP RING
(SELECTIVE)

DRIVING
DISCS

PRESSURE
PLATE

PISTON SPRING

PISTON RETAINER

PISTON SEAL
(INNER)

CLUTCH RETAINER

INPUT SHAFT

SEAL RINGS (2)

SNAP RING

THRUST
WASHER

PISTON SEAL
(OUTER)

PISTON

SPACER RING

WAVE SPRING

CLUTCH
PLATES

PRESSURE
PLATE

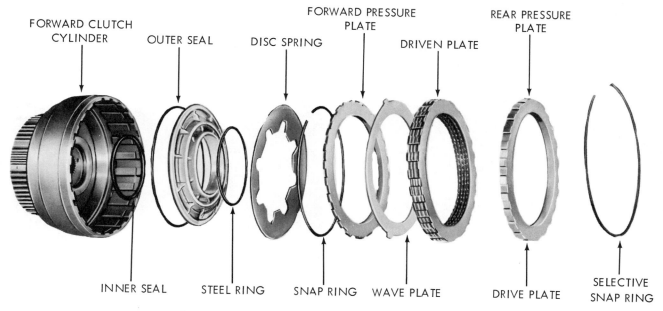

FORWARD CLUTCH CYLINDER — OUTER SEAL — DISC SPRING — FORWARD PRESSURE PLATE — DRIVEN PLATE — REAR PRESSURE PLATE

INNER SEAL — STEEL RING — SNAP RING — WAVE PLATE — DRIVE PLATE — SELECTIVE SNAP RING

Fig. 10-109.   C-6, forward clutch assembly. (Ford Motor Co.)

Fig. 10-110.

Clutch Unit Inspection and Reconditioning Guidelines

To prepare for inspection, clean all metal parts in mineral spirits and air dry. Do not attempt to rinse clean the composition plates if they are to be put back into service. The plate material must retain its oil soak.

• Inspect the drum housing bushing support for wear or scoring (Fig. 10-110). The bushing is a serviceable part and can be replaced.

• Inspect the bore and grooves in which the metal or teflon seals fit (Figs. 10-111 and 10-112). When the oil rings are under fluid pressure, they seal against the ring groove and the bore wall as illustrated in Fig. 10-113. In a rotating drum application, the fluid force seats the ring tightly against the drum bore and the

Fig. 10-111.

Fig. 10-112.

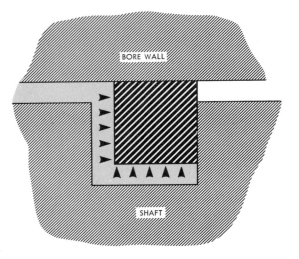

Fig. 10-113.

Fig. 10-117.

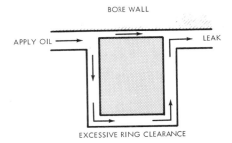

Fig. 10-114.

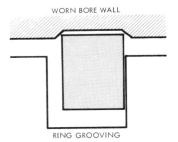

Fig. 10-115.

Fig. 10-116.

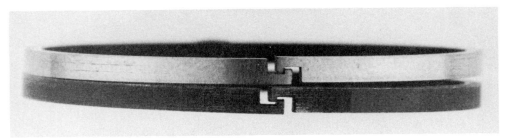

ring rotates with the bore and drum. As can be observed in Fig. 10-113 a sealing action also takes place between one side of the groove and the ring while the ring spins in the groove.

Contaminants in the fluid stream, especially metallic, can cause ring and groove wear. The excessive side clearance that develops results in the failure of the ring to seal (Fig. 10-114). The ring contact to the drum bore can also get upset and develop a wear pattern. During vehicle acceleration and deceleration, the drum unit will move back and forth as allowed by the normal internal transmission endplay. The bore wall, therefore, scrubs across the ring face and eventually polishes away the machine grooves. The scrubbing action is also accelerated by fluid contaminants and excessive transmission endplay. The polished ring will spin in the bore and cause ring grooving and excessive leakage (Fig. 10-115). A polished ring is compared to a new ring in Fig. 10-116.

• A rotating clutch unit will have a check ball in either the drum housing or clutch piston (Fig. 10-117). In some cases, especially when steel stamped pistons are used, the piston and drum combination is not properly matched and neither has a check ball.

The check ball must be free to rattle. If the check ball area is sealed closed by severe varnish or metallic contamination, it must be cleaned out to allow free action of the check ball. Without proper check ball action, the clutch plates will again fail. The check ball operation is described in Chapter 7.

• Inspect the piston bore for score marks. Light scores can usually be removed with crocus cloth. This leaves a polished bore surface. Emery cloth or sand paper produces a scratched surface finish that would quickly wear the piston seals.

• Inspect the piston return springs for distorted or collapsed coils.

• If a single disc spring is used, look for finger wear and distortion, and hairline cracks (Fig. 10-118).

• Inspect the clutch hub for worn splines (Fig. 10-119).

• Inspect the friction and steel clutch plates for possible reuse. When the plates are obviously worn, burned, warped, or coned shaped, replacement is the only answer (Fig. 10-120). Overhaul kits contain replacement plates for all the clutch units and, therefore, it is the common practice to recondition clutch units with all new plates regardless of the reuse value of the original plates. New plates are good insurance for positive clutch action and a long term overhaul.

Reuse of clutch plates is a legitimate service practice and does call for a careful evaluation of the plates. It can, however, become very time consuming when the steel plates need reconditioning.

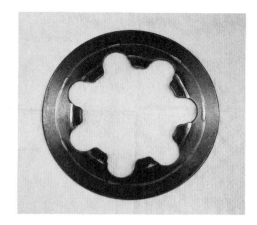

Fig. 10-118.

Fig. 10-119.

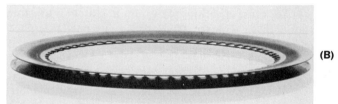
(B)

(C)

(A)

Fig. 10-120. Clutch plate rejects.
(A)Worn and pitted friction plate.
(B)Warped friction plate.
(C)Worn steel plates.

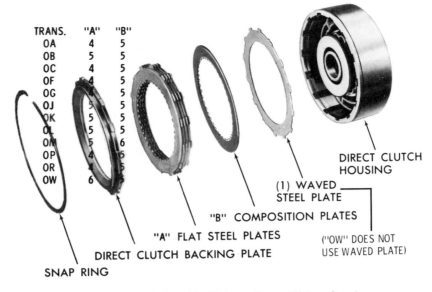

TRANS.	"A"	"B"
OA	4	5
OB	5	5
OC	4	5
OF	4	5
OG	5	5
OJ	5	5
OK	5	5
OL	5	5
OM	5	6
OP	4	5
OR	5	5
OW	6	

DIRECT CLUTCH HOUSING

(1) WAVED STEEL PLATE

"B" COMPOSITION PLATES

("OW" DOES NOT USE WAVED PLATE)

"A" FLAT STEEL PLATES

DIRECT CLUTCH BACKING PLATE

SNAP RING

Fig. 10-121. (Oldsmobile Division, General Motors Corp.)

REUSE OF FRICTION PLATES. When operating in a proper environment, friction plates can give thousands of miles of service without showing significant wear. Even the printed trade numbers and letters may remain visible. They become oil and temperature darkened but can be reused if: (1) the plate is flat and not warped or cone shaped; (2) the fiber material is firm and not pitted, flaked, glazed or loose; (3) when the plate facing is squeezed between the thumb and fingers, oil seeps out of the fiber. A glazed lining sometimes looks awfully good but will not give up oil when squeezed.

To reuse friction plates in a clutch unit, they should all be winners. Do not fuss with partial replacement. Either they can all be reused or they should all be replaced.

REUSE OF STEEL PLATES. If the friction plates pass inspection, the steel plates are usually salvagable. The only requirement is to keep the plates in the same order of removal. This keeps the mating contacting surfaces matched for the right action with the friction plates.

Steel plates can be reused if: (1) the plate is flat and not warped or cone shaped; (2) the plate surface shows no evidence of wear, scuffing, or grooving; (3) at the most, it suffers from only minor hot or oxidation spots; (4) the plate is surface-reconditioned when it is going to be used with new friction plates or a different oil.

Some clutch packs use a waved steel plate on top of the piston to cushion the clutch apply. Do not reject this wave plate because of warpage (Fig. 10-121).

To recondition a steel plate, use a medium-coarse emery or sandpaper grit and lightly work the surface until all the polish is removed (Fig. 10-122). Roughing the surface provides a similar finish of a new steel plate and insures proper application and break-in of the clutch pack. The polished surface of used steel plates matched with new friction plates will cause friction material glazing and drawn-out, lazy shifts.

Steel plate reconditioning is not recommended for the front (direct) clutch in TorqueFlite transmissions.

A study by Borg-Warner was made on the use of grit blasting, sand blasting, and glass-bead blasting as salvage techniques on steel plates. Severe abrasive wear on the clutch pack resulted from the resurfacing using the grit blast and sand blast. These two treatments are not recommended. The refinished surface produced by glass-bead blasting at 90 psi gave satisfactory wear and friction results. Some transmission shops are already using this technique with excellent results.

Fig. 10-122.

• In most cases, the oil ring bore wall shows no significant ring wear except for polish marks. To insure that the new rings will rotate with the drum, the polish surface should be removed from the bore wall with medium-coarse emery or sandpaper grit. For this hand operation, a piece of sponge can be used to work the emery or sandpaper in the bore (Fig. 10-123). Glass bead blasting has also given good results.

Clutch Unit Assembly Guidelines

The technician will be confronted with such items as clutch piston height, clutch plate thickness, required number of clutch plates, and plate clearance. When reassembling a clutch unit, it is important that the assembly parts and service specifications are matched with the transmission model code and engine application. This information is usually provided in the manufacturer's service manual. Chart 10-1 shows a Buick transmission model application for the THM-350.

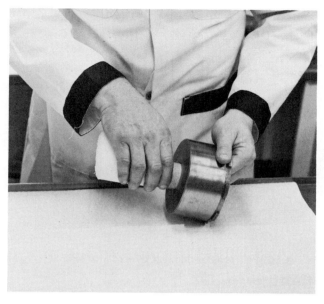

Fig. 10-123.

CHART 10-1 (Buick Division, General Motors Corp.)

Trans. Model	Converter Assembly Information	Engine Cu. In. Displacement	Intermediate Clutch		Direct Clutch		Forward Clutch		Low and Reverse Clutch		Modulator Assembly Note: Refer to PAR 75-35 for Diagnosis Procedure	Engine Usage
			Driven Plate Req'd	Drive Plate Req'd	Driven Plate Req'd	Drive Plate Req'd	Driven Plate Req'd	Drive Plate Req'd	Driven Plate Req'd	Drive Plate Req'd		
JE	Pink Dot of Paint		2	2	3	3	4	4	4	4	Refer to Group 4.205 in the Parts Catalog for Service Part Number	L6 Engine
JH	White Dot of Paint		3	3	4	4	5	5	5	5		350 Engine 2BBL Carburetor Lower Series
JR	White Dot of Paint		3	3	4	4	5	5	5	5		350 Engine 4BBL Carburetor Lower Series
JJ	White Dot of Paint	350	3	3	4	4	5	5	5	5		350 Engine 2BBL Carburetor LeSabre
JS	White Dot of Paint	350	3	3	4	4	5	5	5	5		350 Engine 4BBL Carburetor LeSabre

Fig. 10-124. Inner piston seal, direct clutch THM-200.

Fig. 10-126. Center piston seal, direct clutch THM-200.

Fig. 10-125. Outer piston seal, direct clutch THM-200.

• Lip seals used on the piston must have the lip facing the pressure side. The inner and outer seals are always installed with the lips facing down into the piston cylinder (Figs. 10-124 and 10-125). If the piston is designed with two apply chambers, a center seal is used on the cylinder sleeve hub and the lip must face up or away from the piston cylinder (Fig. 10-126).

The inner seal is sometimes located on the cylinder sleeve hub. A close inspection of the clutch assembly in Fig. 10-127 shows that the inner seal does not fit into the piston and must be installed on the drum cylinder sleeve hub. Failure to replace the seal, especially if the clutch pack was burnt, usually results in another clutch failure. Seals exposed to the heat generated in a burnt clutch pack lose their elasticity and become hard and brittle. They can no longer seal.

Fig. 10-127. Front clutch assembly. (Chrysler Corp.)

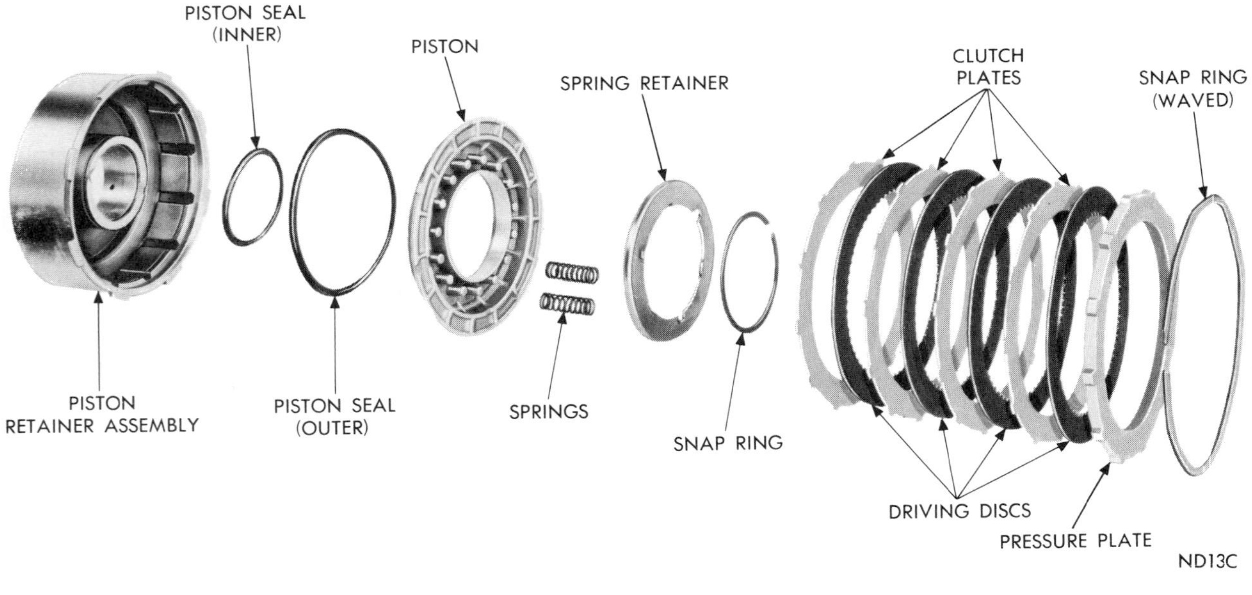

PISTON SEAL (INNER)

PISTON

SPRING RETAINER

CLUTCH PLATES

SNAP RING (WAVED)

PISTON RETAINER ASSEMBLY

PISTON SEAL (OUTER)

SPRINGS

SNAP RING

DRIVING DISCS

PRESSURE PLATE

ND13C

Fig. 10-128.

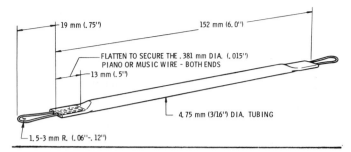

FLATTEN TO SECURE THE .381 mm DIA. (.015'')
PIANO OR MUSIC WIRE – BOTH ENDS

19 mm (.75'')

152 mm (6.0'')

13 mm (.5'')

4.75 mm (3/16'') DIA. TUBING

1.5-3 mm R. (.06''-.12'')

Fig. 10-130.   (Oldsmobile Division, General Motors Corp.)

• Prelubricate the seals with transmission fluid, petroleum jelly, or a silicone wax. Silicone wax (Door Ease®) works especially good on square-cut piston seals. The piston easily slips into the cylinder with light hand pressure. When using this method, the piston cylinder walls must be dry and free from transmission fluid (Fig. 10-128).

• When installing a piston with lip seals, a smooth .010 feeler gauge or piano wire can be worked around the seal to start the lip edge in the cylinder (Fig. 10-129). The piano wire installing tool can be fabricated in the shop (Fig. 10-130). Be careful not to cut the seal and keep a light hand pressure on the piston during this operation.

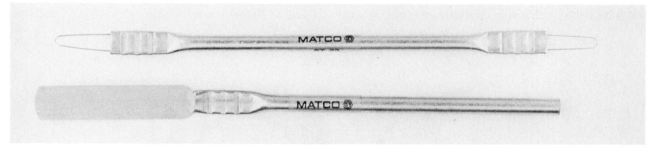

Fig. 10-129.

SPRINGS MUST BE INSTALLED
IN POCKETS MARKED X ONLY

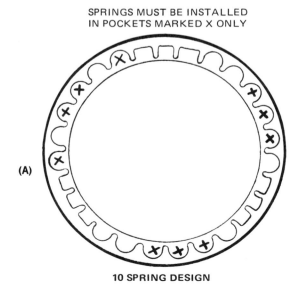

(A)

10 SPRING DESIGN

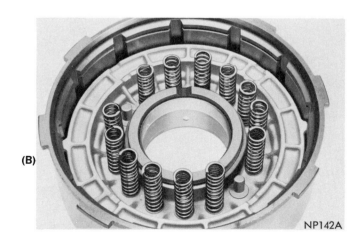

(B)

Fig. 10-131.   (A) (Ford Motor Co.) (B) (Chrysler Corp.)

• Always install the proper amount of piston return springs and in the exact required position. Figure 10-131 shows a Ford C-6 (10) spring design reverse-high clutch and a Chrysler TorqueFlite 727 (13) spring design front clutch.

• New friction plates must be presoaked in automatic transmission fluid for a minimum of 30 minutes and matched with new steel or reconditioned steel plates. The friction plate material must be saturated with oil to prevent glazing or burning during break-up. It requires 10–15 miles of driving before the oil mist surrounding the clutch pack can fully soak the friction plates. When the clutch is applied, the oil squeezed out of the friction lining carries away the heat. It should be obvious that friction plates installed dry or with limited prelubrication can fail within a few miles after an overhaul, especially if bonzani shifts are the customer's immediate criteria for testing.

• Be sure that the correct number of friction and steel plates are installed. There may be a difference in the friction and steel plate thickness between the forward and direct clutch units. As the rule, the thinner plates, whether friction or steel, will always go in the forward clutch.

• Each clutch assembly must be checked for plate clearance. Correct clearance cannot be established if: (1) the clutch plate count is not right; (2) the friction or steel plate thickness is not right; (3) the apply ring width on steel clutch piston applications is not right (illustrated in Fig. 10-132); (4) the clutch parts are not properly assembled.

Some clutch units have no required clearance specification. If the clutch unit has been properly assembled it should have acceptable production clearance. This is the usual requirement for GM transmissions. It is good practice, however, to observe if the clutch pack is too tight or too loose, which would indicate an error. Tight indicates no clearance or a heavy clutch pack drag. Too loose indicates a $\frac{3}{32}$–$\frac{1}{4}$ in. gap or better between the clutch pack and pressure plate.

In the absence of specifications, allow a minimum .010 in. clearance for each friction plate as a guideline.

When the service requirement calls for measuring the clutch pack clearance, the check is usually made with a feeler gauge between the snap ring and pressure plate (Fig. 10-133). The snap ring is selective in several sizes and used for adjusting the clearance. AMC, Chrysler, and Ford use this procedure on the forward and direct clutch units.

In the GM THM-350 and 250, a clearance check is required of the forward clutch and is taken between the pressure plate and clutch pack. The clearance adjustment is made with a selective pressure plate available in 3 sizes.

Always set-up the clutch pack clearance to the minimum side of the given specifications, but never adjust to below the minimum. Adjusting to the low

Fig. 10-132.

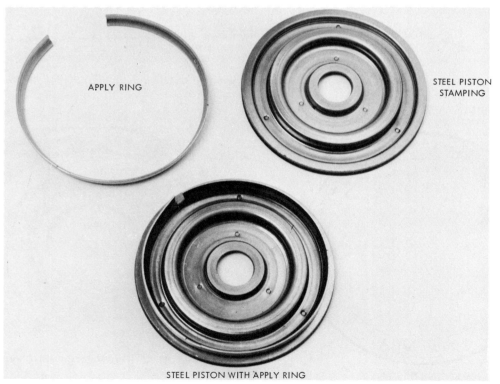

APPLY RING

STEEL PISTON STAMPING

STEEL PISTON WITH APPLY RING

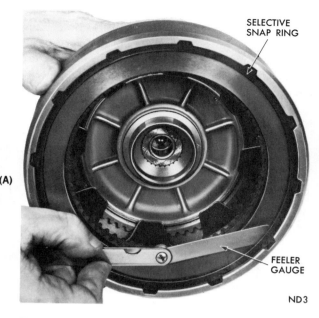

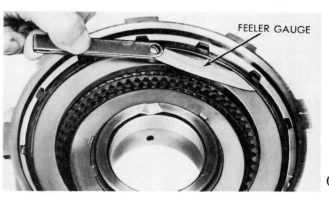

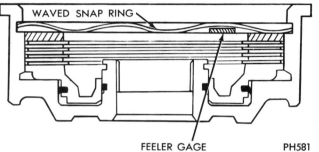

Fig. 10-133. (A) Rear clutch unit. TorqueFlite and (B) Front clutch unit, TorqueFlite. (Chrysler Corp.)

end shortens the piston stroke for longer seal life and crisper shift quality.

Most clearance tolerances allow an army tank to drive through, which can pose some problems. For example, the forward clutch pack clearance on a particular transmission calls for .010–.080 in. What you might have available in a selective pressure plate or snap ring may not get the desired minimum specification. A custom adjustment can be made by one of the following techniques:

(1) Add an extra composition plate and install back-to-back with another composition plate;
(2) Add an extra steel plate and install back-to-back with another steel plate;
(3) Use extra thick steel plates as necessary for replacement. These are available as an aftermarket item.
(4) Use one or two composition plates shaved on one side.

Fig. 10-134.

The plates are easy to shave in the shop (Fig. 10-134) and can be arranged as illustrated in Fig. 10-135 to achieve the desired results. Because the plates are mounted on the same splined hub, the metal sides can face one another.

• Finally, check the reliability of your clutch reconditioning with an air check (Fig. 10-136). This insures that (1) the piston seals were not damaged or incorrectly installed during assembly, (2) the oil rings are right, and (3) mechanically, the piston will apply and release.

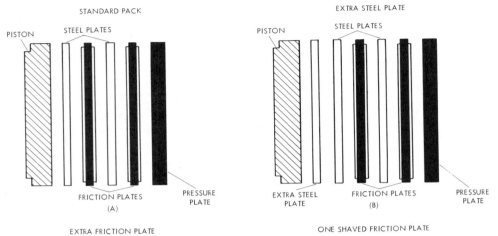

Fig. 10-135.

Fig. 10-136.

Fig. 10-137.

Fig. 10-138.

The air line pressure must be regulated down to 50 psi (Fig. 10-137). Higher pressures will overcome excessive sealing leaks and give a false indication that the clutch unit is OK.

Normal air leakage past oil rings and bushings will be audible during the test. By checking good clutch units, the technician establishes what is normal; then the bad one can easily be detected. The air leakage is more pronounced and the clutch piston action gets lazy even though it may apply and release.

For best test results squirt a liberal amount of trans oil in the clutch apply circuit port hole. This helps the oil rings seal, especially teflon. Also, be sure that the pump assembly is bolted together and torqued. On pump assemblies using a cover, it is advisable to torque several nut and bolt pairs in the case bolt holes (Fig. 10-138). This keeps the clutch circuit tight within the pump assembly and cuts down considerably on internal air leakage.

On clutch units using a center piston lip seal, air to the inner piston apply circuit should provide positive sealing. The center seal holds, as does the inner seal. When air is charged into the outer piston apply circuit, the center lip seal collapses and air exhausts into the inner piston apply circuit, unless the circuit has a check ball in the pump housing. The feed port of the inner apply circuit must be plugged during this test. A positive test result indicates that the outer piston seal is holding.

VALVE BODY SERVICE

Valve body service demands extra clean handling and extra attention to detail. Disassembly, cleaning, and reassembly must have an organized procedure for 100% results. During the transmission overhaul, the technician must evaluate the condition of the valve body for the type of service needed. In most cases, it will not be necessary to take the whole valve body apart, only enough to allow for a thorough flush and inspection of the free movement of the valves. Simply rinse the valve body in mineral spirits (Fig. 10-139).

Fig. 10-139.

Separate the valve body halves and flush out with a gum or varnish cleaner from an aerosol can (Fig. 10-140). Rinse the valve body halves again in mineral spirits and air dry. Oil the valves and check their movement with a miniature screwdriver blade (Fig. 10-141). Always check the tightness of the valve body end plates (Fig. 10-142). Leakage past the plates can cause erratic shifts and repeated clutch/band failures. This is especially important on Chrysler and Ford products.

Valve bodies that are severely contaminated with metal particles should usually be replaced. It is an almost impossible task to recondition a valve body, particularly if it is aluminum. You are never sure that it will work 100%.

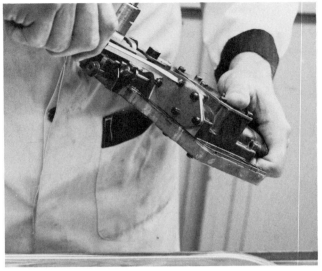

Fig. 10-142.

Fig. 10-140.

Valve bodies that are contaminated with minor deposits of metal particles or suffer with severe sludge or varnish deposits can be overhauled with reliable results. Some valve bodies might look like a disaster but still be serviceable (Fig. 10-143). The following guideline will cover general shop practices and service tips for the successful overhaul.

Valve Body Overhaul Guidelines

For a successful overhaul, the valve body must be completely disassembled to properly cleanout the contaminants and insure that all the valves move freely in their bores. For job efficiency, organize yourself with a clean bench area and equipment.

Fig. 10-141.

Fig. 10-143.

Valves that are severely coated with varnish will need to be sprayed with a gum or varnish cleaner from an aerosol can to unglue them from their bores.

Valves that are stuck in their bores from embedded metal or scratches are sometimes very difficult to remove, but it can be done.

Scratches are caused by fine metallic particles in the fluid stream that work their way between the bore and valve. Each scratch on the valve or the bore forms a groove with flared edges, which results in wedging the valve in the bore. The sticking effect of scratches and embedded metal on the valves is illustrated in Fig. 10-146.

Fig. 10-144.

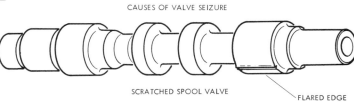

Fig. 10-146.

CAUSES OF VALVE SEIZURE

SCRATCHED SPOOL VALVE

FLARED EDGE

1. Soak the valve body in mineral spirits and clean the exterior with a brush (Fig. 10-144).

2. Using the shop manual, disassemble the valve body over a large parts tray filled with mineral spirits to catch the parts as they are removed; otherwise, the springs, check balls, and valves can easily roll off the bench and get lost, Fig. 10-145. These parts are not normally replaceable items.

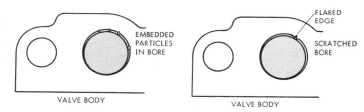

EMBEDDED PARTICLES IN BORE

VALVE BODY

FLARED EDGE

SCRATCHED BORE

VALVE BODY

Fig. 10-145.

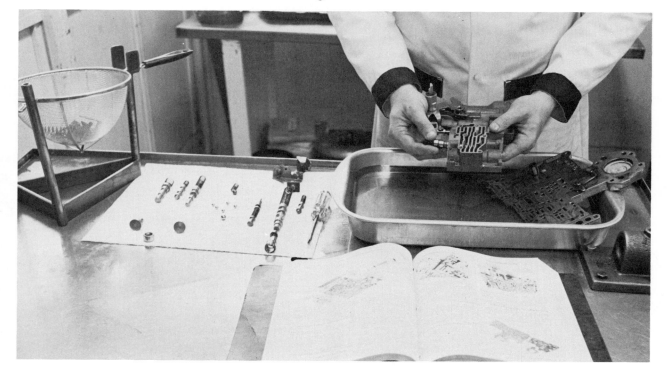

Fig. 10-147.

In most cases, wedged valves can be removed from the bore by carefully prying with a screwdriver blade wherever it can be worked on the valve spools (Fig. 10-147). Using sharp, light blows with a plastic hammer on the end of the bore casting may also work successfully (Fig. 10-148). Should these two techniques fail, then the following shock treatment can be used to eliminate the interference of the flared grooves and embedded particles.

(a) Place a clean shop towel on a flat bench surface. With the flat or passage side facing down, slam the valve body on a flat surface several times, Fig. 10-149.

(b) After the bench slam operation, place a screwdriver blade in the grooved section of the valve. Rap the screwdriver from several positions, top and sides of the valve, with an open end wrench

Fig. 10-148.

Fig. 10-150.

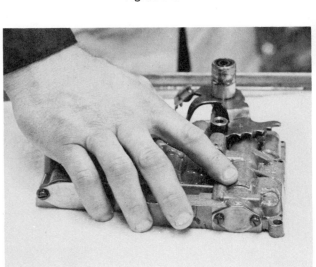

Fig. 10-149.

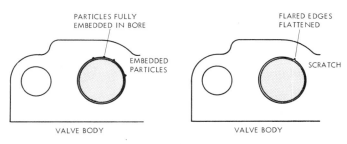

Fig. 10-151. Impact effect on valve body bore to remove interference from embedded particles or scratches.

(Fig. 10-150). The use of a hammer in place of an open end wrench may produce too much force and bend the valve. Fig. 10-151 illustrates the effect of the procedure on the flared edges and metal particles.

3. Keep each valve bore assembly separated and aligned on a clean paper shop towel (Fig. 10-152). Use the manufacturer's pictorial view in the shop manual as a guideline. This practice prevents accidental interchange of look alike springs and valves. It also is a time-saver during reassembly if the parts are properly sorted and organized.

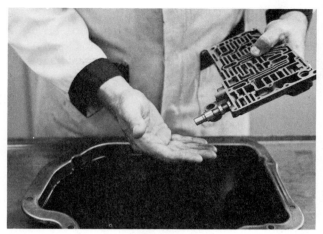

Fig. 10-153.

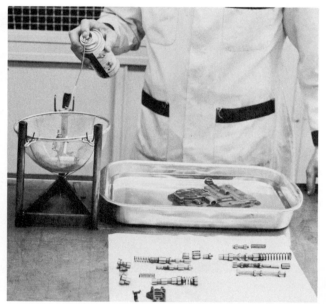

Fig. 10-152.

4. For valve bodies severely contaminated with varnish, sludge, or burnt fluid, soak the valve body castings, bolts, and nuts and cover plates in a transmission cleaner. A carburetor cleaner can be used, but soak only long enough to remove the gum and varnish. Some carb cleaners will etch or pit the castings if allowed to work too long.

After the soak period, flush the castings and parts with detergent soap and hot water, and air dry.

Valve bodies relatively free from varnish and sludge can be sprayed with an aerosol gum and varnish cleaner in place of soaking.

5. The valve bore parts, springs, and valves can easily be cleaned with an aerosol gum and varnish cleaner (Fig. 10-152). This should be followed by a clean, cold solvent flush and air drying.

6. For final reassembly preparation, test the valves that might appear to be a problem. Check for

free movement in their bores under dry conditions Simply insert each suspect valve in its bore. The valve should move freely in its bore as the valve body is tipped back and forth (Fig. 10-153).

Valve bores and valves that suffer from scratches or embedded metal particles can be reconditioned to size in several ways. For most bore diameters, a rolled piece of crocus cloth sheet can be inserted and rotated. By rotating in a direction that unwinds the roll, usually counterclockwise, the crocus cloth hugs the bore and polishes it to size (Fig. 10-154).

Fig. 10-154.

Crocus cloth can also be used to recondition a valve. Place a sheet of crocus cloth on a flat plate surface, such as auto safety plate glass. Just rotate the valve as you scrub it across the cloth. This same operation can be done with a fine honing stone. Both techniques are illustrated in Figs. 10-155 and 10-156. Do not round-off the sharp edges of the valve ends. The razor sharp edges are needed to cutaway any contaminants in the bore that might seize the valve. The rounded edge forms a pocket for the contaminants to gather and the valve easily seizes.

Fig. 10-155.

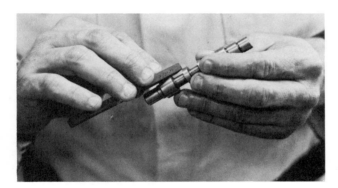

Fig. 10-156.

Fig. 10-157.

Desired results may also be produced by mixing a paste compound of any common household cleanser, transmission fluid, and graphite mix such as Dri-slide® (Fig. 10-157). This technique is especially effective on the small hard-to-get-at valves and bores. Apply the paste with your finger or a brush onto the valve lands and work the valve in and out of the bore. If the valve end permits, a small rubber hose can be attached to the valve for ease of handling. Reapply the paste several times if necessary. This operation is shown in Figs. 10-158 and 10-159. If this does not produce a free moving valve, the valve body is a loser.

Fig. 10-158.

Fig. 10-159.

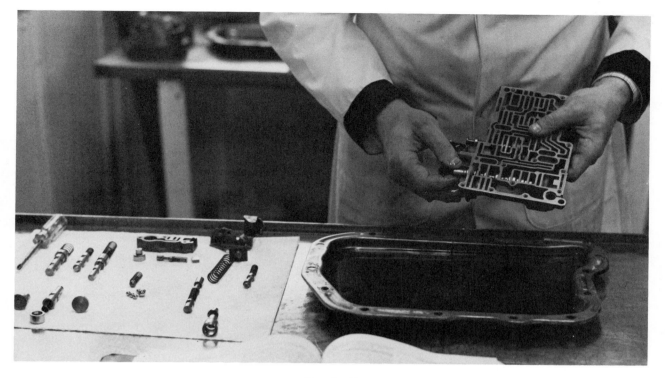

Fig. 10-160.

Always flush the valve and valve body with cold solvent and air dry after removing scratches and embedded particles.

Never remove scratches or embedded particles with emery or sanding paper. This only produces more scratches and adds to the problem you are trying to eliminate.

Worn valves, valve bores, or fatigued springs are not a valve body problem; therefore, there are no formal service checks in this area.

7. Once the valve body and valve bore assemblies have been evaluated and prepared, the valve body unit is ready for assembly. Observe the following tips:

(a) Prelubricate the valves in transmission fluid.
(b) Each valve should slide into the bore free and easy without dragging or binding (Fig. 10-160). Spring-loaded valves can be pushed in their travel range with a wood dowel.
(c) When necessary, check balls can be held in place with petroleum jelly (vaseline).
(d) On two piece valve bodies, it is advisable to completely bolt together and torque-tighten the upper and lower bodies before installing the valves. Some valves, however, will usually need to be installed before bolting. This procedure insures that the valve body has not been distorted by bolt tightening, which can cause valve seizure.

(e) Always torque-tighten the valve body bolts or screws to avoid valve seizure or unwanted circuit leaks (Fig. 10-161). Refer to the manufacturer's shop manual for specifications. Some valve body bolts will require only 35 inch/pounds, just slightly over finger tight.

To avoid stripping threads, be sure to install all the valve body bolts or screws before torque-tightening. This assures alignment of the holes between the valve body halves and separator plate.

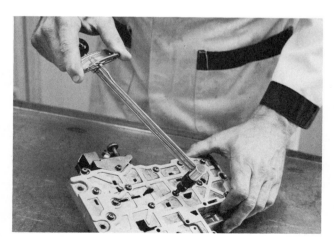

Fig. 10-161.

Fig. 10-162.

(f) There are usually several sets of separator plate gaskets in an overhaul kit. The correct one should match the separator plate configuration and all plate holes should have a matched opening through the gasket (Fig. 10-162). The gaskets are installed dry.

8. Some valve bodies require external adjustments and these should always be checked for accuracy. Figures 10-163 and 10-164 show the line pressure and throttle pressure adjustment checks on a TorqueFlite valve body.

Fig. 10-163. (Chrysler Corp.)

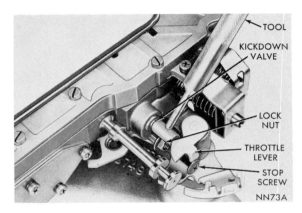

Fig. 10-164. (Chrysler Corp.)

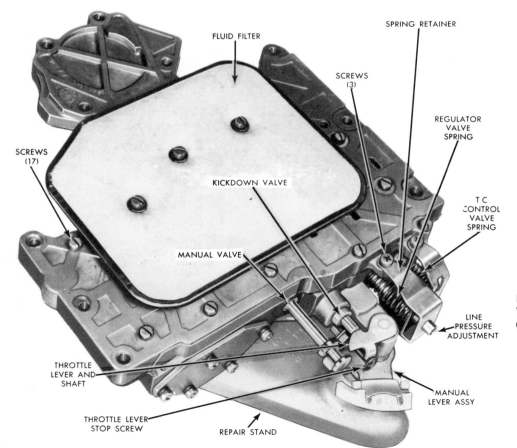

Fig. 10-165.
Valve body assembly.
(Chrysler Corp.)

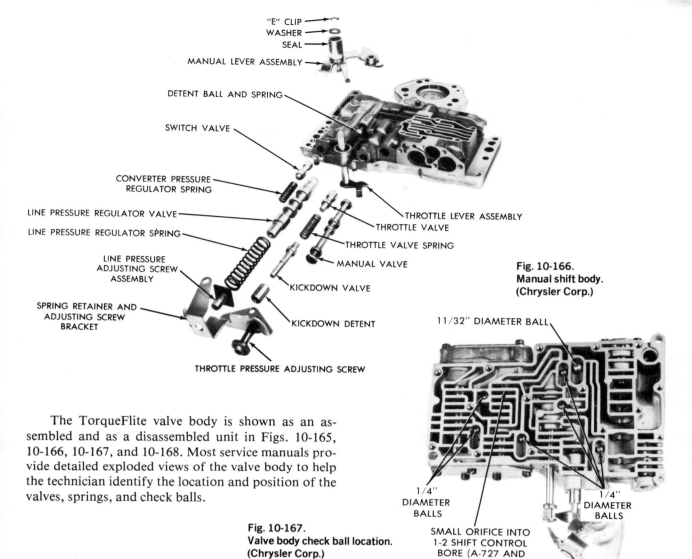

"E" CLIP
WASHER
SEAL
MANUAL LEVER ASSEMBLY

DETENT BALL AND SPRING

SWITCH VALVE

CONVERTER PRESSURE REGULATOR SPRING

LINE PRESSURE REGULATOR VALVE

LINE PRESSURE REGULATOR SPRING

LINE PRESSURE ADJUSTING SCREW ASSEMBLY

SPRING RETAINER AND ADJUSTING SCREW BRACKET

THROTTLE LEVER ASSEMBLY

THROTTLE VALVE

THROTTLE VALVE SPRING

MANUAL VALVE

KICKDOWN VALVE

KICKDOWN DETENT

THROTTLE PRESSURE ADJUSTING SCREW

**Fig. 10-166.
Manual shift body.
(Chrysler Corp.)**

11/32" DIAMETER BALL

1/4" DIAMETER BALLS

1/4" DIAMETER BALLS

SMALL ORIFICE INTO 1-2 SHIFT CONTROL BORE (A-727 AND A-904-LA ONLY)

**Fig. 10-167.
Valve body check ball location.
(Chrysler Corp.)**

The TorqueFlite valve body is shown as an assembled and as a disassembled unit in Figs. 10-165, 10-166, 10-167, and 10-168. Most service manuals provide detailed exploded views of the valve body to help the technician identify the location and position of the valves, springs, and check balls.

Fig. 10-168.   Shift valve body. (Chrysler Corp.)

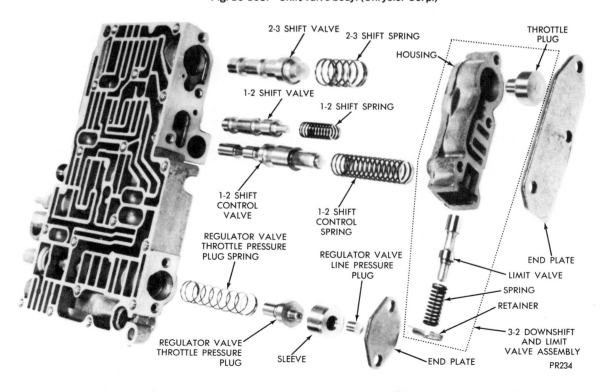

2-3 SHIFT VALVE

2-3 SHIFT SPRING

THROTTLE PLUG

HOUSING

1-2 SHIFT VALVE

1-2 SHIFT SPRING

1-2 SHIFT CONTROL VALVE

1-2 SHIFT CONTROL SPRING

REGULATOR VALVE THROTTLE PRESSURE PLUG SPRING

REGULATOR VALVE LINE PRESSURE PLUG

END PLATE

LIMIT VALVE

SPRING

RETAINER

3-2 DOWNSHIFT AND LIMIT VALVE ASSEMBLY

REGULATOR VALVE THROTTLE PRESSURE PLUG

SLEEVE

END PLATE

PR234

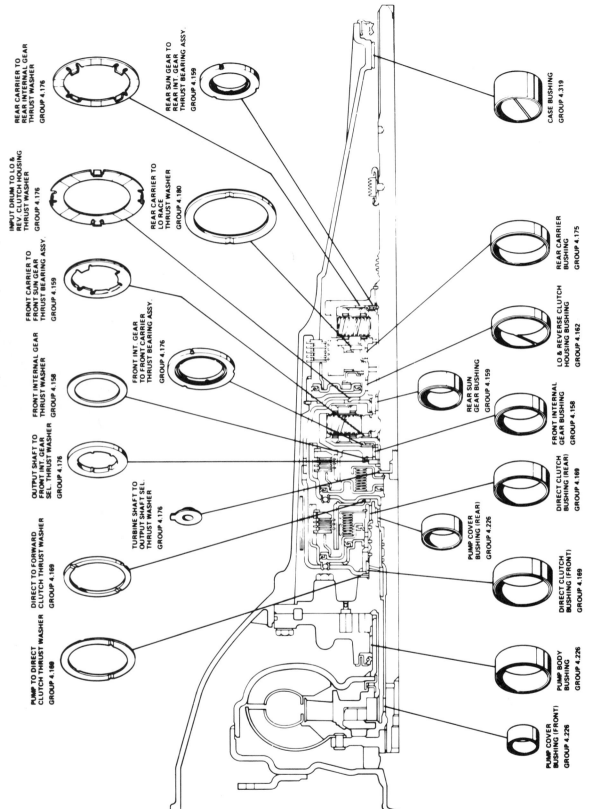

REAR CARRIER TO REAR INTERNAL GEAR THRUST WASHER GROUP 4.176

REAR SUN GEAR TO REAR INT. GEAR THRUST BEARING ASSY. GROUP 4.159

CASE BUSHING GROUP 4.319

INPUT DRUM TO LO & REV. CLUTCH HOUSING THRUST WASHER GROUP 4.176

REAR CARRIER TO LO RACE THRUST WASHER GROUP 4.180

REAR CARRIER BUSHING GROUP 4.175

FRONT CARRIER TO FRONT SUN GEAR THRUST BEARING ASSY. GROUP 4.159

FRONT INT. GEAR TO FRONT CARRIER THRUST BEARING ASSY. GROUP 4.176

LO & REVERSE CLUTCH HOUSING BUSHING GROUP 4.162

FRONT INTERNAL GEAR THRUST WASHER GROUP 4.158

REAR SUN GEAR BUSHING GROUP 4.159

FRONT INTERNAL GEAR BUSHING GROUP 4.158

OUTPUT SHAFT TO FRONT INT. GEAR SEL. THRUST WASHER GROUP 4.176

DIRECT CLUTCH BUSHING (REAR) GROUP 4.169

TURBINE SHAFT TO OUTPUT SHAFT SEL. THRUST WASHER GROUP 4.176

PUMP COVER BUSHING (REAR) GROUP 4.226

DIRECT TO FORWARD CLUTCH THRUST WASHER GROUP 4.169

DIRECT CLUTCH BUSHING (FRONT) GROUP 4.169

PUMP TO DIRECT CLUTCH THRUST WASHER GROUP 4.169

PUMP BODY BUSHING GROUP 4.226

PUMP COVER BUSHING (FRONT) GROUP 4.226

Fig. 10-169. (Oldsmobile Division, General Motors Corp.)

BUSHING SERVICE

The transmission bushings function to align and support shafts, gears, and clutch drums. They must also act as restrictors for the converter and lubrication circuits that are routed between inner and outer shaft members. Figure 10-169 illustrates the bushing locations in a THM-200, which is typical of most Simpson three-speed transmission designs. Worn bushings replaced during overhaul can reduce gear noise, sealing, and ring groove wear, converter drain back, and pressure losses in the converter/lubrication circuits.

Service bushings are available as a dealer or jobber item. They can be purchased individually or in a kit package (Fig. 10-170). The replacement bushings are precision made and have a close tolerance fit. They do not require boring or reaming after installation. On TorqueFlite transmissions, the front stator shaft bushing is eliminated in favor of supporting the input shaft and turbine with a bushing installation in the converter cover (Fig. 10-171). With any TorqueFlite rear stator shaft and/or rear clutch ring and groove wear, you should take into consideration the condition of the converter with a good bench analysis. (Refer to Converter Service.)

During cleaning and inspection of the transmission, most bushings will show little wear and do not need replacement. It is usually obvious when a bushing needs replacement. A visual inspection will easily pickup a galled, scored, or excessively worn condition (Fig. 10-172).

Fig. 10-172.

Fig. 10-170.

Where bushing wear is not obvious but under suspicion, fit the mating part to the bushing and check the looseness with a wire or flat feeler gauge (Fig. 10-173). Although factory recommendations permit clearances up to .008 in., it is best that the limit does not exceed .005 in. Use a .006 in. wire as a no-go gage. Experienced technicians will usually be able to determine excessive looseness by observation.

Fig. 10-171.

Fig. 10-173.   THM-350; measuring sun gear bushing wear.

Fig. 10-174.

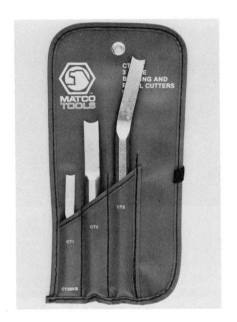

Fig. 10-175. (A) and (B).

Although extensive factory tooling is available for bushing removal and installation, bushing service can be done with some simple tooling and your own innovations. Most bushings can be split and removed with a bushing cutter chisel and hammer (Fig. 10-174). A variety of cutter chisels are shown in Fig. 10-175. Be sure to select the proper chisel for the job and avoid using too light a hammer. Let the weight of the hammer do the work. Because split-type bushings are usually used, drive the chisel on the seam of the bushing split.

On extra small bushings that are located in dead-end bores, a N/C thread tap can do the job. Illustrated in Fig. 10-176 is the use of a 9/16 N/C tap to remove the output shaft bushing in a THM-350. To prevent breaking the tap, a large-size bearing ball must be placed in the bottom of the bushing bore.

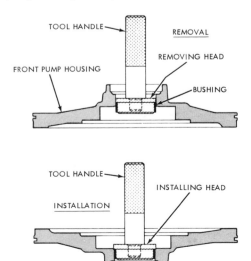

Fig. 10-176.

Fig. 10-177. Pump bushing removal and installation. (Chrysler Corporation)

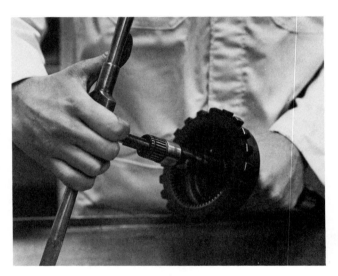

Fig. 10-178. (Oldsmobile Division, General Motors Corp.)

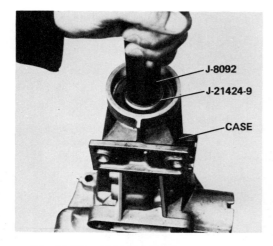

Fig. 10-179. Extension housing. (Oldsmobile Division, General Motors Corp.)

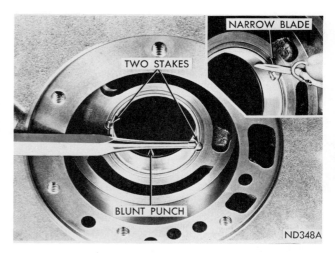

Fig. 10-180. Pump bushing. (Chrysler Corp.)

Fig. 10-181.

Fig. 10-182.

Replacing a bushing requires an exact technique if the job is to be done properly. You will definitely need a bushing installer adapted for the bushing size to drive or press the bushing into place. Otherwise, the bushing will be damaged. Proper bushing installations using adapter heads for removal and installation are illustrated (Figs. 10-177, 10-178, and 10-179). Some bushings must also be staked as required by the manufacturer (Fig. 10-180).

Where case mounted governors are used in the THM 400, 350 and 250 transmissions, the governor bore occasionally gets worn. To salvage the case, special factory tooling is available that permits reaming the bore oversized to accept a governor bushing sleeve. This operation is shown in Fig. 10-181, where the reamer plate guide is centered to the governor bore and in Fig. 10-182 where the governor bore is reamed to size for the new bushing sleeve. Be sure to align the bushing with the governor bore oil holes when driving the bushing into place.

GOVERNOR SERVICE

The governor requires attention during overhaul and is another service item often overlooked. Spending a few minutes to check out the working condition of the governor system will avoid those erratic or no-shift problems after overhaul

Output Shaft Mounted

With output shaft mounted governors, disassemble, clean, and assemble the unit with the same care required of the valve body. A typical unit is illustrated in Fig. 10-183. In this type of output shaft mounted design, be sure to separate the inner and outer weights for cleaning and inspection. The fluid contaminants like to hide in this area and cause improper secondary governor action. The governor body must be removed from its support or distributor to check for a clogged filter (Fig. 10-184). The filter is located on the inlet side of the circuit on both Chrysler and Ford applications (Fig. 10-184).

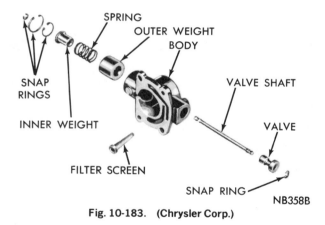

Fig. 10-183. (Chrysler Corp.)

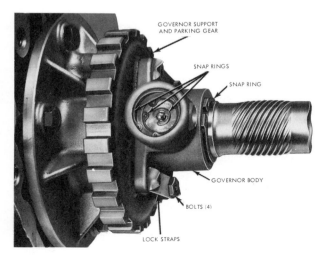

Fig. 10-184. Governor assembly. (Chrysler Corp.)

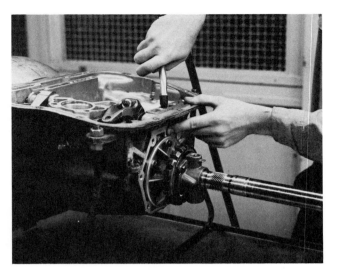

Fig. 10-185. Air checking TorqueFlite governor.

Fig. 10-186. Air checking Ford governor.

When the governor is positioned back in the transmission, it can be checked with a 50 psi air supply for proper action. On all Chrysler and Ford transmissions, apply pressure to the governor out passage located in the transmission case. For best test results, cover the governor case inlet passage with your finger (Figs. 10-185 and 10-186).

• Ford: Listen for a buzzing noise similar to a model airplane engine. This means that the governor valve is properly "hunting" or oscillating.

• Chrysler: The governor must be positioned with the weights working against the valve. A fast acting audible "thud" should be heard. On occasion, however, the valve will prefer to oscillate in a low-keyed tone.

As a counter check on both Ford and Chrysler governors, apply air to the governor case inlet passage. With air charging the circuit, cover the outlet passage temporarily with your finger. The governor valve should snap closed and stay in this position.

Case Mounted

In General Motors THM-400, THM-350, and THM-250 transmission units using case-mounted governors (Fig. 10-187) both the case and the governor need to be evaluated. To check the governor assembly, flush in mineral spirits, air dry, and then make the following inspections.

- Inspect governor sleeve finish for scoring.
- Inspect governor driven gear for damage and looseness.

Fig. 10-189. (Oldsmobile Division, General Motors Corp.)

Fig. 10-187. Case mounted governor assembly and installation. (Oldsmobile Division, General Motors Corp.)

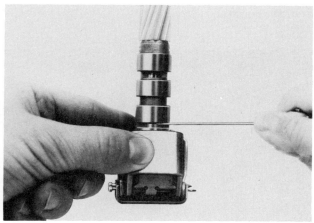

Fig. 10-190. (Oldsmobile Division, General Motors Corp.)

Fig. 10-188.

- Inspect governor weight springs for distortion.
- Check governor weights for free operation in their retainers.
- Check the free movement of the governor valve by moving the weights in-and-out (Fig. 10-188).
- It is very important to check the valve inlet and exhaust port openings. These openings should be at least .020 in. If they are right, the gaps are usually large enough for the technician to make a good judgement without measuring. Should a gap be questionable, use a .020 in. feeler gauge as a go–no-go measurement. To measure the inlet port, the weights are extended completely outward (Fig. 10-189). The exhaust system port opening is checked with the weights completely held in (Fig. 10-190). If the gap openings are not correct, the governor will need to be replaced.
- Check the governor for free rotation in the transmission case bore. If the governor sleeve was

found to be scored on an earlier inspection, then the case bore must be closely examined for scoring.

If the case bore is scored, it can be reamed out and sleeved back to size with a service bushing (see Bushing Service). As another choice, the bore can be lightly polished by hand with a brake wheel cylinder hone (Fig. 10-191) or silicone honing brush (Fig. 10-192). The edges of the honing stones must be rounded off to avoid biting into the aluminum. Oil the stones and turn the hone by hand with a tap handle about ten turns. Both ends of the bore must be conditioned separately and equally. This means that the inner half and outer half are polished with the same amount of turns. Avoid moving the hone in and out when turning. With a silicone brush, rotate the brush using short in and out strokes.

After the honing operation flush and air dry the case. With a new governor, perform the following leak check to test for excessive clearance between the governor sleeve and case bore.

Fig. 10-193. (General Motors Corp.)

1. Place the transmission case on the bench as shown in Fig. 10-193.

2. Install the governor and fill the governor case passages with solvent to the level given in Fig. 10-194.

3. Rotate the governor to remove air bubbles in the circuit and then refill the passages back to level.

4. With the governor at rest, time the leakdown for 30 seconds. If the solvent level falls below point A (Fig. 10-194), then the sealing tolerance between the governor sleeve and the case bore is excessive. This means that the governor case bore must be serviced with a bushing.

Fig. 10-191.

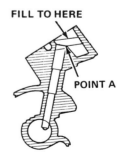

Fig. 10-194. (A) and (B). (General Motors Corp.)

FILL TO HERE

POINT A

Fig. 10-192.

To air check the governor action in the case bore, use the same procedures used for output shaft mounted governors. Governor weights must be in a vertical position (Fig. 10-195). For a good oscillating action, place your finger on the inlet passage while applying 50 psi of air to the outlet.

As illustrated in Fig. 10-196, the case mounted governor can be completely disassembled and serviced if necessary. Small parts replacements are available, including the nylon-driven gear. Consult the manufacturer's service manual for procedures.

Fig. 10-195.

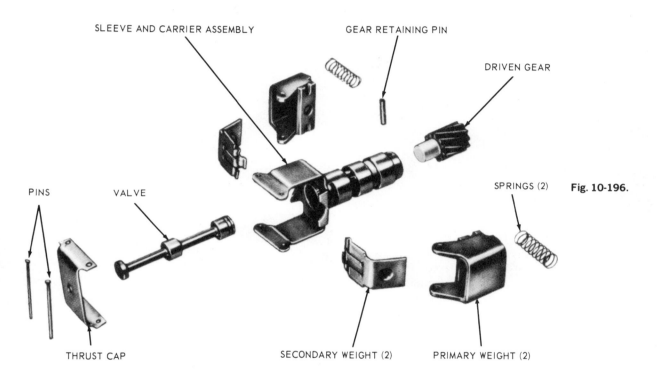

Fig. 10-196.

TRANSMISSION ASSEMBLY

Once the subassemblies and related parts have been evaluated and prepared, they are ready for installation in the transmission case. This basically requires reversing the disassembly procedure. Again, use the manufacturer's service manual or equivalent as a reference. The main concern on installation is to carefully mate the subassemblies together along with the related parts. The transmission should go together with the same care given to a 21-jewel watch; excessive force is not needed. If parts do not assemble freely, find the cause and correct the trouble before proceeding with further assembly.

Assembly Guidelines

Selective illustrations are used to show various key points in general assembly procedures that apply to all automatic transmissions.

- Be sure to replace the manual shaft case seal and throttle shaft seal.
- Presoak new bands and clutch discs for 30 minutes in transmission fluid.
- Careful attention must be given to the placement of thrust washers. They should be tacked into place with petroleum jelly on one side only (Fig. 10-197) Treat the tanged side where applicable. Avoid using white lube or other greases.

Fig. 10-197. (A) and (B).

A thrust washer incorrectly placed or one that drops out of place will cause an eventual assembly bind and prevent snap ring installations on the output shaft.

• Prelubricate all O-ring and case seals with petroleum jelly or transmission fluid.
• Install all paper gaskets dry. Avoid the use of sealers.

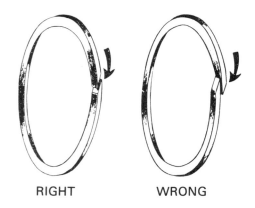

RIGHT   WRONG

Fig. 10-198. (Oldsmobile Division, General Motors Corp.)

• Prelubricate gears, sprag or roller clutch assemblies, shafts, and bushings with transmission fluid. Most parts can be dipped in fluid before installation. The tendency is to neglect lubrication and put the transmission together dry.

Fig. 10-199.   Chrysler 727 TorqueFlite pump.

(A)

(B)

Fig. 10-200.   (A) and (B). THM -200.

• On teflon seal applications, make sure that the cut ends are matched in the same relationship as the cut (Fig. 10-198). Otherwise, the ring will fail to seal. Teflon is a soft material and care must be also taken not to nick the rings.

• Clean or replace governor and oil pump pressure screens.

• Adjust the input shaft endplay to the minimum side of the specifications or even below, close to zero, if it can be attained within the adjustment provisions provided by the manufacturer. Selective thrust washers or shims are provided for this adjustment. Most current automatic transmissions use the number 1 or number 3 thrust washer as selective. The number 1 is located on the back of the pump assembly (Fig. 10-199) and number 3 on the end of the output shaft (Fig. 10-200).

• Be sure to make an output shaft endplay check when required and adjust to the low end of specifications. Figure 10-201 shows the dial indicator set-up for checking the output shaft endplay on the THM-200.

Endplay is controlled by a selective thrust washer on the end of the output shaft.

• A critical part of assembly is the installation of the forward and direct clutch units. The clutch friction discs must all be indexed on their splined hub. If the discs fail to all be indexed, the clutch units will not rest fully in the case and ride high. When the pump is bolted into place, it will wedge against the clutch units and bind the unindexed discs. Front unit endplay is impossible and the input shaft will not rotate.

For ease of handling, index the direct clutch discs onto the clutch hub part of the forward clutch (Fig. 10-202) and install the clutch units together in the case (Fig. 10-203). Manipulate the forward clutch discs into place on their hub by turning and lightly rocking the input shaft.

Fig. 10-202.   TorqueFlite 727.

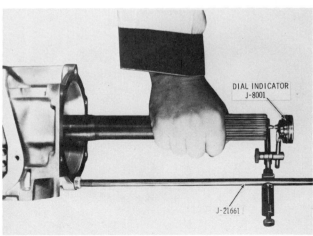

Fig. 10-201.   (A) and (B). THM-200.
(Oldsmobile Division, General Motors Corp.)

Fig. 10-203.   TorqueFlite 727.

If the forward clutch and direct clutch discs are all indexed on their hub, then proper case clearance is attained for pump installation. Some transmission assembly procedures include measurements to insure that the clutch discs are all indexed and the clutch units are at proper case depth (Figs. 10-204 and 10-205).

• Installation of the pump assembly requires extra care. The use of guide pins will ease the operation. Be sure to install a new pump case gasket and to treat the pump body O-ring seal with a lubricant (Figs. 10-206 and 10-207). To avoid stripping pump bolt threads, loosely install all bolts and then draw the bolts down evenly and torque tighten (Fig. 10-208).

Check to make sure the input shaft rotates freely during the tightening process. If the input shaft binds-up, it means that the clutch discs are not all indexed to their hub or a thrust washer is out-of-place.

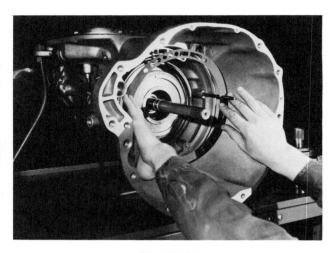

Fig. 10-206.

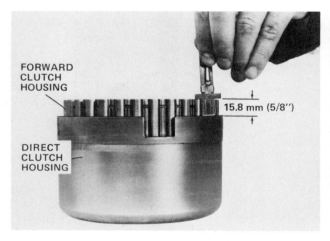

Fig. 10-204. THM-200. (Oldsmobile Division, General Motors Corp.)

Fig. 10-207.

Fig. 10-205. THM-200. (Oldsmobile Division, General Motors Corp.)

Fig. 10-208.

• Where cast iron bands are still used, install the band with the thick end aligned with the case anchor. An early design Ford C-6 with the thick end of the intermediate band facing the case anchor is illustrated in Fig. 10-209. The band adjusting screw acts as the stationary case anchor.

Fig. 10-209.

The heavy anchor end of the band must absorb the thrust of the self-energizing action of the band and the servo piston apply force. The light anchor end could not withstand these combined forces and would break-off.

• Before installing threaded bolts in the aluminum case, dip the bolts in automatic transmission fluid to prevent galling the aluminum threads and to prevent seizing.

• Never use an impact wrench for final tightening.

• Torque tighten extension housing, pump, and valve body case bolts. This prevents stripping of aluminum threads and also prevents internal circuit leaks between the pump and case or valve body and case.

Be consistent on the use of torque specifications; either stay entirely with the high side or the low side of the specifications throughout the transmission assembly. The technician is shown in Fig. 10-210 torquing the valve body to case. Uneven torquing can produce internal circuit leakage or possible valve seizure.

• On band adjustments, the adjustment specifications must match the engine displacement and transmission model. A torque wrench is always used for preloading the band before adjusting the band clearance (Fig. 10-211).

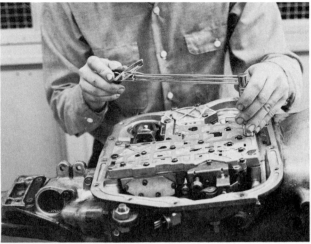

Fig. 10-210.

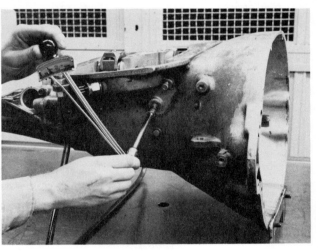

Fig. 10-211.

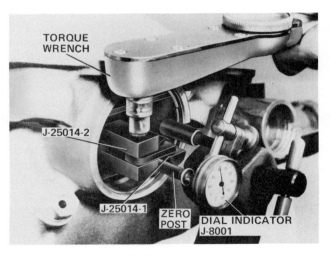

Fig. 10-212. THM-200. (Oldsmobile Division, General Motors Corp.)

Where band adjustment screws are not provided the servo piston apply pin may require a select fit and must be measured for correct length during overhaul. This will be a permanent built-in band adjustment. In Fig. 10-212 a dial indicator set-up is shown for determining the correct intermediate band apply pin, which is available in four sizes.

• For a reliability check on your workmanship, test the clutch, servo, and governor action whenever possible, using regulated compressed air at 50 psi. The TorqueFlite case feed holes to these circuits are illustrated in Fig. 10-213.

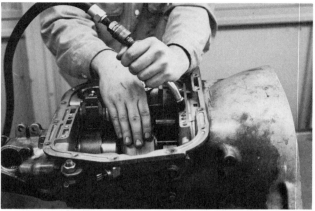

Fig. 10-214.

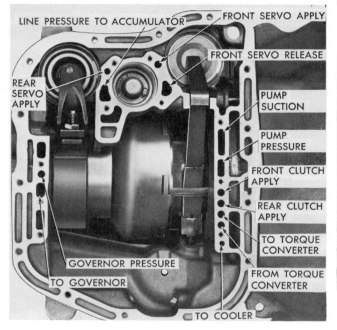

Fig. 10-213.

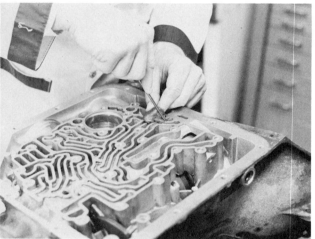

Fig. 10-215.

The technician in Fig. 10-214 is running a check on the rear clutch apply circuit. You should be able to hear and feel the clutch apply and release. The governor circuit and the front and rear servo operation can all be air-tested for operation.

To air-check clutch circuits when the upper valve body channels are part of the case, it may be necessary to form a seal at the feed hole with car body putty (Fig. 10-215). A rubber ball with a metal tube insert can then be used for the air-check (Fig. 10-216).

Air-checking the circuits and units in the transmission takes practice. There will always be a certain amount of air leakage past seal rings and bushings, which you must determine to be normal or excessive. The more checks you make, the more proficient you can become in the art of air-checking in the case. It is normal for teflon rings to bleed more air than metal rings. Under hydraulic pressure, however, they will provide a tight seal.

Fig. 10-216.

• If the transmission is equipped with a vacuum modulator, protect your overhaul longevity with a reliability check-out. (Refer to Chapter 9.)

After installation in the car, always make a road test and perform a final check on the fluid level and for fluid leaks.

Fig. 10-218.

TRANSMISSION MODEL AND PARTS CODE IDENTIFICATION

Every automatic transmission has a model and part code identification usually consisting of groups of numbers or letters. These groups of numbers or letters are codes used for identifying the correct transmission assembly model or part numbers and for manufacturing and warranty claims.

The most important part of the coding system is for the technician to identify the transmission model and part code where applicable. Transmission operating requirements are different for each engine and vehicle combination. This means that some internal parts will be different as well as service and test specifications. When overhauling a transmission, the service manual will often make reference to the transmission parts code. For example, look at the direct clutch plate requirements of various THM-400 models in Fig. 10-217.

404, the numbers and letters are stamped on the rear side of the transmission oil pan flange. The technician is concerned with the seven-digit number that identifies the transmission assembly part number. When ordering parts, refer to this number for exact parts and positive identification of the transmission. The complete coding shown in Fig. 10-218 has the following meaning:

PK4028412—Transmission assembly part number.
5585—Warranty code date.
0651—Daily production number.

The 727 and 904 model type referred to in the service manual can sometimes be identified by embossed letters that stand out on the lower left hand side of the bell housing (Fig. 10-219).

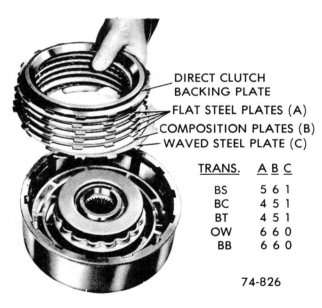

DIRECT CLUTCH
BACKING PLATE
FLAT STEEL PLATES (A)
COMPOSITION PLATES (B)
WAVED STEEL PLATE (C)

TRANS.	A	B	C
BS	5	6	1
BC	4	5	1
BT	4	5	1
OW	6	6	0
BB	6	6	0

74-826

Fig. 10-217. (Buick Motor Division, General Motors Corp.)

Chrysler

On the TorqueFlite 727 and 904, a series of numbers and letters are stamped on the left side of the transmission oil pan flange (Fig. 10-218). On the FWD

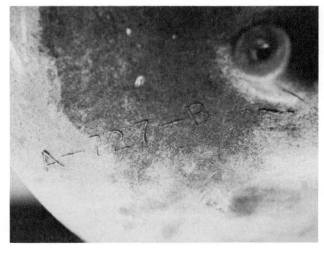

Fig. 10-219.

Ford

Ford Motor Company transmissions use an identification tag with the following code letters and numbers (Fig. 10-220). The assembly part coding on the lower part of the C-4, C-6, AO, and FMX identifies the year model. In this example, the *D* means built in the 1970s and the *9* identifies the year (1979). The tag locations are as follows:

C-4 and C-6—Intermediate servo cover.
AO and FMX*—Lower right side extension housing.
C-3—Lower left side extension housing.
JATCO—Left side transmission case above manual control lever.

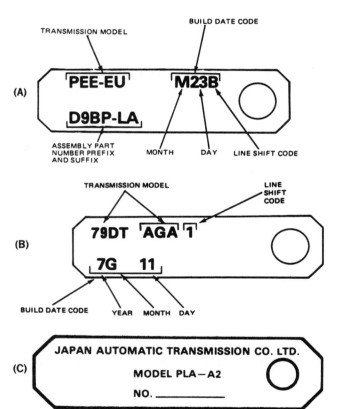

Fig. 10-220. Typical Ford automatic transmission identification tags. (A) C-4, C-6, AO and FMX. (B) C-3. (C) JATCO.

General Motors

250, 250C, 350 AND 350C. TRANSMISSIONS. The transmission model and code numbers are stamped on the governor cover as shown in Fig. 10-221 for the THM-250 and THM-350. Early THM-350 model and code numbers may be found on the accumulator cover (Fig. 10-222), the right vertical sur-

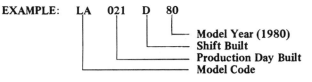

EXAMPLE: LA 021 D 80
— Model Year (1980)
— Shift Built
— Production Day Built
— Model Code

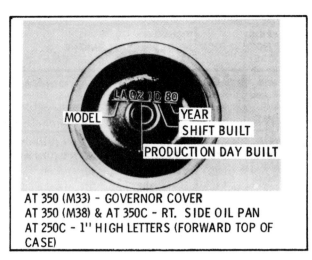

AT 350 (M33) - GOVERNOR COVER
AT 350 (M38) & AT 350C - RT. SIDE OIL PAN
AT 250C - 1" HIGH LETTERS (FORWARD TOP OF CASE)

Fig. 10-221. (Oldsmobile Division, General Motors Corp.)

face of the oil pan, or identified by 1-in.-high inked code letters on the bell housing portion of the case. THM-350C and late THM-350 (M-38) identification is stamped on the right vertical surface of the oil pan. The THM-250C has 1-in.-high code letters on the bell housing portion of the case. The THM-250 and THM-250C also has a band-adjusting screw on the right side of the transmission case.

125, 200, 200C, 200-4R, 325, AND 400 TRANSMISSIONS. All HydraMatic Division transmissions use a serial number plate (Fig. 10-223). The model year is 1980 and the model code OJ in our example. The plate is located on the right side (rear) of the case on the THM-200, 200C, 200-4R, and 400; the 325 serial number plate is located on the left side of the converter housing and, for the 125, next to the manual shaft.

Fig. 10-222.

*Vacuum modulator located left side rear of case.

Fig. 10-223. (Oldsmobile Division, General Motors Corp.)

REVIEW QUESTIONS

CHAPTER 10

Mark the appropriate square ☒ to indicate whether the statement is TRUE or FALSE.

1. Before removing a drive shaft it should be marked for original position.   TRUE ☐   FALSE ☐

2. During transmission removal, it is good practice to mark the flex plate and converter for original position.   TRUE ☐   FALSE ☐

3. Missing engine to trans case dowel pins will cause a cracked flex plate.   TRUE ☐   FALSE ☐

4. Missing engine to trans case dowel pins will cause damage to the converter crankshaft pilot.
TRUE ☐   FALSE ☐

5. All automatic transmissions have an adjustable input shaft endplay.   TRUE ☐   FALSE ☐

6. Transmission gaskets are typically treated with aviation permatex before installation.   TRUE ☐   FALSE ☐

7. The separator or spacer plate gasket is right when all the plate holes have an opening through the gasket.   TRUE ☐   FALSE ☐

8. New clutch plate friction discs should be pre-soaked in transmission fluid for a minimum of 10 minutes before installation.   TRUE ☐   FALSE ☐

9. Emery cloth is an excellent material for polishing valve body bores.   TRUE ☐   FALSE ☐

10. Emery cloth is an excellent material for polishing converter drive hubs.   TRUE ☐   FALSE ☐

11. The passenger side of the transmission is also referred to as the right hand side.   TRUE ☐   FALSE ☐

12. If there is a difference, the forward clutch friction plates are typically thinner than the direct clutch friction plates.   TRUE ☐   FALSE ☐

13. If there is a difference, the forward clutch steel plates are typically thinner than the direct clutch steel plates.   TRUE ☐   FALSE ☐

14. Petroleum jelly is a legitimate lubricant for pre-lubing clutch plates.   TRUE ☐   FALSE ☐

15. When a roller clutch is installed backwards, it will free-wheel in both directions.   TRUE ☐   FALSE ☐

16. A worn or rough governor case bore means that the transmission case must be replaced.
TRUE ☐   FALSE ☐

17. When the fluid sample from the converter has a metallic appearance, the converter should be replaced.
TRUE ☐   FALSE ☐

18. $\frac{1}{16}$ of an inch is approximately .090.
TRUE ☐   FALSE ☐

19. Shaved friction plates can be legitimately used for adjusting clutch plate clearance.   TRUE ☐   FALSE ☐

20. It is acceptable practice to use new friction clutch plates with used steel plates.   TRUE ☐   FALSE ☐

21. O-ring seals should be installed dry with no pre-lube treatment.   TRUE ☐   FALSE ☐

22. It is acceptable practice to use white lube to hold check balls and thrust washers in place.
TRUE ☐   FALSE ☐

23. It is not uncommon for the manufacturer to provide a selective clutch plate retaining ring for adjusting clutch plate clearance.   TRUE ☐   FALSE ☐

24. The #1 thrust washer refers to the thrust washer located on the front pump.   TRUE ☐   FALSE ☐

25. To service a governor, the transmission must be removed from the vehicle.   TRUE ☐   FALSE ☐

26. A suction gun can be used to flush cooler lines.
TRUE ☐   FALSE ☐

27. When the lubrite coating begins to rub off the pump gears, the pump must be replaced.
TRUE ☐   FALSE ☐

28. If the converter drive hub is fully engaged into the front pump, it should fit flush with the flex plate during transmission installation.   TRUE ☐   FALSE ☐

29. It is always standard operating procedure to replace the pump bushing during overhaul.
TRUE ☐   FALSE ☐

30. Converter endplay can be determined by using snapring pliers: TRUE ☐   FALSE ☐

31. As part of an overhaul, all metal or teflon sealing rings are discarded and replaced.   TRUE ☐   FALSE ☐

32. If the sample oil from the converter is heavily varnished or even black, it should be replaced.
TRUE ☐ FALSE ☐

33. Most transmission parts replacement is determined by visual inspection.   TRUE ☐ FALSE ☐

34. Converters without drain plugs must be drilled for thorough flushing.   TRUE ☐ FALSE ☐

35. Sand blasting is excellent for re-conditioning steel plates.   TRUE ☐ FALSE ☐

36. The converter drive hub will not engage an incorrectly installed pump drive gear.   TRUE ☐ FALSE ☐

37. It is acceptable to set the input shaft endplay below minimum specifications.   TRUE ☐ FALSE ☐

38. Emery cloth is an excellent material for removing score marks in clutch piston cylinders.
TRUE ☐ FALSE ☐

39. Silicone wax is acceptable for pre-lubing clutch piston rubber seals.   TRUE ☐ FALSE ☐

40. It is good practice to air check each clutch unit for operation as the transmission gets built-up.
TRUE ☐ FALSE ☐

41. Household cleanser mixed with trans fluid and liquid graphite is an excellent compound for reconditioning a stuck valve in its bore.   TRUE ☐ FALSE ☐

42. When reconditioning stuck valves, it is preferred to round-off the edges of the valve lands.
TRUE ☐ FALSE ☐

43. Severely varnished valve bodies and their assembly parts can legitimately be soaked in carburetor cleaner.   TRUE ☐ FALSE ☐

44. If the forward clutch discs are not all indexed on their hubs then the input shaft will lock-up during pump installation.   TRUE ☐ FALSE ☐

45. (Bench Position) Lip type center piston seals used in some direct clutch units should be installed with the lip facing down.   TRUE ☐ FALSE ☐

46. Governor action can be verified during overhaul with an air check.   TRUE ☐ FALSE ☐

11

SUMMARY REVIEW OF CURRENT AUTOMATIC TRANSMISSIONS

This chapter is a summary study of automatic transmissions in production since 1975. Some of these current transmissions have a long history and predate 1975. In brief, the discussion covers the historical development, transmission description, operating characteristics, mechanical powerflow summaries, and general supporting data. Although automatic transmissions are popularly identified with engine displacements, it can no longer be used as the only criteria. Each manufacturer has a complex system of transmission application based on engine displacement, plus transmission availability, vehicle usage, and vehicle weight. The engine displacements and transmission applications mentioned in the write-ups are to be treated as typical only for the times. By 1985 the standard power plant will be a four-cyclinder with the six-cylinder available as an option. It would not be uncommon to find that a car manufacturer might use two or three different transmissions on the same engine.

CHRYSLER CORPORATION

Aluminum TorqueFlite A-904, A-727 and A-404

The aluminum A-904 TorqueFlite was introduced in 1960 and used with the newly-developed Chrysler slant-six engine. It had replaced the two-speed cast iron PowerFlite. In production year 1962, the cast iron TorqueFlite was phased out in favor of a new heavy duty aluminum A-727 to accommodate V-8 engine applications. Both transmissions are in current production, with the A-904 and A-727 adapted to handle a wide range of the Chrysler engine and vehicle product line. The A-904 and A-727 pioneered the use of the one-piece integrated aluminum case; the converter housing and transmission case are molded as a single casting with a bolt-on extension housing.

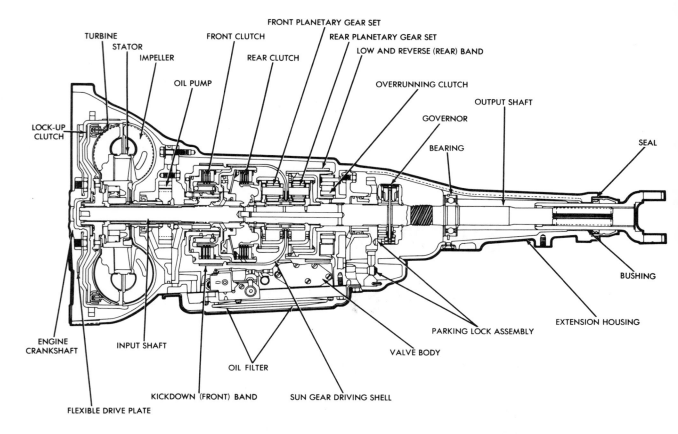

Fig. 11-1. TorqueFlite transmission and torque converter (A-904). (Chrysler Corp.)

Fig. 11-2. TorqueFlite transmission and torque converter (A-727). (Chrysler Corp.)

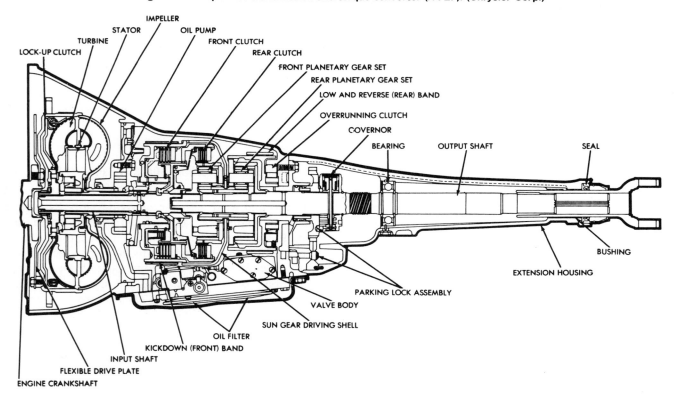

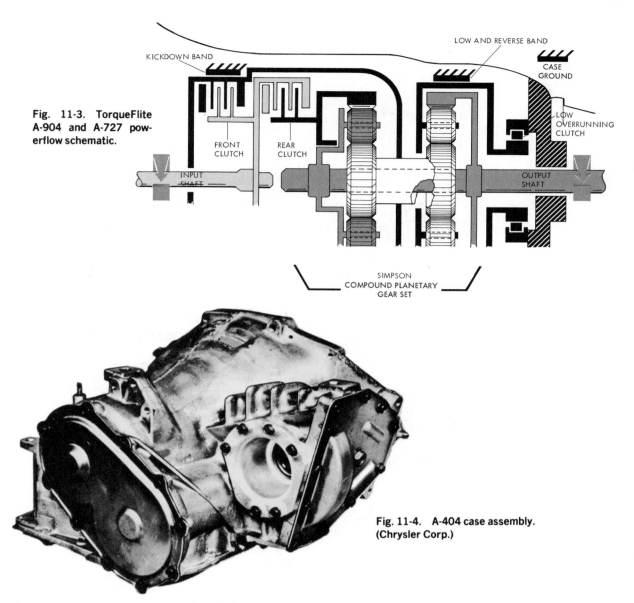

Fig. 11-3. TorqueFlite A-904 and A-727 powerflow schematic.

KICKDOWN BAND

FRONT CLUTCH

REAR CLUTCH

INPUT SHAFT

LOW AND REVERSE BAND

CASE GROUND

LOW OVERRUNNING CLUTCH

OUTPUT SHAFT

SIMPSON COMPOUND PLANETARY GEAR SET

Fig. 11-4. A-404 case assembly. (Chrysler Corp.)

Figures 11-1 and 11-2 show sectional views of the complete A-904 and A-727 assemblies. They differ only in physical size. The TorqueFlite has a three-element torque converter with a maximum stall torque of 2.0 or 2.2, depending on engine application, and a compound Simpson Planetary Set. Two multiple-disc clutches, two bands, and a roller clutch provide the means to control the gear train operation. Figure 11-3 represents a simplified schematic view of the basic gear train and friction control elements. Detailed operation of the gear train is discussed in Chapter 4.

In January, 1978, the basic TorqueFlite design was adapted for use in the automatic transaxle for the Plymouth Horizon and Dodge Omni. Identified as the Omni/Horizon A-404, it combines a three-speed transmission and a differential assembly in one compact front wheel drive unit of metric design (Fig. 11-4). The power train with engine is a transverse or East/West system (Fig. 11-5).

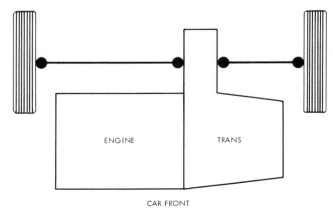

ENGINE

TRANS

CAR FRONT

Fig. 11-5.

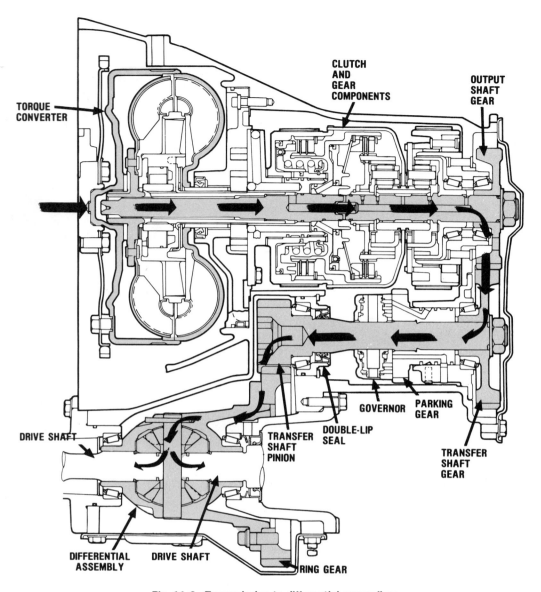

Fig. 11-6. Transmission to differential power flow.

Referring to Fig. 11-6, the powerflow series starts through a nonlockup, three-element torque converter, the transmission clutch and gear components, the output and transfer shaft gears, the transfer shaft, differential, and final drive to the drive shafts. Helical gears are used for transfer of the powerflow from the main centerline to the transfer shaft (Fig. 11-7). A helical pinion gear at the inner end of the transfer shaft drives the ring gear. The final drive uses two gear sets, providing ratios of 3.48 Federal (49 states) and 3.67 California.

The transmission and differential both use Dexron fluid; however, the two sump areas are separate and require their own individual fill level. The differential fill and drain plugs are shown on the right side of the transaxle (Fig. 11-8). Internal seal leakage would result in transmission fluid loss to the differential sump.

For 1981, two new automatic transaxles are avail-

able and almost identical to the A-404 automatic used in the Omni and Horizon. The A-413 is an option on the Aries and Reliant car models equipped with the 2.2-liter engine, while all K cars equipped with the 2.6-liter engine get an A-470 as standard equipment. Servicing either transaxle is very similar to servicing the A-404. There are minor design differences that prevent interchangeability of trans cases.

The converter housing section is shown in a front view of the transaxle (Fig. 11-9).

Typical Engine Applications

A-904	A-727	A-404
6—225 CID (3.7L)	6—225 CID (3.7 L)	4—105 CID (1.7L)
V8—318 CID (5.2L)	V8—318 CID (5.2 L)	A-413
V8—360 CID (5.9L)	V8—360 CID (5.9 L)	4—2.2L
	V8—440 CID (7.2 L)	A-470
		4—2.6L

Fig. 11-7.

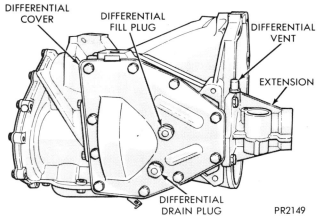

DIFFERENTIAL COVER

DIFFERENTIAL FILL PLUG

DIFFERENTIAL VENT

EXTENSION

DIFFERENTIAL DRAIN PLUG

PR2149

Fig. 11-8.

POWERFLOW SUMMARY AND OPERATING CHARACTERISTICS

N—Neutral: The powerflow dead-ends at the front and rear clutch units. There is no input to the gear train.

R—Reverse gear: A function of the rear planetary unit. Provides a simple planetary ratio of:

- 2.21:1 for all A-904 and A-727 TorqueFlites, including the wide ratio gear train introduced in 1980 production.
- 2.10:1 for A-404

D—Drive range is used for normal driving conditions and maximum economy. Full automatic shifting and three gear ratios are available.

First Gear (Breakaway): A combined function of the front and rear planetary units. Provides a compound gear ratio of:

- 2.45:1 for all A-904 and A-727 TorqueFlites except for A-904 applications using the new 1980 wide ratio geartrain. Wide ratio first gear is 2.74:1. The A-727 is scheduled for the wide ratio gear train after June, 1980.
- 2.48:1 for A-404.

Second Gear: A function of the front planetary unit. Provides a simple planetary ratio of:

- 1.45:1 for all A-904 and A-727 TorqueFlites except for A-904 applications using the new 1980 wide ratio geartrain. Wide ratio second gear is 1.54:1.
- 1.48:1 for A-404.

Third Gear: A direct drive ratio of 1:1, plus converter lock-up for A-904 and A-727.

Fig. 11-9.

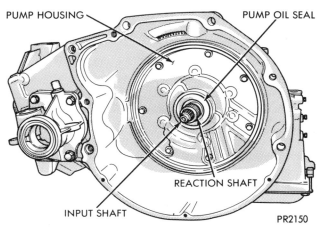

PUMP HOUSING

PUMP OIL SEAL

REACTION SHAFT

INPUT SHAFT

PR2150

Range	Gear	(Direct) Front Clutch	(Forward) Rear Clutch	(Front) Kickdown Band	(Rear) Low-Reverse Band	Low Roller Clutch
Park						
Reverse		On			On	
Neutral						
D—Drive	(Breakaway) First		On			Holds
	Second		On	On		
	Third	On	On			
2—Drive	First		On			Holds
	Second		On	On		
1—Low	First		On		On	Holds

External controls to the transmissions are:

- Linkage Control—To select the transmission operating range.
- Linkage or Cable—To the carburetor for mechanical operation of both the throttle and kickdown systems. Both system control valves are in tandem in the same valve body bore and work from the same single external control.

For added acceleration, full throttle kickdown shifts 3–1, 2–1, and 3–2 are available within the proper vehicle speed and engine torque range. As another performance feature, a 3–2 part throttle downshift is incorporated for controlled acceleration during low speed operation. The closed throttle downshift pattern is 3–1.

The 2 range provides a normal 1–2 shift pattern and keeps the transmission in second gear for extra pulling power or engine braking in hilly terrain. It can also be used for performance in congested traffic. 2 can be selected at any high gear vehicle speed and the transmission will downshift to second. At closed throttle, the shift pattern is 2–1. A full throttle kickdown shift 2–1 is available.

The 1 range maintains first-gear operation for heavy pulling power and engine braking, especially for mountain terrain. 1 range can be selected at any vehicle speed range but will shift to second if the vehicle speed is too high. When the vehicle slows down to a safe speed (approximately 30 mph or 48 km/h), manual low engages and the transmission will not upshift regardless of throttle opening.

Chart 11-1 summarizes the TorqueFlite clutch /band combinations and range operation.

New for the 1978 model year was the development of the lock-up torque converter for A-904 and A-727 transmissions.* This was achieved by modifying the

*See Chapter 2.

valve body and incorporating a lock-up turbine piston in the converter. This means that the converter unit has the capability of internally clutching the turbine element to the impeller cover. The lock-up mode is activated only after the 2–3 shift takes place and the vehicle speed is at approximately 30 mph (48 km/h) or better. This avoids lugging the engine at low rpm's. With the impeller and turbine mechanically locked together, converter slippage is eliminated and fuel economy improved during the coupling phase.

The lock-up torque converter is used on all TorqueFlites except for the following applications: 440 C.I.D. (7.2 L) engine; 225 C.I.D. (3.7 L) California; all high altitude applications; and heavy duty fleet and trailer tow operations. The A-404, A-413, and A-470 models do not use a lock-up converter.

FORD MOTOR COMPANY

The Ford family of Cruise-O-Matic automatic transmissions provides a wide variety of units to meet the requirements of their product line. In current or recent production are the C3, C4, C6, JATCO, AOT and FMX transmissions. The AOT and FMX have their own distinct features while all the others are functionally similar.

C3, C4, C6, and JATCO

The C3, C4 and C6 were introduced respectively in 1973, 1964, and 1966; hence the reference C3, C4 and C6. The JATCO was first used in 1973 for the intercity Courier truck 1800-cc, four-cylinder engines with floor shift. In midyear 1977, it was scheduled for use in the Granada/Monarch with the six-cylinder, 250-CID engine and column shift.

The C3, C4, and JATCO use an aluminum case with bolt-on converter and extension housings. The C6, however, is a one-piece, integrated aluminum case

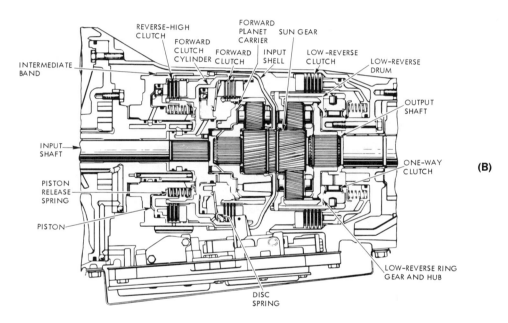

Fig. 11-10. (A). C-6 right side external view. (B). C-6 sectional view. (Ford Motor Co.)

with the converter housing and has a bolt-on extension housing. The C3 and JATCO are all-metric transmissions manufactured overseas in France and Japan. JATCO letters are symbols for the Japan Automatic Transmission Company, LTD.

Figures 11-10, 11-11, and 11-12 show sectional and companion external views of the complete C6, C4, and JATCO assemblies. The C3, with an external view, is shown in Fig. 11-13. The main components of these transmissions are basically the same. They all use a three-element torque converter and a compound Simpson Planetary Set. In the C3 and C4, two multiple-disc clutches, two bands, and a roller clutch provide the means to control the gear train operation. Basically, the C6 and JATCO use these same friction

elements; however, the low–reverse band is substituted with a low–reverse multiple disc clutch. The C3 is fundamentally a small-size version of the C4, and the JATCO is a small-size version of the C6. Figures 11-14 and 11-15 are simplified schematic views of the basic gear train and friction control elements used by these transmissions. Detailed operation of the gear trains is discussed in Chapter 4.

Typical Engine Applications

JATCO	C3
4—108 CID (1.8 L)	4—139 CID (2.3 L)
6—250 CID (4.1 L)	V6—171 CID (2.8 L)

C4		C6
4—139 CID (2.3 L) 6—250 CID (4.1 L)		V8—351 CID (5.8 L)
V6—171 CID (2.8 L) V8—302 CID (5.0 L)		V8—400 CID (6.6 L)
6—200 CID (3.3 L) V8—351 CID (5.8 L)		V8—460 CID (7.6 L)

(A)

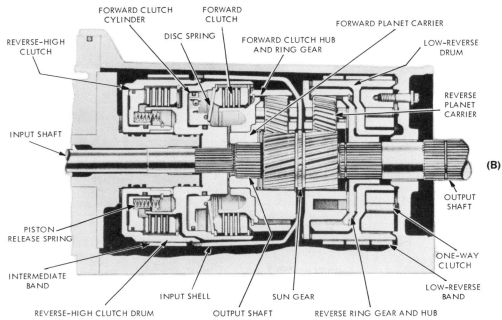

REVERSE-HIGH
CLUTCH

FORWARD CLUTCH
CYLINDER

DISC SPRING

FORWARD
CLUTCH

FORWARD CLUTCH HUB
AND RING GEAR

FORWARD PLANET CARRIER

LOW-REVERSE
DRUM

REVERSE
PLANET
CARRIER

INPUT SHAFT

(B)

OUTPUT
SHAFT

PISTON
RELEASE SPRING

ONE-WAY
CLUTCH

INTERMEDIATE
BAND

INPUT SHELL

SUN GEAR

LOW-REVERSE
BAND

REVERSE-HIGH CLUTCH DRUM

OUTPUT SHAFT

REVERSE RING GEAR AND HUB

Fig. 11-11. (A). Right side external view. (B). C-4 sectional view. (Ford Motor Co.)

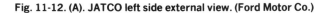

Fig. 11-12. (A). JATCO left side external view. (Ford Motor Co.)

(A)

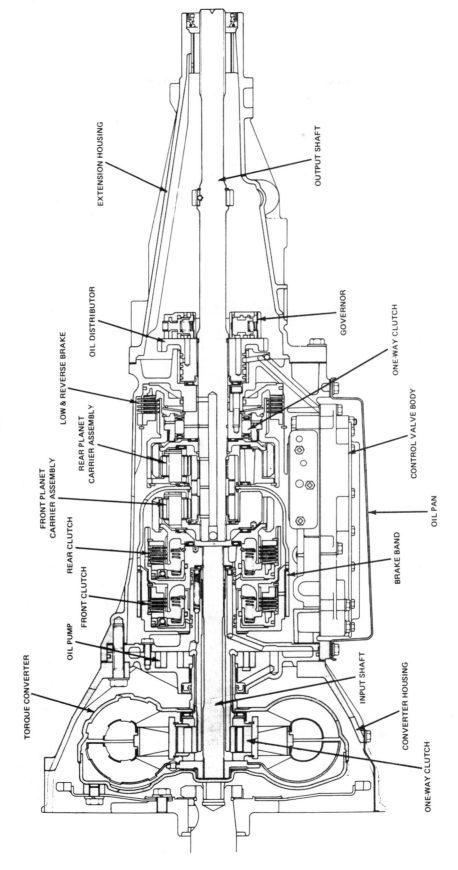

(B)

EXTENSION HOUSING

OUTPUT SHAFT

OIL DISTRIBUTOR

GOVERNOR

ONE-WAY CLUTCH

LOW & REVERSE BRAKE

FRONT PLANET
CARRIER ASSEMBLY

REAR PLANET
CARRIER ASSEMBLY

CONTROL VALVE BODY

REAR CLUTCH

OIL PAN

FRONT CLUTCH

BRAKE BAND

OIL PUMP

INPUT SHAFT

TORQUE CONVERTER

CONVERTER HOUSING

ONE-WAY CLUTCH

Fig. 11-12 (B). JATCO sectional view. (Ford Motor Co.)

Fig. 11-13. C-3 right side external view.

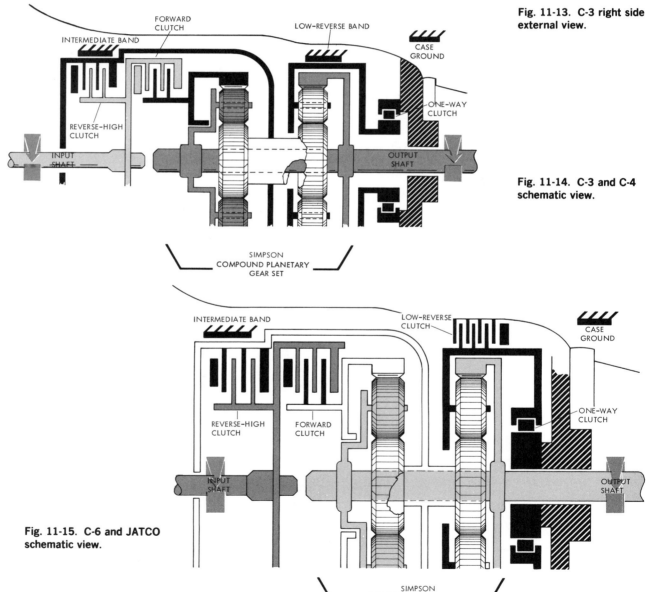

Fig. 11-14. C-3 and C-4 schematic view.

Fig. 11-15. C-6 and JATCO schematic view.

POWERFLOW SUMMARY AND OPERATING CHARACTERISTICS

N—Neutral: The powerflow dead-ends at the forward and reverse/high clutch units. There is no input to the gear train.

R—Reverse gear is a function of the reverse planetary unit. Provides a simple planetary ratio of:

2.11:1 (C3)
2.20:1 (C4)
2.18:1 (JATCO)
2.18:1 (C6)

Note: Ford refers to the rear planetary as the reverse planetary.

D—Drive range is used for normal driving conditions and maximum economy. Full automatic shifting and three gear ratios are available.

First gear is a combined function of the front and reverse planetary units. Provides a compound gear ratio of:

2.47:1 (C3)
2.46:1 (C4)
2.45:1 (JATCO)
2.46:1 (C6)

Second gear is a function of the front planetary unit. Provides a simple planetary gear ratio of:

1.47:1 (C3)
1.46:1 (C4)
1.46:1 (JATCO)
1.46:1 (C6)

Third gear is a direct drive ratio of 1:1.
External controls to the transmission are:

- Linkage—To select the transmission operating range.

- Linkage—To the carburetor for mechanical operation of the forced downshift system on the C3, C4, and C6.
- 12-Volt Solenoid—To electrically activate the forced downshift system on the JATCO only.
- Engine Vacuum—To operate the throttle system modulator unit on C3, C4, C6 and JATCO.

Full throttle forced downshifts 3–1, 2–1, and 3–2 are attained within the proper vehicle speed range for added performance. This will vary according to engine torque design. A 3–2 part throttle downshift feature offers controlled acceleration for low speed operation. The closed throttle downshift pattern is 3–1 at 10 mph (5 km/h) for the JATCO, C4, and C6, and 3–2–1 for the C3, the 3–2 occurring at about 15 mph and the 2–1 at about 5 mph.

In the 2 range, the transmission is manually locked into second gear. It starts in second gear and stays in second gear. If the range selector is moved to 2 from D while in high gear, the transmission downshifts to second. 2 can be used for performance in congested traffic and engine braking on hilly terrain. It also offers better starts on icy road conditions.

The 1 range locks the transmission in first gear for continuous heavy pulling power and engine braking, especially for mountain terrain or steep grades. 1 can be selected at any vehicle speed range but will shift to second if the vehicle speed is too high. When the vehicle slows down below approximately 25 mph (40 km/h), manual low engages and the transmission will not upshift regardless of throttle position or vehicle speed. Some models will need to slow down to 10 mph (5 km/h).

With the 1 and 2 selector positions offering a manual gear lock, the driver has an option to start in 1, then shift to 2 at any speed or peak engine rpm, and then into D for high gear. This arrangement is called Select-Shift by Ford.

The C4 and C6 used a Dual Range Selector arrangement prior to 1967; range pattern P—R—N—D$_2$—D$_1$—L. D$_1$ allows for full automatic shifting with a

CHART 11-2
Ford C-6 & JACTO
Clutch and Band Application (Selector Pattern P R N D 2 1)

Range	Gear	Forward Clutch	Reverse High Clutch	Intermediate Band	Low Reverse Clutch	Low Roller Clutch
Park						
Reverse			On		On	
Neutral						
D—Drive	First	On				Holds
	Second	On		On		
	Third	On	On			
2—Drive	Second	On		On		
1—Low	First	On			On	Holds

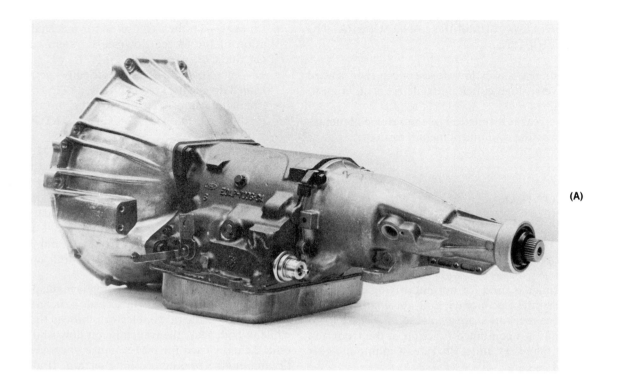

(A)

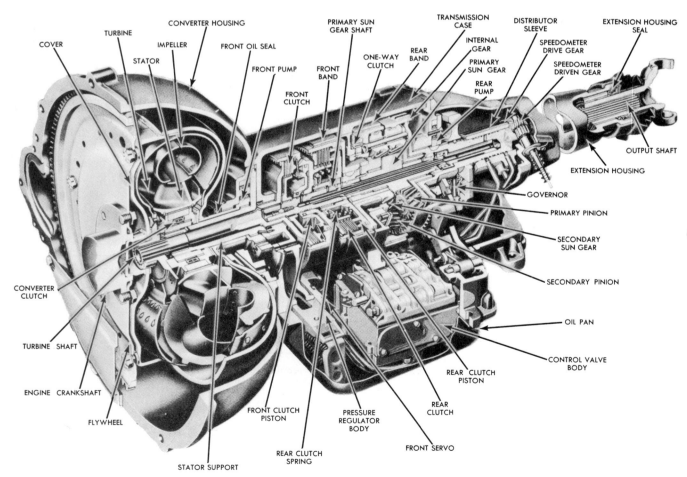

COVER

TURBINE

CONVERTER HOUSING

IMPELLER

STATOR

FRONT OIL SEAL

FRONT PUMP

FRONT CLUTCH

FRONT BAND

PRIMARY SUN GEAR SHAFT

ONE-WAY CLUTCH

REAR BAND

TRANSMISSION CASE

INTERNAL GEAR

PRIMARY SUN GEAR

REAR PUMP

DISTRIBUTOR SLEEVE

SPEEDOMETER DRIVE GEAR

SPEEDOMETER DRIVEN GEAR

EXTENSION HOUSING SEAL

OUTPUT SHAFT

EXTENSION HOUSING

GOVERNOR

PRIMARY PINION

SECONDARY SUN GEAR

SECONDARY PINION

OIL PAN

CONTROL VALVE BODY

REAR CLUTCH PISTON

REAR CLUTCH

FRONT SERVO

PRESSURE REGULATOR BODY

REAR CLUTCH SPRING

FRONT CLUTCH PISTON

STATOR SUPPORT

FLYWHEEL

ENGINE CRANKSHAFT

TURBINE SHAFT

CONVERTER CLUTCH

Fig. 11-16. (A). FMX left side external view. (B). FMX sectional view. (Ford Motor Co.)

CHART 11-3
Ford C-4 & C-3
Clutch and Band Application (Selector Pattern P   R   N   D   2   1)

Range	Gear	Forward Clutch	Reverse High Clutch	Intermediate Band	Low Reverse Band	Low Roller Clutch
Park						
Reverse			On		On	
Neutral						
D—Drive	First	On				Holds
	Second	On		On		
	Third	On	On			
2—Drive	Second	On		On		
1—Low	First	On			On	Holds

low gear start and D$_2$ allows for an intermediate gear start with an automatic shift to high.

Charts 11-2 and 11-3 summarize the clutch/band combinations and range operation. The last production year for both the C6 and JATCO was 1980.

FMX Cast Iron Cruise-O-Matic

The Cast Iron Cruise-O-Matic dates back to 1958 and is the sole survivor from the old line of cast iron transmissions since the age of aluminum took over in the construction of automatic transmission cases in the early 1960s. It was first adapted to the Ford, Mercury, Edsel, Lincoln, and Continental and labelled by the various advertising names Cruise-O-Matic, Multi-Drive, Dual Power, and Turbo-Drive. Several modification changes have occurred since 1958 and various transmission models were designated as FX, MX, and FMX.

The Cruise-O-Matic originally used two case sizes to handle light duty and heavy duty service. An added special HX heavy duty size was developed for the Lincoln and Continental, 1961–65. With the introduction of the C4 and C6 transmissions, the Cast Iron Cruise-O-Matic still remained in production to meet factory output requirements. The light duty 9⅞ in. case size known as the FX was used through production year 1967. A medium duty 10⅞₃₂ in. case size was called the MX and used through 1969 production for passenger cars and continued through 1972 production for light trucks. For current needs, the FMX was introduced in 1968 and is a heavy duty design modification of the FX; the case sizes are the same. Both the FX and MX used rear pump installations through 1967 production, while the FMX original design did not use one.

Figure 11–16 shows a sectional and companion external view of the complete FMX assembly. It has a bolt-on aluminum converter housing and extension

Fig. 11-17. FMX schematic view. (Ford Motor Co.)

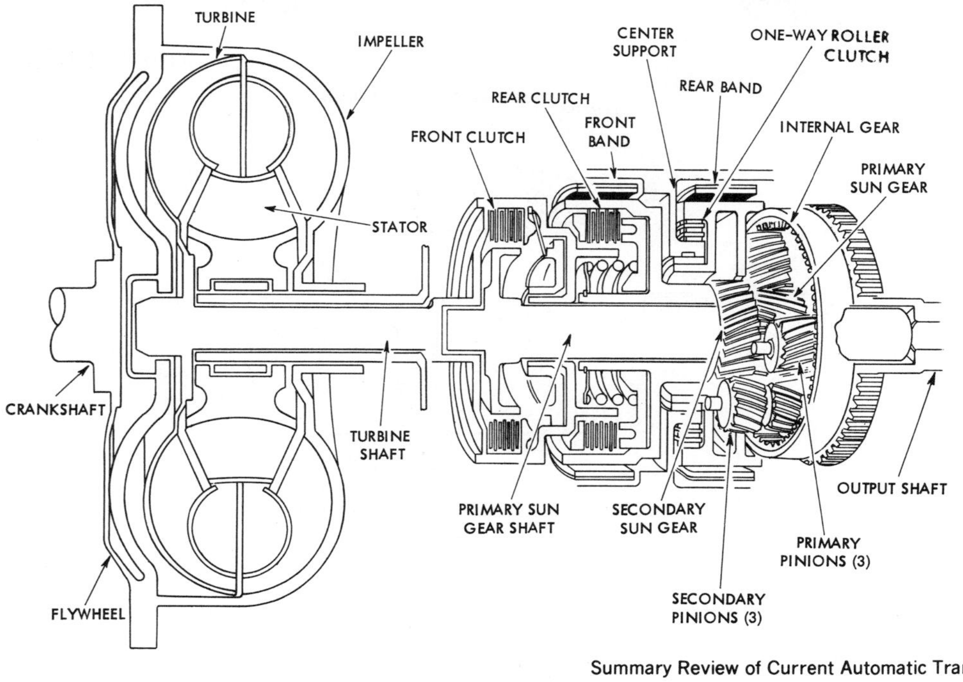

housing to the transmission case. A three-element converter and dual pinion compound Ravigneaux Planetary Set is used for three forward speeds and reverse. Two multiple-disc clutches, two bands, and a roller clutch provide the means to control the gear set. Figure 11–17 is a simplified schematic view of the basic gear train and friction control elements used in the transmission.

TYPICAL ENGINE APPLICATIONS. The Cast Iron Cruise-O-Matic has had a wide variety of applications for cylinder and V-8 engines; however, in more recent years, it has been generally limited to the following:

V8—302 CID (5.0L);
V8—351 CID (5.8 L);
V8—400 CID (6.6 L).

POWERFLOW SUMMARY AND OPERATING CHARACTERISTICS. Simplified gear train sectional views are used to support the powerflow summary. Before attempting to review the illustrations, study the gear set perspective in Fig. 11-18. Note that the short pinions are in mesh with the small diameter primary sun gear and the long pinions but not with the internal gear. The short pinions can, however, drive the internal gear through the long pinions. The long pinions are in constant mesh with the short pinions, internal gear, and large diameter secondary sun gear. The pinion gears are mounted in a dual planet carrier assembly. The output from this gear set is always through the internal gear, which is splined to a flange on the output shaft.

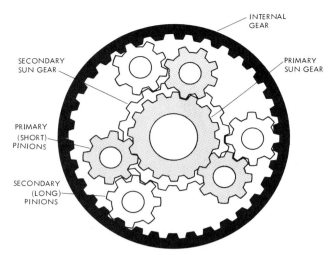

Fig. 11-18. FMX planetary gear set, rear view.

N— Neutral: The powerflow dead-ends at the front and rear clutch units. There is no input to the gear train. Review Fig. 11-19.

R— Reverse gear is a function of the large diameter secondary sun gear driving the output shaft internal gear through the long planet pinions. The planet carrier is held stationary (Fig. 11-20). Provides a simple gear ratio and is computed as follows:

$$\frac{\text{Internal gear} \quad 72 \text{ teeth}}{\text{Secondary sun gear} \quad 36 \text{ teeth}} = 2.0:1$$

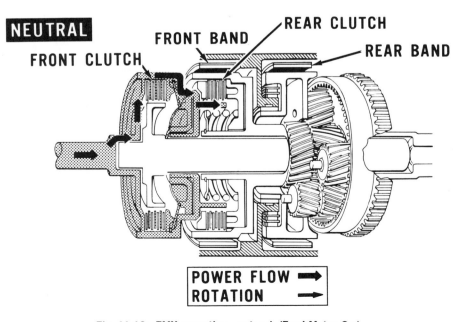

Fig. 11-19. FMX operation—netural. (Ford Motor Co.)

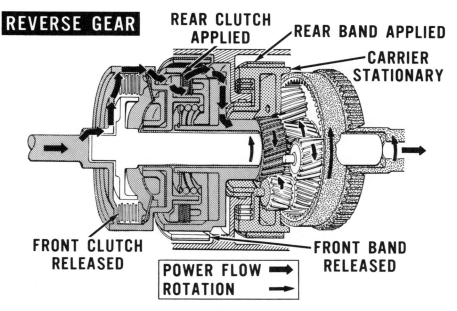

Fig. 11-20. FMX operation—reverse gear. (Ford Motor Co.)

D— Drive range is used for normal driving conditions and maximum economy. Full automatic shifting and three gear ratios are available.

First Gear: A function of the small diameter primary sun gear driving the output shaft internal gear through the planet pinions; the planet carrier is held stationary (Fig. 11-21). Provides a simple gear ratio and is computed as follows:

$$\frac{\text{Internal gear}}{\text{Primary sun gear}} \quad \frac{72 \text{ Teeth}}{30 \text{ Teeth}} = 2.4:1$$

Second Gear: A function of the small primary sun gear driving with the long secondary pinions walking around the secondary sun gear and driving the output shaft internal gear; the secondary sun gear is held stationary (Fig. 11-22). Provides a compound gear ratio, which is computed as follows:

S_1 = Secondary sun gear = 36 teeth

S_2 = Primary sun gear = 30 teeth

I = Internal gear = 72 teeth

$$\frac{I\,(S_1 + S_2)}{S^2\,(I + S^1)} = \frac{72\,(36 + 30)}{30\,(72 + 36)} = \frac{72\,(66)}{30\,(108)} =$$

$$\frac{4752}{3240} = 1.467:1$$

Fig. 11-21. FMX operation first gear, D. (Ford Motor Co.)

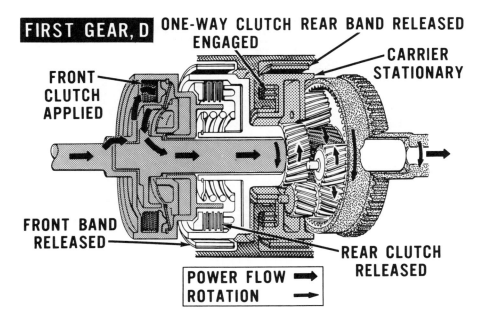

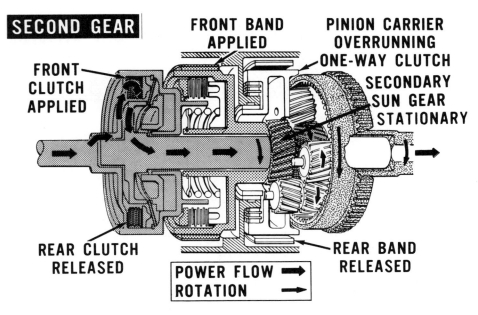

SECOND GEAR

FRONT BAND
APPLIED

PINION CARRIER
OVERRUNNING
ONE-WAY CLUTCH

FRONT
CLUTCH
APPLIED

SECONDARY
SUN GEAR
STATIONARY

REAR CLUTCH
RELEASED

REAR BAND
RELEASED

POWER FLOW ➡
ROTATION ➡

Fig. 11-22. FMX operation—second gear. (Ford Motor Co.)

Third Gear: A direct drive ratio of 1:1. Primary and secondary sun gears are clutched together and driving (Fig. 11-23).

External controls to the transmission are:

- Linkage—To select the transmission operating range.
- Linkage—To the carburetor for mechanical operation of the forced downshift system.
- Engine Vacuum—To operate the throttle system modulator unit.

Full throttle forced downshifts 3–1, 2–1, and 3–2 are attained within the proper engine torque range and vehicle speed. A 3–2 part throttle downshift is also featured. Closed throttle downshift pattern is 3–1 at 10 mph (5km/h)

In the 2 range, the transmission is manually locked into second gear.

In the 1 range, the transmission is manually locked into first gear with the rear band applied for braking action on coast (Fig. 11-24).

The Select-Shift range pattern applies to the FMX and offers the same operating characteristics as for

Fig. 11-23. FMX operation—third gear. (Ford Motor Co.)

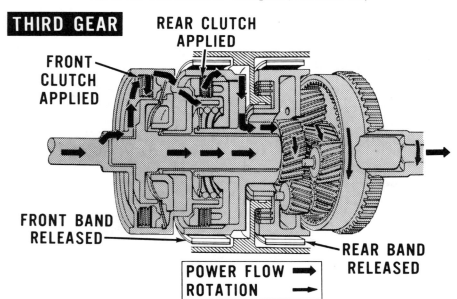

THIRD GEAR

REAR CLUTCH
APPLIED

FRONT
CLUTCH
APPLIED

FRONT BAND
RELEASED

REAR BAND
RELEASED

POWER FLOW ➡
ROTATION ➡

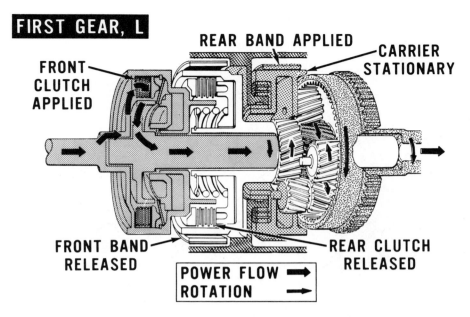

FIRST GEAR, L

REAR BAND APPLIED

CARRIER STATIONARY

FRONT CLUTCH APPLIED

FRONT BAND RELEASED

REAR CLUTCH RELEASED

POWER FLOW ➡
ROTATION ➡

Fig. 11-24. FMC operation—first gear, 1. (Ford Motor Co.)

other Ford Motor Company automatic transmissions. Earlier Cast-Iron Cruise-O-Matics used the Ford Dual Range Selector arrangement; the range pattern P—R—N—D₂—D₁—L. D₁ allowed for full automatic shifting with a low gear start and D₂ allowed for an intermediate gear start with an automatic shift to high.

Chart 11-4 summarizes the church/band combinations and range operation. The last production year for the FMX was 1979.

CHART 11-4
Ford Cast-Iron FMX Clutch and Band Application
(Selector Pattern P R N D 2 1)

Range	Gear	Front Clutch	Rear Clutch	Front Band	Rear Band	Low Roller Clutch
Park						
Reverse			On		On	
Neutral						
D—Drive	First	On				Holds
	Second	On		On		
	Third	On	On			
2—Drive	Second	On		On		
1—Drive	First	On			On	Holds

CW Cast Iron

From 1973-75, Ford Motor Company used a Cast Iron CW automatic transmission manufactured by Borg-Warner. It was limited to application on the 400-2V CID engine. Although it looks similar to an FMX, it is not interchangeable with the FMX, nor are a majority of the service parts.

The operating characteristics are identical to the other Ford automatic transmissions.

AOT (Automatic Overdrive Transmission)

In the 1980 model year, Ford became the first in the automotive industry with an automatic transmission featuring a built-in overdrive. The new transmission is a four-speed in which fourth gear is a 0.67:1 overdrive. Engine rpm in overdrive is reduced by 33% to sustain a given road speed when compared to a conventional high gear ratio 1:1. For 1980, the transmission is standard equipment on the Lincoln Continental and Mark VI, and optionally available on 5.0 L Thunderbirds and Cougar XR-7s, as well as the 5.8 L and 5.0 L Ford LTDs and Mercury Marquis. For 1981 it completely replaces the C6 transmission.

Figures 11-25 and 11-26 show sectional and schematic views of the Automatic Overdrive Transmission. As can be observed, the AOT uses an FMX-type gear train. First, second, and reverse gears have identical powerflows as in the FMX. In third gear, the ratio is 1:1 with the input torque split between two shafts that drive the reverse sun gear and planet carrier. Overdrive is attained by the addition of a band to hold the reverse sun gear while driving the planet carrier. For control of the gear train, the AOT transmission has four multiple-disc clutches, two bands with actuating servos, and two one-way roller clutches.

In close comparison, the AOT is a redesign of the FMX. The overdrive band and direct clutch are new, and the intermediate clutch replaces the front band. The transmission case is a one-piece, integrated aluminum casting with the converter housing and has a bolt-on extension housing.

Bands are nonadjustable, requiring no scheduled maintenance during regular service.

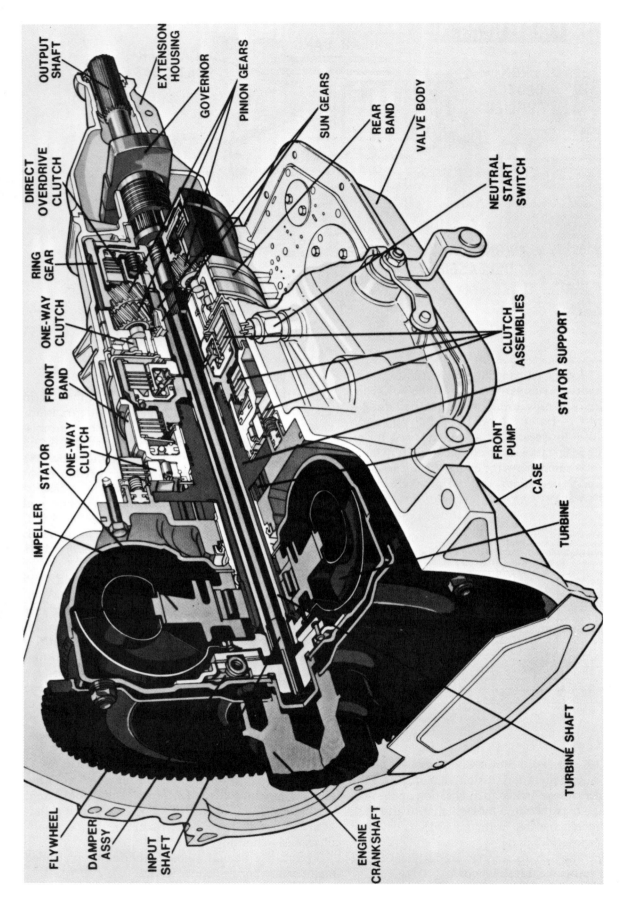

OUTPUT SHAFT

EXTENSION HOUSING

GOVERNOR

PINION GEARS

SUN GEARS

REAR BAND

VALVE BODY

DIRECT OVERDRIVE CLUTCH

RING GEAR

ONE-WAY CLUTCH

FRONT BAND

NEUTRAL START SWITCH

IMPELLER

STATOR

ONE-WAY CLUTCH

CLUTCH ASSEMBLIES

STATOR SUPPORT

FRONT PUMP

CASE

TURBINE

FLYWHEEL

DAMPER ASSY

INPUT SHAFT

ENGINE CRANKSHAFT

TURBINE SHAFT

Fig. 11-25. Ford automatic overdrive cutaway view. (Ford Motor Co.)

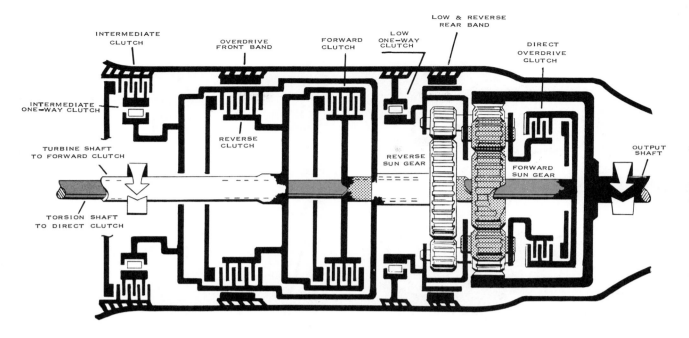

Fig. 11-26. Ford automatic overdrive transmission—schematic view.

The AOT uses a typical three-element torque converter with a new design feature vital to overdrive: a split torque powerflow. Two input shafts provide both hydraulic and mechanical drive. A turbine tube shaft splines into the turbine hub and hydraulically drives the forward clutch cylinder. A solid direct-drive input shaft splines into a torsional damper assembly, which is part of the converter cover. This latter arrangement mechanically links the direct clutch to the engine crankshaft. Input to the gear train will vary from 100% hydraulic drive in low, intermediate, and reverse gears to approximately 40% hydraulic/60% mechanical in third gear (split torque) and 100% mechanical (lock-up) in overdrive. The split torque and lock-up feature of the converter offers additional fuel economy.

POWERFLOW SUMMARY AND OPERATING CHARACTERISTICS. In the following powerflow discussion, you will want to use Figs. 11-25 and 11-26 as a reference with the gearset pictorials that accompany the discussion. For more background, the components of the AOT gearset are individually illustrated, with the "holding" clutches and bands, in Fig. 11-27. Following is a brief summary of each.*

(1) *Reverse Sun Gear.* This sun gear is integral with the input shell. It is driven by the turbine (tube) input shaft when the reverse clutch (10) is applied. [It

*Discussion based on Ford Parts and Service Division Publications, June 1979, 365-464.

turns freely from the forward sun gear (5).] The reverse sun gear also can be held stationary by applying the intermediate clutch (8) or the overdrive band (9).

(2) *Planet Carrier.* Like the FMX, the automatic overdrive transmission has a single planet carrier assembly with long (3) and short pinions (4). The carrier can be held stationary by either the low–reverse band (12) or the planetary (low) one-way clutch (13).

(3) *Long Pinions.* The long pinions in the carrier are in constant mesh with the ring gear (6), with the reverse sun gear (1), and with the short pinions (4).

(4) *Short Pinions.* Short pinions are in constant mesh with the forward sun gear (5) and with the long pinions (3). The short pinions in the gear set do not mesh with a ring gear but can only drive the ring gear through the long pinions.

(5) *Forward Sun Gear.* The forward sun gear is so named because it is driven whenever the forward clutch (11) is applied; that is, in first, second, and third gears. (Physically, it is located behind the reverse sun gear and corresponds to the "primary" sun gear in the FMX). The sun gear meshes with the short planet pinions (4).

(6) *Ring Gear.* The automatic overdrive has only one ring gear, which meshes with the long planet pinions. It is splined to a flange on the output shaft. Thus, the output from this gearset is always through the ring gear.

With the relationship of the planetary gear components, clutches, and bands now established, we are ready to show the powerflow in the various driving ranges.

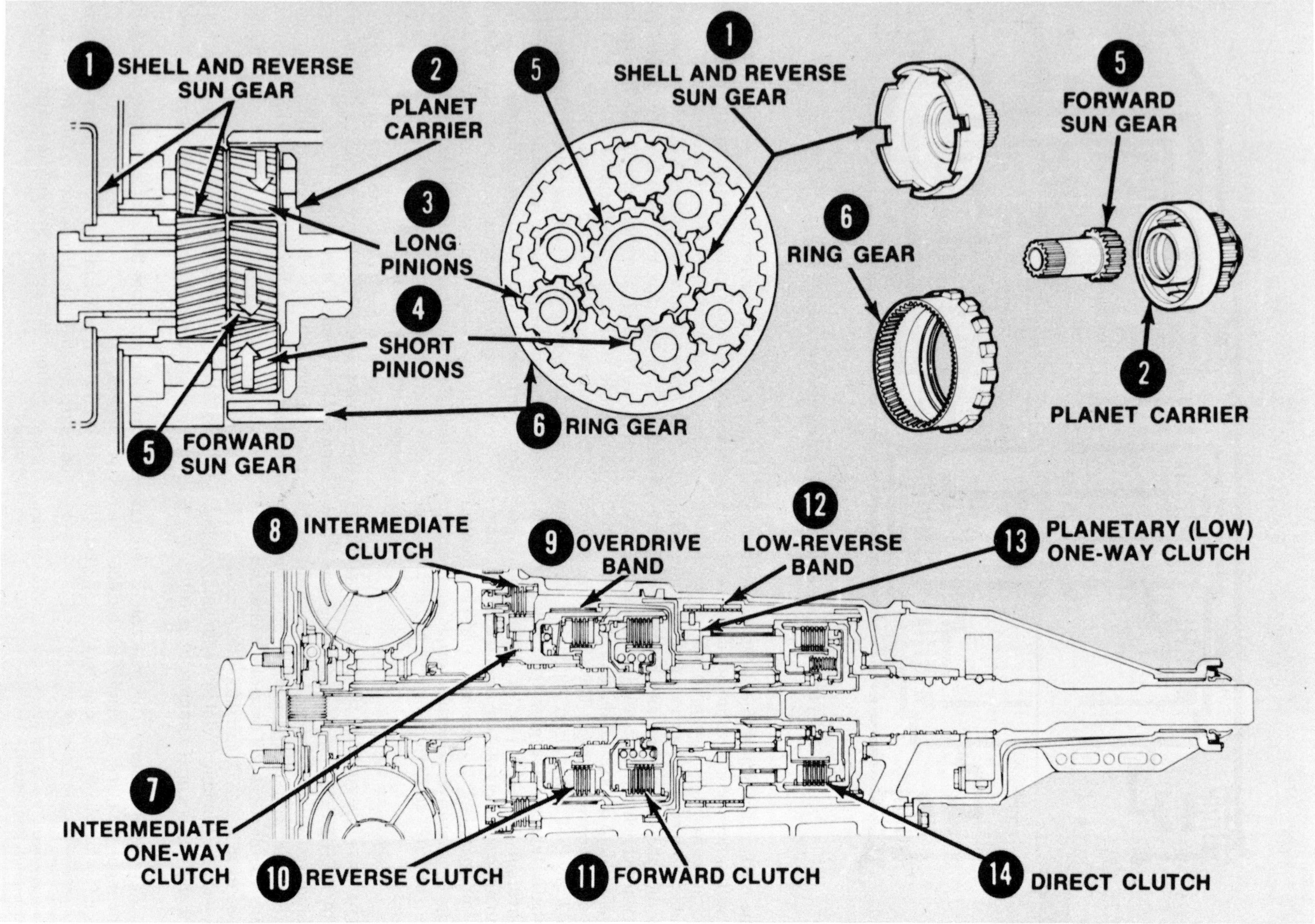

1 SHELL AND REVERSE SUN GEAR
2 PLANET CARRIER
3 LONG PINIONS
4 SHORT PINIONS
5 FORWARD SUN GEAR
6 RING GEAR
5
1 SHELL AND REVERSE SUN GEAR
6 RING GEAR
5 FORWARD SUN GEAR
2 PLANET CARRIER
8 INTERMEDIATE CLUTCH
9 OVERDRIVE BAND
12 LOW-REVERSE BAND
13 PLANETARY (LOW) ONE-WAY CLUTCH
7 INTERMEDIATE ONE-WAY CLUTCH
10 REVERSE CLUTCH
11 FORWARD CLUTCH
14 DIRECT CLUTCH

Fig. 11-27. (Ford Motor Co.)

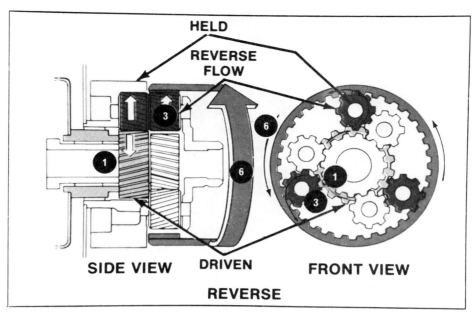

HELD

REVERSE FLOW

3

1

6

6

1

3

SIDE VIEW   **DRIVEN**   **FRONT VIEW**

REVERSE

Fig. 11-28. (Ford Motor Co.)

N/P—Neutral/Park. The forward, reverse, and direct clutches are not applied. There is no input to the gear train (Figs. 11-25 and 11-26). In P, the low–reverse band is applied but does not cause any drive condition.

R—Reverse. In reverse gear (Figs. 11-25 and 11-26), the holding members are:

Reverse Clutch—Locks the turbine input shaft to the reverse sun gear.
Low-Reverse Band—Holds the planet carrier stationary.

The powerflow and gear rotation for reverse is shown in Fig. 11-28.

- The turbine shaft hydraulically drives the reverse clutch, the shell, and reverse sun gear clockwise.[1]
- The reverse sun gear drives the long pinions counterclockwise.[3]
- The long pinions drive the ring gear and output shaft counterclockwise.[6] In effect, the long pinions are acting as reverse idler gears. The gear ratio is 2:1.
- The short planet pinions and forward sun gear also turn but are not involved in the powerflow.

O/D—Overdrive. This is the normal driving range for maximum economy. Full automatic shifting takes place with a fourth-gear overdrive.

FIRST GEAR O/D OR 3 RANGE: The holding members are (Figs. 11-25 and 11-26):

Forward Clutch—Locks the turbine shaft to the forward sun gear.

Planetary (Low) One-Way Clutch—Holds the planetary carrier from turning counterclockwise.

The powerflow and gear rotation is shown in Fig. 11-29.

- The turbine shaft hydraulically drives the forward clutch and forward sun gear clockwise.[6]
- The sun gear drives the short pinions counterclockwise.[4]
- The short pinions drive the long pinions clockwise.[3]
- The long pinions drive the ring gear and output shaft clockwise at a reduced speed.[6] First gear is a 2.4:1 reduction. If the torque converter is at maximum torque output, the combined torque multiplication ratio is about 5:1.

SECOND GEAR O/D OR 3 RANGE: In second (intermediate) gear, the holding members are (Figs. 11-25 and 11-26):

Intermediate Clutch—Locks the one-way clutch outer race stationary.

One-Way Clutch—Prevents the reverse clutch drum, shell, and reverse sun gear from turning counterclockwise.

Forward Clutch—Locks the turbine shaft to the forward sun gear.

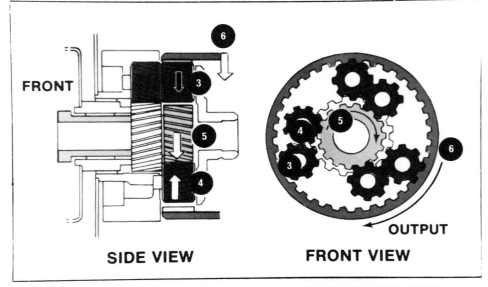

FRONT

6

3

5

4

OUTPUT

SIDE VIEW

FRONT VIEW

Fig. 11-29.
First gear O/D or 3 range.
(Ford Motor Co.)

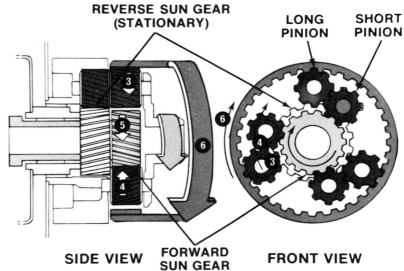

REVERSE SUN GEAR
(STATIONARY)

LONG
PINION

SHORT
PINION

Fig. 11-30.
Second gear O/D or 3 range.
(Ford Motor Co.)

3

5

4
—

6

6

4

3

SIDE VIEW

FORWARD
SUN GEAR

FRONT VIEW

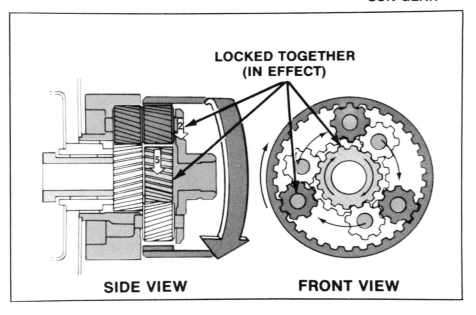

LOCKED TOGETHER
(IN EFFECT)

2

5

SIDE VIEW

FRONT VIEW

Fig. 11-31.
Third gear O/D or 3 range.
(Ford Motor Co.)

The powerflow and gear rotation is shown in Fig. 11-30.

- The turbine and shaft hydraulically drives the forward clutch and forward sun gear clockwise.[5]
- The forward sun gear drives the short pinions counterclockwise.[4]
- The long pinion gears are driven clockwise and "walk" clockwise around the stationary reverse sun gear.[3]

During first gear, the reverse sun gear and shell and the reverse clutch drum are turning counterclockwise, with the intermediate one-way roller clutch remaining ineffective. When the intermediate clutch is applied, it grounds the outer race of the roller clutch, resulting in a lock-up. The reverse sun gear is held stationary against counterclockwise rotation.

- As the long pinions "walk" around the stationary reverse sun gear, they drive the ring gear and output shaft clockwise at a reduced speed.[6] Second gear ratio is 1.47:1.
- The "walking" of the long pinions also drives the planet carrier in a clockwise direction. This releases the low roller clutch when second gear takes over the torque load.

THIRD GEAR O/D OR 3 RANGE: In third gear (direct drive), the holding members (Figs. 11-25 and 11-26) are:

Forward Clutch—Locks the turbine (tube) input shaft to the forward sun gear.

Direct Clutch—Locks the direct-drive input shaft to the planet carrier assembly.

The powerflow illustration in Fig. 11-31 shows the planetary gear system locked together.

- The turbine shaft hydraulically drives the forward clutch and the forward sun gear.[5]
- The direct drive input shaft, splined into the torsion dampner and converter cover, mechanically drives the direct clutch and the planet carrier.[2]
- With two members of the planetary unit driving at the same time, the pinion gears are trapped and cannot rotate on their centers. This locks together the entire gearset and it rotates as a unit with a 1:1 drive ratio.

In actual fact, there is some slip in the converter hydraulic drive and, therefore, an absolute direct drive cannot be attained. The planet pinions do turn on their shafts and within the ring gear to a slight degree. But,

for practical purposes, the planetary system is locked-up. To minimize the slip, the engine torque input splits and takes a dual path through the converter, 40% hydraulic/60% mechanical. Because the planet carrier has a larger turning radius or lever arm than the forward sun gear, it will absorb more of the input torque (Fig. 11-32).

Fig. 11-32. 60/40 third gear split torque.

- The intermediate clutch stays applied; however, with the planetary set lock-up, the input to the roller clutch is clockwise. The intermediate roller clutch freewheels and is ineffective.

FOURTH GEAR O/D ONLY: The holding members are (Figs. 11-25 and 11-26):

Overdrive Band—Holds the reverse clutch drum, the drive shell and reverse sun gear stationary.

Direct Clutch—Couples the planet carrier assembly to the engine.

Overdrive is accomplished by holding the sun gear and driving the planet carrier. The powerflow rotation in the gear set is shown in Fig. 11-33.

- The converter cover and torsional dampner mechanically drive the direct-drive shaft and the direct clutch.
- The direct clutch drives the planet carrier assembly clockwise at engine speed.[2]
- The long planet pinions "walk around" the stationary reverse sun gear in a clockwise direction.[3]
- The ring gear and output shaft are driven by the long pinions at a faster speed.[6] In overdrive, the gear ratio is .667:1. Because the input is 100% mechanical drive, there is no converter slip.

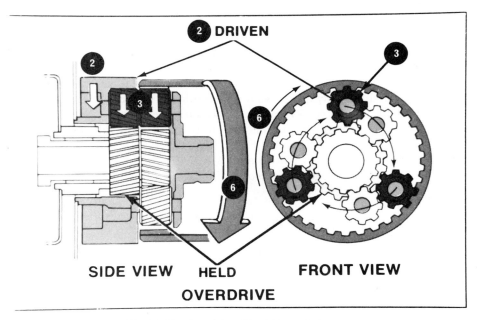

Fig. 11-33. Overdrive. (Ford Motor Co.)

External controls to the transmission are:

- Linkage—To select the transmission operating range.
- Linkage—To mechanically operate both the throttle and kickdown systems with the carburetor. Both system control valves are in tandem in the same valve body bore and work off the same external linkage.

The transmission's gear selector quadrant is similar to those used with other Ford automatics, except that an OD symbol—a D encircled by a O—replaces the conventional D and a numeral 3 replaces the 2 (Fig. 11-34). Because the 2 selector position has been eliminated, second gear starts are not available.

At light throttle, the shift from third to fourth (overdrive) occurs at approximately 40 mph (65 km/h). Full throttle-forced downshifts 4–3. 4–2 and

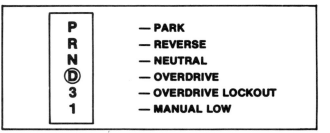

Fig. 11-34. (Ford Motor Co.)

3–1 are attained within the proper vehicle speed range for added performance. In O/D, the transmission will downshift 4-3 when the accelerator is pushed for moderate or heavy acceleration. (At wide-open throttle, the transmission cannot stay in overdrive) The closed throttle downshift pattern shifts through all the gears, 4–3, 3–2, and 2–1.

FORD
AUTOMATIC OVERDRIVE TRANSMISSION
Clutch and Band Application Chart 11-5
Selector Pattern PRN Ⓓ 31

	Interm. Friction Clutch	Interm. One-Way Clutch	Overdrive Band	Reverse Clutch	Forward Clutch	One-Way Clutch	Low-Reverse Band	Direct Clutch
1st Gear Manual Low					Applied	Holding	Applied	
2nd Gear Manual Low	Applied	Holding	Applied		Applied			
1st Gear—O/D or 3					Applied	Holding		
2nd Gear—O/D or 3	Applied	Holding			Applied			
3rd Gear—O/D or 3	Applied				Applied			Applied
4th Gear—O/D	Applied		Applied					Applied
Reverse (R)				Applied			Applied	
Neutral (N)								
Park (P)							Applied	

3—OVERDRIVE LOCKOUT. The objective of the 3 range is to "lockout" the overdrive. It is used to achieve better performance when driving in hilly or mountainous roads. Better engine braking is also realized. The same operating characteristics prevail as in O/D except for the overdrive feature. The selector may be shifted from O/D to 3 or 3 to O/D at any vehicle speed.

1—MANUAL LOW. The objective is to stay in first gear for extra pulling power or maximum braking when the 3 range is not adequate. 1 range can be selected at any vehicle speed, however, if the vehicle speed is too high, second gear is engaged. When the vehicle slows down to a safe speed [approximately 25 mph (40 km/h)], it will downshift to first gear and remains in first gear. Once first gear is engaged in manual low, it stays in first gear with the low-reverse band applied for braking action on coast. Upshifts to O/D and 3 can be made manually for driver select shifting.

Chart 11-5 summarizes the clutch/band combinations and range operation of the Automatic Overdrive Transmission.

AMERICAN MOTORS CORPORATION

Torque-Command

Starting with 1972 model cars, AMC has used Chrysler produced TorqueFlite automatic transmissions. Three Torque-Command transmission models are available; the 904, 998, and 727. The 904 and 998 cases are physically the same size and in appearance except for the reinforcing ribs cast into the top of the rear servo boss on the case for the 998. Internally, the 998 uses a double-wrap rear band and a modified valve body.

Typical Engine Application

A—904	A—998	A—727
4—121 CID (2.0 L)	6—258 CID (4.2 L)	V8—360 CID (5.9 L)
6—232 CID (3.8 L)	V8—304 CID (5.0 L)	
6—258 CID (4.2 L)		

Transmission construction external connections and operating characteristics are the same as those previously discussed under Chrysler TorqueFlite; even the gear ratios are the same. The wide ratio TorqueFlite geartrain, however, is not used. The lock-up converter is utilized in all engine applications, except the 904 with 2.0 l engine and 998 with 4.2 L engine used in the four-wheel-drive Eagle.

The 1980 AMC Eagle is the first U.S. four-wheel-drive passenger car. A version of the system is illustrated in Fig. 11-35. The transfer case is a single-speed case without the low-range feature found in two-speed

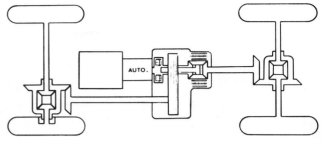

1980 EAGLE FULL—TIME 4WD

Fig. 11-35. (S.A.E.)

cases. The rear driveshaft is driven from the rear of the transfer case. The front driveshaft is off-set to the left, driven by a silent chain. The interdriveshaft differential incorporates a limited slip feature that is controlled by a viscous coupling. There is no mechanical lock-up between the front and rear drives.

GENERAL MOTORS CORPORATION

Turbo Hydra-Matic 400/375, 425, and 475 (Buick, Cadillac, Chevrolet, Oldsmobile, and Pontiac)

Built by Hydra-Matic Division, 1964 was the first production year for the THM-400 when it was introduced in the Buick and Cadillac. For 1965 it was added to Chevrolet, Oldsmobile and Pontiac. In production year 1978, the THM-400 was dropped by Chevrolet in its passenger car models and by Pontiac.

The transmission design as shown in the sectional view (Fig. 11-36) uses a one-piece integrated aluminum case with the converter housing and a bolt-on extension housing. It is a fully automatic three-speed unit consisting of a three-element torque converter and a compound Simpson Planetary Set. Three multiple-disc clutches, two one-way roller clutches, and two bands provide the means to control the gear train operation. Figure 11-37 represents a simplified schematic view of the basic gear train and friction elements.

NOTE: In the early production units, two sprag one-way clutches were used. In late 1965, the low sprag was replaced with a roller clutch. Beginning with 1971 units, a second roller clutch was added to replace the intermediate sprag.

NOTE: Buick, Cadillac, and Oldsmobile used a three-element torque converter with a variable pitch stator through production years 1965–66–67. The maximum stall ratio of the converter was 2.2:1 in the high angle position and 1.8:1 in the low angle position. Current converter units are designed with a maximum ratio of 2.0:1

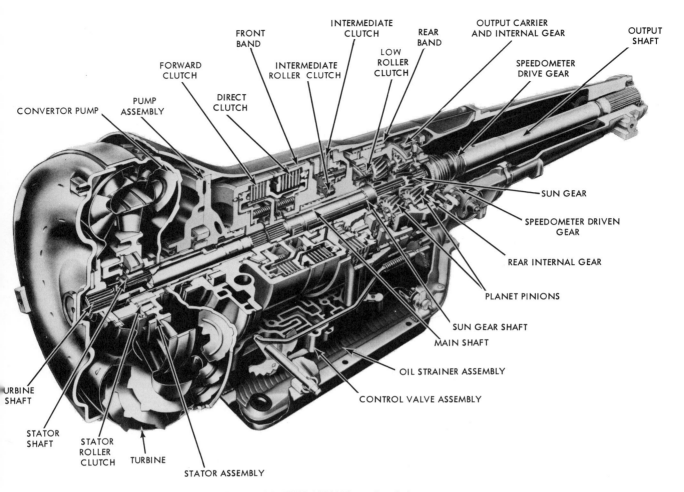

Fig. 11-36. THM 375/400 sectional view.

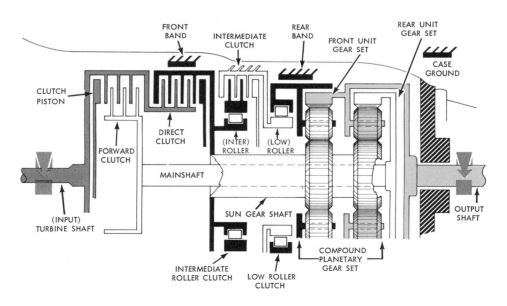

Fig. 11-37. THM-375/400 schematic view.

Adaptations of the basic design have been made to accommodate a wide variety of vehicle and engine applications known as the 375, 425, and 475. The complete THM-400 family is identified in the Parts Book Code by M-40.

The 375 was a 1972 development of the 400 made to handle certain vehicle applications using the 5.7-l (350-CID) V8 engine. The outward physical appearance and size is identical to the basic 400. The internal physical appearance is also identical with the basic dif-

ference being in valve body and accumulator calibrations, plus a decrease in the number of clutch plates used in the forward and direct clutches. Additionally, output shaft and extension housing changes were made to accommodate a different propeller shaft yoke. To identify the 375, raised letters and numbers .6 in. high spell out "375 THM" and are cast on the bottom of the extension housing. The 375 units were used by Chevrolet and Oldsmobile through production year 1976.

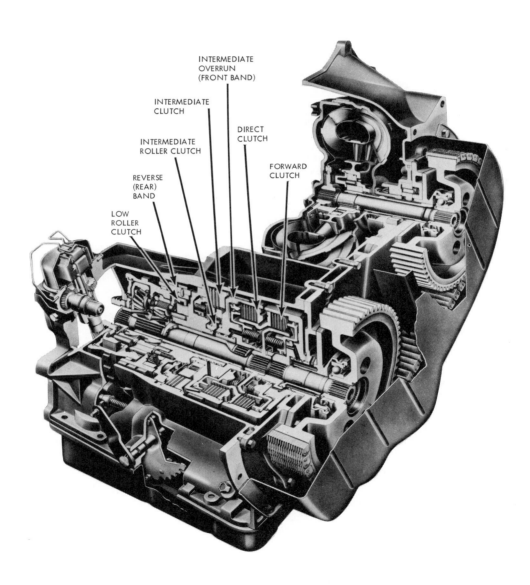

Fig. 11-38. THM-425 sectional view. (General Motors Corp.)

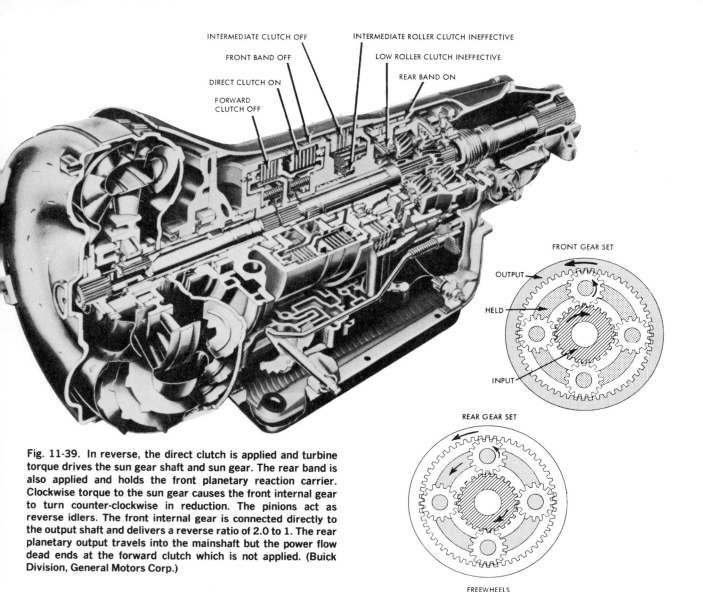

INTERMEDIATE CLUTCH OFF — INTERMEDIATE ROLLER CLUTCH INEFFECTIVE

FRONT BAND OFF — LOW ROLLER CLUTCH INEFFECTIVE

DIRECT CLUTCH ON — REAR BAND ON

FORWARD CLUTCH OFF

FRONT GEAR SET

OUTPUT

HELD

INPUT

REAR GEAR SET

FREEWHEELS

Fig. 11-39. In reverse, the direct clutch is applied and turbine torque drives the sun gear shaft and sun gear. The rear band is also applied and holds the front planetary reaction carrier. Clockwise torque to the sun gear causes the front internal gear to turn counter-clockwise in reduction. The pinions act as reverse idlers. The front internal gear is connected directly to the output shaft and delivers a reverse ratio of 2.0 to 1. The rear planetary output travels into the mainshaft but the power flow dead ends at the forward clutch which is not applied. (Buick Division, General Motors Corp.)

For the front-wheel-drive Cadillac Eldorado and Oldsmobile Toronado, a THM-425 unit used through production year 1978 is shown in Fig. 11-38. Notice that the torque converter couples the engine to the planetary gear set through the use of a drive sprocket, a link belt, and a driven sprocket. Because the transmission front faces toward the vehicle rear, input rotation is counterclockwise. This means that the helical cut of the planetary gears is in an opposite direction of a THM-400 used for rear wheel drive. The roller clutches are also designed to reverse their freewheeling and holding action.

The 475 unit is a heavy duty application used for commercial trucks and buses.

Typical Engine Applications

375	400	425
V8—5.7 L (350 CID)	V8—7.6 L (455 CID)	V8—7.6 L (455 CID)
	V8—6.6 L (403 CID)	V8—7.0 L (425 CID)
	V8—6.5 L (400 CID)	V8—6.5 L (403 CID)
	V8—5.7 L (350 CID)	
	V8—5.0 L (307 CID)	

POWERFLOW SUMMARY AND OPERATING CHARACTERISTICS. Unlike the other Simpson gear trains used in automatic transmissions, the THM-400 uses a third shaft referred to as the mainshaft. When the forward clutch is applied, the power input to the gear train is through the rear planetary ring gear rather than through the front planetary ring gear (Figs. 11-36 and 11-37). You will also notice that the forward, direct, and intermediate clutch units are positioned in reverse order.

N—Neutral: The powerflow dead-ends at the forward and direct clutch units. There is no input to the gear train.

R—Reverse gear is a function of the front planetary unit. Provides a simple gear ratio of 2.0:1. See Fig. 11-39.

D—Drive range is used for normal driving and maximum economy. Full automatic shifting and three gear ratios are available.

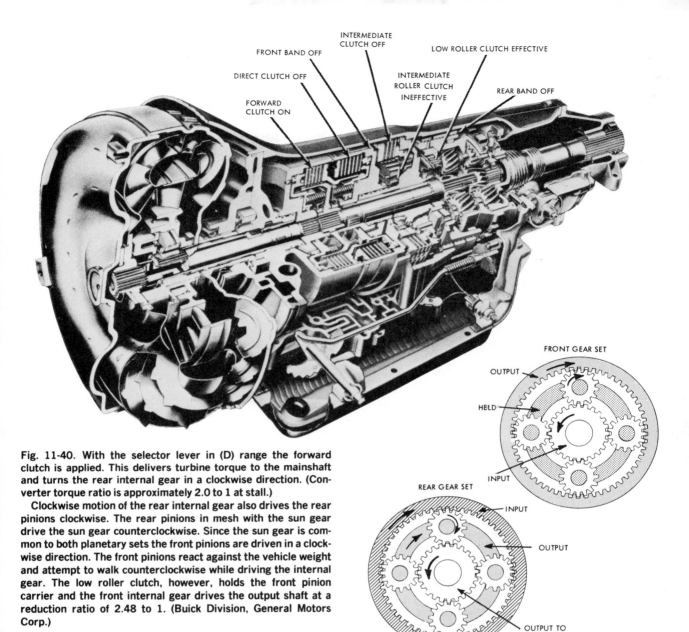

FRONT BAND OFF

DIRECT CLUTCH OFF

INTERMEDIATE CLUTCH OFF

FORWARD CLUTCH ON

INTERMEDIATE ROLLER CLUTCH INEFFECTIVE

LOW ROLLER CLUTCH EFFECTIVE

REAR BAND OFF

FRONT GEAR SET

OUTPUT

HELD

INPUT

REAR GEAR SET

INPUT

OUTPUT

OUTPUT TO REAR UNIT

Fig. 11-40. With the selector lever in (D) range the forward clutch is applied. This delivers turbine torque to the mainshaft and turns the rear internal gear in a clockwise direction. (Converter torque ratio is approximately 2.0 to 1 at stall.)

Clockwise motion of the rear internal gear also drives the rear pinions clockwise. The rear pinions in mesh with the sun gear drive the sun gear counterclockwise. Since the sun gear is common to both planetary sets the front pinions are driven in a clockwise direction. The front pinions react against the vehicle weight and attempt to walk counterclockwise while driving the internal gear. The low roller clutch, however, holds the front pinion carrier and the front internal gear drives the output shaft at a reduction ratio of 2.48 to 1. (Buick Division, General Motors Corp.)

First gear: A combined function of the front and rear planetary units. Provides a compound gear ratio of 2.48:1 (Fig. 11-40)

Second gear: A function of the rear planetary unit. Provides a simple gear ratio of 1.48:1 (Fig. 11-41).

Third gear: A direct ratio of 1:1 (Fig. 11-42).

External controls to the transmission are:

- Manual Linkage—To select the transmission operating range.

- Engine Vacuum—To operate the vacuum modulator unit. On the Oldsmobile Diesel application, the vacuum source comes from an engine operated vacuum pump. Vacuum distribution to the modulator is varied with the engine torque demand by a rotary vacuum valve.

- 12-Volt Electrical Terminal—To energize an internal electrical detent solenoid; all years.

- 12-Volt Electrical Terminal—A second terminal to energize an internal electrical stator solenoid to switch the pitch; for 1965–66–67 car models using the V.P. stator.

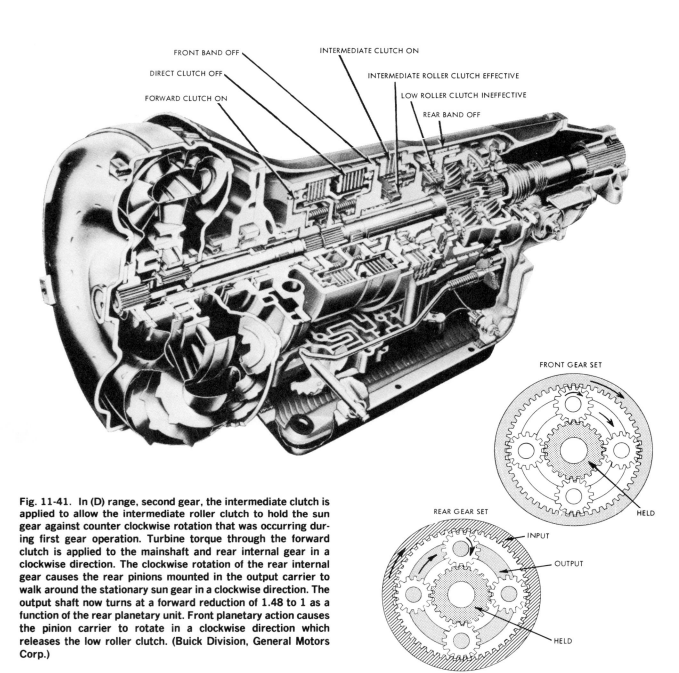

FRONT BAND OFF

DIRECT CLUTCH OFF

FORWARD CLUTCH ON

INTERMEDIATE CLUTCH ON

INTERMEDIATE ROLLER CLUTCH EFFECTIVE

LOW ROLLER CLUTCH INEFFECTIVE

REAR BAND OFF

FRONT GEAR SET

HELD

REAR GEAR SET

INPUT

OUTPUT

HELD

Fig. 11-41. In (D) range, second gear, the intermediate clutch is applied to allow the intermediate roller clutch to hold the sun gear against counter clockwise rotation that was occurring during first gear operation. Turbine torque through the forward clutch is applied to the mainshaft and rear internal gear in a clockwise direction. The clockwise rotation of the rear internal gear causes the rear pinions mounted in the output carrier to walk around the stationary sun gear in a clockwise direction. The output shaft now turns at a forward reduction of 1.48 to 1 as a function of the rear planetary unit. Front planetary action causes the pinion carrier to rotate in a clockwise direction which releases the low roller clutch. (Buick Division, General Motors Corp.)

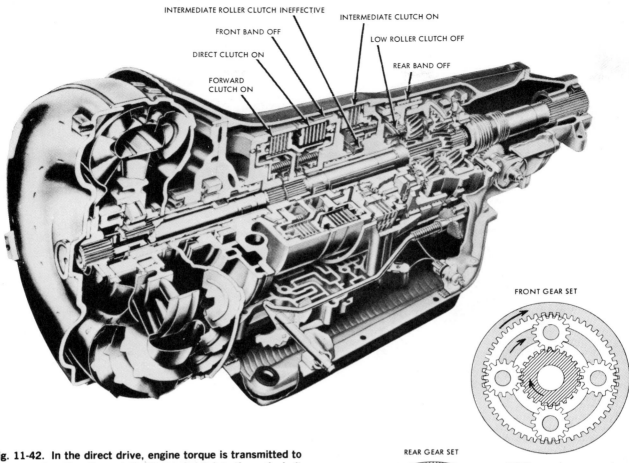

INTERMEDIATE ROLLER CLUTCH INEFFECTIVE

FRONT BAND OFF

DIRECT CLUTCH ON

FORWARD
CLUTCH ON

INTERMEDIATE CLUTCH ON

LOW ROLLER CLUTCH OFF

REAR BAND OFF

FRONT GEAR SET

REAR GEAR SET

INPUT

OUTPUT

Fig. 11-42. In the direct drive, engine torque is transmitted to the converter, then through the forward clutch to the mainshaft and rear internal gear. Because the direct clutch is applied, equal power is also transmitted to the sun gear shaft and the sun gear. Since both the sun gear and rear internal gear are now turning at the same speed, the front and rear planetary units are locked together as one unit for a direct drive ratio of 1 to 1. The clockwise rotation of the locked planetary units releases both roller clutches. (Buick Division, General Motors Corp.)

- 12-Volt Electrical Terminal—A second terminal to operate the (TCS) Transmission Controlled Spark System; a 1971 addition for emission control on certain vehicles only.

The usual downshift features are available:

- Full throttle forced downshifts 3–1, 2–1, and 3–2 for full power performance, which will occur within the proper vehicle speed and engine torque range.
- Part throttle 3–2 downshift for controlled acceleration during low speed operation.
- Closed throttle sequence is 3–2 and 2–1.

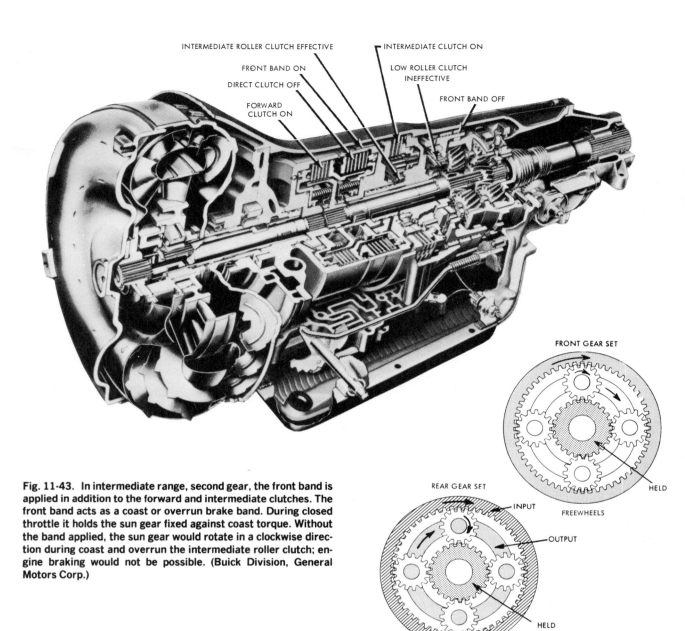

INTERMEDIATE ROLLER CLUTCH EFFECTIVE

FRONT BAND ON

DIRECT CLUTCH OFF

FORWARD CLUTCH ON

INTERMEDIATE CLUTCH ON

LOW ROLLER CLUTCH INEFFECTIVE

FRONT BAND OFF

FRONT GEAR SET

HELD

FREEWHEELS

REAR GEAR SET

INPUT

OUTPUT

HELD

Fig. 11-43. In intermediate range, second gear, the front band is applied in addition to the forward and intermediate clutches. The front band acts as a coast or overrun brake band. During closed throttle it holds the sun gear fixed against coast torque. Without the band applied, the sun gear would rotate in a clockwise direction during coast and overrun the intermediate roller clutch; engine braking would not be possible. (Buick Division, General Motors Corp.)

I—Sometimes Marked D1, S, or L2. Intermediate range allows for performance in congested traffic or hilly terrain. It starts in first gear and has a normal 1-2 shift pattern. The transmission, however, remains in second gear for the desired acceleration and braking requirements. Intermediate can be selected at any high gear vehicle speed and will shift the transmission to second. The closed throttle shift pattern is 2-1. A full throttle-forced downshift 2-1 is also available. Refer to Intermediate Range (Fig. 11-43).

L—Sometimes Marked L1. Low range locks the transmission in first gear for heavy pulling power and engine braking, especially for conditions where continuous first-gear operation is needed, for example,

driving in steep mountain terrain. L can be selected at any vehicle speed range but will shift to second if the vehicle speed is too high. When vehicle speed is reduced to approximately 40 mph (92 km/h), manual low engages and the transmission will not upshift regardless of throttle opening or vehicle speed. On "Hot Dog" packages where the engine peaks out at higher rpms than the stock engines, a 1-2 shift is possible. Refer to Low Range (Fig. 11-44).

Chart 11-6 summarizes the clutch/band applications and range operation. Intermediate range was not included in the original 1964 production transmissions. The manual shift selector takes on the appearance of a two-speed automatic: P-N-R-D-L.

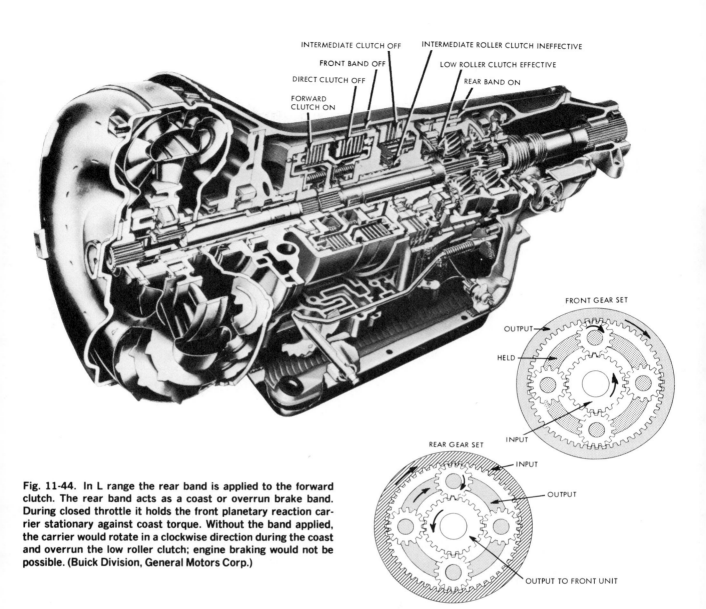

Fig. 11-44. In L range the rear band is applied to the forward clutch. The rear band acts as a coast or overrun brake band. During closed throttle it holds the front planetary reaction carrier stationary against coast torque. Without the band applied, the carrier would rotate in a clockwise direction during the coast and overrun the low roller clutch; engine braking would not be possible. (Buick Division, General Motors Corp.)

TURBO HYDRA-MATIC 375/400
Clutch and Band Application Chart 11-6
Selector Pattern (P R N D S L) (P R N D L$_2$ L$_1$) (P R N D I L)

Selector Position	Gear	Forward Clutch	Direct Clutch	Front Band	Intermediate Clutch	Roller	Low Roller Clutch	Rear Band
Park-Neutral								
Reverse			On					On
Drive	First	On					Effective (Holds)	
	Second	On			On	Effective (Holds)		
	Third	On	On		On			
L$_2$	First	On					Effective (Holds)	
	Second	On		On	On	Effective (Holds)		
L$_1$	First	On					Effective (Holds)	On
	Second	On		On	On	Effective (Holds)		

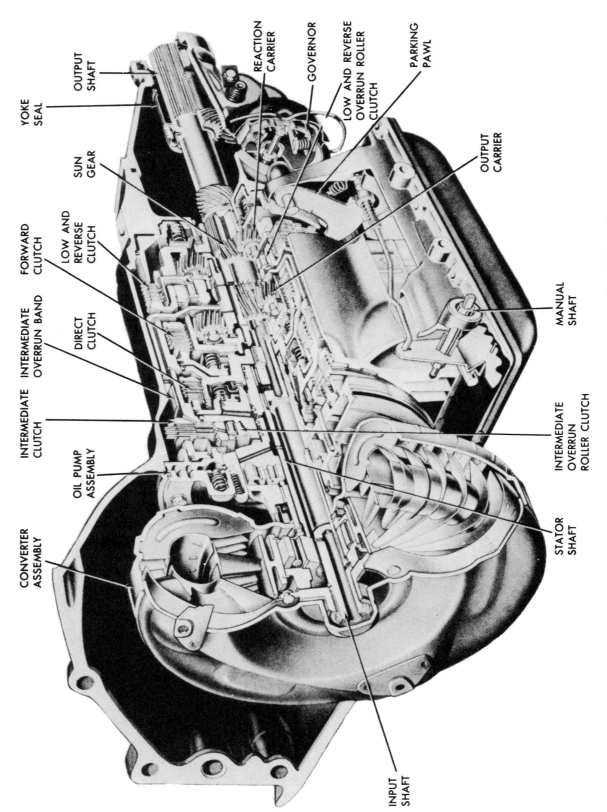

YOKE SEAL

OUTPUT SHAFT

REACTION CARRIER

GOVERNOR

LOW AND REVERSE OVERRUN ROLLER CLUTCH

PARKING PAWL

SUN GEAR

OUTPUT CARRIER

FORWARD CLUTCH

LOW AND REVERSE CLUTCH

INTERMEDIATE OVERRUN BAND

DIRECT CLUTCH

MANUAL SHAFT

INTERMEDIATE CLUTCH

OIL PUMP ASSEMBLY

INTERMEDIATE OVERRUN ROLLER CLUTCH

CONVERTER ASSEMBLY

STATOR SHAFT

INPUT SHAFT

Fig. 11-45. THM-350/375B sectional view. (Oldsmobile Division, General Motors Corp.)

Turbo Hydramatic 350/375B and 350 C (Buick, Chevrolet, Oldsmobile, and Pontiac)

The THM-350 was introduced in 1969 as a three-speed automatic transmission for passenger car and light truck applications. The transmission is built by both Buick and Chevrolet Motor Divisions. For Parts Book Code Identification, the THM-350 is referred to as the M-38 (Chevrolet-manufactured) and M-33 (Buick-manufactured). It continues in production through the model year 1981.

As shown in the sectional view (Fig. 11-45), the transmission design uses a one-piece integrated aluminum case with the converter housing and a bolt-on extension housing. It utilizes a three-element torque converter and a compound Simpson Planetary Set. Three multiple-disc clutches, two one-way roller clutches, and two bands provide the means to control the gear train operation. Figure 11-46 represents a simplified schematic view of the basic gear train and friction elements.

For extra muscle to handle the four-barrel 5.7 L (350 CID) engine for various intermediate and full size car models, the 375B was developed and used from 1972 through 1976 by Buick, Chevrolet, and Oldsmobile. The outward physical appearance and size is identical to the 350. The internal physical appearance is also identical, with the basic difference being in valve body and accumulator calibrations, plus an increase in the number of plates used in the forward and direct clutches.

For 1980, various THM-350 transmission models are equipped with a newly-developed torque converter clutch assembly. These units are referred to as the 350C and identified in the Parts Book Code as MV-4.

TYPICAL ENGINE APPLICATIONS

350	375B	350C
L6—4.0 L (250 CID)	V-8—5.7 L (350 CID)	V6—3.8 L (231 CID)
V6—3.8 L (231 CID)		V8—5.0 L (305 CID)
V8—4.0 L (260 CID)		V8—5.7 L (350 CID)
V8—4.3 L (262 CID)		
V8—5.0 L (305 CID)		
V8—5.7 L (350 CID)		

POWERFLOW SUMMARY AND OPERATING CHARACTERISTICS

N—Neutral. Like other three-speed automatic transmissions, the powerflow dead-ends at the forward and direct clutch units. There is no input to the planetary gear set (Fig. 11-47).

R—Reverse gear is a function of the rear planetary unit. Provides a simple gear ratio of 1.93:1, illustrated in Fig. 11-48.

D—Drive range is used for normal driving and maximum economy. Full automatic shifting and three gear ratios are available.
First Gear: A combined function of the front and rear planetary units. Provides a compound gear ratio of 2.52:1, illustrated in Fig. 11-49.

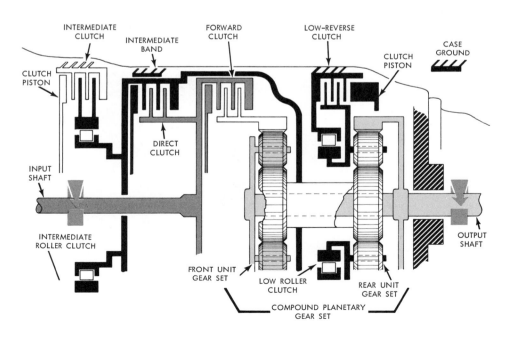

Fig. 11-46. THM-350 schematic view. (Oldsmobile Division, General Motors Corp.)

A Intermediate Overrun Roller Clutch INEFFECTIVE

B Intermediate Clutch OFF

C Intermediate Overrun Band OFF

D Direct Clutch OFF

E Forward Clutch OFF

F Low and Reverse Clutch OFF

G Low and Reverse Roller Clutch INEFFECTIVE

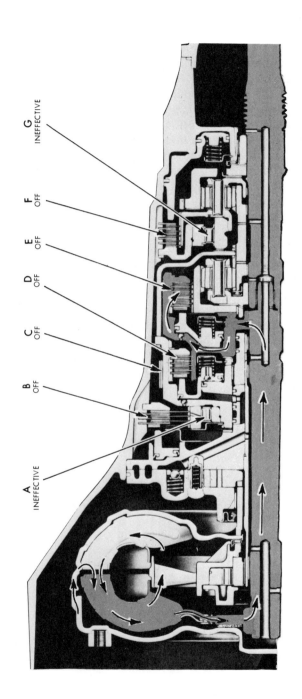

Fig. 11-47. Turbo HydraMatic 350—neutral. In park and neutral, all clutches and the intermediate overrun band are released; therefore, no power is transmitted from the torque converter turbine to planetary gear sets or output shaft. (Oldsmobile Division, General Motors Corp.)

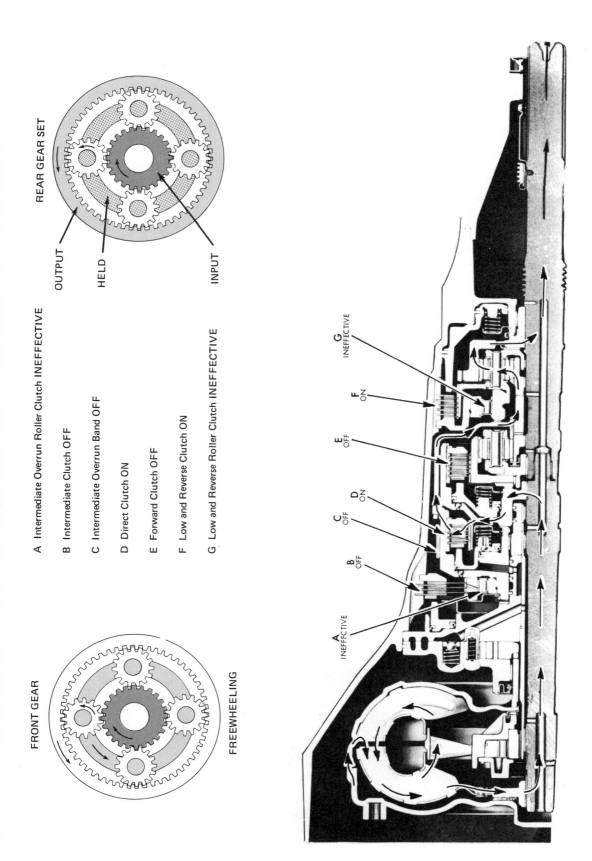

REAR GEAR SET

OUTPUT

HELD

INPUT

FRONT GEAR

FREEWHEELING

A   Intermediate Overrun Roller Clutch INEFFECTIVE

B   Intermediate Clutch OFF

C   Intermediate Overrun Band OFF

D   Direct Clutch ON

E   Forward Clutch OFF

F   Low and Reverse Clutch ON

G   Low and Reverse Roller Clutch INEFFECTIVE

A
INEFFECTIVE

B
OFF

C
OFF

D
ON

E
OFF

F
ON

G
INEFFECTIVE

Fig. 11-48. In Reverse, the direct clutch is applied to transmit torque from the forward clutch housing to the sun gear drive shell and the sun gear. The low and reverse clutch is applied preventing the reaction carrier from turning. Clockwise rotation of the sun gear causes the carrier pinions and output ring gear to turn counterclockwise in reduction. The output ring gear is connected directly to the output shaft and delivers a reverse ratio of 1.93 to 1. The sun gear and output carrier of the front planetary drive the unit at a reverse overdrive but the powerflow dead ends at the forward clutch which is not applied.

REAR GEAR SET

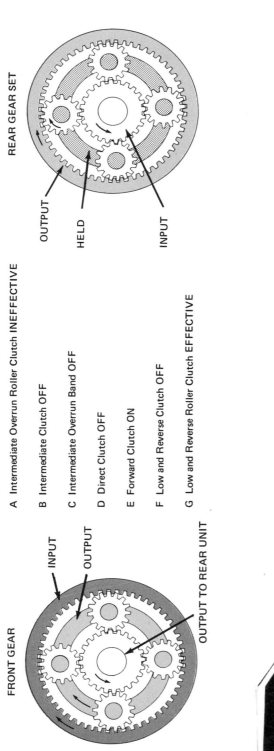

OUTPUT

HELD

INPUT

FRONT GEAR

INPUT

OUTPUT

OUTPUT TO REAR UNIT

A Intermediate Overrun Roller Clutch INEFFECTIVE

B Intermediate Clutch OFF

C Intermediate Overrun Band OFF

D Direct Clutch OFF

E Forward Clutch ON

F Low and Reverse Clutch OFF

G Low and Reverse Roller Clutch EFFECTIVE

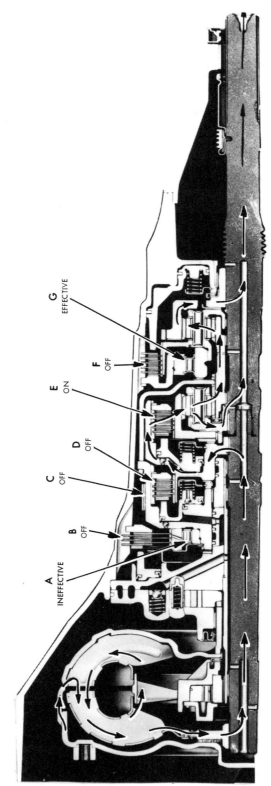

A INEFFECTIVE
B OFF
C OFF
D OFF
E ON
F OFF
G EFFECTIVE

Fig. 11-49. With the selector lever in (D) range the forward clutch is applied. This delivers turbine torque from the input shaft through the forward clutch to the input ring gear in a clockwise direction. Clockwise rotation of the input ring gear causes the output planet pinions to rotate in a clockwise direction, driving the sun gear counterclockwise. Since the sun gear is common to both planetary sets, the pinions in the rear unit reaction carrier are driven in a clockwise direction. The reaction carrier pinions rotate the output ring gear and reaction carrier assembly against the vehicle weight and attempt to walk counterclockwise while driving the output ring gear. The low roller clutch, however, holds the reaction carrier and the output ring gear and output shaft turn at a reduction ratio of 2.52 to 1.

To prepare the transmission for the shift into intermediate (second gear) the sun gear and drive shell, direct clutch housing, intermediate roller clutch and intermediate clutch faced plates are all turning in a counterclockwise direction.

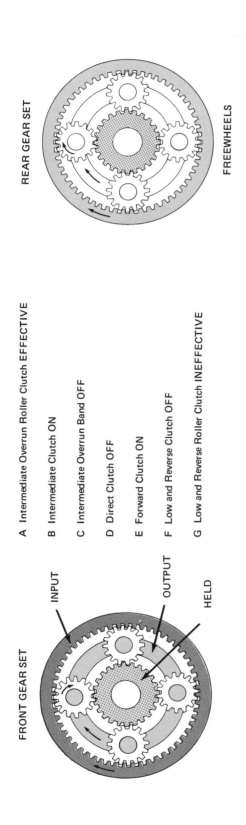

REAR GEAR SET

FREEWHEELS

FRONT GEAR SET

INPUT

OUTPUT

HELD

A Intermediate Overrun Roller Clutch EFFECTIVE

B Intermediate Clutch ON

C Intermediate Overrun Band OFF

D Direct Clutch OFF

E Forward Clutch ON

F Low and Reverse Clutch OFF

G Low and Reverse Roller Clutch INEFFECTIVE

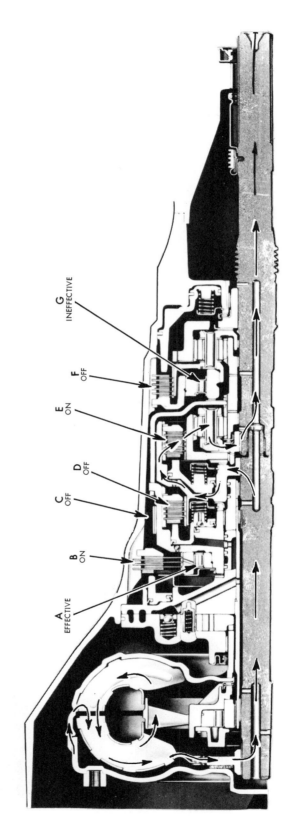

A
EFFECTIVE

B
ON

C
OFF

D
OFF

E
ON

F
OFF

G
INEFFECTIVE

Fig. 11-50. In (D) range, second gear, the intermediate clutch is applied to allow the intermediate roller clutch to hold the sun gear against counter-clockwise rotation that was occuring during first gear operation. Turbine torque, through the applied forward clutch is delivered to the input ring gear in a clockwise direction. Clockwise rotation of the input ring gear causes the output planet pinions to walk around the stationary sun gear and drive the output shaft at a reduction ratio of 1.52 to 1. Second gear is a function of the front planetary unit.

REAR GEAR SET

FRONT GEAR SET

INPUT

OUTPUT

A Intermediate Overrun Roller Clutch INEFFECTIVE

B Intermediate Clutch ON

C Intermediate Overrun Band OFF

D Direct Clutch ON

E Forward Clutch ON

F Low and Reverse Clutch OFF

G Low and Reverse Roller Clutch INEFFECTIVE

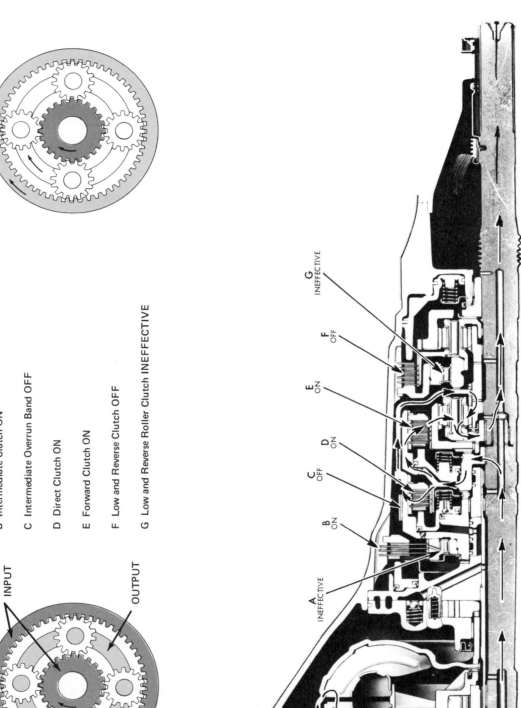

A
INEFFECTIVE

B
ON

C
OFF

D
ON

E
ON

F
OFF

G
INEFFECTIVE

Fig. 11-51. In direct drive, engine torque is transmitted to the converter then through the forward clutch to the input ring gear of the front planetary unit. Because the direct clutch is applied, power is also transmitted to the sun gear drive shell and the sun gear. Since both the sun gear and the input ring gear are now turning at the same speed, the front and rear planetary units are locked together as one unit for a direct drive ratio of 1 to 1. The clockwise rotation of the locked planetary units releases both roller clutches.

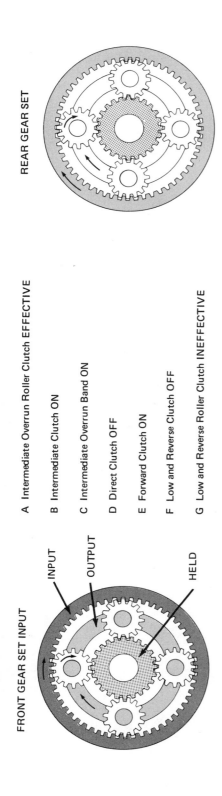

FRONT GEAR SET INPUT

INPUT

OUTPUT

HELD

REAR GEAR SET

A Intermediate Overrun Roller Clutch EFFECTIVE

B Intermediate Clutch ON

C Intermediate Overrun Band ON

D Direct Clutch OFF

E Forward Clutch ON

F Low and Reverse Clutch OFF

G Low and Reverse Roller Clutch INEFFECTIVE

A
EFFECTIVE

B
ON

C
ON

D
OFF

E
ON

F
OFF

G
INEFFECTIVE

Fig. 11-52. In Intermediate range, second gear, the intermediate band is applied in addition to the forward and intermediate clutches. The intermediate band acts as a coast or overrun brake band. During closed throttle it holds the sun gear fixed against coast torque. Without the band applied, the sun gear would rotate in a clockwise direction during coast and overrun the intermediate roller clutch.

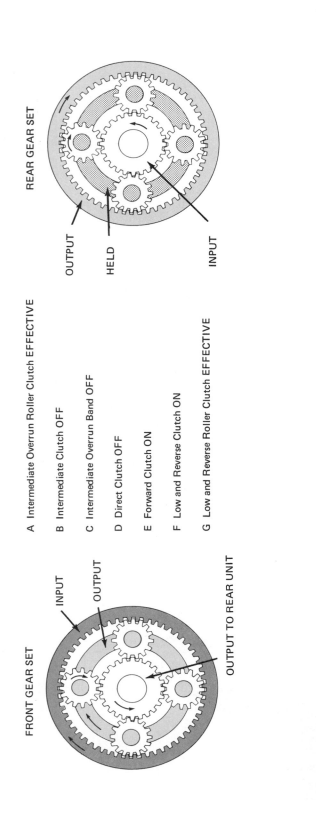

REAR GEAR SET

OUTPUT

HELD

INPUT

A Intermediate Overrun Roller Clutch EFFECTIVE

B Intermediate Clutch OFF

C Intermediate Overrun Band OFF

D Direct Clutch OFF

E Forward Clutch ON

F Low and Reverse Clutch ON

G Low and Reverse Roller Clutch EFFECTIVE

FRONT GEAR SET

INPUT

OUTPUT

OUTPUT TO REAR UNIT

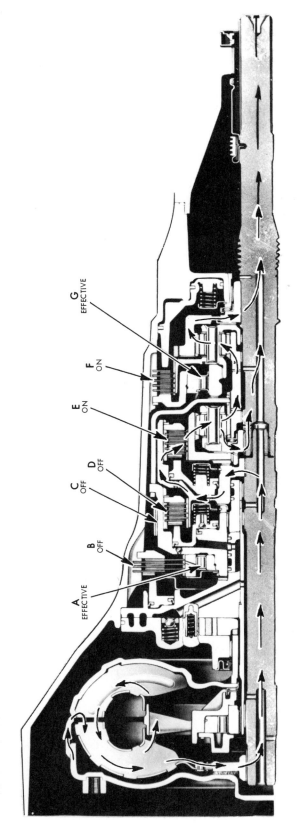

A
EFFECTIVE

B
OFF

C
OFF

D
OFF

E
ON

F
ON

G
EFFECTIVE

Fig. 11-53. In L₁ range the low and reverse clutch is applied in addition to the forward clutch. The low and reverse clutch acts as a coast or overrun clutch. During closed throttle it holds the rear planetary reaction carrier stationary against coast torque. Without the low and reverse clutch applied, the carrier would rotate in a clockwise direction during coast and overrun the low roller clutch.

Second Gear: A function of the front planetary unit. Provides a simple gear ratio of 1.52:1, illustrated in Fig. 11-50.

Third Gear: A direct-drive ratio of 1:1 is illustrated in Fig. 11-51. Converter clutch lock-up occurs in 350C transmission units at the proper vehicle cut-in speed.

External controls to the 350/375B and 350C transmissions are:

- Manual Linkage—To select the transmission operating range.
- Engine Vacuum—To operate the vacuum modulator system.
- Cable Control—To operate the detent forced down-shift system.
- 12-Volt Electrical Terminal (350C)—To energize an internal electrical solenoid for activation of the converter clutch circuit.

The usual downshift features are available:

- Full throttle forced downshifts 3–1, 2–1, and 3–2 for full power performance, which will occur within the proper vehicle speed and engine torque range.
- Part throttle 3-2 downshift for controlled acceleration during low speed operation.
- Closed throttle sequence is 3-2 and 2-1.

L2—Sometimes Marked S. Intermediate range allows for performance in congested traffic and hilly terrain. It starts in first gear and has a normal 1-2 shift pattern. The transmission, however, remains in second gear for the desired acceleration and braking requirements. Intermediate can be selected at any high-gear vehicle speed and the transmission will shift to second.

The closed throttle downshift pattern is 2-1. A full throttle-forced downshift 2-1 is also available. Refer to Intermediate Range (Fig. 11-52).

L1—Sometimes marked L. Low range locks the transmission in first gear for heavy pulling power and engine braking, especially for conditions where continuous first-gear operation is needed. For example, driving in steep mountain terrain. L_1 can be selected at any vehicle speed range but will shift to second if the vehicle speed is too high. When vehicle speed is reduced below 50 mph (80.5 km/h), manual low engages and the transmission will not upshift regardless of throttle opening. Refer to Manual Low Range, Fig. 11-53.

Chart 11-7 summarizes the THM-350 clutch/band combinations and range operation.

Turbo Hydra-Matic 250 and 250C (Chevrolet, Oldsmobile, and Pontiac)

To fill-in for the Powerglide transmission, which was dropped from production after 1973, Chevrolet modified the THM-350. The conversion was introduced for 1974 and called the THM-250. It was used primarily for low-torque engine applications by Chevrolet in 1974–77, Oldsmobile in 1977, and Pontiac in 1976–77. For Parts Book Code Identification the transmission is referred to as the M-31 (Chevrolet-manufactured).

The THM-250 transmission case is physically the same size as the THM-350 and very much identical in external appearance. The 250 is identified by the intermediate band adjusting screw located on the passenger side of the case. In air-cooled converter applications, the housing section of the case will have holes for air circulation. These comparisons are shown in Fig. 11-54. The big internal design change was the elimination of the intermediate clutch and substitution of an adjustable intermediate band for second-gear operation.

TURBO HYDRA-MATIC 350/375B
Clutch and Band Application Chart 11-7
Selector Pattern (P R N D S L) or (P R N D L₂ L₁)

Range	Gear	Forward Clutch	Direct Clutch	Intermediate Clutch	Intermediate Roller Clutch	Intermediate Overrun Band	Low & Reverse Clutch	Low Roller Clutch
Park-Neutral								
Reverse			On				On	
Drive	First	On						Effective (Holds)
	Second	On		On	Effective (Holds)			
	Third	On	On	On				
L₂	First	On						Effective (Holds)
	Second	On		On	Effective (Holds)	On		
L₁	First	On					On	Effective (Holds)
	Second	On		On	Effective (Holds)	On		

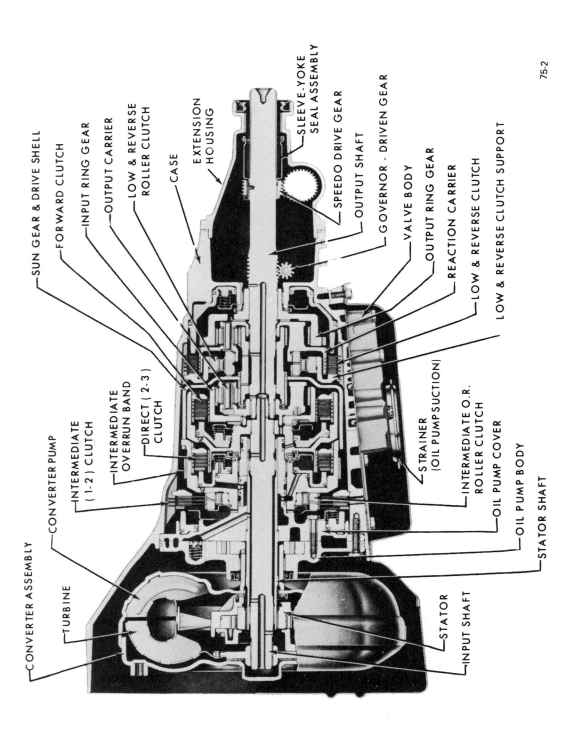

CONVERTER ASSEMBLY
TURBINE
CONVERTER PUMP
INTERMEDIATE (1-2) CLUTCH
INTERMEDIATE OVERRUN BAND
DIRECT (2-3) CLUTCH
SUN GEAR & DRIVE SHELL
FORWARD CLUTCH
INPUT RING GEAR
OUTPUT CARRIER
LOW & REVERSE ROLLER CLUTCH
CASE
EXTENSION HOUSING
SLEEVE-YOKE SEAL ASSEMBLY
SPEEDO DRIVE GEAR
OUTPUT SHAFT
GOVERNOR - DRIVEN GEAR
VALVE BODY
OUTPUT RING GEAR
REACTION CARRIER
LOW & REVERSE CLUTCH
LOW & REVERSE CLUTCH SUPPORT
STRAINER (OIL PUMP SUCTION)
INTERMEDIATE O.R. ROLLER CLUTCH
OIL PUMP COVER
OIL PUMP BODY
STATOR SHAFT
STATOR
INPUT SHAFT

75-2

Fig. 11-54. (A). THM-350.

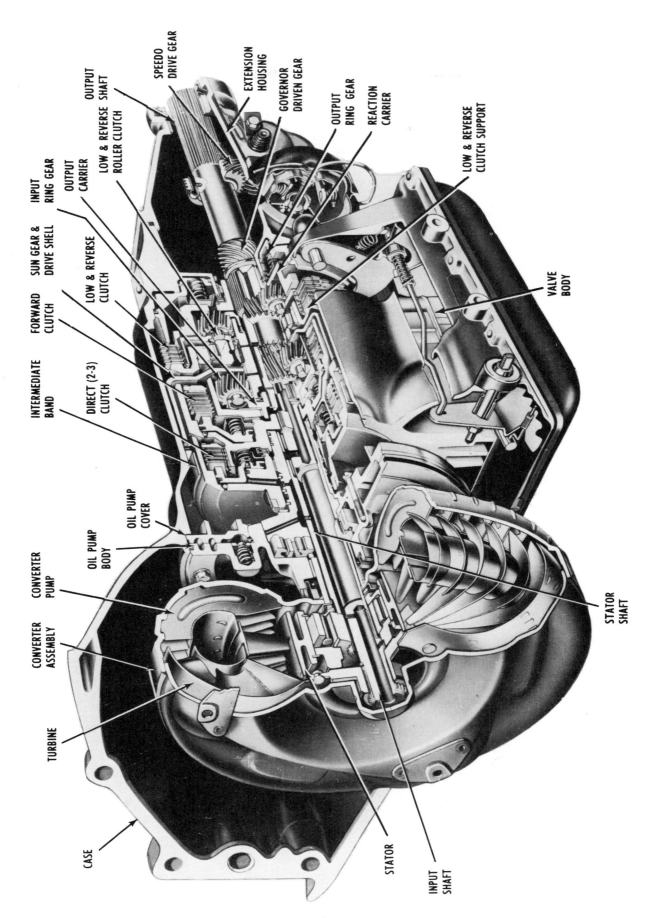

Fig. 11-54. (B) Air-cooled THM-250. (Oldsmobile Division, General Motors Corp.)

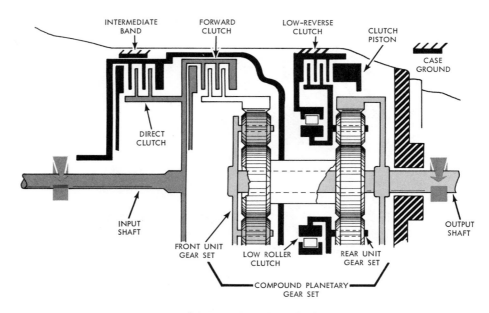

Fig. 11-55. THM-250 schematic view.

Otherwise, the gear ratios and internal make-up remain the same. A simplified schematic view of the 250 basic gear train and control elements is shown in Fig. 11-55.

For 1980, the THM-250 was coupled with the GM torque converter clutch. All production units are equipped with TCC and referred to as the THM-250C. A sectional view of the transmission is shown in Fig. 11-56.

TYPICAL ENGINE APPLICATIONS

250	250C
L4—2.5 L (140 CID)	V8—5.0 L (305 CID)
L6—4.0 L (250 CID)	
V8—4.3 L (262 CID)	

POWERFLOW SUMMARY AND OPERATING CHARACTERISTICS. The planetary gear train operation, external controls, and operating characteristics are similar to the THM-350.

Chart 11-8 summarizes the THM-250 clutch/band combinations and range operation.

Turbo Hydra-Matic 200, 200C, and 325 (Buick, Cadillac, Chevrolet, Oldsmobile, and Pontiac)

The Turbo Hydra-Matic 200 is an all new development by Hydra-Matic Division. Introduced for the car model year 1976 in all GM car divisions except Cadillac, it is an innovative lightweight, all-metric, three-speed automatic transmission capable of han-

TURBO HYDRA-MATIC 250
Clutch and Band Application Chart 11-8
Selector Pattern (P R N D S L) (P R N D L₂ L₁) (P R N D I L)

Range	Gear	Forward Clutch	Direct Clutch	Intermediate Band	Low & Reverse Clutch	Low Roller Clutch
Park-Neutral						
Reverse			On		On	
Drive	First	On				Effective (Holds)
	Second	On				
	Third	On	On			
L₂	First	On				Effective (Holds)
	Second	On		On		
L₁	First	On			On	Effective (Holds)
	Second	On		On		

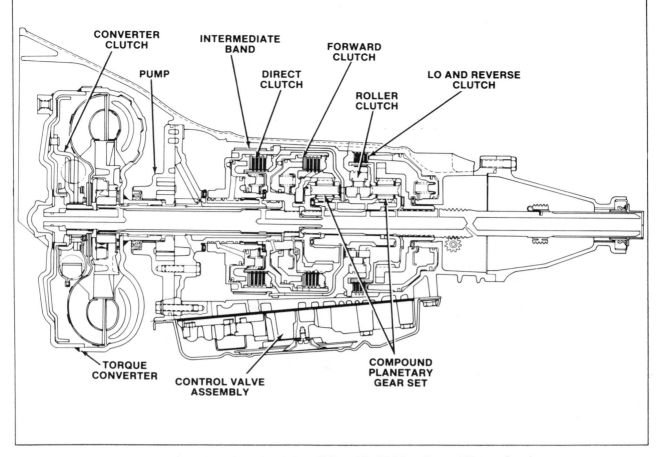

Fig. 11-56. THM-250C sectional view. (Oldsmobile Division, General Motors Corp.)

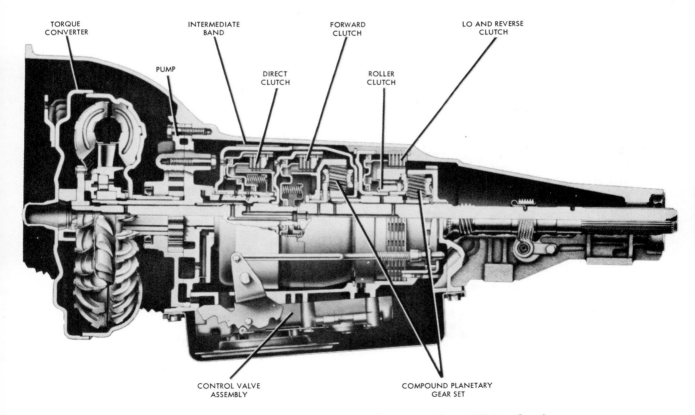

Fig. 11-57. THM-200 sectional view. (Oldsmobile Division, General Motors Corp.)

dling a wide variety of engine and vehicle applications. In 1978. Cadillac adopted the transmission for use in some of its car model lines. For Parts Book Code Identification, the THM-200 is referred to as the M-29. It continues in production through the model year 1981.

Fig. 11-57 represents a sectional view of the THM-200 assembly; it closely resembles the THM-250. New to transmission design is the case structure; the con-verter housing, transmission case, and the extension housing make-up a complete one-piece casting. A three-element torque converter is used with a Simpson Planetary Set. Three multiple-disc clutches, one band, and a one-way roller clutch provide the means to control the gear train operation. A simplified schematic view of the gear train and friction control elements is shown in Fig. 11-58.

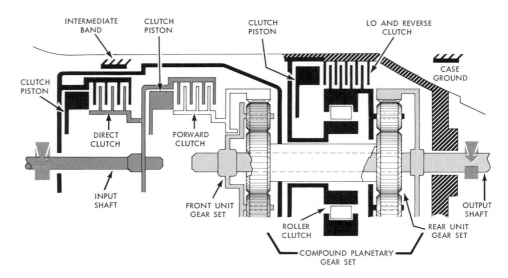

Fig. 11-58. THM-200 schematic view.

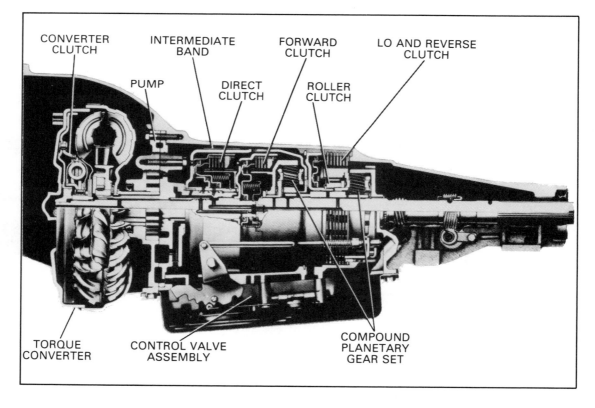

Fig. 11-59. THM-200C sectional view. (Oldsmobile Division, General Motors Corp.)

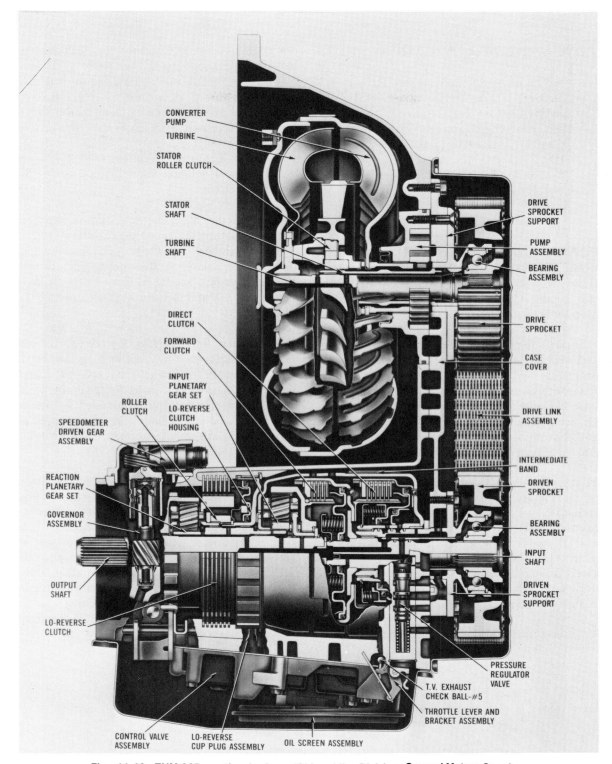

Fig. 11-60. THM-325 sectional view. (Oldsmobile Division, General Motors Corp.)

For 1980, various THM-200 transmission models are equipped with the new GM torque converter clutch. These units are referred to as the 200C and identified in the Parts Book Code as MV-9. A sectional view is shown in Fig. 11-59.

For the front-wheel-drive Buick Riviera, Cadillac Eldorado, and Oldsmobile Toronado, the THM-325

was an engineering development for 1979. It is a heavy-duty adaptation of the THM-200 using the typical set-up of a three-element torque converter and Simpson Planetary (Fig. 11-60). The torque converter couples the engine to the planetary gear set through the use of a drive sprocket, a link belt, and a driven sprocket. The Parts Book Identification Code is M-32.

TYPICAL ENGINE APPLICATIONS

200— Used on all engine applications through 5.7 l (350 CID), 1976-79; L4—2.5 L (151 CID), only for 1980.

200C— Used on all engine applications through 5.7 L (350 CID), for 1980, except L4—2.5 L (15L CID).

325— V8—5.0 L (307 CID) and V8—5.7 L (350 CID), for 1979-80.

325C— For 1982.

POWERFLOW SUMMARY AND OPERATING CHARACTERISTICS. Gear train operation is identical to the THM-350 and THM 250; review the 350 section for details. Chapter 4 can also be consulted for Simpson Planetary operation.

N—Neutral: The powerflow dead-ends at the forward and direct clutch units. There is no input to the gear train.

R—Reverse gear is a function of the rear planetary unit. Provides a simple planetary ratio of 2.07:1.

D—Drive range is used for normal driving conditions and maximum economy. Full automatic shifting and three gear ratios are available.

First Gear: A combined function of the front and rear planetary units. Provides a compound gear ratio of 2.74:1.

Second Gear: A function of the front planetary unit. Provides a simple planetary ratio of 1.57:1.

Third Gear: Both planetary units are locked for direct-drive ratio of 1:1. Converter clutch lock-up occurs in 200C transmission units at the proper vehicle cut-in speed.

External controls to the transmission are:

- Manual Linkage Control—To select the transmission operating range.
- Cable Control—To operate the throttle valve and detent forced downshift systems. Both system control valves are in tandem in the same valve body bore and work from the same single cable control.
- 12-Volt Electrical Terminal (200C)—To energize an internal solenoid for activation of the converter clutch circuit.

Typical operating characteristics are featured in D range. Full throttle-forced downshifts 3-1, 2-1, and 3-2 are attained within the proper engine torque range and vehicle speed. A low-speed, part throttle 3-2 downshift is also available. Closed throttle downshift pattern is 3-2 and 2-1 through 1978 and 3-1 thereafter.

I—Sometimes Marked L_2 or S. Intermediate range allows for performance in congested traffic and hilly terrain. It provides a normal 1-2 shift pattern and keeps the transmission in second gear for the desired acceleration and braking requirements. Intermediate can be selected at any high-gear vehicle speed and the transmission will shift to second. A full throttle-forced downshift 2-1 is available.

L—Sometimes Marked L_1. The transmission is manually locked into first gear for heavy pulling power and engine braking, especially for conditions where continuous first-gear operation is needed. L can be selected at any vehicle speed range but will shift to second gear if the vehicle speed is too high. When the vehicle speed is reduced to approximately 30 mph (48 km/h), manual low engages and the transmission will not upshift regardless of throttle opening.

Chart 11-9 summarizes the clutch/band application and range operation of the THM-200.

TURBO HYDRA-MATIC 200/325
Clutch and Band Application Chart 11-9
Selector Pattern (P R N D S L) (P R N D L_2 L_1) (P R N D I L)

Range	Gear	Forward Clutch	Direct Clutch	Intermediate Band	Low & Reverse Clutch	Low Roller Clutch
Park-Neutral						
Reverse			On		On	
Drive	First	On				Effective (Holds)
	Second	On				
	Third	On	On			
L_2	First	On				Effective (Holds)
	Second	On		On		
L_1	First	On			On	Effective (Holds)
	Second	On		On		

Turbo Hydra-Matic 125 (Buick, Chevrolet, Oldsmobile, and Pontiac)

The Turbo Hydra-Matic 125 is an automatic transaxle transmission engineered for the transverse mounted front-wheel-drive system in GM X-Car Body Models introduced in midyear 1979. Manufactured by Hydra-Matic Division, it is an extra light-weight transmission designed to handle the small L4 (2.5 L) and V6 (2.8 L) engines. It combines a three-speed transmission and a differential assembly in one compact front wheel ''metric'' drive unit (Figs. 11-61 and 11-62). The Parts Book Identification Code number is M-34.

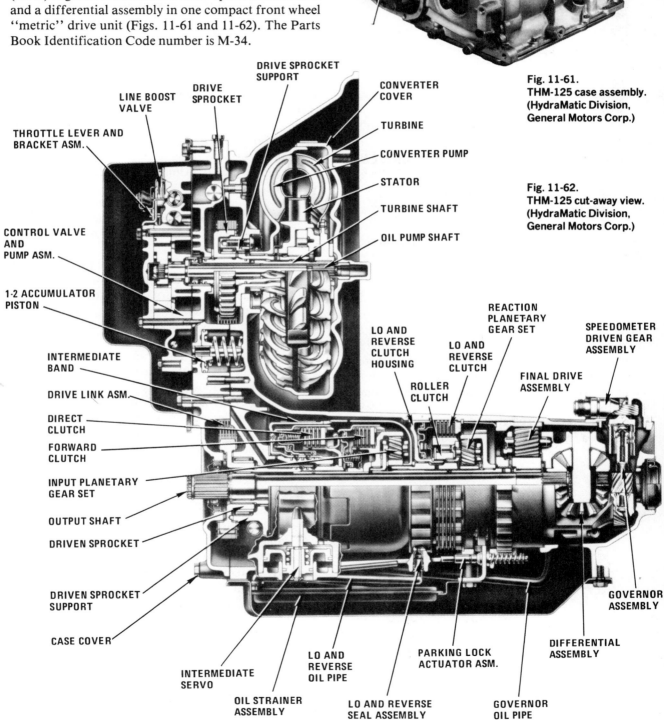

Fig. 11-61. THM-125 case assembly. (HydraMatic Division, General Motors Corp.)

Fig. 11-62. THM-125 cut-away view. (HydraMatic Division, General Motors Corp.)

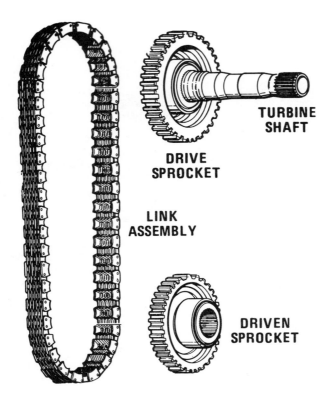

Fig. 11-63. Chain link driven sprocket connects to forward clutch housing, Fig. 11-64. (HydraMatic Division, General Motors Corp.)

The torque converter is a nonlockup, three-element unit that hydraulically drives the gear train through a dual sprocket and drive link assembly (Fig. 11-63). The sprockets are designed with a different number of teeth to accommodate the engine sizes. To connect and disconnect the power output from the converter to the transmission gear train, a forward clutch is used (Fig. 11-64). The gear train components make-up a typical three-speed compound Simpson

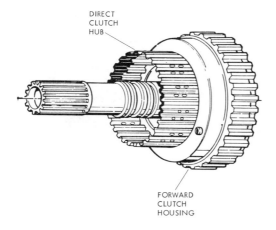

Fig 11-64. (HydraMatic Division, General Motors Corp.)

Planetary Set identical to the set-up used in the THM-200. The same clutch/band combinations control the gear system.

Unique to the transmission is the planetary final drive and differential gears, which are located within the case and on the same main centerline of the power-flow (Fig. 11-65). The final drive assembly is at the output end of the transmission gear train. The gear train output drives the sun gear in the final drive through a shaft drive. The internal gear, shown in Fig. 11-65, is splined to the case and will not rotate. The planet carrier is the output member of the final drive and is mounted to the differential case. The gear set operates in reduction at all times at a fixed ratio of approximately 2.84:1. It performs the same function as the ring and pinion gears in a conventional rear axle drive. The differential assembly also performs the same function and works in identical manner as those used in conventional rear axle drives (Fig. 11-66).

POWERFLOW SUMMARY AND OPERATING CHARACTERISTICS

N—Neutral: The powerflow dead-ends at the forward and direct clutch units. There is no input to the gear train.

R—Reverse is a function of the rear planetary unit. Provides a simple planetary ratio of 2.07:1.

D—Drive range is used for normal driving requirements and maximum economy. Full automatic shifting and three gear ratios are available.

First Gear: A combined function of the front and rear planetary units. Provides a compound gear ratio of 2.84:1.
Second Gear: A function of the front planetary unit. Provides a simple planetary ratio of 1.60:1.
Third Gear: The forward and direct clutches lock-up the gear set for a direct-drive ratio of 1:1.

External controls to the transmission are:

- Manual Linkage Control—To select the transmission operating range.
- Cable Control—From the carburetor for operation of both the throttle- and detent-forced downshift systems. Both system control valves are in tandem in the same valve body bore and work from the same single external control.

For added acceleration, full throttle-forced downshifts 3–2, 3–1, and 2–1 are available within the proper vehicle speed and engine torque range. A part throttle 3–2 downshift feature gives controlled acceleration during low-speed operation. The closed throttle downshift pattern is 3–2 and 2–1.

2—provides a normal 1-2 shift pattern and keeps the transmission in second gear for extra pulling power or engine braking in hilly terrain. It can also be used in congested traffic conditions. The 2 range can be selected at any high gear vehicle speed and will downshift to second. The closed throttle shift is 2–1. A full throttle-forced downshift 2–1 is available.

1—maintains first-gear operation for heavy pulling power and engine braking on steep grades. 1 range can be selected at any vehicle speed range but will shift to second if the road speed is too high. when the car speed slows down to a safe speed [40 mph (64 km/h)], manual low engages and the transmission will not upshift regardless of throttle opening.

Chart 11-10 summarizes the THM-125 clutch/band combinations and range operation.

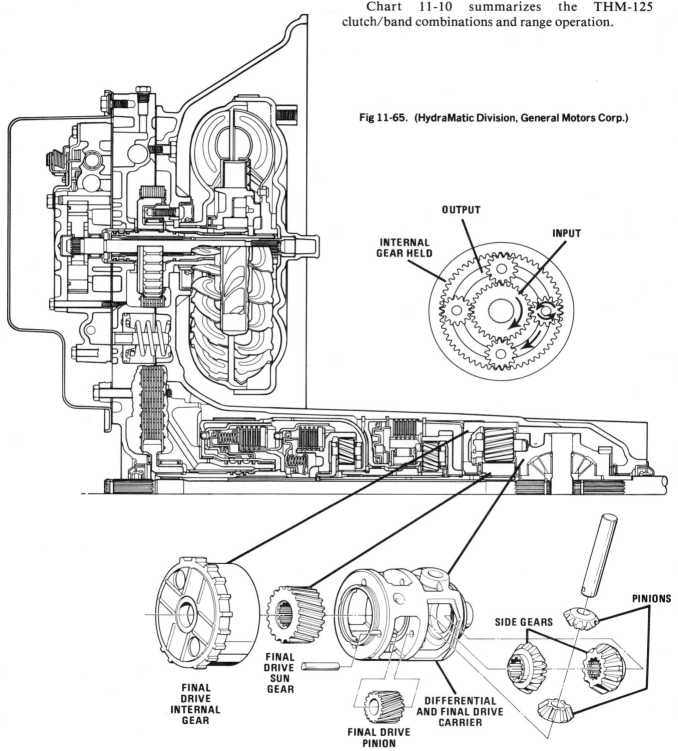

Fig 11-65. (HydraMatic Division, General Motors Corp.)

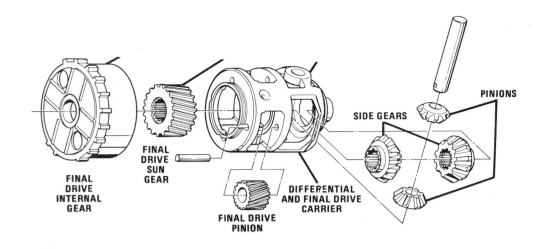

FINAL DRIVE INTERNAL GEAR

FINAL DRIVE SUN GEAR

FINAL DRIVE PINION

DIFFERENTIAL AND FINAL DRIVE CARRIER

SIDE GEARS

PINIONS

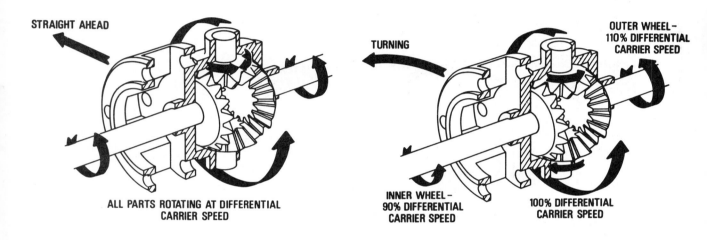

STRAIGHT AHEAD

ALL PARTS ROTATING AT DIFFERENTIAL CARRIER SPEED

TURNING

INNER WHEEL – 90% DIFFERENTIAL CARRIER SPEED

100% DIFFERENTIAL CARRIER SPEED

OUTER WHEEL – 110% DIFFERENTIAL CARRIER SPEED

Fig 11-66. (HydraMatic Division, General Motors Corp.)

TURBO HYDRA-MATIC 125
Clutch and Band Application Chart 11-10
Selector Pattern (P R N D I L) (P R N D S L) (P R N D L_2 L_1)

Range	Gear	Forward Clutch	Direct Clutch	Intermediate Band	Low & Reverse Clutch	Low Roller Clutch
Park-Neutral						
Reverse			On		On	
Drive	First	On				Effective (Holds)
	Second	On				
	Third	On	On			
L_2	First	On				Effective (Holds)
	Second	On		On		
L_1	First	On			On	Effective (Holds)
	Second	On		On		

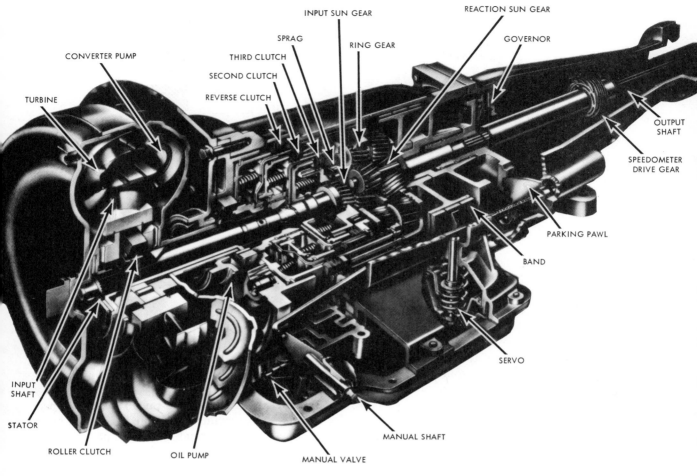

INPUT SUN GEAR

REACTION SUN GEAR

SPRAG

RING GEAR

GOVERNOR

CONVERTER PUMP

THIRD CLUTCH

SECOND CLUTCH

REVERSE CLUTCH

TURBINE

OUTPUT SHAFT

SPEEDOMETER DRIVE GEAR

PARKING PAWL

BAND

SERVO

INPUT SHAFT

STATOR

ROLLER CLUTCH

OIL PUMP

MANUAL VALVE

MANUAL SHAFT

Fig. 11-67. (MD-3) 180, sectional view. (Chevrolet Division, General Motors Corp.)

(MD-3) 180 Automatic Transmission (Chevette)

The 180 automatic transmission is built at General Motors' Strasbourg-Neuhol plant in France and has already been successfully used in GM European-built cars. Beginning in midyear 1977, the 180 was imported for use on Chevettes equipped with the 1.6-L engine and standard federal emission control equipment. Increased popularity of the subcompact necessitated an optional transmission to meet production requirements.

A sectional view of the 180 is illustrated in Fig. 11-67. It uses an aluminum case with bolt-on converter and extension housings. The transmission is a fully automatic three-speed unit consisting of a three-element torque converter and a compound Ravigneaux Planetary Set. Three multiple-disc clutches, a one-way sprag clutch and a band provide the means to control the gear train operation. Fig. 11-68 represents a simpli-

fied schematic view of the basic gear train and friction control elements. Detailed operation of the gear train is discussed in Chapter 4.

N—Neutral: The sprag clutch is locked and, without a reactionary member, all gears are free to rotate on their own centers. No torque is delivered to the planet carrier and output shaft.

R—Reverse is a function of the input sun gear driving and the long pinions walking counterclockwise around the stationary internal gear. The output carrier turns at a reverse reduction and a simple gear ratio of 1.91:1 is provided.

D—Drive range is used for normal driving conditions and maximum economy. Full automatic shifting and three gear ratios are available.

First Gear: A function of the input sun gear driving and the long carrier pinions walking around

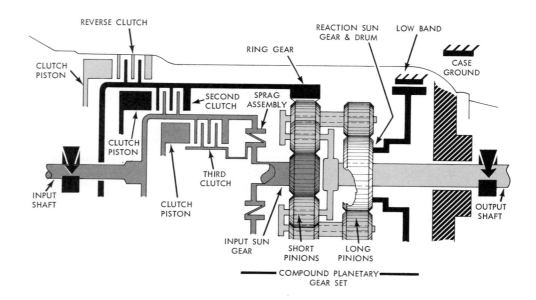

Fig. 11-68. MD-3 transmission, schematic view.

the stationary reaction sun gear. The output carrier turns at a forward reduction and a compound gear ratio of 2.40:1 is provided.

Second Gear: A function of the ring gear driving and the long pinions walking around the reaction sun gear. The output carrier turns at a forward reduction and a simple gear ratio of 1.48:1 is provided.

Third Gear: The ring gear is locked to the input sun gear for a direct-drive ratio of 1:1.

External controls to the transmission are:

• Manual Linkage—To select the transmission operating range.
• Engine Vacuum—To operate the vacuum modulator unit.
• Cable Control—To operate the detent downshift system.

Typical operating characteristics are featured in D range. Full throttle-forced downshifts 3–1, 2–1, and 3–2 are attained within the proper engine torque range and vehicle speed. A low-speed part throttle 3–2 downshift is also available. Closed throttle downshift pattern is 3–2 and 2–1.

L_2 (intermediate or second-range) is used for performance in hilly terrain or congested traffic. It has a first-gear start and normal 1–2 shift pattern. The transmission, however, will remain in second gear for the desired acceleration and braking requirements. Intermediate can be selected at any high gear vehicle speed and the transmission will shift to second. To prevent overspeeding of the engine, do not select L_2 at a vehicle speed that exceeds the owner's manual recommendation.

L_1 (low range) manually locks the transmission in first gear. It can be selected at any vehicle speed and the transmission will shift to first gear immediately.

(MD-3) 180 Automatic Transmission
Clutch and Band Application Chart 11-11
Selector Pattern (P R N D L$_2$ L$_1$) (P R N D 2 1)

Range	Gear	Reverse Clutch	Second Clutch	Third Clutch	Low Band	Sprag
Park-Neutral						Locked
Reverse		Applied		Applied		Locked
D	First				Applied	Locked
	Second		Applied		Applied	
	Third		Applied	Applied		
L$_2$	First					Locked
	Second		Applied		Applied	
L$_1$	First			Applied	Applied	Locked

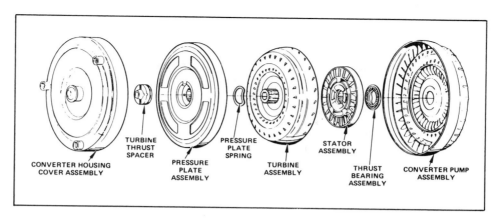

Fig. 11-69. (Oldsmobile Divison, General Motors Corp.)

Note that this deviates from the characteristic operation of other three-speed automatic transmissions. Once first gear is engaged, the transmission will not upshift regardless of vehicle speed or throttle opening. L_1 should not be selected at a vehicle speed that exceeds the owner's manual recommendation. L_1 is used for engine braking or any condition where continuous first-gear operation is desirable for full power.

Chart 11-11 summarizes the clutch/band applications and range operation.

GM Torque Converter Clutch (TCC)

To eliminate converter slippage during cruise conditions and significantly improve fuel economy, General Motors developed a torque converter clutch for its family of automatic transmissions for 1980. The 350C, 250C, and 200C are used on various GM intermediate and full-size cars. The Torque Converter Clutch Assembly is a basic three-element torque converter with the addition of a converter clutch (Fig. 11-69). The converter clutch is splined to the turbine assembly and, when applied, it locks with the converter cover, providing a direct mechanical drive between the engine and transmission input shaft. The direct mechanical hook-up, engine-to-transmission, necessitates

the use of a spring-loaded damper unit in the converter cover. The turbine splines into the damper to reduce converter clutch apply "feel." The converter design is very similar to the Chrysler Lock-Up Torque Converter.

The TCC is applied when the following conditions exist:

- Transmission in third gear, 1980.
- Transmission in second and third gear, on some

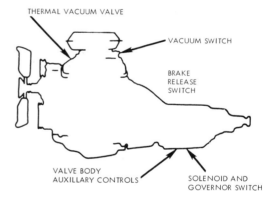

Fig. 11-70.

Fig. 11-71. Gas engine with delay valve (typical). (General Motors Corp.)

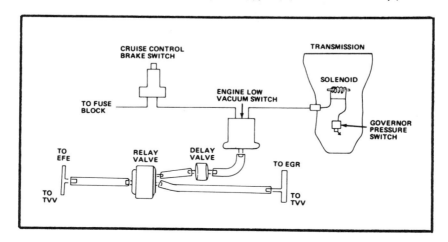

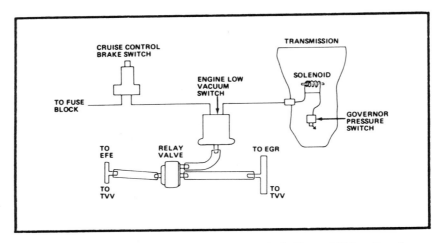

Fig. 11-72. Gas engine without delay valve (typical). (General Motors Corp.)

car models only, 1981.

- Vehicle speed range is 30–45 mph (48–72 km/h).
- Engine coolant is above 130 °F (54 °C).
- Engine vacuum is above 2.5 in.-hg (8 kPa).
- Brake pedal is released.

Engine and transmission sensing devices (Fig. 11-70) indicate when the vehicle is cruising and hydraulic pressure inside the converter engages the lock-up clutch. Representative external control circuits that aid in the apply and release of the converter clutch during various driving conditions are shown in Figs. 11-71, 11-72, and 11-73. The functions of these controls in the circuits are as follows:

1. Brake release switch (all engines)—It is normally closed. Acts to release the TCC when the brakes are applied.

2. Thermal vacuum valve (all gas engines)—It is normally open. Prevents the TCC from applying at low coolant temperatures.

3. Low vacuum switch (all gas engines)—Uses ported vacuum and is normally closed. Releases the TCC when engine vacuum drops below 2.5 in.-hg (8 kPa) prior to low-speed, moderate-acceleration, detent-forced downshifts and during closed throttle coastdown.

4. Low vacuum switch (diesel only)—It is normally open. Releases the TCC when engine vacuum pump reading drops below a preset level during moderate acceleration prior to a part throttle or detent downshift.

5. High vacuum switch (diesel only)—It is normally closed. Releases the TCC during a closed throttle coastdown.

6. Delay valve (4.9 l only)—Slows the vacuum switch response to vacuum changes.

Fig. 11-73. Diesel engine (typical). (Chevrolet Division, General Motors Corp.)

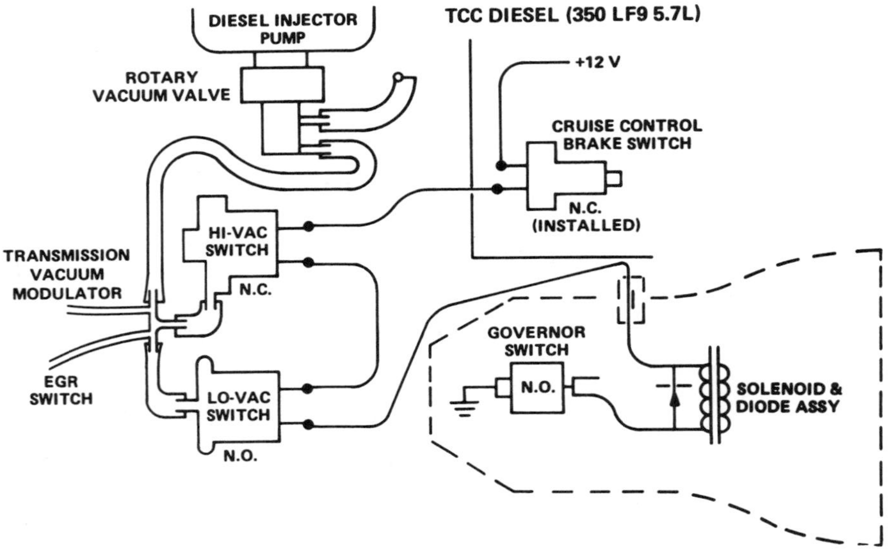

7. Vacuum relay valve (all gas engines)—Prevents ported vacuum from reaching the low vacuum switch at low engine coolant temperatures (when vacuum to EFE stops, vacuum from the EGR port of TVV can pass through the relay valve and on to the low engine vacuum switch).

8. Transmission governor switch—It is normally open. Closes the TCC solenoid circuit by completing the electrical ground with transmission in third gear and car speed range is above 30 mph (48 km/h).

9. Transmission solenoid—It is normally de-energized. When energized, the TCC hydraulic control engages the clutch for lock-up in third gear.

TCC NOTES

- TVV means Thermal Vacuum Valve
- EFE means Early Fuel Evaporation Heat
- EGR means Exhaust Gas Recirculation
- TVV to EFE system is connected to mainfold vacuum. It is normally open when cold and closed when hot.
- TVV to EGR system is connected to ported vacuum. It is normally closed when cold and open when hot.

Two TCC hydraulic control systems are used; however, they both perform the function of oil control to the apply and release sides of the clutch circuit. The

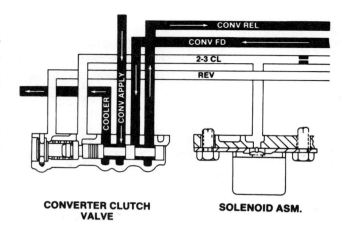

CONVERTER CLUTCH VALVE   **SOLENOID ASM.**

Fig. 11-74. Clutch valve released.(General Motors Corp.)

control valving is either located in the pump cover or an auxiliary valve body.

A representative system in the release mode is shown in Figs. 11-74 and 11-75. The pressure regulator valve converter feed is relayed through a converter clutch valve and charges the release circuit. Converter oil is supplied through a hollow turbine shaft and enters the converter on the front side of the TCC. This moves the clutch away from the converter cover. The charging converter oil continues to fill the converter and exits between the converter hub and stator shaft. The exit oil dumps into the converter apply line and is relayed through the converter clutch valve for cooling and lubrication.

Fig. 11-75. Converter released. (General Motors Corp.)

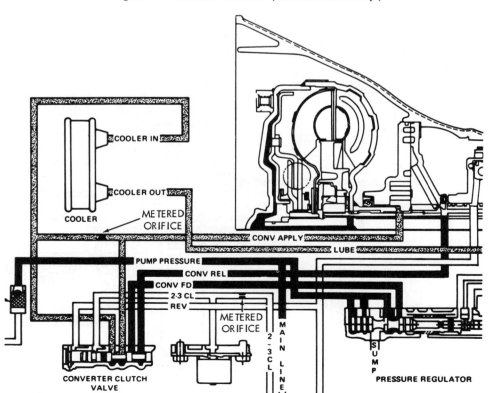

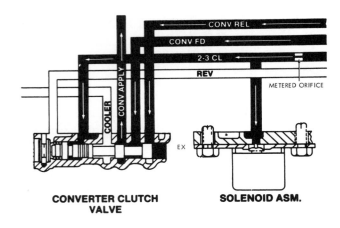

Fig. 11-76. Converter applied. (General Motors Corp.)

is energized when the governor switch is closed between 30–45 mph (48–72 km/h). With the solenoid exhaust closed, the converter valve is switched to TCC apply. The following occurs:

• The converter release circuit is open to exhaust at the converter clutch valve.

• The converter feed from the pressure regulator valve is switched to the converter apply circuit.

• The converter feed oil enters the converter by flowing between the converter hub and stator shaft and charges the apply side of the converter clutch pressure plate.

• A seal is formed between the pressure plate and converter cover; therefore, converter apply oil is not cycled out of the converter for cooling. Converter cooling is not necessary in the lock-up mode.

• To insure continued lubrication, the converter apply circuit meters an oil supply into the cooling and lube line.

NOTE: On some 1981-82 car models, the TCC control circuit is keyed to the computer command control (C.C.C.). The electronic module grounds the TCC circuit externally in place of an internal governor switch to energize the solenoid for lock-up.

In the apply mode (Figs. 11-76 and 11-77) the converter clutch valve must be switched to the apply circuit. This is controlled by the solenoid exhaust valve. In drive range (third gear), the 2–3 direct clutch oil is used for switching the converter clutch valve through a metered orifice feed. The solenoid exhaust valve, however, will bleed off the 2–3 clutch oil until the solenoid

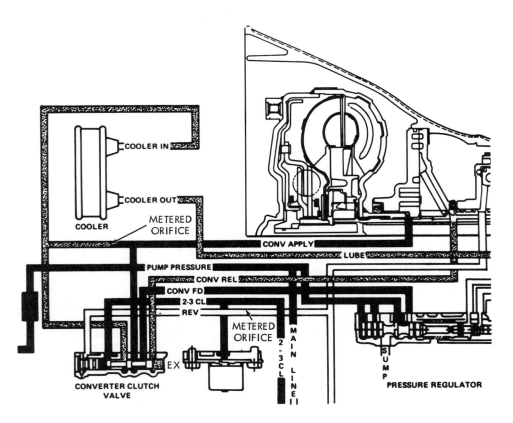

Fig. 11-77. Clutch valve applied. (General Motors Corp.)

1981 HIGHLIGHTS

Ford ATX Transaxle

The ATX Automatic Transaxle offers a new three-speed automatic transmission of metric design as an option on the 1.6-L engine used in the Ford Escort and Mercury Lynx. Front and rear external views are shown in Figs. 11-78 and 11-79. It uses a wide-ratio Ravigneaux-type planetary with a 2.8:1 low, 1.6:1 second, and 1:1 third. The final drive is through a helical gearset differential with a 3.31:1 drive ratio and half-shafts with constant-velocity universal joints. This can be viewed in the sectional pictorial, Fig. 11-80. For control of the gear train, the ATX has three multiple-disc clutches, one band with an actuating servo, and a one-way roller clutch.

A new three-element torque converter uses a patented split-torque concept that greatly reduces converter slippage. A simple planetary gearset is incorporated in the converter and acts as an engine torque "splitter" in second and third gears. Part of the torque is transmitted mechanically, as in a manual transmission, and the remainder by the fluid force on the turbine. In second gear, 62% of the torque is transmitted mechanically and, in third gear, 93%. A torsional damper in the converter cover absorbs engine pulsations to the splitter gearset. In low gear and reverse, full torque is transmitted through the normal converter fluid drive.

Fig. 11-78. ATX front view.

Fig. 11-79. ATX rear view.

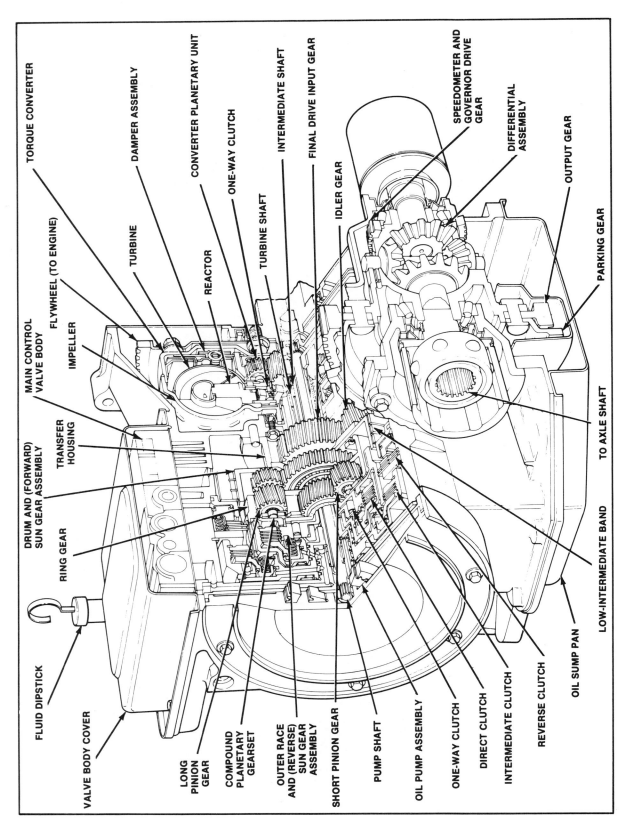

FLUID DIPSTICK

VALVE BODY COVER

DRUM AND (FORWARD)
SUN GEAR ASSEMBLY

RING GEAR

MAIN CONTROL
VALVE BODY

TRANSFER
HOUSING

FLYWHEEL (TO ENGINE)

IMPELLER

TORQUE CONVERTER

DAMPER ASSEMBLY

TURBINE

CONVERTER PLANETARY UNIT

REACTOR

ONE-WAY CLUTCH

TURBINE SHAFT

INTERMEDIATE SHAFT

FINAL DRIVE INPUT GEAR

IDLER GEAR

SPEEDOMETER AND
GOVERNOR DRIVE
GEAR

DIFFERENTIAL
ASSEMBLY

OUTPUT GEAR

PARKING GEAR

TO AXLE SHAFT

LOW-INTERMEDIATE BAND

OIL SUMP PAN

REVERSE CLUTCH

INTERMEDIATE CLUTCH

DIRECT CLUTCH

ONE-WAY CLUTCH

OIL PUMP ASSEMBLY

PUMP SHAFT

SHORT PINION GEAR

OUTER RACE
AND (REVERSE)
SUN GEAR
ASSEMBLY

COMPOUND
PLANETARY
GEARSET

LONG
PINION
GEAR

Fig. 11-80. ATX automatic transaxle. (Ford Motor Co.)

TORQUE CONVERTER POWERFLOW SUMMARY. The powerflow involves an interaction between the converter hydraulic and mechanical drive and the transmission gear train. A study of the relationship between the planetary gearset built into the converter and the hydraulic drive will establish the input to the transmission. The key components and their function are described as follows:

• Cover and Damper Assembly—The cover makes up the usual front part of the converter housing and bolts to an engine-driven flex plate at the end of the crankshaft. A damper assembly is riveted inside the cover to absorb engine torsional pulsations to the gearset (Fig. 11-81).

• Planetary Ring Gear—It serves as the mechanical input member to the planetary gearset. It is splined into the damper assembly and turns at engine speed.

• Planet Carrier Assembly—The planet carrier absorbs the splitter torque in second and third gears and is the output member of the planetary gearset (Fig. 11-82). It is splined to the intermediate shaft for mechanical input to the transmission gear train (Fig. 11-83).

• Sun Gear—The sun gear is the hydraulic driven input member to the planetary gearset. It is splined into the turbine hub (Fig. 11-84) and meshes with the planet carrier (Fig. 11-85). The turbine shaft input to the transmission gear train is splined to the sun gear (Fig. 11-83).

Fig. 11-81.

Fig. 11-82.

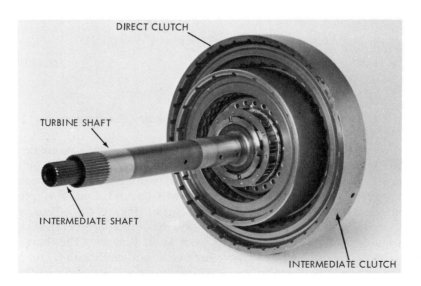

DIRECT CLUTCH

TURBINE SHAFT

INTERMEDIATE SHAFT

INTERMEDIATE CLUTCH

Fig. 11-83.

Fig. 11-84.

Fig. 11-85.

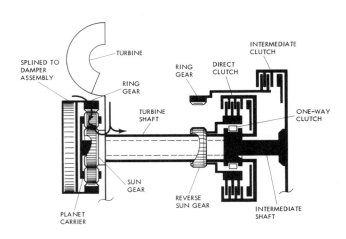

Fig. 11-86.

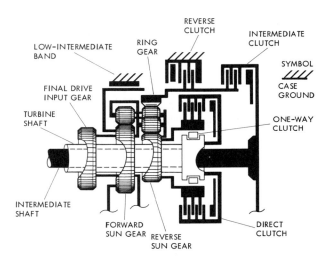

Fig. 11-87.

• Turbine—Provides the hydraulic drive to the transmission gear train (Fig. 11-86).

TRANSAXLE POWERFLOW SUMMARY. The compound planetary gearset in the ATX is a three-speed Ravigneaux with a reverse and neutral. The gear train assembly components and holding members are illustrated in a schematic view, Fig. 11-87. A review of Fig. 11-86 shows the key clutch members that control the converter mechanical/hydraulic drive input to the gear train. Following is a brief summary of each planetary component and gear train clutch/band members. Use Figs. 11-80, 11-86, and 11-87 as references.

Planetary Components

• Planet Carrier—A single carrier assembly is used with three sets of dual pinions (long and short pinions) that are in constant mesh, similar to the AOT and FMX transmissions. It is splined to the final drive input gear (Fig. 11-88). Thus, the planet carrier is always the output member of the gearset.

• Short Pinions—The short pinions in the carrier are in constant mesh with (1) the long pinions (Fig. 11-88) and (2) the reverse sun gear (Figs. 11-89 and 11-90). Essentially, the short pinions act as idler gears between the reverse sun gear and long pinions.

Fig. 11-88.

Fig. 11-91.

Fig. 11-89.

• Long Pinions—The long pinions in the carrier are in constant mesh with (1) the short pinions (Fig. 11-88), (2) the forward sun gear (Figs. 11-91 and 11-92), and (3) the ring gear (Fig. 11-93).

• Reverse Sun Gear—Integral with the one-way clutch outer race and direct clutch hub (Fig. 11-89). It is driven by the turbine shaft when the one-way clutch is effective. The reverse sun gear can also be locked to the turbine shaft by applying the direct clutch. The reverse sun gear is in constant mesh with the planet carrier short pinions (Fig. 11-90).

Fig. 11-92.

Fig. 11-90.

Fig. 11-93.

Fig. 11-94.

Fig. 11-95.

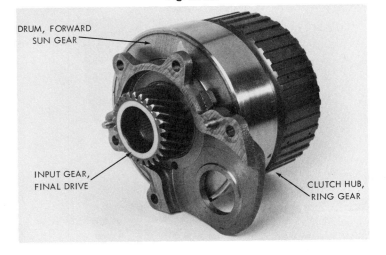

DRUM, FORWARD
SUN GEAR

INPUT GEAR,
FINAL DRIVE

CLUTCH HUB,
RING GEAR

- Drum and Forward Sun Gear—The sun gear meshes with the long planet pinions (Figs. 11-91 and 11-92). The low-intermediate band holds the drum and forward sun gear stationary.
- Ring Gear—Integral with a single clutch hub for the intermediate and reverse clutches (Fig. 11-93). The gear teeth mesh with the long planet pinions (Fig. 11-94).

The gearset components are shown as a complete assembly in Fig. 11-95.

Gear Train Clutch/Band Members

- One-Way Clutch—Locks the turbine shaft to the reverse sun gear when the turbine shaft input drives the sun gear (Figs. 11-96 and 11-97).

Fig. 11-96.

Fig. 11-97.

- Direct Clutch—Locks the turbine shaft to reverse sun gear to prevent one-way clutch freewheeling in manual low (Fig. 11-97).
- Intermediate Clutch—Allows the intermediate shaft to engage and drive the ring gear (Fig. 11-98).
- Reverse Clutch—Holds the ring gear stationary (Figs.11-80 and 11-87).
- Low-Intermediate Band—Holds the forward sun gear stationary (Figs. 11-80 and 11-87).

Gear Train Powerflow. With the assembled relationship of the planetary gearset and clutch/band components now established, the powerflow in neutral, the three forward gears, and reverse can be reviewed. Reference to the basic Figs. 11-80, 11-86, and 11-87 will support the discussion.

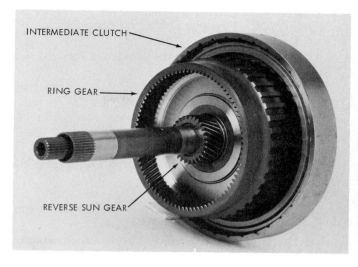

Fig. 11-98.

Fig. 11-99. Final drive input gear and idler gear.

Fig. 11-100. Output gear and differential assembly.

Fig. 11-101. Planet gear rotation, neutral and park.

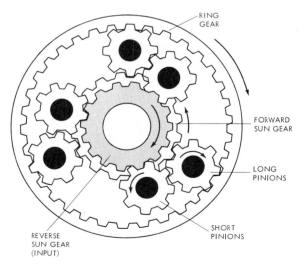

FRONT VIEW ROTATION

The gear train planet carrier is always the output member and turns the final drive input gear (Fig. 11-88). The final drive components are shown as they appear in the transfer gear housing in Figs. 11-99 and 11-100. Note that the helical-cut output gear corresponds to the ring gear in a conventional drive axle. The differential assembly is also identical to those used in other conventional axle differentials.

NEUTRAL/PARK: The one-way clutch is the only holding member. Because the hydraulic turbine drive attempts to turn faster than the reverse sun gear, the one-way clutch locks the turbine shaft to the sun gear (Fig. 11-86). There is, therefore, a powerflow check into the gear train. The planetary gears spin-up but do not transmit power to the final drive because there is no reactionary member (Fig. 11-101).

FIRST GEAR: First gear holding members are:

Low/Intermediate Band—Holds the forward sun gear stationary.
One-Way Roller Clutch—Locks the reverse sun gear to the turbine shaft input.
Direct Clutch—Applied in manual low (1) for engine braking (Fig. 11-86).

First gear is entirely a hydraulic turbine drive (Fig. 11-86).

- The hydraulic turbine drives the converter sun gear and turbine shaft clockwise.
- The turbine shaft attempts to turn faster than the reverse sun gear and the one-way clutch locks the turbine shaft to the sun gear.
- The reverse sun rotating clockwise (Fig. 11-102) drives the short pinions counterclockwise.
- The short pinions drive the long pinions clockwise.
- The long pinions walk around the stationary forward sun gear and drive the planet carrier and final drive input gear clockwise.

First gear is a 2.79:1 reduction. At maximum converter torque, the available reduction in first gear can reach 5.6:1.

The ring gear in mesh with the long pinions rotates clockwise but has no function in the powerflow.

SECOND GEAR: Second gear holding members are:

Low/Intermediate Band—Remains applied and holds the forward sun gear.

Intermediate Clutch—Locks the intermediate shaft to the ring gear (Fig. 11-86).

Second gear input to the gear train is 62% hydraulic and 38% mechanical. The torque split occurs in the converter planet gear assembly (Fig. 11-86). The turbine turning radius acting through the sun gear is much larger than the input radius of the ring gear. The converter planet gear assembly provides for a split torque only and does not multiple torque. It is actually working at a 1:1 ratio.

- The hydraulic turbine torque is transmitted through the planet carrier to the intermediate shaft (Fig. 11-86).
- Mechanical input torque is transmitted from the damper and ring gear, through the planet carrier, to the intermediate shaft (Fig. 11-86).
- The intermediate clutch locks the ring gear to the intermediate shaft. The ring gear rotation causes the long pinions to turn clockwise (Fig. 11-103).
- The long pinion gears walk around the stationary forward sun gear and drive the planet carrier and final drive input gear clockwise.

Second gear ratio is 1.61:1.

The long pinions also drive the short pinions counterclockwise. The effect of the planet carrier rotation causes the short pinions to drive the reverse sun gear at an overdrive speed. The sun gear now overspeeds and the one-way clutch overruns. In second gear, the intermediate shaft provides the input torque to the gear train. The turbine input shaft turns with the turbine but does not transmit any power.

Fig. 11-102. Planet gear rotation, first gear.

Fig. 11-103. Planet gear rotation, second gear.

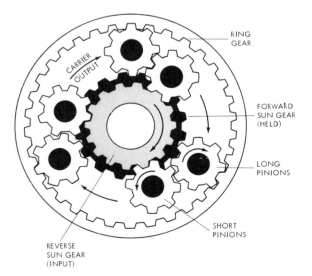

FRONT VIEW ROTATION

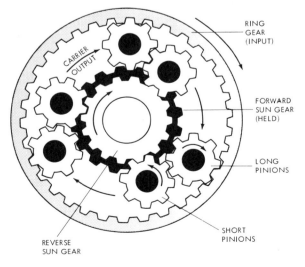

FRONT VIEW ROTATION

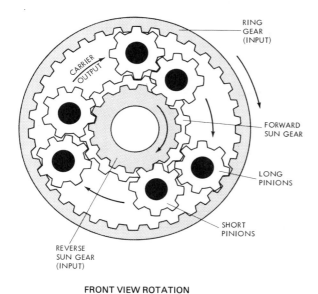

FRONT VIEW ROTATION

Fig. 11-104. Planet gear rotation, third gear.

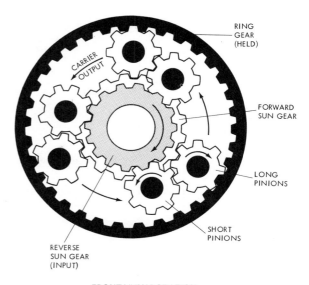

FRONT VIEW ROTATION

Fig. 11-105. Planet gear rotation, reverse.

THIRD GEAR: Third gear holding members are:

Intermediate Clutch—Remains applied and locks the intermediate shaft to the ring gear (Fig. 11-86).
Direct Clutch—Locks the reverse sun gear to the turbine shaft (Fig. 11-86).

Application of the intermediate and direct clutches lock together the converter and transmission gear train planetary units. In effect, the converter and transmission planetary units turn as a unit. The lock-up results in a 94% mechanical and 7% hydraulic torque input.

- The hydraulic turbine torque is transmitted through the planet carrier to the intermediate shaft (Fig. 11-86).
- Mechanical input torque is transmitted from the damper and ring gear, through the planet carrier, to the intermediate shaft (Fig. 11-86).
- In third-gear operation, the converter is in coupling phase and, therefore, the intermediate and turbine shafts are turning essentially at the same speed.
- The reverse sun gear driven by the turbine shaft and the ring gear driven by the intermediate shaft are also common input members to the gear train turning at the same speed (Fig. 11-104). This traps the long and short pinions between the ring gear and reverse sun gear, resulting in a total lockup of the gear train and a 1:1 ratio.
- The planet carrier turns the final drive input gear.

Because the intermediate and turbine shafts are locked to the transmission gear train, this indirectly locks together the converter planetary carrier and sun gear and results in a 93% mechanical direct drive.

REVERSE: Reverse gear holding members are:

Reverse Clutch—Holds the ring gear stationary (Fig. 11-87).
Direct Clutch—Locks the reverse sun gear to the turbine shaft (Fig. 11-86).
One-Way Roller Clutch—Locks the reverse sun gear to turbine shaft input (Fig. 11-86).

Reverse gear is entirely a hydraulic turbine drive.

- The hydraulic turbine drives the converter sun gear and turbine shaft clockwise.
- The turbine shaft attempts to turn faster than the reverse sun gear and the one-way clutch locks the turbine shaft to the sun gear.
- The reverse sun gear rotating clockwise (Fig. 11-105) drives the short pinions counterclockwise.
- The short pinions turn the long pinions clockwise.
- The long pinions in mesh with the stationary ring gear walk around the inside of the ring gear and drive the planet carrier and final drive input gear counterclockwise.

Reverse gear ratio is 1.97:1. At maximum converter torque, the available reduction can reach 4:1.

Chart 11-12 summarizes the clutch/band applications and operating ranges.

Selector Position	Gear	Int-Low Band	Direct Clutch	Intermediate Clutch	Reverse Clutch	One-Way Clutch	Gear Ratio
Park Neutral						Effective	------
Reverse			On		On	Effective	1.97-1
D	1st	On				Effective	2.79-1
	2nd	On		On			1.61-1
	3rd		On	On			1-1
2	1st	On				Effective	2.79-1
	2nd	On		On			1.61-1
1	1st	On	On			Effective	2.79-1

OPERATING CHARACTERISTICS. The automatic transaxle shift selector positions are:

P—Park
R—Reverse
N—Neutral
D—Drive
2—Intermediate
1—Manual Low

The operational highlights for (D), (2) and (1) are as follows:

D—Drive. This selector position is used for normal driving and maximum economy. Full automatic shifting and three gear ratio speeds are provided. The transmission will automatically downshift at closed throttle (coast) 3–2 and 2–1. When coasting in low gear, there is no engine braking action.

For added performance, forced downshifts (kickdown) 3–2, 3–1, and 2–1 are attained at wide-open-throttle, "through-detent," within the proper vehicle speed and engine torque range. A 3–2 part throttle downshift feature offers controlled acceleration for low-speed operation in congested traffic.

External controls to the transmission are:

- Linkage—To select the transmission operating range.
- Linkage—To the carburetor for mechanical operation of both the throttle and kickdown systems. Both system control valves are in tandem in the same valve body bore and work from the same single external control.

2—Intermediate. The transmission starts in first gear and will automatically shift to second; third gear is locked out. There is no engine braking when coasting in low gear. A 2–1 forced downshift (kickdown) is available.

1—Manual Low. The transmission is locked into low gear for extra pulling power or engine braking. If the selector is moved from (D) or (2) to (1) at an excessive speed, the transaxle will downshift to second gear. When a safe road speed is attained, first gear will engage.

General Motors THM 200-4R

The 200-4R Turbo Hydra-Matic transmission is a four-speed automatic transmission that incorporates a 1:1 third gear and an 0.67:1 overdrive fourth gear. It is used in the (B) and (C) full-size car models.

The THM 200-4R transmission unit is illustrated in a cut-away view, Fig. 11-106. It essentially uses a basic THM 200 transmission design with an overdrive planetary gear set located in front of the transmission assembly. Converter output is relayed through the overdrive planetary gear set before driving the three-speed compound (Simpson) planetary unit. Five multiple-disc clutches, two roller clutches, and a band are required to control the gear train operation. A three-element torque converter with a built-in converter clutch provides the input torque.

POWERFLOW SUMMARY. The compound Simpson planetary gearset used in the 200-4R has already been given extensive powerful coverage on a variety of automatic transmissions covered in Chapters 4 and 11. In the 200-4R application it still functions to provide the basic three forward gears plus reverse and neutral. The discussion, therefore, concentrates on the construction and operation of the overdrive assembly and establishes the relationship to the converter and main transmission. The overdrive assembly is illustrated in Fig. 11-107.

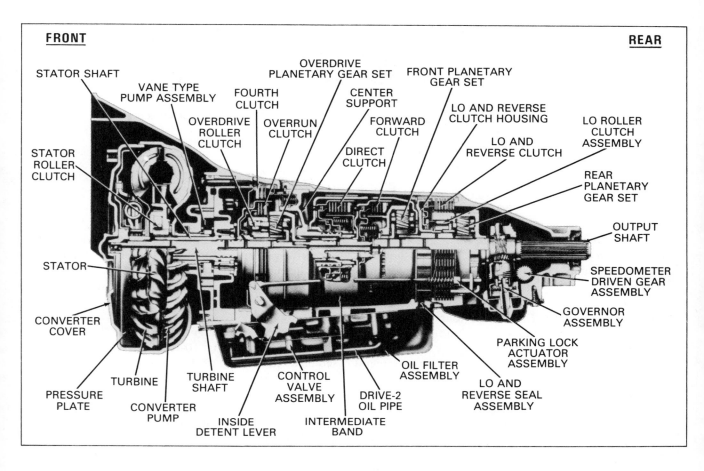

FRONT / **REAR**

Fig. 11-106. Cut-away view THM 200-4R transmission. (HydraMatic Division, General Motors Corp.)

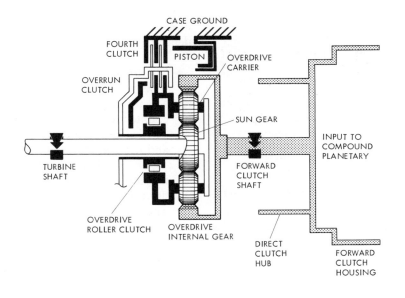

Fig. 11-107. Schematic view—overdrive assembly.

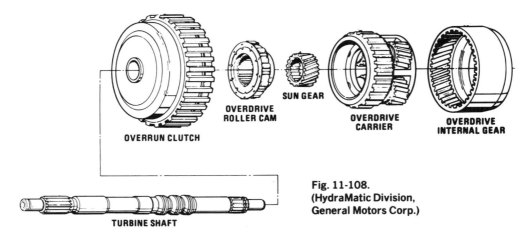

OVERRUN CLUTCH · **OVERDRIVE ROLLER CAM** · **SUN GEAR** · **OVERDRIVE CARRIER** · **OVERDRIVE INTERNAL GEAR** · **TURBINE SHAFT**

Fig. 11-108.
(HydraMatic Division,
General Motors Corp.)

Overdrive Planetary Components. The assembled relationship of the gearset components is shown in Figs. 11-107 and 11-108. The components and their operation are:

- Overdrive Planet Carrier—A four pinion carrier that is splined to the turbine shaft. The carrier is the input to the overdrive planetary and is always turning at converter turbine speed. It is integral with the overrun clutch hub and roller clutch outer race.
- Overdrive Sun Gear—It is in constant mesh with the planet carrier pinions and splines to the overdrive roller cam. It will always be driven at turbine speed through the one-way roller clutch.
- Overdrive Internal Gear—In constant mesh with the planet carrier pinions. The internal gear is the output member of the planetary unit and splines to the forward clutch shaft and housing of the compound planetary (Fig. 11-109).

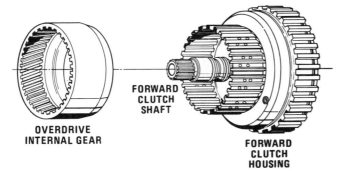

OVERDRIVE INTERNAL GEAR · **FORWARD CLUTCH SHAFT** · **FORWARD CLUTCH HOUSING**

Fig. 11-109. (HydraMatic Division, General Motors Corp.)

Overdrive Holding Members. The clutches that control the overdrive assembly operation function as follows; use Fig. 11-107 as a reference.

- One-Way Roller Clutch—Locks the sun gear to the overdrive planet carrier for direct-drive operation.

- Overrun Clutch—Locks the sun gear to the overdrive planet carrier to prevent roller clutch freewheeling in ranges (3), (2), or (1).
- Fourth Clutch—Holds the sun gear stationary for overdrive operation.

Overdrive Planetary Operation. The overdrive assembly viewed in Fig. 10-107 shows the complete assembled relationship of the planetary components and clutch members and is used as a basic reference in reviewing the operational modes of direct drive and overdrive. The overdrive carrier is splined to the turbine shaft and is the input member of the planetary assembly. The internal gear is the output member and supplies the drive torque to the main transmission.

DIRECT DRIVE: Direct drive holding members are:
   One-Way Roller Clutch—Locks the sun gear to the overdrive planet carrier.
   Overrun Clutch—Applied in Ranges (3), (2), or (1) for engine braking.

The overdrive unit will function in the direct-drive mode in first, second, and third gears, plus reverse and neutral/park.

- The turbine shaft drives the planet carrier clockwise.
- The turning effort of the planet carrier results in a counterclockwise motion of the carrier pinions.
- The carrier pinions want to turn the internal gear and sun gear clockwise.
- The internal gear is connected to the main transmission and resistance of the vehicle weight on the drive line.
- The resistance of the vehicle weight on the internal gear causes the pinions to walk as they rotate, and therefore, the pinions attempt to turn the sun gear faster than the planet carrier. The entire rotational effort of the input forces is shown in Fig. 11-110.
- Because the sun gear wants to turn faster than the planet carrier, the roller clutch locks the sun gear to the carrier.

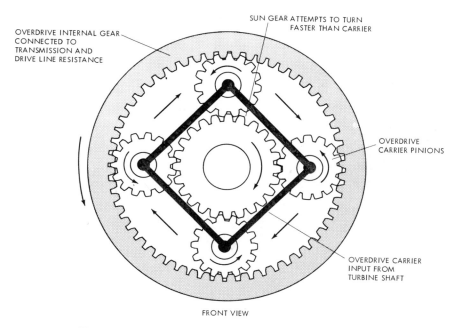

FRONT VIEW

Fig. 11-110. Direct drive directional effort of input forces.

- The pinions are trapped and cannot rotate and force the internal gear to turn with the carrier and sun gear for direct drive (Fig. 11-111).

The operation of the one-way roller differs from most other automatic transmission applications. A one-way clutch is usually used to hold a planetary member stationary; however, in the THM 200-4R overdrive planetary assembly, it is used to lock two planetary members together and transmit drive torque. Also note that a clockwise turning effort by the sun gear locked the roller clutch and not the usual counterclockwise effort.

When the transmission is operated in ranges (3), (2) or (1), it is essential to maintain engine braking for closed throttle stopping or when descending downhill grades. Under these driving conditions, the rear-wheel coast torque from the output shaft drives through the transmission and overspeeds the turbine shaft. With the overdrive internal gear acting as the input to the overdrive assembly, the turning forces in the planetary spin the sun gear counterclockwise and release the roller clutch. This disengages the engine from the driveline (Fig. 11-112). To prevent this action, overrun clutch application locks the sun gear to the carrier and keeps the gear set in direct drive.

Fig. 11-111. Direct drive—roller clutch holding.

Fig. 11-112. Direct drive directional effort during coast.

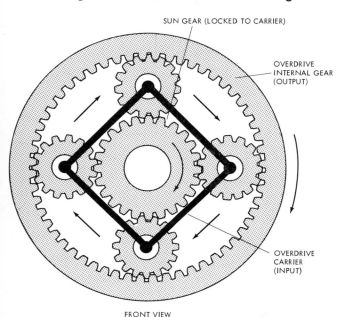

FRONT VIEW

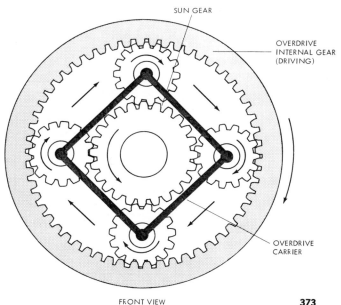

FRONT VIEW

373

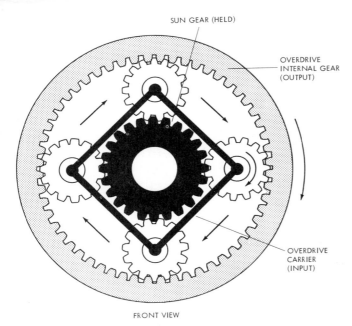

SUN GEAR (HELD)

OVERDRIVE INTERNAL GEAR (OUTPUT)

OVERDRIVE CARRIER (INPUT)

FRONT VIEW

Fig. 11-113. Overdrive.

OVERDRIVE. Holding member in overdrive:

Fourth Clutch—Holds the sun gear stationary.

The overdrive unit switches to the overdrive mode when the fourth clutch is applied for fourth gear with the compound planetary functioning at 1:1.

- The turbine shaft and carrier continue to drive the gear set.
- The pinions turning clockwise are also walking around the stationary sun gear and driving the internal gear at a faster speed than the carrier and turbine shaft (Fig. 11-113).
- The input speed to the transmission compound gear set is now faster than engine speed. Overdrive ratio 0.67:1

Chart 11-13 summarizes the clutch/band applications and operating ranges.

OPERATING CHARACTERISTICS. The Model 200-4R Turbo Hydramatic transmission manual shift selector has seven positions:

PRND321

The operational highlights for (D), (3), (2), and (1) are as follows.

D-DRIVE. Drive range is used for normal driving and maximum economy. Full automatic shifting and four gear-ratio speeds are provided from first gear to overdrive. The shift into fourth gear occurs at a minimum speed of approximately 45 mph (73 km/h). The transmission will automatically downshift at closed throttle (coast) 4–3, 3–2, and 2–1. When coasting in third, second, or low gear, there is no engine braking action.

For added performance, forced "detent" downshifts are available at full throttle. A 4–3 forced downshift can be obtained above 70 mph (112 km/h). Below 70 mph (112 km/h), 4–2 and 3–2 forced downshifts are possible within the proper vehicle speed range. On certain models of the 200-4R, forced downshifts 4–3 and 4–2 are not available. Should the transmission be in third or second gear below 30 mph (48 km/h), forced downshifts 3–1 and 2–1 will occur in all models.

To improve performance during moderate acceleration in overdrive, a 4–3 part-throttle downshift is featured in those transmissions models not designed with 4–3 or 4–2 forced downshifts.

When the vehicle speed range reaches 30–40 mph (48–64 km/h), the converter clutch engages in either second gear or third gear depending on the transmission model.

CHART 11-13
THM 200-4R
Automatic Overdrive Transmission
Clutch and Band Application (Selector Pattern P R N D 3 2 1)

| Selector Position | Overdrive Unit | | | Forward Clutch | Compound Planetary Unit | | | | Gear Ratio |
	Roller Clutch	Overrun Clutch	Fourth Clutch		Direct Clutch	Inter Band	Roller Clutch	L & R Clutch	
Neutral/Park	Holds								----
Reverse	Holds				On			On	2.07:1
1st Gear—D or 3	Holds	(On) 3 Only		On			Holds		2.74:1
2nd Gear—D or 3	Holds	(On) 3 Only		On		On			1.57:1
3rd Gear—D or 3	Holds	(On) 3 Only		On	On				1:1
4th Gear—D			On	On	On				.67:1
1st Gear—2	Holds	On		On			Holds		2.74:1
2nd Gear—2	Holds	On		On		On			1.57:1
1st Gear—1	Holds	On		On			Holds	On	2.74:1
2nd Gear—1	Holds	On		On		On			1.57:1

External controls to the transmission are:

- Linkage—To select the transmission operating range.
- Cable Control—To operate the throttle valve, detent-forced downshift, and part-throttle downshift systems. The system control valves are in tandem in the same valve body bore and work from the same single cable control.
- 12-V Electrical Terminal—To energize an internal solenoid for activation of the converter clutch control circuit.

3—MANUAL THIRD. This selector position is used for city driving, trailer towing, or when engine braking is needed for descending slight grades. The overdrive planetary is locked into direct drive by the overrun clutch and the transmission uses only three gears. Operation of the THM 200-4R is equivalent to the THM 200 in (D) range.

Forced "detent" downshifts 3-2, 3-1, and 2-1 are available within the proper vehicle speed range. If the selector is moved from drive range to manual third, the transmission will downshift to a lower gear depending on the vehicle speed.

Providing the throttle travel is sufficient, the converter clutch engages in either second or third gear depending on the transmission model.

2—MANUAL SECOND. The transmission starts in first and will automatically shift to second; third and fourth gears are locked out. Manual second offers added performance for congested traffic conditions or hilly terrain and provides the availability of engine braking. The overdrive planetary is locked into direct drive by the overrun clutch. Manual second can be selected at any vehicle speed and the transmission will shift to second gear unless throttle or vehicle speed conditions dictate first gear operation.

A forced "detent" downshift 2-1 can be obtained. If the throttle travel is sufficient, the converter clutch engages in second gear on some of the transmission models.

1—MANUAL LOW. The transmission is locked into low gear for extra pulling power and engine braking. Should manual low be selected at an excessive vehicle speed, the transmission engages second gear. When the road speed drops below 30 mph (48 km/h) the transmission shifts to first gear.

General Motors THM 125C

The THM 125C automatic transmission is a basic THM 125 modified to incorporate a Torque Converter Clutch in the converter unit. It was introduced along with the new J-Car Body Models in May, 1981 and is also scheduled for application in X-Car Body Models.

The TCC concept in the THM 125C works identically, hydraulically and mechanically, to the other G.M. converter clutch units discussed earlier in the chapter. The converter clutch will apply in third gear when car speed reaches the clutch engagement speed. Of main concern are the electrical controls used with Computer Command Control and non-equipped Computer Command Control. These two systems are typical of the electrical controls used for 1981-82 TCC General Motors automatic transmissions.

The TCC electrical system used in cars equipped with computer command control (C3) is illustrated in Fig. 11-114. You will note that the governor pressure switch is eliminated and the circuit is completed to ground through the electronic control module when the transmission is in high gear and the combined vehicle speed, throttle position, and engine vacuum is right. This system can be quickly identified by noting the two wires at the transmission junction.

TCC COMPUTER COMMAND CONTROL ELECTRICAL SYSTEM

- Brake Release Switch (Normally closed)—To avoid stalling the engine when braking, any time the brakes are applied the converter clutch is released.
- Electronic Control Module—Energizes and grounds transmission electrical system.
- Vehicle Speed Sensor (VSS)—Sends vehicle speed information to the electronic control module.
- Throttle Position Sensor (TPS)—Sends throttle position information to electronic control module.
- Vacuum Sensor (VS)—Sends engine vacuum (load) information to electronic control module.
- Third Gear Pressure Switch (Normally open)—Permits TCC engagement in 3rd gear only.

In the non-computer command control circuit the usual vacuum switch and governor ground switch is incorporated, Fig. 11-115.

TCC NON-COMPUTER COMMAND CONTROL ELECTRICAL SYSTEM

- Brake Release Switch (Normally closed)—To avoid stalling the engine when braking, any time the brakes are applied the converter clutch is released.
- Thermal Vacuum Valve (Normally closed)—Prevents the converter clutch from applying until the engine coolant temperature has reached 130°F (54°C).

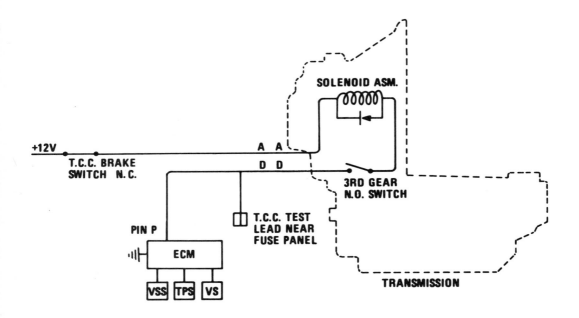

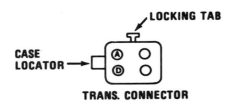

Fig. 11-114. THM 125C torque converter clutch computer command control electrical circuit. (HydraMatic Division, General Motors Corp.)

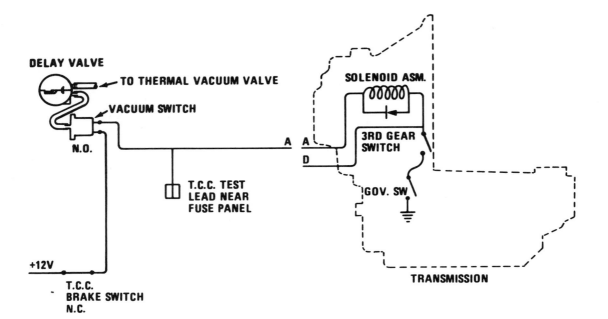

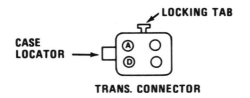

Fig. 11-115. THM 125C torque converter clutch non-computer command control electrical circuit. (HydraMatic Division, General Motors Corp.)

- Engine Vacuum Switch (Normally open)—Releases the converter clutch when engine vacuum drops to approximately 1.5 to 3 inches during moderate acceleration, prior to a part-throttle or detent downshift.
- Vacuum Delay Valve—Slows the vacuum switch response to vacuum changes.
- Ported Vacuum—Source of vacuum to vacuum switch; opens the vacuum switch to release the clutch during a closed throttle coast down.
- Third Gear Pressure Switch (Normally open) - Permits TCC engagement in 3rd gear only.

Note that there is an electrical test terminal at the fuse panel, usually located bottom left. This is common to all TCC electrical circuits. It provides a means to have a check point in the circuit that can test a large segment of the system without making time-consuming individual switch and line connector checks.

For 1981, G.M(TCC) units are standard on all rear-wheel drive vehicles. This includes the new THM 200-4R. On some car models only, the clutch will engage in both second and third gears on the 3-speeds and in both third and fourth gears on the 4-speeds.

REVIEW QUESTIONS

CHAPTER 11 SUMMARY REVIEW OF CURRENT AUTOMATIC TRANSMISSIONS

Complete the following General Information Units as it applies to passenger cars.

PRODUCTION YEAR DATA

1. The following production year data should reflect (1) first year of production, (2) last year of production if no longer used, or (3) identified as currently in production.
   Example: 1966-1980 or 1964/Current
2. Underline all FWD applications.

_____ THM-425	_____ Torqueflite 904
_____ THM-400	_____ Torqueflite 727
_____ THM-350	_____ Torqueflite 404
_____ THM-350C	_____ Torqueflite 413,470
_____ THM-325	_____ Torque Command
_____ THM-250	_____ Ford FMX
_____ THM-250C	_____ Ford AOT
_____ THM-200	_____ Ford ATX
_____ THM-200C	_____ JATCO (Pass. car)
_____ THM-200-4R	_____ C-6
_____ THM-125	_____ C-4
_____ THM-125C	_____ C-3
_____ MD3-180	

GEARSET TYPE

Use the following code letters to indicate which transmissions use the Ravigneaux or Simpson Gearset.

(R) Ravigneaux   (S) Simpson

____ THM-400	____ Torqueflite 904	____ Ford FMX
____ THM-350	____ Torqueflite 727	____ Ford AOT
____ THM-250	____ Torqueflite 404	____ Ford ATX
____ THM-200	____ Torque Command	____ JATCO
____ THM-200-4R		____ C-6
____ THM-125		____ C-4
____ MD3-180		____ C-3

EXTERNAL MODULATOR/THROTTLE CONTROL

Use the letter code (MC), (ML), or (V) as it applies to the transmission.

(MC) Mechanical/Cable
(ML) Mechanical/Linkage
(V)   Vacuum Control

____ THM-400	____ Torqueflite 904	____ Ford FMX
____ THM-350	____ Torqueflite 727	____ Ford AOT
____ THM-250	____ Torqueflite 404	____ Ford ATX
____ THM-200	____ Torque Command	____ JATCO
____ THM-200-4R		____ C-6
____ THM-125		____ C-4
____ MD3-180		____ C-3

EXTERNAL KICKDOWN CONTROL

Use the letter code (E), (IC), (IL) and (CM) as it applies to the transmissions.

(E) Electrical
(IC) Independent Mechanical/Cable
(IL) Independent Mechanical/Linkage
(CM) Combined With Mechanical Throttle Control

____THM-400 ____Torqueflite 904 ____Ford FMX

____THM-350 ____Torqueflite 727 ____Ford AOT

____THM-250 ____Torqueflite 404 ____Ford ATX

____THM-200 ____Torque Command ____JATCO

____THM-200-4R ____C-6

____THM-125 ____C-4

____MD3-180 ____C-3

INTERMEDIATE AND LOW/REVERSE CONTROL

Use the letter code (B) or (C) as it applies to the transmission.

	(B) Band Intermediate	(C) Clutch L & R
• THM-400	——	——
• THM-350	——	——
• THM-325	——	——
• THM-250	——	——
• THM-200	——	——
• THM-200-4R	——	——
• THM-125	——	——
• MD3-180	——	——
• Torqueflite 904	——	——
• Torqueflite 727	——	——
• Torqueflite 404	——	——
• Torque Command	——	——
• Ford FMX	——	——
• Ford AOT	——	——
• Ford ATX	——	——
• JATCO	——	——
• C-6	——	——
• C-4	——	——
• C-3	——	——

FORD AOT POWER FLOW

Label the planetary members in the illustrated Ford AOT planetary unit on facing page.

First Gear In O/D or 3 Range

The _____ clutch locks the turbine shaft to the _____ sun gear. The sun gear drives the short pinions _____ which causes a _____ rotation of the long pinions. The reaction of the long pinions against the ring gear and car weight is taken by the _____ roller clutch which locks the planet carrier to the case. The long pinions drive the _____ gear and output shaft at a reduction ratio of _____ to 1.

During first gear operation, the reverse sun gear and input shell, reverse clutch drum, intermediate one way clutch, and the intermediate clutch faced plates are all turning in a _____ direction.

Second Gear In O/D or 3 Range

In O/D or 3 Range the _____ clutch is applied and locks the roller clutch _____ race to the case. The intermediate _____ clutch is now effective and holds the reverse sun gear against _____ _____ rotation. The forward clutch still drives the forward sun gear clockwise with a resulting CCW/CW rotation of the short and long pinions. The long pinions in mesh with the stationary reverse sun gear walk around the sun gear in a _____ direction while driving the _____ gear and output shaft at a reduction ration of _____ to 1.

Coasting in second gear O/D or 3 range, the intermediate one-way roller clutch _____ and there is no engine braking.

Third Gear (Direct Drive) O/D or 3 Range

Engine crankshaft torque is hydraulically transmitted to the _____ shaft, then through the forward clutch and sun gear. The direct clutch is applied which

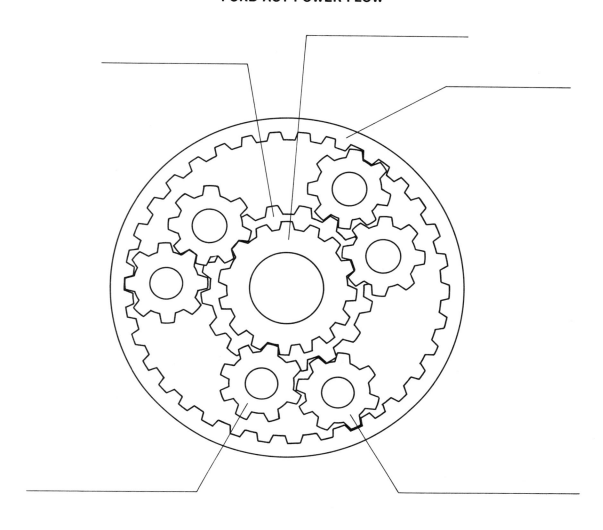

locks the direct drive input shaft to the _____

_____. This permits engine crankshaft torque to be mechanically transmitted to the planetary unit. With the forward and direct clutches applied the _____ sun gear and _____ are essentially locked together and the planetary gearset turns as one unit in direct drive or at a ratio of _____ to 1.

To minimize converter slip, the split torque input feature to the planetary unit is _____ percent hydraulic and _____ percent mechanical. All mechanical torque transmission through the direct drive shaft must pass through a

_____ assembly located internally in the converter cover to absorb engine torsional pulsations to the gearset.

Fourth Gear O/D

The _____ band is applied and locks the reverse sun gear to the case through the _____

_____ clutch drum and drive shell. The direct clutch couples the planet carrier directly to engine crankshaft torque and speed. The carrier input rotation causes the

_____ pinions to walk around the stationary sun gear in a _____ direction while driving the

_____ gear and output shaft at an overdrive ratio of _____ to 1. In overdrive, the input is 100 percent _____ drive, there is no converter slip.

Manual Low (1)

First gear Manual Low works in identical manner as first gear O/D or 3 range. However, when coasting down in first gear O/D or 3 range, the low roller clutch _____ and there is no engine breaking. To provide engine braking in Manual Low, the _____ band is applied to insure that the _____ _____ remains locked to the case.

When second gear is engaged in Manual Low the _____ band is applied to insure that the _____ sun gear remains locked to the case for engine braking.

Reverse

The _____ clutch is applied and locks the turbine input shaft to the _____ sun gear. The _____ band locks the planet carrier to the case. The sun gear drives the long pinions _____ which causes the _____ gear and output shaft to turn counterclockwise at a reduction ratio of _____ to 1.

The AOT can use either _____ or _____ type transmission fluid.

FORD ATX PLANETARY POWERFLOW

Label the planetary members in the illustrated Ford ATX planetary unit.

FORD ATX PLANETARY POWER FLOW

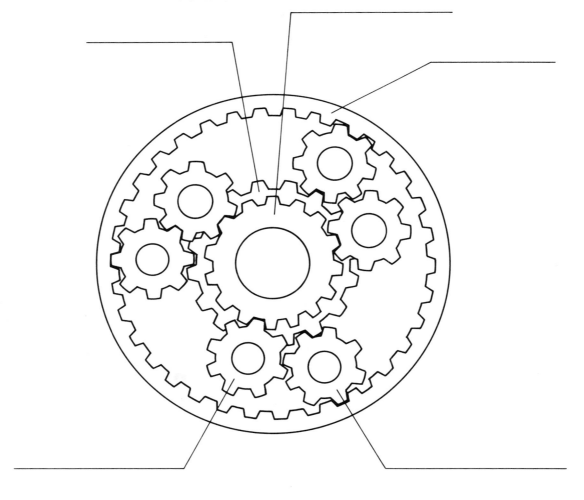

Torque Converter

It contains a _____ gearset that is used for splitting the input torque between mechanical and hydraulic drive in _____ and _____ gears.

There are two input shafts from the converter to the planetary gear set. The _____ shaft transmits the hydraulic torque and the _____ shaft transmits the mechanical torque.

When mechanical drive torque is transmitted a _____ assembly in the converter cover absorbs the engine crankshaft torsional pulsations to the transmission.

Planetary Assembly

From the following groups of planetary components and holding members, select the one best answer to match the question.

GROUP I

A. Reverse Sun Gear   **D.** Planet Carrier
B. Ring Gear   **E.** Long Pinions
C. Forward Sun Gear   **F.** Short Pinions

____ It is coupled to a drum that is surrounded by a band, and is in constant mesh with the long pinions.

____ It has a common clutch hub shared with the intermediate and reverse clutches, and is in constant mesh with the long pinions.

____ It is keyed to the one-way clutch outer race, and is in constant mesh with the short pinions.

____ Houses three sets of dual pinions referred to as the long and short pinions.

____ Splined to the final drive input gear.

GROUP II

A. One-Way Clutch   **D.** Reverse Clutch
B. Direct Clutch   **E.** Band
C. Intermediate Clutch

____ Allows the turbine shaft to lock the drive torque to the reverse sun gear.

____ Allows the intermediate shaft to drive the ring gear.

____ Holds the ring gear stationary.

____ Holds the forward sun gear stationary.

____ Locks the turbine shaft to the reverse sun gear to prevent counterclockwise free-wheeling.

POWERFLOW: FIRST GEAR IN D OR 2 RANGE

- The turbine shaft drives the reverse sun gear through the _____.
- The forward sun gear is held by the _____.
- The output planetary member is the _____.

The clockwise rotation of the reverse sun gear drives the short and long pinions. Clockwise rotation of the long pinions causes the long pinions to walk around the stationary forward sun gear in a _____ direction. This action drives the planet carrier at an output reduction ratio of _____ to 1.

POWERFLOW: SECOND GEAR IN D OR 2 RANGE

- The forward sun gear remains held by the _____.
- The intermediate shaft is locked to the ring gear in the transmission planetary unit by the _____ clutch.
- The drive torque from the engine crankshaft to the intermediate shaft is split at the planet gear assembly in the converter. Power input is _____ percent hydraulic and _____ percent mechanical.
- The output planetary member is the _____.

The ring gear driven by the intermediate shaft in a clockwise rotation drives the long and short pinions. Clockwise rotation of the long pinions causes the long pinions to walk around the stationary forward sun gear in a _____ direction. This action drives the planet carrier at an output reduction ratio of _____ to 1.

The turbine input shaft also turns but does not transmit any power. The effect of the planet carrier rotation causes the short pinions to drive the reverse sun gear at an _____ speed in a _____ direction and overrun the _____ clutch.

POWERFLOW: THIRD GEAR (D)

- The intermediate shaft remains clutched to the ring

  gear by the _____ clutch.
- The reverse sun gear is clutched to the turbine shaft

  by the _____ clutch.
- The output planetary member is the _____

  _____.
- The drive torque off the engine crankshaft is split at the planet gear assembly in the converter. Power input to

  the transmission planetary unit is _____ percent

  mechanical through the _____ shaft

  and _____ percent hydraulic through the _____

  _____ shaft.

Because both the reverse sun gear and ring gear are

driven together in a _____ direction, the long and short pinions are trapped and cannot rotate. This

locks the planetary unit for a third gear ratio of _____ to 1.

POWERFLOW: REVERSE

- The turbine shaft is allowed to drive the reverse sun

  gear through the _____ clutch.
- The turbine shaft is also clutched to the reverse sun gear

  by the _____ clutch.
- The ring gear is held by the _____ clutch.
- The output planetary member is the _____

  _____.

Clockwise rotation of the sun gear drives the short pin-

ions _____ and long pinions

_____. The long pinions "walk around" the inside of the stationary ring gear and drive the planet carrier

_____ at an output reduction of

_____ to 1.

POWERFLOW: FIRST GEAR, MANUAL LOW (1) RANGE

The _____ clutch is applied in addition to the band. This insures that during coast or "de-cel" the planetary unit will not break the powerflow from

the rear wheels to the engine as the sun gear attempts to

overrun the _____ clutch and _____

_____ shaft.

POWERFLOW: FINAL DRIVE

The final drive is made-up of three helical cut gear components.

- The input gear member that splines to planet carrier is

  called the _____ gear.
- The gear member that changes the direction of the gear

  rotation is called the _____ gear.
- The gear member that corresponds to the ring in a con-

  ventional driving axle is called the _____

  gear.

_____

GENERAL MOTORS THM 200-4R

The new automatic transmission with overdrive is

basically the same as the THM- _____ with an overdrive planetary located in front of the transmission case. The con-

verter drive torque always passes through the

_____ planetary before driving the main 3-speed planetary unit. For fourth gear overdrive to engage, the range selector must be in (D) and the vehicle minimum

speed at approximately _____ mph.

Label the planetary members in the illustrated overdrive planetary unit on facing page.

Planetary Assembly

From the following groups of planetary components and holding members, select the one best answer to match the question.

GROUP I

A. Overdrive Sun Gear   **D.** Roller Clutch
B. Overdrive Internal Gear   **E.** Overrun Clutch
C. Overdrive Planet Carrier   **F.** Fourth Clutch

____ Splined to the turbine shaft and always turns at converter turbine speed.

____ Allows the drive torque to lock the planet carrier and sun gear together.

____ Locks the sun gear to the transmission case.

____ It is the output member of the overdrive planetary.

____ Splines to the forward clutch shaft and housing.

____ Locks together the sun gear and planet carrier.

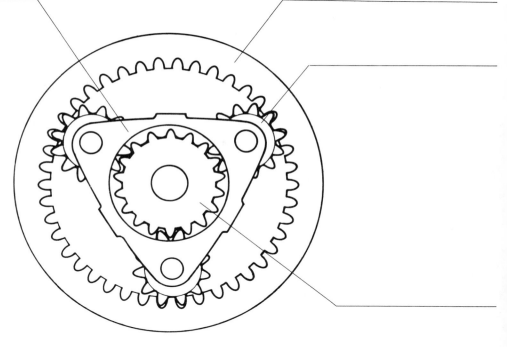

POWERFLOW: DIRECT DRIVE

• The turbine shaft drives the planet carrier. The clockwise rotation of the planet carrier develops a

_____ rotation in the carrier pinions. Under drive torque the rotating pinions work

against the vehicle resistance on the _____

_____ gear. This causes the pinions to _____

_____ as they rotate and attempt to turn the sun gear (faster) (slower) than the planet carrier. This effort locks the sun gear to the planet carrier through

the _____ clutch for a direct drive.

• During "de-cel" when the rear wheel coast torque from the output shaft drives through the transmission and attempts to overspeed the turbine shaft, the overdrive

_____ clutch freewheels and engine braking is lost. When the transmission is operated in Manual Ranges 3, 2 or 1 it is essential to maintain a positive powerflow through the overdrive planetary.

Therefore, the _____ clutch is applied and couples the sun gear to the carrier to insure a positive direct drive lock-up for "de-cel".

POWERFLOW: OVERDRIVE

On the shift into fourth gear overdrive, the

_____ clutch is applied and holds the sun gear stationary to the transmission case. The turbine shaft still drives the planet carrier which cause the rotating planet pinions to walk around the stationary sun gear and drive the

ring gear at an overdrive ratio of _____ to 1.

GM TORQUE CONVERTER CLUTCH

Mark the appropriate square ☐ to indicate whether the statement is TRUE or FALSE.

1. The GM (TCC) component make-up is similar to the Chrysler Lock-Up Converter. TRUE☐ FALSE☐

2. The GM (TCC) was introduced in production year 1980 on some car models only. TRUE☐ FALSE☐

3. For 1981 GM (TCC) units are standard on all rear wheel drive vehicles. TRUE☐ FALSE☐

4. The GM (TCC) can apply in any of the forward gears. TRUE☐ FALSE☐

5. When the GM (TCC) applies it locks the turbine to the stator. TRUE☐ FALSE☐

6. The GM (TCC) circuit controls are similar to the Chrysler Lock-Up converter control.
   TRUE☐ FALSE☐

7. In the lock-up mode, the normal converter feed oil is switched directly to the cooler and lube circuit. TRUE☐ FALSE☐

8. The governor switch grounds the electrical circuit to activate the solenoid. TRUE☐ FALSE☐

9. In the lock-up mode, direct clutch oil charges the converter and applies the (TCC). TRUE☐ FALSE☐

10. The TCC will not apply during engine warm-up. TRUE☐ FALSE☐

11. The TCC control circuit is sensitive to engine vacuum. TRUE☐ FALSE☐

12. When the solenoid is energized, the solenoid exhaust port is opened. TRUE☐ FALSE☐

13. TCC electrical circuits equipped with the computer command control (C3) eliminate the vacuum switch.
    TRUE☐ FALSE☐

14. TCC electrical circuits equipped with the computer command control (C3) eliminate the governor switch. TRUE□ FALSE□

15. TCC electrical circuits equipped with the computer command control (C3) eliminate the brake switch. TRUE□ FALSE□

16. TCC electrical circuits equipped with the computer command control (C3) have a single wire at the transmission junction block. TRUE□ FALSE□

GLOSSARY OF TECHNICAL TERMS

ABSOLUTE PRESSURE: Atmospheric (Barometric) pressure plus the pressure gauge reading.

ACCUMULATOR, HYDRAULIC: A piston operated unit that is employed to absorb a volume of fluid at a controlled rate or interval of time. When incorporated in an apply circuit of a clutch or band in an automatic transmission the accumulator absorbs the apply pressure in relation to engine torque. When the accumulator quits working, the clutch or band is fully applied and the apply pressure jumps to full value. In essence, the accumulator controls shift quality.

ANNULUS GEAR: (*See* Internal gear) Annulus means a ring-like body or figure. Chrysler Corporation uses the term "annulus gear" in reference to the internal gear when describing the planetary gears in the TorqueFlite transmission.

ATMOSPHERIC PRESSURE: One atmosphere is the weight at sea level of an air column one inch square and extending out to the farthest point of the earth's atmosphere. At sea level, the atmospheric pressure is approximately 14.7 pounds per square inch. For simplicity, 15 psi is sometimes used.

AUXILIARY PRESSURE: (*See* Balanced valve and Regulator valve) An added fluid pressure that is introduced into a regulator or balanced valve system. It functions to either increase or decrease the response of the regulator valve to input, or supply pressure. The auxiliary pressure itself can be either a fixed or a variable value.

BALANCED VALVE: (*See* Regulator valve) The same as a regulator valve as regulator valves work on the balanced valve principle. The balanced valve converts a fixed or variable mechanical force into a regulated hydraulic pressure signal known as the output, whereas the input fluid source is referred to as the supply source. In most cases, the transmission line or operating pressure is the supply source.

The force of the regulated pressure itself balances the valve action against the value of the mechanical force. Examples of balanced valve operation in automatic transmissions are the throttle valve and governor valve systems. The throttle valve output balances against a spring force that varies with engine torque while the governor valve output balances against the centrifugal force of a weight that varies with vehicle speed. In some cases, either a fixed or a variable auxiliary fluid pressure is introduced to modify the valve output. The pressure regulator valve is an example of this type of balanced valve design.

BAND: A flexible contracting friction element that tightens around the outside of a drum for the purpose of holding a planetary member stationary to the transmission case and car weight.

BAROMETRIC PRESSURE: (*See* Atmospheric pressure)

BOOSTER VALVE: Refers to the transmission pressure regulator valve system. It is incorporated in the pressure regulator valve system so that auxiliary fluid pressures may be introduced to vary the spring load on the regulator valve and increase the transmission hydraulic pressure to higher values as needed.

Higher transmission operating or line pressures are needed for extra holding torque on the clutches and bands to match any increase in engine torque output. Added transmission line pressure is also needed for reverse operation and is obtained through the booster valve action.

BRAKE HORSEPOWER (bhp): It is the actual horsepower available at the engine flywheel as measured by a dynamometer. In theory, brake horsepower is the available horsepower delivered by an engine after friction horsepower is subtracted from the indicated horsepower developed by the expansion of gases of burning fuel within a piston chamber: Ihp – FhP-Ahp.

BREAKAWAY: A term used by Chrysler Corporation that refers to the actual first gear operation related to the TorqueFlite transmission (drive-breakaway).

CENTRIFUGAL FORCE: The force away from the center of rotation of a revolving weight. The force increases with the square of the speed of rotation. For example, doubling the speed of rotation increases the force by 4 times.

CHECK VALVE (one-way): A spring loaded ball that permits one way fluid flow in a hydraulic line.

CHECK VALVE (two-way): A free floating ball that works in a pocket to permit one-way hydraulic traffic between two circuits sharing a common hydraulic line.

CLUTCH, FLUID: (*See* Fluid coupling) The same as a fluid coupling. A fluid clutch or coupling performs the same functions as a friction clutch by utilizing fluid friction and inertia as opposed to solid friction used by a friction clutch.

CLUTCH, FRICTION: A coupling device that provides a means of smooth and positive engagement and disengagement of engine torque to the vehicle power train. Transmission of power through the clutch is accomplished by bringing one or more rotating drive members into contact with complimenting driven members.

In manually operated transmissions, the clutch is mounted on the engine flywheel and is pedal operated by the driver and usually of a single disc dry-type construction. Spring force from a pressure plate assembly presses the drive and the driven plate surfaces together to produce the necessary friction force to hold against engine torque.

Automatic transmissions favor the use of a hydraulically operated multiple disc wet-type clutch construction to effect gear ratio changes. For rotating or dynamic applications, the clutch disc elements are applied to lock two planetary members together for direct drive or to clutch a planetary member to the drive torque. In static applications the multiple disc clutch is a reaction clutch whereby it locks a planetary member to the transmission case and car weight.

COAST: A condition whereby the vehicle momentum drives the engine, used in retarding or engine braking. The drive wheels, through the power train, try to rotate the engine at a speed faster than its output, therefore engine compression can be used for slowing the vehicle. Coast conditions are brought about by deceleration and when descending steep or long road grades.

COEFFICIENT OF FRICTION: (*See* Friction)

COMPOUND GEAR: A gear consisting of two or more simple gears with a common shaft. The two or more gears may be a one piece forging with the shaft, or may be keyed or splined to the shaft.

CONVERTER: (*See* Fluid torque converter)

CONVERTER LOCKUP: The switching from hydrodynamic to direct mechanical drive usually through the application of a friction element called the converter clutch.

DETENT: A spring loaded plunger, pin, ball, or pawl used as a stop or checking device on a ratchet wheel or shaft. In automatic transmissions, a detent mechanism is used for locking the manual valve in place for the selected operating range by engaging built-in notches on the valve.

DETENT DOWNSHIFT: (*See* Kickdown)

DIAPHRAGM: A flexible membrane, often made up of fabric and rubber, clamped at the edges and usually spring-loaded, used in various pump and control devices such as the fuel pump, distributor vacuum advance, and automatic transmission vacuum modulator.

DIFFERENTIAL AREAS: (*See* Spool valve) When opposing faces of a spool valve are acted upon by the same pressure but their areas differ in size, the ratio of their surface area will be the strength of their relative forces. The face with the larger area produces the differential force and valve movement.

DIFFERENTIAL FORCE: (*See* Differential areas)

DIRECT DRIVE: The gear ratio is 1:1 with no change occurring in the torque or speed input. Torque and speed input equals torque and speed output.

DRIVE LINE: The drive connection between the transmission and the rear axle, consisting of the propeller shaft, universal joints and a slip joint.

DRIVE TORQUE: (*See* Load torque) The torque which is produced by the engine and power train gear ratios to overcome the load torque. Should the drive torque at anytime exceed the vehicle load torque, then acceleration takes place. When the drive torque equals vehicle load torque and there is no drive torque reserve, then maximum vehicle speed has been attained and no further speed increase can take place.

EFFICIENCY: (*See* Mechanical efficiency)

ELEMENT: In reference to a hydrodynamic drive, an element is a single row of flow directing blades. In the simple torque converter the impeller, the turbine and stator each have a row of flow directing blades, thus the phrase, "three element torque converter."

ENERGY: The ability or capacity to do work.

FLUID: A fluid can be either a liquid or gas. In hydraulics, a liquid is used for transmitting force or motion.

FLUID COUPLING: A hydrodynamic drive that transmits power at a 1:1 torque ratio. It does not have the ability to change torque.

FLUID DRIVE: (See Hydrodynamic) Either a fluid coupling, or a fluid torque converter.

FLUID TORQUE CONVERTER: (See Hydrodynamic drive) A hydrodynamic drive that has the ability to act both as a torque multiplier and fluid coupling.

FORCE: A push or pull effort usually measured in pounds or kilograms.

FREEWHEELING: A condition where there is usually a rotating mechanical motion without any power output or distribution.

FRICTION: The resistance that is offered to the sliding or slipping between contacting surfaces of one solid body over another. This relationship is expressed by a ratio called the coefficient of friction (u). Each pair of contacting surfaces has its own coefficient of friction (u). As an example, if it took a 100 lb effort to put a 500 lb block into motion over a flat surface then:

$$u = \frac{\text{Force of Friction}}{\text{Weight}} = \frac{100}{500} = 0.2$$

Should the weight increase to 1,000 lbs the force of friction would be:

$$
\begin{aligned}
\text{Friction} &= (u) \times \text{Weight} \\
&= 0.2 \times 1,000 \\
&= 200 \text{ lbs}
\end{aligned}
$$

FWD: Front Wheel Drive

GEAR: (See Gear ratio) A toothed mechanical device that acts as a rotating lever to transmit power or turning effort from one shaft to another.

GEAR RATIO: The number of revolutions which the input gear makes to one revolution of the output gear. In a simple gear combination, three revolutions of the input gear to one of the output gear gives a ratio of 3:1. The torque and speed changes that take place in a gear set are a function of the gear ratio.

GEAR REDUCTION: Torque is multiplied and speed decreased by the factor of the gear ratio. For example, a 3:1 gear ratio will change an input torque of 180 lb-ft and an input of 2,700 rpm to 540 lb-ft and 900 rpm respectively.

GEAR TRAIN: A succession of intermeshing gears that form an assembly and provide for one or more torque changes as the power input is transmitted to the power output.

GOVERNOR: (See Balanced valve) It is a regulating or balanced valve device that provides a hydraulic pressure which varies in relation to vehicle speed. It senses vehicle speed from the output shaft and sends a hydraulic speed signal to the shift valve body where it acts on the shift valves to cause the upshifts.

G.P.M.: Gallons Per Minute

HORSEPOWER: (See Work) A horsepower is a measure of a definite amount of power: 33,000 foot-pounds of work per minute.

HUNTING: A condition where a hydraulic valve oscillates on either side of its balanced position because of small changes in the balancing forces. For example, a shift valve can't decide to stay open or closed.

HYDRAULICS: A branch of science dealing with the use of liquids under pressure as a means to transfer force or motion.

HYDRODYNAMIC DRIVE: As contrasted with mechanical or electrical, it is a type of drive that transmits power solely by fluid action in a closed recirculation path. The fluid coupling and fluid torque converter are examples of hydrodynamic drives.

IMPELLER: The power input or pump member of a hydrodynamic drive unit.

INDICATED HORSEPOWER: (Ihp) The theoretical horsepower that can be developed by a machine without consideration to frictional power losses inherent to the machine itself. In an internal combustion engine, Ihp is affected by such factors as combustion pressure, number of cylinders, cylinder bore size, piston stroke, and rpm.

INERTIA: The resistance of a mass at rest to movement, or when in motion, its resistance to a change in speed or direction of travel.

INPUT: The power, or energy supplied to a machine. In an automatic transmission, the source of power from the engine is absorbed by the torque converter which provides the power input into the transmission. The turbine drives the input shaft.

INTERNAL GEAR: The ring like outer gear of a planetary gear set with the gear teeth cut on the inside of the ring to provide a mesh with the planet pinions.

IX GEAR PUMP: A popular positive displacement rotary pump design used in automatic transmissions. The pump has a pair of matching gear members that rotate on different centers. The inner or drive gear member has the external gear cut and turns inside the outer or driven gear member with the internal gear cut. Hence the term IX.

IX ROTOR PUMP: (See IX Gear Pump) A popular positive displacement rotary pump design using two rotary members. The inner drive member designed with external lobes turns inside an outer member designed with internal lobes.

KICKDOWN: (detent downshift) A system to force a full throttle power downshift by overruling the shift valve gear selection. When the accelerator is pushed to wide-open-throttle an external control (either linkage, cable or electrical) to the transmission triggers the system within the hydraulic controls. Kickdown shifts 3-2 and 3-1 are available depending on vehicle speed.

KINETIC ENERGY: The energy of motion is called kinetic energy. Within a transmission, the turning of a shaft or gear set, or the movement of fluid is an example of kinetic energy.

LOAD TORQUE: (*See* Drive torque) The amount of output torque needed from the transmission to overcome the vehicle load.

MANUAL VALVE: A valve that derives its name from the fact that it is manually actuated by the driver of the vehicle through a linkage arrangement. In automatic transmissions, the driver selects the transmission operating range by manual selection.

MODULATOR VALVE: (*See* Throttle valve) A regulator valve that is controlled by engine vacuum. It provides a hydraulic pressure which varies in relation to engine torque. The hydraulic torque signal functions to delay the shift pattern and provide a line pressure boost.

ONE-WAY CLUTCH: A mechanical clutch of roller or sprag design that resists torque or transmits power in one direction only. It is used in a planetary gear train to hold a member stationary for gear reduction and in some cases it is used to lock the input shaft drive torque to the planetary gear train.

    The one-way clutch is its own "boss" and needs no external controls.

ORIFICE: A calibrated restriction in a hydraulic circuit line that controls fluid flow and pressure build-up time.

OUTPUT: When referring to power, it is the actual power or energy delivered by a machine. When referring to torque, it is the actual torque delivered by a machine.

    Since power is a function of torque and speed, a machine cannot multiply or decrease power by the factor of the gear ratio, but it can change torque and speed.

OVERDRIVE: (*See* Gear ratio, Gear reduction) A gear ratio that produces the opposite effect of a gear reduction. Torque is reduced and speed is increased by the factor of the gear ratio.

OVERRUNNING CLUTCH: (*See* One-way clutch) Same as one-way clutch.

PISTON: A disc or cup that fits in a cylinder bore and is free to travel. In hydraulics, it provides the means of converting hydraulic pressure into a usable force. Examples of piston applications are found in servo, clutch and accumulator units.

PLANET CARRIER: A basic member of a planetary gear assembly that carries the pinion gears.

PLANET PINIONS: They are the gears housed in a planet carrier and are in constant mesh with the sun gear and internal gear. Because they have their own independent rotating centers, the pinions have capability of rotating around the sun gear or the inside of the internal gear.

PLANETARY GEAR RATIO: (*See* Gear ratio) A planetary gear ratio produces the same results as any simple drive and driven gear set-up. Reduction, overdrive, and direct drive set-ups are attainable. The relationship of the planetary gears in their assembly, however, dictates more complex approaches to gear ratio calculations with gear teeth numbers on the sun and internal gears used in various formula combinations.

    A direct comparison of the input speed to output speed, however, can still be used:

$$\text{Gear Ratio} = \frac{\text{Input Rpm}}{\text{Output Rpm}}$$

PLANETARY GEARSET: In its simplest form it is made up of a basic assembly group containing a sun gear, internal gear, and planet carrier. The gears are always in constant mesh and offer a wide range gear ratio possibilities.

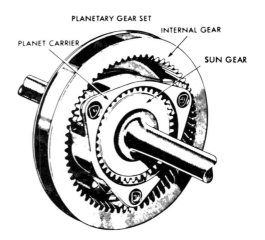

PLANETARY GEAR SET — INTERNAL GEAR — PLANET CARRIER — SUN GEAR

PLANETARY GEAR SET, COMPOUND: A gear set which has more than three elements of the type found in a simple gear set. For example, a Ravigneaux Planetary consists of two sun gears, a dual set of planet pinion gears, and a single internal gear.

PORT: An opening for fluid intake or exhaust.

POUNDS PER SQUARE INCH: This is the unit for measuring pressure of liquids or gases. It is abbreviated psi.

POWER: (*See* Work) The ability to do work per unit of time, as expressed in horsepower: one horsepower equals 33,000 ft-lbs of work per minute, or 550 ft-lbs of work per second. The rate at which work is done (power) is calculated:

$$\frac{\text{Force} \times \text{Distance}}{\text{Time}} = \frac{\text{Work}}{\text{Time}}$$

POWER FLOW: The reference made to the systematic flow or transmission of power through the gears, from the input shaft to the output shaft.

POWER TRAIN: A total automotive power train includes all power transmission components and systems from the end of the engine crankshaft to the drive wheels.

PRESSURE: Pressure is force, divided by area, or force per unit area. Usually, it is measured in pounds per square inch (psi) or kilopascals (kPa).

$$\text{PSI} = \frac{\text{Force}}{\text{Area}}$$

PRESSURE GAGE: An instrument used for measuring the fluid pressure in a hydraulic circuit.

PRESSURE REGULATOR VALVE: In automatic transmissions its purpose is to regulate the pressure of the pump output and supply the basic fluid pressure necessary to operate the transmission. The regulated fluid pressure may be referred to as mainline pressure, line pressure, or control pressure. It regulates according to a fixed spring force and other auxiliary fluid pressures used for modulation.

The pressure regulator valve is sometimes assigned the auxiliary task of controlling the flow of fluid that changes the converter, feeds the oil cooler, and provides a lubrication feed for the transmission.

PUMP TRANSMISSION: Provides the source of hydraulic pressure and is driven in a relationship to engine or crankshaft speed. Types of pumps used in automatic transmissions are the IX Gear, IX Rotor, and Variable Capacity Vane.

PUMP, TORQUE CONVERTER: (*See* Impeller) Means the same as impeller.

RAVIGNEAUX GEARSET: A compound planetary gearset that features matched dual planetary pinions (sets of two) mounted in a single planet carrier. Two sun gears and one ring gear mesh with the carrier pinions. This gearset can function as a 2-speed, or 4-speed planetary with an overdrive.

REACTION MEMBER: In a planetary gear set, reference is made to any one of the planetary members that may be grounded to the transmission case for gear reduction or overdrive. This is accomplished through the use of friction and wedging devices known as bands, disc clutches, and one-way clutches.

In physics, the second law of motion states that for every action an equal and opposite force is exerted. In a planetary gear set, the planet pinions react to a fixed sun gear or internal gear by setting up a walking motion as they rotate on their centers to produce a reduction or overdrive effect. The stator in a fluid torque converter is another example of a reaction member.

REACTION PRESSURE: The fluid pressure that moves a spool valve against an opposing force or forces. The opposing force can be a spring or a combination of spring force and an auxiliary hydraulic force. The area on which it acts is called the reaction pressure.

REACTOR, TORQUE CONVERTER: (*See* Stator) The reaction member of a fluid torque converter more commonly called a stator. The use of the term reactor, however, is descriptive of the function and is commonly used in engineering papers.

REDUCTION: (*See* Gear reduction) Gearing down as in gear reduction.

REGULATOR VALVE: (*See* Balanced valve) A type of valve classification used for various valves in the hydraulic controls that work on the balanced valve principle. It has the capability of providing a constant or variable output pressure.

RELAY VALVE: A type of valve classification used for various valves in the hydraulic controls. They function as circuit switches and have no effect on changing hydraulic pressure. The shift valves in the shift system are typical examples of a relay valve. On the 1–2 shift, the 1–2 shift valve opens and line pressure can apply the intermediate band.

RESERVOIR: (*See* Sump) Same as a sump.

RESULTANT FORCE: It is the single effective directional thrust of the fluid force on the turbine produced by the vortex and rotary forces acting in different planes.

RING GEAR: (*See* Internal gear) Same as an internal gear.

ROLLER CLUTCH: (*See* One-way clutch) A type of one-way clutch design that features cylindrical rollers caged between a cam race and cylindrical race.

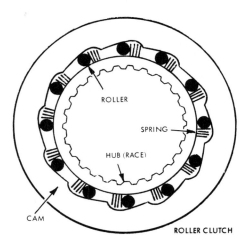

ROLLER CLUTCH

ROTARY FLOW: In a fluid drive unit, it is the rotational inertia effect on the fluid trapped in the bladed sections of the impeller and turbine.

RWD: Rear Wheel Drive

SERVO: In an automatic transmission, it is a piston in a cylinder assembly which converts hydraulic pressure into mechanical force and movement. It is used for the application of the bands and clutches.

SHIFT VALVE: Classified as a relay valve, it triggers the automatic shift in response to a governor and a throttle signal by directing fluid to the appropriate band and clutch apply combination to cause the shift to occur.

SIMPSON GEARSET: A compound planetary gear train that integrates two simple planetary gearsets referred to as the front planetary and rear planetary. Both planetaries share a common sun gear shaft and output shaft. It is popularly used as a 3-speed planetary system. For a 4-speed overdrive application, an overdrive planetary gearset must be added to either the input or output shafts.

SPEED RATIO: Expressed in percentage, it reflects the efficiency of a fluid drive, impeller speed vs. turbine speed.

$$\text{Speed Ratio} = \frac{\text{Turbine Speed}}{\text{Impeller Speed}}$$

SPLIT TORQUE DRIVE: In a torque converter it refers to parallel paths of torque transmission, one of which is mechanical, and the other, hydrodynamic.

SPOOL VALVE: A valve that fits into a cylindrical bore and consists of two or more pistons or spools that are part of a valve stem. Spool valve nomenclature makes reference to lands, valleys or annular grooves, and to faces. The valve itself determines the flow of fluid between two or more possible paths. Spool valve movement can be controlled manually, by hydraulic pressure, or by spring pressure. This type of valve design is used extensively in hydraulic control assemblies.

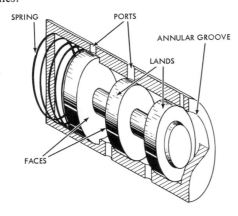

SPRAG CLUTCH: (*See* One-way clutch) A type of one-way clutch design using cams or contoured shaped sprags caged between inner and outer cylindrical races.

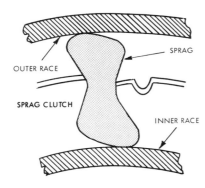

STALL: In fluid drive transmission applications, stall refers to engine rpm with the transmission engaged and the vehicle stationary; carburetor throttle valve can be in any position between closed and wide open.

STALL SPEED: (*See* Stall) In fluid drive transmission applications stall speed refers to the maximum engine rpm with the transmission engaged and vehicle stationary, when the carburetor throttle valve is wide open.

STALL TORQUE: (*See* Stall speed) It is the maximum design or engineered torque ratio of a fluid torque converter and is produced under stall speed conditions.

STATOR: (*See* Reactor) In a fluid torque converter, the stator is the reaction member that changes the direction of the fluid as it leaves the turbine to enter the pump so as to assist the pump to spin during torque phase operation.

SUMP: The storage vessel or reservoir that provides a ready source of fluid to the pump. In an automatic transmission the sump is the oil pan. All fluid eventually returns back to the sump for recycling into the hydraulic system.

SUN GEAR: In a planetary gearset, the center gear which meshes with a cluster of planet pinions is the sun gear.

TACHOMETER: An instrument used for measuring engine revolutions per minute (rpm).

THROTTLE VALVE: (*See* Balanced valve and Modulator valve) It is a regulating or balanced valve that is controlled mechanically by throttle linkage or engine vacuum and sends a hydraulic torque signal to the shift valve body to control shifting in relation to engine torque. Throttle pressure acts to delay shifts, as opposed to governor pressure that causes a shift. Throttle pressure is also used as an auxiliary boost pressure in the pressure regulator valve system to modify line pressure with engine torque requirements.

TORQUE RATIO: (*See* Gear ratio) An expression of the gear ratio factor on torque effect. A 3:1 gear ratio or 3:1 torque ratio increases the torque input by the ratio factor of (3):

Input Torque (100 lb-ft) $\times$ 3 = Output Torque (300 lb-ft)

TORUS MEMBER: Another name for the drive and driven members of a fluid coupling or a torque converter.

TRANSMISSION: A gear box used for power transmission. In passenger cars it provides for torque and speed changes as an assist to engine performance, a reverse, and a neutral. Transmissions are designed for either manual or automatic control.

TRANSMISSION, SYNCHROMESH: A manually operated transmission that permits "clashless shifting" of gears with a minimum of power interruption while the vehicle is in motion. A synchronizing clutch unit acts upon the parts about to be meshed for a gear change and insures that they are turning at the same speed both before and during engagement.

TURBINE: (*See* Fluid torque converter and Fluid coupling) Designates the output or driven member of a hydrodynamic unit.

TURBULENCE: The interference of molecules of a fluid (or vapor) with each other in a fluid flow as when eddies or swirling currents interfere with the linear flow of a system.

UPSHIFT: A shift which results in a decrease in torque ratio and increase in speed.

VACUUM: (*See* Atmospheric pressure) Any pressure less than atmospheric. The pressure valve of a perfect vacuum condition is 0 psi. Atmospheric pressure will support a column of mercury in a perfect vacuum to a height of approximately 30 inches at sea level. For automotive applications, effective vacuum is measured in inches (ability to support a column of mercury). Eighteen inches of vacuum means that the atmospheric pressure will support a column of mercury 18 inches high. At 18 inches of vacuum, the column of mercury is still exposed to 6 psi of pressure in the column.

VACUUM GAGE: An instrument used for measuring the existing vacuum in a vacuum circuit or chamber. The unit of measure is in inches (of mercury in a barometer).

VALVE BODY: A casting that contains the hydraulic valving to provide for the necessary transmission functions.

VARIABLE CAPACITY CONVERTER: A fluid torque converter designed with a two position stator blade angle, high and low. The high angle position gives an increased power input by permitting a higher rate of fluid flow return into the converter pump. This results in an increased engine speed input to the converter pump for improved acceleration. The converter torque output is also changed to a higher value, and thus power performance is achieved. For normal acceleration and cruising conditions, the stator operates in low angle (widest opening) position.

VARIABLE CAPACITY PUMP: As opposed to a positive displacement pump the variable capacity pump has the capacity of providing a variable output depending on the hydraulic needs of the transmission.

VOLUMETRIC EFFICIENCY: Refers to the breathing ability of an internal combustion engine. It is a comparison of the actual volume of fuel–air mixture drawn in on the intake stroke to the maximum volume that it would take to completely fill the cylinder. Volumetric efficiency is related to the carburetor throttle valve opening and other normal restrictions in the engine intake system, and to engine rpm.

VORTEX FLOW: (*See* Rotary flow) In a fluid drive, it is the fluid force generated by the centrifugal pumping action of the impeller or pump. This pumping action on the fluid cycles the fluid between the impeller and turbine members.

Vortex flow and rotary flow are two forces imposed on the fluid as a result of the impeller spin. Their influence on fluid drive operation is dependent on vehicle load and engine output.

WORK: The force exerted to move a mass or object. Work involves motion; should a force be exerted and no motion takes place then no work is done. Work per unit of time is called power.

$$\text{Work} = \text{Force} \times \text{Distance} = \text{ft-lbs}$$
$$33{,}000 \text{ ft-lbs in one minute} = 1 \text{ Horsepower}$$

W.O.T.: Wide Open Throttle

APPENDIX

METRIC—ENGLISH CONVERSION TABLE

Multiply	by	to get equivalent number of:
	LENGTH	
Inch	25.4	millimetres (mm)
Foot	0.304 8	metres (m)
Yard	0.914 4	metres
Mile	1.609	kilometres (km)
	AREA	
Inch²	645.2	millimetres² (mm²)
	6.45	centimetres² (cm²)
Foot²	0.092 9	metres² (m²)
Yard²	0.836 1	metres²
	VOLUME	
Inch³	16 387.	mm³
	16.387	cm³
	0.016 4	litres (l)
Quart	0.946 4	litres
Gallon	3.785 4	litres
Yard³	0.764 6	metres³ (m³)
	MASS	
Pound	0.453 6	kilograms (kg)
Ton	907.18	kilograms (kg)
Ton	0.907	tonne (t)
	FORCE	
Kilogram	9.807	newtons (N)
Ounce	0.278 0	newtons
Pound	4.448	newtons
	TEMPERATURE	
Degree Fahrenheit	(t° −32) ÷ 1.8	degree Celsius (C)

Multiply	by	to get equivalent number of:
	ACCELERATION	
Foot/sec²	0.304 8	metre/sec² (m/s²)
Inch/sec²	0.025 4	metre/sec²
	TORQUE	
Pound-inch	0.112 98	newton-metres (N-m)
Pound-foot	1.355 8	newton-metres
	POWER	
Horsepower	0.746	kilowatts (kW)
	PRESSURE OR STRESS	
Inches of water	0.249 1	kilopascals (kPa)
Pounds/sq. in.	6.895	kilopascals
	ENERGY OR WORK	
BTU	1 055.	joules (J)
Foot-pound	1.355 8	joules
Kilowatt-hour	3 600 000. or 3.6×10^6	joules (J = one W's)
	LIGHT	
Foot candle	1.076 4	lumens/metre² (lm/m²)
	FUEL PERFORMANCE	
Miles/gal	0.425 1	kilometres/litre (km/l)
Gal/mile	2.352 7	litres/kilometre (l/km)
	VELOCITY	
Miles/hour	1.609 3	kilometres/hr. (km/h)

°F
-40 0   32 40 80 98.6 120 160 200 212
°C
-40 -20 0 20 37 40 60 80 100

DIRECT READING METRIC— ENGLISH CONVERSION

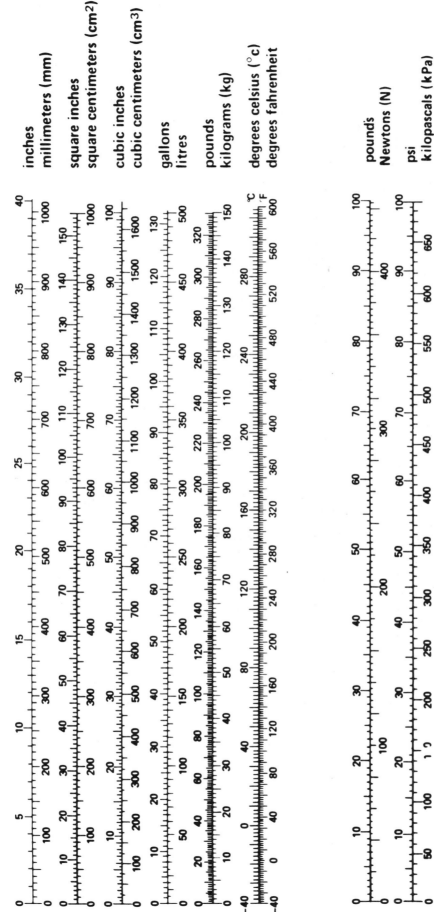
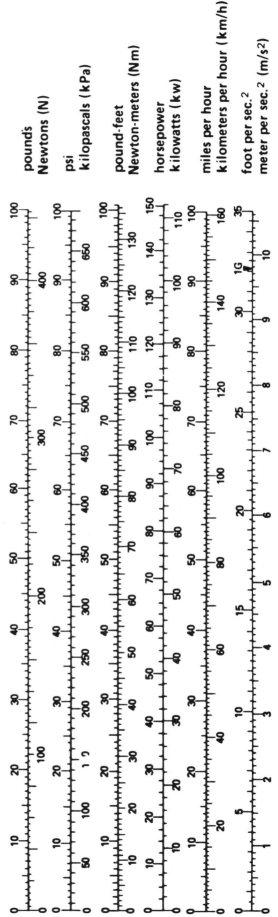

METRIC CONVERSION

DECIMAL AND METRIC EQUIVALENTS

Fractions	Decimal In.	Metric MM.	Fractions	Decimal In.	Metric MM.
1/64	.015625	.39688	33/64	.515625	13.09687
1/32	.03125	.79375	17/32	.53125	13.49375
3/64	.046875	1.19062	35/64	.546875	13.89062
1/16	.0625	1.58750	9/16	.5625	14.28750
5/64	.078125	1.98437	37/64	.578125	14.68437
3/32	.09375	2.38125	19/32	.59375	15.08125
7/64	.109375	2.77812	39/64	.609375	15.47812
1/8	.125	3.1750	5/8	.625	15.87500
9/64	.140625	3.57187	41/64	.640625	16.27187
5/32	.15625	3.96875	21/32	.65625	16.66875
11/64	.171875	4.36562	43/64	.671875	17.06562
3/16	.1875	4.76250	11/16	.6875	17.46250
13/64	.203125	5.15937	45/64	.703125	17.85937
7/32	.21875	5.55625	23/32	.71875	18.25625
15/64	.234375	5.95312	47/64	.734375	18.65312
1/4	.250	6.35000	3/4	.750	19.05000
17/64	.265625	6.74687	49/64	.765625	19.44687
9/32	.28125	7.14375	25/32	.78125	19.84375
19/64	.296875	7.54062	51/64	.796875	20.24062
5/16	.3125	7.93750	13/16	.8125	20.63750
21/64	.328125	8.33437	53/64	.828125	21.03437
11/32	.34375	8.73125	27/32	.84375	21.43125
23/64	.359375	9.12812	55/64	.859375	21.82812
3/8	.375	9.52500	7/8	.875	22.22500
25/64	.390625	9.92187	57/64	.890625	22.62187
13/32	.40625	10.31875	29/32	.90625	23.01875
27/64	.421875	10.71562	59/64	.921875	23.41562
7/16	.4375	11.11250	15/16	.9375	23.81250
29/64	.453125	11.50937	61/64	.953125	24.20937
15/32	.46875	11.90625	31/32	.96875	24.60625
31/64	.484375	12.30312	63/64	.984375	25.00312
1/2	.500	12.70000	1	1.00	25.40000

NOMENCLATURE FOR BOLTS (Ford Motor Co.)

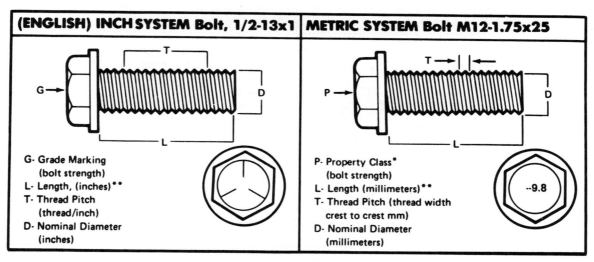

(ENGLISH) INCH SYSTEM Bolt, 1/2-13x1	METRIC SYSTEM Bolt M12-1.75x25
G- Grade Marking (bolt strength)	P- Property Class* (bolt strength)
L- Length, (inches)**	L- Length (millimeters)**
T- Thread Pitch (thread/inch)	T- Thread Pitch (thread width crest to crest mm)
D- Nominal Diameter (inches)	D- Nominal Diameter (millimeters)

*The property class is an Arabic numeral distinguishable from the slash SAE English grade system.
**The length of all bolts is measured from the underside of the head to the end.

BOLT STRENGTH IDENTIFICATION

(ENGLISH) INCH SYSTEM

Grade 1 or 2   Grade 5   Grade 8

English (Inch) bolts - Identification marks correspond to bolt strength - increasing number of slashes represent increasing strength.

METRIC SYSTEM

Metric bolts - Identification class numbers correspond to bolt strength - increasing numbers represent increasing strength. Common metric fastener bolt strength property are 9.8 and 10.9 with the class identification embossed on the bolt head.

HEX NUT STRENGTH IDENTIFICATION (Ford Motor Co.)

(ENGLISH) INCH SYSTEM		METRIC SYSTEM	
Grade	Identification	Class	Identification
Hex Nut Grade 5	 3 Dots	Hex Nut Property Class 9	 Arabic 9
Hex Nut Grade 8	 6 Dots	Hex Nut Property Class 10	 Arabic 10
Increasing dots represent increasing strength.		May also have blue finish or paint daub on hex flat. Increasing numbers represent increasing strength.	

OTHER TYPES OF PARTS

Metric identification schemes vary by type of part, most often a variation of that used of bolts and nuts. Note that many types of English and metric fasteners carry no special identification if they are otherwise unique.

—Stamped "U" Nuts

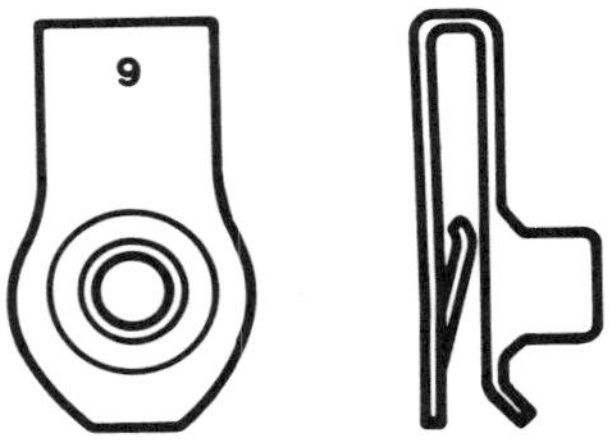

—Tapping, thread forming and certain other case hardened screws

—Studs, Large studs may carry the property class number. Smaller studs use a geometric code on the end.

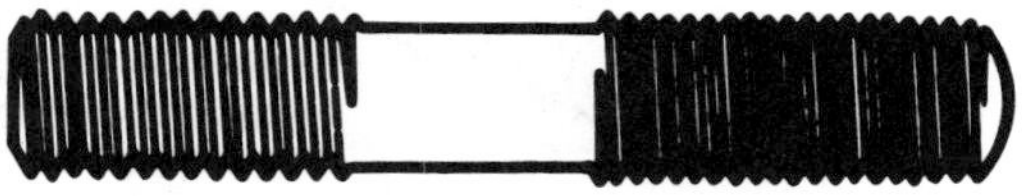

CLASS 10.9   CLASS 9.8   CLASS 8.8

3

INDEX

A

AOD (*See also* AOT, Ford Motor Company)
AOT (*See also* Ford Motor Company)
ATX (*See also* Ford Motor Company)
Accumulator (*See also* Hydraulic control system)
American Motors:
   Torque-Command, 325
Annular groove (*See also* Spool valve)
Annulus gear (*See also* Breakaway; Internal gear)
Atmospheric pressure, 117
Automatic shifting (*See also* Shift system)

B

Balanced valve. *See also* Regulator valve
Bands (*See also* Servo assemblies)
Band adjustments, 295–96
Booster valve, 136–37
Breakaway, 87–88

C

C3, C4, C6, and JATCO (*See also* Ford Motor
    Company)
CW (*See also* Ford Motor Company)
Check valve, 127–28
Chrysler Corporation:
   A-727, A-904, and A-998, 86–92, 301–6, A-404,
      A-413, A-470, 23, 25–26, 303–6
   Gyromatic, Hy-Drive, Prestomatic, and
      Simplimatic, 4–5
Lock-up converter, 23, 25, 57–62
Clutch assemblies, 114 (*See also* Hydraulic control
    system)
Clutch service (*See also* Overhaul)